Management by the Book

Management by the Book

Business Management Lessons from Jesus

ROBERT CASE

WIPF & STOCK · Eugene, Oregon

MANAGEMENT BY THE BOOK
Business Management Lessons from Jesus

Copyright © 2022 Robert Case. All rights reserved. Except for brief quotations in critical publications or reviews, no part of this book may be reproduced in any manner without prior written permission from the publisher. Write: Permissions, Wipf and Stock Publishers, 199 W. 8th Ave., Suite 3, Eugene, OR 97401.

Wipf & Stock
An Imprint of Wipf and Stock Publishers
199 W. 8th Ave., Suite 3
Eugene, OR 97401

www.wipfandstock.com

PAPERBACK ISBN: 978-1-6667-3690-8
HARDCOVER ISBN: 978-1-6667-9576-9
EBOOK ISBN: 978-1-6667-9577-6

JULY 21, 2022 9:03 AM

Scripture quotations are from The Holy Bible, New International Version (NIV) copyright ©2005 by Zondervan. Used by permission. All rights reserved.

The ESV® Bible (The Holy Bible, English Standard Version®), copyright © 2001 by Crossway, a publishing ministry of Good News Publishers. Used by permission. All rights reserved."

Scripture quotations marked (TLB) are taken from The Living Bible copyright © 1971. Used by permission of Tyndale House Publishers, Carol Stream, Illinois 60188. All rights reserved.

Text copyright © 2021 Robert Case. All Rights Reserved. No part of this book may be reproduced in any form or by any means, except for brief quotations for purpose of review, comment, or scholarship, without written permission from the publisher. E-mail: robertcase.43@gmail.com.

Robert Case is the author of:
Esther and Trump: A Commentary on the Book of Esther (2018, Saluda)
David Hume: A Skeptic for Conservative Evangelicals (2021, Wipf and Stock)

Dedicated to all the Christian businessmen and women who are creating wealth and jobs and funds for the kingdom of God, all the while walking by faith in the midst of an increasingly hostile cultural and business environment.

Contents

Preface | ix

Acknowledgments | xxi

Introduction | xxiii

1   Jesus on Management in the Gospels | 1

2   Jesus on Management in the Old Testament | 27

3   Jesus on Management in the New Testament | 54

4   Jesus on Selected Managers in the Old Testament | 103

5   Jesus on Selected Managers in the New Testament | 170

6   Jesus on Specific Responsibilities of a Business Manager | 192

Appendix: Rehoboam: A Study in Failed Management | 369

Bibliography | 393

Subject Index | 423

Scripture Index | 461

Preface

We are in a period of social transition, a period characterized by an unusually rapid rate of change of the most important economic, social, political, and cultural institutions of society. What is occurring in this transition is a drive for social dominance, for power and privilege, for the position of ruling class, by the social group or class of the managers.[1]

JESUS LIKED BUSINESS MANAGERS. I develop the basic premise that Jesus, during "the days of his flesh," taught us how to successfully manage a business. Jesus' lifestyle is the perfect model for the timeless[2] management principles and techniques for any Christian person engaged in the tough endeavor of managing a business in our hostile

---

1. Burnham, *The Managerial Revolution*, 71. James Burnham emerged as a Cold War strategist in 1944 after writing an analysis of Soviet post-war goals for the US Office of Strategic Services. The seeds of his intellectual evolution from Trotskyite to anticommunist cold warrior were planted during the time period between his break with communism and the beginning of the Cold War. It was then that Burnham formulated his "science of politics" and began viewing the world through a geopolitical prism. This intellectual evolution began in 1941 with the publication of his *The Managerial Revolution*, a study in which he theorized that the world was witnessing the emergence of a new ruling class, "the managers." The book was an instant bestseller and was translated into most major foreign languages. It received critical acclaim from the *New York Times*, *Time*, and leading opinion-makers of the day (See Camp, Review of *The Unfinished Presidency*.)

2. Collins and Porras, in their best-selling book on "visionary companies," state, "We set out to discover the *timeless* management principles that have consistently distinguished outstanding companies. Along the way, we found that many of today's 'new' or 'innovative' management methods really aren't new at all" (Collins and Porras, *Built to Last*, xiii).

and post-Christian age.[3] There were personal temptations that Jesus faced, problems that he endured, and barriers that challenged him. In all of these perennial management issues, he was the perfect manager. Furthermore, Jesus loved business managers.

- He knew business managers provided a service to the community by suppling goods, services, and financial employment for the community.
- He knew business managers provided wealth to fund the operations of the kingdom of his Father.
- He knew business managers provided an opportunity for employees to express their gifts and graces.
- He knew business managers encountered unique temptations and problems which provided him with an opportunity to make his name great in the community.

I pin the label of "chamber of commerce supporter" on Jesus. Thus, business managers had an essential role to play in the Lord's teaching. In discussing Jesus as business manager, I first apply the practical approach of Jesus to the culture of his day and how managers are to emulate him. Then I look at the biblical qualities of a business manager. I then apply the Bible to the essential qualities of a Christian manager. Finally, I give an extensive itemization and biblical application of the practical responsibilities of a Christian business manager in today's marketplace environment. In my approach to the material, I start with the gospel teaching, then go to the Old Testament teaching, and ultimately the New Testament teaching. Jesus really loved business managers.

Some years ago, as a pleasant diversion from running my family real estate company, I was reading *The Intemperate Professor*, a volume of essays by one of my favorite thinkers, Russell Kirk (1918–94), the Roman Catholic philosopher, essayist, and political theorist. I was intrigued by the title of one of his pungent essays, "The Inhumane Businessman," in which he lamented that in the American business community, which is so very practical, technical, and innovative and thus prosperous, there is no group of businesspeople being equipped for intellectual and political leadership. Kirk said this educational deficiency resulted in the American businessperson being "inhumane," in that he does not know

---

3. Cf. Joel 1:6.

our "true nature" as human beings and thus our "duty" as human beings.[4] Whether or not one agrees with his assessment, his claim was startling and provocative.

As I read Kirk's essay I was struck with personal embarrassment and conviction, for he was describing me. I considered myself a reasonably well-read businessman, but Kirk was now pinning me to the mat. He was lamenting the fact that American businessmen no longer knew "the arts of *humanitas*, which teach a man his true nature and his duties."[5] Because of this grievous lack, "the American businessman is ill equipped for intellectual and political leadership."[6] Recent American political and economic history seems to confirm Kirk. His words challenged me, as a person of commerce, to engage myself in humane studies, which would teach me, through acquaintance with great writers and thinkers, both the capabilities and limitations of human nature. He wrote that "so far as the understanding of human nature, human intellect, and an orderly society is concerned, most of our businessmen are babies,"[7] that "not one in a

---

4. Kirk, "The Inhumane Businessman."

5. Kirk, "The Inhumane Businessman," 91. There are some fine examples of humanely educated corporate chieftains: Charles H. Murphy Jr., chairman of Murphy Oil Corp.: "All my business decisions are made against the mosaic of literature and history. As Sir Thomas North wrote in his preface to Plutarch's *Parallel Lives*, 'Experience is the schoolmistress of fools; because man's life is so short, and experience is hard and dangerous.'" George W. Mead II, Chairman, Consolidated Papers, Inc.: "A broad base in liberal arts adds to one's basic thinking ability. I find literature very constructive." Donald N. Frey, Chairman, Bell and Howell Company: "It's very easy in business to get too narrow. Management, in the final analysis, is the dealing with human affairs, and literature is human affairs" (Both quotes from Clemens and Mayer, "The Classic Touch," 62).

6. Kirk, "The Inhumane Businessman," 92. In 1909, Charles W. Elliott, past president of Harvard College, was speaking to a group of working men, and he said that while everyone cannot go to Harvard, anyone could "read like a Harvard man" and thus become cultured and educated. All that was needed was a five-foot shelf of great books. Colliers took up the challenge (and potential for profit) and later that year began to publish fifty-one books called "Harvard Classics" edited by Elliott. I have several of these volumes in my library! Richard Stearns of World Vision wrote, "During my career I tried to read a broad spectrum of things, including novels, biographies, historical nonfiction, thrillers, classics, and a couple of newspapers. One year I read *Moby Dick*, *Frankenstein*, biographies of Winston Churchill and Steve Jobs, several good contemporary novels, a couple of books by theologian N. T. Wright, and a book by journalist Malcom Gladwell" (Stearns, *Lead Like It Matters to God*, 176).

7. Kirk, "The Inhumane Businessman," 96.

thousand political or industrial leaders can quote his Cicero, let alone his St. Augustine."[8] Kirk's final sentence riveted my attention:

> If only one percent of our men of business were to begin to pay some heed to the springs of imagination and reason, we might give the lie to the European witticism that America is the only nation to pass from barbarism to decadence without knowing civilization.[9]

For several years I taught both an upper division business principles course and a business ethics course at Central Washington University (along with multiple philosophy courses) and most of my business students were reasonably talented upperclassmen. These young men and women were just months, even weeks away from the post-graduate workforce. Sadly, most were not acquainted with Socrates,[10] Plato, Aristotle, or Adam Smith, to say nothing of Augustine, Aquinas,[11] Calvin, or, even more tragically, Jesus. These were not "humanely" educated people fit for leadership—they are vocationally trained technicians, programmed for prosperity but not posterity. As a teacher of business and philosophy at a state university I was hesitant to get involved in what one academic called "credentialing relevant competencies"[12] in my classes. This book will not teach Socrates, Aristotle, Augustine, Smith, or Calvin. But I would hope it to be a business primer on Jesus.

The gospel of Jesus tells us that our true nature is defined by our bearing the image of God,[13] and our duty is to "glorify God and fully to enjoy him forever."[14] The Bible instructs us as to who we are, where we are, what is out there, and how we are to relate to it. The model Christian

8. Kirk, "The Inhumane Businessman," 96.

9. Kirk, "The Inhumane Businessman," 110. The quote is often attributed to Oscar Wilde (1854–1900).

10. See Case, "Socrates and the Small Businessman."

11 See Case, "Human Resource Management: Aquarius or Aquinas?"

12. "If the schools and churches had taught the people to be honest and conscientious about the good of the community, as Matthew Arnold insisted they should, then there would not be the prevalence of self-servicing sharp practices, profit at the expense of the general good, and outright crime in the business community" (John A. Howard (1922–2015), quoted in Archibald, "Learning from the Liberal Arts").

13. Bryan Bedford, president and CEO of Republic Airways, has the mission statement of his company read in part, "Every employee, regardless of personal beliefs or world views, has been created in the image and likeness of God" (Schrader, "Republic Air CEO Puts His Faith to Work").

14. *Westminster Confession of Faith*, Q & A 1.

business manager of old was a leader schooled in both the best Christian literature (*studia divinitatis*), as well as the great classical literature (*studia humanitatis*).[15] The old businessman had at least a nodding acquaintance with the Bible, the Fathers of the Church (i.e., Augustine, Aquinas, etc.), perhaps even the great theological formulations of Christendom (e.g., Apostle's Creed, Westminster Confession of Faith, Augsburg Confession, Thirty-nine Articles, etc.), and an application of all this transcendental and ethical teaching. That is not to say that these business titans were believing Christians. Not at all, but many of these pioneering captains of commerce had a deep and humane perspective which they gained at home, in school, and in church or synagogue.[16] But not any longer.

My motivation for this book came out of my own ignorance and frustration of working in the business world as a Bible-believing manager and not finding much help in how to deal with the normal stress of management, such as:

- competitors,
- my lack of marketplace skills,
- dishonesty in the marketplace,
- the tendency to do whatever it took to make a profit,
- the internal pressure of the Holy Spirit urging me to lead a pious life,

---

15. Cf. Clemens and Mayer, *The Classic Touch*. The late Charles Murphy Jr. (1920–2002), former chairman of Murphy Oil Corporation, said, "All my business decisions are made against the mosaic of literature and history. As Sir Thomas North wrote in his preface to Plutarch's *Parallel Lives*, 'Experience is the schoolmistress of fools; because man's life is so short, and experience is hard and dangerous'" (Clemens and Mayer, "The Classic Touch"). At the time of this quote (1987) Murphy was reading *Caesar and Christ* by Will Durant and *Great Expectations* and the *Pickwick Papers* by Charles Dickens.

16. Thomas Bulfinch (1796–1867) was a graduate of Boston Latin School, Phillips Exeter Academy, and Harvard College. He was an officer in the Merchant's Bank of Boston and a Latinist to boot. He reorganized the Psalms to illustrate the history of the Israelites and was the author of *Bulfinch's Mythology*, a 1881 compilation of fables and legends. His *Mythology* is a classic work of popularized mythology and continues to be read after all these years. More recently we have captains of commerce like John Campbell, co-founder of Campbell-Lutyens, the international equity fund, and author of the sprawling biography of Richard Haldane, the English political leader of the early twentieth century.

- my hazy understanding of my Christian obligations concerning business methodology.[17]

I wanted easy answers to professional management problems by turning to a verse in Scripture and finding the cookbook solution to a dilemma. Or I wanted to be able to call a trusted friend and have them tell me where to go to get the answers. As retired business executive Robert Stepansky colorfully put it, "Finding the Holy Grail of [management] knowledge would make life easier. There would be a single source from which to draw knowledge and direct my actions."[18] I wanted to know that if I do x then God will do y in a timely fashion so that I could continue to be reassured that God had my back and was still in charge of my business activities—you know, a *quid pro quo* relationship with my "partner in business." However, those expectations were not what I found in my experience. What I discovered was that I didn't get the answers or assurance or confidence I desired and that I was operating in the dark much of the time. Reflecting my frustration, Laura Nash, in her 1994 survey of evangelical business executives, wrote,

> Instead of providing sound theological discussion that is relevant to the complex business problems professional managers face, many evangelical writings offer superficial philosophies of wealth that contradict each other.[19]

Nothing has changed since Nash's description. Furthermore, my lack of assurance was not an insignificant issue. The fact is, this stumbling around cost me money, reputation, personal fulfillment, relationships, and even health.

---

17. I felt like Charles Simeon (1759–1836), the evangelical English pastor who for years looked for others who shared his frustrations and goals in the pastorate but to no avail.

18. Stepansky. *Thoughts on Leadership from a Higher Level*, 2.

19. Nash, *Believers in Business*, 25. In 1684 Puritan preacher Richard Steele wrote a short book entitled *The Tradesman Calling* in which he prefaces the book: "Instead therefore of useless speculations, or perplexing controversies in religion, which neither enrich the mind, nor reform the manners of men, I shall endeavour to direct the conscientious tradesman in the duties of his daily calling, wherein he is surrounded with manifold temptations and difficulties, and stands in need of all the assistance he can obtain from God or man. He hath the same depraved nature to bias him, and the same malicious spirit to tempt him as others, and he hath a much greater variety of trials and temptations from the world, than either the scholar or gentleman" (Steele, *The Religious Tradesman*, vi).

Preface

In trying to answer my questions from a "sound theological" approach, I read books and articles on the Christian in the business world.[20] I attended seminars, classes, lectures, discussion groups, conferences, workshops to gain insight in how I might be a more God-pleasing and successful businessman. Indeed, this book is a part of my doctoral dissertation, investigating a biblical view of managing a small business. What I receive from these efforts made little difference in my thinking. In fact, it is commonly said (by conference presenters!) that if you leave such a gathering with one good idea, it was worth the investment of time and money. I found that justification to be an expensive educational model.

What I found instead of enlightenment was an instructional Christian business environment populated mostly by academics or pastors without real marketplace experience, on one hand, or working (who has time to teach?!) businessmen without serious theological training, on the

---

20. Mike Lindell, the pillow king, tells the story in his biography that he was flipping through the pages of an airline magazine when his eyes fell on a picture of the candidate in his office at Trump Tower. The wall in the office was the same one he had seen in a dream. A little shaken, he stared at the picture for a few seconds, Then he closed his eyes and prayed, "God, I don't know what's going on here. Please show me." In the middle of that prayer, his phone pinged. He opened his eyes and looked at the phone. On the screen was a text message with an invitation. Donald Trump wanted to meet him at Trump Tower in New York (Lindell, *What Are the Odds*, 287). LeTourneau wrote, "Let God's will be done, and the rewards will be so great there won't be room to store them" (LeTourneau, *Mover of Men and Mountains*, 173). Rush comments, "Christian businesspeople everywhere . . . must be committed to knowing and applying biblical principles of doing business. As they do, I believe three things will occur: First, they prosper. Second, the entire business community and society in general will be more prosperous. Third, Satan's effort to control the world by controlling the marketplace will be held back" (Rush, *Lord of the Marketplace*, 26). Armerding concurs: "No one who sticks by his ethical principles really loses." Armerding has a chapter in his book on the Christian in business entitled "Good Ethics Can Make You Rich" (Armerding, *Dollars and Sense of Honesty: Stores from the Business World*, 46). S. Truett Cathy of Chick-fil-A asks, "How do we balance the pursuit of profit and personal character? For me, I find that balance by applying biblical principles. I see no conflict between biblical principles and good business practices" (Cathy, *How Did You Do It, Truett?*, 15). The disgraced George Shinn ("self-made millionaire and the owner of some thirty corporations," according his *The American Dream* dust jacket) stated, "I've met men and women who appear to have become successful without any help from the Lord, but I've noticed that sooner or later life seems to backfire for these people. They make a mistake and lose a lot of money, maybe even their business. Their partnerships go sour. Their marriage falls apart. One of their kids goes bad . . . I believe these happen because the individuals . . . are not shored up by the Lord's blessings, which they can have just for the asking. The proof is in the Bible—John 15:7; Matt 21:22 and Jer 33:3" (Shinn, *The American Dream*, 142–43).

other hand.[21] It is easy to give advice when you've never had your teeth kicked in in the marketplace or had to subject your theological ideas to the demands of earning a living or had to filter your business practices through a biblical grid.[22]

Sixty years ago, business executive and entrepreneur Marion Wade defined the issue: "Many of the men I meet in business are ready to declare that they are Christians if the subject comes up in our conversations. On the other hand, few of them have been able to state that they are applying their religious convictions to their business affairs. Either it hasn't occurred to them that they should, or they haven't figured out how they could. In many cases, these men feel that by attending church on Sundays and perhaps even participating in Bible classes they are fulfilling all of their Christian obligations."[23]

Ironically, after all my exposure to Christians in the marketplace, I found myself returning the life and ministry of Jesus in the New Testament for some practical business advice.[24] Jesus was not only taught the

---

21. Walton, *Sam Walton: Made in America*. Sam Walton, founder of Wal-Mart, was the richest man in America when his biography came out. A Sunday School teacher and practicing Presbyterian, Walton nevertheless failed to mention the importance of a spiritual relationship with God in his 350-page book. Church was somewhat like a spiritual Rotary Club or the Chamber of Commerce (Walton, *Sam Walton: Made in America*, 19–20, 37, 88).

22. I am acquainted with the "health and wealth" gospel, but I don't see it adequately defended in Scripture. I am likewise acquainted with Christian socialism, but I don't see that in God's word either. I am an unrepentant capitalist.

23. Wade and Kittler, *The Lord Is My Counsel*, 2. Wade's (1898–1973) little biography, written in 1966, is one of the best business biographies I have read. Wade is the founder of Service Master Corp. and a deeply biblical business executive.

24. "The book of Proverbs, which incorporates experiential wisdom imported from outside Israel, shows that human beings can still think validly and talk wisely, within a limited field, without special revelation" (Jones, "The Character Education Movement," 91). See McLemore, *Good Guys Finish First: Successful Strategies from the Book of Proverbs for Business Men and Women*. The preexistence of Jesus was a given for New Testament writers: John 8:56; 12:41; 1 Cor 10:4; Heb 11:26; Jude 5; *Westminster Confession Faith* 1.5: "We may be moved and induced by the testimony of the Church to a high and reverenced esteem of the Holy Scriptures. And the heavenliness of the matter, the efficacy of the doctrine, the majesty of the style, the consent of all the parts, the scope of the whole (which is to give all glory to God), the full discovery it makes of the only way of man's salvation, the many other incomparable excellencies, and the entire perfection thereof, are arguments whereby it doth abundantly evidence itself to be the word of God; yet notwithstanding, our full persuasion and assurance of the infallible truth and divine authority thereof, is from the inward work of the Holy Spirit bearing witness by and with the word in our hearts."

Old Testament[25] but he guided the great managers of the Old Testament like Moses and Joseph.[26]

The game in the marketplace is real and the consequences from decisions cannot be underestimated. As a business manager, I'm paid to know the answers, to have a clear view, be confident and assured, and to be right! Saying "I'm sorry" for sloppy service, slipshod products, and unfilled promises isn't good enough when people's money or livelihood is at stake. The marketplace has a different set of punishments for failure than that of non-profits or church or para-church organization work, where opinions and actions are all within certain prescribed boundaries and levels of accountability, many of which seldom touch on livelihood status or have great financial consequences. Compared to the hand-to-hand combat of commerce, these other callings are genteel and deliberative–a safe, secure, and snug harbor; nothing like the rough-and-tumble, ruleless world of competition in today's post-Christian marketplace!

Our post-Christian era means that our once unifying ideologies and values have dissolved. In place of a general Christian consensus in the marketplace are the values of narcissism and materialism.[27] This philosophic and ethical deterioration means that purposefully Christian managers will have to make a courageous habit of acting Christian in their respective organizations. Which will be enough for an authentic testimony.

I wanted serious answers to serious questions, and my study led me to this book and gave me a theological framework for some of those answers.[28]

One final confession: By disposition I am not a manager. I have been in management positions for years and those patient and talented colleagues who worked with my management skills will testify that I am not easy to work for. Probably not easy to work with. And that is not because I have high standards. My difficulty is not understanding management.

25. Jude 5.

26. Heb 11:26.

27. See Rieff, *The Triumph of the Therapeutic*; Lasch, *The Culture of Narcissism*; Hart, *Organizational America*.

28. Doriani found "voluminous management literature" (Doriani, *Work: Its Purpose, Dignity and Transformation*, 202n11) but I was not so fortunate. I agree with Senior's assessment: "Relatively few of these works draw directly on a specific religious tradition such as Christianity, and virtually none connect the specific tasks of administration to the fundamental resources of the Scriptures or Christian theology and Christian faith as such" (Senior, *The Gift of Administration*, xviii).

There is a great difference between leadership, which can be solitary and aloof, and managing people. I am much more comfortable being an entrepreneur or promoter or salesman than a supervisor of other people. My father, who was a successful businessman, was both a good manager and an experienced salesman. But I have my mother's inclinations, which war against a mellow management style. This book is part of my quest to understand good management lessons taught and exemplified in the word of God.

* * *

A note on my approach to this book. I begin with the biblical teaching of Jesus as a role model for the Christian business manager. Chapter 1 of the book is designed to delve into the theology of biblical management and is a bit abstract. I cover the importance of the "days of his flesh," the ambiguous perception of Christ's life, his temptations, and his call for us to follow his management principles. I first look at the modeling aspect of the incarnation itself as a perfect lifestyle to be modeled for Christian business managers in today's pluralistic and paradoxical cultural setting.[29]

In chapter 2 I begin to look at the biblical data concerning the practical functioning of the management of an organization with a focus on principles of management in the Old Testament. In chapter 3 I look at the management principles and lessons contained in the New Testament.[30] Chapter 4 is a survey of Old Testament managers, and chapter 5 covers

---

29. It is worth noting at the outset that the very Christian vocation of "shepherding" (*raah*) was invented by unbelievers (Gen 4:20). The first occurrence of *raah* is in Genesis 29, where it is translated "feed" or "tend." The actual meaning of the root is pasturing or herding livestock. "The Old Testament theological idea of the good shepherd who feed his flock with God's truth (Jer 3:15, etc.) becomes prominent in the New Testament (John 10:11)" (White, "Rosh").

30. Nash looked at the same business environment and came up with an ingenious yet slightly different labeling of what she saw: "I suggest that we can find among [business] evangelicals three basic personal responses to the traditional moral conflicts of business. The first two types of evangelicals, whom I call the 'generalists' and the 'justifiers,' are characterized by their denial of conflicting impulses. These two groups either ignore or rationalize potential discrepancies between business as usual and Christian ethics. The third type of evangelical, whom I call the 'seeker,' has a more complicated response. Rather than seeing business and Christianity as automatically compatible, the seekers find that faith does two things simultaneously: It demands an awareness of conflicting values, while it also becomes the mediating factor in the ongoing tensions between the musts of religion and the musts of business. This is a way of thinking that is best described as a creative paradox" (Nash, *Believers in Business*, xiii).

Preface

some New Testament managers. Finally, in chapter 6, I cover ten critical responsibilities of a manager and the biblical examples of how these responsibilities are fulfilled by Old and New Testament managers.

The book is heavily footnoted with scriptural references, citations,[31] and Hebrew/Greek word definitions. The footnotes are there to make the general reading of the text smoother with fewer diversions. However, if the reader wants to explore more thoroughly the notion of biblical management, the footnotes are designed to provide a more thorough exploration. I have added an appendix in which I explore in some depth a more technical discussion of various views of management with a detailed exegesis of the management style of King Rehoboam.

I offer this book as my own pilgrimage. If it is helpful, I am pleased. If not, then you've only wasted a few bucks and some time.

---

31. I generally put the contributions of the theologians in a footnote as well as extra biblical material for those who want to delve deeper into the subject. Throughout the book I refer to "businessmen" for sake of ease and clarity. Obviously, "businesswomen" exist and are in management positions, and everything I write applies to them as well.

Acknowledgments

A NOTE OF THANKS to the late Ray Anderson of Fuller Theological Seminary and the late David Jones and Robert Reymond of Covenant Theological Seminary, who read portions of this book and offered thoughtful criticisms and suggestions. To Kevin Martin and Tom Norman, remarkably both from WORLD News Group, for providing examples of exemplar Christian business managers. Finally, to the successful businessmen who took the time to read, evaluate, and offer suggestions to the ideas and approaches contained in this book, I thank you. Being a wealth-creating Christian business manager is a high and noble calling and one that I aspired to much of my adult life.

Introduction

HERE IS A BIBLICAL description of good management:

> The people of Judah and Israel were as numerous as the sand on the seashore; they ate, they drank, and they were happy[1] ... During Solomon's lifetime Judah and Israel, from Dan to Beersheba, lived in safety,[2] each man under his own vine and fig tree. (1 Kgs 4:20, 25)

> In the last days ... every man will sit under his own vine and under his own fig tree, and no one will make them afraid,[3] for Yahweh Almighty has spoken. (Mic 4:4)

> In that day each of you will invite his neighbor to sit under his vine and fig tree, declares Yahweh Almighty. (Zech 3:10)[4]

This is a summary judgment of Solomon's management policies for his great organization–the united kingdom of Israel and Judah. This is the goal of all good management: to have happy, productive people enjoying

---

1. *Samech* = joyful, make merry, rejoice, cheer-up, glad, gleeful.
2. *Betach* = confidence, trust.
3. *Charad* = cause to tremble, trouble. See Jer 30:10.
4. "King Solomon was greater in riches (*oshe*) and wisdom (*hokma*) than all the other kings of the earth. The whole world sought audience with Solomon to hear the skill/wisdom (*hokma*) God had put in his heart" (1 Kgs 10:23–24). "The Queen of the South will rise at the judgment with the men of this generation and condemn them, for she came from the ends of the earth to listen to Solomon's wisdom, and now one greater than Solomon is here" (Luke 11:31). The term *hokma* covers all human experience with understanding, insight, intelligence, and skill. It is the wisdom that is required in good leadership, as in David (1 Sam 18:14). It is expressed in secular affairs as well as religious affairs. This term marks technical skill and craftsmanship (Exod 25:3; 31:3, 6) and good management skills, as evidenced by Solomon (1 Kgs 10:4, 24) and by Joseph (Ps 105:16–22; Acts 7:10). Even the Assyrian king Sennacherib promised the good life under your fig tree in Isaiah 36:16–18.

the life God has given them. Just in case we missed it, Yahweh uses Micah and Zechariah, and Luke to tells us that the management results of the messianic kingdom, ushered in by Jesus, will perfectly complete the management results of Solomon's kingdom. And where Solomon was an outstanding manager, with all his faults and sins, Jesus is history's perfect manager. And blessedly for us, he has given us, through revelation, management tips to apply to our own organization.[5]

So, the purpose of my investigation is to see how Jesus does management that results in such a good outcome:

- The workers were happy and enjoyed the good things of life that God provides.
- The workers were safe and secure.
- The workers enjoyed the leadership of excellent managers.
- The workers owned the fruits of their labor.
- The workers enjoyed the fellowship of their colleagues and neighbors.
- The wisdom of the management principles that help create the good life was passed on to others to continue the happy estate.

* * *

The Bible speaks of Jesus taking the form of humanity by way of "enfleshing" himself and thus becoming physically like you and me:

- "The word became flesh (*sarx*) and lived for a while among us" (John 1:14a).
- "... God did by sending his own Son in the likeness (*homoiogeo*) of sinful man" (Rom 8:3).
- "... taking the very nature of a servant, being made in human likeness (*homoiogeo*)" (Phil 2:7).

---

5. Drucker posits the administrative tasks of a manager as two-fold: First, to make effective the very small core of worthwhile activities which are capable of being effective, and at the same time to neutralize those activities which will not yield significant results for the organization. Second, the management task is to bring the business all the time a little closer to the full realization of its potential using already existing resources (Drucker, *Management: Tasks, Responsibilities, Practices*, 46).

- "... who in the days of his flesh (*sarx*)"[6] (Heb 5:7).
- "Every spirit that acknowledges that Jesus Christ has come in the flesh (*sarx*) is from God. And every sprit that does not acknowledge that Jesus Christ is come in the flesh (*sarx*) is not of God" (1 John 4:2–3).
- "For many deceivers have gone out into the world, those who do not confess the coming of Jesus Christ in the flesh (*sarx*)" (2 John 7).

This is the plain teaching of the New Testament. However, the Greek term *sarx* also is used to indicate the worldly environment of sinful "flesh."[7] The point for us is that Jesus lived his sinless life in the midst of a sinful pluralistic culture, and so his teaching and modeling is not abstract but concrete and similar to twenty-first century post-Christian business life. There is nothing heavenly about his parables or his metaphors or his life.[8]

Luke emphasizes the importance of observing Jesus in his day-to-day activities when he notes that the replacement discussion for Judas Iscariot must include the fact that the new man must have been with Jesus the "whole time he went in and out among us" (Acts 1:21). The witnessing of how Jesus lived his life was important for the selection of

---

6. *Os in tas hemerai tas sarkos autou.*

7. Gal 4:29.

8. I suggest the following translation of *sarx* is preferred for our purposes: John 1:14, "The Word of God became *flesh (sarx)* and lived for a while among us. We have seen his glory, the glory of the one and only Son, who came from the Father, full of grace and truth." This is a good translation. Hebrews 5:7, "During the days of Jesus' *life on earth*" should be the Greek literal, "Who in the *days of his flesh (sarx)* . . ." "Behind [Heb 5:7–10] lies the idea of the high priest in the Old Testament liturgy who bore on his shoulders and breasts the names of the twelve tribes of Israel, who had them written on his heart, as he entered within the veil of the holy of holies with the blood of sacrifices in order to intercede for them . . . Of course, Jesus' high priesthood was not a temporary measure like Aaron's, nor was it in symbol or ceremony that he fulfilled his liturgy. He fulfilled it in this very existence and flesh" (Torrance, *Incarnation*, 133). First John 4:2–3, "that does not acknowledge Jesus is *from God*" should be the Greek literal "that does not acknowledge that Jesus Christ is *come in the flesh (sarx)* is from God." Second John 7, "Many deceivers, who do not acknowledge Jesus Christ as coming *in the flesh*, have gone out into the world." A good translation. In sum, the customary translation of *sarx* as "life on earth" or "from God" in these verses drains the power out of Jesus' human testimony by diverting our gaze away from the rough and tumble of the Lord's life in the midst of a "fleshly" environment to theological abstraction. *Sarx* is a powerful word and is not used casually by the writers of the New Testament.

Matthias: "The continuity of exposure to Jesus is central to the special role of the apostles."[9]

> That which was from the beginning, which we have heard, which we have seen with our eyes, which we have looked at and our hands have touched–this we proclaim concerning the Word of life. The life appeared; we have seen it and testify to it, and we proclaim to you the eternal life, which was with the Father and has appeared to us. We proclaim to you what we have seen and heard, so that you also may have fellowship with us. (1 John 1:1–3)

Thus, in addition to being the Savior and the Paraclete,[10] Jesus was also the chief manager, as he provides the perfect observable paradigm for a Christian businessman's lifestyle in today's post-Christian culture. Christian managers are advised to follow the pattern of Jesus in dealing with their coworkers,[11] their suppliers, their customers, their competitors, and their community.

A truly biblical approach to managing one's business will be incarnational in the pattern of the Savior in that it will be ambiguous to what might be customarily expected of a Christian in the first part of the twenty-first century. B. B. Warfield (1851–1921), commenting on Phil 2:5–8 in the first part of the twentieth century, wrote, "The peculiarity of our passage is only that it takes us back of Christ's earthly life and bids us imitate Him in the great act of His incarnation itself."[12]

Our imitation of the incarnational lifestyle,[13] as it relates to business management, is the point of this book. Or putting it in the vernacular, "What would Jesus do as the manager of a business?"

---

9. Bock, *Acts*, 88. In the same vein, Psalm 105:23 refers to Joseph as teaching through his lifestyle as well as his words.

10. John 14:16; 1 John 2:1–2; *paracletos* = helper, advocate, intercessor, one who comes alongside.

11. The New Testament has numerous passages specifically dealing with the intricate relationship between employer/manager and employee/coworker: Eph 6:5–9; Col 3:22–25; 1 Tim 6:1–2; Titus 2:9–10; 1 Pet 2:18.

12. Warfield, *The Person and Work of Christ*, 564.

13. The so-called *kenosis* passage; cf. a Kempis, *Imitation of Christ*. In Book Three, Jesus advises that all is not lost when the result is not as planned; when one thinks that all is lost, it is then that victory is close at hand. Jesus says not to react to a difficulty as if there were no hope of being freed from it.

The Lord's lifestyle was one of ambiguity,[14] forcing the Christian business manager to be humble about following Jesus. Scriptures teach that paradox[15] is interwoven into Christianity;[16] thus, modesty is required and the notion that we can know God's will for certain in our business practices is fraught with peril.[17] Richard Niebuhr (1894–1962) famously argued that there are five answers to the Christian's question of how to interact with the surrounding culture. One of those answers, "Christ and culture in paradox," fairly accurately describes the modern biblical Christian business manager. There is much in Niebuhr's remarkable book (especially his chapter on paradox) to commend reading, but suffice it to quote a couple of pertinent sentences on the paradox of the Christian life: "[The Christian business manager] is under law, and yet not under law but grace; he is sinner, and yet righteous; he believes as a doubter; he has assurance of salvation, yet walks along with the knife-edge of insecurity. In Christ all things have become new and yet everything remains as it was from the beginning. God has revealed Himself in Christ but hidden Himself in His revelation; the believer knows the One in whom he has believed yet walks by faith not sight."[18]

Jesus in "the days of his flesh" unambiguously claimed to be Yahweh. He claimed all the power, all the majesty, and all the attributes of the divine Godhead: "I and the Father are one" (John 10:30).[19] Hardly the claims of a vulnerable human lamb of God. And yet, Scriptures teach that Jesus engaged in a concealed ministry which he selectively revealed to those whom he wished, while to others his life appeared a bundle of ambiguities which continued to confuse those around Jesus, causing them to ask, "Who is this man"? (Luke 5:21).

When I started on this book the thought that it might be a business antidote to a recurrent Marxism[20] was far from my mind. But in the last

---

14. Cf. John 10:24.

15. Clark has colorfully referred to neoorthodoxy paradox as a "charley-horse between the ears" (Douma, *The Presbyterian Philosopher*, 127).

16. Cf. Matt 16:25.

17. Cf. Isa 55:8–9.

18. Niebuhr, *Christ and Culture*, 157.

19. "I give [my sheep] eternal life, and they shall never perish; no one can snatch them out of my hand" (John 10:28). "Anyone who has seen me has seen the Father" (John 14:9); "Believe me when I say that I am in the Father and the Father is in me" (John 14:11).;"You may ask me for anything in my name, and I will do it" (John 14:14).

20. For Marx (1818–83), throughout history there has been a conflict between

couple of years the silly and destructive affection for a sanitized Marxism has become the rage (literally) of the anti-business left. Unlike Jesus, Marx didn't like managers and argued that they should be eliminated from the production cycle. Clearly that is nonsense, because even in a worker's paradise someone is needed to be sure that the work is done. This book has turned out to be more political than I anticipated. It is now an anti-Marxist biblical defense of the managerial class.

But it is not only in his lifestyle but in his teaching that Jesus provides guidance. In various parables Jesus showed he knew how to deal justly and effectively with all individuals, whatever their belief system or social position. At one point, Mark tells us that Jesus usually spoke in parables.[21] He was a storyteller.[22] He taught "many things" to many peo-

---

two commercial classes of people: managers ("bourgeoisie") and the workers ("proletariat"). This clash is particularly violent under modern capitalism. The relations of these two groups to each other rest upon a fundamental contradiction, namely, that although both groups participate in the act of production, the distribution of the fruits of production does not correspond to the contribution made by each group. The products created by worker labor can be sold for more than it costs to hire the worker labor force. Marx agreed with Locke's (1632–1704) view of the "labor theory of value," that is, the value of the product is created by the amount of worker labor put into it. From this point of view, since the product of worker labor could be sold for more than the price of that labor, the non-worker manager would then reap the difference, which Marx called "surplus value" but the manager called "profit." The existence of this so-called "surplus value" or "profit" constituted the contradiction in the capitalistic system for Marx and created what he called the dehumanizing "alienation of labor" for the worker. As early as biblical times, we are seen as alienated from God through the fall of Adam and Eve. In a legal sense, "alienation" means "selling" or "giving" something away, or as Kant (1724–1804) says, "the transference of one's property to someone else is its alienation" (Kant, *Metaphysical Elements of Justice*, 72). In the course of time almost everything became a sellable object. Kant spoke of the process by which a person could be used as a thing.

21. Mark 4:34.

22. "The parables of Jesus are not—at any rate primarily—literary productions, nor is it their object to lay down general maxims ('no one would crucify a teacher who told pleasant stories to enforce prudential morality') but each of them was uttered in an actual situation of the life of Jesus, at a particular and often unforeseen point. Moreover, as we shall see, they were mostly concerned with a situation of conflict— with justification, defense, attack, and even challenge. For the most part, though not exclusively, they are weapons of controversy. Every one of them calls for an answer on the spot. The recognition of this fact indicates the nature of our task. Jesus spoke to men of flesh and blood; he addressed himself to the situation of the moment. Each of his parables has a definite historical setting, Hence, to recover that is the task before us. What did Jesus intend to say at this or that particular moment?" (Jeremias, *The Parables of Jesus*, 21–22).

ple.²³ And so we can take his parabolic teaching and apply it to business management with great profit because it is practical and common.²⁴

In his parables,²⁵ Jesus shows his remarkable sensitivity to human motivation and management. He shows a keen understanding of delegation, of a reward system, of a feedback loop, of managerial relations and prerogatives, of workplace hypocrisy, of separating an employee from his job (firing),²⁶ etc. Studying the Bible is a course in godly and productive organizational management. There is absolutely nothing mystical or other-worldly about the management principles taught by Jesus. In fact, any recognized authority in organizational management or human resource management, secular or religious, will advocate, probably unconsciously, these prudent biblical principles taught by Jesus.²⁷

In the rest of the book, I will bear down on the biblical material on business management itself. There will be no attempt to defend or attack economic systems or philosophies. I will not be noting the merits of capitalism *vis-a-vis* socialism. I embrace capitalism. Nor will I be directly addressing myself to business ethics and vocation. Those important matters will be left to other authors. Obviously, management activities consist of a whole cloth, and so economics, ethics, and vocation will be touched upon, but my primary thrust will continue to be the efficacious management of the resources a Christian businessperson has at his/her disposal in order to be a profitable and, at the same time, faithful Christian manager.

The etymology of the word "management" stems from the French word *manege*, which is a word meaning "leading"²⁸ or "household."²⁹ "Manager," "administrator," "leader," "shepherd," "overseer," "guide" are interchangeable terms, and I will treat them as such. I will make the case that a good manager is a good administrator, a good leader, a good shepherd, and a good guide.³⁰

---

23. Mark 4:2.

24. The same can be said for Paul's teaching as well since he spoke about "everyday life" (Gal 3:15).

25. Cf. the unmerciful servant, Matt 13:21–35; the workers in the vineyard, Matt 20:21–35; the stewardship of the ten minas, Luke 19:11–27; and the stewardship of the talents, Matt 25:14–30.

26. Cf. Matt 7:17–20.

27. Pss 45:1; 119:54.

28. *Mener* = "to lead."

29. *Menagerie* = domestic animal administration.

30. Unlike the de Mirabeau (1749–91) who reputedly said, "There goes the mob,

I will be arguing that a business organization is a community formed around a mission.[31] The manager's primary purpose is to create and sustain a working environment in which the business can carry out its mission effectively and profitably. In doing so, the manager must provide the right atmosphere, the necessary resources and the eliminating of problems so that the workers can carry out their responsibilities in peace, security and enjoyment. The manager is responsible to promote a sense of community where civility, respect, mutual encouragement, shared values, a sense responsibility, trust, creativity, fairness and communication transparency among a diverse workplace group of people is manifest. Indeed, transparency in communication within an organization is the natural corollary of mutual respect and concern between the manager and the workers.

Secular authors have also offered sound advice for the Christian business manager. The secular business world has defined "management" in various ways, using simple or complex formulas,[32] but I will turn to

---

and I must follow them for I am their leader." Or maybe it was Rollin (1807–74). Canadian management scholar Mintzberg summarized the roles of the modern manager as being: 1. extremely busy, 2. working long hours, 3. fighting for time with coworkers, 4. consumed with fragmented responsibilities, 5. under the time clock, 6. non-specialized, 7. anti-intellectual. Mintzberg wrote, "Superficiality is an occupational hazard of the manager's job . . . The manager . . . prefers brevity and interruption in his work. He becomes conditioned by his workload" (Mintzberg, *The Nature of Managerial Work*, 51–52).

31. The concept of community for a business organization is important and a vanishing notion. See Putnam, *Bowling Alone: The Collapse and Revival of American Community*.

32. The Real Estate Brokerage Council defines "management" simply as "Getting things done through people, time, money, and systems." (Real Estate Brokerage Council, "How to Manage a Real Estate Office Profitably"). This seems to touch all the aspects of a daily management routine without going into great detail, but it doesn't address any obligation a manager may have to the people with whom that manager works. The definition is too instrumental. A popular college dictionary of economics gives the classic (and sterile) definition of "management": "Often considered one of the factors of production. It involves the organization and coordination of the other factors—land, labor, and capital—for maximum efficiency in production" (Sloan and Zurcher, *A Dictionary of Economics*, 205). In a standard college textbook on management, "management" is more properly defined as: "The process of managing is the human process of visualizing the future, applied to a collection of individual humans in an organization. Human behavior, human decisions, human relations, and human dreams are at the core. We can hope to comprehend management only by understanding people" (Webber, Morgan, and Browne, *Management: Basic Elements of Managing Organizations*, 5). Geneen (1910–97), the hard-driving business executive who turned

Introduction xxxi

a representative sample of authorities. The premier management ideologue[33] in the western world is still the late Peter Drucker (1909–2005), the Austrian-born, European-educated, American resident who *Forbes* called "the founder of modern management."[34] Drucker wrote extensively on management challenges, theory and responsibilities. It is difficult to pick out one succinct definition for "management" from all his writings, but perhaps his definition can best be summarized in the following words from his magnum opus:

> [Managing] is responsibility for contribution. Function, rather than power, has to be the distinctive criterion and the organizing principle.[35]

Drucker argued that management is first task-oriented and only secondarily definitional. Without specific tasks and functions delineated, there is no management in operation. Deploying his penchant for lists, Drucker defines what functions exist that comprise a management paradigm, and then posits three main functions which constitute the management process:

1. To chart the specific purpose and mission and social function of an organization.[36]
2. To make work productive and the worker an achiever.
3. To manage the social impacts and the social responsibilities of the enterprise.[37]

We have all this advice in the pages of the Bible and in the life of Jesus. As we see the gift of management, the science of management and

ITT into a world-wide industrial powerhouse in the 1960s, defined "managing" as "achieving whatever you commit yourself to ... Good management is when one action fails, you try another, and another until you achieve your goal" (Geneen, *Managing*, 111).

33. There are many newer books on management and leadership. Two of the most prominent are *Good to Great* by Collins and *Leaders Eat Last* by Sinek.

34. Denning, "Best of Peter Drucker." Many management scholars argue that Frederick W. Taylor (1856–1915) with his 1915 book *The Principles of Scientific Management* is the "father of management science." Taylor's basic argument was that there was one best way to perform work. If a task can be specified, then there must be one best way to specify the causal link between means and end.

35. Drucker, *Management: Tasks, Responsibilities, Practices*, 394.

36. The word "mission" comes from the Latin *mittere*, meaning "to send."

37. Drucker, *Management: Tasks, Responsibilities, Practices*, 40–41.

the art of management—all from an incarnations approach—we are able to touch on all the significant areas of application for any Christian manager in the workplace.[38]

Besides, Jesus loved business managers.

While I will be focusing on the management of a small business, everything that is proposed can be applied to any organization in which there is management. I argue that what I call "the theology of ambiguity"[39] can be profitably used by anybody who manages people.

38. Peter Drucker wrote, "Organizing . . . deals with human beings, and therefore stands under the principle of justice and requires integrity" (Drucker, *Management: Tasks, Responsibilities, Practices*, 401). Phil Vischer, founder of Veggie Tales, emphasized that business leaders through their personal character, values, and vision set the tone for the organization for which they work (Vischer, *Me, Myself and Bob*, 135–149). Warren Buffet once wrote, "The attitude and actions of the CEO and other officers of companies are what determine corporate conduct, good or bad" (Cathy, *How Did You Do It, Truett?*, 50).

39. I am familiar with the fact that John Murray once called the neo-orthodoxy of Barth, Torrance, Niebuhr, et al., the "theology of ambiguity," but that is not at all what I mean to say when I repeatedly use the term "ambiguity." Cf. Murray, "The Adamic Administration," in *Collected Writings of John Murray*, vol. 2. Note Page, *Ambiguity and the Presence of God*. One is tempted to use the term "religious" to refer to the unambiguous approach to management. When I use the term "religious," I am referring to that rather long definition of "religion" given by Vernon Grounds in reference to Dietrich Bonhoeffer's preferred "religionless Christianity." Per Vernon Grounds, a "religious" approach to the marketplace is a specific approach held by one who believes, wittingly or unwittingly, that "religion" is a matter of "first . . . speculative metaphysics . . . Second, it is individualistic or privatistic; it concerns itself almost exclusively with inwardness, the subjective, the emotional, and the moralistic. Third, religion, limited as a rule to the 'spiritual,' the other-worldly, the post-temporal dimensions of human experience, is segmented. It does not embrace the whole man and all of life; it does not demand a total response from its devotees. Fourth, religion tends to be magical, viewing God as a *deus ex machina* who intervenes in moments of crisis, answering prayer, solving problems, providing miraculous escape-hatches for an elect in-group. It thus likewise tends to minimize man's responsibility and discourages his self-activity, inculcating a childish dependency hard to distinguish from slavish servility. Finally, religion with its in-group of the elect invariably fosters an attitude of pharisaic superiority. It assumes an aristocracy of true believers separate from the lost world except for occasional evangelistic forays into that God-forsaken territory" (Grounds, "Pacesetters for the Radical Theologians of the 60s and 70s," 263). *Theological Dictionary of the New Testament* maintains that the Greek word *threskos*, translated "religion" or "worship" in the Bible, has both good and bad connotations depending on the context of its usage. Clearly, it does not necessarily refer to Godly worship. In a footnote, Schmidt states, "It was perhaps the only word which could express the general concept of religion in the objective sense, so that neither Israel nor the Christian Church had any need to give it a specific meaning, and yet which could also express the concept of perverted religion. The central clause in this judgment discloses a sound insight into

Introduction

In the 1990s Robert Greenleaf, a nonbeliever, published a couple of books on "servant leadership" which took (and still take) the business community by storm.[40] He argued that an effective manager seeks first to be a servant of his coworkers, and if that is accomplished then the manager can aspire to be a leader. But servanthood comes first, and only then leadership. In other words, good management is focused on service to the employees and not on taking care of the manager's needs and aspiration and goals. Greenleaf argued that a manager is attentive to workers' needs, empowering them to accomplish their goals and a commitment to build a business community.

A personal experience may illustrate my drift. For years I owned one of the oldest real estate companies in central Washington state. My father owned it before me, and his partner and his father owned it before

---

the facts from the standpoint of biblical theology" (Schmidt, "Threskos"). In the New Testament, the word *threskos* appears five times, two of them in a negative context. *Threskos* does not appear in the LXX, but in the Apocrypha we see it in Wisdom of Solomon 11:16; 14:16, 18, 27, always in reference to false worship; see also Acts 26:5 and Colossians 2:18. In Acts 26:5, "They have known me for a long time and can testify, if they are willing, that according to the strictest sect of our religion (*threskos*), I lived as a Pharisee." Paul is bragging about his devotion to his old religion, meaning, among other things, his commitment to the external observance of Jewish laws. Paul's use of the term to describe him is appropriate since the Pharisees were the most scrupulous adherents to the "strict" outward observance of the law (Acts 22:3). In Colossians 2:18 we see Paul warning against worshipping angels (In Rev 22:8–9, the angels themselves repudiate the worship of them and point to the true God): "Do not let anyone who delights in false humility and the worship (*threskos*) of angels disqualify you for the prize. Such a person goes into detail about what he has seen, and his unspiritual mind puffs him up with idle notions." Lightfoot, commenting on the use of *threskos* in this Colossians verse, states, "The word refers properly to the external rites of religion, and so gets to signify an over-scrupulous devotion to external forms . . . Indeed, generally the usage of [*threskos*] exhibits a tendency to a bad sense" (Lightfoot, *St. Paul's Epistle to the Colossians and to Philemon*, 196). Positively, in James 1:26–27, *threskos* is used three times to connote a "pure" religion that is evidenced by a ministry of mercy and justice, and not external ceremonial observations. Richard Trench has a marvelous discussion of *threskos* as it is used in this James passage: "*Threskos* is predominately the ceremonial service of religion, of her whom Lord Brooke has so grandly named 'mother of form and fear'—the external framework or body of which *eusebia* (devout) is the informing soul" (Trench, *Synonyms of the New Testament*, 175). Some commentators have argued that the worshipping of angels was part of a pagan philosophy at Colossae. Colossian worshippers believed that angels determined the course of the events in a man's life, and so they submitted to an angelic cult by performing prescribed acts and by fulfilling certain outward religious rites and regulations. It is a form of legalism. All this to ward off disaster and ensure prosperity.

40. Greenleaf, *The Servant as Leader*; Greenleaf, *The Power of Servant Leadership*.

him. During my time as owner/broker of Thayer-Case Realtors I had several agents who were very successful. They made more money than I did and thus in some respects they were the real leaders of the company. Other agents looked to them for advice, modeling, and encouragement. I, as the owner, consulted with them before any major decisions were made. I needed their buy-in. I still managed the operation, and on the letterhead my name came first, but these high-achieving agents led the organization.

1

Jesus on Management in the Gospels

SCRIPTURE TEACHES THAT THE business manager is to emulate that ambiguous and vulnerable incarnational lifestyle of the Savior in management responsibilities. It is at this point that some uncertainty has arisen in the thinking of the church, for Jesus is not generally looked upon as a modeling big brother for Christians.[1] Rather, the church has been too ready to see Jesus primarily as the "Lamb of God slain for our sins."[2] It might be a natural reaction and pushback to theological liberalism, but that is not the complete, scriptural view of Jesus. Quite the contrary, the exampling life of Jesus is part of what the Bible teaches about our Lord without lessening the emphasis and focus on his redemptive work. Jesus while in the "days of his flesh" was, in fact, the ideal example after which we are to pattern our management obligations. John Calvin called Christ "the one exemplar of right action"[3] and Charles Hodge called Jesus "the ultimate standard."[4]

We need to highlight this temporal, ambiguous modeling aspect of the life of the Redeemer while not detracting from the eternal union with Christians and the glorification of Christians by virtue of our Lord's life, death, and resurrection. The notion of ambiguity is important because

---

1. Despite Rom 8:15–17, 29, and several other passages.

2. John 1:29; such reputable theologians as Berkouwer flatly state, "The fact that Christ did not come to be an ideal example to us is the common confession of the Church" (Berkouwer, *Person of Christ*, 341).

3. Calvin, *The First Epistle of Paul the Apostle to the Corinthians*, 226.

4. Hodge, *Exposition of the First Epistle to the Corinthians*, 226.

that is the pluralistic environment in which Christian business managers find themselves in the current post-Christian age. Thus, the extraordinary importance of the exemplary life of Jesus. From beginning to end the Scriptures teach we are to be like him. John 15:4–5 provides the theological root of our union with him: "Remain in me, and I will remain in you. No branch can bear fruit by itself; it must remain in the vine. Neither can you bear fruit unless you remain in me. I am the vine; you are the branches."

> While Jesus was having dinner at Matthew's [Levi's] house many tax collectors and sinners came and ate with him and his disciples. When the Pharisees saw this, they asked his disciples, "Why does your teacher eat with tax collectors and sinners?" On hearing this Jesus said, ". . . But go and learn what this means: 'I desire mercy not sacrifice.'" (Matt 9:10–13)[5]

Jesus was not afraid to socialize with religious outcasts which offended the religious officials, those very people who should have formed the vanguard and leadership for his spiritual movement and the realization of his religious goals. But that was not his strategy, which was to go to anyone who would receive him.[6] Helmut Thielicke reminds us that part of the "supreme condescension of his majesty" is that Jesus declares his solidarity with publicans and sinners and censors the self-righteous Pharisees.[7] He is the perfect example for a business manager who competes in the secular marketplace. Jesus knew no socio-religio-economic barriers since he did, in fact, recline with seeking and faithful Pharisees. He socialized with the religious aristocracy, the religious powerbrokers, when they would have him. Dinner with the Pharisees seemed to be a habit with Jesus.[8] Jesus treated the Pharisee Simon as he did toll collectors and sinners.[9] He did not have a double standard. Jesus did not spurn

---

5. Ridderbos noted on this verse, "The word 'sinners' here, like 'tax collectors,' refers to people who ignored the religious decrees of the Pharisees [the day of the banquet probably was a fast day, v. 14]; their conduct in general caused legalistic Jews to take a dim view of them. Such were the people with whom Jesus and his disciples shared this meal" (Ridderbos, *Matthew*, 182).

6. Cf. Matt 10:40.

7. Thielicke, *Evangelical Faith*, 3.373; Matt 23.

8. Cf. Luke 11:37; 14:1.

9. "Now one of the Pharisees [Simon] invited Jesus to have dinner with him, so he went to the Pharisee's house and reclined at the table" (Luke 7:36). Fitzmyer, *Gospel According to Luke I-IX*, 688.

socializing with anyone on political, economic, or religious grounds. He was always ready to present himself in person to whomever would receive him. This speaks to the problem of man-made barriers between manager and managed such as salaries, benefits, office accommodations, work schedules, and so forth, to say nothing of the relationship between the Christian manager and customers, suppliers, competitors, and trade associations.[10]

In fact, there are relationships to those outside the kingdom that need to be entered for the sake of justice and peace on earth and glory to God in the heavens.[11] If Scripture does not prohibit the Christian manager from socializing with folks, he or she should not be timid in seeking that social ground to be claimed as occupied territory for the incarnational presence.[12]

Francis Schaeffer makes a great deal of this personal solidarity between all humankind when he discusses the personality of God. Schaeffer calls this solidarity the "mannishness of man," meaning that a personal God has created personal beings in his image to have personality and thus a meaningful communication and fellowship with him. This personal human being is uniquely different from all other creation and is expressed when the personal creator God came to earth as the preeminent expression of humanity's "mannishness" in Jesus. Hence, there is common ground between all humans in order to enjoy bearing God's image and his common grace through rational communication, creative expression, and loving companionship with each other.[13]

---

10. Later, because of the incarnate inclusivity, Paul writes that all barriers are broken down, and there are no religious, cultural, racial, or social borders to cross any longer. "Here there is no Greek or Jew, circumcised or uncircumcised, barbarian, Scythian, slave or free, but Christ is all, and is in all" (Col 3:11); "For there is no difference between Jew and Gentile, the same Lord is Lord of all and richly blessed all who call on him" (Rom 10:12); "There is neither Jew nor Greek, slave nor free, male nor female, for you are all one in Christ Jesus" (Gal 3:29).

11. Cf. Jer 29:4–8; 1 Pet 2:12–17; Gen 18:22–33; Isa 65:8; Ezek 22:30.

12. In *Mere Christianity* Lewis called the world "enemy-occupied territory" (Lewis, Mere Chrsitianity, 46).

13. Schaeffer, *Genesis in Time and Space*. Barth has written, "Solidarity with the world means full commitment to it, unreserved participation in its situation, in the promise given it by creation, in its responsibility for the arrogance, sloth, and falsehood which reign within it, in its suffering under the resultant distress, but primarily and supremely in the free grace of God demonstrated and addressed to it in Jesus Christ, and therefore in its hope" (Barth, *Church Dogmatics*, IV/3:2). Jesus prayed for this solidarity between believers and the world in John 17. At one point, he prayed that

> I am sending you out like sheep among wolves. Therefore, be as shrewd as snakes and as innocent as doves. But be on guard against men. (Matt 10:16–17)

The sending of the managers by Jesus the manager into the marketplace should bring both positive and negative reactions. Positively, the sending should bring comfort because it is Jesus who anoints the Christian manager. Negatively, the manager is being sent into a hostile environment where he or she is to demonstrate intellectual acumen or keenness in the midst of evil. This managerial acumen can be manifest in several ways:

- Jesus the manager wanted his twelve managers to develop managerial insight into the organization's environment.

- Jesus the manager wanted his twelve managers to develop managerial wisdom to do the right thing, at the right time, in the right place, and in the right manner.

- Jesus the manager wanted his twelve managers to develop managerial insight to discover the best means to achieve the mission of the organization.

Christians may be one "as we are one. I in them and you in me. May they be brought to complete unity to let the world know that you sent me" (John 17:22–23). The unity, the solidarity, among Christians and the world, which is founded on Christ's love, will result then in the world believing that God sent Jesus and that God first loves all those who repent and love his incarnate Son. Bonhoeffer comments, "There is no place to which the Christian can withdraw from the world, whether it be outwardly or in the sphere of the inner life" (Bonhoeffer, *Ethics*, 200). The test for truth for Barth in a Christian business manager's life is to what extent "the world" sees Jesus in that manager's life and not necessarily what other Christians see in that manager (cf. John 13:35; 1 John 4:7–21)! The character of the incarnate God simultaneously being above everything and in everything, which leads to a secular Messiah or a heavenly Jesus in which the natural and the supernatural are distinctive but not always separable, is advanced by J. G. Hamann in *Writings on Philosohpy and Language*, who believed that the Christian life was a life of unity, wholeness, experience, and reason, and that God spoke existentially as he illuminated his inscripturated word. In like vein, Bonhoeffer 150 years later writes of a "religionless Christianity," of which the meaning is somewhat unclear. At one point he writes that we should not speak metaphysically or individualistically, but rather we should concentrate on "righteousness and the kingdom of God on earth" because they are the focus of everything in the Scripture (Bonhoeffer, *Letters and Papers from Prison*, 285–86; cf. Rom 3:24).

- Jesus the manager wanted his twelve managers to develop managerial wisdom to know how current decisions will affect the future of the organization.

- Jesus the manager wanted his twelve managers to develop managerial sanctified knowledge to know how current decisions will please God.

While all this shrewdness is going on, the manager must understand that the keenness enjoined never implies compromise with evil because the manager must be as innocent or guileless as a dove. This keenness is demonstrated by Paul in Acts 23:6–8 and the dispute between the Pharisees and the Sadducees, and the innocence of Paul is seen in Acts 24:16. Jesus tells his managers to beware of evil persons who have bad intentions for the organization. The manager should not naively trust all people or unnecessarily make people angry. The manager is not to give people a reason to hate the organization—hate will come naturally if the organization pleases God.

Following Matthew 5:44–48 as God gives sun and rain on non-Christians as well as Christians, the Christian manager is to do good things for "all people" without boundaries. This command may very well mean doing good for the common welfare and not specific individuals. Clearly, doing good for "the family of believers" means doing good things for individual Christians as the manager has the time and the opportunity. But loving care and assistance are to be extended to non-Christians as well. Special care and support are to be extended to Christians who may not have the public support from non-Christian organizations or a hostile government. Christians are to be treated like family members because they are members of the same spiritual family.[14]

---

14. Cf. John 13:34–35; Rom 12:9; Eph 1:15; Phil 2:2; see 1 Macc 12:10, 17; 4 Macc 9:23; 10:3, 15 for the Jewish sense of community of faith. A note on limited liability for the business manager in the spiritual family: The business organization is not a family or a congregation of believers, but rather a select community or organization with limited liability and responsibilities because of its limited mission to serve a customer base and thus to employ workers for that sole purpose, and not carry on eleemosynary endeavors. "The next day he took out two silver coins and gave them to the innkeeper. 'Look after him,' he said, 'and when I return, I will reimburse you for any extra expense you may have'" (Luke 10:35). We see limited liability in the parable of the good Samaritan (Luke 10:25–37), where the Samaritan businessman loved his Jewish neighbor by making a one-time gift of "two silver coins" and "any extra expenses" (Luke 10:35) incurred by the innkeeper for the care of the victim. But there was no continuing obligation for the care of the robbed man. The Samaritan did the loving thing at the point

So, while there must be the continued effort on the part of the Christian business manager to follow the example of Jesus the manager by reflecting an incarnational presence in the world, there should at the same time be the understanding that the world will perceive that Christian presence ambiguously and therefore react inconsistently with either rejection or acceptance or apathy, as it did to Jesus during the "days of his flesh," because "[Christians managers] are not of the world, even as I am not of the world" (John 17:16).[15]

> When evening came, the owner[16] of the vineyard said to his foreman, "Call the workers and pay them their wages, beginning with the last ones hired and going on to the first." (Matt 20:8)

In Matthew 20:1–16, the parable of the workers in the vineyard, we have a wonderful workplace parable. It is also an example of Jesus' artistic management. In this parable, the manager[17] hired unemployed workers

---

of personal contact, establishing for a moment the neighbor relationship. But that caring personal obligation ceased at the moment of departure. Now, the Samaritan did return to the inn as a good "Christian," but that was for the limited purpose of clearing up any debt incurred by the victim in this one incident (Luke 10:30). A racial point to be made here is that this parable also demonstrated the love of one's enemies that is required of all Christians since the businessman was a Samaritan and thus a member of a despised race of half-breeds in the eyes of the Jews ("priest," "Levite," "robbers") at the time. The bigotry of the Jewish church is on full display in this awkward parable. See the discussion of this parable in Bailey, *Poet and Peasant and Through Peasant Eyes*, 48–49. "'But so that you may know that the Son of Man has authority on earth to forgive sins' . . . Then he said to the paralytic, 'Get up, take your mat and go home.' And the man got up and went home" (Matt 9:6–7). Another incident of limited mission is Jesus' healing of the paralytic in Matthew 9:1–8. Jesus heals the man, and rather than say "follow me" Jesus tells him to "take your mat and go home" (Matt 9:6), thus ending the personal, one-on-one, relationship with the man. The point is that Jesus did not feel compelled to prolong every loving relationship he started. The Christian manager has a lifelong obligation for stewardship of the resources God provides, and these resources invariably will include people. But the Christian manager does not have a life-long, continual obligation of care and responsibility for the wellbeing of each employee she has ever managed.

15. Cf. Matt 10:22; John 15:18–25.

16. *Kurios* = master.

17. *Epitropos* = steward, foreman. "Joanna the wife of Chuza, the manager (*epitropos*) of Herod's household" (Luke 8:3). "He is subject to guardians [steward, *epitropos*] and trustees [stewards, managers, *oikonomos*] until the time set by his father" (Gal 4:2). This Greek word is translated "steward" or "guardian." It means someone who is literally caring for something. This Greek term is never employed in the Greek Old Testament (LXX). The word is a combination of "upon" (*epi*) and to "turn" (*trepo*). In Acts 26:12 and Galatians 4:2 the corresponding verb means to "delegate" or

at different times during the workday, promising to pay each worker a certain sum. As it turned out, it was the same sum for all the workers, regardless of time worked. When the first hired workers complained that they should get more because they worked longer, the manager responded,

> Partner,[18] I am not being unfair[19] to you. Didn't you agree to work for a denarius? Take your pay and go. I want to give the man who was hired last the same as I gave you. Don't I have the right to do what I want with my own money? Or are you envious because I am generous?[20] (Matt 20:13–15)

In this instructive parable of management-labor relations and wealth creation, we have a gracious, generous, and kind manager who hired the unemployed so that they could earn a day's wages even when they didn't earn it by a full day's work. And rather than being impressed by the manager's kindness to fellow workers who are more unfortunate than they, the first-hired workers complained that they were treated "unfairly" and that the manager should give them more by adjusting their wages to reflect a longer day's work. Despite the selfish and unappreciative attitude on the part of the first-hired (who were already gainfully employed) the

---

"commission." The usage suggests that the delegated one is a superior agent responsible for the completion of the duties delegated (as it is used in Attic Greek, Homer, Herodotus). The New Testament company followed the Old Testament company in organizing around managers to facilitate their worship, fellowship, military campaigns, and miscellaneous activities. Consistent with Old Testament usage, it has been suggested that Chuza managed the entire royal estate of Herod, just not his house (cf. Josephus, *Ant.* 18.6.6). Nothing much is known about Chuza except that for his name to be mentioned with Herod would indicate a responsible position in the government and probably a wealthy man since his wife was traveling to hear Jesus. We don't even know if Chuza was a Christian, but his wife was, and so, to hazard a guess, perhaps here is another believing manager who handled a multitude of duties for an unbelieving owner (Herod). Joanna wasn't the only member of a prominent political/economic New Testament family to follow Jesus. There were others: Manaen (Acts 13:1), Sergius Paulus (Acts 13:7, 12), and the political officials in Ephesus (Acts 19:31) were all part of this socially prominent group.

18. *Hetairos* = friend, comrade, companion. This is not necessarily a term of endearment like *philos*.

19. *Adikeo* = to do no wrong, damage, hurt.

20. *Agathos* = good, benevolent, useful, profitable.

manager responded with a patient and warm explanation: "Friend, I am being fair[21] to you. Can't I be overly generous to whom I want?"[22]

This is generous artistic business management at work:

- There was generosity in hiring and pay in the first place.[23]
- There was generosity in giving more than was "earned."[24]
- There was generosity with the repeated forays into the unemployment office for more unemployed workers.[25]
- There was generosity in the patient seeking of common agreement between the workers and the manager.[26]
- There was generosity in the wisdom with the absence of managerial demeaning and debilitating charity, but rather the uplifting element of required work for one's wages.[27]
- There was generosity in the transparent managerial communication.[28]
- Finally, there was generosity in the absence of anger and recrimination on the part of the falsely challenged manager as he responded to the workers' anger with kindness by calling them "friends."[29]

As we see the gift of management, the science of management, and the art of management—all from an incarnations approach—we are able to touch on all the significant areas of application for any Christian manager in the workplace. Jesus the manager demonstrated discernment throughout his earthly ministry.[30] While Jesus as the son of God knew the thoughts of all persons,[31] as the Son of Man he was not required to possess supernatural knowledge to know what people around him were thinking. Jesus' perception here is nothing more than being perceptive and

21. *Dike.*
22. Cf. Rushdoony, *Institute of Biblical Law*, and his discussion of wages, 504–10.
23. Matt 20:1–6.
24. Matt 20:12.
25. Matt 20:3, 5, 6.
26. "He agreed to pay them" (Matt 20:2).
27. Matt 20:3; *homo Faber* = man the fabricator, *homo Laborans* = man the worker.
28. "He replied to one of them," "am I not allowed" (Matt 20:13, 15).
29. Matt 20:13; *hetairos*. This is not a term of endearment but rather indicating common purpose and companionship.
30. Matt 4:18–22; Mark 10:35–44; Luke 9:28, 46–50.
31. Cf. Luke 4:23; 5:22; 6:8; 7:40; 9:47; 11:17.

sensitive to the reaction his words and action are causing.[32] We shouldn't lose sight of his keen "fleshly" sensitivity to his surroundings which gave him great wisdom and consequent kindness to his neighbors. Jesus not only exemplified a discerning manager,[33] but he also commanded that we use our God-given discernment.[34] The ability to manage a business in an incarnational fashion is a gift from God. No manager can please God if that manager does not prize the special gift of the position of manager and of the specific people in the organization:

- Jesus the manager tells us that management is a gift because of the opportunity afforded one to manage another person's stewardship and productivity.
- Jesus the manager tells us that management is a gift because of the supernatural power and wisdom needed to lovingly manage.
- Jesus the manager tells us that management is a gift of creational common grace, that all managers have a discerning mind that can, if properly employed, discern how to manage a business.
- Jesus the manager tells us that management is a gift of shepherding and guiding and edifying the persons that God places in the manager's care.

> Listen to another parable: There was a landowner who planted a vineyard. He put a wall around it, dug a winepress in it and built a watchtower. Then he rented the vineyard to some farmers and went away on a journey. (Matt 21:33)

---

32. This is not to be taken as a denial of Jesus' messianic consciousness, but only that the Lord needed to be discerning of what was going on. He needed to be spiritually in tune with his heavenly Father. There is the need to see this ability of Jesus as that supernatural quality of knowing the thoughts of all men (cf. Heb 4:13; Ps 139).

33. The discerning manager asks hard and big questions about the nature of the work being done by the organization. Questions like: Should we, as an organization, be doing this particular project? Should I, as manager, be overseeing this particular project? Should this project be redesigned and staff re-allocated? Should this project be completely dropped from the organization's mission? Does my management contribute to the flourishing of each of my coworkers? Does my management contribute to the common good of the community?

34. Matt 16:3, *diakrino* = discriminate, distinguish, judge; Luke 12:56, *dokimazo* = *diakrino;* in the Greek LXX in many places translated "teach" for decision-making purposes.

Note in the parable of the talents in Matt 21:33–44, Jesus the manager tells us the manager did all the preparation to make the business successful:

- The manager cultivated and planted a new vineyard.
- The manager protected the new vineyard from animals with a wall.
- The manager dug a winepress, ensuring that the grapes would be prepared for wine.
- The manager built a watchtower to protect against marauders.
- The manager leased the entire enterprise to people who knew what they were doing—farmers.

While it is not the focus of this book to discuss a theology of business organizations or to develop a theological rationale for the existence of business organizations, it is necessary to understand that a business organization has a definite calling in the kingdom of God and that managing a business organization must be as reflective of the incarnation management principles as managing the activities and ministry of a church or a parachurch organization. Jesus the manager tells us that managing a marketplace organization is every bit a ministerial function as managing First Presbyterian Church or Youth for Christ. It is biblical and profitable to approach the management of a small business using the same principles of the shepherding paradigm given by Jesus "in the days of his flesh."[35] Throughout the book I will be substituting the terms "organization," "company," "cohort," and even "corporation" for "church" in

---

35. In the marvelous Dickensian allegory *A Christmas Carol*, Ebenezer Scrooge is visited by the ghost of his dead partner, Jacob Marley. Marley is bound, manacled, tortured and remorseful that he cannot make amends for "life's opportunity misused." Scrooge cries out to Marley, "But you were always a good man of business, Jacob." "Business!," cried the Ghost [Marley], wringing its hands again, "mankind was my business. The common welfare was my business; charity, mercy, forbearance, and benevolence, were all my business. The dealings of my trade were but a drop of water in the comprehensive ocean of my business . . . Why did I walk through crowds of fellow-beings with my eyes turned down, and never raise them to that blessed star which led the wise men to a poor abode? Were there no poor homes to which its light would have conducted me!" (Dickens, *A Christmas Carol*). Calvin, in his magnum opus, wrote about the obligation of a Christian in business, or any other occupation for that matter: "Moreover, our mind must always have regard for the Lawgiver, that we may know that this rule [the eighth commandment: 'You shall not steal'] was established for our hearts as well as for our hands, in order that men may strive to protect and promote the wellbeing and interests of others" Calvin, *Institutes of the Christian Religion*, 1.411; cf. Calvin, *Institutes of the Christian Religion*, 1.408–11).

order to make the point that biblical principles of management can and should be applied to a non-ecclesiastical organization, like a business.

> "Teacher, which is the greatest commandment in the Law?" Jesus replied: "'Love the Lord your God with all your heart and with all your soul and with all your mind.' This is the first and greatest commandment. And the second is like it: 'Love your neighbor[36] as yourself.' All the law and the Prophets hang on these two commandments." (Matt 22:36–40)

I want to introduce a key *charismata* of the gift of management—love for the managed—as a gift from God. Loving our coworkers is simply too hard for us alone. This love does not mean the desire to hang out or socialize with an employee. Jesus the manager tells us that this love is a self-sacrificing devotion to the person's wellbeing and flourishing as a human. The Christian manager must continually pray for the love of Christ to be manifested in her actions so that the commandment "tend my sheep"[37] will be manifested. In the business organization there is no closer nor more important "neighbor" to the Christian manager than the coworkers that God has placed under the manager's care:

- The constant daily prayer of any incarnational manager must be "Lord, give me your love for the people you have placed under my management. Make me love them in your sacrificial way so that I might do the best for them."[38]

This exhortation to love may seem a self-evident Christian principle, yet it is a management lesson not often taught in books on management for the Christian. Incarnational love is the key to management harmony within an organization. That doesn't mean there won't be temporary friction within an organization,[39] but it does mean that the

---

36. *Plesion* = fellow man, indicating outward nearness or proximity. There need be no family or tribal affiliation but rather outward nearness.

37. John 21:17.

38. Cf. John 13:34–35; Jesus' example in John 15:12, "Love each other as I have loved you." Stearns, former CEO of World Vision and other national companies, writes, "Most leaders at least give lip service to wanting to help their coworkers develop their skills, grow their capabilities, and achieve greater success. But what if you as a leader first loved them and saw them as people made in the image of God as Christ calls you to do?" (Stearns, *Lead Like It Matters to God*, 75).

39. Acts 15:36–41; Paul and Barnabas separate but later, perhaps, reconcile, Col 4:10, or perhaps not, 2 Tim 4:11.

general atmosphere, attitude, and loving conduct of the manager will set the tone for the organization. And, as a result of the manager's attitude, the organization's atmosphere will be generally edifying for everyone. As one scholar notes, the Christian manager "speaks gently, asks questions, smiles, and drafts schedules for the workers that are fair and accommodate legitimate needs. They love their staff through small acts of kindness and by forgiving minor mistakes. They don't play favorites or disparage socially awkward workers."[40]

> Therefore, keep watch,[41] because you do not know on what day your Lord will come. But understand this: If the owner of the house had known at what time of night the thief was coming, he would have kept watch and would not have let his house be broken into. (Matt 24:42–43)[42]

The theme of this mini-parable is the return of Jesus. But the homespun language of the Lord tells a story of the watchful manager who is constantly surveilling the dangers. The manager is to be ready for the unexpected. When the one who wants to steal from the organization makes his move, the manager had better have the organization prepared and ready to fend off the challenger when he least expects it. Constant readiness is the byword for the discerning manager concerning the competition.[43] The manager will make this preparation in three ways:

- Being alert to individuals outside the organization.
- Avoiding false security and complacency.
- Staying awake.

> Again, it will be like a man going on a journey who called his servants and entrusted his property to them. (Matt 25:14)

Another gospel incarnational example of artistic management is given in the parable of the talents in Matthew 25:14–30. What the manager did was to go to his workers and give each one some responsibility

---

40. Doriani, *Work: Its Purpose, Dignity and Transformation*, 202.
41. *Gregoreo* = be awake, vigilant.
42. Cf. Matt 6:19–20; 12:29.
43. Collins and Porras write in *Built to Last*, 10, "Success and beating competitors comes to the visionary companies not so much as the end goal but as a residual result of relentlessly asking the question, 'How can we improve ourselves to do better tomorrow than we did today?'"

according to the manager's judgment on the gifts and graces ("talents") of each employee and on how well each worker would handle the specific responsibility given. Then, the manager left the workplace, having given the worker the freedom to be creative with the responsibility. The worker had the manager-given opportunity to use all the resources (internal and external) at the disposal of the worker to successfully accomplish the assigned task, with the implicit understanding that the task could be accomplished, and that the manager had the confident expectation that the worker was fully capable of accomplishing the assigned task. There was form and freedom in this Matthew 25 management parable.

> Be on guard! Be alert! You do not know when that time will come. It's like a man going away: He leaves his house in charge of his servants, each with his assigned tasks, and tells the one at the door to keep watch. Therefore, keep watch because you do not know when the owner of the house will come back—whether in the evening, or at midnight, or when the rooster crows, or at dawn. If he comes suddenly, do not let him find you sleeping. What I say to you, I say to everyone: "Watch!" (Mark 13:33–37)

In this short Markan parable the owner of the business ("house")[44] goes away for an indeterminate period of time. He instructs his employees to take care of business.[45] He delegates responsibilities and expects to find them all doing their jobs at the appropriate time—notice the four time intervals (evening, midnight, when the rooster crows, dawn).[46] Three times it is mentioned that no one knows when the employer will return, so everybody must be on their toes doing their job. Five times the employees are told to be alert and to watch:

- The point of all this repetition is that the Christian business manager is to watch over the business enterprise and urge the coworkers to be constantly diligent in doing their jobs.

> When you see a cloud rising in the west, immediately you say, "It's going to rain," and it does. And when the south wind blows, you say, "It's going to be hot," and it is. Hypocrites! You know

---

44. *Oikia* = family, household.

45. *Agrupneo* = to chase sleep, to be sleepless; to be watchful for those who are intent on doing something.

46. Mark 13:35.

how to interpret[47] the appearance of the earth and the sky. How is it that you don't know how to interpret[48] this present time?[49] Why don't you judge for yourselves what is right? (Luke 12:54–57)

Jesus the manager is reminding those assembled that they spend a great deal of attention watching the weather. There is nothing wrong with that, since we are dependent on the weather for our food, our livelihoods, our recreation—all God-given necessities and enjoyments of life. Our weather-watching activity is a gift from God. We "understand"[50] the weather patterns. We can make "right judgments" concerning the effects of observable weather "appearances."[51] We look to the sky, we make a prediction and act accordingly, and the prediction comes true because we correctly "understand" or "discern" or "interpret" the natural world. We base our lives, our behavior, and our income on what we perceive with our senses in the physical world around us. And that is the way God meant it to be. Jesus tells us we have the innate ability to think discerningly. We notice one event and we are able to draw a conclusion that another event will follow.[52] Our minds are so created that we are able to think causally; that is, if this particular event happens, then this particular event will follow.[53]

Jesus the manager now comes to the conclusion of his illustration, and his conclusion can be summarized by the Latin phrase *carpe diem*, "seize the day." Jesus says causal thinking is not only the way business

47. *Dokimazo*.

48. *Dokimazo* = prove, discern, distinguish. Rom 2:18; 12:21; 1 Cor 11:28.

49. The word translated "present time" (*kairon*) is a special Greek word meaning "season," "opportunity," "characteristics of an age." The normal Greek word translated "time" in the New Testament is *cronos*. The word used here is *kairon*, and it means not chronological time, but "features" or "qualities of an era." It is the *Zeitgeist*, the "spirit of an age," as the Germans would say. Jesus is telling his people to "scrutinize the spirit of your age" and make the appropriate decisions. GosThom 91: "You assess the look of the sky and the earth, but you have not recognized what is before you; you do not know how to assess this season."

50. *Dokimazein* = to test, prove, scrutinize. Jesus is saying, "Just like you look intently into the sky to see what the weather is going to be, look intently at my life, and look intently at your culture."

51. *Prosopon* = face, person, countenance.

52. We see clouds off the Mediterranean and we accurately predict rain, cf. 1 Kgs 18:44. We sense the sirocco wind from the southeast, cf. Hos 12:1. And we accurately predict heat, cf. Isa 49:10; Jer 4:11–12; *kauswn* = caustic, holocaust, scorching heat.

53. Cf. Prov 20:27; 1 Cor 2:11.

managers think, but also how they ought to think. In other words, business managers are to use God-given ability to think "discerningly," "judgingly," "discriminatingly," to think about "doing the right thing" in your business just like you think causally and "do the right thing" about the weather. You are so capable about intellectually understanding and interpreting the signs of the natural, physical world, and you correctly notice the regularity and predictability in the natural world, don't be dense about the hidden emotions and aspirations of coworkers and customers.

> The master[54] commended the dishonest manager[55] because he had acted shrewdly.[56] For the people of this world are more shrewd in dealing with their own kind than are the people of the light. I tell you, use worldly wealth to gain friends for yourselves, so that when it is gone, you will be welcomed into eternal dwellings. (Luke 16:8–9)

In the Luke 16 parable of the "shrewd"[57] manager, Jesus the manager is teaching that the world understands the economic and social benefit of prudential marketplace management of employees and the resultant good-will established in that organization. Note how this parable relates to a definition of *oikonomos*, which appears eight times in this single parable and which the ESV translates the occurrences as "manager,"[58] "management,"[59] or "servant."[60] What Jesus is teaching in this parable is not about a dishonest or fraudulent manager, but rather an incompetent manager. The manager is being fired not for stealing or thievery, but rather for mismanagement.

In Luke 16:1–2, Jesus the manager clearly states: "the manager was accused of wasting the rich man's possessions." "Wasting" is a Greek word[61] which means "to scatter" or "to disperse." In our context, we take it to mean "squander" or "mismanage."[62] The manager's action was

54. *Kurios*.
55. *Oikomonos* = steward.
56. *Phronimos*.
57. *Phronimotes* = wise, prudent, practical, shrewd, sensible, and not necessarily spiritual or intellectual.
58. Luke 16:1, 3, 6.
59. Luke 16:2–4.
60. Luke 16:13.
61. *Diaskorpizo*.
62. Cf. Luke 15:13; "Not long after that the younger son got together all he had, set off for a distant country, and there squandered (*diaskorpizo*) his wealth in wild living."

stupid, foolish, and wrong-headed, but it was not illegal or criminal. That is borne out by the fact that the rich man was preparing to only fire the manager ("you cannot be manager any longer") and not arrest him.[63] So, what we have in the first two verses of this parable is a manager who was accused of malfeasance or mismanagement of someone else's resources, but not an evil attempt to embezzle or defraud his entrustment for his personal gain. The result was probably the same, but the intention was not malevolent or illegal.[64] There is no hint that this manager was anything other than an undisciplined "wastrel" in his stewardship duties.[65] In Luke 12:46 the Lord tells us what happens to those managers who are truly malevolent: "He will cut him to pieces and assign him a place with the unbelievers." So far, we only have a manager who is being fired for incompetency, and nothing more.

In the next two verses (Luke 16:3-4), we see the manager not contesting the charge of his untrustworthiness, but rather, by default, admitting it. Furthermore, he began to look to the future so that he would have someplace else to go for work. And he needed a good job recommendation so that he would be "welcomed"[66] and not be a charity hire, or even worse, unemployable. The fired manager laments that he was too old for manual labor and too ashamed to beg.[67]

In Luke 16:5-7, we see what the manager did in order to engender the "welcome" mat for his job-hunting prospects. He discounted the outstanding debts to his rich boss in return for "quick" payment.[68] Only a non-businessman would miss the marketplace practice of getting quick payment for an outstanding debt at a reduced amount (Something less now is better than something more later). This discounting of cash flows for quicker payment was/is a common practice, and the rich man approved. The wisdom of this practice from the rich man's standpoint is that "time is money" and there is time value to money and the investment opportunities now available to him with the lesser amount make up

---

63. Luke 16:2.

64. Lewis Smedes (1921-2002), in *Mere Morality*, wrote about character being what we are at the core, what our intentions are, what our predilections are, what our pattern of behavior is.

65. Luke 16:1.

66. *Dechomai* = receive.

67. Cf. Sir 40:28.

68. Luke 16:6; The word usually translated "bill" in verses 6 and 7 is *grammata* (from *grapho* = "to write"), meaning "something written."

for the diminished return collected from the debtors.[69] So, the manager wasn't necessarily cheating the rich man, but rather implementing a win-win situation for both the debtors and the lender.

Now we come to Luke 16:8, where most translators comment that the rich man "commended the unrighteous[70] manager because he had acted shrewdly."[71] You bet he "acted shrewdly," and even correctly, given the desires and needs of his boss and the debtors. Thus, the translation of *adikos* as "unjust" or "unrighteous" is unwarranted. This translation leaves the reader with the impression that the manager was morally wrong and a despiser of God[72] and the rich man was complicit in the manager's financial shenanigans. Because the antecedent action of the "manager" takes place in the accusation of 16:1, i.e., "wasting the rich man's possessions," a better translation would be "incompetent" or "wasting." What is in view in 16:8 is not sin or a matter of "righteousness," but rather stewardship. Granted, sloppy or lazy stewardship can be a result of a sinful attitude and even lead to a compromised situation, but that is beside the parable's point. The manager fails as a steward, as a manager—not as a "righteous" person (as is the "unfaithful" manager in Luke 12:46).

In Luke 16:13, we see that Jesus the manager told the disciples that "no manager" can serve two bosses. The fact is that every manager serves multiple human bosses as a businessman. The trick always is to navigate the service between demanding human bosses. Jesus said, "Make your choice between Boss God and boss man." But the tension I want to focus on is the tension between being a servant to multiple human bosses: persons above the manager ("master") and persons beneath the manager's employees ("debtors").

> I am the good shepherd. The good shepherd lays down his life
> for the sheep. (John 10:11)

In John 10:11–18 we see that one of the great roles that Jesus modeled for us was that of a shepherd:[73] guiding, protecting, and ultimately dying for the sheep assigned to him.

---

69. Cf. the rich man's investment strategy in Luke 12:16–19: It is better for me to tear down smaller buildings now leaving me without any buildings for a while in order to made room for bigger, better buildings later.

70. *Adikos*.

71. *Phronimos* = prudently, sensibly.

72. Luke 16:13.

73. *Poimen*.

You must follow me. (John 21:22)

After his resurrection, Jesus appeared to several individuals. When he first appeared to Peter, he commanded him to "feed" his followers three different times.[74] And how was Peter to feed the Lord's sheep? By emulating the life of Jesus:[75]

- The charge given to Peter (and to all who would manage an organization) by Jesus the manager was to tend and love the coworkers in the same manner as "the Chief Shepherd" did, but even more than that. The Christian manager is to show the love of Jesus to all his employees as part of his testimony.[76]

> Now that I, your LORD and Teacher, have washed your feet, you also should wash one another's feet. I have set you an example[77] that you should do as I have done for you. (John 13:14–15)[78]

In an extraordinary passage in John 13, Jesus himself set the example for all Christians who would be business managers and tells them to follow him. J. C. Ryle noted that Jesus is teaching us that the "duty of a disciple is to make Christ his example in all things."[79] It was the Lord's humanity that is the business manager's example and guide, for only in his humanity did he "share in our humanity."[80]

---

74. Cf. John 21:15–17. See Case, "Pressures on Presbytery."

75. John 21:22, "Follow me," Jesus commanded.

76. Cf. 1 Pet 5:1–4; John 13:35; Lev 19:18.

77. *Hupodeigma*.

78. Jesus said: "Take my yoke upon you and learn (*manthano*) from me, for I am gentle and humble in heart" (Matt 11:29).

79. Ryle, *Expository Thoughts on the Gospels*, 4.22. Hendricksen stated, "What Jesus had in mind was not an outward rite but an inner attitude, that of humility and eagerness to serve" (Hendricksen, *Exposition of the Gospel According to John*, 236).

80. *Koinoneo* = take part; Heb 2:14. This "sharing in our humanity" by Jesus was noted by Woelfel in his book *Bonhoeffer's Theology*, where he wrote that Jesus is "have-able," "graspable" in the concrete, historical affairs of men, not "eternal non-objectivity," related to the world only "formally and tangentially through bare acts" (Woelfel, *Bonhoeffer's Theology*, 141–42). Karl Barth pointed out that Emil Brunner reminded us that the great truth of the incarnation is that the eternal son of God took upon himself our humanity, and not that the man Jesus acquired divinity. Thielicke related Luther to this notion of Jesus' solidarity with our humanity when he wrote, "This act of divine descent into flesh and history, this condescension, finds expression in the stories of Christ's temptation and passion. Here all transcendence is given up, and Luther's thesis makes sense when he says that God cannot be drawn deeply enough into the flesh"

The angels admonish us: "Men of Galilee, why do you stand here looking into the sky?"[81] To put it into an idiom, if our heads are in the clouds, we may miss the commercial action on earth with our business neighbors. We won't find Jesus in the sky but rather here among us in the office as our perfect role model. The "sky" has come to "earth." In short, we will find the redemptively relevant Jesus here in the world, here in the marketplace, here in the workplace—his lifestyle and accomplishments having been performed among us for all to see! An ancient theologian whose name has been forgotten (Athanasius?) penned, "He became what we are that we might become what he is."[82]

> Anyone who has seen me has seen the Father. How can you say, "Show us the Father"? Don't you believe that I am in the Father, and that the Father is in me? (John 14:9–10)

Hear Jesus' words to Philip. It is instructive for an understanding of the ambiguous perception of the ministry of Jesus that Philip is still seeking proof from Jesus that he is the incarnate Son after being with him for three years! And yet Jesus tells him to have faith and believe his words, and the Lord's lifestyle will become Philip's lifestyle.

> Righteous Father, though the world does not know you, I know you, and they know that you have sent me. I have made you known to them and will continue to make you known in order that the love you have for me may be in them and that I myself may be in them. (John 17:25–26)

This border-destroying work is no more eloquently expressed than by the Lord himself in his priestly prayer recorded in John 17:25, when Jesus

---

(Thielicke, *Evangelical Faith*, 1.289).

81. Acts 1:11.

82. Smith, *Hamann*, 67; "As (*kathos*) you sent me into the world, I have sent them into the world" (John 17:18; cf. John 20:21). Dods comments on this verse, "*kathos* ('as') seems to imply prosecution of the same purpose with similar equipment and *eis ton kosmon* ('in the world') is not otiose but suggests that as Christ's presence in the world was necessary for the fulfillment of God's purpose, so the sphere of the disciples' work is also *ton kosmon*—'the world'" (Dods, *The Gospel of John*, 884). This indeed is the immediate context of John 17. Hermann Sasse maintains that *kosmos* ("world") here is the "great opponent of the Redeemer," and while God loves this *kosmos*, there is unbridled enmity between those "in Christ" and those "in Satan" (Kittel, *Theological Dictionary of the Old Testament*, 894–95). So there can be no friendship with "the world," only incarnational presence in order that the world may know that the Son of Man is, indeed, the Son of God (John 17:21–23).

referred to the rejection of the world. He will suffer, yet that rejection will not deter his ministering to those very people rejecting him. Christ is expressing a solidarity with the world that Paul later repeated.[83] There can be no redemption of the worldly man if Jesus was not worldly.[84] This has huge implications for the Christian business manager. And yet, at the same time, the great ambiguity comes out in the ministry of Jesus when he told his disciples: "If you belonged to the world, it would love you as its own. As it is, you do not belong to the world, but I have chosen you out of the world. That is why the world hates you" (John 15:19).

> You have heard that it was said, "Love your neighbor and hate your competitor." But I tell you: Love your competitors and pray for those who persecute you[85] . . . Be perfect,[86] therefore, as your heavenly Father is perfect. (Matt 5:43, 48)[87]

In this paragraph the Lord commands the Christian manager to be perfect. The most difficult virtue of "perfection" is love extended to our competitors ("enemies").[88] Jesus calls us to moral and ethical

---

83. Cf. Rom 1:14; Col 1:15–20.

84. Thielicke commented on this worldly redemptive effort: "In Christ, God becomes subject to the pressures of history, its finitude, and its nexus of guilt, even to death on the cross. As God's condescension reaches down to the lowest depth of historical existence, there is no secular sphere nor dimension of human existence in the world which is without affinity to God and consequently to transcendence" (Thielicke, *Evangelical Faith*, 1.294). The transcendent yet immanent nature of Jesus is admirably put by Paul in Galatians 4:4: "But when the time had fully come, God sent his Son, born of a woman." Johnston: "Christ can be said to represent the absolute immanence of God . . . The incarnation both demonstrates in fullest measure the immanence of God and was possible because God is not only transcendent, but also immanent. Then, through the consummation of the ministry of the incarnate Son, every believer experiences the immediate immanence of God in the presence of the indwelling spirit" (Johnston, "Incarnation," 267–74).

85. *Kataraomai* = to curse, wish anyone evil or ruin or destruction.

86. In the Old Testament *teleios* is used in the Greek LXX for the Hebrew term *tamin*, which means "complete," "unblemished," "blameless," "perfect": Job 1:1; Ps 37:37; elseshere. The plural form describes the Thummim, the precious stones of Aaron's breast piece. "*Teleios* has the meaning having attained the end or aim; if anything has fully attained that for which it is designed it is perfect. It can refer to the maturity of an adult man—the end or aim to which the boy points. Jesus is calling on his followers to be mature people, attaining the end for which God has made them" (Morris, *The Gospel According to Matthew*, 134).

87. Cf. Lev 19:2; Deut 18:13.

88. Turner notes that the Lord's ethic contradicts fallen human culture in this paragraph expressed in aggressive domination of others, misuse of women by adultery

"perfection"[89] even though he knows we cannot fully attain that in this life. But that must be the manager's aim, the manager's goal. He calls us to be like him, to follow his example.[90] Because that is to be the manager's unreachable goal, no matter how mature the manager might be in the faith, there is always room for growth. That is a blessing because each day brings its own purpose—the striving towards the goal of perfection. Before the manager can influence his company, he must influence himself.

Jesus is teaching that the Christian manager's lifestyle is to be radically different from the lifestyle of the unbelieving manager, because the Christian draws his motivation and inspiration not from the norms of society but from the character of God. The Mosaic law made accommodations to the culture. But for Jesus, perfection was demanded. For our guide we are to look behind the law and see the mind and character of God.[91] And when we see the mind of God, we see love. That is perfection. And how will the business manager manifest that perfect love? By continuing to be kind, welcoming, and encouraging to those coworkers who are obstinate, who oppose him and pursue their own goals.[92] The command for the business manager is that his character must display love and acceptance for everyone with Godly qualities such as patience, tenderness, truthfulness—the fruits of the Spirit.[93] Jesus sets the standard for the faithful Christian manager and sums up the standard by saying simply, "Pattern your live after your heavenly Father—be perfect. By doing so you will please him and be the salt and life in this world." Jesus is teaching here that the Christian business manager speaks and acts with integrity[94] and love his competitors. Nothing to it![95]

In the Gospel accounts we have the example of persons of character in Elizabeth and Zachariah who "were both righteous before God, walking blamelessly in all the commandments and statutes of the Lord".[96]

---

and divorce, integrity of speech, retaliation and finally loving our enemies (Turner, *Matthew*, 178).

89. *Teleios* = carrying out a task. planning. John 19:36 =fulfilled.
90. Rom 5:8.
91. France, *The Gospel of Matthew*, 228.
92. Isa 65:1–5.
93. Gal 5:22.
94. Sinek, *Leaders Eat Last*, 185–97.
95. Turner, *Matthew*, 178.
96. Luke 1:6: "Zechariah and Elizabeth were "righteous (*dikaios*) before God, walking blamelessly in the law of the Lord."

- "Righteous[97] before God" is used to describe a morality that conforms to God's standards, and "blameless"[98] connotes concrete and visible acts which are pleasing to God.[99]
- "Walking"[100] indicates a constant lifestyle in exemplary behavior.

This couple has earned the right to be called "persons of character" in the eyes of God!

If business managers are to emulate Jesus in their management calling they must expect the management temptations that go with that particular calling. The siren call of idolatry of marketplace success never leaves the ear of the business manager.[101] It started in the Garden of Eden and hasn't stopped since. Eve, after all, "looked," "gazed (desired)," "took," and "gave." She was not satisfied with her own capitulation to sin but wanted Adam to join her in her rebellion (Gen 3:6). The business world presents multiple moral and ethical dangers. While not completely unique to the marketplace, the spiritual challenges residing in wealth creation are magnified. "The entrepreneur will be harder pressed in various areas to remain honest and to keep his integrity than a teacher or professor with his fixed salary."[102]

The Lord's three temptations or testings illustrate these dangers. In Matthew 4:1–11 we have the first Matthean expressions of the Lord's ministry after his baptism. "This is the starting point and the foundation for all that Jesus would do later in his public ministry."[103] Yahweh has just christened Jesus as his Son, and now Jesus is sent into the wilderness for forty days without food or water. The contrast between the baptismal waters of the Jordan and the heat of the desert would temp Jesus to ask himself, "What just happened? Am I really the Son of God? If so, where is the proof?" Jesus' hair was still wet from his dunk in the river![104]

---

97. *Dikaios.*

98. *Amemptos.*

99. "Before God."

100. *Poreuo.* This repetitious morality is emphasized by the use of both adjectives "righteous" and "blameless" and the verb "walking."

101. Cf. Deut 13:6.

102. Douma, *The Ten Commandment: Manual for the Christian Life*, 310. Cf. Hodge, *Systematic Theology*, 3.421–37; Dabney, *Lectures in Systematic Theology*, 414–18; Rushdoony, *The Institutes of Biblical Law*, 448–542.

103. Ridderbos, *Matthew*, 62.

104. As Moore points out in his *Tempted and Tried*, 31.

Summarizing the three temptations he is about to face:

- The temptation to distrust/disbelieve Yahweh's providential care (changing stones into bread),
- the temptation to arrogantly presume self-sufficiency about life, forcing God's hand to make his name great (jumping off a high structure),
- the temptation to impetuously grasp world power and benefits by unlawful means (prematurely owning the kingdoms of the world).

As managers go about their business operations they must never forget that the "prince of this world"[105] will not give in to the "Prince of Peace"[106] without a mighty and clever struggle: If the worldly prince had destroyed the first prince (Adam) why couldn't he destroy the second prince (Jesus)?

Notice that Satan attacks Jesus at his weak points:

- hunger (after days of fasting),
- pride (of self-sufficiency),[107]
- ambition (for power, now).

Clever and diabolical.

Capitulating to any one of the particular tests would lead to Jesus' general destruction. Satan is offering quick success versus the long slog of faithful living. With a simple bending of the knee, it could all be Jesus'. The message of patiently waiting for God to act is hard to take! Furthermore, Satan is offering what is not his to give, except temporarily. He cannot provide the personal fulfillment that godly obedience brings. The world is a splendorous place, but a place empty of long-term meaning and satisfaction. The force and attractiveness of the temptations lay not in the temptations but in the personal advantages connected to the temptations.

Ominously, the text seems to present the temptations in a visionary manner as opposed to something physical. That is, the testing came to Jesus in his mind and not in face-to-face combat with Satan. Thus, the application to today's Christian managers. There was not a hideous, monstrous, devilish image to repel Jesus, but the Satan-inspired thoughts

---

105. Cf. John 14:30.
106. Cf. Isa 9:6.
107. Cf. Jer 14:21; Matt 3:17.

in Jesus' thinking. Satan always comes as an understanding friend. If we are not capable of responding to the temptation, there really is no temptation. And if the testing happened to Jesus, be confident that the testing will happen to the business manager.[108]

It is important to see that the temptations are not, in and of themselves, sinful, but rather normal, reasonable, everyday activities and expectations—eating, social influence, and a public demonstration of one's faith. What is wrong with a little bread, or a special display the Father's love, or enjoying his promises now?[109] Satan gets into a battle of the Bible with Jesus as he suggests the Scriptures teach compromise by quoting Psalm 91 to the Lord as a friendly apologetic of accommodation.[110] Satan quotes the Bible to glorify Jesus with the result that Jesus the Son would become Jesus the father of Yahweh, since the Son's faith would compel the Father to act.[111] Satan tells Jesus, "If you really believe in your Father's providential care for you, then publicly demonstrate your trust by a big jump (Jesus' leap of faith!). You can order your own affairs and take care of yourself, thank you. You don't need to wait on God for worldly success."[112] Since the temptations are all in the head of Jesus, he must have Scriptures memorized or else run the risk of being double-minded and defeated: "Is the voice that I am hearing from Satan or from my Father?"

Augustine told us that Satan can only tempt sin; it is up to us to perform sin. Satan was telling Jesus the Son to wink and nod at the requirements of the Father and to come to terms with a pluralistic world ethic: "Look at what you can accomplish by adopting the ways of the world—power to do what you want by simply subjecting yourself to me this once. Do it, Jesus, for God's sake, then just confess if you feel the need."

---

108. Cf. Matt 10:24.

109. Cf. John 17:11.

110. Cf. Matt 4:6.

111. We need to be on guard against our tendency to see in Scripture what we want to see and not what God is saying to us.

112. Only months later James and John were failing the same test: personal ambition (Matt 20:20–28). This later testing isn't the product of the devil's personal action but rather from the disciples' own personal proclivity for personal advancement and improvement. Beware of trifling compromises—like simple seating arrangements!—"little foxes" in Song of Songs 2:15.

We need to understand that being obedient to the word of God may cause material loss (no bread to stave off starvation!).[113] The temptation narrative warns us to be careful about the chimera of being practical, ambitious, and competitive, and thus falling into the sin that the end justifies the means. It is perfectly reasonable to believe that in order to accomplish the goals God has set for us we must have provision, power, and position.[114]

The discouraging fact of life is that Satan never rests, and he and his minions continually will test and tempt the faithful Christian manager. Jesus faced down temptation throughout his life,[115] and so will the Christian manager.

One final application of the temptations of Jesus to today's Christian business manager. I turn to Henri Nouwen (1932–96) for this final biblical/management application.[116] Nouwen combines the temptations of Jesus with the conversation Jesus has with Peter in John 21:15-19: "feed my sheep." The first temptation of Jesus—turning stones into bread—can

---

113. Morris notes that "many who profess to follow Christ have purchased their own empires at the cost of acceptance of the ways of the world" (Morris, *The Gospel According the Matthew*, 77).

114. Filson, *A Commentary on the Gospel According to St. Matthew*, 138–39; cf. Matt 11:12. This reminds me of Louise Bay novel's *King of Wall Street*. Moving from desert temptations, a role model will emerge from the life of Jesus that would be a combination of John Bunyan's "Mr. Great-Heart" and "Mr. Valiant-for-Truth," and "Mr. Steadfast": "Now Mr. Great-Heart was a strong man, so he was not afraid of a Lion; But yet, when they were come up to the place where the Lions were, the boys that went before were glad to cringe behind, for they were afraid of the Lions, so they stept back, and went behind. At this their Guide smiled, and said: 'Now, now, my boys, do you love to go before when no danger doth approach; and love to come behind so soon as the Lions appear?' Now, as they went up, Mr. Great-Heart drew his sword, with intent to make a way for the Pilgrims despite the Lions" (Bunyan, *Pilgrim's Progress*, 257). As "Mr. Great-Heart" guided the pilgrims on their way to the celestial city, he picked up "Mr. Valiant-for-Truth," who singularly fought a victorious battle against three great foes of genuine Christianity: "Wildhead," "Inconsiderate," and "Pragmatick." Valiant's "courage and skill" were bequeathed to the other pilgrims when he entered the city (Bunyan, *Pilgrim's Progress*, 263). A third companion was "Mr. Steadfast, a certainly right good pilgrim" who the pilgrims "saw [as] a man upon his knees, with hands and eyes lift-up, and speaking, as they thought, earnestly to one that was above" (Bunyan, *Pilgrim's Progress*, 263). Bunyan's great allegory can be applied to a small business owner so that that manager can learn to be a courageous, skillful, and prayerful leader of others in the face of marketplace temptation. All for the purpose of helping guide other marketplace pilgrims safely to the celestial city of personal flourishing.

115. Cf. Matt 12:38; 16:1, *peirazo*; 19:3, *peirazo*; 22:18, *peirazo*, 22:35, *peirazo*.

116. Nouwen, *In the Name of Jesus*.

be applied to Peter the manager's shepherding responsibility by Peter's temptation to meet the immediate needs of his coworkers. The manager is tempted to do whatever it takes to meet their needs so that they can become more productive. But what Jesus is telling the managers in the temptation passage is that what the coworkers want is a piece of the manager, not some vocational aid. The point Nouwen makes is that the coworkers want the manager's affection but not his competence.[117]

The second temptation—to be "spectacular" in a jump of faith—is applied to Peter's management shepherding in that the manager wants to do something spectacular in the company rather than the mundane and unspectacular daily duties of shepherding the coworkers. Furthermore, this non-spectacular shepherding is not a lone-wolf exercise but a community effort involving company personnel.[118]

The third temptation—the desire for worldly power and control—is applied to Peter's management shepherding by the giving up of power and control and not accumulating it. That is, the shepherding manager genuinely gives control over aspects of the company to various coworkers to invest themselves in the future of the organization. This is, of course, the most controversial management approach of the three because it takes trust and patience and discernment with coworkers and trust in the sovereign care of the organization by Jesus.[119]

---

117. Nouwen, *In the Name of Jesus*, 15–34.
118. Nouwen, *In the Name of Jesus*, 35–51.
119. Nouwen, *In the Name of Jesus*, 55–70.

2

Jesus on Management in the Old Testament

Do not think that I have come to abolish the Law of the prophets; I have not come to abolish them but to fulfill them. I tell you the truth, until heaven and earth disappear, not the smallest letter, not the least stroke of a pen, will by any means disappear from the Law until everything is accomplished.

(MATT 5:17–18)[1]

Now I want to remind you, although you once fully knew it, that Jesus, who saved a people out of the land of Egypt, afterward destroyed those who did not believe.

(JUDE 5)[2]

NOAH ON MANAGEMENT

IN THE OLD TESTAMENT there is no single word for "character."[3] The best we have is the context for a Hebrew word usually translated

---

1. Cf. Heb 11:26 for Moses and Jesus.
2. 1 Cor 10:4; John 8:56; 12:41; Heb 11:26.
3. See the excellent article by the late David Clyde Jones, "Christ and Character."

"righteousness" or "justice,"[4] and another Hebrew word usually translated "straight" or "upright."[5] It is important to recognize character purified or refined through stress (as in "pure" or "refined" metal coins as valid currency).[6]

> Noah was a righteous man, blameless among the people of his time, and he walked with God. (Gen 6:8–9)[7]

We are given another Old Testament example of a manager of character in Noah who is distinguished from "the people of his time" by his character, which became legend in the Old Testament.[8] Noah is described as:

- "righteous,"[9]
- "blameless,"[10]
- "walking with God."

"Walking with God" makes Noah's life a pattern in integrity and puts him in the company of other Old Testament managers of pure character.[11]

---

4. *Tsedeq*

5. *Yashar*

6. For instance, in Proverbs 25:4, "Remove the dross [Hebrew = *sig*, Greek = *adokimos*] from the silver and out comes material for the silversmith." See also Gen 23:16; 1 Kgs 10:18; 1 Chr 28:18; 29:4; 2 Chr 9:17; Prov 27:21 (*matsreph* = refining vessel, pure); Zech 11:13.

7. *Tamin* = blameless.

8. Isa 54:9–10; Ezek 14:14, 20. Indeed, Josephus writes that the "people of his time" tried to kill him because his blameless life was a reproach to them (Gen 6:5, 11 = Josephus, *Ant.* 1.3.1).

9. *Tsaddiq* is the Hebrew word translated "righteous" which can be translated also as "just," "honest," "right," and "good" and is used by God in Genesis 7:1 to describe Noah as habitually, not occasionally, good.

10. Gen 6:9. *Tamim* is the Hebrew word translated "blameless" which can be translated also as "perfect," "sound," "wholesome," "complete" (Gen 17:1; Deut 18:13; Ps 15:2; 18:24; Prov 11:5; Job 12:4). This attribute indicates a moral uprightness and integrity in one's behavior, but not sinlessness (cf. Gen 20:5–6, "clear conscience"; Deut 18:13; Prov 11:5). "Righteousness" and "blameless" appear together in Job 12:4 as Job protests that he has not done anything wrong to become a laughingstock in the community.

11. Only Enoch and Noah "walked with God." Other patriarchs "walked before God." Cf. Gen 5:22–24; Mic 6:8.

JOSEPH ON MANAGEMENT

> Then Pharaoh said to Joseph, "Since God has made all this known to you, there is no one so discerning[12] and wise[13] as you. You shall be in charge[14] of my palace, and all my people are to submit to your orders. Only with respect to the throne will I be greater than you." And Pharaoh said to Joseph, "I hereby put you in charge[15] of the whole land of Egypt." (Gen 41:39–41)

We have the example of Joseph showing practical discretion and wisdom[16] in his political and administrative dealings. This shrewdness impressed Pharaoh to such an extent that the pagan king of Egypt made the Jewish Joseph "ruler over Egypt and all his palace."[17]

MOSES ON MANAGEMENT

> I am Yahweh your God; consecrate yourselves and be holy, because I am holy. (Lev 11:44)[18]

This call for the individual worker to be holy because God the father is holy is the theme of Leviticus and is repeated in Leviticus five times. Later, God the Son will tell the Christian business manager that his highest duty is to imitate his Creator/Savior: "You, therefore, must be perfect as your heavenly Father is perfect."[19]

> Yahweh said to Moses, "You and Eleazar the priest and the family heads of the community are to count all the people and animals that were captures. Divide[20] the spoils between the soldiers who took part in the battle and the rest of the community. From the soldiers who fought in the battle . . . Give (one out of every fifty, whether persons, cattle, donkeys, sheep, goats, or

---

12. *Bin* = discreet, understanding, intelligent; Gen 41:33.
13. *Hakam* = skillful.
14. *Gal* = over.
15. *Nathan* = to give.
16. *Hakam*; cf. Acts 7:22; Greek = *sophia*.
17. Acts 7:10.
18. Cf. Lev 19:2; 20:26.
19. Matt 5:48: "Be perfect [in your love], therefore, as your heavenly Father is perfect."
20. *Chatsah* = to halve.

other animals) to the Levites, who are responsible for the care of Yahweh's tabernacle. (Num 31:25–28, 30)

Moses defeated the Midianites and was distributing the spoils of war among the Israelites. He divided the spoils between the warriors and those who stayed in the camp. Unlike other cultures in the ancient Near East, where the soldiers keep the spoils of war after giving some to the king and the priest, in the Jewish organization the spoils were distributed to everyone since it was no one man's victory but Yahweh's victory in the first place. This important principle will hold throughout the Bible, and so it must be recognized by the fair business manager who even today operates a business at the pleasure of Yahweh. And it is still controversial.

> When you make a loan of any kind to your neighbor, do not go into his house to get what he is offering as a pledge. Stay outside and let the man to whom you are making the loan bring the pledge out to you. (Deut 24:10–11)

Dignity and respect are important biblical concepts, and in Deuteronomy Moses the manager states that a creditor is not permitted to go into the house of the debtor because of the humiliation it would bring upon the family. This prohibition guards against arbitrary judgment and managerial action. A man's house is his castle, and he is lord over his domain:[21]

- Moses the manager tells employers that they are to treat their employees with dignity and respect due them by virtue of them being created in the image of God.[22] And it doesn't make any difference if the employees are Christian or not. A simple humanitarian concern is required for the Christian business manager.

> Since then, no prophet has risen in Israel like Moses, whom Yahweh knew face to face. (Deut 34:10)

Leadership studies of Moses abound, and books have been written about the character of Moses. However, I want only to highlight a couple character traits which illustrate the fact that character has been essential to God ordained managers from the beginning:

---

21. Deut 24:10.
22. Gen 9:5–6.

- Moses was courageous.[23]
- Moses persevered.[24]
- Moses was humble.[25]
- Moses was patient.[26]
- Moses was discerning.[27]
- Moses was teachable.[28]
- Moses was prudent, practical, and responsible.[29]
- Moses was loyal to his coworkers.[30]

JOSHUA ON MANAGEMENT

> Do not let this Book of the Law depart from your mouth, but you shall meditate on it day and night, so that you may be careful to do everything written in it. Then you will make your way prosperous and successful. (Josh 1:8)[31]

Yahweh tells Joshua that the obedient life of faith—life of character—will lead to a happy achievement of one's goals and prosperity. The Hebrew word translated "prosper"[32] here means the power or ability to live, the ability to accomplish that for which one is oriented. The word translated "success"[33] means to be prudent, wise, circumspect. This is the only passage where both similar Hebrew words are used, and while this verse is often used by Christians to justify business prosperity and wealth,[34] these

---

23. Heb 11:27.
24. Exod 6–12; Heb 11:27.
25. Num 12:3; *anav* = humble.
26. Num 12:1–15.
27. Num 12:1–15; 16:8–11.
28. Exod 18:24.
29. Exod 25:1–8.
30. Num 12:13; 14:19, 16:22, 46.
31. Cf. Col 3:2, 17.
32. *Salah*; Josh 1:7 uses a different word for "prosper": *hiskil* = "to have success, to be prudent."
33. *Sakhal*.
34. Cf. Wade and Kittler, *God Is My Counsel*, 79 (Cf. Deut 6:16–18; Ps 1:3; 34:10;

two words are never used that way in the Bible. The Joshua 1 passage suggests to one scholar that the terms "speak of succeeding in life's proper endeavors. This happens when people's lives are focused entirely on God and obedience to him . . . Thus, in the Old Testament 'prosperity' is not financial in its primary orientation, if at all. Rather, it refers to succeeding in proper endeavors. Also, it comes only when it is not the focus of one's efforts in any case. It comes when one's focus is on God and one's relationship with him. The success is granted by God, not attained by human achievement."[35]

DAVID ON MANAGEMENT

> But David said to Saul, "Your servant has been keeping his father's sheep. When a lion or a bear came and carried off a sheep from the flock, I went after it, struck it, and rescued the sheep from its mouth. When it turned on me, I seized it by its hair, struck it and killed it. Your servant has killed both the lion and the bear . . . Yahweh who delivered me from the paw of the lion and the paw of the bear will deliver me from the hand of this Philistine." (1 Sam 17:34–37)[36]
>
> Then David came to the two hundred men who had been too exhausted to follow him and who were left behind. They came out to meet David and the people with him. As David and his men approached he greeted them. But all the evil men and troublemakers among David's followers said, "Because they did not go out with us, we will not share[37] with them the plunder we recovered" . . . David replied, "No, my brothers, you must not do that with what Yahweh has given us. He has protected us and handed over to us the forces that come against us. Who will listen to what you say? The share[38] of the man who stayed with

---

37:25; Prov 10:15; Job 36:11). In fact, the Bible seems to point us in a different direction. When the Bible speaks of prosperity and success it always uniformly connects worldly success with God's providential blessing based on the individual's obedience to God's word and leading Abraham (Gen 24); Joseph (Gen 39); David (1 Sam 18:5–6, 14–15); Solomon (1 Kgs 2:3; 1 Chr 22:13, 29:23); Hezekiah (2 Kgs 18:56); Jeremiah (Jer 2, 5, 13, 22, 32); Daniel (Dan 3, 6); and the church in exile (Ezra 5, 6; Neh 1, 2).

35. Howard, *Joshua*, 89–90.
36. Cf. 1 Sam 16:18; 18:14–16.
37. *Nathan* = give.
38. *Cheleq* = inheritance.

Jesus on Management in the Old Testament   33

the supplies is to be the same as that of him who went down to the battle. All will share alike." (1 Sam 30:21–25)

King Saul is looking for someone to confront the Philistine man of war, Goliath, and David offers to help in this initial conversation. David is humble before the king by calling himself "your servant." Furthermore, he describes himself as a shepherd and not a "man of war."[39] Earlier, David has been described as a someone who "speaks well"[40] and this is confirmed with this brief conversation as he goes on to detail his valiant duties as a "keeper of sheep." His account of his up-close and personal victorious combat with lions and bears is crisp and riveting.[41] If he can subdue ferocious four-legged beasts, David can handle a two-legged soldier—"Put me in, coach!" But Saul is reluctant since David was just a teenager[42] with no military experience, and Goliath has been fighting since he was David's age. Notice several applications for the business manager from David's plea to be sent in against the larger opponent:

- David the manager prevails over the skeptical and desperate king to fight Goliath.
- David the manager understands that shepherding is good training for a manager because it is a dangerous occupation, requiring constant vigilance and preparedness.[43]
- David the manager not only rescued the sheep (employees) but was ready for a counterattack.[44]
- David the manager did not give up on his sheep because even after the rival took the sheep in his mouth David went after it and rescued it out of the jaws of the lion.[45]
- David the manager did not delegate the responsibilities to attack the lion to his older brothers but took the dangerous duties himself. He had a personal stake in the life of the threatened lamb.[46]

39. 1 Sam 17:34.
40. 1 Sam 16:18.
41. Cf. Prov 18:25; Amos 5:19.
42. *Naar* = youth.
43. 1 Sam 17:34.
44. 1 Sam 17:34.
45. 1 Sam 17:35.
46. 1 Sam 17:34.

- David the manager seems to know what to do with the beasts, and his confidence was sky high. The narrative does not tell us if this beast-battle was a one-off event or if this encounter was a repeated event, but the assumption is that it happened more than once.[47]

David defeated the Amalekites, but after the intense fighting, David's army was so exhausted that two hundred of his warriors stayed behind to guard the supplies as David led four hundred men into battle.[48] As David and the four hundred returned victorious, the two hundred non-fighting brethren came out to welcome him home and celebrate his victory. But there was a handful of "evil"[49] fighting men who did not see Yahweh's hand in the victory but rather attributed it to their skill and prowess.[50] This contingent of evil fighting warriors said to David, "We were on the front lines, they were back peeling potatoes. We were in harm's way and so we deserve the reward. This isn't fair." David, rather than getting furious with the contingent, called them "my brothers"[51] and reminded them that it was Yahweh who protected them and gave them the marauding Amalekite' spoils. Since all the plunder belonged to Yahweh in the first place, "all the [company] will share alike" in the second place (1 Sam 30:25). This equitable stance of David was so important for future plunder distributions that he made it a law and it finally became a custom in Israel henceforth.

> His name was Nabal, and his wife's name was Abigail. She was an intelligent and beautiful woman, but her husband, a Calebite, was surly and mean in his dealings . . . When Abigail saw David, she quickly got off her donkey and bowed down before David with her face to the ground. She fell as his feet and said: "My Lord, let the blame be on me alone. Please let your servant speak to you; hear what your servant has to say. May my lord pay no attention to that wicked[52] man Nabal. He is just like his

---

47. 1 Sam 17:35–37.
48. Cf. 1 Sam 25:13.
49. *Ra* = wicked; *belial* = worthless, evil. Eventually, *belial* will be the name of Satan (2 Cor 6:15).
50. Indeed, the adjective used to describe these men will eventually be used to describe the devil, himself.
51. *Ach* = cousin, fellow countryman, male friend. This is a term of affection.
52. *Belial.*

name—his name is Fool,[53] and folly[54] goes with him. But as for me, your servant, I did not see the men my master sent." (1 Sam 25:3, 23–25)

Through her shrewdness, Abigail the manager averts a slaughter of her husband's retinue and wins the approval of David. Notice Abigail's snake-like wisdom and dove-like gentleness.

> But David said to Abishai, "Don't destroy him! Who can lay a hand on Yahweh's anointed and be guiltless? As surely as Yahweh lives," he said, "Yahweh will strike him; either his time will come and he will die, or he will go into battle and perish. But Yahweh forbid that I should lay a hand on Yahweh's anointed. Now get the spear and water jug that are near his head, and let's go." (1 Sam 26:9–11)

In 1 Samuel 26 we see a short character study of David the manager:

- David is committed to transparent communication with his co-worker, Abishai.[55]
- David is loyal to his employer, King Saul.[56]
- David is committed to the reigning social order of the organization, Israel.[57]
- David is committed to a just relationship with his colleagues, Abishai and Saul.[58]
- David is patient.[59]

> David asked, "Is there anyone still left of the house of Saul to whom I can show kindness for Jonathan's sake?" Now there was a servant of Saul's named Ziba. They called him to appear before David, and the king said to him, "Are you Ziba?" "Your servant," Ziba replied. The king asked, "Is there no one still left of the house of Saul to whom I can show God's kindness"? (2 Sam 9:1–3)

53. *Nabal.*
54. *Nabalah* = emptiness.
55. 1 Sam 26:9–11.
56. 1 Sam 26:9.
57. 1 Sam 26:9–11.
58. 1 Sam 26:9.
59. 1 Sam 26; cf. Job 1:21–22; 2:10; 42:10; (Jas 5:11).

Ziba replied that the son of Jonathan, Mephibosheth, was still alive and living in obscurity in a tiny village named Lo Debar. David summons Mephibosheth, the crippled grandson of David's archenemy, King Saul, and brings him to live with him in the royal court.

- David the manager dignifies the offspring of his deadly enemy, the King of Israel, by endowing him with all the privileges and benefits of royalty. "'I will show kindness[60] to Hanun son of Nahash, just as his father showed kindness to me' . . . Hanun seized David's men, shaved off half of each man's beard, cut off their garment in the middle at the buttocks, and sent them away. When David was told about this, he sent messengers to meet the men, for they were greatly humiliated. The king said, 'Stay at Jericho till your beards have grown, and then come back.'" (2 Sam 10:2, 4–5)

It would take too much space to tell the backstory of the humiliation of David's mighty men at the hands of the Ammonites. Suffice it for our purposes to indicate that David's colleagues were deceived and unfairly shamed, and they slunk back to David thoroughly embarrassed. This was a serious insult to his men because Israelite men, particularly warriors, had a full beard, indicating virility. Exposing their buttocks and genitals was something only done to prisoner of war.[61]

- David the manager, rather than punishing or berating the warriors for being mishandled, exercised kindness, covered their shame and reputation, and brought them back to Jerusalem when they were ready. In short, David the manager had his men's back.

---

60. *Hesed* = loving kindness, goodwill, mercy, benefit, loyalty.
61. Isa 20:3 5.

Jesus on Management in the Old Testament

David summoned all the officials[62] of Israel to assemble at Jerusalem: the officers[63] over the tribes, the commanders[64] of the divisions[65] in the service of the king, the commanders[66] of thousands and commanders[67] of hundreds, and the officials[68] in charge of all the property and livestock belong to the king and

---

62. *Sar.* "David summoned all the managers [*sar*, captains, stewards] of Israel to assemble at Jerusalem: the managers (*sar*) over the tribes, the managers (*sar*) of the divisions (companies) in the service of the king, the managers (*sar*) of thousands and managers (*sar*) of hundreds, and the managers (*sar*) in charge of all the property [*rekush* = substance, that which is gathered together, goods] and livestock belong to the king and his sons, together with the palace managers (*sar*), the mighty men [*gibbor* = men of substance. In this 1 Chronicles verse we find "mighty" men (*gibbor*), but the Hebrew word could just as easily be translated "substantial" or "honored" men, meaning important men in the community and not narrowly restricted to 'warriors,' which will be used in a different context. These 'substantial' men could very well be men of commerce and wealth] and all the brave warriors" (1 Chr 28:1). First Chronicles 28:1 is a golden verse that covers an important term for management. In this list of government officials there is no mention of religious priests or Levites (except perhaps in the phrase "officers over the tribes"). The focus is on secular officials or administrative people ("the affairs of the king," 1 Chr 26:32. The list of the managers of the king's business is a summary of 1 Chr 26:20–32; 27:25–34). All the "officers" and "commanders" in this verse are called *sarim*. The term *sar* applies to the Christian business manager as indicating the power and authority vested in the managerial position and with this position comes the ability to organize, lead, and care for the people by a judicious administration of the means of production and survival (property and livestock). In Isaiah 23:8, *sarim* are "merchants/traders who are "renowned princes/leaders" of Tyre. This 1 Chronicles 28 verse is a good example of David's domestic political management chops: "ministering [*asah* = doing, making, toiling, keeping, handling] justice and righteousness [*sedaqa* = equity] for all his people" (2 Sam 8:15). In this 2 Samuel verse we see King David managing the political apparatus of Israel to accomplish justice and equity for all the members of his organization without prejudice or discrimination. Since the time of Samuel, the leaders of the organization were to govern without favor in order to be fair. David's job was to maintain the welfare of his people. David was a good manager and kept the united Israel together. His son Absalom was not such a unifying manager of the organization (2 Sam 19:41–43), and the Egyptian *sarim* "oppressed" the Jewish cohort for centuries (cf. Exod 1:11).

63. *Sar.*
64. *Sar* = captains.
65. Or companies
66. *Sar.*
67. *Sar.*
68. *Sar* = stewards.

his sons, together with the palace officials,[69] the mighty men,[70] and all the brave warriors. (1 Chr 28:1)

Moving on to another fair management practice, the twenty-eighth chapter of 1 Chronicles tells us that David the manager knew how to delegate and empower his administrators with authority to accomplish their assigned tasks. As 1 Chronicles 28 goes on, notice several features of David's masterful management in his final assembly to the company as he passes the baton to his son, Solomon:

- David the manager's plans to build the temple are out in the open; nothing is done in secret.[71]
- David the manager speaks directly to the people, to his organization.[72]
- David the manager explains his thinking and justifies his actions to his organization.[73]
- David the manager asks the people to participate in the life of the organization at this moment.[74]

---

69. *Saris*

70. *Gibbor* = men of substance, nobles. "Now Naomi had a relative on her husband's side, from the clan of Elimelech, a man of standing (*gibbor*) whose name was Boaz" (Ruth 2:1). *Gibbor* is a borrowed word from Near East languages meaning "to rise" or "restore." It is most commonly used to describe military warriors and champions. But we get a Ruthian hint that the word also had its roots in socially prominent persons—"a man of standing"—of the administrative class of individuals (cf. 1 Sam 9:1, "a man of standing [*gibbor*]"; 2 King 15:20, "wealthy [*gibbor*] man"). Thus, the term, while a minor term, has management implications in that, like *sar* (which we have seen in 1 Chronicles 28), the managerial position carries with it respect and honor which must be earned by the manager. Boaz the *gibbor* was a wealthy businessman, as were the "mighty men" of Israel. The verb *tsawah* gives a sense of the gibbor management practice: "Watch the field where the men are harvesting and follow along after the girls. I have managed (*tsawah*) the men not to touch you" (Ruth 2:9). This Hebrew word means "to command," "to arrange," "to delegate," "to set in order" (1 Sam 13:14; Neh 7:2). It connotes a picture of a superior giving a command to a subordinate to do the right thing. In addition to the communication from Boaz to employees, it is used for the instruction of a father to a son (Gen 49:29, 33; 1 Sam 17:20) and a king to a subject (2 Sam 21:14). There is a moral component to this term.

71. 1 Chr 28:1-3.

72. 1 Chr 28:1.

73. 1 Chr 28:4-10.

74. 1 Chr 28:21.

Jesus on Management in the Old Testament

- David the manager delegates power and authority to his subordinates.[75]
- David the manager defends the organization by being an outstanding warrior.[76]
- David the manager is adroit in diplomacy.[77]

> For Yahweh is righteous, he loves justice; upright people will see his face. (Ps 11:7)

In this verse we have "righteousness"[78] being connected to "upright,"[79] and Yahweh is indicating his interest in the character of a manager, right now, in this life. Yahweh is in his heavenly home, and he is watching the upright business manager in his daily duties. For the manager of action, it is important to note that the growth in confidence in Psalm 11 in Yahweh's provision is not based on prayer but on a conscience remembering that Yahweh is a God of action and will perform his sovereignty.[80] Purity and genuineness are the hallmarks of character quality!

> Yahweh, who may dwell in your sanctuary? Who may live on your holy hill?:

- He whose walk is blameless.
- He who does what is righteous.[81]
- He who speaks the truth[82] from his heart.[83]
- He who has no slander[84] on his tongue.

---

75. 1 Chr 28:10.

76. 1 Chr 28:3.

77. It bears noting that six hundred years after David came the Macedonian leader Alexander, who excelled in managing his organization. Cf. Hammond, *Alexander the Great*.

78. *Tsdaqah* = righteous, justice.

79. *Yashar* = upright.

80. In his article on "tempt" Haarbeck notes that in the Old Testament, "There is always a consciousness of the connection with testing by fire" (Schneider and Brown, "Peirao," *Dictionary of New Testament Theology*, 3.808).

81. *Tsedeq*.

82. *Emeth*.

83. *Lebab*. Words are not enough. Truth must come from inside, from the heart.

84. *Ragal* = to walk along, be a talebearer, backbite.

- He who does his neighbor no wrong.[85]
- He who casts no slur[86] on his fellow man.
- He who despises[87] a vile man.[88]
- He who honors[89] those who fear Yahweh.
- He who keeps his oath[90] even when it hurts.[91]
- He who lends his money without usury.
- He who does not accept a bribe against the innocent.[92]

He who does these things will never be shaken. (Ps 15:1–5)

It is clear from 15:1 that David is addressing leaders who have the power to cause mischief and misery to other people. In short, this is a Psalm for managers. Managers are powerful people in an organization and are subject to temptations that coworkers are not. David is blunt and specific as he discusses what managers must do to enjoy Yahweh's prescence.

> He chose David his servant and took him from the sheep pens; from tending the sheep he brought him to be the shepherd of his people Jacob, of Israel his inheritance. And David shepherded[93]

---

85. *Ra.*
86. *Cherpah* = reproach, shame, scorn.
87. *Bazah* = condemn, distain.
88. *Maas* = loathsome.
89. *Yeremay* = elevates.
90. *Shava* = pledge allegiance, confirm, bind.
91. *Raa* = afflict, dash to pieces, shatter, destroy.
92. *Naqi.*
93. *Raah* = feed. "I am Yahweh . . . who says of Cyrus, 'He is my manager (*raah*) and will accomplish all that I please; he will say of Jerusalem, 'Let it be rebuilt,' and of the temple, 'Let its foundations be laid'" (Isa 44:28). From very ancient antiquity, rulers were described as demonstrating their legitimacy to rule by their ability to pasture their people. Hammurabi and many other rulers of ancient western Asia are called "shepherd" or described as "pasturing" their subjects. God commanded David to manage—*raah*—the Jewish cohort in Israel (cf. 2 Sam 5:2). Failure of the *raahs* of Israel to feed and protect the people either spiritually or physically was deemed a severe transgression (cf. Ezek 24). The Old Testament theological idea of "the good *raah*" who feeds his flock the truth (cf. Jer 3:15) becomes a prominent theme in the New Testament (cf. John 10:11; cf. White, "Rosh"). *Raah* applies to the Christian business manager in that the role of a manager is one of shepherding the workers in the

them with integrity[94] of heart; with skillful[95] hands he led[96] them. (Ps 78:70–72)[97]

We have been given another Old Testament example of an artful discerning episode, this time in David's life. Here David is described[98] as a manager of the Old Testament who is a "servant shepherd" who "tends"[99] or "guides" those who are given to him with "integrity" and "skill" towards the destination that the entire flock will flourish and accomplish the end for which Yahweh intends.[100] The Hebrew word translated "tend" really means "to follow after," so the meaning here is multi-layered. The manager-shepherd watches and guards the coworkers as they seek greener pastures for themselves.[101] The Hebrew word for "integrity" is also translated "simplicity" elsewhere.[102] The Hebrew word translated "skillful"[103] is applied to the patient man[104] and to the man with sound judgment.[105] If David could manage a flock of sheep then perhaps he had the skills to manage a nation. God had gifted him with such talents.[106]

David was a righteous manager.[107] In this key management passage we have the historic example of Yahweh:

---

company in all that the term explicitly and implicitly connotes. In some respects, *raah* is the most important Hebrew term applied to the manager of a business.

94. *Tom* = wholeness, entireness.

95. *Tavunah* = insight, intelligence, wisdom.

96. *Nachah*; Greek LXX = *hodegeo* = guided; cf. Heb 12:7, 24.

97. "As for you [Solomon], if you walk before me in integrity of heart and uprightness, as David your father did, and do all I command and observe my decrees and laws, I will establish your royal throne over Israel forever . . . But if you . . . do not observe the commands and decrees I have given you . . . then I will cut off Israel from the land I have given them and will reject this temple" (1 Kgs 9:4–7).

98. "I have seen the son of Jesse of Bethlehem . . . He is a brave man and a warrior. He speaks well and is a fine-looking man. And Yahweh is with him" (1 Sam 16:18).

99. *Achar;* Greek OT (LXX) = *kubernesis* = guide; Prov 1:5; 11:14; 24:6.

100. *Nachah*; Ps 78:53; Greek LXX = *hodegeo*; Heb 12:7, 24.

101. Cf. 1 Sam 17:34–37.

102. Cf. Josh 24:14; Judg 9:16, 19.

103. *Tovunah.*

104. Prov 14:29.

105. Prov 15:21.

106. Prov 11:12; 28:16. Paul the apostle tells us that if you can manage a family perhaps you can manage an organization of disparate personality and giftedness, 1 Tim 3:4–5. Cf. Piper, "He Must Manage His Household Well."

107. Cf. Redpath, *The Making of a Man of God.*

- Selecting the managed ("Jacob," "Israel his inheritance").
- Choosing the manager ("David").
- Guiding the manager in his management duties ("shepherd").
- Setting the timeline goal of management maturity ("shepherd of his people").
- Training the manager ("took him from . . . and brought him to").

All of this management activity culminates in the manager fulfilling the management task—"shepherding"[108] with character ("integrity"[109] and "skill"[110]). Note that the context of this passage is not ecclesiastical but political, economic and social management. David is not a priest[111] but he is still called a "shepherd"–he is to be a shepherding manager.[112]

> It is well with the man who deals generously[113] and lends; who conducts his affairs with justice.[114] (Ps 112:5)

David gives the manager an example of the virtue of kindness in Ps 112:5 with a generous and benevolent[115] manager being rewarded. After all, David was a kind manager.[116] He describes the Christian business manager as a "trusted" and loyal neighbor.[117]

---

108. *Raah.*

109. *Tom.*

110. *Tovunah.*

111. There is the somewhat complicated relationship between king and priest, but fundamentally the two offices had separate and distinctive duties (cf. Ps 110:4; Gen 14:18).

112. "Management ability is one of the gifts of the Holy Spirit; it is also a science. There is a body of knowledge and principles (acquired through the experience of our predecessors) to be learned. Further, management is an art. There are specific aptitudes and skills to be developer through sustained practice" (Anderson, *Managing Our Work*, 13).

113. *Chanan* = kind, gracious, merciful.

114. *Mispat* = discretion, judgment.

115. *Chrestotes.*

116. 1 Sam 8:3, 7. *Hesed* = kind, loving, mercy; but we have Old Testament examples of unkind managers: the backbiting of Miriam and Aaron towards Moses (Num 12:1–3); the ambition of Diotrephes towards John (3 John 9–10); Jacob's hypocrisy towards Esau (Gen 25:27); Jael's deception towards Sisera (Judg 4:18–23); Delilah's treachery towards Samson (Judg 16:4–22).

117. Ps 15:3; Levite judges are to be "trustworthy" in their judicial judgments, 2 Chr 19:8–11. God the Father is always patient with the business manager (Exod

> One evening David got up from his bed and walked around on the roof of the palace. From the roof he saw a woman bathing. The woman was very beautiful,[118] and David sent someone to find out about her. The man said, "Isn't this Bathsheba, the daughter of Eliam and the wife of Uriah the Hittite?" Then David sent messengers to get her. She came to him, and he slept with her. (She had purified herself from her uncleanness.) Then she went back home. (2 Sam 11:2-4)

The steps David willingly took apply to any temptation facing a manager. David: saw, gazed, sent, inquired, dispatched, summoned, lay. David's bed is probably on the roof to keep cool during the Spring weather. He can't sleep, so he gets up to cool off and enjoy the skyline of the capital city. He sees Bathsheba, probably not for the first time, bathing, probably on her rooftop, as the wife of a prominent warrior. Time to stop, but rather than just noticing her and moving on, David notices that she is beautiful. Time to stop, but his interest is piqued, and he wants to know about her, so he sends one of his attendants to inquire. The information comes back that she is married. Time to stop, but he dispatches an aid to get her, probably under false pretenses. She comes to him perhaps out of curiosity or her own desire. Time to stop, but they have sex. The incident gets worse from then on, resulting in two deaths: Uriah and David's infant son, an unholy marriage, and the shame of being publicly cuckolded.

34:6). Contrarily, we have managerial impatience being displayed time and time again by numerous managers in the Old Testament: Esau (Gen 25:29-34); Moses' lack of self-control resulted in him being denied entrance into the promised land (Num 20:10-12); King Saul's ignoring God's timetable and thus losing the opportunity to have his sons follow him on the throne of Israel (1 Sam 13:8); Solomon equated lack of self-control to a city in collapse (Prov 25:28); Absalom (2 Sam 14:29); Ahab's lack of self-control led to Naboth's murder and Ahab's ultimate death (1 Kgs 21:1); Naaman (2 Kgs 5:11-12); Jonah (Jonah 4:8-9)

118. *Tobat mareh* = literally: "good in appearance," indicating a gazing upon.

THE PSALMIST ON MANAGEMENT

> Good[119] will come to him who is generous and lends freely,[120] who conducts his affair with justice.[121] A righteous[122] man will be remembered forever. He will have no fear of bad news;[123] his heart is steadfast,[124] trusting in Yahweh. His heart is secure, he will have no fear; in the end he will look in triumph on his foes. He has scattered abroad his gifts to the poor, his righteousness endures forever; his horn will be lifted high in honor. (Ps 112:5–9)

Probably David wrote this Psalm,[125] but we have no definite proof. The psalmist is telling us that the manager of character has certain qualities that cause the "wicked man to become angry and gnash his teeth":

- The psalmist manager of character is a generous man with finances.[126]
- The psalmist manager of character is a man of affairs who acts justly with discretion.[127]
- The psalmist manager of character is a man of steadfastness and stability.
- The psalmist manager of character is a man of courage in the face of opposition and bad news.
- The psalmist manager of character shares his expertise with those with whom he works.

---

119. *Tov* = good, virtuous, correct.

120. *Lavah* = to cause to join, Lev 25:35–37. Calvin, *Institutes of the Christian Religion*, 3.7.4–7: "The righteous will manage their affairs with prudence and discernment. And in all their mercantile transactions, they will always be guided by the principles of equity and morality."

121. *Mishpat* = discretion. This is an Old Testament character quality that is to be emulated by all Christian managers: Ps 37:30; Prov 12:5; 21:15; 29:4; Mic 3:1; 6:8.

122. *Tsaddiq*.

123. *Ra* = mischievous, severe, injurious, hurtful, unpleasant, fierce, wild.

124. *Kun* = fixed, firm, established, reliable.

125. Some even say the prophet Haggai or Zechariah.

126. Cf. 2 Cor 9:9.

127. Cf. Ps 101:3–4.

Teach me good judgment[128] and knowledge[129] for I trust your commands. (Ps 119:66)

The Old Testament calls for the discerning artistic wisdom of God in any given management situation. Psalm 119 gives the sense that discernment and discretion come from experience and practice. The word translated "knowledge" can mean technical knowledge (i.e., scientific knowledge of running a business). The word translated "good judgment" can also mean "discretion" or "reasonable." This is the capacity to make insightful decisions, which will be ones which have good outcomes. This verse is a manager's prayer for managerial discernment because without it the manager will make ignorant decisions—"go astray"[130]—and harm the company. Ignorance, unfortunately, is no defense before the Lord.[131]

Asaph lamented the temptation of prosperity in the Psalms three thousand years ago in Jerusalem:

> Their mouths lay claim to heaven, and their tongues take possession of the earth. Therefore, their people turn to them and drink up waters in abundance. They say, "How can God know? Does the Most High have knowledge?" This is what the wicked are like—always carefree, they increase in wealth. (Ps 73:9–12)

The poet is giving us the great material enigma of the Christian faith. This is the providential stumbling block of faith in a materialistic world. The unjust are rewarded and indulged with money, health, and recognition by society, while the faithful groan under hard-to-understand trouble and difficulty and scarcity.

SOLOMON ON MANAGEMENT

Solomon the manager did not leave us with a concise description of a godly manager, nor do we have him exhibiting such a model character for the ages. There is nothing like what Paul or Peter wrote concerning character. But Solomon did leave us with pithy one-liners in Proverbs and Ecclesiastes that have stood the test of time as valuable guideposts to a description of character worthy of a Christian manager's consideration:

---

128. *Taam.*
129. *Daath* = technical know-how, knowledge gained through experience.
130. Laid low, Ps 119:67.
131. Lev 4; Luke 12:48.

- Planning: "Go the ant . . . and consider its ways and be wise! It has no commander, no officer or ruler, yet it stores its provisions in summer and gathers its food at harvest."[132]

- Teachableness: "Instruct a wise man and he will be wiser still; teach a righteous man and he will add to his learning."[133]

- Stewardship: "Lazy hands make a man poor, but diligent hands bring wealth."[134]

- Commitment to God's word: "Righteousness guards the man of integrity, but wickedness overthrows the sinner."[135]

- Love of coworkers: "A friend loves at all times, and a brother is born for adversity."[136]

- Prudent approach: "It is not good to have zeal without knowledge, nor to be hasty and miss the way."[137]

- Discernment: "A prudent man sees danger and takes refuge, but the simple keep going and suffer for it."[138]

- Training: "Do you see a man skilled in his work? He will serve before kings; he will not serve before obscure people."[139]

---

132. Prov 6:6-8. "The ant . . . has no manager (*qatsin*) no officer (*shoter*) or ruler (*mashal*)" (Prov 6:7). The point of this verse is to use the animal kingdom to illustrate the fact that industrious workers, well-trained by the *qatsin*/manager, will do the work assigned to them (cf. Job 12:7; Prov 30:24-30). The significance for the Christian business manager is that the employees are engaged in productive work without direct oversight by the managers. Still, there is generally the need for *qatsin* (cf. Exod 5:13-14, foreman, taskmaster, *sum*; 1 Kgs 6:16, officers, to be set over, *natsah*). *Qatsin* comes from the Arabic root meaning "to judge" or "to cut," so we get the flavor of an official who decides issues and rules on controversy to preserve order and accomplish goals by cutting through the administrative fog to accomplish the administrative goal (cf. Josh 10:24; Judg 11:6, 11; Dan 11:18). Proverbs 6:7 is one of those money verses concerning management in the Old Testament because this one short verse mentions three key Hebrew management terms translated "chief," "officer," "ruler," all of which I translate "manager."

133. Prov 9:9.

134. Prov 10:4.

135. Prov 13:6.

136. Prov 17:17.

137. Prov 19:2.

138. Prov 22:3.

139. Prov 22:29.

Jesus on Management in the Old Testament

- Integrity: "Trusted friends wound each other in love; False friends shower emotion on acquaintances."[140]
- Steadfastness: "Better a poor man whose walk is blameless than a rich man whose way are perverse."[141]
- Humility: "A man's pride brings him low, but a man of lowly spirit gains honor."[142]

> Whoever loves money[143] never has money enough; whoever loves wealth[144] is never satisfied with his income.[145] This too is meaningless. As goods increase, so do those who consume them . . . The sleep of an employee[146] is sweet, whether he eats little or much, but the abundance[147] of a rich man permits him no sleep. (Eccl 5:10–11a, 12)

This is a very interesting passage because it pits the "evils" of the pursuit of wealth with other biblical passages which extol wealth creation. From verses 5:10 to 5:15 Solomon details the snares and deceitfulness of a life of commerce, a theme found elsewhere in the Old Testament.[148] But this pastoral passage is different because it is addressed to the wealth creator himself with several personal applications:

- Solomon the manager asks, Does the wealth creator ever have enough income from his commercial endeavors? There are always more consumers to please, and more hangers-on to endure, and more salaries to pay.[149]

---

140. Prov 27:6.
141. Prov 28:6.
142. Prov 29:23.
143. *Keseph* = silver.
144. *Hamon* = abundance, multitude.
145. *Tebuah* = fruit.
146. *Avad* = to toil, work, serve.
147. *Saba* = satiety, plenty, fulness.
148. The Solomonic authorship of Ecclesiastes is debatable. Prov 11:28; 18:11; Job 31:24; Ps 49:6; cf. Matt 6:19–24; 1 Tim 6:10.
149. Eccl 5:10–11; cf. Prov 14:20; 19:4–6.

- Solomon the manager suggests that the pursuit of wealth can crowd out life's simple pleasures and make the pursuit a ball and chain to be lugged around.[150]
- Solomon the manager says that he pursuit of wealth causes sleeplessness. Insomnia comes from planning on how to get more money, from worry about people stealing your money, from wondering who is really your friend, from personnel problems at work, from the tax bite, from grief over family problems—you get the point. This guy is an Ambien customer. The preacher says that the greedy businessman cannot get a good night's sleep because:
  - He is driven to multiply his wealth so much that that is all he thinks about,
  - He is worried about losing his wealth through personal mistakes,
  - He is worried about losing his wealth though unscrupulous people,
  - He is worried about all the hangers-on who consume his wealth.[151]

However, the personal satisfaction of producing something that others find valuable and are willing to pay for is an affirmation that a manager is doing something right and creating a product or service of value to human beings and therefore is a blessing from God. It must be remembered that the Old Testament many times extols the wealth creator as a blessing.[152] Indeed, Solomon will assert such a bit later:

> When God gives a man wealth and possessions, and enables him to enjoy them, to accept his lot and be happy in his work—this is a gift of God ... God gives a man wealth, possessions, and honor, so that he lacks nothing his heart desires, but God does not enable him to enjoy them, and a stranger[153] enjoys them instead. (Eccl 5:19–6:2)

---

150. Eccl 5:12.

151. Eccl 5:12. The counter is that the wealthy provide goods and services for many "consumers." The "discerning" and "wise" business manager can sleep soundly and sweetly (Prov 3:21, 24).

152. Prov 3:9–10, 16; 8:18; 13:21; 14:24; 15:6; 19:4; 21:21; 24:3–4.

153. *Ish nokri* = a foreigner, man.

The preacher acknowledges that the rich man works hard and long to acquire wealth. That is not the issue. The issue is his idolizing of his wealth creation and acquisitive efforts—he becomes a workaholic. This intense focus crowds out the love of Yahweh, the giver of all wealth, and his coworkers.[154] Wealth is like sand in one's hand; it slips through your figures at the most inopportune time. When one works and plans all one's professional life to hand something over to one's children and the wealth disappears, there is nothing to give them. What a tragedy for the hard-working father who has misplaced his energies and loyalty all these years. The conclusion of this managerial responsibility is that the position of a business manager is a good thing and is a role which has God's blessing, and it is to be seen as a faithful stewardship:[155]

- Solomon argues that the key concept for the Christian business manager in Eccl 5:14 is that the manager's priorities are to be God's priorities and that the business is run according to those priorities, lest calamity strikes, and it is all gone.[156]

ISAIAH ON MANAGEMENT

> He who walks righteously[157] and speaks what is right,[158] who rejects[159] gain from extortion and keeps his hand from accepting

---

154. Cf. example of Scott Rudin: "Broadway producer Scott Rubin steps aside and apologies amid accusation of abusive behavior" to his coworkers. Peter Marks, "Broadway Producer Scott Rudin Steps Aside Amid Accusations of Abusive Behavior Going Back Decades, Apologizes for Pain He Caused."

155. Bruce, in his monumental book on discipleship, *The Training of the Twelve*, wrote on the motivation of an under-shepherd: "He who has a Christian heart must feel that he is strong and wise for the sake of others who want strength and wisdom; and he will undertake the shepherd's office, though shrinking with fear and trembling from its responsibilities, and though conscious also that in so doing he is consenting to have his liberty and independence greatly circumscribed . . . The yoke of love which binds us to our fellows is sometimes not easy, and the burden of caring for them not light; but, on the whole, it is better and nobler to be a drudge and a slave at the bidding of love than to be a free man through the emancipating power of selfishness" (Bruce, *The Training of the Twelve*, 522).

156. Cf. Eccl 12:13; Rom 13:8–10.

157. *Tsedaqah* = rightness, justice.

158. *Mishor* = plain, level land, straightness, honesty.

159. *Maas* = to dissolve, to undo.

bribes, who stops his ears against plots of murder and shuts his eyes against contemplating evil—this is the man who will dwell on the heights, whose refuge will be the mountain fortress. (Isa 33:15–16)

The prophet Isaiah did not hold administrative power in his organization, nor did he manage people. But he set forth for the managers in the organization a template for their conduct and expectations. In this brief, basically one-verse, summary of management, Isaiah laid out six benchmarks for the Christian business manager:

- He who walks righteously.
- He who speaks what is right.
- He who rejects gain from extortion.
- He who keeps his hand from accepting bribes.[160]
- He who won't listen to plans of blood guilt.
- He who shuts his eyes from gazing on evil.

The manager of godly character will be successful and be protected by God. This moral catechism list of six functions is a qualification to enjoy Yahweh's pleasure. The list covers the manager's entire lifestyle. Then Isaiah breaks it down into speech, financial integrity, and, finally, the senses. The prophet tells the manager that his character must be godly in private as well as in public. Godly character involves the organs of receptivity (eyes, ears, hands) and the organs of activity (tongue, feet).[161] God has chosen the kind of persons he wants to dwell with him. What separates a person from Yahweh is incompatibility in terms of character and commitment.[162]

EZEKIEL ON MANAGEMENT

"Suppose there is a righteous man who does what is just[163] and right.[164] He does not eat at the mountain shrines or look to the

---

160. Deut 16:19; Job 31:39; Prov 15:27; 28:16.
161. Young. *The Book of Isaiah*, 2.419–20.
162. Watts. *Isaiah 1–33*, 498–99.
163. *Mispat.*
164. *Tsedaqah.*

Jesus on Management in the Old Testament

idols of the house of Israel. He does not defile his neighbor's wife or lie with a woman during her period. He does not oppress[165] anyone but returns[166] what he took in pledge for a loan. He does not commit robbery[167] but gives his food to the hungry and provides clothing for the naked. He does not lend at usury[168] or take excessive interest.[169] He withholds his hand from doing wrong[170] and judges fairly[171] between man and man. He follows my decrees and by acting faithfully[172] keeps my laws. That man is righteous; he will surely live," declares the Sovereign Yahweh. (Ezek 18:5–9)

Ezekiel provides this code of ethics for the Christian business manager in which the prophet gives a behavior code of honor.[173] The code assumes that the manager has the power and authority to enact the requirements. The prophet gives the manager eleven concrete stipulations after a general statement to live a life of justice and righteousness, of doing what is just and right. The particular ethical stipulations are summarized below:

- He begins with the spiritual principle of worshipping the only true God.
- He then tells the manager to guard his sexual and moral life by being chaste.
- He goes on to command the manager to be a good neighbor by treating all people, particularly the weak, with kindness, generosity, justice, honesty, compassion, and transparency.[174]
- He ends by circling back to a general admonition to live a righteous life by following Yahweh's laws.[175]

---

165. *Yanah* = mistreat, drive away, to wrong someone.
166. *Shuv* = to restore, refresh.
167. *Gezelah* = spoil, violence.
168. *Nesek* = bite, interest.
169. *Tarbit.*
170. *Ewel.*
171. *Emeth* = faithful, stability.
172. *Emeth.*
173. Note the similar structure to other moral catechisms in Ps 24:3–6; Isa 33:14–17; Jer 22:1–5.
174. Exod 20:15; 22; 26–27; Lev 19:13–16, 35–36; Deut 15:11; 23:19–20; 24:6, 19–22; 25:13–16; Isa 58:7; Amos 2:8.
175. Cooper, *Ezekiel*, 13–16.

Interestingly, while this manager loses his son to sin, his grandson comes to the Lord and follows his grandpa. Blessed grandchildren!

ZECHARIAH ON MANAGEMENT

> This is what Yahweh Almighty says, "Administer[176] true[177] justice; show mercy and compassion[178] to one another. Do not oppress the widow of the fatherless, the alien, or the poor. Do not plot evil against one another." (Zech 7:8–10)

Here is another formulation of the manager's creed. The inspired prophet tells the godly manager to do four main things in organization:

- Manage a just workplace. Maintain harmony and peace in the company in the midst of an active work schedule.[179]
- Show mercy and compassion to the employees. Treat coworkers with loyalty and compassion. The manager needs to understand individual circumstances.
- Lift up the workers, particularly the new ones and the less gifted ones. Note the organization's mutuality in the creed: "one another."
- Create a work environment where workers speak kindly and affirmingly to each other. It is not enough to act kindly to each other but genuinely have kind thoughts towards each other.

MICAH ON MANAGEMENT

> He has shown you, O man, what is good. And what does Yahweh require of you? To act justly and to love mercy and to walk humbly with your God. (Mic 6:8)

Micah begins now to define "good":

---

176. *Shaphat* = manage, execute.

177. *Emet* = reliability, permanence, true, faithful.

178. *Rehem* = This word is related to the Hebrew word for "womb" expressing "tenderness toward one another like a mother manifests gentle, devoted feelings toward the fruit of her womb" (Klein, *Zechariah*. 223).

179. Baldwin, *Zechariah, Malachi*, 155–56.

Jesus on Management in the Old Testament

- "Act justly."[180] This means not to just talk the talk but to walk the walk. Practice justice yourself. Justice is a matter of giving back to each coworker what is due him.

- "Love[181] mercy."[182] The Hebrew word for "love" here is usually passed over quickly to get to the important Hebrew word *hesed*, translated "mercy." But "love" here means to show yourself faithful and concerned about your colleagues and sets up the term "mercy." *Hesed* is not a feeling; it is action. It means respect, benevolence, generosity, and fidelity. For our purposes, *hesed* is illuminating, for it connotes "deliverance" in the Old Testament, with the idea that one party is dependent on another party. The superior party is not obligated to deliver, but rather is free not to respond. Thus, when there is response, mercy, grace, kindness is displayed.[183] Clearly, this is the expected action from a manager to his coworkers.

- "Walk humbly."[184] This does not mean humility but rather live a careful life before a watching God. The Hebrew word usually translated "humbly" would better be translated "circumspectly" or "discerningly," "wisely," "prudently."

Micah 6:8 is a "call for the natural consequences of truly forgiven men and women to demonstrate the reality of their faith by living it out in the marketplace. Such living would be accompanied with acts and deeds of mercy, justice, and giving of oneself."[185] Another scholar goes so far as to state that this verse is "the quintessence of the commandments as the prophets understood them."[186]

---

180. *Mispat.*
181. *Ahabat.*
182. *Hesed.*
183. Cf. Gen 20:13; 24:29; 47:29; 2 Sam 16:14.
184. *Sana.*
185. Kaiser, *Hard Sayings of the Old Testament*, 228.
186. Von Rad, *Theology of the Old Testament*, 2.155. As New Testament believers Zechariah, Elizabeth, and Dorcas demonstrated the divine character attributes of justice mercy, humility, and loyalty to God. Dorcas was "always doing good [*agathos* = good] and helping the poor" (Acts 9:36).

3

Jesus on Management in the New Testament

BEREANS ON MANAGEMENT

> Now the Bereans were of more noble character than the Thessalonians, for they received the message with great eagerness and examined the scriptures every cay to see if what Paul said was true. (Acts 17:11)

THE BEREANS WERE DESCRIBED as "noble" or "born well,"[1] meaning they had the characteristics of good breeding—tolerant, generous, well-mannered, and intellectually curious ("great eagerness"). Management lessons to be learned from the Bereans include:

- In contrast to the Thessalonians, the managers of the Bereans were serious about the teaching and training coming into the organization (Acts 17:5).
- The Berean managers did not accept the received wisdom at face value without examining the instruction for themselves. The leadership was diligently examining the evidence, studying every day to accomplish the goal: to confirm Paul's teaching (Acts 17:11).
- Because of the Berean management's careful diligence, "many" Bereans became Christians when only "some" of the Thessalonians

---

1. *Eugenesteros* = character.

became believers. Thus confirming the Berean leadership methodology (Acts 17:12, 4).

PAUL ON MANAGEMENT

While there are no Greek words that absolutely correspond to the English word "character," there is one word that comes close, and that is *dikaios*:

- "But the character (*dikaios*)[2] of him [Timothy] you know, because as a son with his father, he has served with me in the work of the gospel" (Phil 2:22).
- "The reason I wrote you was to know your character (*dikaios*),[3] if you are obedient in everything" (2 Cor 2:9).
- "Out of great character (*dikaios*)[4] through tribulation, their overflowing joy and their extreme poverty welled up in rich generosity" (2 Cor 8:2).
- "Because of the service by which you have shown your character (*dikaios*),[5] people will praise God for the obedience that accompanies your confession of the gospel of Christ, and your generosity in sharing with then, and with everyone else" (2 Cor 9:13).

> For those God foreknew he also predestined to be conformed to the likeness of his Son, that he might be the first born among many brothers. (Rom 8:29)

Romans 8:29 repeats the creation verse of Genesis 1:26 but now requires the redemptive work of Jesus.[6] Charles Hodge was inclusive of other interpretations and saw this verse as including our "likeness" to Jesus in character while in the "days of our flesh." Hodge pointed us to earlier verses in Romans 8 to substantiate his view.[7] This Romans 8:29 verse is a

---

2. Proven worth.
3. Test you and know.
4. Proof, trial.
5. Service, administration.
6. Murray deemed this passage to refer exclusively to the glorified and exalted destination of the believer (Murray, *The Epistle to the Romans*, 318–20).
7. Hodge, *Romans*, 285–93.

natural apostolic transition to the words of the Savior himself, indicating his desire that the business manager be conformed to his worldly image.[8]

Christian business managers can never be a part of the world's value or belief system, nor can they fail to have a distinctive lifestyle from the world based on their incarnational emulation. Separatism, or the call for evangelical monasticism, is not the answer.[9] Rather, prayerful discernment and sensitivity to the ambiguities of the human experience and the absoluteness of the incarnational presence in that experience is what Christian managers are to seek in their lives. Managers do, after all, "see but a poor reflection" and only "know in part"[10] and "walk by faith, not by sight"[11] and cannot know for certain, unambiguously, what reactions their actions will elicit.[12] They cannot even know unambiguously many times what their action should be to please Jesus. Christian business managers are, in a sense, ships without a port destined to continually be at sail until reaching the shore of the promised land.[13] But engagement is the manager's sailing order![14]

> Eat anything sold in the market without raising questions of conscience,[15] for "The Earth is the Lord's and everything in it." If some unbeliever invites you to a meal and you want to go, eat whatever is put before you without raising questions of conscience.[16] (1 Cor 10:25–27)

Paul the manager is urging discernment in any interaction with the surrounding hostile culture. The subject matter is a seemingly trivial one: food. But, in fact, this was a topic of intense debate and disagreement. Thus, Paul felt he needed to address it, and in the course of his comments he shed light on the need for personal discernment on the part of

---

8. Here is another Pauline verse that calls Christian business managers to imitate God: "Therefore, as we have opportunity, let us do good to all people, especially to all who belong to the family of believers" (Gal 6:10).

9. Clapp, "Remonking the Church," 20–21. For a contrary opinion, see Dreyer, *The Benedict Option*.

10. 1 Cor 13:12.

11. 2 Cor 5:7.

12. Cf. 1 Cor 7:16.

13. Like Noah in Genesis 7 and 8.

14. Cf. John 17:18.

15. *Suneidesis* = The faculty of the soul which distinguishes between right and wrong and prompts to choose the right and avoid the wrong.

16. *Suneidesis*.

Jesus on Management in the New Testament

the Christian business manager. The context for Paul's comments is: 1) Early Christians were still considered to be a sect of the Jewish religion and sacred Jewish tradition was against eating food that had any chance of being contaminated by pagan rituals, so there was constant pressure not to eat "gentile" marketplace food.[17] 2) Earlier in chapter 10, Paul sensitizes the Corinthians to the power of the devil in everyday affairs so Satan and idolatry were not far from the Corinthian mind. 3) In 7:13–14 Paul had assured the Corinthian members that marrying a non-believer would not contaminate the believing spouse's faith. 4) The branch offices at Pergamum and Thyatira were both criticized for "eating food sacrificed to idols," so it was a universal concern among the early employees. 5) Jewish workers were particularly sensitive to this issue and argued that even eating with a gentile was condemned.[18] 6) The danger of accommodating to the dominant culture for the Corinthian Christians was always present, just as it is now in our culture, so the sensitivity towards the weaker brothers and sisters in the faith was real and legitimate in the Corinthian office, and the consumption of food was on the front lines of the battle.[19] Francis Schaeffer's (1912–84) last public appearance before his death in 1984 was at the annual convention of the Evangelical Press Association held in 1983 in Minneapolis. He delivered a warning concerning what he saw as the evangelical church's accommodation with the world. His final words to the assembled believers were: "Accommodation leads to accommodation, which leads to accommodation."[20]

So, with this as a background, Paul the manager boldly ventures into the fray by telling the Corinthians not to be overly scrupulous. His message is to eat meat and rejoice in God's goodness. His argument is that when one purchases meat in the market one cannot be expected to know if that meat is pure or not, uncontaminated by pagan sacrifice. So,

---

17. "And you also my son, Jacob, remember my words, and keep the commandments of Abraham, your father. Separate yourself from the gentiles, and do not eat with them, and do not perform deeds like theirs and do not become associates of theirs. Because their deeds are defiled and all of their ways are contaminated, and despicable, and abominable" (*Jubilees* 22:16, Jewish book from the second century BC).

18. Acts 11:2–3, "So, when Peter went up to Jerusalem, the circumcised believers criticized him and said, 'You went into the house of uncircumcised men and ate with them.'" Cf. Acts 10:28, Peter in the home of Cornelius.

19. Cf. 1 Cor 8:9–13. "A Gentile was always ready to contaminate wine through idolatry, if he gets the chance." A Jewish saying quoted by Garland, *1 Corinthians*, 493.

20. Schaeffer, "Transcript and Video of Francis Schaeffer Speech in 1983 on the Word 'Evangelical.'"

feel free to purchase the meat if you want. Let your conscience be your guide. If, however, one knows that the meat has been offered to idols, then that meat is off-limits to the believer since eating that meat would sanction idolatry to the pagan public and weaker Christians, much like Daniel eating Nebuchadnezzar's food.

The message from Paul is that the business manager must use discernment in making practical decisions about cultural involvement. There will always be social pressure to make a decision. The trick is to use discernment and make the right decision. Paul the manager uses the phrase "conscience's sake"[21] three times in making his argument.[22] He emphatically writes, "Eat anything you buy in the market." He continues by telling the Corinthians not to get tangled up in irrelevant navel-gazing about buying meat at Safeway or going to dinner at the local skeptic's house. Use your discerning spirit to decide when accommodation is appropriate and when it is inappropriate. The process of discerning the right solutions is one of examining the choices and asking questions and then making a calculated and biblical decision.[23]

In the exhortation to patronize the local meat market and to accept dinner invitation with non-believers Paul shows that he knows that Christians need social connections in the world and that social relationships are not only important for evangelism but important for the health and wellbeing for the individual Christian business manager. His warning is that in all these social interactions with the world discernment is critical for right judgments and success.

> I gave you milk, not solid food, for you were not yet ready for it. Indeed, you are still not ready. (1 Cor 3:2)[24]

Paul the manager seeks spiritual discernment[25] to be manifested first by him[26] and then by the Philippians[27] and by the Colossians.[28] Practical

---

21. *Suneidesis* = The testimony of one's own conduct borne by consciousness and at the same time one's testimony concerning duty.

22. 1 Cor 10:25, 27–28.

23. *Anakarino* = To distinguish or separate out so as to investigate by looking throughout objects or particulars, hence signifies to examine, scrutinize, and question.

24. Cf. Heb 6:1–3.

25. *Dokimazo* = insight.

26. Cf. 1 Cor 3:2.

27. Cf. Phil 1:9–10.

28. Cf. Col 1:9–10.

discernment is needed to help Paul determine when to tell bad news and how much bad news to tell the Corinthians.

To the Galatian office Paul writes of his desire that the resurrected Christ live in him and in the lives of the Galatian members.[29] And how are Paul and the Galatians to accomplish this Christ-like lifestyle? "Because you are sons, God sent the spirit of his Son into our hearts, the Spirit who calls out, '*Abba*, Father.'"[30] This aspect of the ministry of the Holy Spirit to conform business managers into the image of Christ is even called a "fruit of the Spirit."[31]

> By the grace God has given me, I laid a foundation as a wise[32] builder,[33] and someone else is building[34] on it. But each one should be careful how he builds.[35] (1 Cor 3:10)

In the New Testament, Paul the manager writes about the shrewd manager to the Corinthian office. The master builder[36] contributes knowledge and organization but not necessarily manual labor; he knows what to do because he has the training. The master builder assigned tasks to individual workmen. Paul, as the manager, is telling us that:

- The manager began a work.[37]

---

29. Cf. Gal 2:19–20; 4:19.
30. Gal 4:6.
31. God the Son set the lifestyle example and then laid down his life to make the example possible, and God the Spirit empowers the Christian to reflect the indwelling Christ in the Christian's life. Biederwolf wrote that one of these "fruits" or "communications" or "graces" made over to us through the communion of the Holy Spirit is the gradual making of us into the "likeness of Christ" as the perfect business manager. "Though not called a fruit of the spirit, one cannot analyze the prayer in Ephesians 3:16–19 without seeing that such is the evident result of being strengthened through the Spirit. As Christ in Colossians 1:19 is said to contain all the pleroma of God, so here such is the prayer for us, the pleroma being that with which God is filled—the divine perfections; and notice he says all the pleroma—his love, his knowledge, his power, his goodness, his holiness, etc." (Biederwolf, *A Help to the Study of the Holy Spirit*, 45). Cf. Sanderson, *The Fruit of the Spirit*; and Brunner, *A Theology of the Holy Spirit*.
32. *Sophos* = expert, skilled.
33. *Architekton* = master builder.
34. *Epoikodomeo* = to build upon.
35. *Epoikodomeo*.
36. Cf. LXX Isa 3:3.
37. 1 Cor 3:10.

- The manager installed the utilities.[38]
- The manager poured the foundation for the enterprise.[39]
- The manager insisted that the work should continue to completion under his guidance.[40]

In fact, Paul tells the Christian manager that there are ways the workmen can fail in their tasks:

- If the workmen tamper with the foundation that the manager has laid.[41]
- If the workmen use inferior material in continuing to build.[42]

Every employee must know that he will have to give an account of his labor.[43]

---

38. 1 Cor 3:10.
39. 1 Cor 3:10.
40. 1 Cor 3:10; cf. Matt 7:24–27.
41. 1 Cor 3:11.
42. 1 Cor 3:12–13.
43. Hodgkinson maintains that management is a rational pursuit since it depends for its achievement on value enunciation and the cooperation of persons assembled in purposive organizations. He has written, "The main administrative acts are decisional, and the quintessential form of administration is the making of policy. These acts imply philosophical skills and entail the exercise of power, influence, authority, and leadership" (Hodgkinson, *Towards a Philosophy of Administration*, 99). Hodgkinson believes there are three types of managers: First, there are the managers who come to their office by way of some form of political process, by appointment, election, or patronage. An example of this type of manager can be found in David in the Old Testament and the elders in the New Testament. Second, there are the managers who come to their office by way of a career pattern of preparation and who are permanently affiliated members of their organizations (Case: Solomon). Third, there are the managers who come to their office as professional members of their organization but have no training or preparation in the field of administration, and who are managers for only a specified period (Case: Rehoboam. See Case, "Rehoboam: A Study in Failed Leadership," 67–68). Decker and Decker define administrative functions within an organization as five-fold: One, planning and evaluating organizational services; two, conducting routine business affairs; three, initiating and maintaining personnel services; four, supervising, coordinating, and incorporating auxiliary organizational services, such as plant maintenance; five, providing channels for communication and exchange of information (Decker and Decker, *Planning and Administering Early Childhood Programs*, 47–48). The Marxist philosopher Marcuse argues that every organization needs an authority if there is not to be anarchy. The authority (manager) must be knowledgeable in order to run the organization for the wellbeing of not only the organization but the community. So there must be a rational sense of control or authority for the

> Be imitators[44] of God, therefore, as dearly loved children, and live a life of love, just as Christ loved us. (Eph 5:1)

Paul uses a poetic twist to refer to Christians as being "letters of recommendation from Christ" written on "tablets of human hearts"[45] and an exhortation to follow him: "Be imitators of me, as I am of Christ."[46] Paul elsewhere wrote in the so-called *kenosis* passage of Philippians 2: "Your attitude[47] should be the same as that of Christ Jesus" (2:5).[48] J. G. Hamann, the eighteenth-century German pietist, commenting on the *kenosis* in Philippians 2, wrote, "Christ imitated us, that he might encourage us to imitate him."[49] Not only are business managers to "walk" as Jesus walked, or "follow the example" of Jesus, but they are even to think ("have the same mindset") as Jesus! In sum, Paul tells managers they are to have the same attitude towards life and people as Jesus did! The Christian business manager is to internalize what what theologian Robert Reymond called "the human face of the incarnation" when I had him in seminary[50]

> Managers,[51] take care of your coworkers[52] with what is right[53] and fair,[54] because you know that you also have manger in heaven. (Col 4:1)

The apostle Paul tells the Colossians branch managers to realize that just as their coworkers are accountable to them, so they are managers accountable to the owner. There are several points that Paul the manager is making in Colossians 4:1:

- Managerial accountability is critical in workplace relationships.

---

common good of society in each organization (Marcuse, *Eros and Civilization*, 36).

44. *Mimetes* = "be imitators of me."
45. 2 Cor 3:1–3.
46. 1 Cor 11:1.
47. *Phroneo touto* = your mind.
48. Cf. Eph 4:23; 5:1–2.
49. Kleinig, "Confessional Lutheranism in Eighteenth-century Germany," 115.
50. Cf. Matt 5. Reymond, *A New Theology of the Christian Faith*.
51. *Kurios* = master, owner, superintendent.
52. *Doulos* = servants, slaves.
53. *Dikaios*.
54. *Isotes*.

- Managers are to treat their coworkers just as they want to be treated by those over them. This is a workplace application of the so-called "Golden Rule."[55]
- Paul the manager uses the Greek words for "just"[56] and "fair,"[57] which are basically synonymous for emphasis. This is an important workplace principle which is given to us in Leviticus 25:43: "Do not rule over[58] [your workers] ruthlessly,[59] but fear your God."

55. Matt 7:12. James Cash Penney wrote in a 1949 magazine article, "The same fundamental principles which guided me in the formation of J. C. Penney Company from the beginning are applied to my agricultural and purebred cattle business. Chief among these is the Golden Rule . . . I say with firm conviction, born of many years of experience and observation, that the only sane basis for [human relationships] is the Christian religion. My faith in God, taught me by Christian parents, convinces me that justice, fair dealing, and right are His will for men" (Penney, "The Challenge of Breeding Purebred Livestock").

56. *Dikaios.*

57. *Isotes* = equal, equitable, likeness.

58. *Radah* = subdue, oppress. In the so-called "cultural mandate" in the Old Testament, Moses uses a key Hebrew word for "manager" or "ruler" (*radah*). "Then God said, 'Let us make man in our image in our likeness and let them manage [*radah* = have dominion, lead, subdue] the fish of the sea and the birds of the air, over the livestock, over all the earth, and over all creatures that move along the ground' . . . God blessed them and said to them, 'Be fruitful and increase in number; fill the earth and manage (*radah*) it. Manage (*radah*) the fish of the sea and the birds of the air and over every living creature that moves on the earth . . . Yahweh took the man and put him in the Garden of Eden to work [*avad* = to serve, work] it and take care [*shamar* = to keep, guard, protect, watch over] of it" (Gen 1:26, 28; 2:15; "There is the little tribe of Benjamin leading [*radah*] them," Ps 68:27). *Radah* is a strong verb, meaning "to dominate," "to subjugate," "rule," "subdue," or "oppress" (to tread down as in a winepress, even to walk on a person, Ps 49:14 = "The upright will rule over them [literally, walk on them] in the morning." Psalm 8:6 alludes to the Genesis 1:26 passage but, interestingly, uses another Hebrew term, *mashal*). *Radah* occurs throughout the Old Testament and in many different contexts, but almost always it is limited to human rule over other humans, and not divine rule over humans. Thus, *radah* applies to the Christian business manager (Isaiah uses *radah* in Isaiah 41:2 in reference to the rule of the Messiah, which gives a sense of the word as well as softening the organizational domination of the manager). There is a pecking order in any organization, and *radah* describes the manager of the order. Genesis 1:26–28 teaches that the *radah* is going to: 1. hire ("fruitful and increase in number"), 2. set the ethos of the organization by naming the members and assigning roles in the organization, and 3. care for (lead) the members of the organization. A key Hebrew word employed by Moses in this passage is *shamar* meaning "to guard," "watch over," "retain." The first occurrence of the term connects to the garden of Eden, where careful attention and cultivation is required. It is used to convey guarding against intruders and enemies (Gen 3:24; Job 2:6).

59. Hebrew *perek* = with rigor, severity, harshness; Greek *mochthos* = travail.

Jesus on Management in the New Testament

- Paul the manager's use of the Greek words for "fair" and "just" also suggests that he might be referring to salary. The idea of honest remuneration is implied as in "just" = "grant," or "give." That is, whatever is a "fair" wage should be paid.[60]

- Paul the manager warns that the "fair" and square treatment of the coworker means there is to be no threatening workplace atmosphere: "Treat your coworkers the same way. Do not threaten them since you know what he who is both their Master and yours is in heaven, and there is no favoritism with him" (Eph 6:9). God's impartiality is a special temptation for the manager because the temptation for those in power is to think more highly of themselves and to be more impressed with worldly success than they ought. After all, everything comes from God, and to forget that he is the manager's master is dangerous.[61] Note that Paul stresses the concept of mutual service in the relationship between boss and worker.

- Paul the manager urges that this "just" and "fair" treatment is to be voluntary and cheerful with "a sincere heart," just like the manager's relationship with Jesus[62] and not under any sense of coercion or obligation.

To sum up, this Colossians verse teaches Christian managers to share in the responsibility for the vocational success of the employee by treating them fairly.[63]

There are several key passages which define the elusive concept of character for a Christian manager. First, we have Paul writing to the Romans:

> And we rejoice in the hope of the glory of God. Not only so, but we also rejoice (boast) in our sufferings, because we know that suffering produces perseverance; perseverance, character;[64]

---

60. Matt 20:4, "Whatever is right I will give you."

61. The *Didache* (second-century-AD apostolic writing) tells the masters to have the fear of God before them in their treatment of employees because God "does not come to call people with partiality" (4:10). Sirach 4:30 states, "Be not like a lion in your home and tyrannous and terrible toward your [workers]." The proprietary phrase "your servants" or "workers" (*abuddatak*) appears in Genesis 26:14, Leviticus 25:39, and Job 1:3—all workplace passages.

62. Eph 6:5, 9.

63. Cf. Isa 45:5; Eph 4:12; 2 Tim 3:1; Heb 13:21.

64. *Dokimie.*

and character, hope. And hope does not disappoint us. (Rom 5:2b–5a)[65]

The Greek word translated "rejoice"[66] is better translated "boast." It is the boasting about the God who saves and is utterly dependable. Paul uses the word twice in this short segment to make a point. In 5:3 he tells us why boasting is so important for the Christian manager: Managers are to boast in God's love when they face afflictions and stress in this life. Paul begins his sequence of tribulations in 5:2:

- Tribulations[67] lead to patience.[68] The "patience" mentioned is not the passive quality that we normally think of but rather endurance, steadfastness, constancy, perseverance. This perseverance is the ability to endure difficulties with patience and courage.[69] Sufferings can only lead to praising and rejoicing and boasting if managers see these difficulties and pain coming from God as a means of sanctification and preparation for useful management in this life. While heaven is a great comfort for managers now, pain and suffering in outward circumstances are manifestations of God's benevolent and beneficent character. Christian business managers know this because common experience teaches that trials and testing produce a different mindset in the individual. The manager knows this by personal observation and experience. He doesn't like it, but he knows it to be the truth. "Tribulations, although for the present time not joyous but grievous," change us.[70] After Paul claims that we know that suffering is good for all managers he then gives a chain of sequences in the process of maturing the managers' spiritual walk. This is the development of Christian graces in the individual which flows from the ministry that tribulation brings. It is critical to note that the biblical tribulations which come our way are not normal human

---

65. "Happy is the man whom the Lord remembers with rebuking and protects from the evil way with a whip (that he may) be cleansed from sin that it may not increase. The one who prepares (his) back for the whip shall be purified, for the Lord is good to those who endure discipline" (*Pss Sol* 10:1–2).

66. *Kauchaomai* = to glory, boast.

67. *Thlipsis* = affliction, sufferings that denote the pressure and trouble that Christians face in this life; tribulation.

68. *Hypomonen* = endurance, constancy, patience.

69. Cf. 1 Cor 1:6.

70. Hodge, *Romans*, 134.

sufferings, but tribulations caused by our public commitment to Christ.

- Patience leads to character.[71] The character mentioned by Paul means approvedness or triedness of one's Christian faith which is proven by testing. The important Greek word translated "character" (*dokimie*) is found only in Paul's writings, where it means the approved result of testing and refining through ordeals.[72] It appears that Paul invented this word. *Dokimie* and its cognates have the further meaning of "genuineness" and the experience that one has proven themselves true and trustworthy. In its general usage throughout the New Testament, *dikaios* usually means "to test," "approve," "be genuine," "be pronounced good," "be esteemed," "be trustworthy."[73] Paul is telling us that God renders judgment on character, even during this life![74]

- Character leads to hope.[75] A tested character produces hope in this life. After severe testing one has confidence in one's faith in a sovereign, benevolent God.[76] Furthermore, a gracious God will work through the Holy Spirit to sustain the Christian manager during the days of trouble.

---

71. *Dokimie* = doing away with the dross. In the Greek Old Testament (LXX) *dikaios* is customarily used in passages where *tsedeq* and *yashar* appear. Our English translators have also translated *dikaios* as "just," "straight," "upright." Cf. Isa 1:22 ("Your silver has become dross, your best (*adikaios*) wine is diluted with water"), 2 Cor 2:9; 8:2–3; Phil 2:22; Jas 1:12.

72. Cf. Rom 5:4; 2 Cor 9:13; 13:3; 1 Pet 1:7. In the Old Testament, Job 23:10; Prov 17:3; Apocrypha, *Wis* 3:6.

73. Cf. Rom 2:18. "What matters in testing is that we use God's gifts aright. Timothy, to whom the word of truth had been entrusted, was to show himself an approved (*dikaios*) worker (2 Tim 2:15) by faithful preaching. On the other hand, those who do not honour God according to the knowledge granted them, who reject knowing him, are given over to a base mind (Rom 1:28) and to improper conduct as a punishment" (Schneider and Brown, "Peirao," 3.808).

74. Cf. Rom 15:10.

75. *Elpis* = desire of some good with the expectation of obtaining it.

76. As Schreiner points out: "Moral transformation constitutes evidence that one has really been changed by God. Thus, it assures believers that the hope of future glory is not an illusion. Here is a pattern of growth in the here and how that indicates that we are changing. Believers, then, become assured that the process that God has begun he will complete" (Schreiner, *Romans*, 256).

- Hope does not disappoint.[77] Romans 5:5 tells us that the hope engendered by testing doesn't evaporate. The Greek word translated "disappoint" can also be translated "to put to shame," which gives better meaning that this character-building process is nothing to be ashamed of and that in the final analysis it will be the managers who do not have the refining fire of earthly afflictions who will be the fools.[78] Christians who pass through the affliction will not be ashamed to be called Christian managers because a powerful God has proven himself to be reliable and worthy of their trust.[79] Christian managers will never be in fear of being disappointed or ashamed that they have put their faith in a powerless God because it is God's invaluable love for them, not their valuable love for him, that will complete the process of sanctification.[80]

Among all the lists of the so-called secular character education movement the distinctly Christian virtues of humility, self-denial, forgiveness, and love of enemies are absent. It has been pointed out that Paul's most explicit definitions of Christian character is found in two small verses: Romans 12:2 and Galatians 4:19:

- Do not conform[81] any longer to the pattern of this world but be transformed[82] by the renewing[83] of your mind so that you will be able to test and approve what God's will is—his good, pleasing, and perfect will. (Rom 12:2)

Paul is telling the Christian manager that he is to present his body as a living, breathing sacrifice to Jesus, but he can only do that if his mind is not conformed to the sinful ethos surrounding him. This is another "flee and pursue" exhortation. Resist being conformed to the world's way of life and embrace the biblical way of life. While still living in the old order

---

77. *Kataischuno* = to put to shame, confound.
78. Prov 1:7.
79. Rom 10:11: "Everyone who trusts in him will never be put to shame."
80. Murray writes that Romans 5:5 "is one of the most condensed statements in the epistle. It is a striking example of the combinations in few words of the objective grounds and the subjective certainty of the believer's hope" (Murray, *The Epistle to the Romans*, 164–65).
81. *Suschematizo* = to fashion, Phillips, *The New Testament in Modern English*, "squeezed into the mold."
82. *Metamorphoo* = a change of condition.
83. *Anakainosis* = renovation.

of existence the manager now belongs to a new order in accordance with his new life controlled by the Holy Spirit.[84] The manager is to reprogram his mind through a lifelong struggle of obedience to resemble the standard set for manager by God.

> I am again in the pains of childbirth[85] until Christ is formed in you. (Gal 4:19)

Paul is stating that he will have painful labor with the Galatian manager until the manager's entire being radiates Christ character and ways. This gives a vivid indication of how long and difficult and focused the sanctification of character development is. The Galatian manager will be like Christ in his thoughts and aspirations, and he will reflect the Lord in the words he speaks, in life's attitudes and demeanor, in communication with coworkers. In short, all the aspects of life, including managerial responsibilities, will reflect Jesus.[86]

Christian character is essentially Christ-likeness, which is the goal of all Christians—to have Christ formed in the individual. The goal is realized only in heaven, but even in this life the Christian manager is called to have character transformation into Jesus' likeness.[87]

> Do not be misled: "Bad company corrupts good manners."[88] (1 Cor 15:33)

In a chapter that is highly theological, Paul shifts gears for a moment and gives an exhortation about lifestyle. Making the application to the business manager, Paul tells the Corinthians that evil companions will eventually have a corrosive effect on one's Christian faith. He is not saying, "Don't associate with non-believers." Indeed, he acknowledges dinner parties with non-believers in 1 Corinthians 10:27. What he is saying is that Christian business managers need to be careful about the companionship of non-believers. Such people will have a deleterious effect on one's Christian character.

---

84. Rom 7:6.
85. *Odino* = the pain of childbirth.
86. Hendricksen, *Galatians*, 176.
87. 2 Cor 3:18; Eph 4:24; Col 3:10. For a fuller discussion of the Christian character see Jones, "Christ and Character."
88. *Ethos* = habits, morals.

> But the fruit of the spirit is love, joy, peace, longsuffering, kindness, goodness, faithfulness, gentleness, and self-control. (Gal 5:22)

Paul gives us another description of the Christian manager's character, apart from the life of Christ, in his "fruits of the spirit" portion of Galatians 5. J. B. Lightfoot in 1865 grouped these nine divine endowments into three groups of three each.[89] The first group—love, joy, peace—are spiritual qualities which are to characterize their relationship to God and, while fundamental to the other six, do not arrest our attention as much as the other six. The second group of endowments—patience, kindness, goodness—affect a manager's relationship with his coworkers. The third grouping—faithfulness, gentleness and self-control—describe a Christian manager's internal moral compass.[90] These six characteristics lay the foundation for a harmonious business environment. While there is some dispute over Paul's organization of these gifts, it is helpful for our discussion to use the Lightfoot grouping, so, it is these last six spiritual gifts that warrant some comment:

- Longsuffering[91] is the attitude that Christian managers are to display to their coworkers.[92] The term is related to "patience" and "steadfastness," and refers to the manager who exercises forbearance towards those coworkers who annoy or oppose him. He refuses to give in to passion and anger. New Testament examples of non-patient managers include:
  - The disciples and the Canaanite woman,[93]
  - Peter's impatience by cutting off the servant's ear on the Mount of Olives,[94]
  - James and John about the opposition from the Samaritan village,[95]
  - The farmer in James 5 who is impatient with harvest laws (5:7).

---

89. Lightfoot, *St. Paul's Epistle to the Galatians*, 212.
90. As Paul uses it in Phil 1:9–11.
91. *Makrothymia* = forbearance, patience.
92. 2 Cor 6:6; Eph 4:2; Col 1:11; 3:12; 2 Tim 3:10; 4:2 Heb 6:12; Jas 5:10.
93. Matt 15:23.
94. John 18:10–11; and this was after Peter wanted to put a limit on human patience, Matt 18:21–35.
95. Luke 9:54.

Jesus on Management in the New Testament   69

But Jesus, in the days of his flesh, was patient with all who came into contact with him.[96]

- Kindness[97] is employed only by Paul in the New Testament as an attitude that managers are to show towards their workers. The word is translated also as "good," "gracious," and "gentle." Paul the manager commends his ministry by his kindness[98] and exhorts the Colossian workers to likewise adorn their life with kindness.[99] Thus, a kind business manager uses his position of influence for worthy and "good" acts. As always, our ultimate example is Christ, who was a kind man.[100]

- Goodness[101] is translated from a Greek term also used only by Paul[102] and has a relation to "generosity." It is similar to "kindness" but has more righteousness content in the attitude, as in "good" character. God the Father is good to us.[103]

- "Faithfulness"[104] is a term often used in reference to one's spiritual faith in God, but this particular context suggests that "faith" denotes an attitude of loyalty, dependability, trustworthiness, and fidelity that the manager has towards his colleagues.[105] Paul urged workers to be "trustworthy" towards their employers: "[Employees] are to be well-pleasing, not argumentative, not pilfering, but showing all good faith."[106] Paul may be a bit tender on this attitude, since he complains about the lack of loyalty exhibited by many Galatians.[107] New Testament examples include Timothy, who was a faithful companion to Paul.[108]

---

96. 1 Tim 1:16.
97. *Chrestotes* = good, pleasant, gracious.
98. 2 Cor 6:6.
99. Col 3:12.
100. Mark 10:13–16.
101. *Agathosyne* = moral good in character.
102. Cf. Rom 15:14; Eph 5:9; 2 Thess 1:11.
103. Eph 2:4–10.
104. *Pistis.*
105. Cf. Matt 23:23; 1 Cor 13:7; Titus 2:10.
106. Titus 2:10.
107. Gal 4:16.
108. Phil 2:19–30.

- Meekness[109] or gentleness has "the quality of not being overly impressed by a sense of one's self-importance."[110] This is one of those attitudes that is modeled by Jesus.[111] Meekness is the very opposite of anger, violence, arrogance, and self-assertion, but similar to mildness and gentleness in dealing with coworkers and the embracing of consideration of others. Paul was meek and gentle[112] but Jesus was the model of meekness.[113]

- Self-control[114] is perhaps last in order to stress the contrast between the last two attributes of the works of the flesh: "drunkenness and orgies."[115] Self-control was a prized Greek virtue, emphasized by both Socrates and Aristotle. The Greek word, however, only appears once in the Apocrypha LXX[116] and it only appears three times in the New Testament.[117] Paul applies self-control to our thoughts in 2 Corinthians 10:5 as well as our activities.[118]

> Finally, brothers, whatever is true, whatever is honorable, whatever is just, whatever is pure, whatever is lovely, whatever is commendable, if there is any excellence, if there is anything worthy of praise, think about these things. What you have learned and received and heard and seen in me—practice these things. (Phil 4:8–9)

This Pauline list of virtues is unique for several reasons. It seems to be more reflective of classical lists of virtues that other Classical thinkers wrote.[119] It also has elements of Jewish wisdom. And it is distinctly oriented to the culture in which the Philippians were living at the time. There is nothing quite like it in the ancient world or in other biblical lists. It is important to note that Paul is telling the "brothers" to not just think

---

109. *Praytes* = humble.
110. Bauer et al., "Praytes."
111. Matt 11:29; 21:5.
112. 1 Thess 2:7.
113. Matt 11:29.
114. *Enkrateia.*
115. Gal 5:20.
116. 4 Macc 5:34.
117. Cf. Acts 24:25; Titus 1:8; 1 Pet 1:6.
118. 1 Cor 9:24–27.
119. Epictetus, *Discourses;* Seneca, *Moral Essay.*

noble thoughts but to remember the good things they have "practiced" in the past. There is a political sense to this list because Paul has previously brought citizenship into the letter,[120] and so while the Philippians are citizens of heaven they are also citizens of Rome and must live in that reality while on earth. They are not to abandon their Roman citizenship to concentrate only on heaven. Hendricksen has a nice summary of this exhortation: "You are Roman citizens and proud of it (and so am I, Acts 16:21, 37). But constantly bear in mind that what matters most is the fact that you are citizens of the kingdom of heaven. Continue, therefore, to exercise that citizenship in a manner worthy of gospel of Christ."[121] Here are six "whatever" virtues that Paul emphasizes to the "brother"/managers at Philippi:

- "Whatever is true."[122] While this characteristic has its reference to God and the gospel, here Paul may be stressing the Hebrew wisdom idea of true speech against lies and deceit. The Christian manager is to speak truth to his coworkers.

- "Whatever is noble."[123] In his speech and in his entire behavior, the Christian manager is to be honorable, dignified, and serious. Again, this term may be rooted in Hebrew wisdom in the sense that whatever is worthy of respect, wherever it comes from, is worth considering.[124]

- "Whatever is right."[125] Managers are to take into account what is fair and just for their coworkers. Managers are to realize that they, too, have an employer who treats them justly.[126] This is one of those virtues that is prescribed by what God thinks and not what the world thinks is "right" or "just."

- "Whatever is pure."[127] Managers deal with a constantly secular environment and are therefore constantly being tempted by what is unchaste and impure and immoral, if not illegal. They are to be

120. Phil 1:27; 3:21.
121. Hendricksen, *Exposition of Colossians and Philippians*, 80.
122. *Alethes*.
123. *Semnos* = venerable.
124. Prov 8:6.
125. *Dikalos* = just.
126. Col 4:1.
127. *Hagnos* = freedom from defilement.

steadfast in their faith and not be besmirched by the evil around them.

- "Whatever is lovely."[128] This Greek word only appears here in the New Testament. Here is even a more Hellenistic trait, that of being considered admirable or lovely by the population at large—great art, music, sport feats, etc. Morality takes a back seat to this virtue. It is rooted in God's common grace: appreciation of the beautiful.

- "Whatever is admirable."[129] Here is a concession to the unbelieving culture surrounding the Philippian manager and his organization.[130] The manager is to have a good rapport with those even outside the group.[131]

- "Whatever is excellent"[132] and "praiseworthy." Paul is telling the managers to pick and choose those virtues around them that correspond to the gospel. After all, unbelievers do good[133] and can love.[134] "Excellent" is the primary Greek word for virtue or moral excellence and is not found elsewhere in Paul's writings.[135] "Praiseworthy" is very similar to "excellence," but probably has a more populist meaning in that approval of others is important for a manager's public witness.

Finally, Paul is telling the managers to "practice"[136] these virtues. He is telling them to live an incarnational life to those around him. It is important to embrace the good and virtuous whenever the manager finds it but to do this embracing discernment and care. To help in this lifestyle, the manager is to follow how Paul and Jesus did it.

> But as for you, O man of God, flee these things. Pursue righteousness, godliness, faith, love, steadfastness, gentleness. Fight

---

128. *Prosphiles* = friendly disposition.

129. *Euphemos* = well spoken, reputable, gracious, commendable, decent, honorable, attractive. This word is not found in the LXX.

130. 2 Cor 6:8.

131. 2 Cor 6:8.

132. *Arete* = perfection.

133. Luke 6:33.

134. Matt 5:46.

135. Fee, *Paul's Letters to the Philippians*, 419.

136. *Prasso* = do, perform.

the good fight of the faith. Take hold of the eternal life to which you were called. (1 Tim 6:11–12)

In this short exhortation to Paul's young manager, he separates Timothy from the greedy evildoers of the first part of this chapter, where the love of money characterizes so many in society and even the organization. Paul emphasizes the distinctive character of Timothy by three linguistic devices: "But you," "O man of God," and the "flee/pursue" format. There is the antithesis theme of Timothy's character versus the character of the false believers earlier.[137] This chapter, as all of 1 Timothy, is focused on the characteristics of a company leader and the replacement manager for Paul as he is getting older. However, I see another application for the businessman. Here are some management ideas contained in this brief Pauline exhortation:

"O man of God." Paul calls Timothy "man of God." This is a designation for a person chosen by Yahweh to be entrusted with an important managerial position: Moses, Samuel, David, Elijah, Elisha, Shemaiah (and various prophets), and an angel. Clearly, we have stalwarts in the faith like Moses, Samuel, David, Elijah, and Elisha. But we also have lesser figures like Shemaiah and the prophets in 1 Kings 13 receiving special commissions from Yahweh to be his communicators. I suggest that Timothy, as a manager, qualifies as a unique man of God who was called in like manner (1 Tim 6:12). Paul seems to invest in Timothy a managerial responsibility to be a chosen shepherd whose life is to be an example to all in his organization. Thus, that which follows is directed towards a manager:

- "Flee."[138] This is the first imperative in this exhortation. Timothy is to flee the temptations and allurements of the materialistic impulse of those around him. Here is the great antithesis: not this, but this. Yarbrough helpfully notes that there are times when we fight the sin and other times when we should flee the sin,[139] and Paul thinks this is one of the times, perhaps indicating the draw of greed.

---

137. Towner, *The Letters to Timothy and Titus*, 406.

138. *Pheugo* = Only used three other times in the New Testament, notably in 1 Timothy 2:22.

139. Yarbrough, *The Letters to Timothy and Titus*, 322–23.

- "Pursue."[140] It is not enough to avoid sin. The manager must embrace the good. Paul tells Timothy that he must create and maintain good habits in life. Discard and adopt. And what is Timothy is to run after as a Christian manager. Paul gives a list of good habits. This is the same advice Paul gives Timothy, again, in 2 Timothy 2:22—"flee" and "pursue."

- "Righteousness."[141] This may be the right actions directed towards coworkers. This is moral conduct lived before the community. It is the human relational side of "godliness" which comes next in Paul's list.

- "Godliness."[142] This is the relation a manager needs to have with God. It is on this relationship that the previous virtue of "righteousness" is built. This attribute is so important that Paul mentions it eight times in this letter alone.[143]

- "Faith,[144] love."[145] These two virtues are almost always paired together in the letters to Timothy.[146] "Faith" may be more accurately seen as trust and loyalty to coworkers,[147] and "love" is the outworking attitude towards coworkers. Both of these virtues are built upon "godliness."

- "Endurance."[148] This is the quality of bearing up under adversity. It is steadfastness in all circumstances. If Timothy is to stay and manage in Ephesus[149] he will need this virtue in spades. Paul even points to his own example of "endurance" in his correspondence to Timothy.[150]

---

140. *Dioko* = follow after, run after, constantly strive for.
141. *Dikalosune* = justice.
142. *Eusebia* = devotion, piety to God.
143. 1 Tim 2:2; 3:16; 4:7, 8; 6:3, 5, 6.
144. *Pistis*.
145. *Agape*.
146. 1 Tim 1:5, 14; 2:15; 4:12; 6:11; 2 Tim 1:13; 2:22; 3:10. Cf. Titus 2:2.
147. 1 Tim 1:2; Titus 2:10; Eph 6:21; elsewhere.
148. *Hypomone* = steadfastness, patience.
149. 1 Tim 1:3.
150. 2 Tim 3:10.

- "Gentleness."[151] This virtue is mentioned only here in the New Testament. It means "empathetic" but not meekly weak. It can also mean "to have a generous temperament." Moses is described as gentle, but not with this term, in the LXX.[152] Could it be that gentleness is the last virtue that Paul stresses because gentleness is a defining characteristic of a successful manager as he seeks to lead his organization?
- "Fight the good fight of faith." Paul sums up the pursuit of managerial virtue by stressing that the pursuit is never ending and that it is a contest of wills for the manager to continually corral his own weaknesses in order to lead his organization in the midst of a hostile environment. He calls for daily perseverance on the manager's part against the flesh and the world.

> You [Timothy], however, know all about my teaching, my way of life,[153] my purpose, faith, patience, love, endurance, persecutions, sufferings—what kind of things happened to me in Antioch, Iconium, and Lystra, the persecutions I endured. (2 Tim 3:10–11)[154]

The contrast between the corrosive unbelieving fellowship and the edifying Christian fellowship is given to Timothy. Paul wrote to Timothy while in a Roman prison and getting along in age, so he is reminiscing about his past life for the benefit of Timothy, his younger colleague. Here is the example for the Christian business manager. Live a life before your coworkers ("way of life"),[155] like Paul did, which is attractive and exemplary, full of Christian grace and gifts for their encouragement in you as a leader. Paul gives nine particular virtues which are in no discernable order. The impression Paul leaves is that the Christian business manager must not only know Paul's "teaching" but follow Paul's "way of life" as a model. A small but perhaps significant linguistic point is that before each of the nine items, Paul places the personal pronoun "my," giving emphasis to the item and thus distinguishing them from what would be

---

151. *Praupathia* = meekness. Aristotle uses the term in his *Nicomachean Ethics*, 2.7.1108a: "With regard to anger also there is an excess, a deficiency, and a mean . . . let us call the mean good temper."

152. Num 12:3.

153. *Agoge*, as in 1 Cor 4:17.

154. Cf. Gal 5:22–6:10; 1 Thess 5:12–22.

155. *Agoge*.

expected from a non-believing business manager. Paul is giving a personal testimony of his character to his young manager, Timothy. If one is looking for a personal summary of one's managerial philosophy, Paul gives it here to Timothy. The implication is that Timothy had better be prepared to exhibit those same qualities of life and action as he continues his management calling:

- "My teaching."[156] Paul's doctrine and training was always focused on the mission set out for him by his boss, Jesus. There were no extraneous diversions from that rifle-focus. This passage notes Paul's authoritative doctrinal and practical teaching. Timothy should carry on Paul's teaching.

- "My conduct."[157] Paul's lifestyle, the guiding principles of his life, was available for all to see and judge. His general behavior was a living testimony to other managers and members of the organization. Hendricksen calls this Paul's "walk of life."[158] Future managers should seek to emulate Paul's way of life.

- "My purpose."[159] Paul's singlemindedness, his narrow focus, was always on the charge given to him by his boss. Paul's firm resolution is to accomplish the goals set before him by a sovereign God. Paul's teaching and conduct are in harmony.

- "My faith."[160] Paul's mind and heart were always set on the one unchanging fact in his life, his love for Jesus. This is the emphasis that all Christian managers need to care for their Christian faith.

- "My patience."[161] Paul's life demonstrated a forbearance with those with whom he worked and those with whom he disagreed. This is managerial patience with respect to people, and in an organization it is a non-debatable quality for success.[162] As has been noted before,

---

156. *Didaskalia* = doctrine, refers to the authority of the teacher.

157. *Agoge*; only used here in New Testament, but it is used two times in LXX: Esth 2:20; 10:3.

158. Hendricksen, *I & II Timothy and Titus*, 291. 1 Cor 4:17.

159. *Prothesis*. See "hand to plow" illustration in Luke 9:62 and 1 Corinthians 9:10.

160. *Pistis* = particularly the confidence in divine truths which motivate good works.

161. *Makrothymia*.

162. 2 Cor 6:6.

this "patience" is an attribute of Yahweh (Rom 2:4) and of Jesus (1 Tim 1:16).

- "My love."[163] This forbearance was born out of a love given to Paul by the Holy Spirit since Paul, in his natural state, was not a loving man, but he uses *agape* in every one of his letters for a total of seventy-one times.

- "My endurance."[164] Paul persevered during torture, discouragement, natural disasters, and the ravages of old age imprisoned in a Roman jail.[165] Paul's commitment to the organization was sturdy and he expects Timothy's faith to be as sturdy.[166] This is patience with respect to circumstances and is emphasized as Paul gets to "persecution" and "suffering." Managers: expect to be persecuted and suffer for your Christian convictions.[167]

- "My persecutions."[168] Paul breaks down his trials into persecutions at the hands of enemies. Paul was specific in giving the time and place for these persecutions.[169] This is Paul's active obedience and patience. The persecution will come because the manager is connected to the organization and what it stands for.[170] The fact is, Jesus promises persecution (Matt 13:21).

- "My sufferings."[171] In reminding Timothy of his sufferings, Paul is commending to Timothy one of the hardest and yet noblest aspects of Christian belief: Jesus' followers do not add to what Jesus did for them on the cross, but they are called to live out the implications of the cross in their daily lives. Second Corinthians 11:23–33 gives a list of Paul's "persecutions" and "sufferings."

---

163. *Agape* = charity. Interestingly, this Greek word is not found in classical Greek but only in biblical Greek.

164. *Hypomone*.

165. 2 Cor 6:3–10.

166. 1 Tim 6:11.

167. 2 Tim 3:12.

168. *Diogmos*.

169. Antioch, Acts 13:48–52; Iconium, Acts 14:1–7; Lystra, Acts 14:8–20.

170. 2 Cor 12:10.

171. *Pathema*. Yarbrough, *The Letters of Timothy and Titus*, 421.

> They not only continue to do these very [evil] things but also approve of those who practice them. (Rom 1:32)[172]

Rom 1:32 tells us that there are more than just evil teachers. There are evildoers who will not be satisfied with the freedom to do evil. They will not be satisfied with doing evil in secret, behind closed doors.

- They want public approval for doing evil.
- They want evil out in the open with general approval.
- They want evil to be required by all.
- They want evil to be normal and obligatory.

It is a matter of actions now morally unacceptable becoming acceptable becoming unassailable.[173] This is dueling evangelism: The unbelievers want believers to convert to their lifestyle. While the encouragement by unbelievers for believers to sin is as old as the Old Testament, as David laments ("The wicked freely strut about when what is vile is honored among people," Ps 12:8),[174] Paul gives us the most striking characterization of the evildoers in the phrase "they approve of those who practice them." That is, it is not the "practice" of evil that is as bad as the approval and encouragement and requirement of others to "practice" evil.[175] Isaiah 59:15 thunders, "Truth is nowhere to be found, and whoever shuns evil becomes a prey." The secular forces in the culture set out to ruin anyone who shuns evil. Things have gone way beyond acting against the person who seeks to stand up for what is right and resist that which is wrong.

---

172. Cf. 2 Pet 2:14–19; 1 John 2:26; for contrary, see 1 Cor 13:6; 2 Thess 2:12; Acts 8:1.

173. Cf. Dalrymple, "The Choleric Outbreak," 78–82. "The sexual revolution does not simply represent a growth in the routine transgression of traditional sexual codes or even a modest expansion of the boundaries of what is and is not acceptable sexual behavior; rather, it involves the abolition of such codes in their entirety. More than that, it has come in certain areas, such as that of homosexuality, to require the positive repudiation of traditional sexual mores to the point where belief in, or maintenance of, such traditional views has come to be seen as ridiculous and even a sign of serious mental or moral deficiency" (Trueman, *The Rise and Triumph of the Modern Self*, 21).

174. Cf. Ps 64:5–6. Clarke (1760–1832) in his early-nineteenth-century commentary had it right: "Were we to take this in its obvious sense it would signify that at that time wickedness was the way to preferment, and good men the objects of persecution" (Clarke, "Psalms 12:8").

175. As Bruce noted, "we are not only bent on damning ourselves, but we congratulate others in the doing of those things that we know have their issue in damnation" (Bruce, *The Epistle to the Romans*, 53).

Now even to avoid sin on a personal level makes one a marked man. In our collapsing society those who turn aside from sin will be the losers. John Calvin wrote on Isaiah 59:15, "Whoever wishes to live among people must vie with them in wickedness, according to the common proverb, 'Among wolves we must howl; but he who wishes to live innocently shall be torn in pieces, as a sheep is torn by wolves.'"[176] So the Romans verse (Rom 1:32) tells the Isaiah verse, "You entice the Christian business managers to 'wander away' from a godly management practices by false teaching, you folks lure them to 'stagger' in doing right by wrong teaching, and we will show them what they are doing is the normal and successful thing. And all the while mocking him with laughter behind his back."[177]

176. Calvin, *Commentary on the Book of the Prophet Isaiah*, 4.261: "Whoever shuns vices, exposes himself as a prey to the wicked." Cf. Motyer, *Isaiah*, 416; Oswalt, *The Book of Isaiah, Chapters 40–66*, 524; Young, *The Book of Isaiah*, 3.437

177. Belloc (1870-1953), *This and That and the Other*, 282: "We sit by and watch the Barbarian, we tolerate him; in the long stretches of peace, we are not afraid. We are tickled by his irreverence; his comic inversion of our old certitudes and our fixed creeds refreshes us: we laugh. But as we laugh we are watched by large and awful faces from beyond: and on these faces there is no smile." Rousseau (1712-78), *First Discourse*, 14.6: "What a train of vices must attend upon such uncertainty. No more sincere friendships; no more real esteem; no more well-founded trust. Suspicions, offenses, fears, coolness, reserve, hatred, betrayal, will constantly hide beneath this even and deceitful veil of politeness, beneath this so much vaunted urbanity which we owe to the enlightenment of our century." King David noted Yahweh's protection from these barbarians in Psalm 124:6: "Praise be Yahweh who has not let us be torn by their teeth." Arnold (1822-83), "Dover Beach," describes the eroding of Western civilization: "The Sea of Faith was once, too, at the full, and round earth's shore / Lay like the folds of a bright girdle furled. / But now I only hear / Its melancholy, long, withdrawing roar, / Retreating, to the breath / Of the night-wind, down the vast edges drear / And naked shingles of the world." French novelist Flaubert (1821-80) in an 1872 letter to Russian novelist Ivan Turgenev, wrote: "The bourgeoisie is so stunned that it no longer even has the instinct of self-preservation; and what will follow will be worse! I feel the same sadness experienced by Roman patricians in the fourth century. I feel a wave of relentless Barbarism, rising up from below the ground. I hope to be dead before all is swept away. But in the meantime, it is no joke. Never have affairs of the mind counted for less. Never have hatred of everything that is great, contempt for all that is beautiful, abhorrence for literature been so manifest" (Flaubert, "Thank You for Making Me Read Tolstoy's Novels"). English writer Waugh (1903-66) in his 1939 book, *Robbery under Law*, 278-79: "Civilization has no force of its own beyond what is given it from within. It is under constant assault, and it takes most of the energies of civilized man to keep going at all. There are criminal ideas and a criminal class in every nation and the first action of every revolution, figuratively and literally, is to open the prisons. Barbarism is never finally defeated; given propitious circumstances, men and women who seem quite orderly will commit every conceivable atrocity. The danger does not come

HEBREWS ON MANAGEMENT

> But solid food is for the mature[178] who by constant use have trained[179] themselves to distinguish[180] good from evil. (Heb 5:14)

In Hebrews 5 we see discernment commended. The author of Hebrews refers to theological doctrine as "food" and to those who "have their faculties[181] trained by practice"[182] able to discern the difference between good and evil. This management sensitivity is not easy nor quickly attained, but only comes with patience for the "maturation" process.

In his book on Reformation art, William Halewood notes, "According to the famous Renaissance principles (as stated, for example, by Francis Bacon) art should deliver a 'golden' world of harmony, symmetry, and fulfilled aspiration, a revelation in human terms of universal beauty."[183] Sounds like a great management goal! If art really is a creative activity producing "harmony, symmetry, fulfilled aspirations" and "universal beauty" originating from human relationships over time, then artistry, indeed, is an essential ingredient of successful business management.

Lewis Smedes (1921–2002) wrote that discernment "separates the moral artist from the moral bungler."[184] That is to say, discernment in an organization is the ability to see what is really going on around one and then the ability to make an appropriate response. The discerning manager recognizes the difference between peripheral and central issues. Smedes maintained that the discerning manager is sensitive to "the difference between things that need action now and things that can be put off until tomorrow, between people who need to be confronted and people

---

merely from habitual hooligans; we are all potential recruits for anarchy. Unremitting effort is needed to keep men living together at peace; there is only a margin of energy left over for experiment, however beneficent. Once the prisons of the mind have been opened, the orgy is on."

178. *Teleios* = adult, full grown, complete.
179. *Gumnazo* = use, exercise.
180. *Diakrino* = discern.
181. *Aistheteria* = organ of sense, faculty of perception. Cf. Jer 4:19a, LXX.
182. *Gumnazo.*
183. Halewood, *Six Subjects of Reformation Art: A Preface to Rembrandt,* 19.
184. Smedes, *Choices,* 95.

who need to be comforted, between words that can be taken literally and words that disguise the real message a person wants us to hear."[185]

Management for a Christian is an art because there are no easy answers, no cookbook approaches, no line-by-line manuals, no guarantees when managers are dealing with other humans and their emotions, aspirations, thought processes, psychological makeup, physiological limitations, and sociological backgrounds. It is an art because managers must be sensitive to the creative leading of the Holy Spirit as they apply truth and love to management complexities. And the manager's sensitivity is fallible, time-consuming, and confusing, and so he stumbles, fails, hurts people, and even willfully, to his shame, sins. Managers must remember that as they are developing their artistry of biblical management skills, to give themselves time to mature and develop as under-shepherds of the Great Shepherd so that they can bring forth "harmony, symmetry, fulfilled aspirations, and universal beauty" in their organization.

> Obey your leaders[186] and submit to their authority. They keep watch over[187] you as men who must give an account. Obey them so that their work will be a joy, not a burden, for that would be of no advantage[188] to you. (Heb 13:17)

The context of Hebrews 13:17 is not congregational-specific but rather general exhortations on the Christian life, including marriage, hospitality, prison visitation, avaricious activities, sound teaching, etc. Consequently, while the "managers" in 13:17 refer to company "leaders, who spoke the word of God to you" (13:7), it mustn't be exclusively ecclesiastic. A couple of the words in the Greek text of Heb 13:17 even have application to the marketplace:

Agrupneo is translated "to keep watch." It comes from the combination "to search after" and "sleep" (literally: "to chase sleep"). That is, the managers spend sleepless nights watching over their coworkers. Sleepless nights are part of the business manager's job description! In Mark 13:33–37 the manager is exhorted to keep his accounts short and up to date because he never knows what the future will bring. He has been

---

185. Smedes, *Choices*, 97.
186. *Hageomal* = those that guide.
187. *Arupnousin* = search for.
188. *Alusiteles* = unprofitable.

"assigned tasks"[189] to do by the owner of the business and he needs to stay focused on the work at hand.

Alusiteles is translated "to no advantage," but really it means "unprofitable" or "not making good the expense involved."[190] Spending money for no return is not a good business strategy! If this verse is seen from the viewpoint of one working in the marketplace where a manager's decisions financially affect those working in the organization, then this verse can be readily applied to the shepherding task of the Christian business manager.

Many Christian authors have offered a context for management.[191] Ray Anderson (1926–2009) wrote about parochial church organizations and para-parochial church organizations.[192] Anderson contrasts the parochial church organization with what he terms the "para-parochial" church organization thusly: "The para-parochial form of the church might be termed 'mission specific' as its unique purpose."[193] Further-

---

189. *Ergon* = every many his work, business, deed.

190. Used only here in the New Testament; cf. Luke 17:2, *lusiteleo* = "better," "pay one's expenses."

191. For instance, Engstrom argues that administration leadership carries four basic tasks: 1. the executive ability or skill to lead by developing the gift of leadership, 2. the requirement to appoint people to carry on the work in local congregations, 3. the need to see administration as an essential responsibility, 4. the ability to work with people and develop their skills (Engstrom, *The Making of a Christian Leader*, 54). Many Christian authors have written about management. Engstrom and Dayton define management as simply "the effort to enhance the human potential" (Engstrom and Dayton, *The Art of Management for Christian Leaders*, 37–38). Rush takes a slightly different tack on management when he writes, "Management is meeting the needs of people as they work at accomplishing their job" (Rush, *Management: A Biblical Approach*, 13). John H. Alexander, past president of Inter-Varsity Christian Fellowship and a member of the American Management Association, applies the Christian perspective on management when he writes, "Management ability is one of the gifts of the Holy Spirit. It is also a science. There is a body of knowledge and principles (acquired through the experience of our predecessors) to be learned. Further, management is an art. There are specific aptitudes and skills to be developed through sustained practice" (Alexander, *Managing Our Work*, 13).

192. Parochial church organizations are defined as these organizations which "will always be limited and bound to its geographic and demographic center, which is the church in its sense of being a gathered body of Christians. In this sense, the church as a parish has stability and tends to be what we might call 'community specific' in its nature. By this we mean to suggest that the local church as a gathered congregation has, among its other functions, the unique function of creating and upbuilding a community of people as the body of Christ" (Alexander, *Managing Our Work*, 12–13).

193. Anderson, *Minding God's Business*, 13.

more, there are no geographical boundaries or necessary limitations in a para-parochial organization. While Anderson's definition precludes a marketplace organization from being considered a "Christian" organization, a business organization combines both the geographic dimension and the "mission specific" dimension of a para-parochial organization. So, a business owned and operated by a Christian might legitimately be called a "Christian" organization in the broadest context of its relationship to the kingdom of God, and thus biblical applications would apply.[194] Regardless, Anderson offers helpful ideas along the way for any Christian in business who is seeking a theology for managing a business for the advancement of God's kingdom and the flourishing of the business. At one point, Anderson writes, "The spiritual task of managing Christian organizations is first of all a task of managing an organization with full responsibility for its participation in the created structure of this world as God intended it."[195]

The kingdom of God does not overthrow existing social, economic, or political orders of the culture. The agents of the kingdom of heaven advance within the existing structures, seeking to use the divinely appointed social structure for rational order and human flourishing, while the agents act as "shepherds" and "ambassadors" for the king.[196] Clearly, this shepherding task has application for the Christian manager in the marketplace.

> We do not want you to become lazy, but to imitate[197] those who through faith and patience[198] inherit what has been promised. (Heb 6:12)

F. F. Bruce calls this verse the insistence on "the grace of continuance" for the believers that they should go on exhibiting the same zeal and commitment that marked their first year as Christians.[199] Furthermore, this continuance should persist until the end. The author of Hebrews tells managers that they will need "patience" or "steadfastness" in their Christian walk if they are to persevere until they cross the Jordan,

---

194. Cf. Wade and Kittler, *The Lord Is My Counsel*, 82.

195. Wade and Kittler, *The Lord Is My Counsel*, 23.

196. Cf. Matt 22:15–22, paying taxes to Caesar; Luke 12:13–15, 54–59, inheritance; 1 Tim 6:10; Jas 4:13; Jude 11, greed and profligacy.

197. *Mimetes*.

198. *Makrothymia*.

199. Cockerill, *The Epistle to the Hebrews*, 127.

indicating that being a consistent Christian business manager will not be easy. In fact, the Greek word translated "patience" in Hebrews 6:12 can also be translated "long-suffering" or "steadfast," and it is one of the fruits of the spirit in Galatians 5:22. So, buckle up, being a Christian manager ain't for the faint of heart.

JAMES ON MANAGEMENT

> Brothers, as an example[200] of patience[201] in the face of suffering,[202] take the prophets who spoke in the name of the Lord. (Jas 5:10)

In a parallel passage to the Hebrews 6 exhortation to be steadfast in the face of hostility and patience with those who may persecute them. This is a manager who has the power to avenge himself yet refrains from the exercise of this power. The brother of Jesus knows of what he speaks. Managers are to study the lives and writings of the Old Testament prophets, as well as Jesus, for examples on how to live a life of faith. James saw his brother slaughtered, and he would later be murdered by an angry mob of Pharisees in AD 62 by being thrown off the temple roof in Jerusalem, then stoned, then beat with rods.[203]

> For you know that the testing of your faith produces steadfastness. And let steadfastness have its full effect, that you may be perfect and complete, lacking in nothing. (Jas 1:3–4)

In this brief introductory couplet to his letter to the scattered organization, James tells the believing managers to have the perspective that the trials, temptations, and tribulations that they are surrounded with will produce the best results in their life, even if it doesn't look like it now. They are to consider or count the testing joyful, even if the testing is not a joyful event. Change your attitude, brothers, and your persecution will appear to be better than you expected. From James we have a reiteration

---

200. *Hupodeigma.*

201. *Makrothumia* = self-restraint, forbearance.

202. *Katopatheia* = to suffer misfortune, hardship, or affliction. This Greek word appears only here in the New Testament.

203. According to Hegesippus, which is quoted in Eusebius's *Ecclesiastical History*, 2.23; Manton (1620–77) doesn't stop with James as our model of longsuffering at the hands of others: "Micah was in prison, Jeremiah in the dungeon, Isaiah sawed asunder, and shall we stick at a little suffering? (Manton, *James*, 427).

of the maturation process from testing to perseverance to maturity to ultimate completion. This James passage follows the sequence of spiritual maturity or chain of virtues given by Paul and Peter earlier.[204] The outcome of life's tests is to be steadfast or enduring in one's Christian faith.[205] James is telling the Christian managers that testing is designed by God to produce a wholeness of character that lacks nothing in all the important Christian virtues. But he says, "Buckle up, boys, management is not for the weak-minded."

Some key takeaways for the business manager in this short James passage are several:

- "My brothers" (1:2) is usually interpreted to mean "brothers and sisters" in the organization, but I suggest that "brothers" refers to the male executives of the organization[206] to lead and encourage the branch offices to think rightly about the multitude of tests[207] the organization is enduring, and that these "manager/brothers" are to be example of such biblical thinking.

- James tells the business manager that discernment will come through "testing"[208] and "trials."[209] The Greek word translated "testing"[210] is only used once in the New Testament and twice in the Greek Old Testament, but we get the sense from its use in the Old Testament that the testing is not a one-time event but a process over time. In short, a season(s) of "testings." So the business manager should man up, because tough times are coming. It is important to note that the process of maturity of character which the "trials" are designed to further can be short-circuited or hindered by the lack of endurance or impatience. The "trials" and the "testings" include temptations to leave the faith.[211] In verse 2, James warns the managers not to "fall

---

204. Cf. 1 Pet 1; Rom 8; 2 Cor 1:6; Gal 5; 1 Tim 6:11.

205. Peters talks about "the art of value management" and "symbol management as a source of unparalleled opportunity" for the artistic organization manager" (Peters, "Leadership: Sad Facts and Silver Lining").

206. Notice how often James uses "brothers" in the letter, often in the context of "men": 2:1, 14; 3:1, 10, 12; 4:11; 5:7, 9–10, 12, 19.

207. *Poikilos* = manifold, literally "many colored."

208. *Holokleros* = sound, "may be mature and complete."

209. *Peirasmos* = temptations.

210. *Dokimion*.

211. 1 Tim 6:9.

into"[212] temptation and ruin their leadership witness. This is internal testing.

- There is, however, the external "testing" of persecution that James is probably referring to by using the same word where physical pain is involved.[213] "By stressing that the trials were 'of many kinds,' James deliberately casts his net widely, including the many kinds of suffering that Christians undergo in this fallen world: sickness, loneliness, bereavement, disappointment."[214]

- James tells the manager that she is in for a long management training period ("finish its work").[215] The process of developing "perseverance" is a life-long struggle and doesn't end until glory. That's why perseverance is needed—to stay the course in the face of all the testing coming the manager's way until his character is "finished."[216]

- James uses a Greek word which can be translated "perseverance"[217] but also can be translated "steadfastness," "fortitude," "staying power" and "endurance." But not "patience," because the word indicates how the manager is to deal with external events and not people, since patience is a people-oriented quality.[218] This is a more active set of behaviors which are employed to contend against circumstantial temptations.[219] The Greek word James uses here is that wonderful term *dokimion*, meaning the refining of gold and silver to shed the dross. I have noted that Peter uses the word in the same way,[220] and it is used twice in the LXX[221] to mean that the difficulties of

212. *Peripipto* = NIV has "face trials"; ESV has "meet trials."
213. 1 Pet 4:12.
214. Moo, *The Letter of James*, 54.
215. *Ergon teleion* = have its full effect.
216. *Teleos* = to bring to an end.
217. *Hypomone*.
218. James seems to understand that retribution and retaliation against competitors are not an option for the Christian manager, so an active "perseverance" while waiting for God to act is essential.
219. Trench, *Synonyms of the New Testament*, 278–81. Max DePree, the distinguished business leader, philanthropist, and author, writes, "Leadership is an art, something to be learned over time, not simply by reading books. Leadership is more tribal than scientific, more a weaving of relationships than an amassing of information" (DePree, *Leadership Is an Art*, 3).
220. 1 Pet 1:6–7.
221. Ps 12:6 and Prov 27:21.

life are given us by God to refine our faith in Jesus. James seems to understand that "endurance" is needed in the face of adverse market conditions if the business manager is to mature in her faith. James comes to the penultimate goal of all the testing and trials: active endurance under the difficult circumstances. Of course, Jesus is once again our example of this type of perseverance.[222]

- James's usage of the Greek word translated "complete"[223] tells us the goal for the business manager: integrity. The word is used in Acts 3:16 to contrast it with sickness and is used only once by Paul.[224]

So, the temporal point of James is that the business manager in order to have a healthy character[225] and be fit for service must endure with joy the testing God brings his way through people and circumstances. mature[226] and complete is the ultimate goal of all the earthy tribulations confronting the Christian manager. The term for "mature" is used in the New Testament to indicate a maturity in Christian character.[227] As always, James is hardcore and tells the managers that if they lose their perseverance or begin to complain too much they will not be mature and complete as sons of Jesus.[228] James is stating that Christian managers are born to attain the end of this completeness.

PETER ON MANAGEMENT

> To this you were called, because Christ suffered[229] for you, leaving you an example,[230] that you should follow[231] in his steps. (1 Pet 2:21)

This same reflective nature of the Christian manager's walk being like an image of the original is given expression by Peter. This Petrine admonition

---

222. 2 Thess 3:5.
223. *Holokleros* = entire, having all the parts, intact, undamaged, sound, perfect.
224. 1 Thess 5:23.
225. Cf. Noah as the "complete" man in Genesis 6:9.
226. *Teleios* = complete, mature.
227. 1 Cor 2:6; Eph 4:13; Phil 3:15; Col 1:28; Heb 5:14.
228. Jas 1:6–8.
229. *Pascho* = to suffer, experience, endure.
230. *Hupogrammos* = a writing copy for one to imitate.
231. *Epakoloutheo* = to follow after.

poetically echoes 1 John 2:6 in that it speaks of Jesus being our "example." The Greek word for "example" is the word used to describe forgers as they trace the signature of another person on a document. The Greek word translated "follow" here is unique in the New Testament, but it is used in 2 Macc 2:28 (LXX) to indicate "a following in the footsteps."[232] This particular verse has a primary focus on the individual Christian bearing up under unjust suffering, and as such every Christian manager should keep this passage in mind as he deals with the responsibilities and frustrations of godly management. Managers should walk as Jesus walked, do as he did, and relate to people as he related to people. In short, managers should be the "traced lines" of their Master as they step where he stepped!

> Show proper respect[233] to everyone, love the family of believers,
> fear God, honor[234] the emperor. (1 Pet 2:17)

Peter gives the Christian business manager four imperatives in 1 Peter 2:17: "respect," "love,"[235] "fear," and "honor."[236] The first imperative is the most important for the business manager because it is the most sweeping. The first and fourth imperatives come from the same Greek verb, *timao*. The first two imperatives relate to social groups, and the last two imperatives relate to individuals. Everybody in this verse is in

---

232. Vincent writes on *hupogrammos*: "A graphic word, meaning a copy set by writing masters for their pupils. Some explain it as a copy of characters over which a student is to trace the lines" (Vincent, *Word Studies*, 1.308).

233. *Timao* = esteem, to make heavy.

234. *Timao*.

235. "Dear friends, let us love one another, for love comes from God. Everyone who loves has been born of God and knows God" (1 John 4:7; cf. Rom 5:5; Gal 5:22). Smedes goes word-by-word, phrase-by-phrase through the first seven verses of 1 Corinthians 13 in his little book, *Love within Limits*, which should be on every Christian manager's bookshelf, with personal application notes inside. In his closing comments, Smedes writes, "We have used a simple definition of love: the power that moves us to respond to a neighbor's needs with no expectation of reward" (Smedes, *Love within Limits*, 126). Christian love cannot be self-generated; it is a love which allows for self-sacrifice of the rights and the honor of the manager. It is a love that permits manager vulnerability because it is a love that is not basic to our sinful nature. It is a love that is characterized by the so-called *kenosis* passage in Philippians 2:3–8. It is a love that may require a Christian manager to wait years to receive the honor, prestige, and appreciation due that manager—just as the Master Manager had to wait until his resurrection to receive due recognition and honor from his closest friends (cf. John 20:25–28) and neighbors (cf. Matt 13:57). It is a love that requires Christian managers to turn to God, for this love is the love from God himself.

236. "Honor the king," Prov 24:21.

tension, if not outright conflict with each other. Peter commands us to "love" other Christians and to honor or "show respect" to everybody else.[237] How does this square with the commands of Jesus to "love" our enemies?[238] The answer is that we are to "respect" and "honor" all those to whom "respect" is due. Discernment is needed here. Because fellow Christians are part of the spiritual family, special support and assistance is due them, but all employees are to have the respect of the manager.

> Be shepherds[239] of God's flock that is under your care, serving as overseers[240]—not because you must, but because you are

237. Cf. Jas 3:9.

238. Matt 5:44; Jas 2:8.

239. *Poimaino* = to lead, tend, guide; 1 Cor 9:7. "Again, Jesus said, 'Simon, son of John, do you truly love me?' He answered, 'Yes, LORD, you know that I love you.' Jesus said, 'Manage (*poimaino*) my sheep'" (John 21:16). In this Gospel verse we see that "tending" or "feeding," or better, "managing," involves more than just giving those under one's care food. Jesus is telling Peter that as a manager of the LORD's sheep Peter must guide, guard, discipline, restore, materially assist, exercise authority over, lead to nourishment, and train those under him. Paul adds another dimension to the shepherding role of *poimaino* in 1 Corinthians 9:7 when he states, "Who tends (*poimaino*) a flock and does not drink of the milk?" The point being there is an intimacy between the manager and the managed in that the manager does not take advantage of the managed. They are in the shepherding relationship together.

240. *Episkopos*. "Be managers [*poimaino* = to lead, tend, guide, shepherd] of God's flock that is under your care, serving as managers [*episkopo* = overseers]—not because you must, but because you are willing, as God wants you to be, not greedy for money, but eager to manage [*prothumos* = eager to serve, are ready]; not lording [*katakurieuo* = master] it over those entrusted to you but being examples [*tupos* = a type, symbol, allegory, pattern] to the flock" (1 Pet 5:2–3). *Episkopos* is also translated "guardian," "superintendent," and usually refers to church officers (like Eleazar in LXX Num 4:16; cf. Judg 9:28; 2 Kgs 11:15; Neh 11:9; Isa 60:17, et al.) and "bishop" in Acts 20:28. In a clearly ecclesiastical context, Paul tells Timothy in 1 Timothy 3:1 that this is a "trustworthy saying: If anyone aspires to the office of manager (*episkopos*), he desires a noble task." But the sentiment also can refer to officers in secular organizations as in Num 31:14 ("Moses was angry with the officers [*paqad*, LXX = *episkopos*] of the army—the commanders [*sar*] of thousands and commanders [*sar*] of hundreds—who returned from the battle"). The root of the word means "to care for," "to watch over," "to investigate," "to protect." In this original sense the word has "no religious significance but is used almost exclusively for very secular appointments with technical and financial responsibilities" (Beyer, "Episkopos," 2.599–622). *Episkopos* applies to the Christian business manager in setting the standard for conduct: not greedy, eager to serve, protective, humble, and exemplary in conduct. A high bar for the business *episkopos* (The Greek translators of LXX had a hard time translating the Hebrew term *paqid* and usually went with *episkeptomai*, an overseer [to look over or watch]; Acts 6:3 = appoint). In a clearly secular context, the apostle Paul implies a shepherd-sheep relationship in Ephesians 6:5–9 and Colossians 3:22–4:1 as he uses *episkopos* to refer to

willing, as God wants you to be, not greedy for money, but eager to serve; not lording[241] it over those entrusted to you but being examples[242] to the flock. (1 Pet 5:2–3)

The shepherd paradigm of management is not to be seen as exclusively ecclesiastic. Indeed, in 1 Peter 5:5 there is the extension[243] of the shepherd-sheep mentoring relationship between young and old so that the newer Christian can learn from the older Christian. That same shepherd-sheep relationship is exhorted for the benefit of wives,[244] children,[245]

---

the master-slave relationship as he reflects on the Lord's example to us in our management relationships. Paul encourages Timothy to seek management responsibilities of a cohort. *Episkopos* is used in this context as a "leader" or "manager" of a congregation. The same Greek word is used in the Old Testament (LXX) for "one in charge" (Num 4:16; Ps 108:8, Hebrew = *rosh*, meaning "Ephraim is my helmet") of company duties and is used in the New Testament in the general sense of "manager" (Acts 1:20, "may another take his place of leadership," *episkopos*). Knight, *The Faithful Sayings in the Pastoal Epistles*, 56–61, and Beyer "Episkopos," 2.599–622, give extensive treatment to this word: "In ancient Greece the word *episkopos* was used in many different ways to describe those who held various official positions in respect of their office and work . . . From this it can be seen that *episkopos* involves . . . supervision of the course of work in the interests of the builders, and possibly control of the money allocated to the task. It is along these lines that we are to explain the activity of all the other *episcopoi* who are mentioned in the same connection on Syrian building inscriptions" (Beyer, "Episkopos," 2.611). Furthermore, Paul makes the startling requirement in 1 Timothy 3 that anyone who wants to manage needs to have the respect of all segments of society: "Now the manager (*episkopos*) must be above reproach" (1 Tim 3:2) and "he must also have a good reputation with outsiders" (1 Tim 3:7). Calvin commented on 1 Timothy 3:7: "It seems difficult to think that a godly man should have unbelievers who are most eager to tell lies about us as witnesses to his integrity. The apostles' meaning as far as external behavior is concerned, even unbelievers should be forced to acknowledge that he is a good man. For though they slander all God's children without cause, yet they cannot make a rascal out of a man who behaves honorably and innocently among them" (Calvin, *The Second Epistle of Paul to the Corinthians and the Epistle to Timothy, Titus and Philemon*, 227–28). In short, echoing his letter to Titus, Paul states that the manager needs to be a person of character with the following additional traits: husband of one wife (3:2), temperate (3:2), self-controlled (3:2), respectable (3:2), hospitable (3:2), able to teach (3:2), not given to heavy drinking (3:3), gentle, not violent (3:3), agreeable, not quarrelsome (3:3), not greedy (3:3), manage his own family well (3:45), not be a recent convert (3:6).

241. *Katakurieuo* = master.
242. *Tupos* = a type, symbol, allegory, pattern.
243. I.e., "in the same way" as the "Chief Shepherd."
244. 1 Pet 3:1–7.
245. 1 Pet 1:14.

and neighboring fellow-believers.[246] In 1 Peter 5 Peter tells the manager that the shepherding Christian business manager is to:

- Care for the employees.
- Be a leader of the employees.
- Want to serve as the manager of the employees.
- Have a management style that is firm yet sensitive to the needs of the employees.
- Take a fair compensation package as the manager.
- Be a professional example for the employees.

> Live as free people, but do not use your freedom as a cover-up for evil; live as servants of God. Show proper respect[247] to everyone, [and] love the family of believers. (1 Pet 2:16–17a)

Peter the manager writes to organization colleagues scattered in branch offices throughout the Mediterranean world. The context for this passage is the discussion of the obligations of wives, husbands, slaves, and everyone else. "Master" is not specifically mentioned but implied in these verses, and so slavery is thus the contrast between "masters" (managers) and "slaves" (employees).[248] Applying our business interpretation to this passage, managers ("masters") are free from the constraints of being an employee ("servants"). Peter is telling us that all human beings are to be "honored" and "respected" by us, but there is to be a special relationship between a Christian manager and a Christian employee because Peter describes it in family terms—"brotherhood"—a term found only in Peter's writings.[249] This tenderness towards other Christians in business is born out of an understanding that Christians in the world face unique challenges and opposition.[250]

---

246. 1 Pet 3:8–9.

247. *Timao* = honor.

248. Cf. Titus 2:9. "Slaves" is a stand-in term for employee *vis-a-vis* masters (mangers), and managers *vis-a-vis* owners, because the context is submission in secular institutions: Rom 13:1, 5; 1 Cor 14:34; 16:16; Eph 5:21–22, 24; Col 3:18; Titus 2:5, 9,:3:1; 1 Pet 2:13, 18; 5:5.

249. *Adelphoteta* = family of believers.

250. Cf. 1 Pet 5:9; John 15:18; Jesus uses a warm and tender thought in describing a manager's affection and devotion to one in his organization in Matthew 18:12.

- Peter the manager is calling Christian managers to be courteous and respectful[251] to all people, believers and unbelievers. No matter what the provocation, Christian business managers must not lose respect for their employees or, more profoundly, forget their common humanity.[252]

It seems we can say that, at the very least, Peter the manager sees management:

- As the deliberate and systematic use of all the resources available to the manager.
- As an opportunity for the manager to act prudently and skillfully to create a productive and thus a flourishing work environment for coworkers.
- As the responsibility of the manager to safely guide his coworkers to the common company goals.

In all this leadership activity there must be the awareness on the part of the shepherding manager that God has a special interest in the stewardship of the manager's responsibilities. If Christians are to guide those whom God has given them in a business organization, using his gifts, his *charismata*, to facilitate this guiding to a common destination—then shepherding is a key concept in any biblical definition of business management![253] The Bible insists that the strong (i.e., the managers) have moral obligation to look out for the weak and the poor (i.e., the employees). The employee is always dependent on the manager for wages and even his job, and thus is always faced with the prospect of poverty. It is the moral obligation of the manager to pay the employee his justly earned wages in a timely fashion.[254]

251. *Timao*.

252. 1 Pet 2:13; cf. Jas 3:10–12.

253. Campbell and Reierson, *The Gift of Administration*, 44–58; Anderson, *Minding God's Business*, 76.

254. Paul teaches in Romans 12 that one manifestation of God's gifts to his earthly spiritual body is the gift of "leadership" (*prohistemi* = to stand before). "If it is managing [*prohistemi* = leadership, governing] let him manage (*prohistemi*) diligently" (Rom 12:8). *Prohistemi* is used only eight times in the New Testament and always by Paul and usually for management functions (Rom 12:8; 1 Thess 5:12; 1 Tim 3:4, 5, 22; 5:17). It is important to note that half of the uses of *prohistemi* are to Paul's young lieutenant, Timothy, who is charged with the managing of the young congregations in the region. Engstrom believes that the Greek word *prohisteme* is the operative word in any

> For this very reason, make every effort to add to your faith goodness; and to goodness, knowledge; and to knowledge, self-control; and to self-control, kindness; and to brotherly kindness, love. For if you possess these qualities in increasing measure, they will keep you from being ineffective and unproductive in your knowledge of our Lord Jesus Christ. (2 Pet 1:5–8)

---

definition of administration or management (Engstrom, *Your Gift of Administration*, 24–25). We have *prohisteme* being used concerning the qualifications of a manager of a group of people in 1 Timothy 3 and 5. Note the emphasis on effective management in these verses. It is not enough that a person just manages; the challenge is for a Christian leader to manage "well." Character is important. It is important to note that *prohistemi*, translated "leadership," does not always occur in ecclesiastical contexts. In the Greek Old Testament (LXX) *prohistemi* (with no Hebrew equivalent) occurs two times, both in secular contexts: 2 Samuel 13:17 and Isaiah 43:24. In the Apocrypha *prohistemi* is used in a political sense to "govern" or "manage" a nation (cf. 1 Macc 5:19). But it is in the New Testament where it is used eight times that we get the clearest meaning of *prohistemi*, as it describes a corporate officer ("he that manages"). Coenen comments, "All of these words (i.e., uses of prohistemi) are participles which suggest an activity rather than office" (Coenen, "Episkopos"). The point here is that any organization within the kingdom of God will be given a *prohistemi*, a manager, to help guide and champion that organization.

In Titus 3:8 if one translates the word *prohistemi* as "manage," that seems to get at what Paul is emphasizing. In the preceding verses Paul names several individuals who need help. More than just spiritual activity is needed to accomplish this help. Management of time and resources are required. Guthrie has it right when he translates this phrase "learn to maintain good works" (Guthrie, *The Pastoral Epistles*, 210). Moffatt gets to the point in his translation of the Bible: "practice" (Titus 3:8, MNT). For our purposes Titus 3:8 has the best managerial application of *prohistemi* in the New Testament. In this Titus verse *prohistemi* can be translated as "devote," "commit," "execute," "maintain," or even "practice a profession," as Paul applies it to good works which are beneficial to everyone. This is obviously an important point for Paul since it is a "trustworthy saying." Everyone, customers, suppliers, staff, all benefit from good managerial practices. In Titus 3:14, we have "Our people must learn to manage (*prohistemi*) the doing of good (*kalos*) works, in order that they may provide for daily necessities and not live unproductive lives." Finally, in 1 Thessalonians 5:12, we have: "Now we ask you brothers to respect those who work hard among you, who are over you (*prohistemi*) in the lord and who admonish you." The hortatory context is not ecclesiastic but rather general, and the use of prohistemi could refer to a secular situation. Managers are to warn and admonish coworkers to be good stewards of that which is before them.

A couple of management lessons from this one management verse:

- Managers are to give the example of being the hardest workers in the organization.
- Managers are to care for their coworkers.

With the use of *prohistemi*, we see Scripture stressing management skills in order to lead productive and godly lives, not only for ourselves but also for those under our vocational care.

Not to be outdone by Paul, Peter gives his own definition of the Christian managerial character when he echoes Paul's words. 2 Peter 1:5–8 is rich in character development for any business manager as Peter summons all Christians to a life of virtue.[255] As I have noted and briefly exegeted, there are several lists of Christian virtues in the New Testament, but Peter's list is unique because of its Hellenist and Stoicist content, indicating that Peter is writing to his contemporary pluralistic culture with its social norms. The list of eight virtues is not in any sequential order—only the first ("faith") and the last ("love") are set in concrete. Frankly, the list has more in common with non-Christian lists than the other Christian lists. Peter starts out by claiming that out of our Christian faith, virtue will rise. Peter's Greek does not say "supplement your faith with virtue." This is important to understand because it is wrong to think that one characteristic needs to be mastered before moving on to the next characteristic, which would be a form of moralism.[256] Having reflected the Hellenistic influence, Peter does Christianize the virtues by beginning with "faith" (which is the root of all virtues) and ending with "love" (which is the goal of all virtues) that can only come from the Lord Jesus Christ:

- "Faith"[257] means "faithfulness" or "reliability" in this context. In the Greco-Roman world one was received into the faith of a stronger boss, and so one expected to be under the patron's care and protection. In Peter's case, understood by his readers, the weaker worker

---

255. Aristotle commented on virtues: "The greatest virtues are necessarily those which are most useful to others since virtue is the faculty of conferring benefits... The components of virtue are justice, courage, self-control, magnificence, magnanimity, liberality, gentleness, practical and speculative wisdom" (Aristotle, *Rhetoric*, 1366). The Greek dramatist Menander (342–290 BC) notes, "Always divide the actions of those you are going to praise into the virtues (there are four virtues: courage, justice, temperance, and wisdom) and see to what virtues the actions belong and whether some of them are common to a single virtue" (Menander, *Rhetoric*, 373).

256. "Of [Peter's] selection of virtues, other than 'faith' (*pistos*) and 'love' (*agape*) we can only say that he has chosen virtues familiar from the Stoic and popular philosophical ethics of the Hellenistic world, some of them very general in meaning, to give a general impression of the kind of virtuous life which the Christian faith should foster" (Bauckham, *Jude–2 Peter*, 185). Calvin made the following general observation of 2 Peter 1:7: "Peter's purpose is not only to build up the faithful in patience, godliness, temperance, and love, but he also demands continual progress and improvement to be made in these gifts, and rightly so, for we are as yet far off from the goal We ought, therefore, to be always going on so that the gifts of God increase in us" (Calvin, *Commentary on Hebrews and I & II Peter*, 332).

257. *Pistos*.

was expected to maintain a loyalty to the boss, and to break the loyalty would be a grave moral mistake.[258]

- "Goodness"[259] means "moral excellence" in a social context and is used only here and by Paul in Philippians 4:8. The person of "virtue" or "goodness" demonstrates excellence of character which is demonstrated in generosity and kindness toward others in a surpassing way. It is a key word in this paragraph, for it points to the character of the Christian businessman.

- "Knowledge"[260] is not spiritual knowledge leading to salvation. That's a different word. Peter is using *gnosis* to indicate the knowledge and wisdom a Christian manager needs to employ in order to lead a virtuous life. It is practical and not theoretical knowledge.[261]

- "Self-control"[262] is clearly Hellenistic[263] and means the Christian business manager must minimize his entanglement with material things and physical urges and take hold of himself.[264] This self-restraint is not a sprint, but a long-distance run for all of one's life. This is not patience, but steadfastness, not in the face of persecution, but in the face of daily temptation urged on by the secular teaching of the day![265] Peter warns that the Christian businessman must reject the false teaching of the surrounding secular and pagan culture which emphasizes sensuality,[266] ruthless attitudes and despising (2:10), soft and comforting physical pleasures (2:13), adultery (2:14), corruption (2:19), and the pursuit of profit at all costs.[267] But even more specifically to the business manager, the current business focus is on material success and outcome based management models.

---

258. 2 Pet 1:3–4.
259. *Arete*.
260. *Gnosis*
261. Cf. Phil 1:9.
262. *Egkrateian* = endurance/perseverance.
263. Socrates: "Should not every man hold self-control (*egkrateian*) to be the foundation of all virtue, and first lay this foundation firmly in his soul? For whom without this can learn any good or practice it worthily?" (Xenophon, *Memorabilia* 1.5).
264. Cf. Gal 5:23.
265. Cf. Rom 2:7.
266. 2 Pet 2:2.
267. *Phthora* = bondage, destruction. A bringing into an inferior or worse condition.

- "Perseverance"[268] is one attribute that should characterize a Christian business manager. The need for perseverance (endurance, waiting) is critical for a business manager in the throes of a competitive marketplace since the manager must wait for his coworkers to accomplish their work and then to wait for the results and then to persevere under adverse market circumstance.[269]
- "Godliness"[270] might more correctly translated in our context as "duty." That is, the Christian manager has a "duty" to be loyal to God and his teaching in the face of social opposition.[271] This is an action-oriented adjective and not a speculative armchair virtue.
- "Brotherly kindness"[272] is the penultimate virtue. This is the Christian family of followers of Jesus (2 Peter 1:7), and it is a mark of social solidarity. The Christian community is always threatened by false teachers, so loyalty to the organization is a virtue. The business manager needs to excel in kindness to his fellow believers but be at the same time kind to his business "family."[273]
- "Love"[274] is the last virtue, and it is to be expressed to those outside the Christian community.[275] This is the crown jewel of Christian virtues and summarizes all the other personal values that characterize the Christian business manager.[276] This is the virtue that faces off with the hostility of the competition, the disgruntled employees and the natural tendency to strike out and retaliate, if not to originate.[277] This is a cognitive virtue and not an emotion. There is nothing warm and fuzzy about *agape* love. It is action-oriented and demands doing something. All of this is because *agape* is modeled by God,

---

268. *Hypomene.*

269. As Schreiner, *1, 2 Peter, Jude*, 300, states, "Moral restraint must be combined with endurance and steadfastness for those who hope to win the prize."

270. *Eusebia.*

271. As Green has noted, "One of the principal concerns of Peter is the development of *eusebia* in the lives of his readers." Green, *Jude & 2 Peter*, 194.

272. *Philadelphian.*

273. Gal 6:10.

274. *Agape.*

275. Cf. 1 Thess 3:12.

276. Gal 5 and 1 Cor 13.

277. 2 Pet 2:13–17.

who loved and did.[278] The Christian business manager doesn't even have to like his employees, but he must treat them with love as Peter defines love. This placement by Peter is supremely important, for it tells the Christian manager that he cannot pick and choose which virtue to specialize in because it is easier that the others. There is no cherrypicking of the Peter's virtues. The list hangs together as one. *Agape* encompasses all the other virtues as a unit.[279]

Peter writes that the best way to beat back the bad teaching in secular management theory is continual spiritual growth and increase in moral character.[280] We have seen that the example of Jesus' own life was holiness for managers to emulate, and indeed the call is for that holy emulation. That demonstrated holiness of life is to be worked out in daily managerial duties under the power of the Spirit and guidance of the Scriptures.[281] It is important to stress that a sanctified life is necessary for an edifying, God-pleasing management approach to business. Godliness is the most important issue in a manager's life.

If it is important for a pastor to pray for the sanctification and welfare of his congregants, it is no less important for the business manager to pray for the sanctification and the welfare of his employees. Character is more important than skills, than personality, than experience, than rank. And yet, it is an element in management literature that is given very little coverage because it involves values, judgments, morality, and humble work—all of which are contrary to the value-free managerial climate of the twenty-first century. Nevertheless, a sanctified character is the linchpin for long term management effectiveness.[282]

It seems clear that "character" in the New Testament is a matter of obedience to God's law, of persevering under ethical, spiritual, physical,

---

278. This is a divine virtue given to believers: Mark 1:11; 9:7; 12:30–31; John 3:16; Rom 1:17; elsewhere.

279. For the reverse of godly traits see Herm. *Mand.* 34:4: "But irascibility is first of all foolish, fickle, and senseless. And then, from senselessness comes bitterness, from bitterness anger, from anger wrath, and from wrath rage. Then this rage, which is compounded of such evil things, becomes a great and incurable sin."

280. 2 Pet 3:18. "Peter's point is that having and growing in virtue will make [the Christian business manager] useful and productive as a benefactor instead of being idle in the realm of virtue" (Green, *Jude & 2 Peter*, 197).

281. Cf. Phil 2:12–13; 1 Pet 1:14–15.

282. Green, *More Than a Hobby*, 128–130. Green has a fulltime paid chaplain for his chain of retail stores.

and financial tests in order to emerge on the other side of the tests still faithful to God—in short, it seems that "character" is a result of a life-long and therefore continual process of "working out one's salvation" in one's cultural environment.[283]

> And the Lord said, "Simon, Simon, Satan has asked to sift you as wheat: But I have prayed for you, that your faith may not fail. And when you have turned back, strengthen your brothers." But he said to him, "Lord, I am ready to go with you to prison and to death." Jesus answered, "I tell you, Peter, before the rooster crows today, you will deny three times that you know me"... On reaching the place, he said to them, "Pray that you will not fall into temptation"[284]... And when he rose from prayer, and went back to his disciples, he found them asleep, exhausted from sorrow. "Why are you sleeping?" he asked them. "Get up and pray, so that you will not fall into temptation."[285] (Luke 22:31–34, 40, 45–46)

In this famous temptation and denial story of Peter, notice several things applicable to the business manager:

- The trial, testings, and temptations that come to the manager only come because God has allowed them to come. There is nothing random and chaotic about the temptations that will face a manager ("Satan has asked").
- The temptations will be turbulent and uncomfortable and stressful ("sift you as wheat").
- The temptations are part of the manager's life. They are part and parcel of being a Christian. Jesus doesn't reject Satan's request to test the manager ("I have prayed that your faith will not fail").
- The triumphant manager is commanded to strengthen his coworkers and help them through their own testings and trials and temptations ("strengthen your brothers").
- Peter the manager brushes off Jesus' warning and offer of prayer support for his testings, trials, and temptations with bravado ("Lord, I was born for this!").

---

283. Phil 2:12.
284. *Peirasmos*.
285. *Peirasmos*.

- Jesus responds to Peter with the assurance that his Lord knew him better than he knew himself ("you will deny me three times").

- Jesus tells Peter and the other managers, "Pray that you will not give in to temptation," but they all do by first falling asleep, then Peter's denial, then unbelief after the resurrection. Whatever the temptation is, the disciple/managers fell into it.

- Finally, Jesus repeats the instruction not to "fall into temptation" for emphasis, clearly indicating that more testings, trials, and temptations await them and that they needed to prepare themselves for the coming cultural storm. It wouldn't be long for them to need an attitude change about Jesus. The important conclusion we can draw from this disappointing episode is that, in fact, the managers' faith was sturdy and the Lord's prayer for Peter and the others was answered by subsequent history.

JOHN ON MANAGEMENT

> Whoever claims to live in him must walk[286] as Jesus did. (1 John 2:6)

John had earlier recorded the Lord's words in John 15 concerning the vine and the branches, where Jesus teaches that there is an organic unity between his life and the life of the true believer, i.e., he is the vine and we are the branches.[287] Indeed, Alexander Ross remarks on 1 John 2:6 that every Christian "should feel bound by an inward obligation springing out of a sense of his infinite debt to Christ, to walk even as that One walked."[288] It is instructive to see that the original Greek in 1 John 2:6 has "walking" as the present active infinitive, indicating a continuous performance on the part of the Christian manager, i.e., we must continue to walk as Jesus did.[289]

286. *Peripateo.*

287. Cf. Rom 8:29.

288. Ross, *The Epistle of James and John*, 155–56. In a similar thought, Buswell refers to our "sense of oughtness" that God has given us in order for us to know what is good and what is evil Buswell, *Systematic Theology of the Christian Religion*, 262–63).

289. Thiessen maintains that one of the minor reasons for the incarnation, contra Berkouwer (*The Person of Christ*), is for God to give Christians an example of a holy life: "Christ taught us how to behave toward God, the Scriptures, the religious system

> Love is made complete among us so that we will have confidence on the day of judgment, because in this world[290] we are like him.[291] (1 John 4:17)

In a wonderful verse John teaches that love without the resemblance of the image of Jesus is hollow and a lie. The context of this verse is judgment and the Christian's assurance of salvation. But the verse has a wider meaning. "World" refers to the natural world in which the Christian currently lives. And John is saying that in the same sense that Jesus lived on earth in a pluralistic world Christians are to follow the pattern of their Lord in "the days of his flesh" (1 John 4:2).[292] We are justified in translating this text, "we are in the world in the same way as Jesus was."[293] Christian business managers are with Jesus, up close and personal, and yet in a state of ambiguity. John is stating that you are in your place in the sinful world with all its temptations and challenges and dangers because Jesus put you there, but you do not belong to this sinful world but rather to the spiritual world. The ambiguity is that while you are managers like the perfect Jesus, as you pass through this sinful world you will never be the perfect manager.

Furthermore, this image is a "worldly" image because it is only as Jesus was "in this world" that we can observe and know him, i.e., "in this world we are like him."[294] So, "worldly" in this context means discernible, righteous conduct, and not sinful conduct![295] Indeed, the image of Jesus in us, the reflection of his example, is more than a duty; it is proof of the manager's salvation. As Calvin has written, "For when God's image appears in us, it is, as it were, the seal of His adoption."[296]

> This is how we know what love is: Jesus Christ laid down his life for us. And we ought to lay down our lives for our brothers; if anyone has material possessions and sees his brother in need but has no pity on him, how can the love of God be in him? Dear

---

of our day, lost men, true believers, and enemies . . . It is, therefore, important that we study his character, in order to know the standard, the ideal, of the Christian's walk" (Thiessen, *Introductory Lectures in Systematic Theology*, 293, 307).

290. *Kosmos.*
291. "As he is."
292. Schnackenburg, *The Johannine Epistles*, 223.
293. Kruse, *John*, 168.
294. 1 John 2:6; 3:3.
295. As is customary in many commentaries on 1 Corinthains 3:1 and Titus 2:12.
296. Calvin, *The Gospel According to St. John and the First Epistle of John*, 295.

children, let us not love with words or tongue but with actions and in truth. (1 John 3:16–18)

Solidarity with the world on the manager's part is evidenced by an incarnate love affair with his neighbor in the emulation of Jesus. In this beautiful Johannine passage, we learn the world will never know what true love is until it sees the love that Christians display. And it is precisely this self-sacrificing love that the Christian business manager is to display in his business environment ("all people," "everyone," "neighbor"). John's use of "brothers"[297] has a primary focus on fellow Christians. However, there is little biblical support for the existence of a two-tiered ethic whereby Christians are to receive preferential treatment from each other.[298]

> I am writing these things to you about those who are trying to lead you astray.[299] (1 John 2:26)

The context for this Johannine verse is false teachers ("many antichrists") coming among the flock seeking to "entice" the sheep away from the truth. The key word in this verse is *planao*, which means "to wander,"[300] "stray,"[301] "seduce,"[302] "lure,"[303] "deceive,"[304] "stagger,"[305] "mock"[306]—take your pick. The point is that the deception is not only spiritual but practical.[307] The world will try to seduce the Christian businessman to pursue ungodly goals with the promise of riches, fame,

---

297. *Adelphon*.

298. What is more evident is that the same incarnational ethic of solidarity applies to all men. Passages such as Matthew 5:43–48 and 25:31–46 clearly indicate that even enemies are to receive the incarnational mercies, and Paul rebukes Peter for "drawing back" from the gentiles for fear of believers' censure (Gal 2:11–13). This incarnate love must be displayed during deed and doctrine, "amid tangible realities," as Smith has written on our emulation of Jesus' love for the world: "We get like Jesus by imitating him, and our likeness to him is an irrefragable evidence to ourselves and the world that we are His, as a son's likeness to his father proves their relationship" (Smith, *The Epistles of John*, 187). Cf. 1 John 2:6.

299. *Planao* = seduce, entice.

300. Heb 11:38.

301. 1 Pet 2:25.

302. Greek LXX Jer 23:13.

303. Greek LXX Hos 2:13.

304. John 7:12.

305. Greek LXX Isa 19:14.

306. Greek LXX Judg 16:10, 13, 15.

307. Yarbrough, *1–3 John*.

and power. Sound familiar? John is telling us that Christian business managers are targeted by those who want to see us deny our Lord. In 1 John 3:7 John makes it even more plain: There are folks who are living sinful lives that want to entice us to join them in sin.[308]

* * *

Scripture teaches that God's burden of demonstrating himself to the world, first modeled by his incarnate Son, has now been transferred to the Christian manager, and so if the world is to "know the Father" or "see the Father" it must "know" and "see" the Father through the manager's lifestyle.[309] And all this demonstrating on the manager's part must be done in the world's arena, not "in a corner,"[310] just as Jesus did the Father's work in both the open air of the marketplace and the closed air of the workplace.[311]

It is this going "into the world" by the Christian business manager which draws so much attention for Dietrich Bonhoeffer in his *Ethics*. Bonhoeffer wrote of the necessity of this "worldliness" for the Christian: "Whoever professes to believe in the reality of Jesus Christ, as the Revelation of God, must in the same breath profess his faith in both the reality of God and the reality of the world reconciled. And for just this reason the Christian is no longer the man of eternal conflict, but just as the reality in Christ is one, so he, too, since he shares in this reality in Christ, is himself an undivided whole. His worldliness does not divide him from the world. Belonging wholly to Christ, he stands at the same time wholly in the world."[312] All this "belonging wholly" to Jesus being taught by the Lord and his apostles is empowered only by the Holy Spirit.[313]

---

308. "Dear children, do not let anyone lead you astray. He who does what is right is righteous, just as he is righteous" (Aristotle, *Nicomachean Ethics*). Nobody but a moron believes that our conduct does not form our character. We are as we act and acting badly creates bad character.

309. John 14:7–9.

310. Acts 26:26.

311. Matt 1:6–20, tax collector's booth; Matt 8:19, "law" offices; Matt 19:16–22, trust fund baby; John 4:46, courthouse.

312. Bonhoeffer, *Ethics*, 201.

313. "And we, who with unveiled faces all reflect the Lord's glory, are being transformed into his likeness with ever-increasing glory, which comes from the Lord, who is the Spirit" (2 Cor 3:18). Douty, *Union with Christ*, 191, comments on this spiritual transaction during which we, for our part, contemplate and respond, and God the Spirit, for his part, changes and motivates: "As we are taken up with Christ as reflected

4

Jesus on Selected Managers in the Old Testament

THE BIBLE IS FILLED with exhortations and examples of management because Yahweh employed various managers to advance his kingdom through the Jewish organization in the Old Testament and then the gentile organization in the New Testament. All the biblical managers were flawed but they do provide us with management lessons.

CAIN THE MANAGER

> Cain was building[314] a city and he named the city after his son Enoch ... Adah bore Jabal who was the father[315] of those who live in tents and raise livestock. His brother's name was Jubal, and he was the father of all who play the harp and flute ... Zillah bore Tubal-Cain who forged[316] all kinds of tools out of bronze and iron. (Gen 4:17, 20–21)

Cain is an unlikely candidate for a manager worth looking at, but the fact that he was the first child begotten and born of human parents counts for something. The degenerating effects of sin had not taken full hold of him, even though he was chastised by God at least twice in short order: we

---

in the Bible, the Lord the Spirit will effect the transfiguration that works into us the image of the incarnate Son." Cf. 1 Cor 15:49; 2 Cor 4:10; Col 1:11.

314. *Banah* = to build up.

315. *Av* = biological father, inventor, creator, originator, founder, head, chief, rule, master, teacher.

316. *Latash* = instructor, to sharpen.

see him resentful that his offering was not accepted and then we see him not only lie to God about Abel but dismiss the divine question—"Where is your brother?" Not a good managerial start. But still image bearers of God and directed by the kindness of Yahweh to all, Cain and his (Adah and Zillah) descendants created wonderful contributions to human civilization. Within five generations the Cain family had:

- Built cities,
- Created animal husbandry,
- Invented music,
- Developed metallurgy,
- Created poetry.[317]

While this early Cainite production was primitive, unsanctified, and small, it took organizing effort and efficiency to create a safe environment from the wild outside the city walls. These Cainite cities were shabby, wicked cities and needed to be conquered by the Israelites.[318] Whether or not Cain actually lived in the city we don't know, since the Hebrew narrative is uncertain about the role Cain's son, Enoch, played in this first city. What is important for us is that:

- Cain, as a manager, planned and organized and implemented his plan to build a city for refuge for himself and his family and neighbors. He named the city after his son, "Enoch."[319]
- Cain, as a manager, lived to see and influence his descendants create guilds of musicians and builders of musical instruments.[320]
- Cain, as a manager, lived to see one of his descendants create nomadic communities of herdsmen who lived in tents in the countryside.[321]
- Cain, as a manager, lived to see one of his descendants create and teach the science of metallurgy.
- Cain, as a manager, lived to see his descendants develop a civilization able to produce more than it consumed and thus create the

317. Cf. Collins, *Genesis 1–4*, 212.
318. Num 13.
319. Gen 4:17.
320. Gen 4:21.
321. Gen 4:20.

- Cain, as a manager, lived to see his descendants create the first educational system in order to pass on their knowledge to future generations of humankind, not always with positive benefits.[322]

All of this civilizing activity took management, and it can be assumed that Cain passed along his management skill and expertise to Enoch (who perhaps finished building the first city) and to the rest of his progeny.

NOAH THE MANAGER

> So God said to Noah, "So make yourself an ark of cypress wood... You are to bring[323] into the ark two of all living creatures, male and female, to keep them alive with you... You are to take every kind of food that is to be eaten and store[324] it away as food for you and for them"... Then Yahweh shut him in... After forty days Noah opened the window he had made in the ark and sent out[325] a raven, and it kept flying back and forth until the water had dried up from the earth. Then he sent out a dove to see if the water had receded from the surface of the ground... Noah then removed[326] the covering from the ark and saw that the surface of the ground was dry... Then Noah built[327] an altar to Yahweh and taking some of all the clean animals and clean birds, he sacrificed burnt offerings on it. (Gen 6:14, 19, 21–22; 7:4–5, 16; 8:6–8, 13, 20)

This rather long quote tells us that the common management skills needed to accomplish divine commands are sometimes staggering and simply beyond belief, and we often fail to appreciate the extraordinary management skills needed for these jobs. In this instance, we tend to focus on the sterling character of Noah and not on his management acumen. But let's note the highlights of that management, realizing that Yahweh gave

---

322. Gen 4:21, father or teacher; the tower of Babel in Genesis 11.
323. *Bo* = cause to come in.
324. *Asaph* = gather, collect.
325. *Shalach*.
326. *Sur*.
327. *Banah*.

general instructions and guidelines for the construction and filling of the huge ark:

- Noah managed the details of the construction and filling of the big boat.
- Noah managed the gathering of thousands of animals and birds for the ark. There were no specific instructions as to how exactly Noah was to accomplish this extraordinary herding of live creatures into the confines of a big boat. There had to be male and female, clean and unclean, two of every kind of creature that moves along the ground, seven of every kind of bird, etc.[328]
- Noah managed the gathering and storing of "every kind of food" for his family and for the world's floating menagerie.[329]
- Noah managed the construction and installation of a huge covering over the ark with his limited worker cohort, perhaps during the rain.[330]
- Noah managed the peace between the family and the animals as they were being shut in for forty days with no outside view or fresh air.
- Noah managed the response to the weather conditions several times by sending out birds (ravens, doves) to see if the water had "receded from the earth."[331]
- Noah managed the removal of the giant covering over the ark with his available manpower.[332]
- Noah managed the mass exiting of the boat after a hundred and fifty days of being "cooped" in.

At the appropriate time, Noah the manager determined it was safe enough to depart from the ark and praise Yahweh for his survival by building an altar and sacrificing some of the very animals he had just saved.[333]

328. Gen 6:19–20.
329. Gen 6:21.
330. Gen 7:16.
331. Gen 8:6–11.
332. Gen 8:13.
333. Gen 8:20.

ABRAHAM THE MANAGER

> When Abraham heard that his relative had been taken captive, he called out the 318 trained[334] men born in his household and went in pursuit as far as Dan. (Gen 14:14–16)

Abraham the manager functions as the organizational "trainer" in his domestic organization. The 318 "trained" men would indicate that Abraham had a large private army, big enough to defeat the eastern kings at the Battle of the Siddim Valley. These "trained men" had grown up under the military management of Abraham and so were reliable colleagues that Abraham had personally "trained." In this short episode we see that:

- Abraham the manager led his men in a nocturnal military attack which routed the opposing armies.[335]
- Abraham the manager trained a cadre of fighting men for future contingencies in order to protect his organization.
- Abraham the manager mobilized his men to accomplish the goal of retrieving his nephew Lot.
- Abraham the manager planned an attack at night to successfully defeat armies of the four kings and retrieve Lot and all the other people and possessions.
- Abraham the manager demonstrated personal integrity by not keeping anything for himself. He only took what belonged to him in the first place. There was no plundering of excess booty, only a just reward.[336]

Later:

- Abraham the manager diversified his portfolio by accumulating precious metals in addition to livestock, so he knew something about animal husbandry and mining.[337]

---

334. *Hanik* = instructor.
335. Gen 14:15.
336. Gen 14:23–24.
337. Genesis 12:16 and 13:2 suggest that Abraham's wealth largely came from Pharaoh for sex with Sarai, Abraham's wife. Ill-gotten gain from a pagan source. Still, Abraham knew how to manage and diversify his illicit wealth into a huge estate which colors the rest of Genesis.

- Abraham the manager "directed"[338] and "taught" his enormous domestic organization and joins Cain as a very early biblical example of the Pauline admonition that managers are to govern well one's own family.[339]

- Abraham the manager hosted three visitors and an intercessor for Sodom. He trained the hosts in "righteousness and justice," thus setting the religious, moral, and ethical climate for his organization. He was responsible for the virtuous conduct of his company. In Abraham we see an early example of a manager acculturating his organization.[340]

- Finally, Abraham the manager negotiated with Yahweh over the fate of the Jewish organization in Sodom—the art of the deal! Abraham was defending his organization from destruction. The point to be taken is that Abraham was standing up for his organization and was negotiating for its safety with someone who had the power and justification to harm them.[341]

JOSEPH THE MANAGER

> Joseph found favor in [Potiphar's] eyes and became his personal manager.[342] Potiphar made Joseph his manager[343] of his household, and he entrusted[344] to his care everything he owned.[345]

---

338. *Tsavah* = command.

339. Gen 18:19; 1 Tim 3:4.

340. Cf. Exod 12:25–27; Deut 6:1–7, 20–25; Prov 1:7; 13:1. Hodgkinson, *Towards a Philosophy of Administration*, 196, argues, "The administrator is a philosopher-in-action by *force majeure* and that administration is in large part the clarification, declaration, and objectification of value propositions."

341. Gen 18:18.

342. *Sharath*.

343. *Paqid* = overseer.

344. *Nathan* = put.

345. Literally "all that was to him."

Jesus on Selected Managers in the Old Testament   109

From that time he made him manager[346] of his household and of all that he owned. (Gen 39:5)[347]

346. *Paqid*. "[Potiphar] made him manager [*paqid* = put him in charge] of his household, and he entrusted to his care [*nathan* = give] everything he owned. From the time he made him manager (*paqad*) of the household and all that he owned, the LORD blessed the household of the Egyptian because of Joseph. The blessing of the LORD was on everything Potiphar had, both in the house and in the field" (Gen 39:4–5; "Let Pharaoh appoint commissioners over the land to take a fifth of the harvest of Egypt," Gen 41:34); "Whenever the chest was brought in by the Levites to the king's officials" (2 Chr 24:11); "Eleazar son of Aaron, the priest, is to have charge of the oil for the light, the fragrance incense, the regular grain offering and the anointing oil. He is to be in charge of the entire tabernacle and everything in it, including its holy furnishings and articles" (Num 4:16); "Jehiel [et al.] were supervisors [overseers, inspectors, *paqid*] under Conaniah and Shimei by appointment[mandate, *miphqad*, from the root *paqid*] of King Hezekiah and Azariah the chief officer [ruler, *nagid*] in the temple of God" (2 Chr 31:13); "The chief leader [chief over the chief, one lifted up, *nasi*] of the Levities was Eleazar son of Aaron, the priest. He was appointed over those who were responsible for the care [oversight, *pequaddah*] of the sanctuary" (Num 3:32). *Paqid* has several meanings, such as "to inspect," "charge with," "entrust," and is overwhelmingly applied to military activities (like *gibbor*). The term is used over three hundred times in the Old Testament with the strong underlying meaning of a positive action by a superior in relation to his subordinates. The basic meaning of *paqid* is to exercise oversight over a subordinate in order to cause a considerable change in the circumstances of that subordinate (2 Chr 23:18 = "oversight"; Esth 2:3 = "appoint"; Job 10:12 = "providence/care"). *Paqid* applies to the Christian business manager in that the role requires oversight over many different facets of the operation of a company, and the *paqid* must be conversant with the entire scope of company activities. A Christian business *paqid* should alter the work circumstances of an employee in order to benefit that employee and affect a more positive outcome.

347. So Pharaoh said to Joseph, "I hereby put you in charge [*nathan* = set you over, appointed] of the whole land of Egypt" (Gen 41:41). "So his servants said to him, 'Let us look for a young virgin to attend the king and take care (*sakan*) of him' . . . The girl was very beautiful; she took care (*sakan*) of the king and waited on him, but the king had no intimate relations with her" (1 Kgs 1:2, 4). *Sakan* does not identify an official position in an organization but rather a role the Old Testament manager fulfills—taking care of the boss. The root of this word means "to take care of" (to cherish, minister, to be profitable, treasurer). And it is used to describe the managerial activities of male and female managers. This is the management position responsibilities of ministering to high officials. *Sakan* is akin to *sharath*, which is used to describe Joseph's position in Egypt (Gen 39:4, 80–9) as well as Abishag's position with David (1 Kgs 1:15) and high officials who "served the king" (1 Chr 27:1). *Sakan* applies to the Christian business manager also the same way that *raah*, the shepherd leader, does. Part of the obligation of a biblical manager is to care for the needs of his coworkers and be patient with them as they do their job.

Joseph is, of course, one of the supreme examples of a successful manager given in the Bible.[348] A key and unforgettable point in Gen 39:4 is that Joseph progressed to his ultimate role through gradual stages, all orchestrated by Yahweh:

- Yahweh prospered Joseph's efforts with Egypt.
- Yahweh made Joseph manager in Potiphar's house, and then his royal domain.
- Yahweh turned Potiphar's attention to Joseph's success.
- Yahweh caused Potiphar to add his blessing to Yahweh's blessing.
- Yahweh maneuvered Joseph to take management control of Egypt as prime minister.

Nowhere in the Genesis narrative are the gifts and training of Joseph credited with his advancement or of Pharaoh's kindness. Nor do we see Joseph making changes in Egyptian public policies. Pharaoh was still a bloodthirsty tyrant, and Joseph was just a member of a subordinate tribe. Joseph's political advancement was all Yahweh's doing.[349]

After his managerial ascension, there are two critical roles that Joseph fulfilled:

- Pharaoh's personal manager.[350]
- Pharaoh's political manager.[351]

Joseph probably spent about twelve years in management training, beginning as a seventeen-year-old teenager,[352] before he was ready for significant organizational management responsibilities in Pharaoh's court at the age of thirty.[353] He received his training in the graduate school of hard knocks. No Wharton School for him. A very similar management course to what Moses had.

---

348. In the LXX the translators used the Greek work *episkopos* (bishop) to convey the meaning of *paqid* and the Greek word *kathistemi* (appoint) for *nathan*.

349. Pharaoh's house is the third house which Joseph managed: Potiphar's house, the jailhouse, and Pharaoh's house (Hamilton, *The Book of Genesis 18–50*).

350. *Sharath*.

351. *Paqid* = over his vast business domain, including treasury, judiciary, police, army, navy, agriculture, transportation, etc. (Breasted, *Ancient Records of Egypt*).

352. Gen 37:2.

353. Gen 41:46.

Jesus on Selected Managers in the Old Testament

MOSES THE MANAGER

> Do not be hardhearted[354] or tightfisted[355] toward your poor brothers. Rather be openhanded[356] and freely lend[357] him whatever he needs. Be careful not to harbor the wicked thought . . . Give generously to him and do so without a grudging heart. . . . Therefore, I command you to be openhanded toward your brothers and toward the poor and needy in your land. (Deut 15:7–11)

In this passage, ostensibly teaching generosity, Moses the manager tells the organization that beneath the generous spirit lies a heart of godly character. I have selected verses from the passage which bear on our topic, but the entire section[358] deserves to be read. Notice the qualities that Moses is emphasizing:

- Moses the manager tells the other managers that they are to be generous in spirit as well as in finances to their coworkers who make less that they do. Generosity should mark their attitude and not a narrow, pinched approach to their relationship with their colleagues.

- Moses the manager tells the other managers that there is a reciprocal obligation on the part of the coworkers. The generosity is not one way but rather a mutual covenant between the workers.

- Moses the manager tells the other managers to graciously lend without the prejudiced and "wicked" thought that the coworker may weasel out of the obligation to pay back.

- Moses the manager tells the other managers not to harbor grudges against their coworkers for any reason because Yahweh does not harbor grudges against the managers for their sins.

> So now go. I am sending you to Pharaoh to bring my people the Israelites out of Egypt . . . The next day Moses took his seat to serve as [manager][359] for the people, and they stood around

---

354. *Labab* = heart.
355. literally, "shut your hand."
356. Open your hand wide.
357. *Abat.*
358. Gen 15:7–18.
359. *Shaphat* = to decide, arbitrate, rule, govern. This is the most common word to describe the functioning of an organization. "Then we will be like all the other nations,

him from morning till evening . . . [Moses] chose[360] capable[361] people from all Israel and made them managers[362] of the people, managers[363] over thousands, hundreds, fifties, and tens. They served as [managers] for the people at all times. The difficult cases they brought to Moses, but the simple ones they decided themselves. (Exod 3:10; 18:13–26)[364]

Moses was sent by Yahweh to be the manager and deliverer.[365] All Christian business managers are likewise "sent" by God to manage their organizations. In Acts 7 Stephen describes Moses as a man of "powerful action." Beside leading the Israelites out of Egypt, Stephen has been interpreted by the historian Josephus as referring to a legend that Moses led a military campaign against the Ethiopians.[366] In Exodus 12:35–36 Moses led God's people to plunder the unbelieving Egyptians for their gold, silver, jewels, and clothing, which would later be used for the tabernacle in

---

with a king to manage (*shaphat*) us and to go out before us and fight our battles" (1 Sam 8:20). *Shaphat* is the most common word used in the Old Testament to designate the function of an organization (government) in any capacity, usually in judging. The term is used to indicate ruling (Judg 16:31), leading (2 Kgs 23:22), defending the weak (Jer 5:28). The term comes from the Hebrew *dhin* which essentially means "to govern," whether legislatively, judicially, or as an executive (Zech 3:7). In the New Testament, the term is akin to *katakrino*, meaning "to judge, decide, discriminate" (Luke 12:57), and this Greek term is used in the LXX Greek Old Testament.

360. *Bachar* = to choose after testing.

361. *Chayil* = able, might, strength, virtuous.

362. *Rosh.* "The managers (*sar*) of the people of Gilead said to each other, 'Whoever will launch the attack against the Ammonites will be the manager (*rosh*) of all those living in Gilead'" (Judg 10:18). The basic meaning of *rosh* is to be the "head" of a physical body. The word is translated also as "chief," "leader," or "officer" (cf. Exod 18:23). Although many of the usages of the root word can be traced back to the Sumerian language, the reliance on the nation's "head" as a high official is developed in the Hebrew language. *Rosh* applies to the Christian business manager in that taking the lead in difficult actions when others may faint away goes with the job. The *rosh* has the responsibility to take the lead in all the planning, organizing, and implementing that the head does for the physical body. Accepting the blame goes with the territory of being a *rosh* since a military defeat is always possible, and the head doesn't always lead the body in the right direction.

363. *Sar.*

364. Moses was educated (learned, *paideuo*) in all the wisdom of the Egyptians and was powerful in speech and action (Acts 7:22, 35; cf. Exod 18:13–26).

365. Cf. Acts 7:35.

366. Josephus, *Ant.* 2.10; cf. Num 12:1.

the wilderness.[367] The fact that Moses, as a manager, was highly regarded by the pagan Egyptian officials and general populace was a benefit of the plundering.[368] This entire incident was under the providential kindness of Yahweh to provide for his people. It needs to be understood that Moses did not originate this stripping of the Egyptians, but was used by Yahweh to give the instructions to the Jewish organization and then manage the taking.[369] Unfortunately, God's people have a propensity for misusing God's gifts for their own guilty pleasures, and such was the case in Exodus 32, but that doesn't obviate the biblical teaching that the tools and creations of the unbelievers can be used for God's glory.

After forty years of leading the Jewish organization in all kinds of situations, Moses still needed the wise advice of an outsider to establish a crucial principle of administration for the company.[370] We see this consultant's advice in Exodus 18:13–26, which tells the story of the management duties of Moses and how the business consultant told Moses his system is "not good." Furthermore, the consultant told Moses how he should conduct his administration in a practical way. One needs to remember that Moses was no organizational dullard, for he had already directed large public works projects and organizational endeavors in Egypt[371] and was "educated in all the wisdom of the Egyptians and was powerful in speech and action."[372] In addition to all this practical training, Moses was well over eighty years old when he called in the consultant.[373] Moses was with this consultant a "long period," so he wasn't a newbie as a manager.[374] In order to strengthen his advice, the outside advisor added that Moses should follow his counsel because "God so commands."[375]

367. Exod 25 and 35.

368. Taking; Exod 11:3.

369. God gave the Israelites favor in the eyes of the Egyptians and so all was willingly given to the tribe. This is the only recorded instance in which God gives the Israelites favor in the sight of another nation or tribe.

370. His father-in-law, Midian priest Jethro. Cf. Acts 7:30.

371. Acts 7:36.

372. Acts 7:22. Josephus (AD 37–100) claims that Moses had superior understanding by the age of three (Josephus, *Ant.* 2.9.6); Philo (20 BC–AD 50) claims he received royal instruction and his skill was in every area of knowledge (Philo, "Moses I," V.18–24); Artapanus (second century AD) claims that Moses was a master teacher of Egypt (Artapanus, "Fragment 3 [Moses]").

373. Exod 7:7; Acts 7:30.

374. Exod 2:23.

375. Exod 18:23.

There is no hint in the context of Exodus 18 and 19 that the consultant overstepped his bounds by so stating. Quite the contrary, what we read is that the Canaanite's advice resulted in the quick and effective dispensing of justice for God's people. Here is an early example of Yahweh speaking through an unbeliever![376] Commentators tend to brush past the management implication of Exodus 18:13–26, but there are several important administrative decisions that Moses made that warrant a closer look:

- Moses the manager was diligent and committed to managing the disputes among his coworkers.[377]
- Moses the manager humbly realized he needed help in accomplishing the task set before him, so he took the advice of the consultant.[378]
- Moses the manager realized that being a sole judge worked a hardship on the workers as they hung around waiting for justice.[379]
- Moses the manager realized his health limitation by doing all the work himself.[380]
- Moses the manager knew how to delegate when he chose "capable" and "trustworthy"[381] people to be assistant judges.[382]
- Moses the manager had discernment in choosing good managers and judges.
- Moses the manager divided the population into manageable groups of "thousands, hundreds, fifties, and tens" depending on the legal issue to be decided.[383]

376. Chiles comments on this incident: "Now it has long puzzled commentators that Moses, who had spoken 'mouth to mouth' with God and was his mediator par excellence, should have depended on the practical advice of a foreign priest for such an important element in the life of the nation as the administration of justice ... Yet ... because the world of experience was no less an avenue through which God worked, the narrative can attribute the organization of a fundamental institution of Israel's law to practical wisdom without any indication that this might later be thought to denigrate its importance in the divine economy" (Chiles, *The Book of Exodus*, 331–32).

377. Exod 18:13, 15–16.

378. Exod 18:24. Not always an easy thing for a believing son-in-law to do, particularly from an unbeliever.

379. Exod 18:14.

380. Exod 18:18.

381. *Emeth* = men of truth, stability, firmness.

382. Exod 18:25–26.

383. Exod 18:25–26.

- Moses the manager knew that the more difficult cases demanded his personal attention, so he adjudicated those himself.[384]

In the happy end, Moses' management decisions resulted in thousands of petitioners going home satisfied that justice had been served.[385]

> The leader[386] of the families of . . . (Num 3:24–37, 7:11–84, 34:18–29)

Finally, Moses the manager delegated enormous power and authority to various individuals in the organization to manage the affairs of their respective groups. These were people of community standing, and Moses consulted them on various civic matters (Exod 22:28; 34:31) as did other managers (Josh 22:30). These people were picked from their families so there were built-in relationships and history with their selection.

---

384. Exod 18:26.

385. Exod 18:23, 27.

386. *Nasi*; "Do not blaspheme [*qalal* = revile, be jealous of] God or curse the manager [*nasi* = one who is raised up, to carry, to bear; it is connected to clouds or mist] of your people" (Exod 22:28). Num 17:1–6; Ezek 46:2–8; "From each ancestral tribe send one of its leaders" (Num 13:2); "The chief leader [chief over the chief, one lifted up, *nasi*] of the Levities was Eleazar son of Aaron, the priest. He was appointed over those who were responsible for the care [oversight, *pequaddah*] of the sanctuary" (Num 3:32; cf. 2 Chr 2:1). *Nasi* can be literally translated "a ruler among your people" or administrative "chief," "sheik," "prince," "governor." These people are seen as the legitimate leader in the organization. Moses, the great *nasi*, exhorts us on how to treat people in general. He drills down to how we should treat our lieutenants, those in charge of the community. The Hebrew word translated "blaspheme" in Exodus 22:28 (*qalal* = revile, despise) is the same word usually translated "curse" in Exodus 21:17 as disrespectful speech towards parents. Moses is exhorting the employee about the attitude he needs to have towards the boss. This word is important to note since it can be seen as an attempt to reverse the blessings of the LORD toward the community. Cursing the boss may result in community failure! "Any legitimate leader in God's family . . . leads with God's authority and in God's place as his delegate. Therefore, to curse such a *nasi* is, indirectly but seriously, to curse God" (Stuart, *Exodus*, 1.521). Furthermore, Moses goes on to note in Exodus 22:28–29 that the *nasi*, as well as Yahweh, deserves the full portion of the employee's effort ("do not hold back offerings"). A day's work for a day's pay. *Nasi* applies to the Christian business *nasi* in that the manager should expect his coworker's loyalty and support. There should be no backbiting or slander permitted in the company by the manager's colleagues. Proverbs 27:18 refers to employee loyalty when it states, "He who tends a fig tree will eat its fruit, and he who looks after his master (*adon*) will be honored." Just as the farmer who takes care of his fig trees will be rewarded by the natural course of events, so an employee who takes care of his *nasi*/manager will be rewarded in due course, since the manager is the company's administrative stand-in for God.

BEZALEL THE MANAGER

> Then Yahweh said to Moses, "I have chosen Bezalel . . . and I have filled[387] him with the Spirit of God, with skill,[388] ability[389] and knowledge[390] in all kinds of crafts—to make artistic designs for work[391] in gold, silver and bronze, to cut and set stones, to work in wood, and to work[392] in all kinds of craftsmanship. Moreover, I have appointed Oholiab . . . to help[393] him." (Exod 31:3–6)

Here is a great example of a biblical focus on vocational education. Bezalel's "knowledge" is of the practical and not theoretical type. The Hebrew word connotes technical knowledge gained through experience. It is the same kind of knowledge that Huram-Abi brought to the building project for Solomon.[394] This Spirit-led contractor was given four divine practical gifts to accomplish his task: skill, ability, knowledge, management wisdom:

- Bezalel the manager possessed the skills to do the "work" with his hands.
- Bezalel the manager had the wisdom to know his strengths and weaknesses.
- Bezalel the manager knew what work to delegate to the other "craftsman" working on the tabernacle.
- Bezalel the manager had the wisdom to know what to delegate to his chief lieutenant, Oholiab.
- Bezalel the manager used his trained native abilities under the influence of the Holy Spirit to design, engrave, cut, set, carve, and embroider.
- Bezalel the manager taught his coworkers.[395]

387. *Male.*
388. *Chokhmah.*
389. *Tovunah.*
390. *Dhaath.*
391. *Melakah* = engage.
392. *Melakah.*
393. *Asah* = to deal kindly, to work, labor, toil.
394. 1 Kgs 7:13–14.
395. In Exodus 35:30–35 it states that Bezalel, in addition to all the other

The money phrase of this passage is "to engage all kinds of craftsmanship." The Hebrew word for "engage" is a fancy word for "work."[396] The point being that Bezalel is to be a hands-on manager of the tabernacle construction. "Bezalel, so gifted, is the ideal combination of theoretical knowledge, problem-solving practicality, and planning capability who can bring artistic ideals to life with his own hands."[397]

JOSHUA THE MANAGER

> "I will give you every place where you set your foot, as I promised Moses. Your territory will extend from the desert and from Lebanon to the great river, the Euphrates—all the Hittite country—and to the Great Sea on the west. No one will be able to stand up against you all the days of your life. Be strong and courageous, because you will lead[398] these people to inherit the land I wore to their forefather to give them" . . . Then [the people] answered Joshua, "Whatever you have commanded[399] we will do, and wherever you send[400] us we will go." (Josh 1:4–6, 16)

In Joshua 1, we see that Joshua was a *raah*/manager called to implement the plan of God for the conquest of Canaan. We are told that Joshua was appointed a "manager"[401] of his organization and as such he will lead the organization to the completion of its goal. The Hebrew indicates that this "leading" will involve:

- A just distribution of resources.
- The solving of disputes.
- The organizing of defenses.

---

craftsman-like jobs, also taught others craftsmanship and management.
396. *Melakah.*
397. Durham, *Exodus*, 410.
398. *Nachal* = to allot, distribute.
399. *Tsawah* = arranged, "in charge," a man over.
400. *Shalach.*
401. *Raah* = shepherd, Num 27:15–23.

BARAK THE MANAGER

> At Barak's advance, Yahweh routed Sisera and all his chariots and army by the sword, and Sisera abandoned his chariot and fled on foot. But Barak pursued the chariots and army . . . All the troops of Sisera fell by the sword; not a man was left. (Judg 4:15–16)

While the army general Barak was not a political manager, he lived during the time of Deborah, the fourth judge/manager.[402] Barak led the charge against King Jabin's Canaanite army, commanded by General Sisera and his nine hundred iron chariots. Deborah accompanied Barak and told him that any victory he won over the Midianites would not rebound to his glory. Still Barak went ahead with war preparations knowing there would be no honor for him. He then led the Israelite army of ten thousand chasing General Sisera until Sisera was killed by the woman Jael. Barak's efforts helped usher in forty years of prosperity.[403] Some management lessons from Barak include:

- Barak the manager prepared for the enterprise.
- Barak the manager did not seek the glory or the credit for the enterprise.
- Barak the manager was aggressive in pursuing the enterprise.
- Barak the manager was successful because he followed through in the enterprise.

GIDEON THE MANAGER

> "Watch me," [Gideon] told them. "Follow my lead.[404] When I get to the edge to the camp, do exactly as I do. When I and all who are with me blow our trumpets, then from all around the camp blow yours and shout, 'For Yahweh and for Gideon.'" (Judg 7:17–18)

---

402. *Yasha*, Judg 3:15. Deborah was also called a "leader" (*shaphat*).
403. Judg 4.
404. "Do as I do."

In some respects, the judge/managers are the only true managerial executives in the Jewish organization, since it wasn't long after Judge Samson that King Saul with all his political power was inaugurated.[405] Note the management qualities of Gideon, one of twelve judges, in this short passage, as he leads his organization:

- Gideon the manager got the attention of his coworkers.[406]
- Gideon the manager was prepared to be a role model.[407]
- Gideon the manager was the first one into the endeavor.[408]
- Gideon the manager taught and trained his coworkers.[409]
- Gideon the manager believed that Yahweh had his back.[410]
- Gideon the manager was humble before Yahweh.[411]
- Gideon the manager reduced his company personnel from thirty-two thousand down to only three hundred in order to accomplish the mission with a brilliant strategy against a much larger opponent. (Judg 6–8)[412]

JEPHTHAH THE MANAGER

> Then Jephthah went over to fight the Ammonites, and Yahweh gave them into his hands. He devasted twenty towns from Aroer to the vicinity of Minnith, as far as Abel Keramim. Thus, Israel subdued[413] Ammon. (Judg 11:32–33)

Jephthah, the eighth judge, had a rough young life. His mother was a prostitute, and he was driven away from home by his half-brothers, who were born by the legitimate wife of his father, Gilead. Jephthah led a band

---

405. Although Abimelech, son of Gideon but no judge, was called "king," Judg 9:16.
406. "Keep your eyes on me."
407. "Follow my example."
408. "I will be in front of you."
409. "I will instruct you."
410. Gideon inquired of Yahweh several times for help, and Yahweh kept repeating, "Be confident, I am with you" (Judg 6).
411. "I am the least in my family," Judg 6:15.
412. 1 Sam 12:11.
413. *Kana* = humbled.

of adventurers in Tob when he was recruited by his estranged half-brothers to lead an Israelite army against the conquering Ammonites. Jephthah tried to negotiate a peace by explaining the history between Israel and the Ammonites: "I have not wronged you, but you have wronged me by waging war against me. Let Yahweh, the judge, decide the dispute."[414]

- Jephthah the manager tried conversation and diplomacy before action.
- Jephthah the manager looked to Yahweh to solve the problem.
- Jephthah the manager turned to action when the Ammonite king, Sihon, would not listen to reason, so he crossed the Jordan River and devastated twenty Ammonite towns.

After the victory, the enraged Israelite tribe of Ephraim, full of name-calling, came to Jephthah and said they were going to burn down Jephthah's house with him inside because he had not included them in the war against Ammon, thus depriving them of any booty.[415] Jephthah again responded in peace by saying that they had refused to help when initially asked, and so he had to "take his life into his own hands" and attacked Ammon.[416] To protect his tribe[417] from the angry Ephraimites, Jephthah the manager devised two clever schemes:

- Jephthah's army captured the means of production and transportation from his opponents.[418]
- Jephthah the manager successfully instituted password protection to detect intruders.[419]
- Jephthah the manager would be a manager in Israel for only six years and is known chiefly for his tragically rash vow effecting his daughter, but he should be remembered for some management principles, as well.

---

414. Judg 11:27.
415. Judg 12:1.
416. Judg 12:3.
417. The Gileadites.
418. Judg 12:5.
419. "Sibboleth" vs. "Shibboleth," Judg 12:6.

SAMUEL THE MANAGER

> Samuel continued as [manager][420] over Israel all the days of his life. From year to year, he went on a circuit from Bethel to Gilgal to Mizpah, [managing][421] Israel in all those places. But he always went back to Ramah, where his home was, and there he also [managed][422] Israel. And he built an altar there to Yahweh. (1 Sam 7:15–17)

Samuel stands with David in that royal history of the Jewish organization just a few decades after the last judge/manager, Samson.[423] When the Philistines captured the ark of the covenant,[424] Samuel's management training kicked in:

- Samuel the manager rallied his organization to stay faithful to Yahweh.[425]
- Samuel the manager interceded on behalf of the organization with Yahweh to defeat his opposition.[426]
- Samuel the manager orchestrated internal activities so that the concentration of the members wouldn't be distracted from the goals of the company.[427]
- Samuel the manager travelled to the branch offices as a circuit-riding manager educating and bolstering the spirits of the members of his organization.[428]

---

420. *Shaphat.*
421. *Shaphat.*
422. *Shaphat.*
423. "Samuel, beloved by Yahweh, a prophet of Yahweh, established the kingdom and anointed rulers over his people. By the law of Yahweh he judged the congregation, and Yahweh watched over Jacob" (Sir 46:13–14).
424. 1 Sam 4:11.
425. 1 Sam 7:1–6.
426. 1 Sam 7:5.
427. He determined to place the recovered ark in an obscure place so that it didn't get the attention that belonged to God (1 Sam 7:1–2).
428. 1 Sam 7:13–17.

- Samuel the manager encouraged the gifted members of the organization by establishing professional training and accrediting guilds for coworkers.[429]

In short, when times of trouble came, Samuel stepped into the breech to manage the organization. He has been called "God's emergency man."[430] In his farewell speech to his organization, Samuel said, "I have been your manager[431] from my youth until this day. Here I stand. Testify against me in the presence of Yahweh and his anointed. Whose ox have I taken? Whose donkey have I taken? Whom have I cheated? Whom have I oppressed? From whose hand have I accepted a bribe to make me shut my eyes? If I have done any of these, I will make it right." "You have not cheated or oppressed us. You have not taken anything from anyone's hand," they replied.[432]

- Samuel is laying down the standard of compensation for all managers: Do not deprive the organization of its resources, and act with integrity.

It is worth noting that in this farewell speech Samuel mentions Gideon, Barak (Deborah), and Jephthah along with himself as managers for the company, delivering it from ruthless competitors, thus allowing the organization to "function in safety" and "rest."[433]

---

429. 1 Sam 10:5, 10; 19:20; 2 Kgs 2:3; elsewhere. Because secular songs were so important to Jewish church life, it is probable that secular musicians in the Old Testament church formed themselves into professional guilds to protect their livelihood. In fact, Sendrey notes that for the broad dissemination of music among the Jewish church public, the secular musicians accomplished far more than the Levitical temple musicians. Budde writes, "We possess more than one evidence that already in primeval times Israel had a guild of singers, that is, people well-versed in musical arts, who amassed a treasure of songs, of which they availed themselves at will, just as did the singers of Homer, or the medieval wandering minstrels . . . Num 21:27—'They that speak in parables (proverbs), they are the poet-singer musicians, the folkbards, the wandering minstrels of Israel'" (Sendry, *Music in Ancient Israel*, 539).

430. Fereday, *Samuel: God's Emergency Man and Jonathan and His Times*.

431. "Walked before you."

432. 1 Sam 12:1–4.

433. Judg 5:31; 8:28; 1 Sam 12:11.

DAVID THE MANAGER

> So David reigned over all Israel. And David administered[434] justice[435] and equity[436] to all his people. Joab the son of Zeruiah was over the army, Jehoshaphat, the son of Ahilud, was recorder,[437] Zadok, the son of Ahitub, was a priest, Ahimelech, the son of Abiathar, was a priest, Seraiah was secretary,[438] Benaiah, the son of Jehoiada, was over the Cherethites and the Pelethites, David's sons were chief managers.[439] (2 Sam 8:15–18)[440]

In a passage that is easy to skip if one is reading the Bible for devotion only we find nuggets of information for Christian managers.[441] These

---

434. *Asah* = labor, work, execute.

435. *Mispat*.

436. *Sedaqa*.

437. *Zakhar* = to recollect, remember, 1 Chr 16:4; 2 Chr 24:22.

438. *Saphar* = scribe, to enumerate, recount; Ezra, Baruch (Jer 36:4–32). "On the second day the heads of fathers' houses of all the people, with the priests and the Levites, came together to Ezra the scribe (*saphar*) in order to study the words of the Law" (Neh 8:13). *Saphar* has its roots in the Akkadian language and means "to list" or "to write down." Thus, a chief administrator or secretary who keeps track of official business—a scribe. "From Makir managers (*chaqaq*) came down, from Zebulun those who bear a manager's (*saphar*) staff" (Judg 5:14). "My heart is filled with Israel's managers (*chaqaq*), with the willing volunteers among the people. Praise Yahweh!" (Judg 5:9). *Chaqaq* is a minor title of leaders in the Jewish cohort. The root meaning is to "inscribe," "write," "decree," or "engrave" and can be used to refer to those who inscribe laws and regulations. So the term denotes an administrator, governor, or commander who is a regulator or community leader (Gen 49:10; Deut 33:21; Judg 5:14; Isa 33:22). Deborah the warrior judge loves the *chaqaq*/scribes. This was a professional managerial class who served the ruler in administration (cf. 2 King 25:19; 2 Chr 26:11; Isa 33:18; Jer 37:15; 52:25). The *saphar* became chancellors, commanders, captains, or secretaries of state. Some *saphars* lived in palaces (2 Kgs 18:18) and hobnobbed with the king (Isa 36:3). The most famous biblical *saphar* was Ezra. For the Christian business manager, no detail is too small to warrant his attention (Zech 4:10; Jas 3:4 = small market changes can radically affect the entire business operation). He knows and keeps track of where everything is. The *saphar* fixes all the broken windows. This term belongs to the category of terms defining the Old Testament manager as a secretary or scribe or one who keeps records. Eventually, *saphars* evolved into a powerful sociopolitical force which we see as prominent in the Gospels.

439. *Kohen* = chief ruler, principal officer, priest; 2 Sam 8:18; 20:26.

440. For a parallel list of Davidic royal managers see 2 Sam 20:23–26; 1 Kgs 4:1–6.

441. We will find the same trove with Solomon in 1 Kings 4:1–19. The name of Adoni-ram, in charge of forced labor, is added to this later list of managers. Adoni-ram will serve under Solomon and even Rehoboam.

three verses give us the managerial team for David as he takes control of the organization. David demonstrated his managerial competency in administering justice and righteousness early on by creating positions and appointing quality men to manage the affairs of the organization. The importance of management functions for Yahweh is evidenced by the fact that David's cabinet of managers is repeated three times, giving us the model for future royal reigns.

- Joab, the hero of the Battle of Jerusalem, was a nepotistic hire because he was David's nephew.[442] He was put in charge of the military in order to enforce the just reign of his uncle.[443]
- Jehoshaphat was appointed the crown archivist for David's administration. He remained in office under King Solomon.[444]
- Zadok and Ahimelech (Abiathar) were descendants of Aaron and thus were responsible for oversight of religious observances in the kingdom.[445] Zadok also had the additional responsibilities to be the court prophet,[446] and continued to be the high priest under Solomon.[447]
- Seraiah was appointed "secretary" in charge of disseminating the royal edicts for foreign and domestic consumption. Thus, he functioned as David's secretary of state and was one of the most senior bureaucrats in David's court.[448] His sons succeeded him in office.[449]
- Benaiah was a legitimate military hero and one of David's "mighty men."[450] Thus he was appointed to oversee the mercenary royal guard—the Kerethites and Pelethites. This was the same position that David held under King Saul.[451] Benaiah was to implement David's desire that the military be conducted according to Yahweh's

---

442. 2 Sam 20:23.
443. 1 Chr 11:6.
444. 1 Kgs 4:3.
445. Zadok: Num 25:12–13; 1 Chr 6:3–9. Abiathar: 1 Kgs 2:27.
446. 2 Sam 15:27.
447. 1 Kgs 2:35.
448. Seraiah could be Sheva (2 Sam 20:25) and/or Shisha (1 Kgs 4:3).
449. 1 Kgs 4:3.
450. Benaiah was also born to a priest: 2 Sam 23:20–21; 1 Chr 27:5.
451. 1 Sam 22:14.

wishes.[452] Like Zadok, he continued under Solomon and became general of the army after Joab.[453]

- David's sons played a nebulous role. They were not Levitical priests but priests in the order of Melchizedek, so perhaps in that respect they had sacerdotal responsibilities.[454] It is probable that they did not compete with Zadok and Ahimelech in religious duties. I prefer to see them as royal advisors and trusted consultants to their dad.[455]

> David asked Ahimelech, "Don't you have a spear or a sword here? I haven't brought my sword or any other weapon, because the king's business was urgent." The priest replied, "The sword of Goliath the Philistine, whom you killed in the valley of Elah, is here; it is wrapped in a cloth behind the ephod. If you want it, take it. David said, "There is none like it; give it to me." (1 Sam 21:8–9)

1 Samuel 21:8–9 is interesting for those in the competitive marketplace for David's use of Goliath's sword for advancing God's will. Here we have a believing manager using the tool the unbeliever first used against him. Significantly, the tool[456] used by David was made by unbelievers because the believers didn't have the resources to make their own tools.[457]

---

452. 1 Sam 21:5.

453. 1 Kgs 1–2, 4:4.

454. Like Ira the Jairite who was a non-Levitical priest for David, 2 Sam 20:26.

455. Cf. 1 Chr 18:17.

456. Sword, spear, javelin.

457. 1 Sam 13:19; In 1 Samuel 30:9–18, "David and the six hundred men with him came to the Besor Ravine, where some stayed behind, for two hundred men were too exhausted to cross the ravine. But David and four hundred men continued the pursuit. They found an Egyptian in a field and brought him to David . . . David asked him, 'Can you lead me down to this [Amalekite raiding party]?' He answered, 'Swear to me before God that you will not kill me or hand me over to my master, and I will take you down to them.' He led David down, and there they were . . . David fought them . . . and none of them got away . . . David recovered everything the Amalekites had taken." Once again the organization relies on a competitor to help them accomplish God's will for them. David first feeds the starving Egyptian man and then negotiates in good faith to solve an organizational problem—retrieving David's kidnapped wives and everything else the Amalekite raiding party had taken. David practiced justice in his management responsibilities. 2 Sam 8:15; 1 Chr 18:14.

When one manages[458] men in righteousness,[459] when he manages in the fear of God, he is like the light of morning at sunrise on a cloudless morning, like the brightness after rain that brings the grass from the earth. (2 Sam 23:3–4)

David's last recorded words included a description of his management philosophy. It is important for Christian managers to see David express his humility before his sovereign God, who he called by name—"Who am I, O sovereign Yahweh?"[460]

Much more can be written about David's management of his organization, but I want to move on to other Old Testament managers.

---

458. *Mashal* = reign, have dominion. Management over all the material goods of a master as his steward and management of all the personnel of the enterprise is indicated in the case of Abraham's servant. Also, the term is used of Joseph's administration of Egypt as Pharaoh's prime minister (Gen 15:2; 45:8). "He said to the chief servant (*mashal*) in his household, the one managing (*mashal*) all that he had . . ." (Gen 24:2). In this most interesting verse, Eliezer is referenced as the manager, the administrator (*mashal*) of all of Abraham's possessions. *Mashal* is the primary Hebrew term translated "dominion" and is used to indicate a manager of subordinates (cf. Prov 12:24) and possessions (cf. Ps 8:6). Fundamentally, the term connotes oversight and is the word Moses employed to indicate Joseph's management of Egypt's output in Gen 45:8. The use of *mashal* "demonstrates the importance of the principle of authority, the absolute moral necessity of respect for proper authority, the value of it for orderly society and happy living, and the origin of all authority in God himself" (Culver, "Mashal"). Sounds like an apt description of a Christian business manager, because along with position comes the responsibility of being the chief servant of organization in order to achieve an orderly and productive workplace (Ps 8:6, "You made him manager [*mashal*] over the works of your hands").

459. *Tsaddiq* = Just, right, honest. The term describes a human judge who dispenses true justice (2 Sam 23:3) and portrays an ordinary person who is honest with other men (Prov 29:7).

460. 2 Sam 7:18; 1 Chr 29:14. David's son Solomon will exhibit the same initial humility before his sovereign God (2 Chr 2:6) as did Gideon (Judg 6:15) and even Saul (1 Sam 9:21). A sidenote on David's management skills. In 2 Samuel 9 we read the story of David's kindness towards Saul's grandson, Mephibosheth. Fulfilling a decades-old promise to Jonathan, Mephibosheth's father, David brought the crippled Mephibosheth into the royal residence to live with him. In a tiny notation, the writer notes that "all the members of Ziba's household were servants of Mephibosheth" (2 Sam 9:12). Ziba was a holdover manager of Saul's and had his own large management team ("fifteen sons and twenty servants"). David put Ziba and all his managers at the disposal of Mephibosheth along with his own management team to "farm Saul's land and bring in the crops so that Mephibosheth can be provided for" (9:10). Even though there was later deception on the part of Ziba, David treated him fairly and was generous with him (2 Sam 16).

ADONI-RAM THE MANAGER

> Adoni-ram managed[461] forced labor. (2 Sam 20:24)

Adoni-ram[462] ("Lord high") functioned as the construction manager of the huge public works projects during the reigns of David,[463] Solomon, and Rehoboam. The public works included "Yahweh's temple, Solomon's private palace, the supporting terraces, the wall of Jerusalem, and Hazor, Meggido and Gezer,"[464] which required him to organize and motivate the thousands of workers conscripted from conquered tribes around Israel and short-term workers from Israel.[465] He functioned as the head of the labor department of the Israeli government. Adoni-ram had hundreds of supervisors reporting to him as they managed the construction workers who excavated, shaped, and placed the stones in the growing structure.[466] The workers also harvested the trees and shaped the lumber for the interior work of the temple. All of this activity took the enslaved Canaanite workers away from their homes for years. Even the union workers were on the job for months at a time.[467] All this was under the general management of Adoni-ram. It is not surprising, then, that resentment and anger would be the reaction of the people, and finally, under the inept leadership of Rehoboam, Israelite workers and their families rose up and killed Adoni-ram.[468]

Adoni-ram teaches some important management lessons:

- Adoni-ram the manager was so efficient as a manager of men that David appointed him to the post of secretary of labor, in charge of thousands of construction workers.
- Adoni-ram the manager apparently came from a godly family, since his father's name was Abda, meaning "servant of Jehovah," whom he faithfully served under three difference kings.[469]

---

461. *Al* = above, over.
462. Also Adoram.
463. 2 Sam 20:24.
464. 1 Kgs 9:15.
465. 1 Kgs 5:13.
466. 1 Kgs 5:15.
467. Neh 6:15.
468. 1 Kgs 12:18.
469. 1 Kgs 4:6.

- Adoni-ram the manager was a man skilled in communications, organization, and discipline, since people conquered by Israel were to be spared death but were to be conscripted into labor units to build public works for Israel. It took a skilled and dedicated man to head up this huge multiple-thousand labor force.[470]
- Adoni-ram the manager was sent by King Rehoboam to talk with rebellious workers,[471] but the malcontents, rather than obeying Adoni-ram, killed him, which was a signal event in the history of Israel.[472]

SOLOMON THE MANAGER

> Then they acknowledged Solomon, son of David, as king[473] a second time, anointing him before Yahweh to be manager[474] and Zadok to be priest. (1 Chr 29:22)

Solomon prospered in his managerial duties, as did the entire organization, because the company followed his advice.[475] There are several things to note about Solomon's managerial effectiveness noted in this passage:

- Solomon the manager was given personal prosperity by God.
- Solomon the manager was favored by Yahweh[476]

---

470. Deut 20:10–11.
471. 2 Chr 10:4.
472. 2 Chr 10:18.
473. *Malak*.
474. *Nagid*. "Then they acknowledged Solomon, son of David, as king (*malak*) a second time, anointing him before Yahweh to be manager (*nagid*) and Zadok to be priest" (1 Chr 29:22). Interestingly for our purposes, the word *nagid* has ancient roots meaning "to communicate" (Westermann, "Nagid"). *Nagid* applies to the Christian business manager in that a *nagid* has responsibility to communicate the roles and goals of the organization with those under him. His position is probably like the "captain" (*strategos* = governor, chief magistrate, army commander) of the temple guard in Acts 4:1. So here we have a *nagid* whose job is chief of security of the temple with the responsibilities to keep things moving along in a humming fashion without disruption and being sure that the people know their obligations.
475. 1 Chr 29:23.
476. 1 Chr 29:25.

- Solomon the manager was exalted as one of, if not the best, manager the organization ever had.[477]
- Solomon the manager led the organization, and it prospered under his management.[478]
- Solomon the manager was able to keep all the best managers under his father, David.[479]

The government that Solomon inherited from David had come through some momentous changes. The first king, Saul, had organized the twelve tribes into a loose confederation with a weak central government. Under Saul there was no central corporate headquarters, no strong court system, and no indication of a comprehensive tax authority. The second king, David, established a strong central administrative organization centered in Jerusalem that managed the political affairs of Israel. But political administration was just getting started when the explosive growth of Israel happened. David bequeathed to the third king, Solomon, an administrative state that was successful and ready to govern a powerful nation. As an indication of how much Solomon increased the power of the nation of Israel, note that David's cabinet consisted of approximately eight managers (excluding David's sons),[480] whereas the historian notes that Solomon had approximately eleven capital managers, plus twelve regional managers, in his royal cabinet.[481] Solomon's cabinet is an extraordinary group of managers tasked with the administration of

---

477. 1 Chr 29:25.

478. 1 Chr 29:23.

479. 1 Chr 29:24; "When the priest Pashhur son of Immer, the chief manager (*paqid nagid*) in the temple of the LORD . . ." (Jer 20:1); "Jehiel [et al.] were supervisors [overseers, inspectors, *paqid*] under Conaniah and Shimei by appointment [mandate, *miphqad*, from the root *paqid*] of King Hezekiah and Azariah the chief officer [ruler, *nagid*] in the temple of God" (2 Chr 31:13); "But now your kingdom will not endure; the LORD has sought out a man after his own heart and appointed him leader [*nagid* = captain] of his people, because you have not kept the LORD's command" (1 Sam 13:14). Pashhur was the "governor" or "officer" or *nagid* of the temple, which made him the highest-ranking administrative officer in the Jewish church (2 Kgs 25:18). The use of the Hebrew couplet *paqid nagid* connotes high rank. Pashhur's job was to see that no unauthorized persons entered the temple and that no disturbance occurred within the temple court (Jer 29:26). Pashhur was the temple top cop.

480. 2 Sam 8:15–18; 20:23–25; 1 Chr 18:14–17.

481. 1 Kgs 4:1–19.

a huge organization to efficiently manage labor, taxes, defense, and provisions. The verdict on Solomon's management was:

> The people of Judah and Israel were as numerous as the sand on the seashore; they ate, they drank, and they were happy... During Solomon's lifetime Judah and Israel, from Dan to Beersheba, lived in safety, each man under his own vine and fig tree. (1 Kgs 4:20, 28)[482]

In addition to his capital command staff, Solomon organized twelve district offices to govern the company. It is instructive to see the great overlap between the two reigns. Many of David's men took jobs in Solomon's organization. The Egyptian influence is present in these names, and we know that Solomon asked his Egyptian father-in-law, Pharaoh, for advice in managing his realm.[483] Based on 1 Kings 4:1-19, the following is a quick run through Solomon's key managerial staff of high officials,[484] secretaries,[485] recorders,[486] officers,[487] army commanders,[488] priests,[489] friends,[490] one in charge of the palace,[491] one in charge of forced labor,[492] twelve district officials,[493] and one governor over everything.[494]

---

482. "King Solomon was greater in riches (*osher*) and wisdom (*hokma*) than all the other kings of the earth. The whole world sought audience with Solomon to hear the skill/wisdom God had put in his heart" (1 Kgs 10:23-24). *Hokma*—This term covers all human experience with understanding, insight, intelligence, and skill. It is the wisdom that is required in good leadership, as in David (1 Sam 18:14). It is expressed in secular affairs as well as religious affairs. This term marks technical skill and craftmanship (Exod 25:3; 31:3, 6) and good management skills, as evidenced by Solomon (1 Kgs 10:4, 24) and by Joseph (Ps 105:16-22; Acts 7:10). "In the last days... Every man will sit under his own vine and under his own fig tree, and no one will make them afraid, for Yahweh Almighty has spoken" (Mic 4:4).

483. 1 Kgs 3:1.

484. *Sar.*

485. *Saphar.*

486. *Zakar* = to cause to remember.

487. *Natsab.*

488. Over the hosts (*tsaba*).

489. *Kohen* = chief ruler, principal officer, confidential advisors.

490. *Reeh.*

491. *Al* = most high.

492. *Mas* = tribute, levy.

493. *Natsab* = one set up.

494. *Netsib* = one set up.

- Azariah was the high priest. He was probably the grandson of Zadok and the son of Ahimaaz who served under David, so he was an experienced religious leader with good family training.[495] Azariah, as the royal chaplain, was probably the most trusted advisor to the king. Thus, his name comes first in the list.[496]

- Elihoreph and Ahijah, managers, the sons of Shisha (Seraiah), were secretaries.[497] These two managers may have split the secretary of state duties between them, one dealing with foreign affairs the other dealing with domestic affairs. They inherited their positions from their father who also worked in David's company as a high-ranking administrator.[498]

- Jehoshaphat the manager was the recorder[499] and as such was probably akin to our chief of protocol. He was another holdover from the Davidic reign.[500]

- Benaiah took Joab's place as general of the army.[501] His leadership over David's mercenary king's guards (Cherethites and Pelethites) was probably subsumed under the general Israeli army.[502]

- Azariah the manager was chief of staff.[503] This position was new and had the responsibility of managing the twelve district managers, a highly important position in the Solomonic regime. He was probably a grandson of David, being the son of Nathan, David's son.[504]

- Zabud was a priest[505] and Solomon's personal advisor.[506] Zabud was also a son of Nathan and so he was also David's grandson. He joined

---

495. 1 Chr 6:9; 2 Sam 15:29, 36.

496. 1 Kgs 4:2.

497. *Saphar.*

498. 2 Sam 8:17.

499. *Zakar* = to cause to remember.

500. 2 Sam 8:16, 20:24.

501. over the hosts (*tsaba*).

502. General Benaiah, after all, had assassinated Joab under Solomon's orders, 1 Kgs 2:35.

503. *Natsab.*

504. 2 Sam 5:14–15. "Nathan" was a common name in Israel at the time, 2 Sam 4:5.

505. *Kohen* = chief ruler, principal officer, confidential advisors. Mostly, the term is translated "priest," and so it is not included in my list of managers, but see 2 Samuel 8:18 and 1 Chronicles 18:17 for "royal advisors" or "chief ministers."

506. *Reeh.*

Azariah in joining his uncle Solomon's government. The Hebrew term translated "friend" is a synonym for "chief advisor."[507]

- Ahishar the manager was in charge of the palace, meaning he was something like the prime minister. He would work with Ahijah, administering domestic affairs, including real estate, trade, and mining.[508] This was to be a common position in future governments.[509]

- Adoni-ram the manager continued to manage the forced labor. He was a holdover from David probably because he was good at his job in the construction of all Solomon's public works projects. He would be a carryover to Rehoboam's court.[510]

Solomon the manager divided up the land into administrative districts, each with its own manager and branch office. He seems careful to divide the land according to tribal boundaries, thus averting rebellion in the tribal population.

- Ben-Abinadab the manager managed the region of Dor and was married to Taphath the daughter of Solomon, so he was the king's son-in-law. He was also Solomon's first cousin.[511]

- Ben-Geber the manager managed the fortified towns once ruled by King Og of Bashan.[512]

- Ahinadab the manager was in charge of managing the city of Mahanaim[513] which had been the capital of Israelite kings Ish-baal[514] and Absalom.[515]

---

507. Hushai the Archite held the job before (2 Sam 15:37; 16:16). Interestingly, Hushai was a Canaanite. David's grandson would not be called "friend," 2 Sam 4:5.

508. 1 Kgs 16:9; 18:3; 2 Kgs 10:5; 15:5; 18:18–37; 19:2; Isa 22:15; 36:3; 37:2.

509. 2 Sam 4:6.

510. 1 Kgs 12:18. Samuel had specifically warned the nation that the institution of enslaved labor would be the result of a king, 2 Sam 4:6; 1 Sam 8:10–18.

511. 2 Sam 4:1; 1 Sam 16:8; 17:13.

512. 2 Sam 4:13; Deut 3:4.

513. 2 Sam 4:14.

514. 2 Sam 2:8.

515. 2 Sam 17:24.

- Ahimaaz the manager managed the region of Naphtali and was married to Basemath the daughter of Solomon, so he was another son-in-law.[516]
- Geber the manager was the son of Uri and managed the region of Gilead, the country of Sihon king of the Amorites and of Og king of Bashan.[517]
- Azariah the manager probably managed all the district managers as well as Judah.[518]

Interesting from the standpoint of management is the fact that land in Judah was not divided into districts, only Israel's land. The reason may be that Judah was understood to be managed by the capital clique and it is the provinces that need to be managed with district offices.

> Yahweh gave Solomon wisdom[519] just as he had promised him. There were peaceful relations between Hiram and Solomon, and the two of them made a treaty. (1 Kgs 5:12)

Probably no Hebrew word describes management any better than *hokma*. The basic meaning of *hokma* and its cognates is to describe a manner of thinking and attitude towards life. It is worldview thinking with the dominant characteristic being prudency in the practical affairs of life.[520] It is shrewdness. A "wise man," a "*hokma* man," is seen in the Old Testament as constituting almost a third office in the Jewish organization, along with priest and prophet.[521] That is because of the wide range of wisdom displayed by the *hokma* man:

- We see the managerial political shrewdness of Solomon with foreign leaders.
- We the see the management skills to motivate others.[522]

---

516. 1 Kgs 4:15.

517. 1 Kgs 4:1–19.

518. 1 Kgs 4:5. "And Solomon managed (*marshal*) all the kingdoms from the River to the land of the Philistines, as far as the border of Egypt. These countries brought tribute and were Solomon's subjects all his life" (1 Kgs 4:21).

519. *Hokma*.

520. Prov 90:12.

521. Jer 18:18.

522. Prov 8:33; 23:19; 27:11.

- We see time management skills.[523]
- We see prudential management skills used for the safety of the group.[524]
- We see technical management skills used to accomplish a finished product.[525]
- We see management skills in strategic operation.[526]
- We see management skills used in political and operational matters.[527]
- We even see management stills being used by those outside the Jewish organization, like Egypt,[528] Babylon,[529] Tyre,[530] and Persia.[531]

Solomon the manager gave great management advice in his proverbs and one of those valuable proverbs is 1:5: "Let the wise[532] listen and add to their learning, and let the discerning[533] get management advice."[534] In Proverbs and Job[535] there is a strange Hebrew word that is translated "good advice" or "guidance" or "skill": *tachbuloth*. The word is only used six times in the Old Testament,[536] and commentators trace the word back to the binding or the tackling of a ship and thus the rope pulling or steering or directing a ship's course. *Tachbuloth* is managing a group of people as the pilot manages a ship. Involved in piloting or guiding the crew is

---

523. Ps 90:12.
524. 2 Sam 20:22.
525. Exod 28:3; 31:3; 35:10, Jer 10:9.
526. Isa 10:3.
527. Deut 34:9; 2 Sam 14:20; 1 Kgs 5:7.
528. Gen 41:8.
529. Isa 44:25.
530. Ezek 28:4–5.
531. Esth 6:13.
532. *Chakham*.
533. *Bin* = understanding, perceive.
534. *Tachbuloth* = counsel.
535. "At his direction (*tachbuloth*) [the clouds] swirl around over the face of the whole earth to do whatever he commands them" (Job 37:12).
536. Cf. Prov 1:5; 11:14; 12:5; 20:18; 24:6; Greek LXX = "generalship," Job 37:12.

learning,[537] discernment,[538] and wisdom.[539] Speaking to the importance of this Hebrew term is that the Greek Septuagint (LXX) translates *tachbuloth* into the Greek word *kubernao* ("to guide," "govern") in five of those Old Testament places.[540] Suffice it to say here that in the Old Testament, Yahweh taught the business manager that it was the manager's responsibility to guide and pilot the company, particularly during tough times, i.e., crisis management. This was really the major responsibility given to the manager by the Great Manager. Unfortunately for the Jewish organization, Solomon's son Rehoboam failed to take his dad's exhortation for multiple advisers.

Solomon the manager excelled in the understanding of non-philosophical and non-theological subjects such as "plant life, the cedars of Lebanon, the hyssop that grows out of walls, animals, birds, reptiles, and fish,"[541] and construction: "Solomon had seventy thousand carriers and eighty thousand stonecutters in the hills, as well as thirty-three hundred managers[542] who managed[543] the project and managed[544] the workers."[545]

The verdict: Solomon was a "wise son endowed[546] with intelligence and discernment."[547] The record of Solomon is one of wise action, administration, and construction.[548] We again see that God's world is to be understood by the Christian business manager, and that understanding takes time to apprehend. Solomon was twenty when he ascended to the throne and fifty-nine when he died, so his managerial training indicates he was an immature man when he became king. Hence his royal training began immediately as he prayed for practical wisdom.[549]

---

537. *Lamad.*

538. *Bin.*

539. *Chakham.*

540. Prov 1:5; 11:14; 12:5; 20:18; 24:6; cf. Acts 27:11; Rev 18:17, "pilot"; 1 Cor 12:28, "administration."

541. 1 Kgs 4:29–34.

542. *Natsab* = foremen.

543. *Paqad* = supervised.

544. *Radah* = directed.

545. 1 Kgs 5:16.

546. *Yada* = knowing.

547. 1 Chr 22:12; 2 Chr 2:1–14.

548. Cf. 1 Kgs 3:16–4:34; 7:1–12.

549. 1 Kgs 3:7–9.

In 2 Chronicles 2, Solomon's future managerial leadership and instincts are clearly enunciated for our benefit:

- Solomon the manager, having decided to build his massive public works project, acquired[550] the necessary labor pool to complete the work.[551]
- Solomon the manager honored his heritage and continued the legacy of a winning managerial example through nepotism.[552]
- Solomon the manager gives us an early example of international relations between two sovereign kings: Solomon and Hiram.[553]
- Solomon the manager was humble in his building project: "Who is able" and "who am I"[554] to undertake such an endeavor?[555]
- Solomon the manager knew his limitations and managed accordingly. He knew that the building project could only accomplish a limited amount, "a place to burn sacrifices," and not the entire residence of Yahweh.[556]
- Solomon the manager wanted the best-trained people in the known world to work on his "magnificent" building complex.[557]

---

550. *Saphar* = conscripted, assigned, enumerated.

551. "Solomon gave orders to build a temple . . . He conscripted seventy thousand men . . . and 3600 construction managers over them" (2 Chr 2:1-2). "The temple I am going to build will be great . . . large and magnificent" (2 Chr 2:5, 9).

552. "You did for my father" (2 Chr 2:3).

553. 2 Chr 2:3-10.

554. Exod 3:11; 1 Sam 18:18; 2 Sam 7:18; 1 Chr 29:14.

555. "Who is able to build a temple for him? Who then am I? . . . except as a place to burn sacrifices before him" (2 Chr 2:6).

556. 2 Chr 2:6.

557. "Send me then a man skilled (*chakham*) to work . . . and experienced [*yada* = learning] in the art . . . to work . . . with my skilled (*haham*) craftsmen" (2 Chr 2:7). *Chakham* = clever. "I am sending you Huram-Abi, a man of great skill . . . he is trained to work . . . he is experienced in all kinds of engraving and can execute any design given to him" (2 Chr 2:13-14). Huram-Abi could work on the outside construction as well as the inside finish work (cf. Gen 23:5-6; King Huram shrewdly calls Solomon's father David "my Lord" as a sign of respect from one merchant to another). Huram-Abi is subtly compared to the tabernacle craftsmen Bezalel and Oholiab (Exod 31:1-6; 35:30—36:2). Solomon wanted only the best to work with.

- Solomon the manager looked for talent wherever it could be found. He was a networking manager.[558]
- Solomon the manager knew what needed to be done to build the temple and he knew the individuals who could accomplish the task.[559]
- Solomon the manager knew that Huram-Abi was not only an expert craftsman but an expert construction manager as well.[560]
- Solomon the manager took the initiative in salary negotiations by offering the workers a generous remuneration. He is being sure that his employees get paid.[561]

The Chronicler emphasizes that Solomon's skill and wisdom was given to him by Yahweh and was thus perfectly suited to build this huge complex. Solomon is portrayed as a man in charge, taking responsibilities for the entire project, from design and planning to recruiting the best available workers to determining the compensation for the laborers.

And the beat goes on: Ecclesiastes 2 tells us more of Solomon's managerial accomplishments:

- Solomon the manager found joy in doing the work. His pleasure came from the physical, hands-on management of all his projects ("I undertook," "I built," "I planted," "I made," "I bought," "I acquired," "my work, "my labor," "my toil"[562]).
- Solomon the manager exercised "wisdom"[563] in his management of Israel. He repeats this fact four times in Ecclesiastes 2. What is this "wisdom" that he is so proud of owning? The Hebrew word used here is the "wisdom" that is seen in the management skill of technical work,[564] craftsmanship,[565] military strategy,[566] and government

---

558. "I know that your men are skilled in cutting timber" (2 Chr 2:8).
559. "He will work with your craftsmen and those of David" (2 Chr 2:7, 14).
560. "To work with my skilled craftsmen" (2 Chr 2:7).
561. "I will give your servants twenty thousand cors" (2 Chr 2:10).
562. "There is nothing better for a man than to enjoy his work because that is his lot" (Eccl 2:4–8).
563. *Chokhmah*.
564. Exod 28:3.
565. Exod 31:3, 6.
566. Isa 10:13.

administration.[567] This is knowledge gained from experience and practice and is always used in a positive way. And you add to all these skills what Solomon has used his "wisdom" to create in our passage and one gets the impression that this wisdom is management wisdom.[568]

- Solomon the manager created viticulture ventures that were commercially successful and not for private use. They also were huge and profitable and personally designed and managed by him.[569]
- Solomon the manager uses the language of Ecclesiastes 2 to resemble the creation narrative in Genesis 1:26–28 for aggressive management of natural resources to be faithful to the creation mandate.[570]
- Solomon the manager dug his own mines for silver and gold and imported treasures for foreign nations.[571]
- Solomon the manager took personal oversight over his animal breeding.[572]
- Solomon the manager made "gardens and parks" with many "fruit trees" commercially valuable to Israel.
- Solomon the manager created political districts for better governing. So he was a political reformer, as well.[573]
- Solomon the manager created and sustained a society of culture in Israel, with music and poetry. Since his choirs were mixed they were secular musical events and not religious, Levitical, male-only choirs.[574]

One scholar summed up the extent of Solomon's managerial creativity as "remarkable and includes cuisine, architecture, farming, gardening, relationships, and gathering antique and other treasures."[575]

---

567. Deut 34:9; 2 Sam 14:20; Ezek 28:4–5.
568. Eccl 2:3, 9,12,13.
569. Eccl 2:4.
570. Eccl 2:5; cf. 1 Kgs 4:33; Neh 2:8.
571. Eccl 2:8.
572. Eccl 2:7.
573. Eccl 2:8; cf. 1 Kgs 7–19.
574. Eccl 2:8; cf. 1 Kgs 4:32.
575. Bartholomew. *Ecclesiastes*, 137.

Solomon himself gave us his management resume in Ecclesiastes 2:9–11. This is Solomon at his most hedonistic transparency:

> I became greater by far than anyone in Jerusalem before me. In all this my wisdom[576] stayed with me. I denied myself nothing my eyes desired; I refused my heart no pleasure. My heart took delight in all my work, and this was the reward for all my labor. Yet when I surveyed all that my hands had done and what I had toiled to achieve, everything was meaningless, a chasing after the wind; nothing was gained under the sun.

Solomon the extraordinary manager had a dark side in his powerful male obsession with sex, which would presage the future decline of the company.[577] Clearly, Solomon is not to be praised for his indulgence of his fleshly desires. Indeed, he gives his motivation six times in Eccl 2:9–11: "for me." The personal toll that quality management can take on the manager is evident as Solomon's personal life began to descend into religious declension and chaos:[578] "Yahweh became angry with Solomon because his heart had turned away from him, who had twice warned him."[579]

OBADIAH THE MANAGER

> Now the famine was severe in Samaria, and [King] Ahab had summoned Obadiah who managed[580] his palace. (1 Kgs 18:3)

Obadiah was the "manager of the king's palace," which means he was one of the most powerful individuals in the country. During the reign of evil King Ahab of Israel, godly Obadiah had ascended the political ladder to where he was a powerful official in Ahab's government. That this ascent took place in any government is remarkable, but given the tremendous religious decline and apostacy of Ahab's reign the ascent of Obadiah was quite spectacular! While Ahab was not the first Israelite king to fall short of God's stated standard for righteous rule, he was the first king to

---

576. *Chockmah* = skill.
577. Eccl 2:8; cf. 1 Kgs 11:1–3.
578. 1 Kgs 11:9–14.
579. 1 Kgs 11:9.
580. *Mashal* = "was in charge," governor. There were several other royal palace managers mentioned in the Bible: Ahishar (1 Kgs 4:6), Arza (1 Kgs 16:9), unnamed administrator and city manager (2 Kgs 10:5), Eliakim (2 Kgs 18:18, 37; 19:2).

systematically depart from Jehovah and to embrace the Phoenician deities of Baal and Ashteroth.[581] It was in this downward slide that faithful Obadiah was elevated by Yahweh to serve the disreputable royal court. Notice some of his management decisions:

- During the first state persecution of believers recorded in Scripture, Obadiah courageously hid one hundred of the corporate leaders. Obadiah was a godly manager who was able to husband small resources to accomplish a great rescue mission.[582]
- At the same time Israel's first lady, Jezebel, was slaughtering God's people, her husband King Ahab was ordering Obadiah to help relieve the effects of the long famine on the royal cows by hunting for good grazing grass.[583] And away went the dutiful Obadiah looking for grass to preserve royal animals when fellow company members were being killed and starved to death by Ahab. A good manager picks his fights with the boss in order to create the best available outcome for the organization given all the circumstances.

Obadiah's faith in Jehovah was evident when he met Elijah, and the prophet told him to go tell Ahab that Elijah would finally meet the king after hiding for three years during the famine. Obadiah's natural response was to say, "Why me? What have I done to you to cause you to make such a request of me? I don't know if you're going to stick around to meet Ahab. And if you don't stay, he'll think I'm lying and kill me!"[584] Even though Obadiah had not previously met Elijah, after the prophet had given his word,[585] Obadiah was obedient and left to tell the volatile Ahab. Obviously, Obadiah had Ahab's respect and confidence because the king, in turn, left immediately to meet Elijah.

In sum, Obadiah was a faithful manager, an obedient manager, and a bold and effective manager in a very delicate and ambiguous situation.

---

581. 1 Kgs 16:30–32. In assessing the radical apostasy of Ahab, Stanley wrote, "The change from a symbolical worship of the one true God, with the innocent rites of sacrifices and prayer, to the cruel and licentious worship of the Phoenician divinities was a prodigious step downwards and left traces in northern Palestine which no subsequent reformations were able to entirely obliterate" (Stanley, *Lectures on the History of the Jewish Church*, 2.245. Cf. Kirk and Rowlinson, *Studies in the Book of Kings*).

582. The murder by their own government (a Jewish pogrom!). Cf. 1 Kgs 18:4

583. 1 Chr 18:5.

584. 1 Chr 18:7–9.

585. "As the LORD Almighty lives."

Obadiah shows what is possible when a believer is working for an unbelieving boss.

UZZIAH THE MANAGER

> Then all the people of Judah took Uzziah (Azariah) . . . and made him king . . . He was the one who rebuilt[586] Elath and restored[587] it to Judah . . . His fame spread far and wide, for he was greatly helped until he became powerful. (2 Chr 26:1-2, 15)

Uzziah needs to be mentioned in this hall of fame of Old Testament managers because he was an example of wise managers surrounding him in his early years of leadership. Uzziah was a gifted man and pretty much everything he put his hand to succeeded. Second Chronicles 26 is devoted to him and tells of his success in war, in construction projects, in agriculture, and in the military:

- Uzziah the manager recaptured the plains from the Philistines and turned it into a garden. After all, "he loved the soil."[588]

- Uzziah the manager repaired Jerusalem after the previous regimes let capital improvements and maintenance fall by the wayside. He fortified the capital city.

- Uzziah the manager trained,[589] equipped, and organized the army into an efficient fighting force. He even invented weaponry.[590]

---

586. *Banah* = to build up.
587. *Shub* = to cause to turn back.
588. 2 Chr 26:10.
589. *Koach* = power.
590. 2 Chr 26:11-15. King Uzziah delegated "Jeiel the *shoter*" in his administration to have administrative authority, that is, to be a manager (2 Chr 26:11). "That same day Pharaoh gave this order to the slave drivers and managers (*shoter*) in charge of the people" (Exod 5:6). *Shoter* is a common Semitic word with a basic meaning of "to write" or "document." The word morphed into those involved in the scribal arts or arrangers or organizers. In short, those who were trained in administration. In the Bible *shoter* is used to denote a taskmaster or overseer. During the Egyptian captivity it was used to refer to those Israelite managers who reported to their Egyptian superiors. These *shoters* drove their fellow Jewish members hard because they were responsible for the quality and output of the work (Exod 5:10-14). Moses appointed *shoters* to be minor judges and administrators in the organization (Deut 1:15; 31:28; elsewhere).

- Uzziah the manager surrounded himself with capable managers in all these important public policy areas. The implication of 2 Chronicles 26:15 is that Yahweh helped him by using experienced and wise counselors[591] to guide the young king.[592]

Unfortunately but predictably, all of this excellent work resulted in Uzziah's over-weaning pride which led to his downfall.[593]

HEZEKIAH THE MANAGER

> This is what Hezekiah did throughout Judah, doing what was good[594] and fair[595] and faithful[596] before Yahweh his God. In everything that he undertook in the service of God's temple and in obedience to the law and the commands, he sought his God and worked wholeheartedly. And so he prospered. (2 Chr 31:20)

We get to Hezekiah as an Old Testament manager: "this is what Hezekiah did . . . " The Hebrew verb for "fair" is actually used to describe Hezekiah. When he assumed the throne at age twenty-five, Hezekiah was already described as doing what was "right" or "fair" in the eyes of Yahweh.[597] It is clear that Hezekiah was a faithful follower of Yahweh, but what specific management activities did Hezekiah do to earn such accolades?

- Hezekiah the manager honored the organization's history and important symbolism and refurbished the organization's meeting places.[598]

---

591. Amaziah, Zechariah, Jeiel, Maaseiah, Hananiah, Azariah.
592. 2 Chr 26:7.
593. Noted in 2 Chr 26:16.
594. *Yashar* = right.
595. *Tob.* The Hebrew word *tob* is most commonly used in a utilitarian or functional context. That is, someone is "fair" or "good" because they are objectively judged to be so. Someone is "good" for something. A proper evaluation of a "fair" person will be the provable evaluation. *Tob* is most commonly translated *agathos, isotes, kalos,* or *chrestos* in the Greek LXX.
596. *Emeth* = steadfast.
597. 2 Chr 29:2.
598. 2 Chr 29:3–36.

- Hezekiah the manager led by example in the organization's public celebrations.[599]
- Hezekiah the manager communicated with his people.[600]
- Hezekiah the manager showed compassion to his competitors.[601]
- Hezekiah the manager encouraged the leaders of the organization and took time to understand their roles.[602]
- Hezekiah the manager was generous with his people.[603]
- Hezekiah the manager organized his organization into management units.[604]
- Hezekiah the manager delegated responsibilities to those under him and gave them special duties.[605]
- Hezekiah the manager provided tools and resources to the organization's leaders so that they would be successful in their assigned responsibilities.[606]
- Hezekiah the manager made sure that the organization's leaders were sufficiently paid for their work.[607]
- Hezekiah the manager planned and prepared for the future.[608]
- Hezekiah the manager consulted with the leaders of the organization to find solutions to problems.[609]
- Hezekiah the manager was boldly strategic in his actions when decisiveness was important.[610]

---

599. 2 Chr 29:28–30, 36.
600. 2 Chr 30:1–2; 6, 22–23.
601. 2 Chr 30:6–12; 18–19.
602. 2 Chr 30:22; 32:7–8.
603. 2 Chr 30:24.
604. 2 Chr 31:2.
605. 2 Chr 31:2; 32:6.
606. 2 Chr 31:3.
607. 2 Chr 31:4–8, 16–19.
608. 2 Chr 30:4; 31:11; 32:5, 28–29.
609. 2 Chr 32:3.
610. 2 Chr 32:3–4, 30.

The biblical conclusion of Hezekiah's managerial leadership: "He succeeded in everything he undertook."[611] We should be so blessed as managers.

However, a note of warning to all managers about Hezekiah. The Chronicler notes that God brought the Babylonians to Judah to test Hezekiah's commitment to Yahweh, but "Hezekiah's heart was proud[612] and he did not respond to the kindness shown him [by Yahweh]."[613] Happily Hezekiah repented, and the anger of Yahweh subsided, and the king was buried in the best grave Israel had.

JOSIAH THE MANAGER

> King Josiah said, "Have him get ready the money that has been brought into the temple of Yahweh, which the doorkeepers[614] have collected from the people. Have them entrust it to the men appointed to supervise[615] the work[616] on the temple. And have these men pay the workers who repair[617] the temple of Yahweh—the carpenters, the builders and the masons. Also have them purchase timber and dressed stone to repair the temple. But they need not account for the money entrusted to them because they are acting faithfully. (2 Kgs 22:4–7)

Look at the specific activities of Josiah concerning the management of the organization:

- Assigned people to collect the taxes in order to run the national organization.

---

611. 2 Chr 32:30.

612. *Gabah* = lifted up, to be high and haughty.

613. 2 Chr 32:25. Pratt continues, "As the record of Kings demonstrates, [Hezekiah] failed the test. Once again, the Chronicler revealed his interest in the inner motivations of his characters. Fidelity grew out of a whole-hearted commitment to God" Pratt, *1 & 2 Chronicles*, 460).

614. *Shamar* = guard, protect, retain. The first occurrence of this term is in Genesis 2:15, which has the sense of tending or managing the garden of Eden. There is thus the sense that care and commitment to watching over something is implicit in the word. Cf. Zech 3:7.

615. *Asah* = to do.

616. *Melakhah* = This is a flexible word meaning the actual activity of work, the skills in order to work, or the fruits of one's labor.

617. *Chazaq* = fix, strengthen, harden.

- Assigned people to competently distribute the taxes among the organization's operations.
- Appointed men to "supervise"[618] the construction of the organization's buildings.
- Hired craftsmen of various specialties who can restore the beauty of Solomon's temple.
- Hired purchasing agents to acquire lumber and stone who are honest men.

DANIEL THE MANAGER

> Are you more shrewd[619] than Daniel? (Ezek 28:3)[620]

Daniel joins Nehmiah and Esther as the only managers in the Bible to have books named after them. In the Old Testament we have the example of Daniel as being a "shrewd" and discerning manager of the boss's affairs. In a prophecy against the king of Tyre, Yahweh unfavorably compares the king to Daniel in Ezekiel 28:3. "Shrewd" is the same adjective that is used to describe Solomon.[621] The main meaning of this Hebrew term is to be "wise" or "pious" or "righteous," but there is its use in the Old Testament meaning "shrewd" or "smart" or "creative." Thus, Daniel is seen as a smart, clever, and shrewd manager of Nebuchadnezzar's affairs:[622]

---

618. *Paqad* = "oversight"

619. *Chakham*.

620. See Appendix for my chapter on Daniel in Doug Bond's book *Hold Fast*, 2.69–80. There is some dispute over whether or not this is Daniel of the Bible book, but I hold that it is the same Daniel.

621. *Chakham*, 1 Kgs 5:7.

622. And Belshazzar's affairs, Dan 2:5.

Then the king placed[623] Daniel in a high position[624] and lavished many gifts on him. He made him manager[625] over the entire province of Babylon and placed him as manager[626] of all

623. *Yehab* = to give high honors.

624. *Rabrab* = abundant, very great. There is no evidence that this Babylonian term was used outside of Isaiah to refer to an official position in a foreign government. Always an adjective with the Jews. "Then all the officials (*sar*) of the king of Babylon came and took seats in the Middle Gate: Nergal-Sharezer of Samgar, Nebo-Sarsekim, a chief officer (*rab-saris*), Nergal-Sharezer, a high official (*rab-mag*) and all the other officials (*sar*) of the king of Babylon" (Jer 39:3). *Rab* is a Babylonian term designating a chief or executive of a group. It is used in 2 Kings 25:8 to refer to a Babylonian commander of an army unit. It is used in Daniel 1:3 to refer to Ashpenaz, the chief Babylonian eunuch. It is always used to refer to non-Israelite officers (Isa 36 and 37).

625. *Shalat*. "Now Joseph was manager [*shalat* = administrator] of the land, the one who sold provisions to all its people" (Gen 42:6) ("[The ant] has no commander [administer = *qatsin*] no overseer [*shatlar*] or manager [*mashal*]," Prov 6:7). "There is an evil I have seen under the sun, the sort of error that arises from a ruler (*shatlar*)" (Eccl 10:5). The root of *shalat* means to exercise administrative control and dominion, most often autocratically (cf. Neh 5:15). So the term designates a governor, a magistrate, even a tyrant who provides for his subjects. We have a cognate form of the term in Daniel 4:17 where Yahweh is "sovereign" (*shatlar*) over men and dispenses political power to whomever he wants. Montgomery, *A Critical and Exegetical Commentary on the Book of Daniel*, 236, calls 4:17 "one of the immortal sentences of the Hebrew Scriptures." But it was not just Yahweh who exercised sovereign administrative control (shalat) over the earth. Joseph was a sovereign administrator. Joseph was the second most powerful man in the most powerful nation on earth—Egypt—and he controlled the resources of the entire country (Cf. Gen 41:43, 55-57). It was his job to provide for those under him.

626. *Sagan*. "The managers (*sagan*) did not know where I had gone or what I was doing, because as yet I had said nothing to the Jews or the priest or managers (*chor*)" (Neh 2:16). "So [Jezebel] wrote letters in Ahab's name, placed his seal on them, and sent them to the elders" (Lev 27:1-8). *Zaqen* means age, old, ancient, elderly. The age of sixty separated the seniors from the rest of Israelite society. The context of the passage determines whether the term refers to an organized body of elders or just a group of older men. Such a group would sit at the city gate and debate issues and decide questions (Deut 19:12). A quorum of ten men was necessary to settle an issue (Ruth 4:2). This group of older, distinguished men had great influence in the life of post-exilic Israel and managers (*chor*) who lived in Naboth's city with him (1 Kgs 21:8). *Chor* means "freeborn" and refers to a "leader" or "noble" who is free to govern cities (cf. Jer 39:6 = nobles of Judah). This is a borrowed word from Aramaic and is used extensively in Nehemiah. The *chor* helped in the reconstruction period after the Babylonian exile (cf. Neh 4:14). Sometimes they seem to be administrators who managed people's schedules and activities, and sometimes just influential people. But whatever the role was, nobility in all its finest permutations is applied to *chor* and thus to the Christian business manager as he governs the commercial metropolis. In short, the *chor* is the company prince and representative of the owner or managers (*sagan*) or any others who would be doing the work (*malakhah* = work, labor, performance, trade; Gen

its wise men. Moreover, at Daniel's request the king appointed Shadrach, Meshach, and Abednego as managers over[627] the province of Babylon, while Daniel himself remained at the royal court. (Dan 2:48–49)[628]

In Daniel 1, we see Daniel, showing an "aptitude for every kind of learning" and a quick mind, being trained in the court of Babylon so that he would be "qualified to serve in the king's palace."[629] Daniel accomplished three major administrative victories in the court of the Babylonian, Nebuchadnezzar:

- Daniel the manager was appointed to head up the Babylonian "wise men."

39:11; Prov 18:9; Neh 2:16). *Sagan* is another ancient Akkadian term meaning "ruler," "officer," or "superintendent" as one who is a deputy of the king. We find it in Jeremiah referring to a governor of Babylonia and in Nehemiah as a ruler of the Israelites in Jerusalem. This term is used extensively in post-exilic Isaiah, Jeremiah, Ezekiel, and Nehemiah. *Sagan* applies to the Christian business manager in that he is a working manager and not just a paper pusher. The *sagan* roles up his sleeves and "works" alongside of his colleagues. *Sigenin* is related to *sagan* and is found only in Daniel: "Then the king made Daniel a great [*rebah* = to make great] man, and gave him many great gifts, and made him manager (*shalat*) over the whole province of Babylon, and chief [*rab* = great one] of the managers (*sigenin*) over [*al* = above] all the wise men [*chakkim* = skillful] of Babylon" (Dan 2:48). *Sigenin* is an Akkadian loanword and is found only five times in the Old Testament and always in Daniel as "ruler" or "superintendent" (Dan 2:48; 3:2, 3, 27; 6:7). *Sigenin* applies to the Christian business manager in that the manager is the CEO or "governor" of the company, and all the other managers report to him. Thus, the manager wears two hats: one is *capo dei capi* (boss of the bosses) and the other is manager over his coworkers. There is the implication in Daniel that the *sigenin* has been given the gifts of leadership who is capable of governing the smartest people ("wise men") in the company.

627. *Al* = over, above the affairs.

628. "Then [Nebuchadnezzar] ordered Ashpenaz, chief of the court officials . . . to teach (*lamad*) [Daniel] the language and literature of the Babylonians" (Dan 1:4).

629. Dan 1:4. Fausset commented on this verse: "That the heathen lore was not altogether valueless appears from the Egyptian magicians who opposed Moses; the Eastern magi who sought Jesus, and who may have drawn the tradition as to the 'King of the Jews' from Dan 9:14, etc., written in the East. As Moses was trained in the learning of the Egyptian sages (Acts 7:22), so Daniel in that of the Chaldeans, to familiarize his mind with mysterious lore, and to develop his heaven-bestowed gift of understanding visions" (Fausset, *Bethany Parallel Commentary on the Old Testament*, 1765). The word translated "to be in charge" or "to govern" (*sagan*) in Daniel 2:48 is Akkadian and only occurs in Daniel (Dan 2:48; 3:2–3, 27; 6:7). However, Daniel is also described as a ruler (*shalat*) and this word connotes autocratic control and is formed from the same Arabic root as "sultan."

- Daniel the manager got his three Jewish friends appointed leading managers in the Babylonian kingdom.
- Daniel the manager convinced the king to keep him in the capital, close to the boss, so that he would have the king's ear.

Daniel the manager was in formal management training for at least three years as a "young man." He accepted a student position in the court of Nebuchadnezzar in order to "learn the language and literature of the Babylonians" and to be "trained for three years, and after that he was to enter the king's service" in which he stayed for decades.[630] If John Whitcomb's historical reckoning is correct, then Daniel could have been an old man (at least sixty, maybe even seventy-five to eighty years old) when he became one of the three court managers to the pagan king.[631] The book of Daniel clearly indicates that Daniel did not feel learning and understanding the ways and methods of the pagan Babylonians compromised his loyalty or effectiveness to the founder of the company[632] but rather afforded him the opportunity to serve the greater population of Babylon and Persia, including his captive organization.

---

630. Dan 1:4–5.

631. Whitcomb, "Darius the Mede." King Darius of Persia; *sarekh* = presidents. This Aramaic word may have been a loanword from the Persian language. It refers to the royal ministers of the Persians, i.e., an emir. "It pleased Darius to appoint 120 satraps to rule throughout the kingdom, with three administrators [*sarekh* = presidents, high officials, ministers. The word is derived from the Old Persian word for "head"] over them, one of whom was Daniel. Now Daniel so distinguished himself among the administrators and the satraps by his exceptional qualities that the king planned to set him over the whole kingdom" (Dan 6:2–3). This is one of those Aramaic terms which is used only in the last part of the Old Testament. The role of these three *sarekh* is to oversee the 120 district administrators in Persia, an extraordinary political position for a Jew in Persia. These district managers would give an account of their activities and the taxes raised and collected so that there would be an accurate accounting of Persian revenue. The three would also be checking on district corruption and malfeasance. Daniel had proven himself reliable and loyal to Nebuchadnezzar so the new government under Darius wanted him to continue in governmental service. It didn't hurt that Daniel had a fine reputation with the Babylonian citizens. Daniel 6:3 tells us that Darius was so impressed with the work of the Jew Daniel that he planned to make him the *sarekh* over all of Persia. Greek LXX = *taktikos* = "to set over." Dan 6:1–3;.

632. God of Abraham.

> But Daniel resolved[633] not to defile[634] himself with the royal food and wine, and he asked[635] the chief official[636] for permission not to defile himself this way . . . So the guard took away their choice food and the wine they were to drink and gave them vegetables instead. (Dan 1:8, 16)

In this short vignette about life in Babylonia, we get a glimpse of the discerning character of Daniel the manager.[637] The story is well-known: Daniel and his three friends (Shadrach, Meshach, and Abednego) were to be given rich Persian food from the king's table as part of their indoctrination into Babylonian ways. Daniel proposed another trial diet, not from the king's table. The Babylonian official at first resisted Daniel's suggestion but eventually relented as long as the results were healthy for the quartet and the official. That's the outline of the story, and now for a deeper dive into the management narrative.

Let's clear up the "defilement" issue. Many commentators maintain that Daniel did not want to eat the king's food because the content of the diet was contrary to Mosaic law.[638] Furthermore, because at least some of the food had been offered to Babylonian idols, it was idolatrous. Maybe, but there are at least three incidents in the Old Testament where observant Jews ate pagan food without reproach: King Jehoiachin,[639] Queen Esther,[640] and Nehemiah.[641] This is an important point because a better reason for abstinence is that to eat the king's food in these troubled circumstances would be a sign of cultural solidarity, of allegiance with Nebuchadnezzar and his pagan gods. The Hebrew word translated "defile"[642] does not necessarily restrict its meaning to religious or moral defilement. It is also used in the Old Testament to indicate political or cultural

---

633. *Sum* = purposed.
634. *Gaal* = pollute, stain.
635. *Baqash* = request, inquire.
636. *Sar* = head, captain, prince.
637. The name of a Daniel appears in Ezekiel (14:12–23, "Noah, Daniel, and Job," and 28:3, "Are you wiser than Daniel? Is no secret hidden from you?") and there is some controversy because of the spelling of the name as to whether or not it is the Daniel of the book. I believe it is the same Daniel.
638. Lev 11, elsewhere.
639. 2 Kgs 25:27–30.
640. Esth 5:4–5.
641. Neh 2:1.
642. *Gaal* = repudiate, stain, soil, desecrate.

defilement.[643] What Daniel the manager did amounted to a principled and discerning stand, without the backing of Mosaic law, to bolster his convictions. The chief official wants to diminish the cultural divide by giving the Judean teenagers Babylonian names in their new Babylonian context, and yet Daniel is still asserting a non-negotiable marker of Judean identify by refusing the Babylonian king's food.[644] Apparently there were other young Jewish boys taken captive by Nebuchadnezzar who did not have the discernment of Daniel.[645]

Daniel the manager in a tactful and respectful manner "asked" the "chief official" for a different diet. The Hebrew word translated "ask" is a gentle seeking or pleading, not an urgent demanding. There are many things about Babylonian assimilation that Daniel cannot change, but he can ask for a different food regimen. However, he must be very political how he asks because the food he rejects is from Nebuchadnezzar, himself, so he needs to nuance how to frame the rejection.

The chief official's response challenged Daniel the manager to come up with an alternative diet that was acceptable to Daniel's scruples and preserve the goal of Nebuchadnezzar to have healthy Judeans to serve him; this was a win-win solution. Additionally, the chief official and steward wanted to live another day in Babylon and thwarting the king's food "allocation"[646] was not guaranteed to do that. The Babylonian official's fear was well-founded because Nebuchadnezzar had a volcanic and mercurial temper.[647] Notice that the chief official gave a non-responsive response to the concern for defilement ("I am afraid of my lord and king").[648] It was left up to the steward to agree to Daniel's proposition—all the while keeping his boss in the dark about the deal. This royal diet was not an insignificant thing. Royal eyes were watching.

---

643. Ezra 2:62, "excluded from the priesthood because they were unclean"; Mal 1:7, 12. Ernest Lucas notes, "In this context it is understamable that [Daniel] decides to make a stand that symbolizes his intention not to assimilate and simply to become like the Babylonian subjects of Nebuchadnezzar, but rather to remain loyal to the God of Israel above all other claims on his allegiance" (Lucas, *Daniel*, 55).

644. Cf. Newsom, *Daniel*, 47.

645. Dan 1:10.

646. *Manah* = to number, count, prepare, ordain. This word is used to stress the numbering or appointing of a thing, as in arithmetical, precise computations.

647. Cf. Dan 2:12; 3:19–20.

648. Dan 1:10.

Jesus on Selected Managers in the Old Testament   151

The steward told Daniel that he would approve a diet change if Daniel could come up with an alternative that would do the four things: maintain the boy's scruples, keep his heath, satisfy Nebuchadnezzar's demands, and save the officer's life. Daniel responds now to the steward[649] who was officiating the food allocation in the place of the chief official (Ashpenaz): "Please test your servants for ten days. Give us nothing but vegetables to eat and water to drink. Then compare." Almost every word in this brief response shows that Daniel discerned the issue before him and structured his response accordingly, thus giving the Christian business manager some helpful hints:

> Please test your servants for ten days: Give us nothing but vegetables to eat and water to drink. Then compare our appearance with that of the young men who eat the royal food and treat your servants in accordance with what you see. (Dan 1:12–13)

- Daniel the manager begins with a humble and beseeching request—"please."[650] The Hebrew word used here is used in submission and modesty before a superior.

- Daniel the manager calls himself a "servant," a "subject of the king," "a man in bondage,"[651] clearly indicating he knew his place in the hostile political hierarchy and submitted to it.

- Daniel the manager suggests a test, a trial with the understanding that it could fail. "Put the burden on me to prove[652] that my suggestion is a good one."

- Daniel the manager suggests a time limit for the trial of only ten days. This is short enough not to arouse suspicion from the court and yet long enough to see the results. You can stand on your head for ten days! Daniel is scrupulous in protecting the chief office and his steward.

- Daniel the manager said to give them only vegetables and water. No meat and no wine. This no meat, no wine[653] diet would even save the court costs for feeding.

649. *Melzar* = overseer.
650. *Na* = a particle of entreaty.
651. *Eved*.
652. *Nasah* = In most cases this verb carries with it the idea of testing the quality of someone or something through a demonstration or stress.
653. Dan 10:3. The food from Nebuchadnezzar's table no doubt included food

- Daniel the manager leaves the verdict up to the guard, a low-level official: "Look and judge for yourself. Compare us with the other Judeans who have been eating the king's food. You decide." This gave the guard a sense of genuine importance and organizational power.
- Daniel the manager was given a "keen mind and knowledge and understanding" and the ability to "solve difficult problems."[654]
- Daniel the manager was made chief executive officer over the entire organization, including headquarters staff.[655]
- Daniel the manager was made chief advisor and counsellor to the president of the organization—he had the ear of the boss.[656]
- Daniel the manager was given authority to choose vice-presidents over the organization.[657]
- Daniel the manager ran the day-to-day operations of the government since his office was in the capital building.[658]
- Daniel the manager did not enrich himself through his political position.[659]
- Daniel the manager was transparent and honest with his boss.[660]
- Daniel the manager was loyal to his boss.[661]
- Daniel the manager was ruthless with his competitors.[662]
- Daniel the manager was discrete in organizational matters.[663]

---

offered to the Babylonian idols and thus a sentence from Bel and the Dagon has applicability: "Now the Babylonians had an idol called Bel, for which they provided every day twelve bushels of fine flour, forty sheep, and fifty gallons of wine. The king held it to be divine and went daily to worship it" (*Bel* 3–4).

654. Dan 5:12.
655. Dan 2:48; 6:1, 28.
656. Dan 2:48.
657. Dan 2:49; 3:12, 30.
658. "King's court," Dan 2:49.
659. Dan 5:17.
660. Dan 5:22–23.
661. Dan 6:22.
662. Dan 6:24.
663. Dan 7:28.

- Daniel the manager was diligent in his assigned duties in the organization.[664]

Of course, behind all of Daniel the manager's discerning response is the gracious hand of God causing him to be successful in his actions. After all, it is Yahweh who caused Daniel to enjoy the "favor and sympathy" of the Babylonian chief official.[665]

Before we leave Daniel the manager it is worth noting the constant temptations that the surrounding culture presented to Daniel and his buddies, Shadrach, Meshach, and Abednego. The boys needed all their faithful shrewdness to thwart the cultural enticements as they managed the affairs of Babylon while still worshipping Yahweh.[666] We find the narrative in Daniel 3:

- The first temptation was to "bow down and worship" the man-made idol. The boys, as the lead managers, were expected to lead the false worshippers and provide an example for the people, especially the other Judeans. As chief administrator, the king looked to them to be role models.[667]

- The second temptation came with the "malicious accusation" by high-ranking government officials of treason on the part of the boys by not submitting to the cultural pieties. Undoubtedly these accusers were persons of influence and had the ear of the king. The threat was the fiery furnace, and the boys could easily have publicly proclaimed loyalty to the reigning creed of their boss, Nebuchadnezzar, and quiet the dangerous threats.[668]

- The third temptation came when the king personally questioned the boys about the truthful change that they would not agree to the politically correct mantra of royal heresy. The king was hoping to change their mind, so he personally confirmed the reports and give

---

664. Dan 8:27.

665. "Then the king placed Daniel in a high position and lavished many gifts on him. He made him ruler over the entire province of Babylon and placed him in charge of all its wise men. Moreover, at Daniel's request the king appointed Shadrach, Meshach and Abednego administrators over the province of Babylon, while Daniel himself remained at the royal court" (Dan 2:48–49).

666. Dan 2:48–49.

667. Dan 3:4–7.

668. Dan 3:8–12.

the boys a chance to repudiate the charges. They did not take the opportunity to renounce their decision and change their minds.[669]

- The fourth temptation came when the boys realized that Nebuchadnezzar was seriously angry with them and threatened to kill them. This was an important issue for their political patron, and they publicly humiliated him by refusing to go along with his publicly proclaimed code of conduct. There was still time to adopt the culturally approved lifestyle.[670]

- The fifth temptation came when the boys were actually bound and readied for the furnace. The furnace was so hot that the soldiers taking the boys to their fiery death were themselves killed by the heat of the furnace. There was still time to recant their intransigence and be loyal to the reigning cultural orthodoxies that their boss wanted.[671]

Yahweh had permitted the multiple temptations to renounce him in order to survive as chief administrators of the hostile government, but the managers stayed firm in their convictions and thus not only survived but prospered: "Then the king promoted Shadrach, Meshach, and Abednego in the province of Babylon."[672]

NEHEMIAH THE MANAGER

> Moreover, from the twentieth year of King Artaxerxes, when I was appointed[673] to be the company manager[674] in the land of Judah, until his thirty-second year—twelve years. (Neh 5:14)[675]

669. Dan 3:16–18.
670. Dan 3:19.
671. Dan 3:20.
672. Dan 3:30.
673. *Tsawah* = instructed to be, as in 2 Sam 21:14.
674. *Pechah* = governor, deputy. "How can you repulse one manager (*pechah*) of the least of my master's servants [*ebed* = servant, doer, tiller, slave], even though you are depending on Egypt for chariots and horsemen?" (2 Kgs 18:24). *Pechah* is a borrowed ancient Near East term from Babylonia or Persia and means a "governor" or "captain" or "pasha." The word was used during the reign of Solomon to denote the governor of Judea (1 Kgs 10:15) and of Syria (1 Kgs 20:24). We see it used several times during the Persian reign of Esther (Esth 8:9; 9:3) and Malachi (Mal 1:8) to refer to an official. Nehemiah is called a *pechah* (Neh 5:14) and Zerubbabel is called a *pechah* (Hag 1:1). So, clearly, a *pechah* is a manager with great authority and responsibility for organizing the company into flourishing units.
675. Neh 2:1–6.

Jesus on Selected Managers in the Old Testament

The book of Nehemiah tells us that Governor Nehemiah the manager distinguished himself from his exiled predecessors by key management actions directed towards the common good of the organization in Judah:

- Nehemiah the manager rebuilt the Jerusalem wall.[676]
- Nehemiah the manager refrained from purchasing more land for royal benefit.[677]
- Nehemiah the manager kept control of the royal guard and had them do national guard duties.[678]
- Nehemiah the manager did not use tax receipts for personal expenses.[679]
- Nehemiah the manager drained the royal administrative swamp of corruption by young royal retainers.[680]
- Nehemiah the manager extended generosity and hospitality to all who came to Jerusalem to help the organization.[681]

Furthermore, as we look at Nehemiah, we can see numerous characteristics of a Christian business manager:

- Nehemiah the manager was a man of integrity. He led other managers by example.[682]

---

676. Neh 3:1–16.

677. Neh 5:7–12, 16.

678. Neh 3:12, 17–19, 29; 4:13–23; 7:3.

679. Neh 5:12–15, 18.

680. Neh 5:8, 15; *achim* = brethren, assistants. The term is used to connote a member of the same tribe (Lev 25:46; Deut 24:7), so it is possible that Nehemiah is here referring to his lieutenants in the government (Neh 5:8).

681. Neh 5:17; cf. 1 John 3:17. Fensham nicely summarizes Nehemiah's approach to managing Judah: "Nehemiah set an example as a Persian official without precedent in the Persian empire, as far as we know. He wanted to stress the fact that, contrary to what the Jewish leaders did, he himself endeavored to promote the welfare of his people" (Fensham, *The Books of Ezra and Nehemiah*, 198–99).

682. Neh 4:23; 5:9–12, 14–19; 8:9–10; 10:1, 32–39; 13:4–28. Stearns, *Lead Like It Matters to God*, 93–103, maintains that there are three types of integrity: Personal integrity, which means that a leader with integrity provides her staff with the confidence that she will always strive to do the right thing, the fair thing, no matter what. Relational integrity, which mean that all our relationships require that we deal with others honesty, sincerely, transparently, considerately, and fairly. Corporate integrity means that integrity should characterize the culture of an entire organization led and defined by its leaders.

- Nehemiah the manager had a commitment to God's word.[683]
- Nehemiah the manager was loyal to his unbelieving boss.[684]
- Nehemiah the manager was stable, persevering, humble, and entrepreneurial.[685]
- Nehemiah the manager had a genuine concern for others.[686]
- Nehemiah the manager was a man of discernment.[687]
- Nehemiah the manager was a motivator with enthusiasm for the task set before him.
- Nehemiah the manager set goals for his organization.[688]

MORDECAI THE MANAGER

> Mordecai was sitting at the king's gate ... All the royal officials at the king's gate knelt down and paid honor to Haman, for the king had commanded this concerning him. But Mordecai would not kneel down or pay him honor ... When Haman saw that Mordecai would not kneel down or pay him honor, he was enraged ... Haman looked for a way to destroy all Mordecai's people, the Jews, throughout the whole kingdom of Xerxes ... And all the nobles of the provinces, the satraps, the governors and the king's administrators helped the Jews, because fear of Mordecai had seized them. Mordecai was prominent[689] in the palace; his reputation spread throughout the provinces, and he became more and more powerful ... Mordecai the Jew was second in rank[690] to King Xerxes, preeminently[691] among the Jews,

---

683. Neh 8:9.

684. Neh 2:1–8; 6:8.

685. Neh 2:12–13; 11:1–3, 9, 19, 24. In Nehemiah 11, we see Nehemiah appointing "leaders" (*sar*), "chiefs" (*rosh*), "officers" (*paqid*), "gatekeepers" (*shamar*), and royal "agents" (*yad*) for the Jews.

686. Neh 1:4–11; 5:1–6, 9–10, 13:18.

687. Neh 2:5, 12–17; 6:2–4; 10–13.

688. Neh 2:17–18; 4:6, 14; 6:1. Cf. Barber, *Nehemiah and the Dynamics of Effective Leadership*; Redpath, *Victorious Christian Service*.

689. *Gadol* = great.

690. *Mishnah*.

691. *Gadol* = great.

Jesus on Selected Managers in the Old Testament 157

and held in high esteem[692] by his many fellow Jews, because he worked for the good of his people and spoke up for the welfare of all the Jews. (Esth 2:21; 3:2; 3:9:3–4; 10:3)

In Esther 8:2 we are told that Mordecai assumed the governmental position that Haman had occupied, that is, second in command in the world's greatest empire. We have seen other Old Testament believers ascend in management responsibilities in pagan kingdoms.[693]

While we are not exactly sure what Mordecai's responsibilities were, we think of a secretary of state but that is not confirmed by Persian, Babylonian or Egyptian records. Interestingly, the narrative indicates that he was a Jewish champion and focused his attention on "working for the good" of the Jewish Persians. So we are not sure what Mordecai's administrative role was in the Persian Empire, other than the fact that King Xerxes trusted him and held him in high regard and gave him power over Persian gentiles. Even our brief exposure to Mordecai the manager shows us noteworthy management traits:

- Mordecai the manager was a man obedient to the structure of the organization for which he worked.[694]
- Mordecai the manager, clearly an ambitious man, put family before career as he carved out time to raise an orphan cousin, Esther.[695]
- Mordecai the manager shrewdly knew the intricacies of organization politics.[696]
- Mordecai the manager was as man of principle. He continually chose to risk everything, including his life, for the sake of truth and the survival of the church.[697]
- Mordecai the manager was a man of boldness. He publicly refused to bow to Haman, and he made his civil disobedience public.[698]

---

692. *Ratsah* = to be pleased with, take pleasure or delight in, be favorable towards.
693. Like Joseph becoming the second in Egypt, Gen 41:43, Obadiah was second to Ahab in Israel, 1 Kgs 18:3; Daniel becoming third in Babylon, Dan 5:29.
694. Esth 2:22; 8:7–8.
695. Esth 2:7, 11, 19–20.
696. Esth 2:10.
697. Esth 3:2–4; 5:9, 13.
698. Esth 4:8–14.

- Mordecai the manager was a man of patience. Despite the silence from Yahweh and the overwhelming power of the Persian government, he never gave up in despair or anger.[699]
- Mordecai the manager was a man of intelligence. It is argued that Mordecai ushered in the age of the rabbis and the Talmud with their faulty understanding that the word of Yahweh now rested in the hands of human scholars and not revelation.[700]
- Mordecai the manager used his shrewd personal public front to so enrage the volatile Haman that Haman pursued a self-destructive agenda to his death and Mordecai's political advancement.

AHIKAM THE MANAGER

> [King Josiah] gave these orders to Hilkiah the priest, Ahikam son of Shaphan, Acbor son of Micaiah, Shaphan the manager[701] and Asaiah the king's attendant.[702] (2 Kgs 22:12)

Ahikam[703] was a prominent official for decades in Judah's political history and thus was named first among political operatives in King Josiah's list of political appointees, indicating the most important political position in the government—secretary of state. Nepotism was at work in the royal court, since Ahikam was the son of Shaphan, secretary or scribe to King Josiah. Ahikam was a genuine man of integrity who impressed Hilkiah the high priest.[704]

- Ahikam the manager deserves our perpetual thanks and gratitude because he supported and protected the prophet Jeremiah and intervened to save him from death during the reign of Jehoiakim.[705]
- As a high-ranking manager in Josiah's and Jehoiakim's governments Ahikam was able to influence the thinking of two kings of Judah,

---

699. Esth 6:1–3.
700. Esth 8:9–10; 9:20–23. See Hazony, *God and Politics in Esther*, 169–82.
701. *Saphar* = to cypher, number, write, record. Secretary.
702. *Ebed* = servant, slave, tiller.
703. Katzenstein, "The Royal Steward."
704. 2 Kgs 22:19–20.
705. Jer 26:24.

- and at the same time raised a son, Gedaliah, who would influence at least one Babylonian king and then rule Judah as governor.[706]
- Ahikam the manager was chosen by King Josiah to be a part of a five-man delegation to Huldah the prophetess concerning the book of the Law.[707]
- Ahikam the manager was so trusted by Judean king, Josiah, that he was appointed to be one of three Judah officials to inquire of Yahweh as to the future of the country.[708]

GEDALIAH THE MANAGER

> Nebuchadnezzar king of Babylon appointed Gedaliah son of Ahikam, the son of Shaphan, to manage[709] the people he had left behind in Judah . . . Gedaliah took an oath to reassure them and their people, "Do not be afraid of the Babylonian officials. Settle down in the land and serve the king of Babylon, and it will go well with you" . . . (2 Kgs 25:22–24)
>
> [Nebuchadnezzar] the king of Babylon appointed [Gedaliah] over the towns of Judah.(Jer 40:5)

Gedaliah was from the prominent Jewish family of Ahikam and Shaphan.[710] Nebuchadnezzar appointed Gedaliah governor of Judah because the king appreciated the prophet Jeremiah's message of commitment and loyalty to Babylonian peace and stability.[711] However, Gedaliah was governor for only two months. Archeological information tells us that before being appointed governor, Gedaliah managed King Zedekiah's estate.[712] So Gedaliah was a manager who got his job through family

---

706. Nebuchadnezzar king of Babylon appointed Gedaliah son of Ahikam, the Son of Shaphan, to be over the people he had left behind in Judah.

707. 2 Kgs 22:14.

708. 2 Kgs 22:11–13.

709. Al = to be above/over.

710. 2 Kgs 34:14–21. Shaphan was King Josiah's secretary of state and protected Jeremiah (Jer 26:24).

711. Jer 29:4–14; Lam 3:26–27: "It is good to wait quietly for the salvation of Yahweh. It is good for a man to bear the yoke while he is young."

712. "Over the house of." Zedekiah's managers had a tough time. Nebuchadnezzar king of Babylon had many of the Judean managers killed (Jer 52:9–11; 24–27). It was

connections and a good management record. Leaders of roving bands of Jewish soldiers who had not surrendered to the Babylonians came to Governor Gedaliah for support for the Jewish resistance to the Babylonians. Gedaliah tried to assure them that Jeremiah's policy of cooperation with their Babylonian captors was the proper course of conduct for Jews that would lead to their survival and even an Egyptian-like prosperity. The foreign king had even given the Jews towns to control.[713] But the Jewish rebels were not convinced to lay down their arms. The general Jewish population, however, hearing the restoration message of Jeremiah and Gedaliah, rejected the rebels and flocked back to Judah from around the Babylonian empire, and the organization began to prosper.[714] Not satisfied, Gedaliah was eventually assassinated by one of the leaders of the "open country" rebel units,[715] but he was a faithful follower of Yahweh and Jeremiah and politically managed Yahweh's message to the dispersed Jews. One scholar offers a summary of Gedaliah's management: "He possessed the confidence alike of his own people and their conquerors; a man of rare wisdom and tact, and of upright, transparent character, whose kindly nature and generous disposition would not allow him to think evil of a brother; a man altogether worthy of the esteem in which he was held by succeeding generations of his fellow-countrymen."[716]

ZERUBBABEL THE MANAGER

> Now these are the people of the province who came up from the captivity of the exiles, whom Nebuchadnezzar king of Babylon had taken captive to Babylon (they returned to Jerusalem and Judah, each to his own town, in company with Zerubbabel). (Ezra 2:1–2)

Zerubbabel was the Persian Jewish governor of Judah under the Babylonian King Nebuchadnezzar and then the Persian King Cyrus.[717] He

---

dangerous being associated with a defeated king. The principle bears remembering.

713. Jer 40:10, 12.

714. LXX Jer 43:25, but not in the Hebrew Old Testament. Gedaliah was one of three high ranking officials to implore Jewish King Joakim to listen to Jeremiah's preaching.

715. 2 Kgs 25:25.

716. Crichton, "Gedaliah."

717. Hag 1:1–15.

Jesus on Selected Managers in the Old Testament

was also the grandson of Jewish King Jehoiachin.[718] In 538 BC he led a group of Jewish exiles back to the promised land in order to complete the construction of the temple. During his time in Jerusalem, he was part of a tripartite Judean leadership executive group.[719] The prophets Haggai and Zechariah both encouraged and stiffened the spine of Governor Zerubbabel when he faced opposition and was faint of heart.[720] Some of the most well-known verses in the Bible come from Zechariah's encouragement to the governor: "Not by might nor by power, but by my Spirit."[721] and "Who despises the day of small things?"[722] Zerubbabel was the last great Old Testament manager[723] as he worked to complete the reconstruction of the temple in Jerusalem.[724] "It is clear from Haggai and Zechariah that Zerubbabel was the most important person in Judah."[725]

---

718. 1 Chr 3:17—5:26. Zerubbabel is elsewhere called "son of Shealtiel": Ezra 3:2, 8; 5:2; Neh 12:1; Hag 1:1, 12, 14; 2:2, 23. His name may mean "offspring or seed of Babylon," connoting no religious affiliation but rather a cultural grounding in Babylon.

719. The group was composed of Tattenai the military leader, Joseph the religious leader of Judah, and Zerubbabel the political leader who managed the administration of Judah.

720. Zech 4:10. Indeed, in Zechariah 9:7 the prophet announces that as Yahweh is punishing the organization's opponents he will raise up a remnant of clan leader-managers (*allups*) from Philistia to join Judah. "Those who are left will belong to God and become managers [*allup* = clan leader, governor, dignified person, governor, chief] in Judah" (Zech 9:7). Of all the managers in the Old Testament, the group that seems to earn the ire and condemnation of the Jewish cohort is the Edomite group of managers called *allup*. The root of this word is used as an adjective to describe an object which is gentle, tame, or familiar (Jer 11:19), but is used as a noun indicates a ruler of a thousand. The basic sense of this term is management over political affairs or military activities (cf. Exod 18:21; Num 1:16; 31:4; 1 Chr 13:1; 27:1; Amos 5:3). Thus, it is used exclusively to refer to a chief or manager of the warring tribe of Edom (cf. Gen 36:15–19; Exod 15:15; 1 Chr 1:51–54). Harrison notes, "Of all the neighbors of Israel, Edom, as a nation, was the only one who was not extended any promise of mercy from God" (Harrison, "Edom"). The prophets universally condemn and denounce the tribe of Edom in the most vociferous language. The entire book of Obadiah is given over to denouncing Edom. The men that managed the Edomites were men of savage brutality and betrayal. It all stemmed back to the founder of the tribe, Esau (Gen 27: 1—28:9).

721. Zech 4:6.

722. Opposition to building the temple is described as a "mighty mountain" facing Zerubbabel, but it will become "a plain" by the power of the Holy Spirit (Zech 4:7).

723. Sirach 49:11 refers to Zerubbabel as a man of renown: "How shall we magnify Zerubbabel? Even he was as a signet on the right hand." Zerubbabel had a loyal entourage (associates) who accompanied him (Eccl 3:2).

724. Zech 4:8.

725. Fensham, *The Books of Ezra and Nehemiah*, 78.

The atmosphere in Judah in which Zerubbabel was to begin his huge public works project of building the temple was hostile, tempestuous, and fraught with danger and poverty.[726] Strangely, Zerubbabel disappears from Scripture after Ezra 5:2 and is not mentioned in the inauguration of the temple.[727] However, there are management lessons to be gleaned from the administration of Zerubbabel as noted by Ezra:

- We are not sure of the identity of the "governor" in Ezra 2:63, but if it is Zerubbabel the manager,[728] the reference indicates that he refrained from making administrative decisions until he inquired of God and correctly understood the will of Yahweh. We will see that this confidence was needed as the manager faced fierce opposition and challenges even from members of the organization.

- Zerubbabel the manager dedicated the work to Yahweh by constructing an altar before the construction project even begins, in the midst of opposition by the surrounding culture.[729]

- Zerubbabel the manager practiced incrementalism as he wisely began the construction work gradually because of the hostility of the culture, first the altar, then the temple building itself, so as not to unnecessarily antagonize the "people around them."[730]

- Zerubbabel the manager had to negotiate the massive construction project in the midst of a culture that was not sympathetic to the work of the newly arrived Jewish corporate exiles from Babylon. He faced opposition from hostile tribes ("peoples around them" = Ashdod, Samaria, Ammon, Moab, Edom) and even from settled members of the organization who had given up the faith.[731]

- Zerubbabel the manager knew that any organization[732] needs social guidelines or norms for proper functioning. So such cultural

---

726. Zech 8:10: "Before that time there were no wages for man or beast. No one could go about his business safely because of his enemy, for I had turned every man against his neighbor."
727. Ezra 6:14–18.
728. *Natsach*.
729. Ezra 3:2.
730. Ezra 3:6; 4:4.
731. 2 Kgs 17:24.
732. "Company," "assembly," Ezra 2:64.

conventions were established early, even before the first foundation stones were laid.[733]

- Zerubbabel the manager hired only the best people to do the work with the best materials for the temple. He had high standards of workmanship and materials.[734]

- Zerubbabel the manager took great pains to plan and to record the construction activity on the temple. He was efficient and orderly and kept statistics on his work. The careful planning of the construction is evident in that the shipping of the timber from Lebanon would take time, so first came the stone altar, taking just a few stones, then the stone foundation, taking more stones from the quarry, then finally the wood from Lebanon. Eventually, this second temple would take about seven years to build, but everything had to be coordinated by a small but dedicated group of managers.[735]

- Zerubbabel the manager was careful to delegate and manage the other managers.[736] He chose the managers carefully from among the best trained Jews in Jerusalem—the Levites.[737]

- Zerubbabel the manager had trained Joshua the Levite in managerial skills to such an extent that even after the governor was out of the picture the high quality of temple construction continued to completion.[738] Supervisors were to be at least twenty years old, lower than the thirty-year-old standard for the first temple,[739] thus indicating the scarcity of available managers. This indicates that

---

733. Ezra 3:6.

734. "Talented masons and carpenters" and the "best grade wood from Lebanon," Ezra 3:7.

735. Ezra 3:7–9.

736. *Natsach* = to be set over, be preeminent, establish. "The priests and the Levites and all who had returned from the captivity to Jerusalem began the work appointing Levites twenty years of age and older to manage (*nasah*) the building of the house of Yahweh" (Ezra 3:8). This word denotes brilliant, pure, preeminent, set forward, reliable, and thus supervisory leadership. In 1 Chronicles 15:21 it is used to describe the lead or "chief" musicians (Hab 3:19). Specifically for the managerial class, the title is used to connote "superintendent" or "director" in Ezra. It is used twice in Ezra 3:89 to suggest managerial oversight of the workers and of the work to rebuild the temple (cf. 1 Chr 23:4).

737. Ezra 3:8–9.

738. Ezra 6:15.

739. 1 Chr 23:2–3.

Zerubbabel was adapting to the circumstances on the ground, getting the best managers available to him.[740]

- Under Zerubbabel the manager the work on the temple was characterized by efficient administration and excellent cooperation and unity in the organization.[741]
- Zerubbabel the manager had to be a shepherd, as he had to encourage his people amid the disappointment of many of the senior members of the organization who had worshipped at the old Solomonic temple and now saw the new, smaller, less elegant and magisterial Zerubbabel temple.[742]
- Zerubbabel the manager was not afraid to exclude those members of the surrounding community—the "enemies of Judah and Benjamin"—from participation in the mission. He was prepared to publicly shame his opponents for the cause of Yahweh.[743]
- Zerubbabel the manager stayed faithful to the mission—"we alone will build it for Yahweh, the God of Israel." The organization faced coordinated opposition from the surrounding competitors in Judah (some unbelieving Jews as well), but Zerubbabel was perceptive enough to know that offers to help from these "enemies" were disguised to hinder the mission of the work.[744] The temptation to accept the local help was real, because the rebuilding project needed money and people to complete the work.[745]
- Zerubbabel the manager knew that if he agreed to assistance from those outside the mission statement of the organization, the mission itself would be compromised and the effort to accomplish the mission would be diluted by those who had not really bought into the mission statement. This political decision to publicly decide who is for the organization and who is against the organization was

---

740. A semi-job description is given in 1 Chronicles 23:4–5 for the building of the first temple.
741. Ezra 3:8–9.
742. Ezra 3:12–13; Hag 2:3; Zech 4:10.
743. Ezra 4:1–3.
744. Cf. 2 Kgs 17:33.
745. Ezra 1:6; 4:3; Hag 1:6, 9–11; 2:15–17.

difficult and took courage; Friends and acquaintances may have been involved in the rejection.[746]

- Zerubbabel the manager enthusiastically returned to the work after a sixteen-year hiatus caused by three factors: opposition of "enemies,"[747] selfish priorities,[748] and harsh economic conditions in Judah.[749] He courageously stayed committed to the mission of the organization and eventually laid the material and motivational foundation for the completion of the task.[750]

ELIAKIM THE MANAGER

> In that day I will summon my servant,[751] Eliakim son of Hilkiah. I will clothe him with your robe and fasten your sash around him and hand your authority over to him. He will be a father[752] to those who live in Jerusalem and to the house of Judah. I will place on his shoulder the key to the house of David; what he opens no one can shut, and what he shuts no one can open. I will drive him like a peg into a firm place; he will be a seat of honor for the house of his father. All the glory of his family will hang on him: its offspring and offshoots—all its lesser vessels, from the bowls to all the jars. In that day, declares the Yahweh of hosts, the peg that was fastened in a secure place will give way, and it will be cut down and fall, and the load that was on it will be cut off, for Yahweh has spoken. (Isa 22:20–25)

God speaks to Shebna, the second highest ranking official in the Hezekiah regime, and tells him he is banished ("deposed") and is to be replaced by Eliakim, a member of a prominent family. There is palace intrigue in Hezekiah's reign because in Isaiah 37 it was reported that Eliakim was

---

746. Ezra 4:3–4; cf. Mark 9:40; 1 John 2:19.

747. Ezra 4:4–5, 24; 5:2, "set out to discourage" is literally "relaxing the hands," telling us the opposition had practical ramifications in the construction work (cf. Jer 38:4). The enemies hired "counsellors" who may have been Persian governmental apparatchiks or "advisors" with direct contact to the king (Ezra 7:14–15, 28; 8:25).

748. Ezra 4:23.

749. Hag 1.

750. Zech 4:9.

751. *Eved* = officer, manager, ambassador, laborer.

752. *Ab* = ancestor, source, inventor.

"palace manager"[753] at the same time that Shebna was the "royal secretary." Clearly roles were changed and then changed again with Eliakim coming out on top of the internecine warfare. Being designated as the "son of Hilkiah," a previously high-ranking official, is a means of legitimizing Eliakim to any governmental doubters. All that was important to Shebna is now publicly given to Eliakim, including the very vestments of authority. In a wonderfully descriptive management phrase, Yahweh says that Eliakim will be a "father" to those of Hezekiah's kingdom.[754] In order to accomplish his "fatherly" responsibilities, Eliakim will be given worldly authority—Shebna's official governmental position of secretary of state—but also divine power. The role of being over the house of the king was not divinely instituted but rather a human invention to serve the organization at this particular time in its history. The promised job is for Eliakim only and not for his descendants. Thus, the biblical definition of the exact duties of this position is somewhat obscure. Whatever the exact duties of the position, it was a burdensome responsibility. This is a terrific example of a godly role given to a biblical manager that was conceived in a time of organizational need. Eliakim took it upon himself to pass along his royal position to his descendants who predictably failed in their responsibilities, thus warning managers to adhere to the tasks at hand and not seek organizational preferments. Management lessons to be taken from Eliakim:

- Eliakim the manager is to handle the wealth and resources of the king with almost complete autonomy.
- Eliakim the manager acknowledged that his position and responsibilities were due to God's providential calling and placement.[755]
- Eliakim the manager governed the organization in such a way that there was a flourishing of the individual workers.[756]

---

753. NIV = "administrator," "over the house" = *al* = over, above. "Over the house" is the Old Testament name given to a political office of great importance in both Israel and Judah. It was probably the highest office in the political world and one that was so important that heirs to the throne were jealous of their advancement. The person who occupied this political position ran the entire domestic agenda for the king. He stood next to the king (Delitzsch, *Commentary on Isaiah*, 398–99). Cf. Mettinger, *Solomonic State Officials: A Study in Civil Government Officials of the Israelite Monarchy*, 186.

754. Cf. Gen 20:2, 8 (Abimelech = "my father the king"); Job 29:16.

755. Isa 22:20.

756. Isa 22:21.

Jesus on Selected Managers in the Old Testament

- Eliakim the manager had his fingers in all aspects of the organization; nothing was too small or insignificant for his attention.[757]
- Eliakim the manager was firm and resolute in his responsibilities and did not shirk from the difficult duties.[758]
- Eliakim the manager knew that management is difficult work and fraught with heavy burdens.[759]
- Eliakim the manager supported and affirmed all the workers, not just the supervisors.[760]
- Eliakim the manager understood that his success depended on God's blessing and not on his sufficiency to do the job. He did not let organizational power corrupt his thinking.[761] However, he unwisely passed along his governmental sinecure to his relatives who failed in the job.

Not all of the prominent Old Testament managers were "servants of Yahweh." Some were selfish, self-centered scoundrels like Rehoboam and Shebna, who misused their high office.

REHOBOAM THE MANAGER

> "Your father put a heavy yoke on us, but now lighten the harsh labor and the heavy yoke he put on us, and we will serve you"... Then King Rehoboam consulted the elders who had served his father Solomon during his lifetime... But Rehoboam rejected the advice the elders gave him and consulted the young men who had grown up with him and were serving him... "My father laid on you a heavy yoke; I will make it ever heavier." (1 Kgs 12:4, 6, 8, 11)

See the Appendix for an in-depth look at the management style of Rehoboam. But now note that nothing is more indicative of Rehoboam's management style than early decisions:

---

757. Isa 22:22, 24.
758. Isa 22:23.
759. Isa 22:24.
760. Isa 22:24.
761. Isa 22:25.

- Rehoboam the manager rejected the measured advice given him by his experienced senior managers.[762]
- Rehoboam the manager consulted and then took the advice of less qualitied and experienced advisers on difficult problems.[763]
- Rehoboam the manager dispatched his veteran department of labor manager, Adoni-ram, to meet with the people whom he has subjugated for years, eventuating his death.[764]

What is remarkable about Rehoboam is that he initially had the support and loyalty of the senior managers of the organization. In 2 Chronicles 11:13–17 we are told that the religious leaders sided with him over Jeroboam and "even abandoned[765] their pasturelands and property" to join him. For three years they supported Rehoboam before they turned their back on him because of his bad management practices. It was his reign to lose, which he did.[766]

SHEBNA THE MANAGER

> Go say to this manager[767] to Shebna, who manages[768] the palace . . . I will depose you [Shebna] from your office,[769] and you will be ousted from your position.[770] (Isa 22:15, 19)

Here the LORD is referring to "Shebna, the manager of [King Hezekiah's] palace" (vs. 15).[771] The office of "steward," the highest office in the na-

762. 2 Chr 10:8.
763. 2 Chr 10:10–11.
764. The people took out their rage against the crown and their labor policies by killing Adoni-ram, 2 Chr 10:18.
765. *Azav* = to forsake, relinquish.
766. 2 Chr 10:16.
767. *Soken* = steward, treasurer, server.
768. *Al* = be above, over.
769. *Matzov* = place, station.
770. *Maamad* = station.
771. "Azra, the man in charge of the palace at Tirzah" (1 Kgs 16:9); "palace administrator" under King Ahab (2 Kgs 10:5). "Eliahim . . . the palace administrator" under King Hezekiah (2 Kgs 18:18, 37; 19:2); "Jotham, [King Azariah's] son had charge of the palace and governed the people of the land" (2 Kgs 15:5); "Ahishar—in charge (*oikonomos*) of the palace; Adoni-ram, son of Abba—in charge (*oikonomos*) of forced labor" (1 Kgs 4:6); "They wrote out all Mordecai's orders to the Jews, and to the satraps,

tion at the time, puts Shebna "in charge of the palace,"[772] which was a royal position probably instituted by Solomon in 1 Kings 4:6. By Isaiah's time, the governmental position of "steward" had attained a great significance.[773] Interestingly, Shebna was appointed governor over the house of King Hezekiah, and he was not even a vested member of the company. The name "Shebna" may come from the Aramaic or Egyptian, and since we don't have his father's name, it might indicate foreign (probably Egyptian) birth.

- Shebna the manager had responsibilities to manage Israel while Hezekiah was sick.

- Shebna the manager had responsibilities to prepare Jewish Jerusalem to defend herself against the forces of Gentile King Sennacherib and the Assyrians.

- Shebna the manager rather than doing what Yahweh had called him to do as a steward, was preparing an elaborate tomb for himself. He is said to be "hewing your grave on the height and chiseling your resting place in the rock" in Jerusalem[774] apparently among the graves of the Jewish nobility, towering above the common folk.[775]

As one commentator wrote, the proud Shebna's life "stands as an example of the accountability God requires of his servants in positions of leadership."[776] Samuel Storms, past president of the Evangelical Theological Society, calls Shebna "a worthless steward."[777] He was clearly a self-seeking bureaucratic manager.

---

governors (*pechah*) and nobles of the 127 provinces stretching from India to Cush" (Esth 8:9).

772. Literally "over the house."

773. The term *sokan* ("steward") occurs only with reference to Shebna in Isaiah 22:15. The root apparently means "to be of service," "benefit," "use" (Young, *The Book of Isaiah*, 2.105–106). Job 15:3; 22:2, 21; 34:4; 35:3; Isa 40:20; Ps 139:3; Num 22:30. The form is also found in Ugaritic at Tell el-Amarna all with a business or official context. It is a common ancient Near Eastern term meaning "servant" or "to care for" or "to be of use." The royal position lasted decades, until Governor (*pequddah* = over the house, 2 Kgs 25:22) Gedaliah under Nebuchadnezzar eliminated it.

774. Isa 22:16.

775. Cf. 2 Chr 32:33. If he were Jewish he would have his own ancestral burial place in the land. Second Chronicles 16:14 refers to a tomb of the royal steward and it is thought to be the tomb of Shebna.

776. Smith, *Isaiah 1–39*. 392.

777. Storms, "Jesus: God the Son."

5

Jesus on Selected Managers in the New Testament

THE NEW TESTAMENT HAS its own, admittedly smaller, cast of managers who provide examples for today's managerial class.

Jesus the Great Manager will be extensively covered in the next chapter, which deals with various management responsibilities.

PILATE THE MANAGER

> The [chief priests and the elders of the people] bound [Jesus], let him away and handed him over to Pilate, the manager.[1]
> (Matt 27:2)

Pilate may seem like an unusual person to highlight as a manager because of his relationship with Christianity and because most of what we know about him (which is very little) comes from non-Christian sources.[2] Still, even if the sources of our information are a bit suspect and the information is scant we have enough to note several management decisions made by Pilate. Pilate was an upper-middle-class military brat from a Samnite family.[3] We know almost nothing about his early life. In AD

---

1. *Hegemon* = governor, leader, guide, one going before.

2. Wroe, *Pontius Pilate*. xiii.

3. The Samnites were an ancient southern Italian people who lived in Samnium. They became involved in wars with the Roman Republic until the first century AD. Later they became enemies of the Romans and were soon involved in a series of three wars against the Romans. The Samnites were eventually subjugated. The Samnites later helped Pyrrhus and some went over to Hannibal in their wars against Rome. They

26, Roman Emperor Tiberius (reigned AD 14–37) appointed him *prefectus* of Judea.[4] He later would be titled *procurator*. As procurator Pilate had complete control of the Judah province. After a particular dispute with the inhabitants of Judea, Pilate was recalled to Rome by Tiberius for investigation. We don't know the results of the investigation, but the historian Eusebius reported that Pilate was forced to commit suicide sometime under Emperor Gaius (reigned AD 37–41) who succeeded Tiberius.[5] So, based on non-biblical sources, Pilate ruled Judea for approximately ten years. During that decade of management, here are some of the takeaways:

- Pilate the manager was in charge of the army of occupation which meant the calvary and the infantry up to five thousand soldiers.

- Pilate the manager had life-and-death authority over the inhabitants and could reverse any decision of the Sanhedrin.

- Pilate the manager appointed the high priest and controlled the activities of the temple in Jerusalem, which included temple revenue and even the vestments of the priests.

- Pilate the manager, totally misreading the sense of the local population, set up Roman military shields in Jerusalem upon assuming his position as procurator, naturally antagonizing the religious officials. After a week of conflict, Pilate removed the standards from Jerusalem and reinstalled them in Caesarea, where the army was garrisoned. Pilate also created a set of gold shields for his Jerusalem residence but again the Jewish managerial executives complained, this time to Emperor Tiberius, and Tiberius had the shields reinstalled in Caesarea.

- Pilate the manager constructed a long aqueduct from a spring to Jerusalem some thirty miles long. While the project was impressive, the people revolted because Pilate used temple funds to pay for the construction. A riot ensued and many Jews were killed, including many of Herod's subjects.[6] Thus the animosity between Pilate and

---

were eventually assimilated by the Romans and ceased to exist as distinct people.

4. This is the title used by Felix (Acts 23) and Festus (Acts 26). Agrippa may have done the same thing (Acts 25).

5. Eusebius, *Church History*, 2.7.100.

6. Luke 13:1–2.

Herod[7] and the olive branch attempt by Pilate to Herod in the trial of Jesus.[8]

- Pilate the manager minted copper coins for local consumption in Judea. Unfortunately for him, he had the coins stamped with pagan Roman religious insignia and not the usual flora and fauna designs acceptable to the Jews. To solve the problem, Marcus Felix, the procurator, took some of the Pilate coins and over-stamped them with ears of corn and local trees.

- Pilate the manager tried to keep the peace again when a large group of Samarians gathered on Mt. Gerizim under a false understanding relating to Moses. Pilate jailed many in the group and then killed its ringleaders. The people again complained to the higher authorities (Lucius Vitellius, governor of Syria, reigned AD 34) and he ordered Pilate to answer the charges to Emperor Tiberius. This is the Eusebian investigation the outcome of which is unknown.

Pilate's management can be summarized thusly: While Pilate has never had good press with the Christians, the Jews also hated him because he had little understanding and affection for them. Philo the Jewish historian could find no good thing about Pilate: "He is by nature ridged and stubbornly harsh and of spiteful disposition and an exceeding wrathful man who engaged in bribery, the acts of pride, the acts of violence, the outrages, the cases of spiteful treatment, the constant murders without trial, the ceaseless and most grievous brutality."[9] Note the mockery of the Jewish executive in the wording of the superscription on the cross in John 19:19–22.

JOSEPH OF ARIMATHEA THE MANAGER

> When it was evening, there came a rich[10] man from Arimathea, named Joseph, who was also a disciple of Jesus. He went to Pilate and asked for the body of Jesus; then Pilate ordered it to be given to him. So Joseph took the body and wrapped it in a clean linen cloth and laid it in his own new tomb, which he had

---

7. Luke 23:12.
8. Luke 23:6–7.
9. Philo, *On the Embassy to Gaius*, 38.299–301.
10. *Plousios*

hewn in the rock. He then rolled a great stone to the door of the tomb and went away. (Matt 27:57–60)

With a little sanctified speculation, we can come up with some management principles from Joseph of Arimathea. Interestingly, all four Gospels mention Joseph, a rarity in the Gospel accounts, so he must have played an important role in the mind of God. Here are some management points of interest:

- Joseph the manager was a rich agribusinessman. The village of Arimathea[11] was in the hill country northwest of Jerusalem and not on the coast or on a major trading route, so Joseph's wealth was probably from vineyards and orchards. Thus, he knew how to schedule and manage workers.

- Joseph the manager was a prominent and wealthy member of the antagonistic Sanhedrin, yet he publicly disagreed with the Sanhedrin decision to murder Jesus. He had access to the governor, Pilate, so he was used to speaking his mind and being listened to. When he made up his mind he was stubborn in the face of opposition.

- Joseph the manager was more than a follower of Jesus. He was a disciple. He was looking for the coming of the Messiah, and he was the first prominent businessman to be discipled by Christ. Joseph the manager, unlike Peter, was not afraid to identify himself as a disciple of Jesus, and he boldly went to Pilate and asked for the body of his Lord, which probably indicated his social and economic standing.[12]

- Joseph the manager was wisely discreet in his devotion to Jesus since he kept his allegiance secret, but the murder of Jesus was too much for him and forced him out in the open. His discretion indicated that he was used to negotiation and success in a hostile environment.

- Joseph the manager may have been the only disciple to believe in the resurrection since he had no provision for the body of Jesus until it was certified that Jesus had died. Since he thought there was no need for a grave at Jesus' death he had to plan quickly and purchase

---

11. A small rural town approximately twenty-five miles outside of Jerusalem. The exact current name and location of Arimathea is in some dispute, but many scholars think that the village was perhaps Ramah (1 Sam 1:1–20).

12. Mark 15:43.

new expensive linen clothes to wrap Jesus' unresurrected body.[13] Joseph actually touched the body of the dead Jesus, making him almost utterly unique among humans.[14]

- Joseph the manager buried Jesus in a new tomb just carved out for him, probably indicating that Joseph was an older man, having made his money already.[15]
- Joseph the manager had direct supervision and approval over the burial plot. Joseph's men probably cut the tomb into the rock.[16]
- Joseph the manager was rich enough to have employees to help him take Jesus' body to his tomb, which had to be carved out and then help in rolling the stone over the entrance. Joseph rolled a big stone in front of the cave, which took the assistance of men, probably men in his employ.[17]
- Joseph the manager supervised the planning and preparation of the tomb from getting the dead body to rolling the huge stone in front of the cave.
- Joseph the manager acted with the body of Jesus, indicating that he was used to giving to the poor and disadvantaged.
- Joseph the manager was forced to bear the cost of another expensive burial chamber because Jewish law forbade another body from being buried in Joseph's tomb.[18]

DIVES THE MANAGER

> There was a rich[19] man [Dives] who was dressed in purple and fine linen and lived in luxury every day. (Luke 16:19)

We have another businessman who apparently managed his business affairs effectively and successfully. The fact that he was "rich" is emphasized

13. Mark 15:45.
14. Matt 27:59; the gentile Roman centurion was the other human.
15. Matt 27:60.
16. Matt 27:60.
17. Matt 27:60.
18. Morris, *The Gospel According to Matthew*, 729.
19. *Plousios*.

by mentioning his wealth three times and "luxury" once. But this business manager failed to manage his personal affairs successfully. This is a tragic warning to all businesspeople to watch that their professional life doesn't consume their private life. Here was a man who was prosperous and enjoyed all the "good things" of life: fine clothes, fine food, fine companionship, enjoyable family relationships, good health, pleasant amusements, and even a sense of religious heritage. The text from Luke indicates several points in the life of this business manager:

- Dives the manager had clothes which were expensive and elegant. He dressed in expensive clothes made purple by dye from snails. Even his underwear was expensive linen. Luke's narrative does not indicate that his man was unusual or corrupt in his comfortable lifestyle, but rather typical of a successful man.
- Dives the manager was properly buried in his own grave, signifying prominence in the community.
- Dives the manager constantly indulged himself in making merry, that is, celebrating his prosperity with feasts and epicurean delights. He apparently came to this lifestyle naturally since his younger brothers needed to be warned by Abraham lest they too follow his example. It appears that this extravagance was a family trait.
- Dives the manager knew of poor Lazarus but did nothing to ameliorate Lazarus's poverty and hunger, indicating that he was dedicated to social and class distinctions. He learned his lesson in compassion, but it was too little, too late.
- Dives the manager had compassion, but it was limited to his sphere of influence—his five brothers. Nothing for those around him in society.
- Dives the manager was obtuse about his personal relationships, thinking that Lazarus would help him in his rough condition. "He thought the old order would be the eternal order and even in Hell he imagines Lazarus to be his servant."[20]
- Dives the manager was familiar with the Old Testament and Abraham, but he was not a serious student of the Scriptures and failed to understand them.

---

20. Edwards. *The Gospel According to Luke*. 470.

- Dives the manager appealed to Abraham with self-justification, complaining, and victimization.
- Dives the manager believed that if he had been given material signs he could have saved himself from his current state. There is no repentance, only self-preservation of his earthly lifestyle.
- Dives the manager had success in business due, in part, to his perseverance and pragmatism: If it works, it is true. And even a second request avails himself nothing (probably a new experience for him). He perseveres even in hell by approaching Abraham to relieve him of his discomfort.

PETER THE MANAGER

> In those days when the number of disciples was increasing, the Grecian Jews among them complained against those of the Aramaic-speaking community because their widows were being overlooked in the daily distribution of food. So the Twelve gathered all the disciples together and said, "It would not be right for us to neglect the ministry of the word of God in order to wait on tables. Brothers, choose seven men from among you who are known to be full of the spirit and wisdom. We will turn [management] responsibility[21] over to them and will give our attention to prayer and the ministry of the word." This proposal pleased the whole group. They chose[22] Stephen . . . also Philip, Porcorus, Nicanor, Timon, Parmenas and Nicolas from Antioch, a convert to Judaism. (Acts 6:1–5)

The Acts passage covering the "choosing"[23] of the seven is full of management insights ripe for an application of the problem-solving technique known as "Five Whys" implemented by Toyota.[24] After Acts 6:1 comes

21. *Kathistemi* = to set, place, to make somebody something, to put into a position.
22. *Eklego* = to lay out.
23. *Episkeptomai* = to look at something, examine, inspect, observe, to take care of, regard.
24. The so-called "Five Whys" could look something like this: Problem: Certain widows were being overlooked in "daily distribution" (Acts 6:1). Why: The organization was trying to do too much with the current staff. A decision needed to be made as to reduce obligations or increase staff. Increasing staff was the decision the apostles made. Thus, increasing staff was mandated, but that was a problem. After Acts 6:1 comes a "Why," but before that, the first "Why" would be the following: Why: There

the first new "why" point: There was racial tension between the Hebrew believers and the Hellenistic believers. Then comes the 2nd "why" point, which is not noted.

The background is that the organization was growing so rapidly[25] that certain goals were not being met.[26] It was a potentially destructive situation. In the beginning, the day-to-day management of the Jerusalem organization was the responsibility of the apostles, led by Peter.[27] In the course of perhaps only five years the organization had attracted ethnically diverse groups who had a hard time integrating with each other. There is no hint that there was racial discrimination at the corporate headquarters, but the danger of non-assimilation was there, and the need for good management of the organization was evident to all. The solution to the problem was to appoint more hands-on managers, and this seemed to satisfy the employees.[28] The leaders could have split the company into two smaller groups—Aramaic-speaking Jews and Greek-speaking Jews—but they chose to work together to counter the ethnic divisions in the society around them, unlike the old company, which was split along ethnic lines.[29] Here are some Petrine management points hidden in this interesting paragraph:

---

is ethnic tension between the Jerusalem Jews and the Hellenistic Jews in the church.

1. Why: Only the twelve apostles were staff empowered to do the "daily distribution" (carry on the "apostolic ministry," Acts 1:25; 6:2).

2. Why: "The apostolic ministry" was limited to those who had an experience with God through the Holy Spirit (Acts 1:21).

3. Why: That's the way the early organization was set up (Acts 1:24–26, 6:2).

Solution: Increase the number of staff in the early Jewish organization who had an experience with God to do the "apostolic ministry" (Acts 6:3–4).

25. Lenski suggests that there were approximately twenty-three thousand disciples at this time (Lenski, *The Acts of the Apostles*, 239).

26. E.g., the goals of caring for all the needy among them (Acts 4:34).

27. Acts 4:35; cf. Luke 22:32.

28. Acts 6:5.

29. Acts 6:9.

- Peter's management team saw that the murmuring, complaining gossip[30] from the Hellenist widow segment of the organization[31] needed to be addressed quickly lest it get out of hand.[32]
- Peter's management team of the organization respected the fact that the Greek-speaking employees were in the minority in the company, probably only about 15 percent.[33]
- Peter's management team called a staff meeting. Shared leadership.[34]
- Peter's management team must have had an executive session to discuss a sensitive plan to suggest appointing seven Greek-speaking men to handle the management of company affairs.[35]
- Peter's management team told those "complainers" ("the disciples") who raised the problem of distribution of services[36] to solve the problem themselves.[37] It was to be their delegated duty to implement and oversee this organization "business."[38]
- Peter's management team had the "complainers" appoint seven Greek-speaking men from their own ranks to solve the problem.[39] Who would know the needs of the Greek-speaking members better than other Greek-speaking members? This is an example of internal promotion.[40]

---

30. Acts 6:1; *gongysmos* = mutter, complain in a low voice, grumble.

31. Cf. the Greek widow Dorcas (9:39) and the group of widows referenced in 1 Timothy 5.

32. "So, the Twelve gathered all the disciples together" (Acts 6:2).

33. "The Hellenistic Jews among them" (Acts 6:1).

34. Acts 6:2.

35. Acts 6:2-3.

36. E.g., food, clothing, money.

37. Acts 6:3-4.

38. Acts 6:3-4; *chreia* = duty, affairs.

39. Acts 6:5. The seven appointed men all had Greek names, probably coming from the Hellenic segment of the church. If the men were to be assistants to the apostles then they would have suggested twelve men, and not only seven. So these men were to act independently of the apostles. Besides, the apostle would have chosen their assistants themselves, like Paul did (Acts 15:36-41).

40. Just as with the replacement for Judas in Acts 1.

- Peter's management team warranted that the Greek-speaking men appointed were qualified men—they were to have "good judgment"[41] and be "godly." It was not just a popularity contest.[42]

- Except for Stephen and Philip, these prominent Greek-speaking men are all lost in the mist of history. The names are all Greek, but they probably were not gentiles but Greek-speaking Jews, since Nicolas is a gentile, uniquely noted for converting the Judaism.[43] Nicolas may have been the leader of the pack as an ethnic Greek,[44] although Stephen is likely the leader since he is named first.[45]

- Peter's management team's decision to prioritize their activities and not do everything themselves reflected good leadership and management skill.[46]

- Peter's management team, once chosen, apparently solved the problem, since Luke doesn't mention the issue again, proving that the apostles' management instincts were correct.

- Peter the manager seemed to have a formal management role in the early organization. His management authority was used to hold the nascent organization together during several contentious challenges:

- Peter the manager called the organization together to select the replacement for Judas.[47]

- Peter the manager explained what happened at Pentecost to the assembled organization.[48]

---

41. *Sophos* = practical wisdom and know-how necessary for the proper management of the church.

42. Acts 6:3.

43. Acts 6:5.

44. Irenaeus, *Against Heresies*, 1.26.3. Some scholars feel Nicolas may have been Luke's primary source of information about the Hellenists, who later seem to have centered around Antioch (Acts 11). Cf. Polhill, *Acts*. However, some of the church fathers, such as Irenaeus and Tertullian, believed that Nicolas became apostate later and founded the gnostic sect of the Nicolaitans (Rev 2). That is why Luke mentions him last, as a traitor.

45. Like Peter in Acts 5:29.

46. Bock. *Acts*, 259.

47. Acts 1:15–26.

48. Acts 2:14–36.

- Peter the manager handled the Ananias/Sapphira situation and explained it the organization.[49]
- Peter the manager solved the Simon bribe situation.[50]
- Peter the manager dealt with the Cornelius situation of outsiders joining the organization.[51]
- Peter the manager was a key figure in the Council of Jerusalem in Acts 15 and the question of outsiders joining the company. He played a vital role in mediating the disagreement among the leaders of the company.[52]
- Peter the manager was the first reputable leader of the organization to seek an ill-advised accommodation between Jews and gentiles in order to further the gospel. Confronted by Paul for his hypocrisy,[53] Peter continued to thread the management needle in order to advance Christianity.[54]

BARNABAS THE MANAGER

> Joseph, a Levite from Cyprus, whom the apostles called "Barnabas" (which means "son of encouragement"), sold a field he owned and brought the money and put it at the apostles' feet. (Acts 4:36–37)

Following Peter, Barnabas is the first post-resurrection manager in the New Testament. His great contribution to the fledgling organization was his mediating skills and management style. Luke calls Barnabas "a good man, full of the Holy Spirit and faith."[55] In all of Barnabas's effort we see his unifying and harmonious management techniques at work to accomplish the unity of the new organization. The Jerusalem Council

---

49. Acts 5:1–11.
50. Acts 8:14–25.
51. Acts 10:1–8.
52. Acts 15:6–21.
53. Gal 2: 11–14; Greek, *hupokrisis* = hypocrisy, feigning.
54. 1 Pet 2, elsewhere. 1 Cor 8:1–13; Paul would later relax his absolutist attitude.
55. Acts 11:24.

called Barnabas our "beloved Barnabas."[56] We see his management approach in several incidents:

- Barnabas the manager was the one selected by the apostles to introduce the new management trainee Paul to the headquarter's staff after his conversion. Clearly, Barnabas had the trust of the executives of the mother ship of the new organization.[57]
- Barnabas the manager was commissioned by the Jerusalem headquarters to go to Antioch to see what was happening with the branch office there. There were reports that new and unique members were joining the organization. Barnabas reported back to the mothership that all was well in Antioch.[58]
- Barnabas the manager is called by God to take Saul/Paul and set off for the work to which they were commissioned. This is the first recruiting trip for Paul.[59]
- Barnabas the manager was selected by the head office in Jerusalem, along with Saul, to organize a relief mission to Judea to provide famine assistance to the branch offices in that region.[60]
- Barnabas the manager played a decisive role in the Jerusalem national convention in Acts 15. The issue was the gentile members coming into the organization run by Jews. Barnabas gave a report on his first trip with Paul, and it was well received. The executive committee of the convention then sent a letter to all the branch offices that gentiles should be welcomed into the organization without prejudice. The Convention chose men of reputation and integrity—Barnabas and Paul—to carry the missive to the outlying posts.[61]

---

56. Acts 15:25.
57. Acts 9:27.
58. Acts 11:20–24.
59. Acts 13:1–3.
60. Acts 11:27–30.
61. Acts 15:22–29.

PAUL THE MANAGER

> When [Paul and Barnabas] had preached the gospel to [Derbe] and had made many disciples,[62] they returned to Lystra and to Iconium and to Antioch, strengthening[63] the souls of the disciples, encouraging[64] them to continue[65] in the faith . . . And when they had appointed[66] elders[67] for them in every [branch office], with prayer and fasting they committed[68] them to the Lord. (Acts 14:21–23)

In Acts 14:21–23 we have Paul and Barnabas "appointing" managers of the branch offices in Derbe, Lystra, Iconium, and Antioch after training them in their duties.[69] In these four cities Paul and Barnabas staffed, taught, encouraged, motivated, and organized coworkers into functioning units.[70] The two senior managers (Paul and Barnabas) exemplified boldness and resolve to their community when they returned to the very cities that had endangered them.[71] It was important that the new members of the organization were encouraged during the early times of getting to know the ropes of their new associations, and the courageous examples of Paul and Barnabas helped. This is the first example of Paul appointing managers in the organization. This is another instance where the Greek term for "appointing" suggests that perhaps the group voted

---

62. *Matheteuo*. The Greek literal translation reads "made many disciples" using the Greek word *matheteuo*, which means to learn or instruct with the result that the student becomes a follower in thought and action. The term means more than just learning information (Matt 28:19).

63. *Episterizo* = to support, lean upon, confirm, establish.

64. *Parakaleo* = exhort.

65. *Emmenein* = remain, abide.

66. *Cheirotoneo* = to elevate by stretching out the hand (2 Cor 8:19).

67. *Presbyteroi* = elder, sometimes just an old, bearded person, Acts 4:5, 8, 23, 6:12; 23:14; 24:1; 25:15. This corresponds to the Old Testament use of "elders" (*zaqen*) in Josh 20:4; Ruth 4:2; Isa 24:23. Sometimes it is an official position, as in Acts 14:23; 15:2, 4, 6, 22,23; 16:6; 20:17; 21:18.

68. *Paratithemi* = commit, commend, entrust, prove, provide.

69. This "appointing" is a different Greek term from the "appointing" of the seven in Acts 6.

70. Senior, *The Gift of Administration*, 30, maintains that Paul did not exercise any management leadership over any of the churches in Asia Minor or Macedonia. I disagree.

71. Acts 14:19–20.

on who the managers would be, and senior managers endorsed their vote. Paul made sure that the right managers were installed. This will be a common practice and routine for Paul as he established branch offices throughout the Mediterranean region.[72] In this instance, the managers apparently followed the practice used by Peter in Acts 6 where the issue was presented to the group for discussion and action, then Paul made the appointment. These early group managers were undoubtedly Jewish since only the Jews knew the Old Testament Scriptures well enough to lead a group of new members. So Paul was recruiting his trained people for the job. Also, note that again deacons were not chosen in these new congregations since the corporate need had not yet risen.

So to summarize the management activities of Paul and Barnabas:

- Paul and Barnabas recruited for the organization and made managers out of some of the new members.[73]
- Paul and Barnabas personally supervised the activities of the organization.[74]
- Paul and Barnabas trained the new hires.[75]
- Paul and Barnabas motivated them to embrace the mission of the organization.[76]
- Paul and Barnabas delegated managers to supervise the activities of the organization.[77]
- Paul and Barnabas handled the finances of the new organization.[78]
- Paul and Barnabas prayed for the success of each of the new managers.[79]

---

72. Cf. Acts 20:17; 1 Cor 16:13–18; Phil 1:1; 1 Thess 5:12–24; 1 Tim 5:17; Titus 1:5; perhaps James in Jas 5:14; Peter in 1 Pet 5:1; and John in 2 John 1 and 3 John 1.
73. "Made disciples" (Acts 14:21).
74. "They returned" (14:21).
75. "Strengthening the souls" (14:22).
76. "Encouraging them to continue in the faith" (14:22).
77. "Appointed elders" (14:23).
78. Acts 11:30.
79. "They committed them to the Lord" (14:23).

This is why I [Paul] left you [Titus] in Crete, so that you might put what remained into order,[80] and appoint[81] managers[82] in every town as I directed[83] you. (Titus 1:5)[84]

This one Pauline verse is rich in management principles. In Titus 1:5, Paul tells Titus to "appoint" managers in every town in Crete that Paul had visited. Titus is simply a good and reliable manager appointed by Paul to run the Cretan organizations.[85] Embracing multiple responsibilities on the island of Crete, Paul tells Titus it is essential that all branch offices are to be managed "well":

- Titus the manager is to finish what Paul began. We don't know what the unfinished business was, but for our purposes it is not important

---

80. *Epidiorthoma* = to set right, to correct, to complete unfinished reform.

81. *Kathistemi* = to appoint a person to a position of authority (Luke 12:14).

82. *Presbuteroi.* "From that time on Jesus began to explain to his disciples that he must go to Jerusalem and suffer many things at the hands of the city managers (*presbuteros*), chief priests and teachers of the law, and that he must be killed and on the third day be raised to life" (Matt 16:21, Cf. Matt 26:3; 27:41; Mark 8:31; 11:27; Luke 9:22; 20:1; Acts 6:12). This Greek term has become so associated with ecclesiastical structure that the secular use has been diminished. The term means "older" or "senior" (although the history of the term indicates that men as young as thirty are called "elder managers"), as in "elder men" or "older ones." In the New Testament it is also "ambassador," as in 2 Corinthians 5:20 and Ephesians 6:20. But the word carries with it not only age but experience and organizational position. We see it used this way in the LXX Joshua 20:4 and Ruth 4:2 where it refers to town managers who lead the secular affairs of the Israelites. In the Gospels we see the town managers lumped together with the chief priests and the teachers of the law in unified opposition to Jesus, thus covering the religious, political, and social powers. As Bornkamm notes in the Septuagint: "As representatives of the whole people the managers go with Moses when he punishes Dathan and Abiram (Num 16:25). The managers also stand by Joshua when the theft of Achan is expiated (Josh 7:6). With Joshua they lead the people in the attack on Ai (Josh 8:10). Joshua summons them when he calls all the people together to a national assembly at Shechem . . . Instructive is the unmistakable tendency to set the established authority of the managers, which needs neither validation nor legal definition, in the service of the guidance of the whole people (Josh 24:1)" (Bornkamm, "Presbus," 6.655). What the use of this term means is that we can find lessons of wisdom, experience, judgment, boldness, and loyalty when it is employed in the character of *presbuteroi.*

83. *Diatasso* = appoint, order, command; direct, binding, and authoritative instructions, Luke 3:13; Acts 20:13.

84. Cf. 2 Tim 2:2

85. Titus is never given the title of "bishop" or any ecclesiastical role in the church.

except that Paul directed Titus to finish the matter.[86] The Greek word for "correct" or "order" the unfinished business indicates that Paul had already started to organize the congregations but had to leave for other assignments. Obviously, Paul thought that Titus could manage whatever problems arose.

- Titus the manager is charged with "appointing" managers for each group on the island. The task was not ordaining, but rather, by using sound judgment, to select leaders for each group.[87] Crete was known as a region with many villages, so the task given to Titus was time-consuming and thus needed time management skills. Probably because the branch officers were new and small (maybe even home office units) the employees were asked for suggestions as to who their leaders would be, and Titus would endorse these local suggestions.

- Titus the manager is given a set of clear instructions by Paul as to the qualifications for leaders in each branch. There was order and priority to Paul's instructions, for he doesn't tell Titus to appoint administrative managers but only executive managers.[88]

- Titus the manager is to appoint deacons later as the need arose but for now Paul's instructions are to do first things first. The Greek term used here for "appointing" is a very strong verb, signifying the importance of organizing the Cretan branches quickly. This is the direction given by a senior manager to a subordinate manager to work with dispatch to accomplish the efficient and peaceful organizing of a multifaceted organization. Organizational management authority was important to these people.

Titus the manager joined Paul in the managerial responsibilities of staffing, planning, encouraging, evaluating, acculturating, and engaging in the community, in addition to handling the finances.[89]

The fact that Paul asserted his managerial authority over Titus, while stark, is not unusual. John, an old man and the last surviving apostle,

---

86. Paul the manager was used to giving orders and directions, and we have him "enjoining" or "ordering" (*epitasso* = to put upon one as a duty) Philemon to take back Onesimus and treat him with respect (Phlm 8).

87. Cf. Luke 12:14.

88. Titus 1:6–9.

89. Titus 1:5. For financial management note 2 Corinthians 8:19.

begins his second and third letter by reminding the readers that he has an authoritative position in the organization—he is the "senior manager,"[90] a fact that everyone in the multinational organization at that time was no doubt aware.

> From Miletus, Paul sent to Ephesus for the managers[91] of the organization. When they arrived, he said to them, "You know how I lived the whole time I was with you, from the first day I came into the province of Asia ... You know that I have not hesitated to preach anything that would be helpful[92] to you but have taught you publicly and from house to house ... For I have not hesitated to proclaim to you the whole will of God. Guard yourselves and all the flock of which the Holy Spirit has made you managers.[93] Be managers[94] of the organization.[95] So be on your guard. Remember that for three years I never stopped warning each of you night and day with tears. (Acts 20:17–18, 20, 27, 31)

Luke has left us with this extraordinary report of a meeting between Paul and the Ephesian managers which, if looked at with management eyes, is fundamentally a management training seminar. Looking at the report contained in Acts 20:17–35; note that in the meeting of the managers Paul emphasized his management practices to his colleagues:

- Paul the manager reminded his Ephesian branch managers that he practiced management by wandering around ("MBWA"). He knew the workplace and the members of the organization.[96]

---

90. *Presbyteros.*
91. *Presbyteros.*
92. *Sumphero* = profitable, advantageous, expedient, that which confers benefit.
93. *Episkopos.*
94. *Poimaino.*
95. Church of God.
96. Acts 20:18. "MBWA" refers to a style of business management which involves managers wandering around, in an unstructured manner, through the workplace(s), at random, to check with employees, equipment, or on the status of ongoing work. The emphasis is on the word "wandering" as an unplanned movement within a workplace. The expected benefit is that a manager, by random sampling of events or employee discussions, is more likely to facilitate improvements to the morale, sense of organizational purpose, and productivity and quality of the management. The origin of the term goes back to Hewlett-Packard for management practices in the 1970s. Peters and Waterman used the term in their 1982 book *In Search of Excellence: Lessons from America's Best-Run Companies.*

- Paul the manager noted that his lifestyle was transparent the entire time he was in Ephesus.[97]
- Paul the manager reminded the Ephesian managers that he conducted the manager development program with humility and personal attachment.[98]
- Paul the manager reminded the Ephesian managers that he told them everything that he believed would "help" make them successful managers of the group. He did this publicly and privately, corporately and personally, for three years.[99]
- Paul the manager reminded the Ephesian managers that every manager was to receive training. There was no discrimination in the executive management training program.[100]
- Paul the manager told these leaders that they were managers of the group because God had made them such; they were divinely appointed as far as he was concerned.[101]
- Paul the manager was transparent in discussing the difficulties laying ahead for him and the organization and that the managers needed to be prepared for serious competition from other groups.[102]
- Paul the manager once again emphasized the importance of being steadfast in accomplishing the mission of the organization.[103]
- Paul the manager told them to watch their own spiritual walk with God since it is his group of which they are managers.[104]
- Paul the manager stressed the importance of choosing the right people for the organization and that there was the need to watch over the staffing of the organization.[105]
- Paul the manager emphasized planning and preparation.[106]

97. Acts 20:18.
98. Acts 20:19, 31, 35.
99. Acts 20:20, 27, 31.
100. Acts 20:21.
101. Acts 20:17, 28.
102. Acts 20:23, 28–31.
103. Acts 20:24.
104. Acts 20:28.
105. Acts 20:30.
106. Acts 20:31.

- Paul the manager told them that they had to guard their spiritual walk because they had to guard the Ephesian organization against enemies that would come against them.[107]
- Paul the manager reminded them that during the training program he did not take an exorbitant salary at the expense of the organization. Paul was careful of finances.[108]
- Paul the manager reminded them that he did not ask them to do anything that he hasn't done or wouldn't do. He worked with them side by side.[109]

No group of managers in the New Testament got as much personal training from Paul as the Ephesian managers. Paul's training was not just in theology but also in organization development to keep the fledging groups together in the face of the coming challenges.[110] How did the Ephesian elders/managers do? Well, John writes of the Ephesian organization several decades after Paul's farewell address in Revelation 2:1–7. It is the only follow-up report we have of any New Testament congregation, and it makes for interesting reading from a management standpoint. Without quoting the entire seven-verse narrative (you can do that on your own), there are several points to note about the management effectiveness of the Ephesian overseer/managers:

- The Ephesian organization was active in community "works" and eleemosynary efforts in Ephesus.[111]
- The Ephesian organization had a reputation for hard work and diligent efforts on behalf of its mission, advancing the kingdom of God. The hard work and perseverance are of the same coin, one side active and one side passive.
- The Ephesian organization persevered in loyalty to the mission.
- The Ephesian organization did not tolerate the practice of sin in its midst (Nicolaitans).

---

107. Acts 20:31.
108. Acts 20:33–34.
109. Acts 20:35.
110. Cf. 1 Cor 12:7, "common good."
111. "I know your deeds" (Rev 2:2).

- The Ephesian organization tested those who would be their leaders. This testing was to protect against the wolves that Paul warned them against in Acts 20.[112]
- The Ephesian organization has persevered and endured hardship and not been found wanting.

However, the Ephesian organization had fallen away from its first enthusiastic love affair with Jesus, as commended by Paul in Acts 20. While they had been diligent in maintaining correct orthodoxy, their Christian life had devolved into arid duty and works, and they had lost the love they initially had, which devalued all the rest of their faithfulness. "Good works and pure doctrine are not adequate substitutes for that rich relationship of mutual love shared by persons who have just experienced the redemptive love of God."[113]

John mentions six marks of faithfulness for the organization in Ephesus. Many scholars believe that John was at one time the manager of this important branch office. Clearly doctrinal purity seemed to be a peculiar distinction of this group. As one scholar noted, the congregation knew that her theology had to be right or "toil would lose its spring, patience its encouragement, shrinking from evil men its intensity, and perseverance its support."[114] Jesus knows what's going on in Ephesus and picks three things to encourage: their deeds, their hard work, and their steadfastness, all in part due to Paul's management seminar in Acts 20.

AQUILA AND PRICILLA THE MANAGERS

> After this, Paul left Athens and went to Corinth. There he met a Jew named Aquila, a native of Pontus, who had recently come from Italy with his wife Pricilla. (Acts 18:1–2)

Aquila and Pricilla had been expelled from Rome and moved to Corinth, where they assumed leadership in the fledgling organization.[115] They were probably members of the organization before they left Rome, so they quickly became leaders in the Corinthian branch. They were

---

112. The early congregations tested the leaders for their orthodoxy: 1 Thess 5:21; 1 Cor 14:29; 1 John 4:1.
113. Mounce, *The Book of Revelation*, 88.
114. Milligan, *The Book of Revelation* 45.
115. 1 Cor 16:19.

important enough in the organization that Paul sought them out. The couple were engaged in a business of making leather goods, and Paul needed to network with them for his own income.[116] Furthermore, Paul stayed with them while he was in Corinth. Here is the management of interpersonal relations in an organization on full display. Clearly, the couple was a favorite of Paul's, because he honors them in Romans 16:3 by calling "Priscilla"[117] her more formal name, "Prisca."

- Aquila and Pricilla understood the dynamics of organizational planting enough that Paul took them to Ephesus with him and then left them there to manage the Ephesian branch.[118]
- This power couple bought a home which functioned as the Ephesian headquarters.
- Aquila and Pricilla hosted Apollos, the well-educated and exuberant teacher from Alexandria, when he came to Ephesus in order to manage his gifts and enthusiasm.

PHOEBE THE MANAGER

> I commend to you our sister Phoebe, a manager[119] of the branch in Cenchrea. I ask you to receive her in the Lord in a way worthy of the saints and to give her any help she may need from you, for she had been a great help to many people, including me. (Rom 16:1–2)

Paul is commending Phoebe, a manager of the branch office in the seaport city of Cenchrea, which services Corinth. He describes her with an adjective which means "a servant leader." Paul tells the recipients of his letter to honor Phoebe for at least three reasons:

- Paul has entrusted Phoebe to deliver this important letter to the Roman branch of the organization. She will probably read and explain the contents of the letter to the Roman organization.

---

116. Acts 18:2–3.
117. It is Luke who uses the conversational name of "Priscilla."
118. Acts 18:19.
119. *Diakonos*.

Jesus on Selected Managers in the New Testament

- Phoebe is the Cenchrea branch manager in the organization, and her coworkers in the greater Corinthian region are to give her what she needs to conduct her responsibilities.
- Phoebe, the Cenchrea manager, has been a great benefactor[120] to many in the organization, including Paul himself.

---

120. *Prostatis* = succor, patron, assistant.

6

Jesus on Specific Responsibilities of a Business Manager

- Staffing
- Planning
- Organizing
- Motivating
- Evaluating
- Peacemaking
- Training
- Competing
- Acculturating
- Witnessing

THE STAFFING MANAGER

> [Yahweh] changes times and seasons; he sets up kings and deposes them. He gives wisdom to the wise and knowledge to the discerning. (Dan 2:21)[1]

---

1. Dan 4:17; 1 Sam 2:7–8. Good Christian managers attract good workers; or, "talented leaders attract bold people" (Doriani, *Work: Its Purpose, Dignity and Transformation*, 10).

THE STAFFING MANAGER IN THE GOSPELS

Jesus the staffing manager

> When morning came, [Jesus] called his disciples to him and chose twelve of them, whom he also designated apostles. (Luke 6:13)

Nothing is more important in an organization than hiring the right people.[2] In the life of Jesus, we see God's sovereignty over personnel decisions in this Lukan passage. Early in the morning, first thing, Jesus picked[3] twelve men from a larger group of male followers to be his intimate companions.[4] We don't know the number of these initial "disciples"[5] but it probably was rather small because it was early in the Lord's ministry, and it took a substantial commitment to give up everything to follow and obey Jesus at this point in his ministry.[6]

Many disciples were not chosen, and that had to hurt some feelings, but Jesus chose anyway. The Lord's staffing decision was calculated and deliberate. Then he took the Twelve and calls them "apostles,"[7] further elevating them above the larger pool of "disciples." This select group of twelve is usually referred to in a nontitular manner, but Jesus called them "apostles," thus commissioning them to be his messengers in a cultural sense. Later, the term "apostles" would be used to refer to a small elite group of organizational executive managers and include many more post-resurrection individuals, such as Paul and Barnabas.

We find Jesus making other personnel decisions from the very beginning. From the discriminating call of certain men and not others,[8] to the visit to the mount of transfiguration for some and not others,[9] to a

---

2. Cf. The principle is given in Ps 1:1; 26:4–5; 119:115; Prov 13:20; 14:7; 1 Cor 5:11; 15:33; 2 Cor 6:14; Titus 3:10.

3. *Eklexamenos* = elected, choose.

4. Acts 1:21, "the men who have been with us the whole time."

5. *Mathetes* = a follower of one's teaching, adherent.

6. Luke 14:26–27, 33.

7. This appellation is only used in Mark 3:2 and Matt 10:2 (maybe) for the Twelve.

8. Matt 4:18–22.

9. Luke 9 28–36.

visit to the synagogue leader in the aftermath of the raising of the Jairus's daughter. Some would follow, some would not.[10]

In an interesting short parable Jesus is talking about eating food and the ripe harvest, and then he gives a short exhortation about teamwork in the field:

> Even now the reaper draws his wages, even now he harvests the crop for eternal life, so that the sower and the reaper may be glad together. Thus, the saying "One sows and another reaps" is true. I sent you to reap what you have not worked for. Others have done the hard work, and you have reaped the benefits of their labor. (John 4:36–38)

The focus of this passage is the spiritual harvest of evangelism. But Jesus uses an illustration from agribusiness reminiscent of Amos 9:13.[11] Jesus gives a natural staffing relationship: a reaper may reap where she has not sown,[12] and a sower may never experience the joy of reaping what he has sown.[13] In any endeavor, especially a business endeavor, management and teamwork are essential. One worker is paid[14] in advance even while a coworker is finishing his job, and the reason is because both sides of the process can rejoice together in a completed job well done.[15] In John 4:37 Jesus quotes a well-known saying, "One sows and another reaps" to summarize John 4:38 while referring to the unity of life and the diversity of gifts in a business enterprise.[16] The managed work of all employees is essential to success.[17] One gets a sense of urgency in each other's work. After all, wages are being paid to the sowers even before the harvests are finished. Time is of the essence. Sowing, being there first, is hard work[18]

---

10. Mark 5:37.

11. "'The days are coming,' declares Yahweh, 'when the reaper will be overtaken by the plowman and the planter by the one treading grapes.'"

12. Cf. Deut 6:11; Josh 24:13.

13. Cf. Deut 28:30; Mic 6:15.

14. *Misthon* = payment; cf. Matt 20:1, 16; Luke 10:7; 1 Cor 3:8, 14; 1 Tim 5:18; Jas 5:4

15. Cf. Deut 16:13–14.

16. The diversity of the workplace is evident in various biblical environments: 1 Kgs 5; Dan 1:3; Gal 3:28; Col 3:11; Rev 5:9.

17. Carson, *The Gospel According to John*, 230.

18. In John 4:38 Jesus uses three different Greek terms for "labor": *kekopiakate, kekopiakasin, kopon*.

Jesus on Specific Responsibilities of a Business Manager

and underappreciated and must be recognized by the reapers and encouraged by the manager.

THE STAFFING MANAGER IN THE OLD TESTAMENT

Asaph the staffing manager

> No one from the east or the west or from the desert can exalt[19] a man. But it is God who judges:[20] He brings one down,[21] he exalts another. (Ps 75:6–7)[22]

Asaph, the staffing manager, is telling us in Psalm 75 that we humans cannot successfully exalt ourselves to achieve the goals we strive for. It is God who will decide who is successful. It is Yahweh who ultimately evaluates.[23] The theology behind this bold statement is given in Psalm 75, where it is stated that it is Yahweh who created and sustains the world, not man, and that Yahweh is the one who will establish and sustain leadership in the world. It is Yahweh who establishes the stability and moral order of the world. If either stability or order is challenged by man, chaos may erupt, and the steady hand of God will be needed to re-establish order and tranquility. So those who exalt the individual over God are engaging in a frontal assault on the very fundamental nature of reality. Thus, it is God who makes the final staffing decision about who gains power and who loses power in the world order, including organizations within that order.[24] Clearly there will be short-term gains made by the most talented and ambitious of people. But in the long term, it is Yahweh who decides winners and losers.

---

19. *Rawm* = promote, extol, bring up, sets up.
20. Evaluation.
21. *Shaphel* = puts down, to make low, humble.
22. Hannah prayed that "The LORD sends poverty and wealth; he humbles, and he exalts" (1 Sam 2:7).
23. Cf. Isa 31:1–3.
24. 1 Sam 2:7; Isa 2:11, 16; 5:15. Spurgeon on Ps 75:6–7: "Men forget that all things are ordained in heaven; they see but the human force, and the carnal passion, but the unseen Lord is more real than these. He is at work behind and within the cloud" (Spurgeon, *The Treasury of David*, 2.294).

Samuel the staffing manager

> Samuel said to [Saul], "Yahweh has torn the kingdom of Israel from you today and has given it to one of your neighbors—to one better[25] than you." (1 Sam 15:28)

Note the famous biblical example of firing someone in 1 Samuel 15:28. Yahweh fired Saul as king and hired David, giving the Christian business manager the following lessons:

- Saul the manager's firing was decisive ("torn") and permanent (Yahweh will not change his mind).
- Saul the manager's firing was immediate ("today"), and he immediately gave up his keys and his parking place and was escorted from the building. There was no two-week grace period after being fired!
- Saul the manager's replacement had already been chosen (one of Saul's subjects—David)[26]
- Saul the manager's replacement is a "better" fit for the organization.[27]
- Saul the staffing manager received no explanation because he already knew the reasons for his firing.[28]

David the staffing manager

> Now, Hiram, king of Tyre, sent messengers to David, along with cedar logs and carpenters and stonemasons, and they built a palace for David. (2 Sam 5:11)

Speaking of great managers attracting great people, note that when David had to flee from King Saul, David had so impressed his "mighty men" coworkers that hundreds of them followed him (2 Sam 23:8–39). That is company loyalty at display: "All those who were in distress or in debt or discontented gathered around him, and he became their leader/manager"[29] (1 Sam 22:2):

25. *Tob.*
26. 1 Sam 16:21–22.
27. 1 Sam 16:18.
28. "You have rejected the word of Yahweh," 1 Sam 15:23; 1 Sam 15:24.
29. *Sar.* "So, David and his men, about six hundred in number, left Keilah and

Jesus on Specific Responsibilities of a Business Manager

- David the staffing manager asked the busy Sidonian king, Hiram, for workers to be sent to Jerusalem to build his royal home. Does not the prophet Isaiah exult that all the nations of the world will pay homage to the kingdom of God through service,[30] workmanship[31] and performance[32]? What is important in hiring people is quality of workmanship, of personal training, and performance—not necessarily philosophical or spiritual convictions. A theistic worldview of performance should, and often does, go hand in hand with excellence, but religious convictions are secondary when staffing for marketplace work performance is concerned.[33] Obviously, there must be a core commitment to business community values (e.g., honesty, integrity, and loyalty), but these attributes are not uniquely biblical.

Solomon the staffing manager

> And Solomon ruled[34] over all the kingdoms from the River to the land of the Philistines, as far as the border of Egypt. These countries brought tribute[35] and were Solomon's subjects all his life. (1 Kgs 4:21)[36]

- Solomon the manager hired unbelieving Canaanite workers and supervisors from the Sidonian city of Tyre to come to Jerusalem and construct the most important of the organization's buildings—the national headquarters.

---

kept moving from place to place" (1 Sam 23:13).

30. *Sharath* = to serve, minister. The word is always used of a servant of higher rank, like Joseph.

31. *Barah* = build.

32. Isa 60:3–13; *paar* = beautifying.

33. Penney refused to hire anyone who gambled, drank, used tobacco or did not profess belief in a supreme being. "Creed were not discussed, and I made no great point at that time of a church connection either. But I would never have an atheist in a store of mine" (Penney, *Fifty Years*, 58).

34. *Mashal*.

35. *Minchah* = offering.

36. "And God gave Solomon wisdom [*chokmah* = skill] and very great insight [*tavun* = discernment], and a breadth of understanding [*leb* = mind, heart] as measureless as the sand on the seashore" (1 Kgs 4:29, 30–34).

- Solomon the staffing manager hired these foreign pagan workers because they were more "skilled"[37] and "experienced"[38] than the local workers.[39] The foreign workers could do a better job building God's house than the residents! Huram-Abi, the Phoenician builder and architect (whose father was from Tyre), was able to build any "design"[40] given to him by the Israelites.[41] Yahweh himself gave the design to the pagan Sidonians.[42]
- Solomon the staffing manager assigned[43] 153,300 Canaanites ("aliens") to work on the temple, 3600 of them being assigned managerial responsibilities[44] over the Hebrews.

Interestingly, Huram-Abi, the Phoenician architect mentioned earlier in 2 Chronicles 2, is said to have possessed "wisdom, understanding, and knowledge."[45] These Hebrew terms have a practical connotation and express "empirical wisdom,[46] practical insight, and sagacity"[47] and describe the common grace skill ("wits") given by Yahweh to the seaman,[48] Shalmaneser the successful Assyrian military general and king,[49] and Bezaleel the skillful artisan.[50]

- Solomon the staffing manager confirms the orderly nature of God's sovereign vocational and staffing plans that our sinful nature continues to batter, but never prevails against: "In his heart a man plans his course, but the Lord determines his steps."[51]

---

37. *Yada* = knowledgeable.
38. *Chakham* = understanding.
39. 2 Chr 2:5–14.
40. *Mahashaba* = plan.
41. 1 Kgs 5:5–6: "We have no one so skilled in felling timbers than the Sidonians."
42. Cf. Exod 25:8–9; 1 Chr 28:11–18. Yahweh gave the design first to Moses and David and it was passed on to the pagan builders.
43. *Asah* = set, use.
44. 2 Chr 2:17–18; *menatskheem* = leader, taskmaster.
45. 2 Chr 2:13–14.
46. *Hokma* = skill.
47. Gray, *1 and 2 Kings*, 183.
48. Cf. Ps 107:27.
49. Isa 10:13.
50. Exod 28:3.
51. Cf. Prov 16:1, 9; 19:21; 21:1.

But Solomon wasn't the last Israelite to ask for heathen workers to achieve organizational goals.

Jonah the staffing manager

God's sovereignty over personnel decisions is evident in the dramatic events recorded in Jonah. In Jonah 1:7 when the pagan sailors want to find out who was responsible for the violent sea storm, God's sovereignty caused the "lots"[52] to fall on Jonah.[53] Even the pagan sailors make a major theological assumption in casting lots: God communicates through the rolling of dice. Throughout the Old Testament personnel decisions for the organization were made by the casting of lots, which depended on God's endorsing the action:

- Choosing a king.[54]
- Choosing who sinned.[55]
- Choosing leaders in a battle.[56]
- Choosing the one who broke an oath.[57]
- Choosing guards for security.[58]

Examples of the competitors using lots to confirm Yahweh's personnel decisions include:

- Philistia dividing up Israelite prisoners.[59]

52. Hebrew = *goral*; Greek = *kleros*.

53. The church father Jerome (347–420) writes, "[Jonah] is taken by lot, not from any virtue in lots themselves, least of all the lots of heathens, but by the will of Him who governs uncertain lots" (Jerome, *Commentary on Jonah*, 1.7).

54. 1 Sam 10:20–21.

55. Josh 7:14.

56. Judg 20:9.

57. 1 Sam 14:42–43.

58. 1 Chr 26:13–19. Most famously in the New Testament the apostles choosing a replacement for Judas (Acts 1:15–26). Hodgkinson argues that "formal authority [in an organization] may be designed, legislated, structured, but [management] authority is different in that it appears to be something which is conceded from the followership" (Hodgkinson, *Towards a Philosophy of Administration*, 94). Solomon the manager writes in Proverbs 16:33, "The lot is cast into the lap, but its every decision is from Yahweh," and Proverbs 18:18, "Casting the lot settles disputes."

59. Joel 3:3; Nah 3:10.

- Pharaoh hiring Joseph.[60]
- Nebuchadnezzar hiring Daniel.[61]
- Ahab hiring Obadiah.[62]
- The Persians "hiring" Cyrus the Zoroastrian.[63]
- Xerxes hiring Mordecai.[64]

Daniel the staffing manager

> He changes times[65] and seasons;[66] he set up kings and deposes them. He gives wisdom[67] to the wise and knowledge[68] to the discerning.[69] (Dan 2:21)

In Daniel 2:21 we have an interesting reference to Yahweh's sovereignty over persons, times, and opportunities for staffing changes. This is political talk, and kingdoms are the focus of Daniel the manager's statement. However, what is true for the royal courtroom is true for the corporate boardroom:

- "Times": God is sovereign over short time spans and involve worker activity.
- "Seasons": God is sovereign over long-range planning and the vagaries of the marketplace.
- "Sets up," "disposes": God is active in the selection of who, when, and where persons work.

---

60. Gen 41.
61. Dan 2.
62. 1 Kgs 18.
63. Isa 44:28.
64. Esth 8.
65. *Iddan* = an appointed time or season.
66. *Zeman* = an Aramaic term meaning appointed times, periods.
67. *Chokmah* = skill.
68. *Mandha* = Aramaic term used only in Daniel, meaning intelligence.
69. *Biynah* = meaning, understanding; cf. Dan 2:21; 4:17, 32; see also the OT passages on the arm of the Lord not being shortened (i.e., power limited) in any given situation or structure: Gen 18:14; Num 11:23; Job 5:12; Isa 50:2; 59:1; Jer 32:17, 27.

- "Wisdom," "knowledge": God provides wisdom and insight for decision making.

Ezra the staffing manager

> And you, Ezra, in accordance with the wisdom[70] of your God, which you possess, appoint[71] magistrates and judges to administer[72] justice to all the people of Trans-Euphrates—all who know the laws of your God. (Ezra 7:25)

In Ezra 7, the priest Ezra is referring to the Persian king Artaxerxes and the king's permission to Ezra to travel to Jerusalem in order to re-establish worship at the temple. This royal staffing responsibility from Artaxerxes was the most important responsibility that Ezra the manager was given by the Persian king.[73] It is the Zoroastrian king Artaxerxes, under the control of Yahweh, who appointed Ezra to lead the corporation back to national headquarters. What we have is God sovereignly at work, staffing people to organizations and determining the actions of people, even unbelievers ("times and seasons"), to accomplish God's plan for the advancement of his kingdom.[74]

Esther/Mordecai the staffing managers

> Do not think that because you are in the king's house you alone of all the Jews will escape, for if you remain silent at this time, relief and deliverance for the Jews will arise from another place, but you and your father's family will perish. And who knows but that you have come to royal position for such a time as this? (Esth 4:13–14)

- In Esther 4:13–14, we see another example of divine staffing sovereignty at work when Mordecai, the staffing manager, chastises

---

70. *Chokhmah* = Aramaic term meaning experience, insight, intelligence.
71. *Mena* = appoint, set.
72. *Dhin* = rule, sway, plead, govern. This is the only time used.
73. Clines, *Ezra, Nehemiah, Esther*, 105.
74. Ezra 7:27–29.

Esther, the Jewish queen in the Persian court of Xerxes, to do the job that she may have been appointed by Yahweh to do.[75]

Nebuchadnezzar the staffing manager

> For the king of Babylon will stop at the fork in the road, at the junction of the two roads, to seek an omen: He will cast lots[76] with arrows, he will consult his idols, he will examine the liver. Into his right hand will come the lot for Jerusalem, where he is to set up battering rams, to give the command to slaughter, to sound the battle cry, to set battering rams against the gates, to build a ramp and to erect siege works. (Ezek 21:21–22)

Another Old Testament example of God sovereignly working with "lots" and unbelievers to accomplish his will is given in Ezek 21:21-22 where Babylon will be used by God to judge Israel's rebellious spirit:

- God will have the pagan Babylonian king Nebuchadnezzar, the staffing manager, "cast lots with arrows" with the result that "into his [king's] right hand will come the lot for Jerusalem."

Consequently, Jerusalem is attacked and destroyed by the heathen hordes all because of cast lots.[77] There is probably no area of greater confusion in a Christian manager's mind than in hiring policies, and in creating and maintaining a God-honoring hiring culture. The impulse of a Christian manager is to hire only believers, thereby ensuring a common ground for harmony, excellence, and integrity for the organization.[78] But that is not necessarily the result, because Christians are at different understandings of biblical truth, Spirit sensitivity and endowments by the Creator. Besides, the secular culture is fraught with legal problems and challenges. Because the business corporation has a mission of profitability and marketplace performance, the criteria for hiring into a business

---

75. Henry, *Commentary on the Whole Bible in One Volume*, 861, commented on this Esther passage: "We should, every one of us, consider for what end God has placed us in the place where we are, and when any particular opportunity of serving God and our generation offers itself, we must take care that we do not let it slip. These things Mordecai urges to Esther."

76. Qesem = divination.

77. Cf. Ezek 21:27.

78. An illustration of this is found in Vischer's book *Me, Myself and Bob*, 164–66.

organization must be performance based, and not religious convictions. As much as we might want there to be a correlation between redemption and stewardship the two concepts may, unfortunately, have little in common, to say nothing of today's legality of preferential hiring. Everyone in the manager's flock, all his coworkers, believers and unbelievers, are in that organization at that moment because a sovereign God has placed them under that manager's care for that period.[79] In short, the Christian manager believes there are no eventual personnel mistakes.[80] When the time comes to retire, transfer, fire or promote an employee, the timing is always in the hands of a sovereign God.

THE STAFFING MANAGER IN THE NEW TESTAMENT

Paul the staffing manager

> From one man he made every nation of men, that they should inhabit the whole earth; and he determined[81] the times[82] set for them and the exact places[83] where they should live. (Acts 17:26)

In Acts 17:4, we have Paul preaching and teaching in Thessalonica, with the result that "some of the Jews were persuaded and joined[84] Paul and Silas." Now "joined" in this passage is better translated "were assigned" or "were allotted to" or "were gathered to" Paul and Silas. God was sovereignly positioning his people for a specific purpose. While this is the only

---

79. Matt 20:23; Rom 9:21.

80. An interesting Old Testament example of untimely and ill-advised human promotion is given in Numbers 22–24, where Balak king of Moab, during the time of Moses, hired the prophet Balaam to curse the Israelites with Balak's final inducement to Balaam that [Balak] "will reward you handsomely and do whatever you say" (Num 22:17). Balaam saw power, promotion, and riches, and did what the king [manager] wanted. But, rather than power and riches as promised by Balak, Balaam got the end of a vengeful Israelite sword (Num 31:8). And King Balak got only the centuries-old obloquy of a fool who tried to thwart God's will by rewarding an individual against God's will.

81. *Horizo* = to set a boundary, put limits on, determining that one is something.

82. *Kairos* = seasons.

83. *Katoikia* = residence, habitation.

84. *Prosklarothasan*.

use of this Greek verb in the New Testament, it is used in classic Greek to convey the passive voice of "going where they are told to go."[85]

Paul the staffing manager appreciates Yahweh's organizational sovereignty and tells the Areopagus that times, seasons, and places are in the hands of the God of Abraham. While the focus of Acts 17 is on a global scale, involving nations and nationalities, the principles apply to the micro-world of company staffing. In Acts 17:4 we find sovereign placement, timing, and personnel management being taught. We may not discern or understand it, but God's providential care over the staffing of our organizations is a fact of life. Acts 17 provides us several key management bullet points:[86]

- The Christian business manager knows that basic human nature is the same and that he can rely on certain human attributes to be present in each company colleague.
- The manager can count on the fact that, for the moment, each worker is in his right place because the Creator has so ordained it. Human affairs are not capricious.
- The manager understands that each worker is at his place in the company for as long as God wills it. No longer and no shorter.
- The manager accepts the fact that the job description and responsibilities of each coworker are under the sovereign control of God, and, when it is appropriate for both the individual and the company, the description and responsibilities will change ("times, seasons and places").
- The manager knows that God allots[87] to the Christian manager the specific people to manage.

---

85. Cf. Eph 1:11; Knowling, *The Acts of the Apostles*.

86. Lenski wrote, "God's hand has ever been and still is in history. Nations begin, rise to full development, finally decline. Historians trace out their courses, and thousands of natural causes are found to be at work. But these are but the surface. Underneath, over, within is the unseen Hand that guides and careers according to the supreme will, we see the pattern from below, as it appears on the wrong side of the cloth; someday we shall see it as God weaves it, the right side, which is beautiful and perfect" (Lenski, *The Acts of the Apostles*, 720). For a different view, consult Haenchen's mammoth *The Acts of the Apostles*.

87. *Kleros*.

Jesus on Specific Responsibilities of a Business Manager

We don't have to like it and the situation doesn't have to be easy, but there is simply no aspect of any organizational life that is bereft of God's gracious sovereignty. If God is not sovereign over our staffing decisions, he is not sovereign over anything. An important Greek word is *kleros*, which is translated in the Scriptures as "allotted," or "inheritance" or "called," whether there is a clear ecclesiastical context or not.[88] In the New Testament, *kleros* is used in one of the under-shepherd passages, 1 Peter 5:3: "Be shepherds[89] of God's flock . . . not lording it over those entrusted (*kleros*) to you but being examples to the flock." As usual, this is primarily an ecclesiastical passage, but the sovereign allotment of specific humans to specific organizations is taught here.[90]

> Each one should remain in the situation (*klesis*) which he was in when God called (*klesis*) him . . . Were you a slave when you were called (*klesis*)? Don't let it trouble you—although if you can gain your freedom, do so . . . Brothers, each man, as responsible to God, should remain in the situation (*klesis*) God called (*klesis*) him to. (1 Cor 7:20-24)

In 1 Corinthians 7, we have Pauline passages which teach several staffing lessons, and one of those repeated lessons is that God is sovereign over our earthly station, i.e., organizational relationship. The Greek word Paul uses in this passage is *klesis*. John Calvin, perhaps the greatest expositor of a theology of vocation, writes on this 1 Corinthians 7 passage: "Therefore, lest through our stupidity and rashness everything be turned topsy-turvy, He has appointed duties for every man in his particular way of life. And that no one may thoughtlessly transgress his limits, he has named these various kinds of living 'callings.' Therefore, each individual has his own kind of living assigned to him by the Lord as a sort of sentry post so that he may not heedlessly wander about throughout life."[91]

---

88. Cf. LXX 1 Kgs 7:14; Mark 13:34, "assigned task."

89. *Poimaino*.

90. Barclay, commenting on this passage, wrote: "*Kleros* means something which is allotted man; it is something which has been specially assigned to him . . . That must mean that the whole attitude of the elder, or of anyone who takes up any service, to his people must be the same as the attitude of God to his people. Here we have another great thought . . . Peter says to the elders, 'Shepherd your people like God.' Just as Israel is God's special allotment, the people we have to serve in church or anywhere else are our special allotment; and our whole attitude to them must be the attitude as God; we must shepherd them like God" (Barclay, *The Letters of James and Peter*, 317-18).

91. Calvin, *Institutes of the Christian Religion*, 2.724.

Rather than a prescription for a life of striving to improve one's situation in life, this passage teaches that freedom is better than slavery, so if one has the God-given opportunity to be free, one should take it. Still, we are enjoined to enjoy whatever "calling" of life one is currently in because all of life is a gift of God and one is where one currently needs to be. First Corinthians 7:17–24 is oriented more to the employee who believes that now that he has become a Christian and has freedom in Christ, he no longer is under any social, economic, or political arrangement. Consequently, freedom in Christ means freedom in society. Paul the manager is saying, "Hold on. Not necessarily so." If freedom comes, well and good. But, if freedom doesn't come, the redeemed employee is to be content and godly in the "calling"[92] in which he finds himself. All stations or employments in life for all persons, however temporary, are still under God's sovereignty and we are to use that "place in life"[93] to "keep God's commands because that is what counts."[94] One is not to advance oneself at the expense of another or to engage in revolutionary activity to benefit oneself.[95]

Paul the staffing manager notes the competition of ethical goods when he speaks to God's marriage bond in 1 Corinthians 7:15–16. A note of uncertainty in 7:16 is worth mentioning. Paul states, "how do you know"[96] what will be the result of maintaining peace through love within the marriage relationship? Salvation comes from God, and who knows the mind of God when it comes to his redeeming activity? Once again, the "who knows" what will happen in an unequal yoking within a business relationship forces the Christian manager to pray and to treat unbelieving coworkers with love and integrity and respect. The "who knows" uncertainty is used elsewhere in Scripture to express the ambiguity of life.[97] This ambiguity is a critical consideration in staffing a business organization in today's cultural environment because it speaks to the efforts of the Christian manager to influence the culture of a business organization in a secular environment. Proper behavior and conduct by the manager

---

92. *Klesis.*
93. *Klesis.*
94. 1 Cor 7:19b.
95. Cf. Onesimus in Phlm 10–13.
96. *Ti hodas.*
97. David and his infant son, 2 Sam 12:22; confession before Yahweh, Joel 2:14; the overthrow of Nineveh, Jonah 3:9.

are important for the life and stability of the business organization as a role model for the employees.[98]

The Bible teaches repeatedly that one of the great comforts afforded to Christian managers is the gracious good will of God unremittingly bestowed on them in all their professional staffing relationships. God sovereignly guides history to accomplish his will. The fact that Christian business managers don't always perceive or understand the movement of history does not diminish the gracious control of the Lord.[99] In short, God sovereignly works in the company to staff organizations and therefore the people a Christian manager works with are to be seen as divinely appointed for that time to be where they are.[100] A Christian manager must therefore shepherd the staffing makeup of an organization as a gift from God according to "his good pleasure."[101]

Christians are to be one with their culture and endorse an intimate identity with their culture as God the Father did in his incarnate identity of Jesus. The role of the business manager is not only to apply a set of shepherding skills to the management task but also to accept a rank or station or calling in an organization, and that secular calling is variously described in the Bible as "manager," "steward," "leader," and "shepherd." It follows:

- First, that both the moral and leadership criteria that are attendant to those responsibilities would flow to management of a business organization.
- Second, the general management skills and personal attributes of the position would be the same, regardless of the organization being managed.

---

98. Cf. 2 Thess 3:6; 14–15; 1 Tim 5:20.

99. Hodge wrote, "A large part of the predictions, promises, and threatenings of the word of God are founded on the assumption of this absolute control over the free acts of his creatures, without this there can be no government of the world and no certainty as to its issue. The Bible is filled with prayers founded on this assumption. All Christians believe that the hearts of men are in the hand of God; that He works in them both to will and to do according to his good pleasure" (Hodge, *Systematic Theology*, 1.589).

100. Cf. Mark 3:13.

101. Phil 2:13.

THE PLANNING MANAGER

> The plans of the diligent lead to profit[102] as surely as haste leads to poverty.[103] (Prov 21:5)

Planning for the future is a consequence of a biblical view of history. At the heart of Christianity is the teaching that Christians are to live with an eye on the future, that Christians are only strangers and aliens in this world. The Christian manager is to focus his attention and marshal his resources on the coming kingdom of God in the present. So, planning for unwelcome realities in the future is an act of discipleship.[104] Planning is prudent in that it protects the organization from the "prodigality of the dreamer."[105] It is part of human nature to plan.[106]

Because planning is such a high form of stewardship ("inquiring of Yahweh"), God is pleased with the planning process and allows us discretion to plan and seek the best method to accomplish his will.[107] In any

---

102. *Mothar* = that which is left over, plenteousness.

103. *Machsor* = want, lack.

104. Cf. Senior, *The Gift of Administration*, 61–65, "unwelcome realities."

105. Cf. Jude 8, "on the strength of their dreams these ungodly people"; Eccl 5:7, "much dreaming and many words are meaningless"; 1 John 4:1, "test the spirits." Vischer puts it bluntly: "Finally, and I am very serious when I say this, beware of your dreams, for dreams make dangerous friends . . . dreams are misplaced longings. False lovers. Why? Because God is enough" (Vischer, *Me, Myself and Bob*, 250).

106. Planning is all over the Old Testament: the Egyptians plan (Isa 19:3, *etsah* = to plan, consult, counsel). Rehoboam rejected the plans of his senior advisors (1 Kgs 12:8), and Absalom rejected Ahithophel's plans (2 Sam 17). Even Yahweh "planned (*etsah*) wonderful things long ago" (Isa 25:1) and "brought them to pass" (Isa 37:26).

107. Cf. 2 Cor 8:10–21. There is a sense, albeit understated, in which consultation with God and the personal apprehending of God's approval is really the only important step in marketplace decisions. The "inquiring" of God before decisions are made is absolutely essential in a Christian life. Rush quotes Steve Crane (a banker in the southeast US) as Crane seeks to make financial decisions for his bank in concert with some of his vice presidents: "I'm sure they think I'm nuts when sometimes I tell them I have to pray about it before I can give them my answer" (Rush, *Lord of the Marketplace*, 23). It is an oft repeated claim that when faced with difficult decisions the business operator seeks God's guidance, and rejects human advice, and goes it alone on the perceived divine guidance. I know a prominent Christian in Colorado who insisted that she sought God's approval alone, and that was enough for her. Galatians 1:16 ("But when God . . . called me . . . I did not consult any man") is used to justify this highly personal and inner leading and illumination by the Holy Spirit when faced with decisions. Indeed, it often appears that God and the Christian businessman have a private understanding of what will please God. Years ago, Stanley Tam, founder of US

Jesus on Specific Responsibilities of a Business Manager

marketplace organization there is never the perfect plan to accomplish God's will; there are only thoughtful business plans, attempting to accomplish God's perfect will.[108] By virtue of establishing a plan of action, a set of objectives for an organization, a Christian business manager takes a decisive step to deliberately and intentionally start or stop an event by not giving birth to a course of action.[109] Thus, planning is very conservative; it is both negative and positive; by its very nature planning seeks stability and reliability and effectiveness. The point of systematic and strategic long- and short-range planning is that planning is required in order to be a good steward of the scarce resources God has given that manager,

---

Plastic Corporation (b. 1915), wrote a book entitled *God Owns My Business*. Stanley Tam legally gave his entire business to God and the profits that have been generated ever since have gone to the spread of the gospel across the world. To date, the business Stanley Tam built (which is wholly owned by a non-profit organization) has generated more than $140 million towards the work of the Lord. In particular, much of the resources have been poured into world evangelism, and just one of the ministries it supports is in over forty-two counties, with 1,600 men going door-to-door sharing the gospel. Mr. Tam considers giving his business to the Lord as simply an act of obedience. R. G. LeTourneau said he had a "partnership with God" in his huge machinery business, R. G. LeTourneau, Inc., and Myron Rush had a divine "business partner." The late corporate executive of Godfather's Pizza, Herman Cain, wrote that his failed campaign for the US presidency in 2012 was part of "God's plan" and that if one joined the "Herman Cain train" then he and his wife would be living in "the People's House at 1600 Pennsylvania Avenue in January 2013" (Cain, *This is Herman Cain*, 96, 157). This terminology is typical of popular business books written by evangelical Christians. LeTourneau wrote, "Now I ask you, what's the use of having a religion that won't work? If I had a religion that limped along during the week, and maybe worked only on Sunday, or while you're in church, I don't think I'd be very sold on it" (LeTourneau, *Mover of Men and Mountains*, 203). Even the fabulously wealthy and culturally Roman Catholic David Koch, after surviving a plane crash in 1991, told ABC's Barbara Walters in 2014, "Thinking back on it later, I felt that the good Lord was sitting on my shoulder and that He helped save my life because He wanted me to do good works and become a good citizen" (ABC News, "David Koch on the Plane Crash That Helped Change His Life"). I applaud the Koch brothers for the many "good works" they have done.

108. Cf. Jas 4:13–16. Drucker, *Management: Tasks, Responsibilities, Practices*, maintains that a manager undertakes five basic responsibilities in an organization: 1. Sets objectives for the organization; 2. Organizes the workers; 3. Motivates and communicates with the workers; 4. Measures performance of the workers and the organization; 5. Develops the workers, including himself. Under "setting objectives" Drucker would place planning, both long-range and short-range. He also believes that any objective setting must consider a balancing judgment between business results and the realization of the philosophic principles one holds dear.

109. Cf. 1 Cor 5:11, "You must not associate with anyone who . . ."; Num 16:20–21, "Separate yourself from this assembly."

and so expert and experienced advice on planning should prayerfully be sought by the manager.[110]

Because of its need for cooperation, a plan, by necessity, involves the organization members, whereas the dreamer can be solitary, and therefore, isolated from reality. One of the duties of a good manager is to help answer the fundamental questions of:

- What is the organization's purpose?
- Why does it exist?
- What impact should it have on the broader community?
- What are the values and principles that guide the decisions and operating procedures of the organization?

THE PLANNING MANAGER IN THE GOSPELS

Jesus the planning manager

> After this, Jesus went around in Galilee, purposely[111] staying away from Judea because the Jews there were waiting to take his life. (John 7:1)

When Jesus was threatened with death, he wisely protected himself by escaping, and when he needed help, he asked for it.[112] There was no mystical *deus ex machina* for a solution or escape; just rationally plausible actions. Jesus believed in long-range planning organized around the accomplishment of a specific set of goals with detailed action steps along the way to help gauge the progress towards reaching those goals.[113] He understood there is a cause-and-effect relationship in God's economy that governs

---

110. Lindell: "I had just turned south on I-35 when I heard an almost audible message: Go to church tomorrow. You are done with gambling. Four days ago, you played your last card. Mind you, I didn't hear a voice. Call it an impression, direction or a guiding hand. Call it whatever you want, but it was clear as a bell . . . By now I understood that these premonitions I'd had all my life weren't premonitions at all. They were God whispering to my heart in that still, small voice spoken of in Scripture. How could I be hearing from God if I didn't have a relationship with Him?" (Lindell, *What Are the Odds*, 271, 280).

111. He would not go to Judea.

112. Cf. John 7:1.

113. Cf. Luke 6:46–49.

Jesus on Specific Responsibilities of a Business Manager

every thought and action, such as, whoever undertakes a project should first of all make sure whether he will be able to finish the project, i.e., short- and long-range planning.[114] He also understood the social costs of not reaching publicly-identified goals.[115] In the normal course of human affairs Jesus did as we would do. He interacted with people as we would interact with people. However, at the same time, he never rationalized his heavenly Father out of his planning and interaction and considerations. And yet Jesus was always available and ready to receive the miraculous intervention of a loving heavenly Father who sent him.

> James and his brother John were in a boat with their father Zebedee preparing[116] their nets. (Matt 4:21)

The brothers were "preparing their nets" to accomplish that for which the nets were designed and made.[117]

---

114. Cf. Luke 14:28–33.

115. Cf. Luke 14:28–33. The miraculous incidents of the feeding of four and five thousand hungry people with only a handful of small fish and a few loaves of bread shows an other-worldly power. This is clearly not the normal way of food preparation for a large convention! In Matthew 10:19–20 Jesus gives some hard-to-understand advice and comfort: "But when they arrest you, do not worry about what to say or how to say it. At that time, you will be given what to say, for it will not be you speaking, but the Spirit of your Father speaking through you."

116. *Katartizo*.

117. "When the soldiers crucified Jesus, they took his clothes . . . with the undergarment remaining. This garment was seamless, woven in one piece from top to bottom" (John 19:23). Employing literary license, but still with some theological truth in evidence here, this seamless robe is indicative of how Jesus in "the days of his flesh" appeared to those around him: Whole, of one piece, unified, no additions, no attachments, no separations—nothing to show a divided mindset, a divided approach to the problems and questions of mankind as Jesus observed them and answered them. Our incarnational approach to others must be of the same whole cloth that Jesus wore. A seamless cloth precluded any danger that two unsuitable or unmatched or incompatible materials had been joined together (double-mindedness)—not totally unlike Matthew 9:16. There ought not to be man-sewn patches of this lifestyle here and there, but rather one unified lifestyle to all people which is consistent with the Master's seamless lifestyle. Paul had this unified lifestyle approach in 1 Cor 1:12–13; 2 Cor 6:14–15; Col 2:6–8; Eph 4:14. As did James in James 1:6–8, and David in Psalm 119:113.

> Watch out[118] for false prophets.[119] They come to you in sheep's clothing, but inwardly[120] they are ferocious wolves. By their fruit you will recognize them. Do people pick grapes from thorn bushes, or figs from thistles? Likewise, every good tree bears good fruit, but a bad tree bears bad fruit. A good tree cannot bear bad fruit, and a bad tree cannot bear good fruit. Every tree that does not bear good fruit is cut down and thrown into the fire. Thus, by their fruit you will recognize them. (Matt 7:15–20)

The focus of Matthew 7:15–20[121] is on bad teachers, and the Lord is contrasting false teachers with true teachers. Clearly, the point of the parable is that false theology leads to a false life, but the principle is applicable to training in business: Bad teaching leads to an unproductive career. Indeed, the Lord's language is sharp: Bad teachers are like "ferocious wolves" who come as harmless "sheep." It is important for the company that the employees get the best training and professional education possible and appropriate for them. Their very income may depend on it. Untrained or poorly trained employees will suffer professionally and economically and not be able to competently do what the Lord has assigned them to do. Bad teachers will present themselves as experts and masters of success so the Christian manager must guard his coworkers from these profiteering charlatans. Unfortunately, these bad teachers are in the business themselves; they are "thorn bushes" and "thistles" and grow abundantly in the business community. When they are exposed by the discerning manager they are to be quickly discarded before they can cause trouble in the business organization. But this discernment will not be so easy, since these false trainers present themselves as solvers of business problems.[122] Bad teaching affects not only the individual worker but the entire organization as a whole.

> Then the king will say to those on his right, "Come, you who are blessed by my Father; take your inheritance, the kingdom

---

118. *Prosecho* = beware, hold towards oneself.

119. "False prophets"; The Greek word translated "bad" (*sapros*) can also be translated "rotten," "worthless," poor quality," "unfit for use." "False prophets" = *pseudoprophetes* = persons who appear on the surface to be something they are not. As a wolf is known for its ferocity it is the natural enemy of the sheep. These false teachers, deceivers, are the natural enemies of the truth and godly productivity.

120. *Esothen*.

121. Cf. Luke 6:43–45.

122. Ps 78:70–72; Matt 25:15; *dunamis* = ability, power.

prepared[123] for you since the creation of the world." (Matt 25:34)[124]

This extraordinary verse lays the foundation for salvation of all Christian managers and their Christian coworkers. All the management good deeds have been planned from before the foundation of the world by a sovereign Creator. While this verse is open to small interpretation differences I see it as telling managers that before they were born God determined that they would be managers of people and that they, therefore, had the responsibility to act accordingly and be faithful to their divine calling. As one scholar has noted, management has been in the plan of God from the very beginning. "Jesus is not speaking of some afterthought but of what God had always planned to bring about."[125] Calvin provides pastoral comfort for the foreordained manager: "In case our minds are cast down by the haunting price of the ungodly, in case our own miseries weaken the strength of our hope, let us always turn our thoughts to our inheritance, which awaits us in heaven: for it does not depend on any uncertain outcome, but was prepared for us from God even before we had been born."[126]

> Therefore, everyone who hears these words of mine and puts them into practice[127] is like a wise[128] man who built his house on the rock. (Matt 7:24)

Jesus compares two contractors. One plans and builds a house on a solid rock foundation, and the other doesn't plan but builds his house on the first type of ground that is convenient. The two houses are indistinguishable from the street, but when trouble comes the builder who planned for trouble is safe and secure and the builder who was expedient is in trouble and will lose everything. When the rains come, when the floods come, when the gales come, it is the manager who thoughtfully planned for the guaranteed storms who will save the organization.

---

123. *Hetoimazo.*

124. "But to sit at my right or left is not for me to grant. These places belong to those for whom they have been prepared (*hetoimazo*)" (Mark 10:40).

125. Morris, *The Gospel According to Matthew*, 637.

126. Calvin, *Matthew, Mark, and Luke*, 3.114.

127. *Poieo* = to do.

128. *Phronimos.*

The entire creation has come into existence by one who has a divine plan to implement. God the Father doesn't give authority even to his son to deviate from his plan. From start to finish Jehovah is a planning God:

> But understand this: If the owner of the house had known at what hour the thief was coming, he would have kept watch[129] and not let his house be broken into. You also must be ready.[130] (Matt 24:43)

In this mini-parable about the misplaced request of James and John, Jesus is telling us that prudent homeowners plan for safety against intruders. Obviously, the application for business managers is that planning provides a modicum of safety for the business. We can't plan for every contingency, but we can make general plans that can minimize problems. Notice that Jesus begins by a strong pro-planning statement: "Understand this!"—literally "Know this!" Furthermore, the Lord urges us to follow the plan ("watch" and "be ready"). Burglaries happen when one least expects it, so the homeowner needs to be constantly on the alert and following his plan for protection. Make a plan and then work the plan for success.

> Then he sent some more servants and said, "Tell those who have been invited that I have prepared[131] my dinner:[132] My oxen and fattened cattle have been butchered, and everything is ready.[133] Come to the wedding banquet." (Matt 22:4)

The focus for us in this parable of the wedding feast is the preparation that the king made for the banquet. "Everything" was done according to a plan; nothing is left to chance or last-minute surprises. The "animals[134] have been slaughtered and the feast has been prepared."[135] The uniqueness of this extensive planned meal is heightened by the unique terms employed. The extensive plans for this banquet get little attention

---

129. *Phulake* = guard.

130. *Hetoimos* = prepared; Luke 12:20; Acts 23:23. Paul tells Philemon to prepare (*hetoimazo*) a guest room for him as he plans to visit Philemon in the near future (Phlm 22).

131. *Hetoimos*.

132. *Aristao* = "meal" occurs in Matthew only here.

133. *Hetoimos*.

134. *Tauros* = "bulls" occurs in the Gospel only here, and *sitistos* = "fattened cattle" occurs in the New Testament only here.

135. Hagner. *Matthew 14–28*, 629.

from the commentators but for us it is a crucial endorsement of the importance of careful and thoughtful planning.

> But while they were on their way to buy the oil, the bridegroom arrived. The virgins who were ready[136] went in with him to the wedding banquet. And the door was shut. (Matt 25:10)

This short parable teaches the importance of preparedness: have a plan and stick to it. There was a festival going on in a small village and the girls were asleep. But before they go to sleep five of the girls worked their plan to have enough oil for their lamps. These girls prepared their lamps by trimming the wicks and adding oil when they could still buy oil. Five girls did not do so. In a last-minute surprise, the groom arrived at night and the wedding was to begin. The unprepared girls scrambled around to find oil for their darkened lamps. They asked the prepared girls for oil for their empty lamps but there was "no oil to spare." Consequently, the foolish girls had to go into the village at night looking for an oil merchant, losing valuable time in the process. The virgins who had planned for all contingencies, including the surprise arrival of the groom, went into the wedding celebration free to enjoy themselves. The girls with a plan were prepared because they had the oil they needed and their appointed inclusion in the festivities was rewarded. On the other hand, the foolish virgins were "a day late and a dollar short" and were excluded from the celebration. They failed because they had no workable plan. Matthew 25:9 teaches the importance of a single-mindedness in being prepared to accomplish the task set before us. Notice that the unprepared girls were not accused of sin or unfaithfulness, but unpreparedness, which still had them being left out of the festivities!

> Jesus said, "Go tell that fox, 'I will drive out demons and heal people today and tomorrow, and on the third day I will reach my goal.[137] In any case, I must keep going today and tomorrow and the next day—for surely no prophet can die outside Jerusalem.'" (Luke 13:32–33)[138]

---

136. *Hetoimos*; cf. Matt 24:44.

137. *Teleloo* = completed, perfected, finish.

138. "The wisdom of the prudent is to give thought [Hebrew = *bin*] to their ways, but the folly of fools is deception . . . A simple man believes anything, but a prudent man gives thought [Hebrew = *bin*] to his steps" (Prov 14:3, 15). The plans (Hebrew = *mahashaba* = thought, intention; Job 5:12; 21:27; Ps 94:1; Prov 20:18; 15:22; 19:21. Note the reference in Jer 18:12 for "plans" [*mahashaba*] which displease) of "the diligent lead to profit as surely as haste leads to poverty" (Prov 21:5); cf. Prov 13:11; 15:22;

In this lament over Jerusalem, Jesus the planning manager sets for himself and his struggling band of disciples a goal of him being crucified in Jerusalem on the Passover. Several planning points are worth mentioning in Jesus' laments over Jerusalem:

- Jesus the planning manager sets the goal for the fledgling organization even though the loose-knit organization didn't even know what the goal entailed.
- Jesus the planning manager knows what his responsibilities are.
- Jesus the planning manager assumes those responsibilities.
- Jesus the planning manager planned a timetable for finishing the task he was sent to do.
- Jesus the planning manager plans to be unstoppable from achieving his goal.
- Jesus the planning manager knows he answers to a higher authority.

> Suppose one of you wants to build a tower. Will he not first sit down and estimate[139] the cost[140] to see if he has enough money to complete it? For if he lays the foundation and is not able to finish it, everyone who see it will ridicule him, saying, "This fellow began to build and was not able to finish." (Luke 14:28–30).

Another couple of short planning parables occur in Luke 14, where Jesus talks about counting the cost in management. The lesson here is to look before you leap.[141] The type of tower being contemplated is irrelevant. What is important is that the Christian business manager needs to count the cost before engaging in any project. Be committed to reality against one's dreams. Interestingly, the cost enunciated by Jesus is not the loss of money on a badly planned tower or faulty construction because of trying to limit the costs, but rather public humiliation and ridicule for the developer, thus diminishing future business opportunities.[142] The picture here is someone sitting down, taking the time to go over the books and

---

19:21; 20:25; 22:3.

139. *Psephizo* = to calculate, to use pebbles, count. Cf. Rev 13:18.

140. *Dapano* = spend, consume.

141. Hendricksen, *Exposition of the Gospel According to Luke*, 736.

142. Being a laughingstock in the community was "far worse in the honor-shame culture of Jesus' day than whatever the capital losses might be" (Edwards, *The Gospel According to Luke*, 428).

reasonably execute a careful plan so that after laying the foundation, one doesn't run out of money to complete the job. Construction planning is not limited to New Testament parables. Yahweh "planned"[143] and executed a construction blueprint of his own in 1 Kings 5 and 6. Just to be sure a businessperson gets this parable Jesus uses two Greek monetary terms: *dapane*, which refers to the expense or cost of a given enterprise, and *psephizo*.

> Or suppose a king is about to go to war against another king. Will he not first sit down and consider[144] whether he is able with ten thousand men to oppose the one coming against him with twenty thousand? If he is not able, he will send a delegation while the other is still a long way off and will ask for terms of peace. (Luke 14:31–32)

In this parable our king must make a plan. The builder of the tower in the previous parable doesn't have to start on his foundation, but the king is forced to make a tough decision. His plans to make war are upset by, after investigation, the realization that the enemy is twice as big and is on the move towards him. There will be conflict. He has two options: to engage and probably be defeated or surrender. He has to change his initial plans and do it quickly. Time is of the essence. The consequences of a bad plan in this case are more disastrous than public ridicule; they are annihilation of his army and probably his death.

The accent of both these little parables is that one must make deliberate and reasonable plans ("first sit down") but be prepared for the unexpected and change those plans ("if he has enough," "is able") to accomplish success.[145]

> And [Jesus] told them this parable: "The ground of a certain rich man produced a good crop. He thought to himself, 'What shall I do? I have no place to store my crops. This is what I will do. I will tear down my barns and build bigger ones, and there I will store all my grain and my goods. And I'll say to myself, 'You have plenty of good things laid up for many years. Take life easy; eat, drink and be merry.' But God said to him, 'You fool! This every night your life will be demanded from you. Then who will

---

143. Isa 22:11 = *yatsar* = fashion, devise, produce. *Yatsar* implies initiation as well as building. It can also refer to constructed thoughts and purposes, i.e., planning.

144. *Bouleuomai* = consult, take counsel, decide, deliberate. Cf. Acts 27:39.

145. Cf. Prov 24:3–6.

get what you have prepared[146] for yourself?' This is how it will be with anyone who stores up[147] things for himself but is not rich toward God." (Luke 12:16–21)

In the parable of the rich foolish farmer, Jesus speaks to business priorities. The money verse for our purposes is 12:16: "The ground of a certain rich man produced a good crop." Here is common grace in action:

- The man was given by God good ground to produce his crops.
- The man was given good health by God to work the ground.
- The man was given intelligence by God to know how to work the ground.

In Luke 12:17–18 we are told that God blessed the man with planning skills: his good ground and hard work created a nice problem, and he investigated how to solve it. In fact, his prosperity outstripped his initial planning, which left him too few barns for storage, so he needed more barns. So far so good. The man was making prudent and intelligent decisions about what to do with his abundance. There is no hint of dishonesty or wickedness. There may be a hint of trouble with all the "my's" and "I's" in 12:17–18, since the farmer is confused about ownership versus stewardship. In 12:19 he said to himself, "I'm going to kick back and relax and enjoy the results of my farming operation.[148] I've got good grass and livestock and vineyard and orchards and money in the bank and I want to enjoy my success and eat, drink, and be merry."[149] Commentators universally condemn the man for his self-indulgence. I don't see it that way, unless one interprets "eating, drinking, and being merry"[150] as a life of sin, indolence, and debauchery. There is nothing to suggest that this man wasn't generous with his money towards his neighbors or synagogue worship, although the repeated use of the first-person pronoun and the phrase "stores up things for himself" in Luke 12:21 implies selfishness, but could just be prudency.

---

146. *Hetoimazo* = provided, to make ready.
147. *Thesaurizo* = to treasure, lay-up; origin of "thesaurus."
148. Cf. Jas 4:13–14.
149. *La dolce vita* = "the good life." Eccl 2:24; 3:13; 5:18; 8:15; Judg 19:4–9; Isa 22:13.
150. *Euphraino* = to be merry, glad, cheerful; 2 Cor 2:2.

Jesus on Specific Responsibilities of a Business Manager

But in Luke 12:20, Jesus calls this rich, successful, hardworking farmer "a fool." In what way is he "a fool"?[151] Not in his planning.[152] Not in his hard work. Not in his foresight. Not in his wanting to relax a bit. He has, though, returned to the wilderness of temptation and believed that he can live by bread alone, for Yahweh does not appear in his thinking.[153] The rich have a tough time getting into heaven because of the iniquitous seduction that invariably comes from the ability to amass wealth which distracts the rich from considering what life is all about.[154] The problem for the rich farmer was that this organization member trusted more in his hard work and earthly wealth than in the God who enabled him to accumulate this wealth.[155] A story is told that a man said to his friend, "I hear that George died. How much did he leave?" His friend replied, "Everything."

Later in Luke 12:47 we read the Lord's warning about not planning: "That servant who knows his master's will and does not get ready[156] or does not do what his master wants will be beaten with many blows." Here the coworker first plans to accomplish what the employer wants but then fails to implement the plan. The implication is that the coworker creates the plan but doesn't follow through. He has the knowledge of what to do but just doesn't do it. This coworker who has the plan and doesn't do it is more culpable than the coworker who hasn't developed a plan out of ignorance. We are reminded that "the presumption in this [parable] is that [coworkers] entrusted with tasks have also been given the wherewithal [by God] to carry them out."[157]

---

151. Kendall notes, "It is God's privilege to call somebody a fool. Only he has the prerogative to do so. You may recall that in the Sermon on the Mount, Jesus warned the people against calling anyone a fool. God, however, can do this because he knows all things . . . When God used this phrase in Jesus' parable, he was speaking to a person who should have known better" (Kendall, *The Parables of Jesus*, 184–85).

152. *Hetoimazo* = provided, to make ready; Acts 23:23; Phlm 22. In the Old Testament *koon* is in Prov 24:27; 30:25.

153. Edwards. *The Gospel According to Luke*, 371.

154. Fitzmyer. *The Gospel According to Luke X–XXIV*, 972.

155. Cf. Matt 6:33.

156. *Hetoimasia* = to prepare, make ready.

157. Fitzmyer. *The Gospel According to Luke X–XXIV*, 992.

The Planning Manager in the Old Testament

> The plans[158] of the diligent[159] lead surely to abundance but everyone who is hasty comes only to poverty. (Prov 21:5)

The proverbial planning manager

This proverb tells us that planning leads to abundance but warns against shortcuts and impulsive actions on the part of the Christian business manager. To succeed in business, one must plan and not act hastily; after all, in the agrarian economy of the Old Testament, the farmer had to be patient with his land. Planning is a hard discipline, and the sage is saying the diligent manager will be wise to plan and follow the plan, in contrast to the impetuous and rash manager. It is important to note that being "hasty" is not equated with being sinful, just unprofitable.[160]

Our God is a planning God.[161] He is a foreordaining God.[162] And he knows that we are planning creatures because we are made in his image. Our plans are to be edifying plans which reflect God's will for us. He warns the organization coworkers not to plan[163] evil against another member of the company.[164] The Jewish organization, after all, had the example of evil plans for Joseph in her tradition.[165] The Bible is full of planning managers.

Solomon the planning manager

> The Proverbs of Solomon . . . for giving prudence to the simple, knowledge and discretion[166] to the young. (Prov 1:4)

---

158. *Machashavah*; Prov 20:18.
159. *Charuts* = sharp, pointed, determined.
160. Like it is in Proverbs 28:20, 25.
161. Gen 50:19.
162. Ps 40:5, "The things you have planned (*machashavah*) for us no one can recount to you."
163. *Machashavah*.
164. Zech 7:10.
165. Gen 50:19.
166. *Mezimma* = shrewdness, cleverness, caginess.

Jesus on Specific Responsibilities of a Business Manager

> The wisdom of the prudent[167] is to give thought[168] to their ways, but the folly of fools is deception . . . A simple man believes anything, but a prudent man gives thought to his steps. (Prov 14:8, 15)

These two verses describe the "prudent" Solomonic planning manager as one who "gives thought" to his actions ("ways," "steps"). In fact, the book of Proverbs is centered around the message contained in these two verses. In Proverbs 1:4 we read that the purpose of the book of Proverbs is to give "prudence," "knowledge," and "discretion" to the young and naïve in order to avoid a superficial analysis of life. The Hebrew word for "discretion" in 1:4 means to "plan" or "devise," the point being that when the "prudent" business manager "gives thought" to his actions he is planning and devising his approach to the problem. 14:8 tells us that wisdom calls for planning and prudence to be present in decision making,[169] and 14:15 tells the business manager that cautionary prudential action will keep him from making mistakes.[170] In fact, Proverbs 17:2 tells us that a prudent manager will save the bacon of a foolish business owner.[171]

- The wisdom of the prudent[172] is to give thought to their ways, but the folly of fools is deception. (Prov 14:8)
- A simple man believes anything, but a prudent[173] man gives thought to his steps. (Prov 14:15)
- He who works his land will have abundant food, but the one who chases fantasies[174] will have his fill of poverty. (Prov 28:19)

---

167. *Aram* = crafty.

168. *Bin* = the faculty of intellectual discernment and interpretation, reason, explicate and internalize the meaning of something. Cf. Waltke, *The Book of Proverbs*, 1.176–177, 2.588–595.

169. Cf. Prov 8:12. Prudence describes one's ability to use reason to navigate the problems of life. It is cautious and deliberate.

170. Cf. Prov 13:16.

171. "A wise servant will rule over a disgraceful son and will share the inheritance as one of the brothers." Longman, *Proverbs*, 343, says ability outweighs birthright. Also see the following passages from Solomon extolling the virtues of planning: Prov 13:11; 15:22; 19:21; 20:25; 22:3.

172. *Arum* = crafty, cunning, sly, subtle.

173. *Arum*.

174. *Req*.

The sage of Proverbs writes to the dreamer. The Hebrew word translated "fantasies" is elsewhere translated "vain" or "empty" or "worthless" or "nothing." "Fantasies" are not defined, but it means anything that is a distraction from the responsibilities at hand, in this case, farming. The writer is warning the reader not to fritter away the current time and resources in daydreams amounting to nothing but a waste of God's provisions.[175] Theologically, Proverbs 28:19[176] joins Proverbs 12:11[177] in exhorting the worker to adhere to Yahweh's social structure of honest, productive work in order to be a contributing member of the community. Dreamers need not apply.[178]

> Be sure you know the condition of your flocks, give careful attention[179] to your herds; for riches do not endure forever and a crown is not secure for all generations. When the hay is removed and new growth appears and the grass from the hills is gathered in, the lambs will provide you with clothing, and the goats with the price of a field. You will have plenty of goat milk to feed you and your family and to nourish your servant girls. (Prov 27:23–27)

The focus of this passage is that "careful attention"[180] to details and long-range planning can help anticipate future reverses in finances. Replace the broken windows lest there become broken walls through negligence. There are no guarantees of long-term wealth or power, but

---

175. Breton writes of the surrealistic attraction to dreams is that the dreamer is able to be whoever he wants to be in whatever kind of world he chooses: "The mind of the man who dreams is fully satisfied by what happens to him. The agonizing question of possibility is no longer pertinent. Kill, fly faster, love to your heart's content. And if you should die, are you not certain of reawakening among the dead? Let yourself be carried along; events will not tolerate your interference. You are nameless. The ease of everything is priceless" (Breton, *Manifestoes of Surrealism*, 13).

176. "He who works his land will have abundant food, but the one who chases fantasies [*req* = vain, empty, vanity] will have his fill of poverty."

177. "He who works his land will have abundant food, but he who chases fantasies lacks judgment."

178. A good example of the lack of discernment or just plain street smarts in the dreamer is the case of Joseph and his relationship with his brothers in Genesis 37 as he tells them of his dreams. Joseph should have kept his dreams to himself.

179. *Yada* = be acquainted with, to know, diligent.

180. "[Steve Jobs's] management mantra was 'focus.' He eliminated excess product lines and cut extraneous features in the new operating system software Apple was developing . . . Thus Steve Jobs became the greatest business executive of our era" (Isaacson. *Steve Jobs*, 359, 566).

prudent planning will pay off in a sustainable condition. Every business manager must take heed to this admonition. Notice that by caring for the health of part of the manager's entrustment (flock, herds, hay, grass) the necessities of life (clothing, food, household goods, place to live) will be taken care of. And not just for the manager's family but for all the families in the organization ("servant girls").

Uzziah the planning manager

> Then all the people of Judah took Uzziah (Azariah)... and made him king... He was the one who rebuilt[181] Elath and restored[182] it to Judah. (2 Chr 26:1–2)

In a brief chapter of only twenty-two verses, the reign of Uzziah, the second longest reigning king in Israel (fifty-two years),[183] details the extraordinary plans put into place by this long-reigning king.[184] And in a remarkable, pro-manager phrase, the Chronicler tells us that the king was "greatly helped until he became powerful."[185] Who "helped" the young king? It was his managerial team[186] and Yahweh.[187]

We get two sources for our information on Uzziah: a government source[188] and a spiritual source.[189]

- Uzziah the planning manager had the wisdom to have as his chief advisor a wise man named Zechariah (not the prophet) "who instructed him in the fear of God" and as long as Uzziah followed Zechariah's advice "God gave him success."[190]

---

181. *Banah* = to build up.
182. *Shub* = to cause to turn back.
183. Shared alternately with his father (twenty-four years) and his son (ten years).
184. Uzziah is mentioned in Isa 1:1; 6:1; Hos 1:1; Amos 1:1; Zech 14:5; 2 Kgs 15.
185. 2 Chr 26:15.
186. 2 Chr 26:5, 10, 11–13, 15.
187. 2 Chr 26:7.
188. 2 Kgs 15:6.
189. 2 Chr 26. Apparently, Uzziah was made king by unanimous acclamation (2 Chr 26:1).
190. *Tsaleach* = to prosper, to go on. Uzziah followed in his grandfather's (Joash's) footsteps by having a wise counsellor: "Joash did what was right in the eyes of Yahweh all the years of Jehoiada the priest" (2 Chr 24:2). When Jehoiada died so did Joash's piety.

- Uzziah the planning manager rebuilt Elath and restored it to Judah.[191]

- Uzziah the planning manager waged successful wars against the Philistines, the Arabs, the Meunites, and the Ammonites on the southwestern border.[192] Uzziah's fame even reached Egypt.[193]

- Uzziah the planning manager rebuilt the towns he destroyed in the territory of the Philistines by colonizing Philistia.

- Uzziah the planning manager strategically built fortified towers at the Corner Gate, the Valley Gate, and the "angle of the wall" in Jerusalem.[194]

- Uzziah the planning manager built fortified towers in the desert to protect his huge livestock herd and to store his produce.[195]

- Uzziah the planning manager dug many cisterns for watering his large livestock herd. Uzziah "could with justice be considered the patron saint of farming."[196]

- Uzziah the planning manager mobilized the people to work in all his vineyards and fields.[197]

- Uzziah the planning manager trained, organized, and equipped a huge army. His army was a well-oiled military machine.[198]

---

191. Elath was an important port city at the head of the Red Sea and gave access to the maritime commerce to the east. Once subdued by Solomon, it had revolted under Jeroboam.

192. Jabneh probably became Jamnia centuries later and was the site of Jewish scholarship for centuries.

193. He even fought the powerful Assyria under Tiglath-Pileser far from home in 742 BC. The northern border fronted on Israel under Jeroboam, who was too strong for Uzziah. Control of the northern city of Jabneh gave Judah control of the area through which Israel would attack Judah as well as the major coastal highway—the "Via Maris" (1 Chr 14:17).

194. This building project was prompted by the destruction caused by the famous earthquake during Uzziah's time, 760 BC (Amos 1:1).

195. 2 Chr 26:10.

196. Dillard, *2 Chronicles*, 209.

197. 2 Chr 26:10.

198. No longer did the soldiers have to provide their own arms as in earlier days, indicating Uzziah's prosperity and planning (1 Sam 13:19–20).

- Uzziah the planning manager made weapons of war to protect Jerusalem.[199]

And all this activity is recorded in just the first fifteen verses of 2 Chronicles 26.

Uzziah the planning manager's great pride led to his downfall, but still "he did right in the eyes of Yahweh."[200] His pride is interesting and understandable. Uzziah's spiritual crime was wanting to offer a sacrifice to Yahweh himself and not to go through the priests. His pride brought him to the point of usurping the honor of the priests' role. He committed a process crime! This was not worship to a false god.[201] Uzziah was enormously successful in multiple endeavors as king with Yahweh's help, so why shouldn't he personally thank God by entering the temple to burn incense to him.[202] Uzziah, however, violated the worship process handed down by Moses by which the priests alone are to govern temple worship, including the rather minor rite of offering incense of thanks. Uzziah can be forgiven for this rule-breaking action at this point. However, his reaction to the priests' chastisement and warning for him to stop indicated that his pride had taken over, and he became angry and insolent.[203] It is unfortunate that his wise advisor, Zechariah, was no doubt dead by this late stage in Uzziah's life, for Uzziah himself was sixty-eight.[204] Yahweh was in turn angry with Uzziah because he did not worship him in the way God has proscribed, so he inflicted the king with a skin disease and Uzziah spent the remainder of his days in royal quarantine. Despite all that Uzziah accomplished in his illustrious reign his funeral obloquy was, tragically, "he had leprosy."[205]

The first part of Uzziah's life was one of godly success and planned accomplishments, but the end of Uzziah's life is a warning that Christian

---

199. 2 Chr 26:15.

200. 2 Chr 26:4; 27:2.

201. Although Uzziah did not destroy the "high places" of worship which Yahweh detested (2 Kgs 15:4).

202. It was the offering of incense that formed the condemnation of King Jeroboam (1 Kgs 12:33).

203. 2 Chr 26:19.

204. 2 Chr 26:3.

205. 2 Chr 26:23.

business managers are to "hold firmly until the end the confidence [in the living God] we had the first."[206]

Jeremiah the planning manager

> But they will reply, "It's no use. We will continue[207] with our own plans;[208] each of us will follow the stubbornness of his evil heart." (Jer 18:12)

The prophet Jeremiah was not a company administrator, but note the reference in Jeremiah 18:12 to management "plans" which displease God. This is a repetition of Jeremiah 2:25 in which the managers tell themselves their plans are useless to accomplish their goals, but they will pursue them nevertheless.[209] In 18:12 we get the admission that the managers know the condition of their thinking and personality ("stubbornly evil") but that doesn't stop them from destructive planning. This is a particularly poignant verse for this admission.

- Jeremiah the planning manager tells us that bad planning managers continue to be bad managers even after they recognize their errors.

Josiah the planning manager

> Prepare[210] yourselves by families in your divisions, according to the directions[211] written by David king of Israel and by his son Solomon. (2 Chricles 35:4)

Josiah king of Judah was a planning king because he told his subjects to prepare for the future. In this one sentence we see several aspects of royal planning and preparation:

---

206. Heb 3:14.
207. *Halak* = to go on.
208. *Mahashaba* = plan, purpose, intentions. Cf. Job 5:12; 21:27; Ps 94:11; Prov 20:18.
209. "Do not run until your feet are bare and your throat is dry. But you said, 'It's no use! I love foreign gods, and I must go after them'" (Jer 2:25).
210. *Kun* = establish.
211. *Kethab* = writings, register.

Jesus on Specific Responsibilities of a Business Manager

- Josiah the planning manager tells the company executive to plan for the future by organizing themselves into workable units.
- Josiah the planning manager directs the planning to follow the written instructions by David and Solomon so there would be unity in the community.[212]
- Josiah the planning manager emphasizes the continuity and authority of David's preparations by mentioning David and Solomon together.

THE PLANNING MANAGER IN THE NEW TESTAMENT

Paul the planning manager

> But one thing I do: Forgetting what is behind and straining[213] toward what is ahead, I press[214] on toward the goal[215] to win the prize for which God has called me heavenward in Christ Jesus. (Phil 3:13–14)

- Paul the planning manager tells the Philippian members of the organization that he has a goal for which he has planned. His planning involves several features:
- Paul the planning manager is aggressive and forceful in his pursuit of the goal. He presses and he takes hold or seizes the sanctification that was given him by Jesus (3:12).
- Paul the planning manager plans to act like he is running a foot race in which he will not look back, presumably at the other runners, but concentrate on his own performance.
- Paul the planning manager plans to "strain" his body so that he will give his all to accomplish his goal. He is prepared to pay the cost for such "straining."

---

212. Now lost, but we do get a hint in various OT passages.
213. *Epekteino* = to reach out, to stretch out.
214. *Dioko* = to pursue, push, drive.
215. *Skopos* = something to look at, fix the eye, to aim at the mark.

- Paul the planning manager adds to his straining by saying that he is driving himself towards his personal goal.[216]
- Paul the planning manager doesn't want just to compete, he wants to win for himself by reaching his goal. The point being not that he wins and others lose, but that he has high expectations for himself.

> Remember this: Whoever sows sparingly[217] will also reap sparingly, and whoever sows generously will also reap generously. (2 Cor 9:6)

Paul the planning manager now addresses the Corinthian branch office, and he uses an agriculture illustration that will be familiar to all his Corinthian readers. Every successful farmer will plan to sow as much seed as he is able in order to reap as much harvest as the ground, weather, and labor will allow. Careful planning in the sowing season will reap benefits in the harvesting season. Tightfisted sowing to save money will result in small return. Plan accordingly. This is a biblical theme from beginning to end: Plan and expect God to bless your sowing.[218]

- Paul the planning manager notes the principle of causation here: Plan for a particular action to result in a particular outcome.
- Paul the planning manager reminds us that faithful sowing may not rebound to the sower but rather someone else in the organization, which is all good under God's sovereign management.[219]

Hebrews and the planning manager

> God had planned[220] something better for us so that only together with us would they reach their goal.[221] (Heb 11:40)[222]

---

216. Life's finish line.
217. *Pheidomenos* = to refrain. Only here in the New Testament.
218. Solomon—Prov 22:8; Hos 8:7; Job 4:8.
219. Cf. Job 31:8; Mic 6:15; John 4:37.
220. *Problepo* = look forward.
221. *Teleloo* = be made perfect.
222. Cf. Ps 37:13.

- The planning manager in Hebrews notes that one generation of workers without the previous generation of workers is imperfect and will not accomplish the original mission of the organization.

This wonderful promise tells us that Yahweh is the master of plans and has planned salvation history so that there is unity between those in the organization in bygone years and the current employees, all sharing in the same tradition and mission statement. There is organic unity in the generations in that the current employees need the example of the perseverance of those that came before them, and those old timers need the benefits of the current workers won for all through the work of the Great Manager.

James the planning manager

> You see that was active along[223] with his works, and faith was completed[224] by his works. (Jas 2:22)

James the planning manager is concerned that his readers do not think that Abraham's faith was mere intellectual assent but rather that the great Old Testament manager put his faith to work in action.

There was intimate synergy or intermingling between Abraham's faith and his works. There is no hint that Abraham was saved by his works, only that you can't have one without the other in order to be a genuine believer. James seems to be suggesting that Abraham's faith accomplished the divinely planned goal when he did what Yahweh wanted him to do.[225] The Jewish commentator Philo seems to get the intent when he writes that Jacob "was made perfect through practice.[226]

- James the planning manager tells us the Christian planning manager needs to realize that words and attitudes taken in the workplace need to be backed up by a plan of action in the marketplace:

---

223. *Synergei* = working with.
224. *Teleioo* = completed, perfected.
225. Cf. Moo, *The Letter of James*, 136–37.
226. Philo, *On the Confusion of Tongues*, 181.

> Now listen, you who say, "Today or tomorrow we will go to this or that city, spend a year there, carry on business[227] and make money."[228] Why, you do not even know what will happen tomorrow. What is your life? You are a mist[229] that appears for a little while and then vanishes. Instead, you ought to say, "If it is the Lord's will, we will live and do this or that." (James 4:13–15)

This Jamesian passage is a warning to business managers about presumptively planning for the future. There seem to be four plans of action coming from the planning managers: we will go to a city, we will spend a year in a city, we will conduct business in a city, we will be successful in a city. These plans involve a map, a calendar, an entrepreneurial spirit, and an optimistic attitude. So far, nothing wrong with these plans. But James is about to lower the boom on these boys. He reminds these corporate capitalists what Solomon wrote in Proverbs 27:1, "Do not boast about tomorrow, for you do not know what a day may bring forth."[230] It is the stated ambiguity and uncertainty of life that needs to be factored into the manager's plans, but in this passage that ambivalence is not a part of the process. Indeed, James will implore the managers to the Lord's sovereignty and providence in their schemes.

These confident planning managers are sure that they can forecast the future and determine the outcome of their actions. While there seems to be bit of uncertainty and waffling about their plans for timing and location there is no lack of confidence in what they can earn by their entrepreneurial labors. This is not a screed against long-range planning or stewardship or profit making. This is a rebuke against not inquiring of the Lord about the future because only he has determined future events. James closes in for the kill in 4:14 when he rhetorically asks the managers how can they presume to know the future a year from now when they

---

227. *Emporeuomai* = trade, emporium, buy and sell. In 2 Peter 2:3, the only other place in the New Testament this term appears, it has the connotation of deceit and cheating. However, there is nothing intrinsic about the morality of commerce resident in this Greek word.

228. *Kerdaino* = gain.

229. *Atmis* = atmosphere. Acts 2:19; LXX Gen 19:28.

230. What Job said in Job 7:7, 9, 16; what David said in 1 Chronlicles 29:15 and Psalm 39:5–6; and Moses said in Psalm 90:4–6. McKnight notes a document from the Dead Sea Scrolls which reads: "Surely a man's way is not his own; neither can any person firm his own step. Surely justification is of God; by His power is the way made perfect. All that shall be, he Foreknows, all this is, his plans establish; apart from him is nothing done" (McKnight, *Letters of James*, 375).

don't know what will happen a minute from now. That is because their humanness is a "mist," a whiff of smoke, an insubstantial and transitory bit of flesh.

And then we come to what some call the "Jacobian condition": "If it is the Lord's will." This is the clear expression of the sovereignty of God and the contingency and dependence upon Jesus to order our activities in a way that pleases him:[231]

- The planning manager must plan with an eye on the Lord's will and in accordance with his word in the Bible.

THE ORGANIZING MANAGER

> For God is not a God of disorder[232] but of peace . . . But everything should be done in a fitting[233] and orderly way.[234] (1 Cor 14:33, 40)

THE ORGANIZING MANAGER IN THE GOSPELS

Jesus the organizing manager

> After this the Lord appointed[235] seventy-two others and sent[236] them two by two ahead of him to every town and place where he was about to go . . . "When you enter a house . . . When you enter a town . . ." (Luke 10:1, 5, 8)

---

231. Matt 6:10; 26:42; Acts 18:21; 21:14; Rom 1:10; 15:32; 1 Cor 4:19; 16:7; Phil 2:19, 24; 1 Pet 3:17. Calvin wrote on the "Jacobian condition": "Let us, however, say it is right and useful, when we make any promise for future time, to make a habit of these expressions, 'God willing,' or, 'God permitting.' . . . the holy servants of God spoke of future events without qualification, although all the time they were sure in their minds that they could do nothing without God's assent" (Calvin, *Matthew, Mark and Luke*, 3.303).

232. *Akatastasia* = confusion, unsettled, tumult, commotion.

233. *Euschemonos* = decently.

234. *Taxis* = arrangement, regularity.

235. *Anadeiknynai* = show up for assignment.

236. *Ekballein* = cast out, dispatched = a stronger term than just "send." It signifies workers not volunteering for the job.

The market for the gospel was growing and so Jesus "appointed" another bigger group to go to the people with his message. Jesus the organizing manager was delegating responsibility for the mission. There were simply too few workers to handle the demand. Whether or not it is seventy or seventy-two is beside the point for us. Whatever the number, the manager was sending out representatives to thirty-five different locations and giving his coworkers the tools they needed to accomplish the assigned tasks. The coworkers must also be aware that they are going into hostile territory and would meet with opponents of their message.[237] The manager gave them the blunt instructions to shake the dust off their feet if they faced rejection, clearly indicating that they were not to try a hard sell to the people.[238] It was a regional effort, and there were communities that needed to hear the message. Luke 10:4 contains four prohibitions given by the manager: Do not take a purse; Do not take a bag; Do not take an extra pair of sandals; Do not greet anyone on the road. This mission was friendship-selling, setting-the-stage promotion. In Luke 10:7 "wages" are mentioned as a reward for their effort, but the manager warns them not to seek better housing. They are to focus on the task at hand: evangelizing. Because the cities undoubtedly contained gentiles, the coworkers were not to worry about dietary restrictions lest insult and humiliation get in the way of the purpose of the trip. In sum:

- Jesus the organizing manager gave his coworkers the instructions as to what they are to do on the trip to the assigned towns.

- Jesus the organizing manager gave his coworkers instructions as to what they were to take on the journey.

- Jesus the organizing manager gave his coworkers instructions as to what they were to do when they entered the assigned town.

- Jesus the organizing manager gave his coworkers the tools[239] needed to accomplish the assigned task.

237. Cf. Matt 10:16.

238. Luke 10:10–11. Edwards comments: "The instruction to shake dust from their feet is a searing judgment. Jews traveling outside Palestine were required to shake themselves free from Gentile dust when returning home, lest they pollute Israel" (Edwards, *The Gospel According to Luke*, 309).

239. John 21:11: "Simon Peter climbed aboard and dragged the net ashore. It was full of large fish, 153, but even with so many the net was not torn." The symbolism here has been interpreted as the unbroken net telling us that the number of Christian converts is unlimited, and the net of the gospel has many more spiritual fish to catch.

Jesus on Specific Responsibilities of a Business Manager 233

- Jesus the organizing manager gave his coworkers instructions as to their conduct during the sales trip.
- Jesus the organizing manager gave his coworkers instructions as to how they are to leave each assigned home and city.
- Jesus the organizing manager gave his coworkers the reasons for their assigned mission and what the general message was to be.

> He called his twelve disciples to him and gave the authority to drive out evil spirits and to cure every kind of disease and sickness. These are the names of the twelve disciples: . . . These twelve Jesus sent out with the following instructions: . . . "He who receives you receives me, and he who receives me receives the one who sent me." After Jesus had finished instructing[240] his twelve disciples, he went on from there to teach and preach in the towns of Galilee. (Matt 10:1–2a, 5a, 40; 11:1)

In yet another executive seminar, Jesus gives instructions to the original twelve managers. In a sketchy fashion, Matthew 10 records the beginning of Jesus' initial organizational principles:

- Jesus the organizing manager hand-picked the hiring of the executive team. It was a personal concern for the manager.[241]
- Jesus the organizing manager built the organization around his vision,[242] and he personally communicated that vision to the twelve managers of the organization.[243]
- Jesus the organizing manager assigned the twelve managers a specific task with specific and detailed instructions and a reporting

---

While this interpretation may be true, what is undeniable is that the tools needed to accomplish the Lord's mission are provided by the Lord. So it is in business. A prayerful manager can rely on Jesus to provide the tools needed to accomplish his business mission. In Luke 5:6 the fish catch breaks the net, but not in John 21. The difference is not explained, since both incidents come about after the Lord told the fishermen what to do.

240. *Diatasso* = command, order.
241. "He called."
242. To drive out evil spirits and to cure every disease and sickness.
243. "Sent out with the following instructions."

time frame.[244] Jesus marked the various aptitudes of his managers and assigned to each the office for which he was fitted.[245]

- Jesus the organizing manager delineated lines of authority, i.e., from God the Father to Jesus the manager to the executive team. And it was understood by them that there was a continuous line of authority[246] whereby if they were rejected, the entire chain of command was rejected. In short, there was a command staff loyalty within the organization.

- Jesus the organizing manager had appointed an executive committee in the leadership structure of the organization because in Matthew 17:1 the manager chose three in the organization to accompany him on a special assignment.

- Jesus the organizing manager delegated the responsibilities, gave the authority, power, message, and loyalty needed to accomplish the tasks, and then he let them go on their own without him looking over their shoulders.[247]

> (About five thousand men were there.) But he said to his disciples, "Have them sit down in groups of about fifty each."[248] (Luke 9:14)

In the narrative of the great feeding of the thousands we have an illustration of that Jesus the organizing manager understood the importance of being organized on a daily basis. This organizational principle of smaller groups of fifty takes us back to Obadiah and Elijah in 1 Kings 18:13 where the exact phrase is used in the Greek LXX.[249]

- The groups of fifty individuals each will give Jesus one hundred such groups to feed, making it easier to distribute food.

---

244. "He who welcomes you welcomes me."

245. He entrusted Philip with the business of supply officer (John 6:5, 8), and, since Judas had an aptitude for finance, he made him treasurer (John 12:4–6; 13:29) (Smith, *The Days of His Flesh*, 153).

246. "One who sent me" to "me" to "you."

247. "After Jesus had finished instructing his twelve disciples, he went on from there to preach and teach."

248. *Ana pentekonta.*

249. I take the 1 Kings reference as a prefigure of Christ.

- Jesus the organizing manager requires that the people in the groups sit down and not wander around, thus making the distribution fair to all and not preferential to some, to say nothing of being easier to count and manage.

THE ORGANIZING MANAGER IN THE OLD TESTAMENT

Moses the organizing manager

We have rudimentary organization management being expressed in Exodus 20. Management authorities have found five key organizational values in the Ten Commandments, as the company organizes herself.[250]

- Moses the organizing manager gives us the first value for any healthy organization: the need to have a clear objective.[251]

- Moses the organizing manager gives us the second foundational value of any organization: the need to establish and maintain a clear line of authority within the organization.[252]

- Moses the organizing manager gives us the third fundamental value that must be expressed in any business organization: committed loyalty from the members to their organization.[253]

---

250. Johnson, "A Biblical Philosophy Girds Godly Organization."

251. That is, any organization needs a central purpose, a mission statement, a reason for existence. The organizing manager must continually set forth that mission, thereby continuing to root the organization to its central *raison d'etre*. Exod 20:3, "You shall have no other gods before me."

252. We see authority both in a position (Elohim = "God") and in a person (Yahweh = "LORD"), combining the formal with the informal; Exod 20:4–6, "no idols." Note also Exodus 18:17–24 for Jethro's advice to Moses for establishing the internal organizational structure for dispensing justice, wisdom, and mercy to Israel.

253. We find this value in Sabbath keeping. Cf. Exod 20:8–12. Green, *More Than a Hobby*, 133–138. For another view from the pew: "The store largely consumed [James Cash] Penney's life and that of his wife; their infant son, Roswell, typically slept beneath the sales counter, and despite their religious convictions, neither gave a thought to shutting down on Sunday even for a church service, as Sundays were typically their busiest day for agricultural trade" (Kruger, *J. C. Penney: The Man, the Store, and American Agriculture*, 21). Penney would later deeply regret this early behavior. The prominent eighteenth-century New York Sabbatarian businessman Arthur Tappan (1786–1865) established a business newspaper, *Journal of Commerce*, and hired an editor who controversially worked on the Lord's Day: "In order that [Tappan] could certify from his own knowledge that, in regard to the Sabbath, the day was not

- Moses the organizing manager gives us the fourth value that is basic to any biblical organization: a sense of responsibility and therefore accountability between the organization and its members, and the members to each other.[254]
- Moses the organizing manager gives us a fifth value that is basic to a genuine biblical organization: prohibitions as part of its core nature.[255]

---

infringed upon by any work connected with the paper, he made it an invariable practice to stand by and see the printing office and editors' office closed at 12 o'clock every Saturday night, and opened every Sunday night at the same hour" (Tappan, *The Life of Arthur Tappan*, 93). The Enlows relate a World War II incident at Correct Craft in Florida where the company made an amazing four hundred boats in fifteen days without working on Sunday in order to fulfill a US government wartime emergency need. They conclude, "visitors from all parts of the United States, for many weeks thereafter, came to see the place where a company could build four hundred boats in fifteen days without infringing on the Lord's Day." The Meloons attributed all honor to God who had led and strengthened them: "To us it was simply an indication that the Lord honors the obedience of His children" (Enlow and Enlow, *Saved from Bankruptcy*, 15). It is ironic that the Meloons' company went bankrupt years later and, after revitalization, the main ministry of the Meloon family business evolved into successful bankruptcy counselling for Christian businesspeople—Kingdom Advisors. Perhaps the most famous Sabbatarian national business in contemporary America is Chick-fil-A. From its beginning, the restaurant has been closed on Sunday out of principle and practicality. Truett Cathy, the founder of the restaurant chain and a serious Christian, has stated that people don't eat at Chick-fil-A because the restaurant is closed on Sunday. They eat there because the "food tastes good and we honor our customers" (Cathy, *How Did You Do It, Truett?*, 42). See Cathy's discussion of Sunday closing for his restaurants, Cathy, *How Did You Do It, Truett?*, 55–60. The organization must have clear methods of evaluation of performance and clear rewards and consequences for the level of stewardship among its membership. This principle is found in Exodus 20:7 ("you shall not misuse the name"; cf. Matt 10:40–42). Loyalty within a business organization is a two-way street, though. The individual must be loyal to the organization's goals and mission, but the organization must likewise be loyal to meet the individual's needs and goals. The Christian organizing manager must attempt to increase the degree of overlap between the organization's goals and the member's goals. To the degree that the goals are different there is a dysfunctional relationship between the individual and the organization; for such dysfunction, note Korah and the prominent men opposing Moses in Numbers 16:1–3, 19–21.

254. 2 Cor 9:3. Miller and Bedford, *Culture without Accountability*. Cf. the parable of the talents in Matthew 25:14–30. Paul wrote to the Galatians, "The one who is throwing you into confusion will pay the penalty [*krima* = judgment, punishment], whoever he may be," clearly indicating that the concept of accountability shows no partiality (Gal 5:10).

255. Cf. Exod 20:13–17. The organization must set limitations on permissible activities of its members and permissible expenditures of God-given resources available

There is a theology of Old Testament management change called "appointment history" which covers four transitions of organizational leadership by sovereign "appointment" from Yahweh:

1. Moses and Jethro.[256]
2. Managers appointed to help Moses.[257]
3. Joshua is appointed to succeed Moses.[258]
4. Managers appointed to lead the organization into the promised land.[259]

David the organizing manager

> A larger number of leaders were found among Eleazar's descendants than among Ithamar's . . . They divided them impartially by casting lots. (1 Chr 24:4–5)

David was prohibited by Yahweh from building the temple because of his past military actions. But that didn't stop him from organizing the temple activities, and in 1 Chronicles 24 we have him organizing the leading priest for temple worship. Of interest for us is the way he organized the personnel. Two brief verses tell us his methodology. In 24:4 we have him picking the best or chief[260] priests for the more extensive duties. The Hebrew term used to describe the Levites from the family of Eleazar means "captain," "best," "head."[261] In the Greek LXX the word is used by Jesus[262]

---

to the organization. In short, self-control is part of any effective organization (cf. the Ten Commandments reiterated in Rom 13:8–10—"do nots").

256. Exod 18:13–26; "select," "appoint," Hebrew = *chazah*; Greek LXX = *episkeptomai*.

257. Num 11:1–25.

258. Num 27:12–23; "appoint," "set over" Hebrew = *paqad*. Greek LXX = *episkeptomai*.

259. Deut 1:9–18.

260. *Rosh*. Some commentators translate the word "numerous" meaning greater number but that usage is not employed elsewhere in the Bible.

261. In 1 Chronicles 24:5 we see the phrase "officials of God" or "governors of the sanctuary" or "sacred officers." The Hebrew term us here is the familiar *sar* meaning "chief," "ruler," "manager," or "steward."

262. Matt 21:42.

and Paul[263] to signify "head." Eleazar was given the management of the Levites and had charge of the tabernacle and all within it.[264] On the death of his father, Aaron, Eleazar became chief religious manager (high priest) of the church. The Levitical family of Eleazar is the dominant priestly family in the post-exilic church. Ezra was of the family of Eleazar,[265] and a descendent of Eleazar was the chief religious manager up to the time of the Maccabees. In 1 Chronicles 24:5 we read that despite the excellence of the Eleazar managers causing them to have more responsibilities, the Ithamar managers were not excluded from exercising their gifts in temple management.

Management lessons to be learned in this 1 Chronicles 24 Davidic episode:

- From among the leadeing managers in the organization, David chose the most excellent managers to carry the burden of the organization.
- After choosing the best managers to organize company responsibilities, David made sure that all the managers had roles to play and were given the recognition of leadership.

> This is the list of the Israelites—heads of families, managers[266] of thousands and managers of hundreds, and their managers,[267] who served[268] the king . . . David summoned all the officials[269] of Israel to assemble at Jerusalem: the managers[270] over the tribes, the managers of the divisions in the service of the king, the managers of thousands and managers of hundreds, and the managers[271] in charge of all the property and livestock belongs to the king and his sons, together with the palace managers.[272] (1 Chr 27:1; 28:1)

---

263. Eph 5:23.
264. Num 3:32.
265. Ezra 7:1.
266. *Sar* = commander, leader, stewards.
267. *Saris* = officers.
268. *Sharath*.
269. *Sar* = officers.
270. *Sar*.
271. *Sar* = stewards.
272. *Saris*.

Jesus on Specific Responsibilities of a Business Manager

In this important chapter on the organization of the Old Testament company we have David organizing the three major facets of secular company life in a hostile environment: the miliary managers (27:1–15), the community managers (27:16–24), and the administrative managers (27:25–34). David's administration is summed up in 28:1. The Chronicler uses the noun *sar* repeatedly to refer to the company managers who had leadership responsibilities. The army managers (commanders) and the tribal managers (chiefs) don't concern us as much as the administrative managers. These seven verses detailing the commercial managers of the organization are unique in the Old Testament. The advisory role of the five individuals in 27:32–34 seem to be less institutional and more informal in the administration of the government. Then we have the general of the army, Joab, mentioned in 27:34, tying the earlier verses to David's royal cabinet. This chapter is, by far, the most extensive list of managers in David's government.[273] Not much information to go on about David's managerial team. We will get much more about the maturing of the administrative state under Solomon.[274] But in 1 Chr 27:25–34 we do get some intriguing information about David's managerial actions. David set up storehouses in the capital city (royal Jerusalem) and in the flyover country (outlying districts). David appointed a manager of his workforce (field workers). And he appointed different field managers over not only the vineyard but the produce of the vineyards and did the same with the orchards and the produce of the orchards. And then he divided his livestock managers into those who managed his herds in the rich coastal fields[275] and those that managed in the loamy valleys. He hired managers with specialized expertise over their particular animals: a manager for the camels,[276] one for the donkeys, and one for the fowls. Finally, we get a brief look at the various governmental advisors surrounding the chief operating officer, David.

Managerial lessons to be learned from 1 Chronicles 27:25–34:

- There are four spheres of managerial responsibilities outlined in this chapter: those managers responsible for the company's wealth, those managers responsible for the company's agriculture production,

---

273. Previous to this we only have the snippets of 2 Samuel 18:15-18; 20:23–26; and 1 Chronicles 18:14–17.

274. 1 Kgs 4–5 and 9–10.

275. "Sharon," which was managed by a local Sharonite. Cf Isa 65:10.

276. *Obil* means "Camel driver." Obil was not an Israelite but an Ishmaelite!

those managers responsible for the company's livestock care and maintenance, and those managers responsible for the efficient running of the company.

The Organizing Manager in the New Testament

Peter the organizing manager

> Now those who had been scattered by the persecution in connection with Stephen traveled as far as Phoenicia, Cyprus, and Antioch, telling the message only to Jews. Some of them, however, men from Cyprus and Cyrene, went to Antioch and began to speak to Greeks also, telling them the good news about the Lord Jesus. (Acts 11:19–20)

The organizing manager must manage for future change. This organizing is a critical aspect of management, and it is highlighted in Acts 11. With the growth of the company and the accompanying persecution, and with the conversions of gentiles, the company had to make organizational changes in structure and thinking. These changes took management leadership and so the Council of Jerusalem (Acts 15) was called to deal with the issue. The organization rapidly became a regional operation and not just a local one, and this necessitated branch offices with managers and structures and procedural manuals. Adaptation was required and so the managers had to develop organizational structures that would enable the community to survive and prosper. There is even a hint that physical structures needed remodeling to fit the growing organization.[277]

Paul the organization manager

> And in the church God has appointed those . . . with gifts of administration. (1 Cor 12:18)[278]

[277]. The fourth-century pilgrim Egeria visited this church and described it (as preserved by Petrus Diaconus in 1137) as follows: "The house of the prince of the Apostles in Capernaum was changed into a church; the walls, however, are still standing as they were" (Early Church History, "Peter's Home in Capernaum Found"). This house-church would further go under modification in the fifth century AD. The old churches were filled in with dirt and an octagonal church was built on its new platform.

[278]. Kubernesis = directorship, governments (1 Cor 12:28). This is one of those key verses for those looking at management in the Bible. But the exact meaning of

- Paul the organizing manager tells us of the spiritual gift of "administration." As noted elsewhere, the Greek word Paul uses here is *kubernesis*, meaning a pilot of a ship or guide.[279] Hodge translates this Greek word as "governments," which is the spiritual gift of governing an organization.[280] To counter the claim that the Greek word means "administration" or "management" is too modern to be applied to the first century organization one only needs to see

---

kubernesis is a bit cloudy. It is used elsewhere in the New Testament for steering or guiding a ship (cf. Acts 27:11; Rev 18:17) but that is about it. In the Greek Old Testament this term is translated in Proverbs as "guidance," as in guiding a ship (Prov 1:5; 11:14; 12:15; 24:6). In his 1 Corinthians 12 list of spiritual gifts, Paul does not attach supernatural endowments to the gifts of management. Notice that management gifting is plural, "gifts." For Paul, management is a gift of service. Fee maintains that a better translation of kubernesis is "acts of guidance" (as it is in the Greek LXX) and not "administration" or "management." It doesn't make any difference if the captain is the actual one doing the steering, since he is ultimately responsible for his senior management team for the direction of the ship. Beyer, writing in the *Theological Dictionary of the New Testament* on *kubernesis*, states, "The importance of the helmsman increases in a time of storm. The office of directing a congregation may well have developed, especially in emergencies, both within and without... No society can exist without some order and direction, it is the grace of God to give gifts which equip for government" (Beyer, "Kubernesis," 3.1035–37). The gifts of management are unique in several ways from the list of spiritual gifts in 1 Corinthians or in Romans 12:8. While the management gifts are from God, they are gifts that can be improved upon through training, experience, and education. It is noteworthy that the gift of helps (*antilepsis* Acts 20:35; 1 Thess 5:14 = "helping the weak") immediately precedes the gifts of management, since they are locked together in managing an organization. The management duties of those with the gift of helps probably include care for the finances and arranging for services of the organization. The gifts of management are used to help others accomplish their mission and to lead and manage the organization's affairs. Christian business managers are not primarily the teachers, nor necessarily the spiritual leaders, of the organization, but the intelligence and morality of the managers' lifestyle is critical in leading a company. Beyer points out that if necessary, "any member of the congregation may step in to serve as ruler. Hence these offices, as distinct from those mentioned in 1 Corinthians 12:29, may be elective. But this does not alter the fact that for their proper discharge the 'charisma' of God is indispensable" (Beyer, "Kubenesis," 3.1036).

279. LXX Prov 1:5; 11:14; 24:6.

280. Hodge, *Exposition of the First Epistle to the Corinthians*, 262. Morris suggests that the Greek term has the meaning of direction, but it is too vague to really pin down (Morris, *The First Epistle to the Corinthians*, 173). Grosheide thinks that 1 Timothy 5:17 "indicates that there were elders who ruled without laboring in the word and in doctrine. Those men were charged not so much with the administration of external things as perhaps the 'helps' were, but rather with the spiritual leadership" (Grosheide, *Commentary on the First Epistle to the Corinthians*, 299).

company-planting endeavors in the New Testament to notice that some management was needed in the young congregations.

- Every act of appointing, calling together, arranging, strengthening, being sent, is an act of organizing or administration, and is found throughout the history of the New Testament organization.[281]

THE MOTIVATING MANAGER

> Whatever you do, work at it with all your heart,[282] as working for the Lord, not for men. (Col 3:23)

The manager's job has always been to keep the organization focused on point and progressing towards her goal and to get his coworkers to move forward to accomplish the mission of the organization. Yahweh is the Great Motivating Manager.

> So Yahweh stirred[283] up the spirit[284] of Zerubbabel son of Shealtiel, governor of Judah, and the spirit of Joshua, son of Jehozadak, the high priest, and the spirit of the whole remnant of the people. They came and began to work on the house of Yahweh Almighty, their God. (Hag 1:14)

Notice that Yahweh started with the managers of the organization and worked down to the members. First the leaders, then the followers. There was complete buy-in in the organization. After being "stirred up" by God the people:

- "Came" to Jerusalem ready to work on the goal of the organization.
- "Began to work" on the goal of the organization.

---

281. Cf. Acts 11:26; 14:23, 27; 15:2, 41; 16:5; 20:13; 1 Cor 7:17; 9:14; 16:15–18; 2 Cor 8:19; Phil 1:1; 1 Thess 5:12; 1 Tim 5:17; Titus 1:5; 1 Pet 5:1–2; 2 John 1; 3 John 1; among others.

282. *Psuche* = animal spirit.

283. *Oor* = wake up, lift up. Yahweh used his power to "stir up" unbelievers as well: 1 Chr 5:26; 2 Chr 21:16; Ezra 1:1; Isa 41:2; Jer 50:9; 51:1, 11.

284. *Ruah* = wind.

THE MOTIVATING MANAGER IN THE GOSPELS

Jesus the motivating manager

> His master replied, "Well done, good and faithful [employee]![285] You have been faithful with a few things; I will put you in charge[286] of many things. Come and share your [manager]'s[287] happiness!" (Matt 25:23)

In the parable of the talents, Jesus shows us the difference in results in ownership versus non-ownership of the manager's objectives (Matt 25:14–30). The five-talent and two-talent workers each return their entrustment to the manager with the words, "Master, you have entrusted me with two [or five] talents. See, I have gained two [or five] talents more." Each of these workers considered the manager's talents to be his own talents.[288] On the other hand, the one-talent worker considered the money to be "his master's" alone[289] and returned it as such.[290] Matthew marks the personal investment of the first two workers in generating a "profit" for the business manager.[291] Even though the first two workers received a different amount to invest their accolade from the owner/manager was the same.[292]

- The motivating manager expected them to work whatever was given to them, regardless of the risk, in the most responsible way without jealousy or envy of others.

---

285. *Doulos*.

286. *Kathistemi* = ruler, to make somebody something, to set in place, to place in an office; cf. Acts 6:3.

287. *Kurios* = boss, lord.

288. "His own money," Matt 25:16–17.

289. Matt 25:18.

290. "See, here is what belongs to you," Matt 25:25.

291. France calls this "a model for enthusiastic discipleship" (France, *The Gospel of Matthew*, 954).

292. "Well done, good and faithful servant," Matt 25:21, 23.

The Motivating Manager in the Old Testament

Abraham the motivating manager

> When Abraham heard that his relative had been taken captive, he called out the 318 trained[293] men born in his household and went in pursuit as far as Dan. (Gen 14:14)

We have already seen this important notation of Abraham being a manger in his organization. And we will look at this verse later as a training manager. But note here Abraham being a motivating manager. His domestic cohort probably numbered a thousand if he can muster 318 fight men out of his domestic group. In this short episode we see that:

- Abraham the motivating manager prepared for future contingencies by recruiting and training a cadre of fighting men to protect his organization.

- Abraham the motiving manager mobilized and led his 318 trained warriors in a nocturnal attack which routed the four opposing armies.[294]

- Abraham the motivating manager was successful. Witness the fact that his sizable but still small private army could defeat the combined forces of four kingdoms, which indicates the level of motivation with which the army of Abraham fought. Genesis 14:16 indicates how deep the motivation of Abraham's army was because they "recovered," "brought back" "goods," "possessions," "woman," "other people." Notice all the duplication.

Moses the motivating manager

> Then Yahweh said to Moses, "Why are you crying out to me? Tell the Israelites to move on."[295] (Exod 14:15)

Yahweh is telling Moses to man up, quit whining, tell the organization to quit whining (14:10), and move on to the next stage of his purpose. And

---

293. *Hanik* = instructor, found nowhere else in the Bible.
294. Gen 14:15.
295. *Naca* = to go forward, to start, to pull up stakes.

Jesus on Specific Responsibilities of a Business Manager 245

move out the organization did! Whether Yahweh is addressing Moses personally as the motivating manager of the group or as the spokesman for the group, the message is the same: Get the group off their rears and move on in obedience towards the goal of the organization.

> When you are harvesting in your field and you overlook a sheaf, do not go back to get it. Leave it for the alien, the fatherless and the widow, so that Yahweh your God may bless you in all the work of your hands. When you beat the olives from your trees, do not go over the branches a second time. Leave what remains for the alien, the fatherless and the widow. When you harvest the grapes in your vineyard, do not go over the vine again. Leave what remains for the alien, the fatherless and the widows. Remember[296] that you were slaves in Egypt. That is why I command you to do this. (Deut 24:19–22)

- Moses the motivating manager gives six gleaning commands to the farmer in this passage: two concerning wheat, two concerning olives, and two concerning grapes. The point is that when the farmer is harvesting his crop he is going to miss stuff. He will be inefficient in gathering his crop. But he is not to go back over the field and clean it bare. Moses the motivating manager tells the farmer that he is to leave the results of his lack of complete harvesting to his poor neighbors. This leaving behind is to remind the Jewish farmer that the land and the produce belong to Yahweh in the first place and the farmer is blessed to have use of it. Turning to the poor, Moses tells them that the remainder is theirs if they go get it. No hand-outs. They have to engage in a mini-harvest themselves. A hand-up, not a handout.

- Moses the motivating manager reminds the wealthy that what he has comes from a beneficent God.

- Moses the motivating manager reminds the poor that a gracious God provides for him by giving him a healthy body to do the work.

- Moses the motivating manager reminds everyone that the basic idea of this law is that all members of the community are to share in the blessings of Yahweh through work and effort. Ultimately, the resources of the company (land, produce, etc.) are a gift from God,

---

296. *Zakar* = imprint.

and it is up to the manager to see that all employees participate in the goodness of God.

> Then Moses went out and spoke these words to all Israel: "I am now a hundred and twenty years old and I am no longer able to lead you. Yahweh has said to me, 'You shall not cross the Jordan.' Yahweh your God himself will cross over ahead of you. He will destroy these nations before you, and you will take possession of their land. Joshua also will cross over ahead of you, as Yahweh said. And Yahweh will do to them what he did to Sihon and Og, the kings of the Amorites, whom he destroyed along with their land. Yahweh will deliver them to you, and you must do to them all that I have commanded you. Be strong[297] and courageous.[298] Do not be afraid[299] or terrified[300] because of them, for Yahweh your God goes with you; he will never leave[301] you nor forsake[302] you." Then Moses summoned Joshua and said to him in the presence of all Israel, "Be strong and courageous, for you must go with this people into the land that Yahweh swore to their forefathers to give them, and you must divide[303] it among them as their inheritance." (Deut 31:1–7)

This passage is a long but very interesting look at how a motivating manager leads his company. The setting is that Moses is about to die and the management of the company is about to change hands to Joshua. Moses is giving his final speech to the organization:

- Moses the motivating manager immediately begins by publicly recognizing his failing abilities and the effect of old age on his leadership.[304]
- Moses the motivating manager is utterly transparent with the organization by saying that he is too old and frail to continue as CEO.

---

297. *Chazaq* = firm, valient.
298. *Amats* = strong, hard, steadfast.
299. *Yare* = tremble.
300. *Arats* = frightened.
301. *Raphah* = relax, fail, feeble.
302. *Azar* = set free, loosen, abandon.
303. *Nathan*.
304. Moses was a grandfather.

- Moses the motivating manager is transparent in his relationship with Yahweh who has told him that because of his past sins he will not lead the organization into the next phase of its existence.[305]
- Moses the motivating manager formally announces his endorsement of Yahweh's chosen replacement, Joshua.
- Moses the motivating manager tells the organization what to expect from Joshua: he will go before the group to the next phase so that there will be no lapse in godly leadership.
- Moses the motivating manager tells the organization that the mission will be accomplished under the new leadership just like it was under him.
- Moses the motivating manager assures the organization that the help and support given during the time of Moses will continue unabated so that there is no reason to be anxious or worried.
- Moses the motivating manager tells the organization to be strong and courageous because there is nothing to fear about the future because of Yahweh's continued presence and the new leadership of Joshua.
- Moses the motivating manager tells the organization that Joshua will not only be the leader in battle but also the leader in managing the domestic affairs of the group once settled.

With such a handoff and motivating speech from the great lawgiver, it is no wonder that during the lifetime of Joshua the organization was largely true to its mission and accomplished its goals.[306]

Joshua the motivating manager

> Yahweh said to Joshua . . . "Be strong and courageous, because you will lead these people to inherit the land I swore to their forefathers to give them. Be strong and very courageous. Be careful to obey all the law my servant Moses gave you; do not turn from it to the right or to the left, that you may be successful wherever you go. Do not let this Book of the Law depart from your mouth; meditate on it day and night so that you may be

---

305. Radical transparency and honesty.
306. Josh 24:31.

careful to do everything written in it. Then you will be prosperous and successful. Have I not commanded you? Be strong and courageous. Do not be terrified; do not be discouraged, for the LORD your God will be with you wherever you go" . . . So Joshua ordered the officers of the people: "Go through the camp and tell the people, 'Get your supplies ready. Three days from now you will cross the Jordan here to go in and take possession of the land the LORD your God is giving you for your own.'" Then the people answered Joshua, "Whatever you have commanded us we will do, and where you send us we will go." (Josh 1:6–11, 16)[307]

Still another long example of excellent organizational communication. Joshua is doing some pretty effective and direct organizational communicating in Joshua 1:10–11:

- Joshua the motivating manager is telling his organization what to do, with whom to do it, where to do it, when to do it, and the personal benefit for doing what it was going to do.

Solomon the motivating manager

Acquitting[308] the guilty and condemning[309] the innocent—Yahweh detests them both. (Prov 17:15)

It is not good to be partial[310] to the wicked or to deprive[311] the innocent of justice. (Prov 18:5)

Solomon the motivating manager is telling the business manager not to be partial in treatment of his employees. Partiality is a sure way of killing motivation. He says that showing partiality is literally "lifting up (raising) the face" of the employee showing underserved favor. The setting is that one who has authority and is superior in rank reaches down to the worker and causes him to rise up and be recognized. What an encouragement for the worker. Yet, if the praise is underserved and the praiseworthy are unrecognized, havoc will reign in the organization and the structure will

---

307. Cf. Num 14:5–9; Judg 7:15–18, 21; Neh 4:14.
308. *Tsadaq* = to clear oneself.
309. *Rasha* = to vex, act mischievously.
310. *Nasa* = to lift up, raise.
311. *Natah* = stretch out, incline, overthrow.

Jesus on Specific Responsibilities of a Business Manager   249

eventually collapse. No one will be motivated to give their best effort to the company. This proverb shows the power of partiality. The Proverbs are filled with admonitions not to praise the worthless employee while neglecting the worthwhile worker. The context is almost always in a courtroom, so the point is for a legal judgment. However, the principle is applicable to the workplace setting of treatment of employees.[312] Proverbs is filled with negative stir-up passages.[313] A great challenge for the motivating manager is to be a calming influence in the company. All this negative motivation is offset by the beautiful Psalm 45:1: "My heart is stirred[314] by a noble theme."

Nehemiah the motivating manager

> Then [Nehemiah] said to them, "You see the trouble[315] we are in: Jerusalem lies in ruins, and its gates have been burned with fire. Come, let us rebuild the wall of Jerusalem, and we will no longer be in disgrace."[316] I also told them about the gracious[317] hand of my God upon me and what the king has said to me." They replied, "Let us start rebuilding."[318] So they began this good[319] work. (Neh 2:17–18)

Nehemiah confronts the complacent organization that has grown used to a shameful situation and learned to live with a city in shambles. But here comes Nehemiah the motivating manager from outside the city seeking to stir up the troops to restore the glory of the capital. Note the motivating aspects of Nehemiah's marvelous speech to the organization:

- Nehemiah the motivating manager is utterly transparent and honest: "It is plain to see that our organization is in trouble. It is up to us to repair the damage."

---

312. Cf. Prov 17:15; 18:21; "A hot-tempered man stirs up [*garah* = This strong word is used in a military context of stirring up for battle] dissension [*madon* = strife, contention], but a patient man calms a quarrel" (Prov 15:18).

313. Prov 10:12; 15:1; 28:25; 29:22.

314. *Rachash* = to prompt, to boil over.

315. *Ra* = distress, sadness.

316. *Cherpah* = shame, scorn, dishonor.

317. *Tob*.

318. *Barah* = rise up and build.

319. *Tob* = literally: strengthened their hands.

- Nehemiah the motivating manager tells the current organization that it has a debt to those who went before them to solve the problem. "Our headquarters is a disgrace and a reproach to our mission."
- Nehemiah the motivating manager, assures the organization that God has the back of the manager and has commissioned him to solve the problem.
- Nehemiah, the motivating manager assures the organization that the secular authorities have given the company the permission to solve the problem.

The result of Nehemiah's management was that the workers responded to his leadership and marched forth to do a good work and accomplish the goals of the organization.

Rehoboam the motivating manager

> But Rehoboam rejected the advice the elders gave him and consulted the young men who had grown up with him and were serving him. (1 Kgs 12:8)

A stunning example of bad managerial motivation through an ill-advised organizational communication is given in 1 Kings 12 and King Rehoboam's communication methodology with the organization which he managed. When the organization's members spoke to Rehoboam the motivating manager they felt like he didn't listen to them, much less treat their ideas with integrity.[320] Rehoboam failed to be sensitive to what was being communicated to him by the people, and he failed to use discernment in communicating his concerns and desires for the company when he spoke and dealt with his organization. Thus, the organization was fractured and ceased to accomplish the goals for which it was created.

THE MOTIVATING MANAGER IN THE NEW TESTAMENT

Paul the motivating manager

> Do you not know that in a race all the runners run, but only one gets the prize? Run in such a way as to get the prize. Everyone

---

320. See Case, "Rehoboam: A Study in Failed Leadership." Cf. Appendix.

Jesus on Specific Responsibilities of a Business Manager 251

who completes[321] in the games goes into strict training. They do it to get a crown that will not last, but we do it to get a crown that will last forever. Therefore, I do not run like a man running aimlessly; I do not fight like a man beating the air. No, I beat my body and make it my slave so that after I have preached to others, I myself will not be disqualified[322] for the prize. (1 Cor 9:24–27).

This is an interesting passage on motivation. The motivation for engaging in a business enterprise is to become profitable and pleasing to God in the process. Paul the motivating manager is obviously primarily referring to living a Christian life now in light of eternity. But as he makes his points applicable, principles jump out at us if we are sensitive to a business application:

- Paul the motivating manager begins this paragraph by taking for granted that the Corinthians knew the ground rules of Christian living ("Do you not know?"). No ignorance can be claimed. Christian business managers know what is expected of them by the Lord.

- Paul the motivating manager reminds the Christian business managers to conduct their business practices as if they are winners. Managers are to run their business as if they are the victors in the Grecian games, even if they lose.

- Paul the motivating manager tells the business managers they are to conduct their professional lives with necessary discipline[323] and training[324] because they know the goal of their business has eternal ramifications as well as the monthly profit-and-loss statement. They know, with certainty, where they are headed.

- Paul the motivating manager tells the business manager that in the process of self-discipline, they know who the real enemy is—their own sinful mindset. God has given them all they need to succeed.

- Paul the motivating manager tells the managers that it is up to them to marshal what God has given them to accomplish the task he has set before them. They know the goal. They know the kind of focus

321. *Agonizomai* = contend, fight, wrestle.
322. *Adokimos* = unapproved, unworthy.
323. *Egkrateuetai* = training, mastering, controlling, 1 Cor 7:9.
324. Plato noted that ten months of rigorous training were required to compete in the games (Plato, *Laws*, 840a).

needed to accomplish the goal. They have met the enemy and the enemy is them.[325]

- Paul the motivating manager reminds the managers that while they are to run their companies as victors and champions, there is no guarantee that they will not fail and disappoint Jesus. Paul tells them that just by entering the race they will get a prize.[326] So there is no connection between entering the race and winning. The Christian business manager races because that is the only option he has.

- Paul the motivating manager acknowledges that the Christian managers are constantly evaluating and judging themselves and comparing themselves to the marketplace competitors in order to improve their game.

- Paul the motivating manager knows that in order to motivate members of a business organization the manager must communicate the goals and mission and aspirations of the organization to the members in such a way that the members adopt those organizational goals as their own—with personal buy-in and accountability attached to their individual stewardship.[327]

In motivating a business organization, justice and integrity are more important than analysis and efficiency. The most critical aspect of motivating a work force within an organization is the transference of vision and mission from the manager to the managed. If the worker is to be motivated to full potential stewardship that worker must accept ownership and buy-in of the manager's objectives for the organization. This acceptance can come as a result of jointly arriving at the organizational objectives, or it can be transferred from the top down, or it can be transferred from the bottom up, but in any case it must be accepted and internalized as the objective of both the managed and the manager. The goals must be seen to be just and fair to all concerned, and the employee must believe that his/her contribution is vital to the success of the organization.

The greatest motivating message a Christian business manager can impart to that manager's organization is the idea of personal

---

325. Cf. Rom 7.

326. Cf. Phil 3:12–21.

327. See Walton, "Communicate, Communicate, Communicate," *Sam Walton: Made in America*, 282–85; Vischer, "Lesson 7: Build a Team that Rows in the Same Direction," *Me, Myself and Bob*, 222–23; Zabloski, "Communication," *The Twenty-five Most Common Problems in Business*, 35–55.

Jesus on Specific Responsibilities of a Business Manager

stewardship—"Be all you can be." If a worker performs with the view that she never wants to have to say, "If only I had done that at that time," then stewardship will have been accomplished for both the managed and the manager. For the Christian worker, the reward should be one of no regrets, and to hear those wonderful words, "Well done, good and faithful employee."[328] The manager must be an encourager, giving out verbal and material rewards at the drop of a hat![329]

Paul, the motivating apostle, had the Romans' back with these encouraging words:

> I myself am convinced, my brothers, that you yourselves are full[330] of goodness,[331] complete[332] in knowledge and competent[333] to instruct one another. (Rom 15:14)[334]

- Paul the motivating manager could hardly give a more fulsome encouragement to his employees than that they are "full of goodness," "complete," and "competent."
- Paul the motivating manager makes sure that his compliment is not seen as second-handed but rather first-hand—he stands behind his words ("I myself").
- Paul the motivating manager makes the content of his compliment specific and tailored to the Roman cohort.
- Paul the motivating manager makes his compliment full of meaningful content. The Romans are "good," they are "knowledgeable," and they are ready to do what they are called to do ("teach").

---

328. Matt 25:23; cf. Rom 16:1–2; Heb 11:2; elsewhere.

329. Obviously, salary (Cf. Jas 5:4; Mal 3:5; Lev 19:13; Deut 24:15), work schedules, financial bonuses, office space are legitimate expressions of appreciation and encouragement, but they may be limited by external forces. Stearns of World Vision maintains that "a leader's number one job is to help release the unique abilities of each member of his or her team so that they can realize their full potential" (Stearns, *Lead Like It Matters to God*, 195).

330. *Mestos* = replete, stored.

331. *Agathosune* = active goodness.

332. *Pleroo* = to fill.

333. *Dunamai* = able, power, ability.

334. Cf. Rom 1:8.

Second Corinthians 9:2 has an instructive observation: The Corinthian branch's "enthusiasm"[335] has stirred up[336] the Macedonian branch office "to action." The Christian manager needs to be a cheerleader for the company. In Philippians 1:10 Paul urges all employees to up their game in whatever duties they are responsible for. He tells the Philippians to concentrate on the "best"[337] in life because Christ did just that—he was "superior"[338] and "better"[339] by far than anything that had gone before.[340]

Barnabas the motivating manager

> Barnabas took [Saul] and brought him to the apostles. He told them how Saul on his journey had seen the Lord and that the Lord had spoken to him, and how in Damascus he had preached fearlessly[341] in the name of Jesus. So Paul stayed with them and moved about freely in Jerusalem. (Acts 9:27–28)

Nothing supplants encouraging words for motivating people—the Barnabas effect—his name means "son of encouragement." Barnabas the motivating manager told the doubting assembled saints in Jerusalem that they could trust the new brother because, after all, Saul had not only seen Jesus but had spoken to him! Furthermore, Barnabas editorialized a bit when he said he had seen and heard Saul, now Paul, preach in Damascus, and he was "fearless" in his preaching. Barnabas had Paul's back in this crucial meeting:

- The charge to all Christian business managers is to be the company cheerleader and supporters of all the employees.
- The charge to all Christian employees is to work as a good and faithful steward, using all the gifts and graces that God has given that individual.[342]

---

335. *Zelos* = emulation.
336. *Erethizo* = provoke, excite.
337. *Diaphero* = more excellent, be of more value.
338. *Ta diaphorota* = surpassing, more excellent.
339. *Kreisson* = stronger, dominant.
340. Heb 8:6. Finally, Paul tells Timothy to hold out for the very best among us to be the leaders of the militant company (1 Tim 3:2–7; Titus 1:6–8).
341. *Parresiazomal* = boldly, frankly.
342. Cf. 2 Cor 5:9; 1 Thess 4:12; 2 Tim 2:15.

Hebrews and the motivating manager

> And let us consider how to may spur[343] one another on toward love and good[344] deeds. (Heb 10:24)

The incarnational motivating manager will always be looking for opportunities to inspire and motivate his colleagues to do better than they've done in the past. The writer of Hebrews gives all Christian business managers this challenge: "Let us consider how we may spur one another on toward love and good deeds" (Heb 10:24). While the context is ecclesiastical there is the application of "good deeds" to the business operation. The Greek term for "good" here is a Greek adjective used for something that is well-adapted to its circumstances or goals. The term is not always infused with spiritual intent.[345] Sometimes the adjective refers to personal "works" which benefit those who receive them, such as generosity, hospitality, empathy, and contentedness.[346] It is important to note that "love" or "affection" comes before the "stirring up," indicating that an internal attitude expressed in kindness must come before successful motivation. The preacher of Hebrews exhorts us to press on to "the complete accomplishment of our goal."[347] He obviously is speaking of our theological understandings, but the principle of improving one's mind and habits is stressed. He adds that our lives are lived out in a stadium setting where we have an obligation to perform at our best before the "great cloud of witnesses" watching us:[348]

- All told, Hebrews 10:24 instructs managers to understand that a flourishing organization has mutual concerns which create and sustain an organization in difficult circumstances.[349]

---

343. *Paroxysmos* = provoke, stimulate, incite, persuade, arouse. A very strong verb used only here and in Acts 15:39.
344. *Kalos.*
345. Cf. Matt 3:10. As opposed to the Greek term *agathos*.
346. Heb 13:1–6.
347. Heb 6:1–3; *teleiotes* = perfection, maturity.
348. Heb 12:1.
349. Cockerill, *The Epistle to the Hebrews*, 478–79.

Peter the motivating manager

> Dear friends, this is now my second letter to you. I have written both of them as reminders to stimulate[350] you to wholesome[351] thinking. (2 Pet 3:1)

Peter the motivating manager adds a comment that motivation doesn't begin with actions or conduct. No, it begins in the mind: I have written you "to stimulate you to wholesome thinking." (2 Pet 3:1) Notice that motivating was so important to Peter that he writes two letters to spur the organization on. The Greek word translated "wholesome" or "pure" does not have a moral definition by itself. It needs a context. In itself it means to have discernment, understanding, clearness, or perspicuity of mind or the ability to see all things intelligently and proceed without mistake; the phrase could be translated "arouse your sincere understanding." Lots of meaning here.

In sum, any motivation from the manager to the worker in a business organization must meet at least four communication needs:

- Peter the motivating manager reminds the manager that the worker needs to know where the organization is heading.
- Peter the motivating manager reminds the manager that the worker needs to know how the organization will get there.
- Peter the motivating manager reminds the manager that the worker needs to know how important he is to the organization's mission.
- Peter the motivating manager reminds the manager that the worker must mentally buy in to the company mission statement and have

---

350. *Diegeiro* = arouse, awaken from sleep.
351. *Eilikrine*.

that positive attitude affect their work habits.[352] After all, "Do two

[352]. "Jesus said, 'Everything is possible [dunatos = able, capable, powerful] for him who believes'" (Mark 9:23b). But this statement has been taken to cautionary lengths by some Christian writers. Jeremiah suggests the brainwave synaptic power of habitual thinking and action in a famous verse: "Can the Ethiopian change his skin or the leopard his spots? Neither can you do good who are accustomed to doing evil" (Jer 13:23; cf. Gen 6:5; Jer 17:9; 31:33; John 8:34). The point of this verse is to warn that the practice, the custom (lomad = "to learn, become accustomed to") of sin is so deeply ingrained in the heart and mind of a person that his very identity, his very character, is defined as evil, and that state is as stable as the spots on a leopard or the skin color of an African. Deep-seated wickedness caused by years of learning and practice of sin have made evil virtually a fixed feature of one's life and behavior. He has become a willing slave to sin. He can do nothing but sin without direct intervention of Yahweh (Rom 6:19–20; Jer 31:18, 20, 31–34; 33:8). In short, the "synapsis" (*sunapto* = "to join together, unite, to bind or tie") of the mind are wired for sin. N. T. Wright famously calls this process the "electronic pathway in the brain." This doctrinal emphasis is a Christianized version of Maltz's cybernetics (Maltz, *Psycho-Cybernetics*) in which you program yourself to succeed through mental images. A basic premise is the recognition that the human brain is a programmable computer, and the power of positive thinking or using our moral muscle (cf. Wright, *After You Believe*, 39) changes the brain's synapses firing to create success. Christian self-help books on business are filled with this type of thinking. Older but still informative: Cook, *Success, Motivation and the Scriptures*; McLemore, *Good Guys Finish First*; Ringer, *Winning through Intimidation*; Korda, *Power: How to Get It, How to Use It*; Greenleaf, *Servant Leadership*; Wanamaker, *Maxims of Life and Business*; Jones, *Life is Tremendous*; Bland, *Success: The Glenn Bland Method*; Ziglar, *See You at the Top*; Johnson, *The Success Principle*; Shinn, *The Miracle of Motivation* and *The American Dream Still Works*; Green, *More Than a Hobby*; DeVos, *Believe*; Conn, *The Possible Dream*; Hill, *Think and Grow Rich*; Carnegie, *How to Win Friends and Influence People*. Full disclosure: I am a fan of these self-help Christian writers. Sooner or later the Christian motivational writers refer to Reformed pastor Norman Vincent Peale (*The Power of Positive Thinking*). Amazingly enough, some of these Christian authors even refer to the philosophy of the secularist William James (1842–1910) for support for this motivational self-help theology! James, an American philosopher, wrote, "Ideas become true just so far as they help us to get into satisfactory relations with other parts of our experience" (James, *Pragmatism*, 28). Nevertheless, the proof of the pudding is in the eating. For the idea to be truly "true," it must "work" not merely by being pleasing in itself, but by anticipating or producing the satisfactory experiences it promises. As long as it continues to "work" in this way, it remains true. When it ceases to yield satisfactory results and no longer works, the idea becomes false and goes into the garbage can of outworn creeds, outgrown hypotheses, and discredited theories. James asks his famous question about truth: "What, in short, is the truth's 'cash value' in experiential terms? What does it do for you?" (James, *Pragmatism*, 88). Unfortunately, there is a large and growing body of religious literature that exhorts Christian business managers to put faith in themselves and their ability to succeed—with God's help, of course. But one must tread lightly with self-affirmation and motivation. Jim Collins, in his best-selling book on business management, *Good to Great*, relates a story about the famous Vietnam War US Navy admiral and vice-presidential candidate in 1992, James Stockwell, in what he calls "the

walk together unless they have agreed to do so?"[353]

THE EVALUATING MANAGER

> Examine[354] yourselves to see whether you are in the faith; test[355] yourselves. (2 Cor 13:5)

Scriptures teach the importance of testing for the skill needed in the organization. It is important that the employees are adequately trained for their jobs and do not fear failure or defeat in their work efforts. The manager's job is to give the coworkers cover to make mistakes and take risks in the job. The workers need to have the freedom to make decisions.

THE EVALUATING MANAGER IN THE GOSPELS

Jesus the evaluating manager

> Well done, good and faithful servant! You have been faithful with a few things,; I will put you in charge of many things. Come and share your master's happiness! . . . You wicked, lazy servant! So, you knew that I harvest where I have not sown and gather where I have not scattered seed? Well then, you should have put my money on deposit with the bankers, so that when I returned I would have received it back with interest. (Matt 25:23, 26–27)

Stockdale paradox." Stockdale was the highest-ranking United States military officer in the "Hanoi Hilton" prisoner-of-war camp during the height of the Vietnam War. He was "tortured over twenty times during his eight-year imprisonment from 1965 to 1973" and he "lived out the war without any prisoner's rights, [with] no set release date, and no certainty as to whether he would even survive and see his family again." Admiral Stockdale told Collins of how he and others survived in the camp. Collins asked Stockdale, "Who didn't make it out?" "Oh, that's easy, the optimists." Collins was confused: "The optimists? I don't understand." Stockdale responded, "The optimists were the ones who said, 'We're going to be out by Christmas.' And Christmas would come, and Christmas would go. Then they'd say, 'We're going to be out by Easter.' And Easter would come, and Easter would go. And then Thanksgiving, and then it would be Christmas again. And they died of a broken heart" (Collins, Good to Great, 83–85).

353. Amos 3:3.
354. *Peirazo* = prove.
355. *Dokimazo* = prove, distinguish.

Jesus on Specific Responsibilities of a Business Manager

In the parable of the talents the issue is how does the Christian business manager deal with competing biblical injunctions for excellent "stewardship" and "forbearance" when supervising slothful workers? In this parable:

- We have a presumption of adequately hired and trained staff.[356]
- We also have the staff possessing a clear job description and agreeing to it.[357]
- We have the judgment of Jesus on the non-excellent worker, i.e., "You wicked, lazy worker."[358]
- We see the manager "throwing the worthless[359] servant outside."[360] The Christian evaluating manager is not responsible for the worker forever.

What did the manager do with the lazy workers who diminished the organization's resources after adequate training and delegation and time? The manager fired that worker (25:30). The conclusion to be drawn from this parable is that the calling for a high degree of stewardship of God's resources is not mitigated by God's longsuffering mercy, and that after adequate training, clear communication, and warning, and time, the lazy worker is separated from the business organization lest the entire organization continue to suffer resource loss because of the obstacles posed by that "profitless" worker.

There is a battle going on in today's marketplace about the need for excellence in service and product by the business community and the cost of such excellence. As in the tension over a competitive attitude, there is a balancing to achieve quality control for a Christian evaluating manager with the expense of such evaluation.

There is no room in the Christian work ethic for laziness, slipshod work or mediocrity. The grace and mercy of God do not condone poor stewardship of his resources. God expects and demands strict accounting and a return on that with which he gives us to work. And yet, sometimes the manager finds himself working with and managing people who are

---

356. Matt 25:15.
357. Matt 25:14, 24–25.
358. Matt 25:23.
359. *Acherios*, "unprofitable," "useless."
360. Matt 25:26–30.

poor stewards of their time and resources. They are, in fact, wasting God's resources, whether they recognize it or not. The result is that coworkers of the sloppy workers can lose their opportunity to achieve their own workplace excellence. And this is to say nothing about the financial costs of poor stewardship.

The biggest problem in the evaluating task, and it may be the hardest task of a manager, is to make evaluation a vehicle for self-control of the employee and not external control by management.[361] However, there must be some external control if sin is to be correctly recognized and mitigated. Employees need more than just words to change their behavior.[362] Getting employee buy-in is critical to the flourishing of an organization. Any evaluation done by the manager must be none according to existing company standards. That is, ad hoc standards are not fair and conducive to growth in the employees. Concerning the parables of the workers in the vineyard[363] and the parable of the talents,[364] although this is not the point of these two parables,[365] the manager could have done a better job in communication.

In any kind of measurement system, there are two basic types of reward paths:

361. Eckerd: "It is said there are two ways to motivate people—rewards and punishments. Of the two, I would much rather have the ability to reward people than to punish them . . . If I can reward an individual for good work, I don't need to worry about punishing people for bad work. That usually takes care of itself" (Eckerd and Conn, *Finding the Right Prescription*, 178). The late Ray Miles (1932–2019), in his important book *Theories of Management*, posits three theories of workers that any manager holds: 1. The traditional model that assumes that work is inherently distasteful for most workers; 2. The human relations model that stresses the need for social gratification, acceptance, and recognition; 3. The human resource model that rejects manipulation, denies the distastefulness of work, and bases its understanding of human nature on Maslow's (1908–70) highest level of needs (Miles, *Theories of Management*, 32–46). Similarly, management psychologist Herzberg (1923–2000) distinguished between lower-level and higher-level needs. At the lower level, Herzberg saw hygiene needs, organizational supervision, pay, and working conditions. At the higher level, he saw motivational needs like organizational promotion, achievement, responsibilities, and challenge (Herzberg, *Work and the Nature of Man*).

362. Prov 29:19. Apparently the workers understand the instructions but are resistant to obey. Something more than words is needed to motivate them. Actions speak louder than words!

363. Matthew 20:1–16 tells us that as long as the employer pays what is due the individual employee he remains free to do what he chooses with the rest of his money, but always keeping in mind the dignity of the worker.

364. Matt 25:14–30.

365. Cf. Gal 5:7–8.

Jesus on Specific Responsibilities of a Business Manager

- One path is internal to each person; it is intrinsic.[366] "Where one's treasure is, there one's heart is."[367]
- One path is external to each person; it is extrinsic.[368]

The internal path to rewards is based on a person's effort being translated into a person's performance, which in turn leads to certain internal rewards, such as a degree of self-satisfaction and fulfillment.[369] This sense of self-worth is inherent in the human soul and is dependent on how close the worker's performance level is to the worker's own sense of personal standards. The discerning manager needs to foster and encourage in his coworkers this innate sense of satisfaction those workers. The manager also needs to gently and discerningly press the worker to raise her own standards of stewardship, to up their game.[370]

The extrinsic reward path is based on a worker's effort being translated into worker performance, which in turn leads to certain external rewards.[371] On this measurement path of labor, the degree of worker self-satisfaction, of fulfillment, is dependent on how coincidental the worker performance is to the organization's expectations, or the manager's expectations and public recognition of good works. The greater the coincidence, the greater the external reward, and therefore the greater the degree of worker satisfaction. External rewards exist within the life of an organization. Again, we see Jesus being observant in the parable of the talents in Matthew 25:14-29.

---

366. Prov 16:26, Living Bible. Cf. Luke 12:34; Matt 12:35.

367. Lencioni writes about two basic motives for management: internal and external. "At the most fundamental level, there are only two motives that drive people to become a leader. First, they want to serve others, to do whatever is necessary to bring about something good for the people they lead. They understand that sacrifice and suffering are inevitable in this pursuit and that serving others is the only valid motivation for leadership . . . The second reason why people choose to be a leader—the all too common but invalid one—is that they want to be rewarded. They see leadership as the prize for years of hard work and are drawn by its trappings: attention, status, power, money." Obviously, Lencioni finds reward-based management to be flawed and destructive to an organization (Lecioni, *The Motive*, 131–133).

368. The power of public judgment = Matt 18:15-17; 1 Cor 5:11-13; 2 Cor 2:6-7.

369. Cf. Ps 139:14; 1 Cor 11:28; Eph 1:4-6; 1 Pet 2:9. "Conscience is clear."

370. Cf. Matt 4:18-19.

371. "Take the talent from him and give it to the one who has the ten talents. For everyone who has will be given more, and he will have an abundance. Whoever does not have, even what he has will be taken from him" (Matt 25:28-29).

Who then is the faithful[372] and wise manager,[373] whom the

372. *Pistos*

373. *Oikonomos/doulos*. Later in the parable, *oikonomos* will be substituted by *doulos* ("manager/servant") to refer to the same position and responsibilities, signally servant leadership (Luke 12:43, 45, 46, 47). "Erastus, who is the city's manager [*oikonomos* = director] of public works" (Rom 16:23). The usual Greek word for "management" used by the Greek Old Testament LXX translators is *oikonomia* and all its derivatives (1 Chr 26:27; 2 Kgs 12:11; Ps 111:5; Isa 22:19; 1 Kgs 4:6; Ps 101:7; Exod 16:35). The duties of Erastus in Rome are in dispute, but they probably involve being in charge of the city streets, buildings, and finances. If so, this is a highly responsible individual with important management duties in a major city in the ancient Near East, not all that different from a city manager (cf. Moo, *The Letter to the Romans*, 951; Dunn, *Romans 9–16*, 911). This Greek word is a combination of "house" (*oikos*) and "distribute" (*nomia*); consequently, one who assigns or dispenses household responsibilities and benefits. This family of words can be translated "manager," "officer," "overseer," "steward," "administer," "governor," "planner," and almost always refers to an official position or rank (cf. 1 Kgs 4:6; 2 Kgs 18:18; Esth 1:8; Isa 36:3. *Oikonomia* is first mentioned as an office of manager in 1 Kings 4:6 and literally means "over the house." Our understanding of the position is in conflict, but I take it to mean that it is someone "in charge of royal property, including supervision of royal trade and mining, and was equivalent to the Egyptian *mr pr wr*, the chief of the royal private estate, including supervision of royal trade and mining. A hugely important position in the government" [Jones, *1 & 2 Kings*, 138]). Paul wrote of the high qualifications necessary for God's "manager" (*oikonomos* = overseer, bishop, elder) in his organization: "Since a manager (*oikonomos*) is entrusted with God's work, he must be blameless—not overbearing, not quick tempered, not given to much wine, not violent, not pursuing dishonest gain" (Titus 1:7). For an Old Testament list of management virtues, see Psalm 15. The qualification for a manager of a congregation applies to the managerial virtues of a commercial enterprise. Senior, *The Gift of Administration*, spends a great deal of time on "institutional" management and doesn't draw a distinction between religious and non-religious organizations: managers should be blameless. By being first, Paul gives this as the overarching quality needed to be an effective manager. The manager is God's representative to the company and thus must have godly characteristics.

- Not be overbearing. The quality of being arrogant and self-willed must be put to death by the manager. Wright comments on Colossians 2:12: "What we need to grasp, as being of the essence of Paul's summons to Christian virtue is the moral effort involved: 'Put to death,' 'put away,' 'put on.' The main thing to notice is that none of these things comes naturally . . . This is how virtue works . . . Practice the skills in the present which will gradually enable you to do and be what will go to make up that complete character" (Wright, *After You Believe*, 142–43,148). The manager is not to ride roughshod over employees.

- Not be quick tempered. The manager is not to be quick to anger with an explosive lack of control which destroys personal relationships.

- Not prone to drink too much. The manager must be reliable and dependable both in action and in temperament. Booze destroys that ability and leads to violence.

master puts in charge[374] of his servants to give them their food allowance at the proper time? (Luke 12:42)

In Luke 12:35–48, the parable on watchfulness, we see more of the Lord's teaching on managerial evaluation. The Greek word *pistos* can be translated "trustworthy," "steadfast," or "faithful" without the spiritual connotation.[375] Thus, we find Jesus teaching that management responsibilities, whether delegating down or delegating up, are a separate office within an organization, and that "manager" and "servant" refer to the same position. In Luke 12, faithful stewardship is required not only of material possessions but also of persons assigned to the manager by a sovereign God. Jesus gives us some criteria for all managers:

- The evaluating manager needs to train the coworker and give him the resources need to accomplish the task assigned.[376]
- The evaluating manager needs to set aside a time of accounting for the work of the coworker.[377]
- The evaluating manager expects that the stewardship of the resources given to the coworker will result in "profit" for the organization. Stewardship requires that there is an expected "profit"[378] from the coworker's use of resources given him.[379]
- The evaluating manager has the responsibility of communicating clear objectives and expectations to the coworker. Clear objectives and expectations are the responsibility of the manager to the coworker.[380]

What we have then is the Lord teaching that ignorance of management skills is no excuse or protection for a Christian evaluating

---

- Not violent. As far as Paul is concerned, alcohol leads to violence.
- Not greedy. The manager must have monetary integrity and be fiscally responsible.

374. *Oikos*
375. "Trustworthy," as in Matthew 25:21.
376. Luke 12:47.
377. Luke 12:47–48.
378. *Polus* = much, Matt 26:9.
379. Luke 12:48.
380. Luke 12:47.

manager.[381] Those Christian managers who desire to increase their management responsibilities and authority and who study the principles of godly management will be rewarded with increased responsibilities. To those Christian managers who are trained in the art of evaluation, the standard of faithful stewardship is now greater than before being trained![382] The principle is given by James: "Not many of you should presume to be teachers, my brothers, because you know that we who teach will be judged more harshly."[383]

The evaluating manager in the Old Testament

The principle of evaluation is present early in the Scriptures, and while Yahweh is a gracious and forgiving God in his covenant approach to Abraham and the Israelites, he nevertheless institutes curses and blessings depending on behavior.

Abraham the evaluating manager

> [Abraham] said to the chief[384] servant[385] in his household, the one in charge[386] of all that he had … (Gen 24:2)

Abraham, the evaluating manager, has evaluated his retinue and determined that Eliezer is the best of his employees, so he makes him his second in command of the extensive organization. The first biblical manager of exceptional diligence is Abraham's trusted servant, Eliezer of Damascus, who would have inherited Abraham's fortune if Ishmael and

---

381. "Does not know," Luke 12:48.

382. "Much will be demanded," "much will be asked," Luke 12:48. Etzioni wrote, "Most organizations most of the time cannot rely on most of their participants to internalize their obligations, to carry out their assignments voluntarily, without additional incentives. Hence, organizations require formally structured distribution of rewards and sanctions to support compliance with their norms, regulations, and orders" (Etzioni, *Modern Organizations*, 59). Managers are the persons who fulfill this leadership "distributive" function of Etzioni's.

383. Jas 3:1.

384. *Zagan* = eldest, experienced.

385. *Eved* = officer, laborer, ambassador; Zerubbabel (Hag 2:23).

386. *Mashal.*

Isaac had not been born.[387] Eliezer was the same "chief servant" in charge of all Abraham's possessions who, many years later, was commissioned by Abraham to go and find a wife for his son, Isaac. Eliezer traveled an astonishing 450 miles, where he found Rebekah and then returned with her to marry Isaac.[388]

Pharaoh the evaluating manager

> Settle your father and your brothers in the best[389] part of the land. Let them live in Goshen. And if you know of any among them with special ability,[390] put them in charge[391] of my own livestock.[392] (Gen 47:6)

Pharaoh the evaluating manager tells his chief manager to evaluate his family members for leadership abilities in order that they might do royal service. Joseph's brothers were to be officers of the crown, enjoying all the privileges attendant to that position.[393] So we have Joseph's brothers who so impressed Pharaoh with their skill and trustworthiness in agribusiness that he was willing to make them managers of all his livestock. They were men with "special abilities" or "competencies." Pharaoh the evaluating manager also evaluated his land and cattle.

Moses the evaluating manager

> But select capable[394] men from all the people—men who fear God, trustworthy men who hate dishonest gain—and appoint[395]

---

387. Gen 15:2.
388. Gen 24.
389. *Metab* = good.
390. *Chayil* = might, strength, power, valor. Used in a military context.
391. *Sar.*
392. Gen 47:6; *miqneh* = cattle, possessions.
393. Hamilton notes that "an Egyptian pharaoh requesting the services of Hebrew herdsmen to tend his animals may be compared with a Hebrew Solomon requesting the service of Phoenician craftsmen to help him build the temple" (Hamilton, *The Book of Genesis 18–50*, 608).
394. *Chayil.*
395. *Sum* = to set over, to erect.

them as officials[396] over thousands, hundreds, fifties and tens. (Exod 18:21)

This Exodus verse shows Moses evaluating his organization for important posts in management. The Hebrew phrase translated "special abilities" literally means "men of competence" and is used in Exod 18:21 for shrewd officials. It is unusual that a foreigner would be brought in for administrative advice to help shape the judiciary of God's people. This is evidence of common wisdom and insight given to all people by Yahweh. It is also noteworthy that financial corruption should be mentioned as a disqualifier for being a judge.

Moses the evaluating manager only selected the best men. There is the indication these selected managers:

- Needed to know the legal precedents.
- Needed to understand the law's application.
- Needed to be honest enough to be unprejudiced.[397]

> But those who hate[398] him he will repay[399] to their face by destruction;[400] he will not be slow to repay to their face those who hate him. (Deut 7:10)

In evaluation, turnabout is fair play. God is constantly evaluating and keeps his covenant of steadfast love to those who keep his commandments. But to those who reject him he will reject.

David the evaluating manager

> One thing God has spoken, two things have I heard: that you, Yahweh, are strong and that you, Yahweh, are loving. Surely you will reward[401] each person according to what he has done. (Ps 62:11–12)

---

396. *Sars.*
397. Durham, *Exodus*, 250–52.
398. *Sane* = reject, become unloving, alienated.
399. *Salam.*
400. *Avad* = perish.
401. *Salam.*

David notes that he has heard that Yahweh is characterized by two attributes: strength and love. Consequently, it is important to note that Yahweh blesses the individual when that individual does not deserve blessing. The Old Testament is full of baseless blessings. And Yahweh doesn't always punish faithlessness. He is, after all, a God of compassion, grace, and forgiveness and slow to anger.

However, as Moses told the Israelites hundreds of years before, God is always evaluating what is being "done" on earth and will judge accordingly. Those that recompense God's "love" with love will be blessed, and those that refuse to recompense God's love will be harshly judged. "What is more fair than that a man's life and character should furnish the rule of the divine distribution?"[402]

Solomon the evaluating manager

> Let your eyes look straight ahead, fix your gaze directly before you. Make level paths for your feet and take only ways that are firm. Do not swerve to the right or the left; keep your foot from evil. (Prov 4:25–27)

Critical in evaluating organizational performance and worker productivity are key performance indicators. "KPIs" are a set of quantifiable measures that an organization uses to gauge its performance over time. We see this implied in Proverbs 4:25–27, where attention to detail and measurement of activity is called for. The manager is to help the worker not be distracted from the organization's mission. Or as Fox puts it, "unswerving directedness towards a goal."[403]

- To show partiality[404] is not good—because a man will do wrong[405] for a piece of bread.[406]
- To show partiality[407] in judging[408] whoever says to the guilty, "You are innocent"—peoples will curse him and nations denounce him.

402. Plummer, *Psalms*, 626.
403. Fox, *Proverbs 1–9*, 187.
404. *Nakhar* = respect, honor, to scrutinize, to look intently.
405. *Pasha* = to break away, trespass, transgress. Cf. Prov 6:30; 30:9; Isa 8:21.
406. Prov 28:21; cf. Prov 17:15; 18:5.
407. *Nakhar*.
408. *Mispat*.

But it will go well with those who convict the guilty, and rich blessing will come upon them.[409]

We have looked at partiality before when motivating employees was the focus of attention. However, there is the matter of simple justice towards the individual and the group in correctly evaluating the worker. In Proverbs 28:21 the "lifting up of a worker's face" (partiality) is usually seen in the context of giving a bribe. However, there can be another interpretation. That interpretation will see this parable as saying if one shows unwarranted partiality to one worker in the form of compensation ("piece of bread")[410] another disadvantaged worker will wrongly seek compensation somewhere else—perhaps theft. Proverbs 24:23–25 clearly teaches the destructive consequences of unwarranted praise and emoluments given to a worthless worker. Company divisions and conflict will needlessly arise and group cohesiveness will vanish. Evaluations must be based on evidence and not favoritism. This partiality amounts to managerial malfeasance.

> One who is slack[411] in his work is brother to one who destroys.
> (Prov 18:9)[412]

Proverbs 18:9 tells us that the result of lethargy is ruin and "destruction," akin to robbery, which naturally leads us to doing things in an excellent manner. The principle of rewarding the productive and chastising the unproductive is a biblical principle found throughout the Old Testament. And when individual workers waste resources, they will, by definition, cause the business organization to waste God's resources, which is akin to robbing God. The organization becomes less excellent, less profitable, and less pleasing to God. Lack of good stewardship is serious business.

We see the *quid pro quo* of evaluation and consequences throughout the Old Testament: Exodus 8:1–2, refusal = plague;[413] Judges 7–8, refusal

---

409. Prov 24:23–25.

410. Cf. Prov 28:19.

411. *Raphah* = slothful, remiss, weak. The basic idea of the term seems to be a relaxing of the hands or a letting down.

412. Cf. Prov 6:6–11; 10:26; 12:24, 27; 13:4; 14:23; 19:15, 24; 20:4; 22:13; 26:13–16; 28:19; 24:30–34; "the sluggard," Matt 12:30.

413. "Then Yahweh said to Moses, 'Go to Pharaoh and say to him, "This is what Yahweh says: Let my people go, so that they may worship me. If you refuse to let them go, I will plague your whole country with frogs."'"

Jesus on Specific Responsibilities of a Business Manager

= punishment;[414] Proverbs 10:4-5, diligence = wealth, lazy = poor;[415] Proverbs 12:24, diligence = ruling, laziness = slavery;[416] Proverbs 13:4, diligence = satisfaction, laziness = emptiness;[417] Proverbs 3:27, doing good = reward;[418] 2 Samuel 7:14, doing wrong = punishment.[419] Then there is the command and example to do all things in an excellent manner in order to have management authority: Genesis 41:39-40, discerning and wise = in charge;[420] Daniel 6:3, distinguished and exceptional = oversight;[421] Esther 10:3, esteemed and doing good = vice-president;[422] Proverbs 22:29, skill = executive service:[423]

---

414. "While each [Israelite] held his position around the [Midianite] camp, all the Midianites ran, crying out they fled... Gideon and his three hundred men, exhausted yet keeping up the pursuit, came to the Jordan and crossed it. He said to the men of Succoth, 'Give my troops some bread; they are worn out and I am still pursing the kings of Midian.' But the officials of Succoth said... 'Why should we give bread to your troops?'... From there [Gideon] went up to Peniel and made the same request of them, but they answered as the men of Succoth had... Gideon went up... and fell upon the unsuspecting army. The two kings of Midian fled, but he pursued them and captured them, routing their entire army. Gideon then returned from the battle by the pass of Heres. He took the elders of the town and taught the men of Succoth a lesson by punishing them. He also pulled down the tower of Peniel and killed the men of the town."

415. "Lazy hands make a man poor, but diligent hands bring wealth. He who gathers crops in the summer is a wise son, but he who sleeps during harvest is a disgraceful son."

416. "Diligent hands will rule, but laziness ends in forced labor."

417. "The sluggard craves and gets nothing, but the desires of the diligent are fully satisfied."

418. "Do not withhold good from those who deserve it, when it is in your power to act."

419. Yahweh says to Nathan concerning David, "I will be his father, and he will be my son. When he does wrong, I will punish him and the rod of men, with flogging inflicted by men."

420. "Then Pharaoh said to Joseph, 'Since God had made all this known to you, there is no one so discerning and wise as you. You shall be in charge (*yether*) of my palace, and all my people are to submit to your orders. Only with respect to the throne will I be greater than you.'"

421. "Now Daniel so distinguished himself among the administrators and the satraps by his exceptional qualities that the king planned to set (*yattir*) him over the whole [Babylonian] kingdom."

422. "Mordecai the Jew was second in rank to King Xerxes, preeminent among the Jews, and held in high esteem by his many fellow Jews, because he worked for the good of his people and spoke up for the welfare of all the Jews."

423. "Do you see a man skilled [*mahir* = diligent, ready. Ezra 7:6; Ps 45:1] in his

- Biblical wisdom is concerned not with piety alone but with responsible excellence in one's work. God is telling us that good is the enemy of the best and the Christian evaluating manager should push on to the highest standard.
- Proverbs bluntly tells us that those Christian managers who work hard with skill will end up successful and working for the most powerful and influential people in society.[424] Stewardship counts for something in secular society.

Jeroboam the evaluating manager

> Now Jeroboam was a man of standing,[425] and when Solomon saw how well[426] the young man did his work,[427] he put him in charge[428] of the whole labor force of the house of Joseph. (1 Kgs 11:28)

Solomon the evaluating manager evaluates Jeroboam and rewards him with a position of influence and power over other people in the organization.

We have the example of Jeroboam and his work ethic. Jeroboam was a trustifund baby, his father having died and left the estate to his wife, Jeroboam's mother.[429] He was in the service of King Solomon as a construction manager in charge of building the Millo or "supporting terraces" of the temple.[430] Specifically, he was in charge of the seventy thousand carriers of stone and wood.[431] He was industrious, energetic, and ambitious, and Solomon liked him. In fact, Solomon "put him in charge of the

---

work [*Malakhah* = business, employment]? He will serve before kings; he will not serve before obscure men."

424. Prov 22:29.
425. *Gibbor* = mighty men of valor.
426. *Asah* = skillful, accomplish, industrious.
427. *Asah* = build, create, accomplish, prepare.
428. *Paqad* = ruler.
429. 1 Kgs 11:26.
430. 1 Kgs 11:27; 9:15, 24.
431. 1 Kgs 5:15.

whole labor force of the house of Joseph," meaning the tribes of Ephraim and Manasseh.[432]

The results of Jeroboam's management efforts: The prophet Ahijah gave him ten tribes to rule over as king, leaving Solomon only one tribe (1 Kgs 11:31, 37).

Isaiah the evaluating manager

> Woe to those who call evil good and good evil, who put darkness for light and light for darkness, who put bitter for sweet and sweet for bitter . . . who acquit the guilty for a bribe but deny justice to the innocent. (Isa 5:20, 23)

To repeat: Isaiah was not an administration official, but he had things to say to the administrators. In this powerful passage the great prophet pronounces a "woe" on a business manager who would subvert moral and ethical distinctions in the pursuit of utilitarianism. Notice that the evaluating manager knows the difference between good and evil but still insists that "good" be called "evil." I would prefer if the translators had the terms in quotation marks. Isaiah is warning that when words lose their meaning and are devalued then an organization is corrupt. Truth, accuracy, and integrity are necessary for a company's health.[433] It could be that the distinction is not primarily in speech but in actions ("put"); that is, the business managers act like there is no difference between the moral characteristics. It seems moral perversion will not coexist with ethical rightness and that the "darkness" and "bitterness" will overtake the "light" and the "sweet." Isaiah takes us back to Proverbs 17:15: "Acquitting the guilty and condemning the innocent—Yahweh detests them both."

---

432. 1 Kgs 9:23.
433. Watts, *Isaiah 1–33*, 93.

Jeremiah the evaluating manager

> I, Yahweh, search[434] the heart and examine[435] the mind, to reward[436] a man according to his conduct,[437] according to what his deeds deserve.[438] (Jer 17:10)

- Jeremiah the evaluating manager tells us that the evaluating manager treats the worthless employee as if the employee is worth something and the worthy employee is worthless. This managerial action is a perversion of the very essence of moral distinctions and thus fundamentally sinful.[439]

- Jeremiah the evaluating manager tells us the evaluating manager must, therefore, be consistent in his treatment of coworkers lest the organization be swallowed up by sin.

- Jeremiah the evaluating manager sets down the Old Testament principle that God's economy for the world dictates that eventually one is repaid for one's deeds. This evaluation is serious business and God searches and examines the entire worker to arrive at a correct assessment and reward.

- Jeremiah the evaluating manager enunciates the assumption that everyone does something, good or bad, and thus leaves a record to evaluate. No one gets out of life with a free lunch.[440]

---

434. *Chaqar* = to penetrate, examine, seek out.
435. *Bachan* = to try, prove, test, examine, investigate.
436. Give.
437. *Dherekh* = walk, journey, path, way, manner.
438. *Peri* = fruit.
439. Young, *The Book of Isaiah*, 1.219–23.
440. Cf. 1 Kgs 8:39.

THE EVALUATING MANAGER IN THE NEW TESTAMENT

Paul the evaluating manager

> Therefore, it is necessary to submit to the authorities, not only because of possible punishment[441] but also because of conscience.[442] (Rom 13:5)

Romans 13:5 tells us that evaluation, if it's to be productive and growth-producing, must be both external and internal with a reward system attendant.[443] If the performance is coincidental to the standards of the organization, then there is a match up, and faithful personal stewardship has been achieved, and the worker will enjoy a great deal of satisfaction. This kind of worker motivation/evaluation comes from within the person and is usually hidden from all but the most discerning managers. It is this kind of internal motivation that drives an individual to do good when there is no apparent external reward: "Workers, obey your managers not only to win their favor when their eye is on you, but like servants of Christ, doing the will of God from your heart."[444] However, Paul the evaluating manager was sensitive to giving credit where credit is due and practiced honoring the work of colleagues.[445]

One of the points of Romans 13:5 is that Christians should submit to the authorities because they recognize in their conscience that God has ordained an authority structure to rule in his stead on earth. Paul's mention of "conscience" points to a sense of moral responsibility to obey earthy authorities, including business managers. Our motivation to obey the authorities is to avoid a guilty conscience for disobedience. Paul

---

441. *Orge* = wrath, anger.

442. *Suneidesis* = to know intuitively. This Greek word is found more often in Paul than in the rest of the New Testament. For Paul the conscience was a human faculty by which a person approves or disapproves his actions. Paul gives a pretty good definition of "conscience" in 1 Corinthians 2:11. Origin commented on "conscience" in his commentary on Romans: "Conscience is the spirit which the apostle says is with the soul, according to which we have been instructed in the higher things. This spirit or conscience is linked to the soul as a teacher and guide" (Origen, *Commentary on the Epistle to the Romans*, 5.100).

443. Cf. Gal 6:4; 1 Tim 1:20; Rev 20:12.

444. Eph 6:6; cf. "eye-pleasers," Gal 1:10; Col 3:2; cf. 1 Cor 11:28; 2 Cor 13:5; 1 Thess 2:4; 5:21.

445. 2 Cor 10:16.

has moved us from obeying the authorities out of fear of their external wrath[446] to obeying out of fear of our internal conscience.[447]

Paul the evaluating manager adds an evaluation comment in 13:7: "Give everyone what you owe him: If you owe taxes, pay taxes; if revenue, then revenue; if respect, then respect; if honor, then honor." Here is a general exhortation to give an individual what they deserve. Paul applies this principle to the relationship between the individual Christian and the state, but the principle is the important point: Give the coworker what the coworker deserves. Evaluating managers have the obligation to give back to a coworker what that person has earned, good or bad.[448]

John the evaluating manager

> Behold, I am coming soon! My reward[449] is with me, and I will give to everyone according to what he has done.[450] (Rev 22:12)

John the evaluating manager has the final evaluating word from Jesus.

THE PEACEMAKING MANAGER

> Blessed are the peace makers[451] for they will be called the sons of God. (Matt 5:9)

---

446. Rom 13:4.

447. "Conscience! Conscience! Divine instinct, immortal voice from heaven; sure guide for a creature ignorant and finite indeed, yet intelligent and free; infallible judge of good and evil, making man like to God! In you consists the excellence of man's nature and the morality of his actions; apart from you, I find nothing in myself to raise me above the beasts—nothing but the sad privilege of wandering from one error to another, by the help of an unbridled understanding and a reason which knows no principle" (Rousseau, *Emile*, 254).

448. "Remember this: Whoever sows sparingly will also reap sparingly, and whoever sows generously will also reap generously" (2 Cor 9:6). Stepansky notes that organizations must set performance parameters against which employees will measure their effort. The parameters should measure the internal production (worker satisfaction) and external production (management satisfaction) (Stepansky, *Thoughts on Leadership from a Higher Level*, 67).

449. *Misthos* = wages.

450. *Ergon* = work, performance.

451. *Eirenopoios*.

> Do not repay anyone evil for evil. Be careful to do what is right in the eyes of everybody. If it is possible, as far as it depends on you, live at peace[452] with everyone. (Rom 12:17–18)

The primary focus of managerial responsibilities is on peacemaking in the organization, with the manager acting as the mediator/peacekeeper. Peacemaking between two parties was evident from the earliest history of God's organization. In fact, the examples of managers seeking peace with others is a prominent attribute of God's children and is frequently noted in the Bible. There is a minor but significant difference between "peacekeeping" and "peacemaking." In a diverse company the manager must be proactive in making peace, since there may not be real peace between the workers.

THE PEACEMAKING MANAGER IN THE GOSPELS

Jesus the peacemaking manager

> If you are offering your gift at the altar and there remember that your brother has something against you, leave your gift there in front of the altar. First go and be reconciled[453] to your brother; then come and offer your gift. Settle[454] matters quickly with your adversary who is taking you to court. Do it while you are still with him on the way. (Matt 5:23–25)[455]

This passage is focused on reconciliation between two parties without a moderating manager, but it does have application to a peacemaking manager in a mediating situation:

- One management lesson is the priority of reconciliation within an organization. Organizational harmony is important to our Lord. Before worship comes peace with members.
- The peacemaking manager's responsibility is to get involved in worker relationships. Drop everything to effect comity among member of the organization.

---

452. *Eireneuo* = be peaceable.
453. *Dialiasso*, only here in the New Testament.
454. *Eunoeo* = agree, well-minded.
455. Cf. Matt 18:15–20.

- Another lesson is that in a dispute there is enough blame to go around. Jesus tells the peacemaking manager it is not enough that one's temper be tamped down but that one must not arouse the temper of another. No member skates free in peace keeping responsibility.
- Another lesson is that the peacemaking manager is to take whatever steps are necessary to restore harmony in the organization.

A peacemaking lesson from Matthew 18:15-19:

- The peacemaking manager needs to be willing to separate the obstreperous employee from the company if peace cannot be achieved.
- The peacemaking manager needs to be willing to give the contending parties several opportunities to reconcile.
- The peacemaking manager needs to be willing to go through several stages of mediation to achieve harmony between the employees.

The Peacemaking manager in the Old Testament

Jacob the peacemaking manager

An attitude of peacemaking is evident in the relationship between Jacob and his brother Esau in Genesis 32–33, where Jacob assiduously pursues peace with a supposedly enraged brother.[456] Jacob makes the move to "find favor in Esau's eyes." We are not told what Esau's motivation was as he approached brother Jacob. Did he have evil intent? We are not told if Jacob's olive branch changed Esau's mind, but we do know that in response to Jacob's blandishments Esau came "running" to embrace his estranged brother.[457] Jacob's attitude seems to have been that no price was too great to pay for reconciliation with his brother. Jacob humbled himself, and God's organization was spared a horrific conflict of sibling rivalry. A couple of lessons for the peacemaking manager:

- The peacemaking manager should note which of the warring parties is prepared to make the first conciliatory move.

---

456. Gen 32:8.
457. Gen 33:4.

- The peacemaking manager shouldn't underestimate the desire for peace between the employees.

Joseph the peacemaking manager

Another early example of a peacemaker seeking reconciliation with offended parties was Joseph with his brothers in Genesis 45. Joseph had been estranged from his brothers for over two decades and apparently had learned to speak fluent Egyptian,[458] and we see him changing languages in just a couple of verses, first Egyptian to his Egyptian attendants and then Hebrew to his brothers.[459] Joseph the peacemaking manager is so Yahweh-saturated that in just six chapters God is mentioned as the motivating factor in his life at least seventeen times. Joseph was quick to forgive and make preparations for reconciliation.[460] It is interesting that Joseph did not forget brotherly treatment and remembered it to the very end. But he was able to genuinely forgive them, thus "reassuring" them that peace would reign in the patriarchal family.[461]

Moses the peacemaking manager

> And I charged your managers at that time: Hear the disputes between your brothers and judge fairly,[462] whether the case is between brother Israelites or between one of them and an alien. You shall not be partial[463] in judgment. You shall hear the small and the great alike. You shall not be intimidated[464] by anyone, for the judgment is God's. And the case that is too hard for you, you shall bring to me, and I will hear it. (Deut 1:16–17)

---

458. Gen 41:39–45.

459. Gen 45:1–3. For the third time in this family encounter Joseph "weeps," Gen 45:2; 42:24, and 43:30. He will weep again in 45:15 and 46:29.

460. Gen 42:24.

461. Gen 50:15–21.

462. *Tsedeq* = straight, honest, integrity.

463. *Nakar* = to discern, literally: acknowledge faces.

464. *Ghur* = be afraid, to turn aside.

Justice in the organization was to be impartial and evenly extended to all, even to those non-members of the organization.[465] Moses the peacemaking manager is telling his vice-presidents not to be impressed with the social or economic standing of those appearing before them for adjudication. Be fair with everyone so that peace reigns in the company. If peace could not be found then the vice-presidents were to send the issue up the chain of command to Moses. As a peacemaker the phrase "judgment is God's" is critical in that it put the conciliation between two parties in the lap of an impartial authority, so the manager is doing righteous work by his mediation as he inquires of God. Peace and justice are not always the province of a peacemaking manager but of the manager's God.

Gideon the peacemaking manager

> Now the Ephraimites asked Gideon, "Why have you treated us like this? Why didn't you call us when you went to fight Midian?" And they criticized[466] him sharply.[467] But he answered them "What have I accomplished compared to you? Aren't the gleanings of Ephraim's grapes better than the full grape harvest of Abiezer? God gave Oreb and Zeeb, the Midianite leaders,[468] into your hands. What was I able to do compared to you?" At this, their resentment[469] against him subsided.[470] (Judg 8:1–3)

This brief narrative is pretty self-explanatory. Several peacemaking ideas to note about this passage are:

- Gideon the peacemaking manager cut out of the initial attack against the Midianites the fractious and powerful Ephraimites, for whatever reason,[471] when on the surface of things, it seemed strategically appropriate for them to be involved. Thus, any spoils of the battle would not come to them.[472] The Ephraimites were furious at

---

465. "Alien," Deut 1:16.
466. *Riv* = quarrel, contest, feud.
467. *Chozqah* = forcefully, violently, strongly.
468. *Sar.*
469. *Ruach* = anger, spirit.
470. *Raphah* = abate, loosen, abandon, desist.
471. Perhaps Gideon was jealous of his role as manager coming from a small tribe and feared pushback from the most powerful tribe in Israel.
472. Judg 6:35; 7:24.

Jesus on Specific Responsibilities of a Business Manager 279

Gideon the peacemaking manager for the snub and were locked, loaded, and ready to contend for their share of booty and respect.

- Gideon the peacemaking manager, from the rival and smaller tribe of Manasseh, commends the Ephraimites' capture of the two Midianite leaders. He assures them of their importance.

- Gideon the peacemaking manager downplays his accomplishment and exalts those of the Ephraimites. He doesn't let his ego get in the way of a peaceful solution to a tense situation.[473]

- Gideon the peacemaking manager metaphorically tells the Ephraimites that the dregs of their grape harvest (the capture of the Midianite leaders Oreb and Zeeb) is superior to the vintage harvest of his,[474] referring to the general night-time attack. After all, the battle against the Midianites still needs to be won, and there is military work to do and spoils to be gained.

- Gideon the peacemaking manager, while a warrior at heart, turns to diplomacy and smooth words to avert a violent confrontation with a division in the organization.

- Gideon the peacemaking manager demonstrates the success of his masterful diplomacy when the Ephraimites are satisfied with his response.[475]

David the peacemaking manager

> When Eliab, David's oldest brother, heard him speaking with the men, he burned[476] with anger[477] at him. (1 Sam 17:28–31)

The story here is that Yahweh rejected David's brother Eliab as the replacement for Saul, even though Eliab was the oldest son, better looking and bigger than the young David. Being considered but passed over for the royal job by God stuck in Eliab's craw, and so he naturally was intensely jealous of David. Eliab's royal prospects were his to lose, and he

---

473. Later in Judges 8 Gideon will show his ruthlessness in battle.
474. Abiezer refers to Gideon, Judg 6:11.
475. Judg 8:3.
476. *Charah* = kindled, glow with anger.
477. *Aph* = flared nostrils in anger.

did. The scene is that David is about to go against Goliath, and he is talking with the soldiers around him about the battle. Eliab takes the tense occasion to publicly ridicule his younger brother:

- "You are only qualified to shepherd a small number of our sheep and not the family's main flock. You are not even man enough to be the main shepherd."
- "Why have you left the sheep fold to come down here and watch men battle?"
- "Your being down here shows you are conceited and a teenager who thinks he can be warrior like real men. You are a conceited and insolent follower of Yahweh, and your presence proves it."

The young David responds to his big brother:

- "Now, what have I done to make you unhappy with me? All I have done is respond to Dad by bringing you food as he asked."[478]

A couple of management tips for the peacemaking manager:

- David the peacemaking manager did not reply to Eliab in anger but with a teasing rhetorical question: "Can't I even discuss the battle scene with these soldiers?"[479]
- David the peacemaking manager diffused an awkward situation by responding gently to his brother who was clearly hurt and offended by David's choice.[480]

The result of David's public peacemaking role was an audience with the king.[481]

> Be still before Yahweh; trust in him and wait patiently for him;
> do not fret[482] when men succeed[483] in their ways, when they

---

478. 1 Sam 17:17. Apparently, Eliab had a habit of belittling and criticizing David.

479. 1 Sam 17:29. This was a very mild rebuke given the public humiliation of David attempted by Eliab.

480. Cf. Prov 26:4–5.

481. 1 Sam 17:31.

482. *Sharah.*

483. *Tsalaeach* = prosper.

Jesus on Specific Responsibilities of a Business Manager

carry out their wicked schemes.[484] Refrain[485] from anger and turn from wrath; do not fret—it leads only to evil.[486] (Ps 37:7–8)

While this Davidic Psalm is about patience, as always there is more to it:

- David the peacemaking manager tells the peacemaking manager to fundamentally relax in marketplace competition.
- David the peacemaking manger tells us not to be lax, but not fret because God has our backs. Fretting and anger only causes harm and will not change your competitors' actions.
- David the peacemaking manager reminds us that striking out at the "wicked" competition only causes you to descend to their level of evil.
- David the peacemaking manager tell us the peacemaking manager needs to be patient with the parties in dispute and give them time to calm down.

Jonathan the peacemaking manager

> Then David went to Jonathan and asked, "What have I done? What is my crime? How have I wronged your father, that he is trying to take my life?" "Never!" Jonathan replied. "You are not going to die! Look, my father doesn't do anything, great or small, without confiding in me." (1 Sam 20:1–2)

- Jonathan the peacemaking manager couldn't bring the two conflicting parties, David and Saul, in the organization together. In short, he failed as a peacemaker. But his effort was commendable and worthy of notice.

> Then Jonathan said to David, "By Yahweh, the God of Israel, I will surely sound out[487] my father by this time the day after

---

484. *Mezimma* = plot, device, plan, intrigue, crafty, mischief. Prov 12:2; 14:17.
485. *Raphah* = cease.
486. *Raa* = to spoil by breaking into pieces, to make something valuable worthless.
487. *Chaqar* = searched, investigate.

tomorrow! If he is favorably disposed toward you . . . but if my father is inclined to harm you . . ." (1 Sam 20:12–13).

The issue, of course, is that King Saul, Jonathan's father, wants to kill David because Saul perceives him as a threat to his crown. So David is hiding from Saul in a field outside of Jerusalem. Saul wants to deceive David to join him at court so that he might kill him. Jonathan has made a covenant with David to protect him, or at least inform him of his dad's murderous intentions. Saul looks around for David but doesn't see him, so he asks Jonathan if he knows where David is. Saul assumes that some religious reason is dictating David's absence from the dinner table. Jonathan tells his dad that David's absence is not from religious conviction but rather out of fear, and that he wants the freedom to go to Bethlehem to see his family on a special occasion.

> Saul's anger flared up at Jonathan, "Don't I know that you have sided with [David] to your own shame and to the shame of the mother who bore you?" Jonathan asked his father, "Why should he be put to death? What has he done?" But Saul hurled his spear at him to kill him. Then Jonathan knew that his father intended to kill David. (20:30, 32)

Jonathan may have been a bit slow on the uptake about his father's hatred of David, but he finally saw that murder was on his dad's agenda. Saul's anger was fueled out of the knowledge that if David was made king as Saul's successor, Jonathan would not be king. How could Jonathan throw in with David and deny himself the royal treatment?

- One management lesson here seems to be that the peacemaking manager needs to really know the parties involved in the dispute.

Abigail the peacemaking manager

> "Now since Yahweh has kept you [David] from bloodshed and from avenging yourself with your own hands, as surely as Yahweh lives may your enemies and all who intend to harm [you] be like Nabal . . . Let no wrongdoing be found in you as long as you live. Even though someone is pursuing you to take your life, [your life] will be bound securely in the bundle of the living by the Yahweh your God. But the lives of your enemies he will hurl away as from the pocket of a sling . . . [David] will not have on

his conscience the staggering burden of needless bloodshed or of having avenged himself" ... "May you [Abigail] be blessed for your good judgment and for keeping me [David] from bloodshed this day and from avenging myself with my own hands." (1 Sam 25:26, 28–31, 33)

This passage relates the effort of perhaps the most effective peacemaking manager in the Bible. In this remarkable story of Abigail, David, and Nabal, we see the dark and volcanic temper of David in full display, as well as Yahweh tempering his attitude towards Nabal. We are interested in David's and Abigail's reaction. This is a story of a competitive mindset run amok but for the peacemaking intervention through another party. The story is that Nabal, a rich rancher, refuses to help David feed his six hundred troops.[488] David's reaction to Nabal's rejection: "Saddle-up, boys, and put on your swords!" Abigail the peacemaking manager sees all this huffing and puffing and runs to David with the plea quoted above. With that summary in mind let's look at a couple of key verses. First, Abigail's counsel to David:

> Now since Yahweh has kept you [David] from bloodshed and from avenging[489] yourself with your own hands, as surely as Yahweh lives may your enemies[490] and all who intend to harm[491] [you] be like Nabal. (1 Sam 25:26)

David is the stand-in for the Christian business manager who has enjoyed the blessing of God in his marketplace activity. The manager is being told by the peacemaking Abigail not to throw the blessings away by taking "revenge" into his own hands. The fruitless saving of one's company by one's one hand will defeat the blessing of God and not accomplish the goal.[492] Abigail comforts David by telling him that God will continue to sustain him against those who seek to "harm" him, his "enemies," if he relies on him for protection. The way the word is used in the Old Testament connotes a subjectivity of defining what "harm" is. The "harm" intended doesn't necessarily mean physical attack but rather to visit misfortune on

---

488. "Who is this David? Who is this son of Jesse?" (1 Sam 25:10).

489. *Yasha* = to be free, to push back against confinement, to preserve, to give victory, to take vengeance.

490. *Oyeb* = enemy.

491. *Ra* = evil, bad. Isaiah threatens those whose moral judgments are distorted (Isa 5:20) so marketplace "harm" will be specific to the manager's business.

492. Cf. Judg 7:2.

the competitor. The word is used in several places to describe dishonest business practices.[493] However, the Hebrew word "harm" basically means "hostility." It is used in a legal context,[494] and it is used even when one's "enemies" change their ways in order to please![495] The Christian manager must be on guard not to bring the guilt ("bloodshed") of competitive vengeance into the company ethos.

> Let no wrongdoing[496] be found in you as long as you live. Even though someone is pursuing you to take your life, [your life] will be bound securely in the bundle of the living by the Yahweh your God. But the lives of your enemies he will hurl away as from the pocket of a sling. (1 Sam 25:28–29)

The competitive business manager is cautioned by the peacemaking manager not to retaliate even in the face of dishonest and unethical competition. Let God handle the vengeance side of marketplace battle.[497] In 1 Samuel 25:28 revenge is termed "wrong-doing" or "evil," which is the term used to describe the competitor's action against the manager. In other words, Abigail's plea is, don't lower yourself to the same level as the opponent, but enjoy comfort and safety of your just God. The Christian manager should expect his ruthless competition to be flung away like a stone in a sling shot.

> [David] will not have on his conscience[498] the staggering burden of needless bloodshed or of having avenged himself. (1 Sam 25:31)

Abigail the peacemaking manager tells David that the bonus of not retaliating against an unethical business competitor will be a clear conscience. The avenging Christian competitive manager will have numerous opportunities to implement revenge, but all will be of no satisfaction in the end because only God can deal out justice that lasts. Do the right thing and be patient and wait for the Lord. The somewhat rare Hebrew word translated as "conscience" in 1 Samuel 25:31 means "to stumble" and is used to refer to opponents to lose sleep thinking about how to

---

493. Gen 31:7; 41:21; 44:5; Num 16:15; Deut 15:9; Ps 22:16; Prov 20:14.
494. Num 35:21–22.
495. Prov 16:7.
496. *Ra*.
497. Prov 25:21–22; Rom 12:15–21.
498. *Miktab* = troubled heart, offense of heart, a stumbling (Prov 4:16).

Jesus on Specific Responsibilities of a Business Manager

make someone "stumble" or idols who make one stumble in their spiritual walk.[499]

> May you [Abigail] be blessed for your good judgment and for keeping me from bloodshed[500] this day and from avenging[501] myself with my own hands. (1 Sam 25:33)

Success! Here the manager is praising Abigail the peacemaking manager for helping him see that personal revenge will get him nowhere. "bloodshed" here clearly refers to physical violence and shedding of Nabal's blood, but the word is used figuratively elsewhere in the Old Testament. It can simply mean "to pour out" or "heap up" or "throw out." Reciprocity begets reciprocity, and the cycle only ends when one competitor loses heart. The Christian peacemaking manager breaks the cycle. Here is a recognition that God uses individuals to accomplish his will, even in the most unlikely circumstances. Personal vengeance is pointless in the marketplace.

Solomon the peacemaking manager

> And [Solomon] said, "Divide the living child in two, and give half to the one and half to the other." Then the woman whose son was alive said to the king, because her heart yearned for her son, "Oh, my lord, give her the living child, and by no means put him to death." But the other said, "He shall be neither mine nor yours; divide him." Then the king answered and said, "Give the living child to the first woman, and by no means put him to death; she is his mother." And all Israel heard of the judgment that the king had rendered, and they stood in awe of the king, because they perceived that the wisdom of God was in him to do justice. (1 Kgs 3:25–28)[502]

Enough said.

---

499. Cf. Jer 18:15.

500. *Shaphakh* = to bare one's personality in anger (1 Sam 1:15).

501. *Yasha* = to give ease.

502. Cf. Prov lo:12; 15:1, 18; 16:7, 28; 18:13, 19; 19:11; 25:8, 21–22; 28:25; 29:2, 25.

Jehoshaphat the peacemaking manager

> Jehoshaphat lived in Jerusalem, and he went out again among the people... and turned them back to Yahweh, the God of their faithers. He appointed judges in the land, in each of the fortified cities of Judah. He told them, "Consider carefully[503] what you do... Judge carefully, for with Yahweh our God there is no injustice or partiality[504] or bribery." (2 Chr 19:4–7)

Several features of this short passage bear noticing from a peacemaking perspective:

- King Jehoshaphat the peacemaking manager continued to establish and administer a national system of branch offices for the organization.[505]

- Jehoshaphat the peacemaking manager personally visited each of the branch offices. He was a hands-on manager. This was public evidence that the managing director of the organization cared for the peace and welfare of his coworkers. He reached out to them and did not expect them to come to him in the head office.[506]

- In each of the branches, Jehoshaphat the peacemaking manager appointed managers to conduct business in that region. These branch managers were carefully chosen from the leaders of the region, and they were given the charge to be "careful" in their administration. Implied in Jehoshaphat's exhortation is to administer quickly.

- The purpose of the visits of Jehoshaphat the peacemaking manager was to "turn back" the thinking of the members of the organization to the original mission of the company.[507] The people had adopted the thinking of the world around them, and the stability, progress, and peace of the organization was in danger.

---

503. *Raah.*

504. *Masso* = respect of persons.

505. "Away from the temple," 1 Chr 26:29; cf. 1 Chr 23:4; 2 Chr 1:2. Both David and Solomon had established a national network of branch offices for the organization (1 Chr 26:29).

506. Pratt argues that Jehoshaphat did not go out personally but rather sent representatives (Pratt, *1 & 2 Chronicles.* 330).

507. 2 Chr 20:32–33; Rev 2–3.

- Jehoshaphat the peacemaking manager gave his branch managers the reminder that their appointment was really from Yahweh and that they were doing Yahweh's bidding in their offices. Another example of God doing the staffing work for the manager.
- Jehoshaphat the peacemaking manager gave each branch manager the instructions that they were to conduct company business with justice, impartiality, and integrity. This charge was not easy since bribery and corruption were common in the culture, including the culture of the organization, so the managers had to be people of character and courage.

Amos the peacemaking manager

> Do two walk together, unless they have agreed to meet? (Amos 3:3)

Amos is not an Old Testament peacemaking manager of the organization. He was a prophet, so he doesn't provide us with an example of peacemaking management, but he does gives us a goal of peacekeeping: unity in the organization:

Amos the peacemaking manager tells us that the conditions for traveling together are that both parties need:

- To agree to meet.
- To agree on a destination.
- To agree on departure date.
- To agree on the duration of the journey.
- To agree on the route to be taken.
- To agree on provisions for the journey.

Lots of agreeing going on here, but without these agreements there will be no peace, no unity between the parties.[508] The point is that companionship involves a level of agreement, compromise, and graciousness to put aside certain disagreements. The peacemaking manager has his work cut out for him.

---

508. Smith, *Amos, Obadiah, Jonah*, 72–73.

The Peacemaking Manager in the New Testament

James and the Council of Jerusalem peacemaking managers

> Some men came down from Judea to Antioch and were teaching the brothers: "Unless you are circumcised according to the custom taught by Moses, you cannot be saved." This brought Paul and Barnabas into sharp dispute and debate with them. So Paul and Barnabas were appointed, along with some other believers, to go up to Jerusalem to see the apostles and elders about this question . . . "It seems good to the Holy Spirit and to us not to burden you with anything beyond the following requirements: You are to abstain from food sacrificed to idols, from blood from the meat of strangled animals and from sexual immorality. You will do well to avoid these things." (Acts 15:1–2, 28–29)

Luke narrates a critical meeting of the organization in the early days of its new era. As we look at this brief passage in the historical narrative we can discern several peacemaking management lessons at work:

- Paul and Barnabas, two key but relatively new peacemaking managers in the company, publicly and "sharply" contest some proposed office policies from Antioch managers.
- Paul and Barnabas, peacemakers, led the split Antioch delegation to Jerusalem in order to hash out the differences before the company national leaders.
- The national convention of the company, after debating the issue, came up with three proposals, with the justification that these proposals will be "good" for all concerned, as well as inspired by the company founder. The three proposals are:
    1. Abstention from eating food sacrificed to idols.
    2. Abstention from eating from blood from the meat of strangled animals.
    3. Abstention from sexual immorality.
- The initial issue was forcing the new members of the organization to adopt some old practices that warred against company harmony. The concern of the assembled coworkers believed that the issue being debated in Antioch was symptomatic of bigger issues outlined

by the chief executive officer, James.[509] The vote to follow the gentle leading of James was a stinging defeat for the Antioch conservatives, but they graciously accepted the vote and company harmony was achieved.

Paul the peacemaking manager

> Let us therefore make every effort to do what leads to peace[510] and to mutual edification.[511] Do not destroy the work of God for the sake of food. All food is clean, but it is wrong for a man to eat anything that causes someone else to stumble. (Rom 14:19–20)[512]

Most commentators miss the management lesson being taught in the passage by Paul the peacemaking manager because it is not the primary theme of these verses. The general focus of this chapter in Romans is on the relationship between the weak in the faith and the strong in the faith and the tendency to judge each other.

- Paul the peacemaking manager teaches us that the peacemaking manager is not to let a minor issue disrupt the harmony and unity of the organization. It is easy and even natural to have strong convictions about weak issues, and the manager's job is to be sure that such conviction doesn't get out of hand and divert the mission of the company.

- Paul the peacemaking manager tells us the peacemaking manager's job is to keep the eyes of the workers on the overarching corporate mission of the company and not let small and petty issues divide the workforce.

- Paul the peacemaking manager tells us the goal of corporate peace is not just for the institutional success but for the individual worker as well. Company peace and employee edification go hand in hand, and the peacemaking manager is responsible.

---

509. Acts 15:19–20.
510. *Eirene* = unity.
511. *Oikodome* = build.
512. Col 3:13–14.

THE TRAINING MANAGER

> So that the man of God may be thoroughly equipped[513] for every good work. (2 Tim 3:17)

Christianity has been a training religion since its very foundation. Education has always been critical for the believer.[514] The Christian manager is responsible for training coworkers for productivity, professional satisfaction, and protection. Managers create healthy work environments that include the proper training and equipment for worker success. Furthermore, the training of employees, even silly and irresponsible employees, is a critical part of the manager's Christian responsibility.[515] It has been pointed out that Christian training managers must take special interest in coworkers with few skills because the worker cannot negotiate from professional weakness. Once again, a shepherding heart is needed for the manager to keep emphasizing the value of further training,[516] all with the vocational purpose of beautiful work by the hands of employees.[517]

THE TRAINING MANAGER IN THE GOSPELS

Jesus the training manager

Jesus was the best training manager the world has ever seen. He knew all the responsibilities that a good manager needed to master in order to make an organization successful. That he trained the apostles in theology and administration and personnel relations is evident in Acts 2:14, "But Peter, standing with the eleven, lifted up his voice and addressed them: 'Men of Judea and all who dwell in Jerusalem, let this be known to you, and give ear to my words.'"

And off Peter goes in the first post-resurrection sermon. It is, of course, a masterful explanation of the gospel, with numerous citations from the

---

513. *Exartizo* = furnished, to put in appropriate condition.

514. Deut 6:6–7.

515. Genesis 22:8 is interesting in this regard since a roof parapet is designed to protect the foolish, the irresponsible, and the self-destructive person. The manager understands that without God's help we will all destroy ourselves. Once again, Doriani tells it straight: "God loves people who fall off buildings" (Doriani, *Work: Its Purpose, Dignity and Transformation*, 16, 141).

516. Cf. Phil 3:13.

517. Ps 90:17.

Old Testament incorporated into the life and message of Jesus of Nazareth with application to the new growing group of "Christians." What is so startling about this apostolic sermon is that:

- This is the same Peter, now filled with the Holy Spirit, who only weeks earlier rebuked Jesus for saying that he was going to Jerusalem to die.
- This was the same Peter who cowardly ran away on the night of Jesus' arrest.
- This is the same Peter who inspired Mark to write his Gospel account and in that account admitted to his own discredit that he did not understand Jesus' teaching that he was God, or that God was triune, or that there was to be a resurrection.[518]
- This is the same Peter who couldn't explain the gospel message to people "during the days of Jesus flesh."
- Peter and the rest of the uneducated apostles, who were clueless about the fundamental facts of Jesus of Nazareth, came to write the four Gospels, Acts, James, Peter, John, and Jude.

So what can explain the stunning turnaround in wisdom, eloquence, and managerial authority? It was the fifty days of teaching between the resurrection and Pentecost in which Jesus "opened the minds of the apostles to understand the Scriptures" (Luke 24:45). The well-educated Paul had his own lengthy training session in Arabia which mirrored what the apostles had gone through.[519] These men recruited, organized, managed, counseled, and trained other people to establish the world-wide organization in less than seventy years. The nineteenth-century Princeton theologian Charles Hodge wrote, "What then were the apostles? It is plain from the divine record that they were men immediately commissioned by Christ to make a full and authoritative revelation of his religion; to organize the organization; to furnish it with officers and laws; and to start it on its career of conquest through the world."[520]

> While Jesus was having dinner at Matthew's house, many tax collectors and sinners came and ate with him and his disciples.

---

518. Gen 36:15–29; Exod 15:15; 1 Chr 1:43–54.

519. Gal 1:12, 17–18.

520. Hodge, *What Is Presbyterianism?*, 53. Cf. Rayburn, "A Neglected Chapter in the History of Redemption: The Forty Days."

> When the Pharisees saw this, they asked his disciples, "Why does your teacher[521] eat with tax collectors and sinners?" On hearing this, Jesus said, "It is not the healthy who need a doctor, but the sick. But go and learn what this means: 'I desire mercy not sacrifice.' For I have not come to call the righteous, but sinners." (Matt 9:10–13)

Part of what angered Jesus so much in Matthew 9:10–13 is that with all the talent and training the scribes[522] and Pharisees enjoyed, they squandered their lives on their own self-aggrandizement.[523] Professional training for the manager should advance the flourishing of the managed as well as the manager. It should be other-directed.[524]

Christian training managers must seek their coworkers' good, and that good always involves further training, education, and resourcing of their vocational calling so that they might be more fulfilled workers in the image of the Creator and provide for the needs of themselves and their families.[525] With the result that in their fulfillment they might be the best stewards of the gifts, talents, and graces that God has given them.

> He also told them this parable: "Can a blind man lead a blind man? Will they not both fall into a pit? A student is not above his teacher,[526] but everyone who is fully trained[527] will be like his teacher." (Luke 6:39–40)

---

521. *Didaskalos*.

522. *Grammateus* = "teachers of the law." Ross notes, "In the New Testament period, the scribes were learned teachers and authoritative leaders, who were drawn from the priests and Levites, as well as the common people. Mark portrays them as high officials, advisors to the chief priest, and teachers of the Law. As such they were part of many types of officials opposed to Jesus. Matthew presents them as the learned of Judaism, leaders of the community. Luke portrays them as an appendage of the Pharisees, learned men who were protecting Judaism and leaders who were associated with the chief priests. It is clear from the many witnesses that the scribes had authority because they had knowledge. And whatever level of government they served they sought to preserve Judaism against opponents like Jesus" (Ross, "7. The Scribes").

523. Cf. Matt 2:4; Luke 18:9–14.

524. As Thielicke, *The Evangelical Faith*, 2.373, stated, "What matters is that the Pharisees do not use their superiority to understand love and hence to accept solidarity with the despised and to draw near to them in service. Because the one who is truly superior acts differently in this respect, or better because he is different.".

525. Eph 4:28; 1 Thess 4:11; 1 Tim 5:8; Titus 3:14.

526. *Didaskalos* = master.

527. *Katartizo* = to set up, establish, arrange. *Katartizo* comes from the root word *artios*.

Jesus on Specific Responsibilities of a Business Manager

Jesus gives an incarnational call for continuing education on the part of all Christian training managers to understand as much as possible about shepherding their organizational flock.[528] Indeed, in the Matthew parallel to Luke 6, Jesus commands his disciples to leave the blind leaders[529] lest the disciples be destroyed by taking a dangerous path, leading to demolition.[530] The Christian training manager must not be a "blind" manager, but rather an "enlightened" manager through the best training of management practices he can gather. The Greek word translated "trained" means "to put a thing in its appropriate place." It is used in the Gospels to mend and repair nets so that they can accomplish what they are designed to accomplish.[531] In this short Lukan parable, Jesus the Great Training Manager tells all his managers that "training" is a modeling lifestyle activity they need to emulate. The Christian training manager understands that the Greek word for training carries with it the signification of "appropriateness," "suitability," "usefulness," or "fitting a situation or requirements." So when "training" is used it means that the manager employs for his instruction for his coworkers that is "perfectly fitting and appropriate."

- The training manager knows his coworkers. The coworkers will not be successful if they are "blind." They need to follow a sighted manager who can show them how to arrive at their professional destination.

- The training manager is being told by Jesus not to be hasty in promoting coworkers to positions of responsibility. Their training must be suitably long and appropriate for the needs of the company.

- Luke 6 warns employees not to attach themselves to an ill-equipped teacher/trainer because it will be hard to overcome the limitations of that teacher.

- This parable advises the employees to look for a manager who can not only teach information, but life skills as well. Someone worth emulating ("be like").[532]

528. Luke 6:39–40.
529. *Hodegos.*
530. Matt 15:14.
531. Matt 4:21; Mark 1:19.
532. Acts 4:13, "When the secular society saw the courage of Peter and John, they realized that while the fishermen were unschooled, ordinary men, they were

Jesus grew[533] in wisdom[534] and stature,[535] and in favor with God and man. (Luke 2:52)

Jesus had his own "training" or "internship" period. In short, he grew and improved in discernment. The incarnate Word himself spent fifteen years beyond being a "young man" in management training before his heavenly father anointed him into management responsibilities at the age of thirty.[536] Luke, the gentile physician, noted the satisfactory results of Jesus' early training in Luke 2:52. Jesus' years of training under Joseph were in not only the construction of objects but in the financing, marketing, and planning needed to conduct business at a carpenter shop.

> But to sit at my right or left is not for me to grant. These places belong to those for whom they have been prepared.[537] (Mark 10:40)

In Mark 10:40, we see the Lord announcing that "preparation" for certain responsibilities is essential for selected individuals. Jesus tells James and John that placing them at his right and left hands is not up to him but rather up to God the Father. Needless to say, the other disciples were "indignant" over the brothers' request. The point for us is that the assignment of places will be according to those who have been "prepared" by the Father for those places. It is worth noting that their request comes late in the ministry of Jesus, and the brothers have been with him for several years, and still Jesus is not ready to make a commitment to them. This hesitation on the part of Jesus is due to his continued submission to the Father's will; the choice of organizational responsibilities will be up to the Father.[538] However, it also speaks to the fact that the Christian life is one of continual "preparation" for responsibilities. In the parable of the talents, we read that the manager gave each worker the number of talents "according to his ability."[539] This manager had trained his people

---

astonished as they took note that these men had been with Jesus."
533. *Prokopto*.
534. *Dokimazo*; Luke 4:22.
535. *Helikia* = greatness, length, age.
536. Luke 3:23.
537. *Hetoimazo* = to make ready.
538. Cf. Mark 13:32.
539. Matt 25:15; *dunamis* = "power," "strength."

Jesus on Specific Responsibilities of a Business Manager

to handle responsibility commensurate to that which was eventually delegated to them.

Then in Matthew 16 we have a most interesting parable:

> [Jesus] replied, "When evening comes, you say, 'It will be fair weather, for the sky is red,' and in the morning, 'Today it will be stormy, for the sky is red and overcast.' You know how to interpret[540] the appearance[541] of the sky, but you cannot interpret the signs of the times."[542] (Matt 16:2–3)

Jesus is reminding those assembled, many of them faithful God's people, that they spend a great deal of attention watching the weather. There is nothing wrong with that. We should notice the weather conditions. After all, we are dependent on the weather for our food, our livelihoods, our recreation—all God-given necessities of life. Weather is a gift from our Lord. Jesus just makes note of our weather-watching activity. This is elementary science, and we will and should practice it.

Jesus is saying we "understand" or "discern" the weather patterns. We make "right judgments" concerning the effects of observable weather "appearances." We look intently into the sky, we make a prediction and act accordingly, and the prediction comes true because we correctly "understand" the natural world. We base our lives and our behavior on what we perceive with our senses in the physical world around us. This is our basic scientific nature, and that is the way God meant it to be.[543]

Jesus reminds the training manager that he has the innate ability to think causally. He notices one event and he is able to draw a conclusion that another event will follow. He sees clouds off the Mediterranean and he accurately predicts rain.[544] He senses the sirocco wind from the southeast[545] and he accurately predicts heat.[546] His mind is so created that he is able to think causally—if this particular event happens, then this

---

540. *Dokimazein* = interpret.

541. *Proswpon;* Luke 12:56.

542. *Kairon* = season, opportunity, features, qualities of an era, time.

543. Is it any wonder why the great founders of modern science were all Christians? People like Copernicus, Galileo, Kepler, Newton, Boyle, Harvey, Beeckman. They were observant men who saw the face of God in the natural world. So it is a good thing that we are scientific creatures.

544. Cf. 1 Kgs 18:44.

545. Hos 12:1.

546. *Kauswn* = caustic, holocaust, scorching heat; cf. Isa 49:10; Jer 4:11–12.

particular event will follow.[547] The Greek word translated "times" is a special Greek word meaning "characteristics of an age."[548] It is the *Zeitgeist*, the "spirit of an age." Jesus is telling his managers to "scrutinize the spirit of your age" and make the appropriate management decisions.[549]

> They worship me in vain; their teachings[550] are but rules[551] taught by men. (Matt 15:9)[552]

The Greek word translated "rules" conveys the cultural pieties of the age. This is received wisdom which has the power of public acceptance.[553] By the time of Jesus there was growing body of oral tradition which was treated as authoritative by the Jewish cohort.[554] It was customary to be guided by these human rules and preferences which were learned by rote and memory. The point is that human rules and business customs have the power to override biblical teaching, and the business manager must always be on guard to vet business practices with the word of God. Christian training managers need to be constantly training themselves in shrewd conduct.

> "How is it you don't understand that I was not talking to you about bread? But be on your guard against the yeast of the Pharisees and Sadducees." Then they understood that he was not telling them to guard against the yeast used in bread, but against the teaching[555] of the Pharisees and Sadducees. (Matt 16:11–12)

Later in Matthew 16 Jesus instructs the thick-headed disciples about the ideas of false teachers using the metaphor of the influence of leaven:

547. Cf. Prov 20:27; 1 Cor 2:11.

548. The normal Greek word translated "time" in the New Testament is *cronos*.

549. Jesus now comes to the conclusion of his illustration which can be summarized by the Latin phrase *carpe diem* = "seize the day." He appeals to the manager to judge for themselves what is right. The Greek word translated "right" (*diakion*) means "just," "discerningly," "discriminatingly," to think about "doing the right thing" for his business, just as he thinks causally and "does the right thing" about the world around him. The manager is so capable about intellectually understanding and interpreting the signs of the natural, physical world, and he or she is to be as smart as the marketplace.

550. *Didasko*.

551. Greek = *entaima*; Hebrew = *mitswah* = doctrines (Cf. 1 Sam 17:20; Ruth 2:9; 2 Sam 21:14; Gen 49:29, 33).

552. Isa 29:13.

553. Cf. Col 2:22.

554. Which finally came to be the unbiblical Jewish Mishnah and Gemara.

555. *Didache* = doctrine.

"Beware of the leaven of the Pharisees and Sadducees" (Matt 16:11–12). The point of the short parable is not that leaven is bad because it is not by nature. Rather, leaven is used by Jesus to indicate the quick pervasiveness of one part to alter the whole. False ideas cannot be contained or compartmentalized or siloed away from other ideas. Once embraced and introduced into one's worldview everything else can be corrupted.[556] It is the same with management practices from non-believers. Some practices may be worthy of adoption, but many practices may be dangerous to the Christian training manager's walk with God. So be careful, because bad ideas could morph into bad company policy. Train to be shrewd.

> The master commended the dishonest manager[557] because he had acted shrewdly.[558] For the people of this world are more shrewd[559] in dealing with their own kind than are the people of the light. I tell you, use worldly wealth to gain friends for yourselves, so that when it is gone, you will be welcomed into eternal dwellings. (Luke 16:8–9)[560]

Jesus commands us to be wise in our management duties as he opens up the window to view the world's methodology *vis-a-vis* revealed truth with the parable of the shrewd manager.[561] Rather than being diplomatic and sensitive like the "dishonest manager" in dealing with people, "people of the light" are too often undiplomatic and unwise in their conduct toward others. Instead of acting in an endearing, binding way, in a

---

556. Cf. 1 Cor 5:6–8.

557. *Oikonomos* = steward.

558. *Phronimos* = wisely.

559. *Phronimos*.

560. Geldenhuys commented on this intriguing passage: "The master did not praise the manager's unjust and fraudulent act as such but the worldly wisdom with which he had acted towards the debtors. It was His object to use the parable to call attention to the wise and diplomatic manner in which worldlings generally act towards their fellow men in order to achieve their own selfish aims" (Geldenhuys, *Commentary on the Gospel of Luke*, 415–16).

561. Paul wrote: "Be very careful, then, how you live—not as unwise [fools, *aso-phos*] but as wise (*sophos*)" (Eph 5:15). He also wrote in 1 Timothy 4:7 for us to "train (*gumnazo*) [ourselves] to be godly." And yet, Jesus also taught that his heavenly Father was prepared to do miraculous things for the sake of his children's faith, and his glory: "I tell you the truth, if you have faith as small as a mustard seed, you can say to this mountain, 'Move from here to there,' and it will move. Nothing will be impossible for you" (Matt 17:20); "Jesus looked at them and said, 'With man this is impossible, but with God all things are possible'" (Matt 19:26).

way that commends association with them, Christian managers act in such a way that people of the "world" are unnecessarily repulsed. Christian managers are to have a "good reputation" to those outside the faith.[562] In the world, but not of the world—a difficult and dangerous ambiguity to embrace faithfully. This notion of using our trained rational faculties to shrewdly solve practical and everyday problems of the operation of a business was an established fact of God's economy by the time of Jesus. But it is a tightrope on which to walk the fine line between accommodation and differentiation.

The Training Manager in the Old Testament

Moses the training manager

> The Israelites did as Moses instructed[563] and asked the Egyptians for articles of silver and gold and for clothing. Yahweh had made the Egyptians favorably disposed toward the people, and they gave them what they asked for; so they plundered[564] the Egyptians. (Exod 12:35–36)

In Moses the training manager we see the personal welfare of every person assigned to him by God being important to God: "manservant," "maidservant," "alien,"[565] "city"[566]—even animals![567] The tools and resources created by unbelievers, sometimes in opposition to God's people, are to be used by Christian managers to further the will of Jesus. The principle is laid down for us by Moses in Exodus 12:35–36 when the Israelites, obedient to the instructions from Moses, "plundered the Egyptians" as they left Egypt for the promised land.

---

562. "I am sending you out like sheep among wolves. Therefore, be as shrewd [*phronimos* = wise] as snakes and as innocent as doves" (Matt 10:16; cf. 1 Tim 3:7–8; 1 Pet 2:15–17).

563. *Dabar* = word.

564. *Nasal* = spoiled, to snatch away, to free.

565. Exod 23:9.

566. *Shalom*, Jer 29:7.

567. Exod 20:10.

Joseph the training manager

> [Pharaoh] made [Joseph] master[568] of his household, ruler[569] over all the possessed, to instruct[570] his princes as he pleased and teach[571] his elders[572] wisdom. (Ps 105:21–22)

The psalmist gives us a glimpse of Joseph's management training regimen for Egyptian workers. In this one rich couplet the sage of the Psalms tells us the management style of Joseph the trainer includes the following:

- Joseph the training manager had earned the trust of his boss, Pharaoh. The Egyptian Pharaoh delegated enormous and intimate training responsibilities to the Jewish Joseph—"master of Pharaoh's household."

- Joseph the training manager had earned the respect and confidence of the owner of the company. There are seven personal pronouns

---

568. *Adon.* "Adoni-ram son of Abda—manager [was over, in charge of] forced labor" (1 Kgs 4:6; 5:14; 12:18). *Adon* is translated "lord," "in charge of," "master," "owner," "father." Famously, the term is applied to God, as in Exodus 34:23, "the Lord (*adon*), Yahweh, the God of Israel." But it also is used to not only designate human managers but is even part of their name, as in 1 Kings 4:6 (like "Lord Jim" in Conrad's *Heart of Darkness*). There were several Old Testament leaders who used *adon* in their name: cf. Adoni-jah ("my Lord is Jehovah"), the oldest living son of David after the death of Amnon and Absalom. This Adoni-jah wanted to become king after David instead of Solomon (2 Sam 3:4, 1 Kgs 1). Adoni-jah is described as a handsome and showy man but incompetent as a manager. He had no real command of the respect of the leading citizens who shouted, "Long live King Adonijah." When the people heard that Solomon had been crowned they "rose in alarm and dispersed." Adoni-jah admitted the inevitable but later engaged in political intrigues which led to his death by the command of Solomon (1 Kgs 2). "Adonijah, the leader (*rosh*) of the people during Nehemiah's governorship" (Neh 10:16); Adonijah was a Levite and teacher for King Jehoshaphat who delegated to him the task of teaching the law (2 Chr 17:8). There is also Adoni-kam ("my Lord has risen up") who led a group of exiles back to Jerusalem (Neh 7:8). Adoni-ram ("my Lord is exalted") was a manager in the kingdom of David, Solomon, and Rehoboam. He was a political survivor. Interestingly, there was Adoni-zedek ("Lord of righteousness"), the Canaanite king of Jerus at the time of the conquest, who was defeated by Joshua at the battle of Gibeon (Josh 10). Joseph is called an *adon* (Gen 42:10), as is Boaz (Ruth 2:13). Perhaps the most charitable way to defined managerial qualities in an *adon* is to note that the character of Yahweh is encompassed in *adon* (*adonai* = LORD of lords) (Deut 10:17).

569. *Mashal.*
570. *Asar* = to gird, bind, imprison, discipline. Isa 11:5; Eph 6:14.
571. *Hakam.*
572. *Zaqen.*

in these two verses, and only one can reasonably refer to Joseph. It is really quite astonishing that Pharaoh would delegate some much authority and freedom to an individual outside the organization, and a young one at that, to train the managers of Egypt.

- Joseph the Jewish training manager was made "ruler over all" the Egyptian king possessed. Nothing was kept from Joseph's oversight. The earned trust was total. The president of the corporation gave the running of the corporation over to his CEO: Joseph. Two words bear mentioning before I move on: "master" and "ruler." The Hebrew word translated "master" has enormous weight. It connotes ownership. Indeed, the word is used to describe the pharaoh himself.[573] The Hebrew word translated "ruler" is a familiar word meaning to rule, have dominion, or govern. Part of Joseph's responsibilities was to train the administrative staff of the Egyptian government.

- Joseph the Jewish training manager is the trainer of all Egyptians! The money clause: "to discipline his princes as he pleased and teach his elders wisdom." The Hebrew term translated "discipline" or "bind" can also be translated "imprison" or "gird." The LXX, Jerome, and Leslie Allen all translate the term "instruct" based on the Hebrew.[574] The context doesn't seem to make sense in order to warrant the translation of "binding" or "imprisonment." I prefer the translation of "instruct," but using "gird" or "discipline" to color "instruct" does give us a sense of Joseph's management style—tough love—and the goal of his training program: to standardize the administrative process.

- Not only is Joseph the training manager a tough taskmaster and a disciplinarian, but he is a teacher of leadership. Here is another management principle being exercised: authority. Furthermore, the translated phrase "as he pleased" or "at his pleasure" or "personally" is literally "by means of his life" or "in his throat." The point being made here by the psalmist is that Joseph the training manager was personally involved in the instruction, no delegation here, and that part of the instruction was the conduct of Joseph's life. He was a living lesson in wisdom and leadership to the leader of Egypt.

---

573. Gen 40:1.
574. Allen, *Psalms 101–150*, 38; Jerome, *Homilies*, 1.1–59.

- Joseph the training manager was to teach the Egyptian managers in the art of leadership and administrative details, and he was do this by exemplifying what a manager looks like. He was to model leadership and management aplomb.

- Joseph the training manager "taught" the elders of Egypt. This Hebrew word means practical wisdom and skill. This is what Joseph is "teaching." So he was teaching them political science, economics, ethics, and leadership principles. The Hebrew term translated "wisdom" was not speculative but practical. The psalmist uses a form of a Hebrew term[575] which tells us that the wisdom teaching of Joseph the training manager was to convey an intelligent approach to life's experiences. The word is also used to describe the construction skills of the tabernacle workers.[576] Joseph was teaching skills and prudential decisions. No doubt Joseph was even smuggling in God's word since Hebrew "wisdom" was really nothing more than what Yahweh had revealed to Joseph. And all this Egyptian teaching and discipline and being done by a thirty-year-old Jew.[577] The word translated "elders"[578] often refers to an experienced ruling body of men. This was the governing council of managers for Pharaoh. So here we have Joseph training the senior managers of Egypt.[579]

- Joseph the training manager was to train the Egyptian managers in the concept of Hebrew wisdom, meaning prudential living, practical skills, and ethical behavior.

David the training manager

> He chose David his servant and took him from the sheep pens; from tending[580] the sheep he brought him to be the shepherd[581] of his people Jacob, of Israel his inheritance. And David

---

575. *Chakham.*
576. Exod 35:10.
577. Gen 41:46.
578. *Zaqen.*
579. Deut 21:19; Prov 31:23; elsewhere.
580. *Achar* = following after.
581. *Eved* = servant.

shepherded[582] them with integrity[583] of heart; with skillful[584] hands he led[585] them. (Ps 78:70–72).

In Psalm 78:70–72 we see the time element of management training noted by Asaph in that David progressed from being a shepherd of sheep in contained pens to being a shepherd of sheep in the open field to being a shepherd of God's people. This progression took time and stages.[586]

It is difficult to know exactly how long David was in management training, but we know he ruled Israel for forty years[587] and we know he was a "young man" when he left the pasture for the palace,[588] so he probably was a young teenager when he began his training. We have the account from Josephus that David was seventy when he died.[589] With these assumptions we can say that David's divine management training lasted approximately fifteen years, more if we count his youthful shepherding years as training.[590]

> Blessed be Yahweh, my rock, who trains[591] my hands for war
> and my fingers for battle. (Ps 144:1)

In Psalm 144, David is praising God for training him in the art of war. The Hebrew word for "training" is used for more than just instruction and learning. There is the physical element to the term which is seen in its use in Hosea 10:11 where Ephraim is likened to a "trained cow" that loves to be doing what they were created to do—working in the field. In fact, the word comes from the family of words referencing a prod for

582. *Raah* = feed.
583. *Tom.*
584. *Tovunah.*
585. *Nachah* = guide.
586. As Plummer has noted, "God . . . chose the neglected David and raised him, step by step, till his throne was settled and his kingdom established. He had been faithful over a few things and God made him faithful over many things" (Plummer, *Psalms*, 761). On this same passage. Spurgeon made note: "To the man thus prepared, the office and dignity which God had appointed for how often divine wisdom so arranged the early and obscure portion of a choice life, so as to make it a preparatory school for a more active and noble future" (Spurgeon, *Treasury of David*, 2.347).
587. 1 Kgs 2:11.
588. 1 Sam 17:55—18:2.
589. Josephus, *Ant.* 7.15.2; Scott, "David."
590. I.e., seventy years old at death - forty years of reign = thirty years old when he became king - fifteen years of training = fifteen years old.
591. *Lamad* = instruct, practice, learn.

oxen. The point for us is that God uses all manners of things to get us to do what he wants because training is important. The principle stands: the training manager needs to use available resources to train his coworkers to do the job they are hired to do.

Solomon the training manager

> The proverbs for attaining wisdom and discipline; for understanding words of insight; for acquiring a disciplined and prudent life, doing what is right and just and fair; for giving prudence to the simple, knowledge and discretion to the young—let the wise listen and add to their learning, and let the discerning get guidance. (Prov 1:2–3)

The principle of training for success is given in Proverbs 1. Indeed, this brief passage covers all the bases that good training affords the employees: wisdom, discipline, understanding, insight, prudence, righteousness, justice, fairness, knowledge, discretion, learning, guidance. Solomon continues in his proverbial gems. In Proverbs we see many verses that Solomon copied from pagan sources to make a spiritually relevant point on prudential living.[592] It is crucial that the employee has the necessary resources to complement her training. The proper tools, diligent preparation, and a sense of priorities for the worker are seen as crucial to the worker's welfare, all of which a wise manager should provide. We see the mention of the "training" of individuals as keenly important to their personal success:

> Train[593] a child in the way he should go, and when he is old he will not turn from it. (Prov 22:6)

You can discern three simple steps to this early "training" effort:

- The manager needs to understand and support the training.
- The manager needs to review the results of the training.
- The manager needs to follow-up to be sure that the training is being implemented.

---

592. Cf. Prov 30:1, "Agur son of Jakeh"; Prov 31:1, "King Lemuel"; and Egyptian influence in earlier Proverbs.

593. *Chanik*.

Non-believers have this God-given attribute of prudency and practical wisdom on "the way they should go," even if that "way" doesn't involve Yahweh.[594]

- Iron sharpens iron.[595]
- Whoever loves discipline loves knowledge.[596]
- Every prudent man acts out of knowledge.[597]
- Listen to advice and accept instruction,[598] and in the end you will be trained.[599]
- Finish your outdoor work and get your fields ready; after that, build your house.[600]

Proverbs famously puts the value of training in work before the individual in Proverbs 22:

> Do you see a man skilled[601] in his work? He will serve before kings; he will not serve before obscure men. (Prov 22:29)

This "wise saying" puts it bluntly: If one works hard with skill one will succeed in his career and do important work. If one is lazy and untrained one will fail in their career and work only in the lowest of jobs. The Hebrew word translated "skill" is used in related terms in Near East texts to mean "able," "craftsman-like," "experienced and learned," and "prudent."

---

594. Egyptians, Gen 41:8; Babylonians, Isa 44:25; Persians, Esth 6:13, "Hanukkah" comes from the root of *chanik*.

595. Prov 27:17.

596. *Dhaath*, Prov 12:1.

597. *Dhaath*, Prov 13:16.

598. *Musar*.

599. *Chanik* = wise; Prov 13:18.

600. Prov 24:27; cf. Prov 27:23–27.

601. *Mahir*. The Old Testament uses the term in three other places: Ezra 7:6; Ps 45:1; Isa 16:5. Jesus picks up the theme of the proverb in Matt 25:14–30. where trust in small responsibilities leads to trust is big responsibilities.

Isaiah the training manager

> Listen and hear my voice; pay attention and hear what I say. When a famer plows for planting, does he plow continually?[602] Does he keep on[603] breaking up and harrowing the soil? When he has leveled the surface, does he not sow caraway and scatter cummin? Does he not plant wheat in its place, barley in its plot and spelt in its field? His God instructs[604] him and teaches[605] him the right way.[606] Caraway is not threshed with a sledge, nor is a cartwheel rolled over cummin; caraway is beaten out with a rod, and cummin with a stick. Grain must be ground to make a bread; so one does not go on threshing it forever. Though he drives the wheels of his threshing cart over it, his horses do not grind it. All this also comes from Yahweh Almighty, wonderful in counsel[607] and magnificent in wisdom.[608] (Isa 28: 23–29)

In this extended but extraordinary passage, Isaiah tells us that Yahweh is, along with everything else, a vocational ag teacher in how to make a living.

- Isaiah the training manager presents Yahweh as training ("instructing," "teaching," "counselling") an agri-businessman on how to raise a profitable crop, from the cultivating of the soil to the sowing of the various seeds, to the harvesting methods of the various crops, to the timing of the entire process. God is in the business of training his people to be discerningly productive.

- Isaiah the training manager points out that the good training manager knows when to stop and move on to the next stage of production.

---

602. All day.

603. Open and break.

604. *Yasar* = to reprove, disciple, teach. The Hebrew root of this word has the definite connotation of either physical enforcement or verbal reinforcement. One becomes educated when the proper amount of training and correction are imposed.

605. *Yarah* = to case, show, direct.

606. *Mispat* = discretion.

607. *Etsah* = plan, advice, consultation. Rehoboam rejected the *etsah* of the older men of Israel (1 Kgs 12:8, 13) and Absalom rejected Ahithophel's good *etsah* in 2 Sam 17.

608. *Tushiyah* = counsel, understanding.

The Training Manager in the New Testament

The disciples as training managers

To repeat: In a little recognized historical situation, the disciples underwent an extraordinary period of training in the forty days between the resurrection and the ascension. At the time of the resurrection the people were clueless about the life and ministry of Jesus, but by the time of the ascension they were sophisticated and experienced preachers of the gospel as evidenced by Peter's extraordinary sermon in Acts 1:15–17. What happened during that time? The Bible is silent, but intensive training obviously happened! We get a hint of this training in Luke 24:45–49 when Jesus "opened their minds so they could understand the Scriptures." And ten days later at Pentecost, Peter delivered his great sermon recorded in Acts 2. Fifty days after the resurrection, God used these ill-equipped disciples to begin to change the world after they underwent the most extraordinarily intensive training in history.

Paul the training manager

> [Mangers], provide[609] your [coworkers] with what is right[610] and fair,[611] because you know that you also have a [manager] in heaven. (Col 4:1)

Here Paul the training manager is telling the manager to treat his employee with equality. This is not social equality but rather professional equal and evenhanded treatment. No worker should get preferential training. Fairness is demanded by God. Thus, the principle of coworker justice and fairness is laid down for all business managers:

> You must teach[612] what is in accord[613] with sound[614] doctrine . . . encourage the young men to be self-controlled.[615] In everything set them an example of doing what is good. In your

---

609. *Parecho* = to hold alongside, give.
610. *Dikaios*.
611. *Isotes*.
612. *Laleo* = speak at random.
613. *Prepei*.
614. *Hugiaino* = healthy.
615. *Sophroneo* = moderate, sober.

teaching[616] show integrity,[617] seriousness and soundness of speech that cannot be condemned ... Teach coworkers[618] to be subject to their managers[619] in everything, to try to please them, not to talk back to them, and not to steal from them, but to show that they can be fully trusted. (Titus 2:1, 6–10)

One can learn "sound" business principles from the world. J. G. Hamann laid a great deal of importance on the fact that God communicated truth and illumination of revealed truth not only through unbelievers but also through nature and experience. Hamann stated that God has revealed himself in nature and his word and that "both revelations explain and support one another, and cannot contradict one another, however much the explanations of our reason would like to show contradictions."[620] Obviously, Paul is referencing theologically sound doctrine in the midst of heresy detailed in Titus 1. The Greek word translated "accord" can also be translated "become," meaning that integrating faith and behavior is critical to the Christian manager. Paul the training manager has a habit of connecting doctrine to godly living.[621] Furthermore, the Greek word for "sound" can also be translated "healthy."

So, to apply this verse to the managerial responsibility, in order to create a healthy environment in an organization it is important that fitting and appropriate training for the employees be a part of a manager's business practice. Paul the training manager is encouraging business managers to be aware of the best practices in their field and endeavor to integrate these "sound" business practices with "sound" theology.

616. In all things.
617. *Typos kalos ergon* = pattern of good works.
618. *Doulos* = slaves.
619. *Despotes* = despot, unlimited authority.
620. Hamann, 119. If "science" can be defined as "knowledge acquired by study which is concerned either with a connected body of demonstrated truths or with observed facts systematically classified and more or less colligated by being brought under general laws, and which includes trustworthy methods for the discovery of new truth within its own domain" (*The Compact Edition of the Oxford English Dictionary*, 2668), then the incarnational manager is to seek a better understanding of the "science" of management from any source which will aid that manager's shepherding performance. The anvil of Scripture is the judge of all management theory and principles and practices, so if our knowledge is bedrocked on the revealed word and knowledge of God then our duty is to aggressively seek knowledge for more management insight.
621. Eph 5:3; 1 Cor 11:13; 1 Tim 2:10.

> We are taking pains[622] to do what is right,[623] not only in the eyes of the Lord but also in the eyes of people. (2 Cor 8:21)

Paul the training manager is stating that as a financial manager his conduct must be open to the scrutiny of everyone, members or not.[624] If he is slipshod in financial matters his leadership will be ruined, so everything must be "above board."

In the leadership qualifications given to us in 1 Timothy 3:2–7 and Titus 1: 6–9 we see that one of the main attributes for the manager of the company is that he needs to be teachable, not quarrelsome, and already a holder of a track record in managing people, his family.

> Managers,[625] provide[626] your coworkers[627] with what is right[628] and fair,[629] because you know that you also have a master in heaven. (Col 4:1)

In this Colossians 4 passage, Paul the training manager enjoins managers to provide their employees with what is right and fair, because they know that they have a Manager in heaven who provides them with all they need for success. Paul uses a Greek word translated to "provide," or better, "hold alongside of as equal" to indicate that employers are to treat employees as equal. Even sinners are to be accorded respect and honor as human beings. Following the commandment to honor one's parents,[630] the Old Testament has coworkers calling their superiors "father."[631] In fact, the same respect and honor that should be given to the emperor should be given to all employees.[632] "If employers always did this, there would be no labour problems."[633] Jesus tells all Christian managers to do the loving thing for all those with whom the manager is associated, even

---

622. *Pronoeo* = to plan, to think before.

623. *Kalos* = honorable, honest, excellent, good; Phil 4:8; 1 Pet 2:12; Rom 14:18, "approved by men."

624. 2 Cor 8:19.

625. *Kurios* = owner, master.

626. *Parecho* = to furnish, supply, equip, provide.

627. *Doulos* = servants, slaves.

628. *Dikaios* = just.

629. *Isotes* = equal, likeness in proportion.

630. Exod 20:12.

631. 2 Kgs 2:12; 5:13.

632. Cf. 1 Pet 2:13–17.

633. Robertson, *Word Pictures in the New Testament*, 4.509.

if they are not Christians, or are not even sympathetic or tolerant of the manager's faith convictions.

> It was he who gave . . . pastors and teachers to prepare[634] God's people for works of service, so that the body of Christ may be built up. (Eph 4:12)

While this Ephesians verse is preeminently used in an ecclesiastical context, it can also supply us with a business organization maxim for the Christian training manager as that manager attempts to cause each co-worker to fully "prepare themselves for works of service" in pursuit of the company mission. Paul uses another cognate version of the Greek word translated "prepare" in 2 Timothy 3:17, "so that the man of God may be thoroughly equipped[635] for every good work." The point here is that incarnational training managers have the responsibility to see that every person Jesus gives them to work with is equipped to do the job assigned to that person in the best stewardship fashion possible.[636]

Hebrews and the training manager

> No discipline seems pleasant at the time, but painful. Later on, however, it produces a harvest of righteousness and peace for those who have been trained[637] by it. Therefore, strengthen[638] your feeble arms and weak knees. (Heb 12:11–12)

Management is a long-term, continual process, the complexities of which can't be learned outside the rough-and-tumble world of human experience and relationships. It is not prudent to be a manager before one's time.[639] In Hebrews 12 we read of God's discipline for our spiritual benefit. Couldn't this thought be applied to management education as a

---

634. *Katartizo*.

635. *Exartizo*.

636. Cf. 2 Cor 9:8–10; In Ephesians 4:11–12 and 1 Thessalonians 5:14 we see the training for success being delegated to other coworkers and not just the province of the managerial class. Interestingly, the church father John Chrysostom (347–407) argued that this 1 Thessalonian passage refers to managers ("brothers") in the church (Chrysostom, *Homilies on the Epistles of St. Paul the Apostle to the Philippians, Colossians, and Thessalonians*, 13.366–67).

637. *Gumnazo* = exorcized, to use.

638. *Anorthoo* = lift up, to erect again.

639. Cf. Rehoboam's eagerness in 1 Kgs 12; Jas 3:1.

step of obedience on the path of being a more effective godly shepherd of an organization? Effective management training will not be pleasant and easy because new skills are being taught and old skills are being discarded. Even though such management education may be tedious, inconvenient, sometimes misguided, costly, and time-consuming, won't it be richly rewarding if we endure? I believe so.

Peter the training manager

> Live as free people, but do not use your freedom as a cover-up for evil;[640] live as servants of God. Show proper respect to everyone: love the Brotherhood of believers, fear God, honor the king. (1 Pet 2:16–17)

Peter the training manager instructs Christian training managers not to use their management position to mistreat those around them in the organization, but rather to treat every person with dignity and respect: "Do not use your freedom as a cover up for evil." I expand this to mean managers are not to use their managerial position to do malice to their coworkers.[641] So Peter is not necessarily referring here to moral evilness or debauchery, but rather to "a personal mischievousness which hurts" those in the organization by not adequately preparing them to flourish in their job. Clearly the context deals with interpersonal relationships between people of varying social, economic, and political positions, which aptly describes any organization.[642]

---

640. *Kakia* = mischievousness.

641. *Kakia* can mean "bad quality," and William Vine maintains it is the opposite of "excellence" (Vine, *Expository Dictionary of New Testament Words*, 94).

642. Calvin commented in a fitting way: "In the first place, Peter denies that there is any cloak or pretext for wickedness by which he means that we are not given liberty to hurt our neighbors, or to do any harm to others. True liberty is that which harms or injures no one . . . Peter's commands that honor is to be rendered to all, I explain as an order that none are to be neglected. It is a general command, which refers to the fostering of human fellowship. The word, *giddail* . . . conveys to me the simple idea that regard ought to be had for all men, since we ought to cultivate, as far as we can, peace and friendship with all; there is, indeed, nothing more inimical to concord than contempt" (Calvin, *Commentary on Hebrews and I & II Peter*, 272–73).

THE COMPETING MANAGER

> Do nothing out of selfish ambition or vain conceit, but in humility consider others better than yourselves. Each of you should look not only to your own interests, but also to the interests of others. (Phil 2:3–4)

In market economies like that which still exists in the United States, competition fosters innovation, efficiency, and surplus. As I have previously stated, I am a running dog capitalist and happily so. However, as a Christian, there needs to be reflection about competition. This is not the book to do that, except to say that Jewish sociologist Amitai Etzioni has posited a helpful distinction about competition in that he argues for an "I and we" approach to the marketplace as opposed to an "I and I" approach.[643] Other writers have called this approach "covenantal thinking."[644] The basic question to be answered by the covenantal approach to competition is "How is what the manager is doing benefiting his coworkers and customers?" and not the self-interested notion of how is it benefiting the organization. This personal management approach should color every decision the manager makes.

THE COMPETING MANAGER IN THE GOSPELS

Jesus the competing manager

> But I tell you who hear me: Love your enemies, do good to those who hate[645] you. Bless those who curse[646] you, pray for those who mistreat[647] you. If someone strikes[648] you on one cheek[649] turn to him the other also. If someone takes[650] your cloak,[651] do

---

643. Etzioni, *The Moral Dimensions*.

644. DePree, *Leadership Is an Art*. I had the pleasure of siting in Mr. DePree's lectures while getting my doctorate at Fuller Theological Seminary in the late 1980s.

645. *Misco;* cf. Luke 1:71; Ps 18:17; 106:10.

646. *Kataraomai* = to give over to ruin, to wish anyone ruin.

647. *Perezone* = abuse, to act spitefully.

648. *Typtein* = to hit.

649. *Siagona* = jaw.

650. *Airol* = to lift up.

651. *Himation/chiton* = outer garment/inner garment.

not stop him from taking your tunic. Give to everyone who asks you and if anyone takes what belongs to you, do not demand it back . . . But love your enemies, do good to them, and lend to them without expecting to get anything back. (Luke 6:27-30, 35)

In Luke 6:27-36 we have Jesus' exhortation to show integrity and moral courage under duress and unfairness.[652] The point of this parable for us is that Christian competing managers will show themselves to be God's children by their imitation of Jesus' character. Private marketplace revenge is strictly forbidden![653] The manager's response to his competitors is not to be reciprocal or proportionate but radically different. Samson reflected the moral standards of the world when he responded in a reciprocal fashion: "I merely did to them what they did to me."[654] The manager's ruthless competitors are those that are defined as:

- Those who "hate" you.

- Those who "curse" you. The Greek word for "curse" means "to wish someone ruin or extinction." For the competitors of the Christian manager, their enemies in anger will wish to harm or destroy them in the name of an unnamed god indicating the depth of their hatred. The idea of blessing a competitor is to invoke God's favor on that person, particularly enemies, as both Jesus[655] and Stephen did.[656] It bears mentioning that Paul, in an apparent momentary weakness, "cursed anyone who does not love the Lord."[657]

- Those who "mistreat" you. The mistreatment or abuse at the hands of the competitors will be borne out of malice and spite. The pagan Greek writer Lysias (445-380 BC) enunciated the world's approach: "I consider it established that one should do harm to one's enemies."[658] The Christian manager must not so respond but follow Jesus.

652. Peter reiterates the exhortation in 1 Peter 2:19-21.
653. Marshall, *Commentary on Luke*, 264.
654. Judg 15:11.
655. Luke 23:24.
656. Acts 7:60.
657. 1 Cor 16:22; cf. Gal 1:8-9; 2 Thess 3:14-15. The rejection is not of Paul's teaching, but rather of Jesus.
658. Lysias, *Against Eratosthenes*, 9.20. Cf. Simonides, "Plato Republic," paragraph 642; Hesiod, *The Works and Days*, lines 340-57; Pindar, "Ode #2," line 83.

- Those who "take your coat/tunic." The competitors will seek to steal from the Christian manager, but the appropriate response is to exercise charity, expecting no return. In fact, the Christian manager should expect repeated stealings. The risk is that the manager will become naked, figuratively and literally, as the competitor takes everything from him.

- Those who "strike your cheek." The opportunity to be struck on the cheek is greater when a manager exposes himself by reaching out a helping hand to assist a competitor. The risk is for more abusive attacks because the rival knows there won't be a counterattack because the Christian manager has become vulnerable with an outstretched hand. There is the hint of this because the Greek word translated "strike" suggests that the hit is more than just a ltender tap but rather a full-blown blow to the face. To return the blow is anti-Christian and restraint requires supernatural self-discipline.

- Those who refuse to follow the so-called golden rule. The context of this phrase can mean to give money without expecting to be paid back or to give money without expecting credit. Either way, it goes against human nature and requires spiritual maturity on the part of the Christian competing manager.

To sum up the Luke 6 passage: The Christian competing manager will alter not only his behavior but his very character as he follows Jesus the competing manager.[659] The morality of the world expects commensurate responses to actions. Christian morality requires the manager to not expect commensurate good response to doing good and warns the manager not to despair when he doesn't receive good for doing good.[660] Furthermore, the competing manager is not to respond to ruthlessness by being ruthless. The Christian competitor must respond with the leaven of love.

---

659. As Edwards notes, even the most righteous among us is a debtor to the grace of Christ (Edwards, *The Gospel According to Luke*, 200). Cf. Luke 17:7–10.

660. Luke 6:35.

THE COMPETING MANAGER IN THE OLD TESTAMENT

Job the competing manager

> If I have rejoiced[661] at my enemy's misfortune[662] or gloated[663] over the trouble[664] that came to him—if I have not allowed my mouth to sin by invoking a curse[665] against his life . . . (Job 31:29-30)

The Hebrew grammar of these verses is a bit difficult, but for our purposes the grammar is not too important. What is being stressed here by Job is that he does not rejoice in the troubles which beset his competitors.[666] *Schadenfreude* is out! Furthermore, he has not invoked God's displeasure on his competitors. Job the competitive manager is showing compassion on his foes. "Rejoicing" is a strong verb, and it indicates that Job the competitive manager is not happy that Yahweh is giving his competitor some tough waters to go through. It would only be natural for there to be a bit of joy, a smirk to see a competitor suffer a bit, but there is not to be any vengefulness or ecstatic feelings. Yahweh warned the Edomites to watch their gloating: "You should not look down on your brother in the day of his misfortune, nor rejoice over the people of Judah in the day of their destruction, nor boast so much in the day of their trouble" (Obad 12). Being glad can be a fleeting feeling but not a sustained and deliberate attitude towards the misfortunes of a manager's competitors.[667]

---

661. *Sameach* = shine, be glad.
662. *Pid* = disaster, ruin, destruction.
663. *Ur* = lifted or stirred me up.
664. *Ra* = evil, unpleasantness.
665. *Alah* = a promise.
666. Still, there are biblical examples of rejoicing over the troubles of the wicked competitors: Job 22:19-20; Ps 52:6; 58:11; 107:42; 109:6-20; 118:7; 137:8-9; 143:12; 144:6; Prov 1:26; Jer 11:20; 12:3.
667. Nah 3:19.

Moses the competing manager

> Do not have two differing[668] weights in your bag—one heavy, one light. You must have accurate[669] and honest[670] weights and measures, so that you may live long in the land Yahweh your God is giving you. For Yahweh your God detests[671] anyone who does these things, anyone who deals dishonestly. (Deut 25:13–16)[672]

This early admonition about unscrupulous business practices is often seen to be an ancient Hebrew Federal Trade Commission missive to treat customers honestly. That is true, but it also has a competitive interpretation as well: The Christian competing manager must not seek to unscrupulously undercut competition by falsifying his product or services. This law obviously speaks to the tenth commandment against coveting, which is an attitude that all Christian competing managers must guard against. The danger is that the businessman could obtain more than he paid for by using a large weight or measure and when selling use a light weight[673] or measure,[674] thus providing less product than what the customer paid for. All of these schemes allow for a lower price that the customer pays for the goods obtained, and fewer goods sold to the customer for the price paid. Thus stealing customers from competitors while keeping the stock of goods for future sales. The Christian competitive manager's God "detests" such practices.

David the competing manager

> Now here is the man who did not make God his stronghold but trusted in his great wealth and grew strong by destroying[675] others. (Ps 52:7)

---

668. *Eben* = literally: a stone upon a stone, weight.
669. *Shalem* = whole, complete, perfect.
670. *Tsedeq* = just, fair, truth.
671. *Toebah* = abomination.
672. Cf. Lev 19:35–37; Prov 11:1; 16:11; 20:10, 23; Amos 8:5; Mic 6:11; Hos 12:7.
673. *Eben* = stone.
674. *Ephah* = a unit of capacity in vessels designed to hold grain.
675. *Hawwah* = wicked, mischievous, perverse.

Psalm 52 speaks of the man who "plots destruction," "works deceit," "lies with words that devour," and is summed up as one who "craves to be strong in order to be destructive."[676] Enough said.

Solomon the competing manager

> Do not gloat when your enemy falls; when he stumbles, do not let your heart rejoice, or Yahweh will see and disapprove and turn his wrath away from him. (Prov 24:17–18)[677]

Solomon the competing manager warns against a Psalm 52-type of thinking for the business manager in Proverbs 24:17–18. Money, power, and sin are a temping combination to exercise ruthless competition on an opponent. Another warning against *Schadenfreude*.[678] Yahweh commends and praises Solomon for not asking for the death of his competitors in 1 Kings 3:11: "So Yahweh said to [Solomon], 'Since you have asked for this and not for long life or wealth for yourself, nor have asked for the death of your enemies,[679] but for discernment in administering[680] justice,[681] I will do what you have asked.'" Here treating one's competitors or enemies with care is equated with treating them with justice and divine compassion.

Isaiah the competing manager

> Woe to you who add house to house and join field to field till no space is left and you live alone in the land . . . Surely the great houses will become desolate, the fine mansions left without occupants. A ten-acre vineyard will produce only a bath of wine, a homer of seed only an ephah of grain. (Isa 5:8–10)

Isaiah 5:8–10 is a powerful passage in defining limits to a competitive attitude. Yahweh, through his prophet, is condemning the greedy land-grabbing activity of the clever rich who crowd out the poor homeowners until the wealthy have complete control of entire urban blocks of

---

676. For "craving," see Prov 10:3.
677. Cf. Prov 17:5.
678. A bit of divine *Schadenfreude* in Micah 2:4.
679. *Oyeb.*
680. *Shama* = hear, listen.
681. *Mispat.*

Jerusalem or acreage in the country. The result of such ruthlessness is that there is no room left for anybody but the opportunistic entrepreneur. These evil managers[682] now have so much land that they cannot even cultivate the acreage that they have accumulated. Isaiah is not condemning "fine mansions"[683] nor multiple acreage tracks.[684] Indeed, Yahweh is not accusing these rich folks of breaking the Mosaic law. If one needs those things to adequately and appropriately provide for themselves and their family, then those possessions are delightful in the eyes of God.[685] But when one uses one's economic power to force others into being homeless, landless, and dispossessed to the point of not being able to provide shelter and sustenance for their families,[686] then God will condemn that competitive spirit. Isaiah the competing manager is saying that unredeemed marketplace competitiveness seeks to destroy the livelihood of other persons by removing them from the marketplace entirely, leaving the field of economic battle to the winner, alone, in his/her own little world. They are literally king of the mountain.[687] The ruthless competitive manager has no need for other persons, so he attempts to drive them into financial extinction as he runs the risk of being devoured himself.[688]

Micah the competing manager

> Woe to those who plan iniquity,[689] to those who plot evil[690] on their beds! At morning's light they carry it out because it is in their power to do it. They covet fields and seize them, and

---

682. Men, women—"cows of Bashan," Amos 4:1.
683. Isa 5:9.
684. Isa 5:10.
685. Cf. 1 Tim 5:8.
686. Isa 5:8, "until no space is left."
687. "'Milton was right,' said my Teacher. 'The choice of every lost soul can be expressed in the words "Better to reign in Hell than serve in Heaven." There is always something they insist on keeping even at the price of misery . . . There are only two kinds of people in the end: those who say to God, "Thy will be done," and those to whom God says, in the end, "Thy will be done"'" (Lewis, *The Great Divorce*, 71, 75).
688. Isa 5:10; Amos 3:15; 5:11; 6:4–7. In the New Testament, Gal 5:15.
689. *Awen* = the major Hebrew term for sin.
690. *Ra* = inferior.

houses, and take them. They defraud[691] a man of his home, a fellowman of his inheritance. (Mic 2:1–2)

Here Micah the competing prophet/manager unloads on the grasping, avaricious competitive business manager who is so consumed with greed that he lays awake at night planning on how to increase his wealth. This is not a sudden, spontaneous, opportunistic act but rather a thoughtful, deliberate plan of malpractice. This is not a momentary acquiescence to temptation but a careful strategy to accumulate more. The evil competing manager can hardly wait until morning to begin his assault on his competitor, the little man. This can almost be seen as a rich city slicker fleecing a country bumpkin in the name of efficiency and profitability. Success is almost guaranteed, since "the graspers have the power to do it."[692] Micah puts us in the mind of the negotiation between Naboth, King Ahab, and Jezebel in 1 Kings 21. During Micah's time, King Uzziah had ushered in a time of prosperity and wealth through trade, and many Judean businessmen had become wealthy and wanted to indulge themselves. The Hebrew word translated "defraud" in Micah 2:12 means taking something away from another through an advantage or position or power. In Israel's social order in Micah's time a person's identity and dignity rested on his ownership of property. Take that away and the person had no place in the community. He would become a slave to others. So the taking of a house and a piece of land was more than just real estate theft. It was stripping away the legitimate status of another human being. And this could be all done legally and in the open because "it is in their power to do it."[693] The rich controlled the social and political structures, so getting what they wanted was relatively easy. They dominated the flow of commerce in society.[694] Not so different from today.

---

691. *Asaq* = oppress, wrong, extort.

692. Mic 2:2. As Lightfoot puts it, "There is a sort of religious purpose, a devotion of the soul to greed, which makes the sin of the miser so hateful" (Lightfoot, *Saint Paul's Epistles to the Colossians and to Philemon*). Cf. Prior, *The Message of Joel, Micah & Habakkuk*, 125–26.

693. Cf. Mic 3:1, 9; Amos 5:12.

694. "This text describes a classic case of the kind of imbalance of power between two parties that, humanly speaking, is almost guaranteed to lead to might prevailing over right. However, as a result of God's intervention in favor of the weaker party, whose labor has been unjustly exploited by the one in power, justice prevails" (Van Gemeren, *New International Dictionary of Old Testament Theology and Exegesis*, 1.399). Cf. Neh 5:5.

In short, unfettered competitiveness is anti-human and sub-Christian because it seeks economic murder.[695] It is this insatiable appetite for economic conquest that is the root of the condemnatory aspect of competition.[696] Providing for oneself and one's family is godly, but to cross over to rapacity is not! To determine the cross-over point is the artistic, discerning task of the Christian competitive manager. Tough decisions, but required!

The competing manager in the New Testament

> Bless those who persecute[697] you; bless and do not curse.[698] Rejoice with those who rejoice; mourn with those who mourn. Live in harmony with one another. Do not be proud but be willing to associate with people of low position.[699] Do not be conceited.[700] Do not repay[701] anyone evil for evil.[702] Be careful[703] to do what is right[704] in the eyes of everybody. If it is possible, as far as it depends on you,[705] live at peace with everyone.[706] Do not take revenge, my friends, but leave room for God's wrath, for it is written: "It is mine to avenge;[707] I will repay," says the Lord . . . Do not be overcome by evil but overcome evil with good. (Rom 12:14–19, 21)

---

695. A violation of Matthew 5:21–26.

696. Cf. Isa 57:17.

697. *Dioko* = to drive away, put to flight.

698. Matt 5:44; Luke 6:27–28; Mark 13:9; Luke 21:12; John 16:2.

699. Jesus, in the days of his flesh, again sets the model. Cf. Matt 5:3–5; 11:29; 18:4; 23:12; Mark 10:42–45.

700. Do not be wise in your own estimation. Collins, *Good to Great*, 17, argues that the best leaders in business are marked by personal humility.

701. *Apodidomi* = to give back, render, recompense.

702. Jesus, as our business role model, tells us the same thing. Cf. Matt 5:44, 38; Luke 6:28.

703. *Pronoeo* = provide, plan. Jesus, again, in the days of his flesh, tells us the same thing and provides the role model (Matt 5:16).

704. *Kalos* = honest, admirable, becoming (1 Pet 2:12).

705. *Pronoeo*. "Take thought for what is right in the eyes of all people," "respect what is right," "provide honest things."

706. Jesus tells us the same thing (Mark 9:50).

707. *Ekdikeo* = vindicate, justify.

The challenge for the Christian businessperson is to be lovingly competitive.[708] The English terms, "competition" or "strive" are translated from the Greek *athleo* in 2 Timothy 2:5 and Philippians 1:27, from which we get the word "athletics."[709]

Paul the competing manager

This Romans passage from Paul is the distillation of Old Testament wisdom, New Testament wisdom, Greek wisdom, and most especially Gospel wisdom from the mouth of Jesus. It is the classic Pauline statement against an unbridled competitive spirit:

- "Bless those who persecute you; bless and do not curse." Jesus promised persecution, but we don't usually apply that to marketplace persecution. Jesus also told the competitive manager to love his enemies. The Greek word translated "persecute" doesn't necessarily imply physical or judicial persecution but can just as easily be applied to economic opposition and social ostracism. Furthermore, there is to be no cursing, that is, imprecatory prayers, asking God to bring disaster on a competitor.[710]

- "Rejoice with those who rejoice; mourn with those who mourn." It is easier to sympathize with those who mourn than to celebrate with those who succeed, especially if they are our competitors. But Paul,

---

708. Eckerd: "I love to compete; I always have. I think that was probably the most enjoyable part of business to me, beating my competitors. I have been quoted as saying that when I was active in business, I hated my competitors. Well, I think I was misquoted on that. I didn't mean that I hated them personally, but I did hate the idea of losing to them, and that comes pretty close sometimes" (Eckerd and Conn, *Eckerd: Finding the Right Prescription*, 181).

709. Three other Greek words give us roughly the same aggressive meaning: *agonizornai* = "to contend, strive" (cf. 1 Cor 9:25–26; Luke 13:24; John 18:36, "fight"; 1 Cor 9:25; Col 1:29; 4:12; 1 Tim 6:12, "fight"; 2 Tim 4:7, "fight"), *erizo* = "to strive, wrangle" (only in Matt 12:19); *mache* = "to strive, fight, quarrel" (It appears eight times in New Testament: John 6:52; Acts 7:26, "fighting"; 2 Cor 7:5, "fighting"; 2 Tim 2:23–24, "quarrel"; Titus 3:9; Jas 4:1–2, "fight"). But none of these individual words are particularly helpful in assisting us to arrive at an adequate understanding of incarnational competition.

710. Cf. Ps 58. As Murray points out, "It is not the mere abstinence [of vindictiveness] that is here required nor is it simply endurance of the persecution, but the entertainment of the kindly disposition expressed in blessing" (Murray, *The Epistle to the Romans*, 134).

the competing manager, presses the competitive manager for this attitude. The manager is to take pleasure in others' victories as if they were his own! And lest he take comfort in half of Paul's admonition, he tells him that he is not to be glad at someone's misfortune or calamity, which is his bent.[711] It is one thing to be sad with another when difficulty strikes. It is quite something else to be pleased when a competitor enjoys success. Nothing is harder than to ask Jesus to prosper and bless the competitor who is nasty towards the manager.

- "Live in harmony with one another." Literally the Greek says, "think the same thing." This phrase can apply to the relationship between Christians and non-Christians in the marketplace in the sense that the ethical testimony of the Christian manager can positively influence the local marketplace. We will see hints of this later in this passage.

- "Do not be proud but be willing to associate with people of low position. Do not be conceited." This is especially *apropos* for the Christian manager with non-Christian employees and competitors. The exhortation is to be spiritually humble.

- "Do not repay anyone evil for evil." This negative exhortation is paired with the positive exhortation immediately following. There is to be no vindictive retaliation to "anyone."

- "Be careful to do what is right in the eyes of everybody." While we are not to repay evil for evil we should be careful not to needlessly antagonize our neighbor.[712] The Greek word means "take into consideration" or "think beforehand." So the emphasis is on thinking about how the manager is to act in the midst of non-believing employees and competitors. As Paul the competing manager tells the gentile Corinthian cohort, "commend ourselves to every man's conscience in the sight of God."[713] The Greek word translated "right" can mean more than moral or ethical right. It also connotes "honor" or "beauty," which, because of common grace, non-Christian

---

711. Cf. Prov 17:5.

712. Moo comments, "We should take Paul's words at face value: he wants us to commend ourselves before non-Christians by seeking to do 'what is right' that non-Christian approve and recognize. There is, of course, an unstated limitation to this command, one that resides in the word 'right' itself" (Moo, Letter to the Romans, 785).

713. 2 Cor 4:2.

competitors will appreciate. In this admonition Paul is saying to do what is right for our competing neighbor!

- "If it is possible, as far as it depends on you, live at peace with everyone." In this admonition, Paul the competing manager is saying to the competing manager, don't unnecessarily stir up your competing neighbor. Don't be pig-headed. This double qualification to "live at peace" tells us that Paul realizes how difficult this will be. There will be hostility and bias and cruelty in the marketplace that the Christian manager can do nothing about, but Paul is still setting forth the goal. Paul clearly sees social and economic conflict that awaits the Christian competitive manager, and so he lathers his admonitions to his qualification: "Be at peace, if it is possible, when it depends on you!"

- "Do not take revenge, my friends, but leave room for God's wrath, for it is written: 'It is mine to avenge; I will repay,' says the Lord." There is a sense in which Paul recognizes that taking "revenge" is the province of those who have the power to take revenge. Often the Christian competitive manager is not in a position to take revenge but only deal with putting up with nasty action on the part of a competition. However, for those managers in a position to wreck revenge Paul gives the admonition—Don't do it. "Revenge" has a spiritual component of self-righteousness that "repaying" doesn't have. The concept has a tinge of theological judgment, putting the vengeful manager in the place of God. After all, Paul the competing manager tells the manager in Romans 1:18 that God's judgment doesn't wait for heaven but is applicable right now in this life. So taking "revenge" is even more sinful for the Christian manager than a tit-for-tat repaying because the evil competitor may have his comeuppance in this life.

- "Do not be overcome by evil but overcome evil with good."[714] Stephen provides a great example in Acts 7:60. This sentence summarizes the entire paragraph. Paul isn't saying that by being a "good" Christian competitive manager, salvation will come to the competitor. No, only that shame may come to the ruthless competitor.[715] And the business manager has to be satisfied with that ambiguity.

714. Jesus again sets the Pauline tone for the Christian manager by demonstrating this attitude in Luke 23:34. Cf. Luke 6:27–28, 35.

715. "Burning coals on his head" (Rom 12:20).

Jesus on Specific Responsibilities of a Business Manager

This Romans paragraph is tough medicine designed for a minority Christian community in a powerful dominant community of Roman pagans. While Paul does not quote directly from the Lord, the words and thoughts of Jesus are apparent in the entire passage. Paul is telling us that by doing good competitive Christian managers are to be instruments of quenching the animosity and ill-doing of competitors and rivals. Paul the competing manager has no illusions about competing in the world's arena. He is stating that the Christian manager cannot respond to marketplace malevolence in kind lest evil simply feed on itself and spawn greater evil and good be vanquished and the Holy Spirit be quenched.[716]

> We work hard[717] with our own hands. When we are cursed,[718] we bless;[719] when we are persecuted,[720] we endure it;[721] when we are slandered,[722] we answer kindly.[723] Up to this moment we

---

716. 1 Thess 5:19; Dunn, *Romans 9–16*, 756.

717. *Ergazomai* = to be employed, to get by laboring; Matt 25:16; John 6:27; Rev 18:17. "Who through faith conquered kingdoms, managed [*ergazomai* = administrated] justice, gained what was promised; who shut the mouths of lions, quenched the fury of the flames and escaped the edge of the sword . . . who became powerful in battle and routed foreign armies?" (Heb 11:33–34). In this most interesting couplet, management is portrayed as an example of "faith" in Yahweh and raised to the heights of the eight other glorious achievements of faith. The preacher of Hebrews lists six Old Testament leaders plus "the prophets" as outstanding men of faith who were "managers of justice." The expression is used for doing what is right with reference to personal integrity and justly managing an organization for the people (LXX Ps 15, "practicing justice," v. 2); cf. Acts 10:35 ("doing what is right"). Good character = good management. The Greek word translated "managed" in this couplet comes from the Greek word *ergon*, meaning "work" or "labor" and could very well refer back to those two great Old Testament managers: David (2 Sam 8:15) and Solomon (1 Kgs 10:9). It is the word from which we get "ergonomics." Among the nine active verbal triumphs coming right after "conquered" and before "shut" is "managed." Jesus uses the word in the parable of the talents to put the money to "work" for an increase (Matt 25:16) and in John 6:27 as a warning not to "work" for food that spoils. The preacher of Hebrews tells us that these six named individuals (Gideon, Barak, Samson, Jephthah, David, and Samuel), in addition to other accomplishments, "managed or administered justice" to their communities. This was not a spiritual activity but an organizational activity, and justice is required not only in government but in business. So the preacher is talking not only to the political class but to the business manager class.

718. *Loidoreo* = to revile, reproach, blaspheme.

719. *Eulogeo* = to speak well of.

720. *Dioko* = pursue, to drive away, put to flight.

721. *Anechomai* = to hold up against, to bear with.

722. *Blasphemeo* = revile, to hurt the reputation or speak evil of.

723. *Parakaleo* = to call to one's side usually for encouragement, comfort,

have become the scum of the earth, the refuse of the world. (1 Cor 4:12–13)

Obviously, Paul is speaking here of his ministry among the Corinthians. He laments the abuse ("cursed," "persecuted," "slandered") he received at their hands. Indeed, he probably means to extend the received abuse to all the provinces and cities in which he labored. Despite all his hard and careful work, the abuse, from whatever locality it came, came at the hands of those who opposed him and the gospel, yet he persevered in the business of founding and managing branch offices of the organization. The point to be taken by the competing business manager is that in the face of competing worldviews Paul was steadfast ("endured") and loving ("bless," "answered kindly"), but in the end he still remained "scum" and "refuse" to his opponents. Paul the competing manager was competing against secular worldviews for the minds and loyalties of the people;[724] so does the competitive business manager.

This notion of loving our competitors and seeking their welfare ("We work hard with our own hands. When cursed, we bless, when slandered, we are kind.") is not a new idea of Paul's but rather is found throughout the Old Testament.[725] Paul and Peter continue this divine command to love our enemies and do good to them for their benefit, and to leave the bottom line to God's judgment.[726] In summary, the Pauline competitive attitude of a Christian manager must be characterized by:

- A focus on personal stewardship of what God has given that manager.
- A love for those managed as well as those competitors who seek their enrichment at the manager's expense.[727]

---

consolation; Holy Spirit (John 14:16).

724. Acts 17.

725. Exod 23:4–5; 2 Kgs 6:21–23; 2 Chr 28:9–15; Job 31:29–30; Ps 35:11–16; Prov 17:5; 25:21–22.

726. "Do not repay evil for evil . . . Do not take revenge, my friends, but leave room for God's wrath . . . On the contrary, if your enemy is hungry, feed him; if he is thirsty, give him something to drink" (Rom 12:17–21; cf. 1 Pet 3:9). "Alexander the metal worker did me a great deal of harm. The Lord will repay him for what he has done" (2 Tim 4:14).

727. And all of this loving our marketplace enemies and doing good for them so that they might prosper is patterned after the action of our God and Savior: "When we were God's enemies, we were reconciled to him through the death of his son" (Rom 5:10), and "We love because he first loved us" (1 John 4:19).

Jesus on Specific Responsibilities of a Business Manager

- A trust in God's justice and mercy to reward the faithful competitive manager with just deserts as well as the unscrupulous competitor.

If the marketplace is economic warfare and only the fittest survive and prosper, if the operating emotion in the marketplace is hostility (i.e., "hostile takeover") towards competing firms,[728] if in a world of scarce and expensive resources only a few businesses can continue to operate,[729] if self-interest is the guiding ethic of the marketplace, if the big guys are squeezing out the small guys, and the international firms are squeezing out the nationals, and the nationals are squeezing out the regional firms, and the regionals are squeezing out the locals—if all this is true, then the temptation for the Christian manager to achieve marketplace viability or even leadership is overwhelming, and the tendency to gloat over the failure of a competitor is overwhelming and near irresistible.[730]

> If you keep on biting[731] and devouring[732] each other, watch out or you will be destroyed[733] by each other. (Gal 5:15)

While Paul is clearly speaking about infighting among Christians, the principle holds true for any community, including the business community. This is an allusion to animal behavior, with the "biting" being done by snake-like creatures and "consuming" being done by everything. All with the result that everyone will be "destroyed" as in a conflagration.[734] This is a true picture of a marketplace dog-eat-dog atmosphere. Paul the competing manager is warning that a lot of people are going to get chewed up as some managers strive to get rich and satisfy their hunger for power and craving. The point of this verse is to warn the competitive

---

728. Matt 10:16.

729. Although I don't believe creation is a zero-sum reality.

730. *Schadenfreude is* German for "joy in someone's harm"; Job 31:29; Prov 17:5; 24:17–18. Buchanan, the writer and former White House advisor, recorded a pertinent incident illustrative of this gloating attitude: "One night I heard Dick Cavett speaking at the White House correspondents' dinner, and at the end of his monologue, he dropped this wisecrack: 'In order to be truly happy, it is not only necessary to succeed in life; one's friends must also fail.' A penetrating remark, and everyone laughed" (Buchanan, *Right from the Beginning*, 194).

731. *Dakno.*

732. *Katesthio.*

733. *Analisko.*

734. Wade, *The Lord Is My Counsel*, 129, calls ruthless competition "cannibalism in the marketplace."

manager to keep his eye on company quality and customer service and not on the competition.

> Each one should test his own actions. Then he can take pride in himself, without comparing[735] himself to somebody else, for each one should carry his own load.[736] (Gal 6:4–5)

Paul is exhorting the Christian competitive manager to reevaluate their own actions and take justifiable pride in what they accomplish. Managers are not to obsess over what the competition is doing. Focus on the managerial responsibilities given to them by Jesus, and let the results be in his hands. The Greek word translated "burden" or "load" in Galatians 6:5 has a commercial sense because it means goods or merchandise.[737] Paul the competing manager is telling the managers to judge themselves by themselves and not competitively with others. They are not to advance themselves at the expense of other managers. The apostle is attempting to reduce rivalry and competitive boasting. In Galatians 6:5 he nails the warning with the command: handle your own responsibilities and don't worry about another manager's burden. Given this vocational environment; many Christians leave this field of battle and simply go into another line of work in which competition for wages and survival is not a major consideration. The problem with this exodus from the marketplace is at least three-fold:

- Only the private sector pays net taxes to fund proper government services. And so, eventually, the responsibility for generating and maintaining our national economic and social wellbeing comes back to the private marketplace where competition, now on a global scale, reigns supreme. If there are no wealth creators, who will fund the kingdom of God?

- If Christians leave the arena of marketplace battle, who will be the "salt," "light," and "leaven" of that arena of competitive endeavor in order to "bring justice, mercy, and faithfulness?"[738]

735. *Phortion* = load, burden.
736. It is used for taxes in Romans 13:6–7.
737. Acts 27:10.
738. Matt 23:23. The nineteenth-century Scottish divine Fraser, commenting on Matthew 23:23–24, wrote that the Lord's reproof must be brought against those who "combine a very punctilious Christian profession with a lax or unprincipled morality" (Fraser, *Metaphors of Christ*, 182–83). He went on to state that Jesus is emphasizing two points for consideration in Christian doctrine and morality: 1. Inward qualities

- If God is calling an individual to be a wealth creator, then the marketplace is the only place to do that, and to refuse to engage is to grieve the Holy Spirit.[739]

Thus, the divine gauntlet is thrown down to all Christians in business to be incarnational in their actions for their own sake, for their neighbor's sake, as well as for God's sake.

If escape and retreat from the marketplace is not a valid alternative, and if an unbridled and unfettered competitive attitude with the destruction of the economic enemy as a goal is not a valid alternative, where then do Christian competitive managers in the marketplace turn to for some guidance on competition? Paul the competing manager provides a suggestion:

> Do nothing out of selfish ambition[740] or vain conceit,[741] but in humility[742] consider[743] others better than yourselves. Each of you should look[744] not only to your own interest, but also to the interests of others. (Phil 2:3–4)

---

count for more than outward observance. Fraser calls this outward theological emphasis "barren externalism." 2. A just sense of proportion is essential to a well-regulated Christian mind (Fraser, *Metaphors in the Gospel*, 185).

739. Eph 4:30; Acts 5:1–11; 24:17; 1 Cor 16:1–3; 2 Cor 8:13.

740. *Eritheia* = strife, faction, self-seeking, rivalry.

741. *Kenodoxia* = vainglory, empty pride. Only here in the New Testament.

742. *Tapeinophrosyne* = brought low, cast down.

743. *Hegeomai* = consider, prefer. "He gave Joseph wisdom (*sophia*) and enabled him to gain the good will of Pharaoh king of Egypt; so, he made him manager [*hegeomai* = ruler] over Egypt and all his palace" (Acts 7:10). The Greek *hegeomai* is used in both a spiritual context and in a temporal context, with the primary meaning being "to guide" or "to lead," "to be over." In the Greek Old Testament, the term is used in Exod 13:17; Neh 9:12; Isa 63:14; elsewhere for *nachah*. This is a seldom-used term in the New Testament, but in Acts 7:10 the term is used in reference to Joseph "managing" Egypt with wisdom and skill. This is management with accountability. The Christian business manager prays for wisdom and skill to handle the responsibility of managing because he knows there will be a day of reckoning on his leadership role. In Hebrews 13:7 we see the word used to describe managers who live exemplary lives, worthy of emulation by coworkers. Character counts for a business manager. The word also means "governor" and is used to describe Jesus (Matt 2:6), Joseph (Acts 7:10), Pilate, Felix, and Festus. *Ethnarch* is translated "governor" for an unnamed person in 2 Corinthians 11:32. It has a nice managerial ring to it because it literally means "people ruler" (cf. Jas 3:4).

744. *Skopountes* = aim, goal. Keeping an eye out for the benefit of others.

The context for this passage is unity in the Philippian branch office and Paul's exhortation to be humble with each other. But the principles apply to a business operation not only within the operation but in a relationship with marketplace competitors. In fact, this is a passage often quoted in relation to competitors:

- "Selfish ambition" or "vain conceit." The passage begins with an exhortation not to engage in unholy rivalry. Paul harkens back to Philippians 1:17 and "selfish ambition" where it is used to describe Paul's rivals for the hearts of the Philippians. For emphasis he adds "vain conceit," meaning someone who is ambitious for his own reputation and jealous of competitors.[745] It has the sense of a commitment to prevail over competitors.[746]

- "In humility, esteem others better than yourself." Competitive managers are to give serious thought to consider others (i.e., competitors) better than yourself. This is hardcore stuff because Paul is not saying to just think about others as being better than you but to care for them and act towards them as being better than you. The Christian competitive manager is to help carry the burden of your competing neighbors. Managers are to put the authentic needs and concerns of competitors equal to theirs.[747] Paul's concept of humility does not mean self-disparagement. Both Paul and Jesus defended themselves and took care to provide for themselves.[748] But Paul does teach that the manager is not to devalue the competition.

- "Each of you should look" describes the action. The word translated "look" means "to look out for" or "to keep your eyes on." In other words, have it as a goal to be diligent to see opportunities to help a competing colleague. Combined with "esteem" used earlier, this is a powerful injunction for the manager. Christian competitive

---

745. Gal 5:26.

746. Fee interprets this phrase as saying "eating and devouring one another!" (Fee, *Paul's Letter to the Philippians*, 187).

747. The motivation for this attitude is Jesus himself (Phil 2:5).

748. Hendricksen has a helpful thought on Paul: "Paul himself had grown in this grace of humble-mindedness. He who during his third missionary journey called himself 'The least of the apostles' (1 Cor 15:9) styled himself 'the very least of all saints' during his first Roman imprisonment (Eph 3:8), and a little later, during the period that intervened between this first and second Roman imprisonments, climaxed these humble self-descriptions by designating himself 'chief of sinners' (1 Tim 1:15)" (Hendricksen, *Philippians*, 101). Contrast this with Acts 22:3–5.

Jesus on Specific Responsibilities of a Business Manager

managers are to look for the good and positive qualities in their competitors; even the competitors that are less obviously praiseworthy. This is counterintuitive for aggressive competitive managers. Indeed, in classic Greek, to be humble and generous of spirit was considered shameful, pusillanimous, and to be avoided and overcome, as it can be in today's post-Christian marketplace activities.[749] But that is what is called for in the Christian manager.[750]

A practical example might help illustrate. In the marketplace, the most valuable asset to a company is people—the workers who develop and maintain the economic organization. Every business is always looking for good people to fill specific organizational slots. As in every scarce commodity, there is a shortage of good people for any given position. So proselytizing is rampant at all levels of marketplace competition. Invariably, when one good person leaves an organization to join a competing organization, that person's departure is traumatic to the organization. That person is missed positively because their contribution to the economic welfare of the organization is gone,[751] and negatively because the training, the trade secrets, the success methodology—all the things that made the one organization successful—are now in the hands of a competitor. There is the opportunity for great anger and vindictiveness to be expressed from the losing organization.[752]

It is at this point that an incarnational attitude will dictate an approach that supports the individual who left the organization as the appropriate thing for that person to do at that time, even if there is disagreement on the rightness of the action. The leaving individual's judgment must be treated with freedom and respect, and the Christian competitive manager of the bereft organization must depend on God to

---

749. And yet there is a limit to taking abuse, as Jesus hints in Matthew 10:14–15 ("shaking the dust off your feet").

750. Barth has stated that these two verses in Philippians 2 contain the heart of Paul's ethics (Barth, *Epistle to the Philippians*, 49).

751. LeTourneau mentions a *quid pro quo* between tithing and prosperity, even God's blessing, when he wrote about his own experience: "Right then I had the thought that I had failed to share with the Lord the year before when I had my first big profit, promising to share with Him this year when my profits would be big pickings. Certainly, in dropping me a hundred thousand in debt He had shown me the error of my ways" (LeTourneau, *Movers of Men and Mountains*, 187).

752. See David among the Philistines in 1 Samuel 27 and 29. Cf. Acts 15:36–41; Gal 2:11–13; 1 John 2:19.

mitigate marketplace damages beyond the leader's control (cf. the father continues to manage the farm after the prodigal son leaves;[753] the disciples continue to manage the ministry after Judas leaves;[754] life goes on after giving away your coat[755]).

Hebrews and the competing manager

> For we do not have a high priest who is unable to sympathize with our weaknesses, but we have one who has been tempted in every way, just as we are[756]—yet was without sin. (Heb 4:15)[757]

In Hebrews 4:15 we see the writer stressing the total identification of Jesus with the actual human situation. Jesus had to resemble the "brothers" in reality, as one brother resembles another.[758] Being incarnationally competitive means being in love with your economic enemy. Jesus told us not only to love your enemies but to do "good"[759] to them without any expectation of returned kindness! So our attitude towards our competition is to be not only not negative (withholding hate) but also positive (doing good things). As Paul told the Galatians, "Therefore, as we have opportunity, let us do good to everyone, especially to those who belong to the family of believers."[760]

---

753. Luke 15:11–13.
754. John 13:27.
755. Luke 6:29–30.
756. *Kata homoiotes.*
757. Heb 2:17.
758. Lane notes that the emphatic statement that Jesus was "tested in every respect, in quite the same way as we are," implying that he was susceptible to all the temptations that confront the individual (Lane, *Hebrews 1–8*, 64).
759. *Kalos.*
760. Gal 6:10.

Jesus on Specific Responsibilities of a Business Manager

Peter the competing manager

> Do not repay[761] evil with evil or insult[762] with insult, but with blessing,[763] because to this you were called so that you may inherit a blessing. (1 Pet 3:9)

After focusing on the relationship between believers in 3:8, Peter now changes direction and focuses on the relationship between a Christian competing manager and his nasty non-Christian competition. Peter the competing manager uses "blessing" to mean that the Christian manager is to proactively ask God to show favor on those competitors who have insulted and abused the manager and his organization. Furthermore, the manager is asking for divine grace for the competition, which eliminates slander and vicious gossip—bad talk—from the manager. This asking for blessing for a competitor is real and actual and will benefit the competitor, and the manager had better be prepared for a blessed competitor! It is not just words. Why would a Christian manager ask God to bless a ruthless competitor?

- Theologically the blessing makes sense because blessings came from the priest in the Old Testament[764] and Peter has already called the Christian competing manager a "priest."[765]
- The motivation for this managerial blessing confirms the salvation of the manager and passes along the unmerited blessing to a competitor, just as the competitive manager received the unmerited blessing from a gracious Redeemer.

THE ACCULTURATING MANAGER

It is the manager's responsibility to create a workplace environment that furthers the flourishing of the organization and the individual members of the organization.[766] Christianity believes that the culture of an

---

761. *Apodidomi* = to give back, render.

762. *Loidoria.* Paul uses the same language in 1 Corinthisans 4:12; cf. Lev 19:18; Prov 20:22; 24:29; Rom 12:17; 1 Thess 5:15.

763. *Eulogeo* = good words.

764. Num 6:22–26.

765. 1 Pet 2:9.

766. As Doriani, *Work: Its Purpose, Dignity and Transformation*, 10, noted, "an

organization sets the religious and moral temperature of the group and that the manager sets the perimeters of the culture. This is expressed in a covenant between the members of the organization.

> Then God said, "Let us make man in our image, in our likeness, and let them rule over the fish of the sea and the birds of the air, over the livestock, over all the earth, and over all the creatures that move along the ground." (Gen 2:25)

The principle of acculturation was given to us with Adam in the Garden of Eden.

> Acknowledge and take to heart this day that Yahweh is God in heaven above and on the earth below. There is no other. Keep his decrees and commands, which I am giving you today so that it may go well with you and your children after you and that you may live long in the land Yahweh your God gives you for all time. (Deut 4:39–40)

The cultural agreement gets more specific with Moses.

> Samuel told all the words of Yahweh to the people who were asking him for a king.[767] He said, "This is what the king who will reign[768] over you will do." (1 Sam 8:10–11)

Seven verses later God finished telling the organization what a ruler would do to them. The biblical organization had leaders before the king;[769] not until the kings came along did the chief manager have the authority to fire and hire with the power of the sword.

The Acculturating Manager in the Gospels

> Do not conform[770] any longer to the pattern of this world but be transformed[771] by the renewing of your mind. Then you will be able to test and approve what God's will is—his good, pleasing and perfect will. (Rom 12:2)

---

executive shapes a company, and even society, in a way that a [coworker] never will, and it's ludicrous to pretend otherwise."

767. *Melek* = counsellor.
768. *Malek*.
769. Abraham, Moses, Joshua, the Judges, Joseph, Samuel.
770. *Suschematizo* = fashioned.
771. *Metamorphoo* = "metamorphose."

Jesus the acculturating manager

> Some pharisees came to him to test him. They asked, "Is it lawful for a man to divorce his wife for any and every reason?" (Matt 19:3)

A look at the Lord's instructions concerning divorce in Matthew 19 has some management application. In response to the question by the Pharisees concerning the legality of divorce, Jesus quoted the Old Testament law forbidding divorce.[772] The Pharisees then responded,

> Why then did Moses command that a man give his wife a certificate of divorce and send her away? (Matt 19:7)

In other words, if divorce were prohibited by Yahweh, who is Moses to permit it under any circumstances? Jesus replied,

> Moses appropriately permitted you to divorce your wives because your hearts were hard. (Matt 19:8)

In short, to keep the social good of civil peace and tranquility in the community and to keep from a total breakdown of civil law and order, Moses permitted that which was not pleasing to God. God's prohibition against divorce is absolutely binding on believers because they are the only ones to submit themselves to the divine teaching and ethic. Those outside God's family are given reluctant provision to destroy the outward semblance of a sacred institution—marriage—because of the specific sinfulness of their lives which will wreak havoc on society in general. God was not pleased with their action, but social harmony was preserved by a modification of this prohibition, caused by the rampant sin evidenced in society ("because your hearts were hard"). The unregenerate hardness of heart causes there to be unfaithfulness on the part of one spouse or the other; the marriage covenant is broken, and thus divorce is officially permitted since the marriage is in fact already dissolved.[773]

In this conversation Jesus seems to be saying to us that we need to recognize that the culture of the world will be fundamentally different and unalterable from that of the company's culture.[774]

---

772. Deut 24:1–5.

773. The leniency given in divorce is not applicable to serious sin condemned by God, Matt 18:15–17; cf. Jones, *Biblical Christian Ethics*, 125–53.

774. Cf. Luke 11:7, 23; Matt 22:21. Stearns maintains that good managers need to have a vision for the organization. He defines vision casting as having four parts:

> When King Herod heard [the king of the Jews has been born] he was disturbed[775] and all Jerusalem with him. (Matt 2:3)

A New Testament example of an acculturating manager may be found in Herod in Matthew 2:3. This is an interesting sentence by Matthew, for it portends the opposition of the capital city of Jerusalem to the coming Messiah, all of which has been fed by Herod's insecurity to his throne.[776] To the extent that Herod had poisoned the populace or at least the leaders of the city the king/manager had acculturated the members of the organization to reject Jesus. The attitude of the king was communicated to the members of the organization, and everyone was upset. The history of the world of business is replete with examples of acculturating managers who provided direction and vision to coworkers which enabled them to accomplish great goals, goals they couldn't have achieved by themselves.[777]

THE ACCULTURATING MANAGER IN THE OLD TESTAMENT

Moses the acculturating manager

> Hear, O Israel: Yahweh our God, Yahweh is one. Love Yahweh your God with all your heart and with all your soul and with all your strength. These commandments that I give you today are to be upon your hearts. Impress them on your children. Talk about them when you sit at home and when you walk along the road, when you lie down and when you get up. Tie them as symbols on your hands and bind them on your foreheads. Write them on the door frames of your houses and on your gates. (Deut 6:4–9)

Notice how Moses the acculturating manager is setting the cultural framework for the organization:

A manager must define the current reality, articulate a desired future, identify a way forward, and personally own the vision (Stearns, *Lead Like it Matters to God*, 106).

775. *Tarasso* = troubled, agitated. Bruce notes, "The spirit of the city was servile and selfish. They bowed to godless power and cared for their own interest rather than for Herod's. Few in that so-called holy city had healthy sympathies with truth and right. Wither the king's fears were groundless or not they knew not nor cared. It was enough that the fears existed" (Bruce, *The Synoptic Gospels*, 71).

776. Cf. Matt 15:1; 16:21; 20:17–18; 21:1, 10; 23:37; 27:24–25.

777. A secular lesson of 1 Corinthians 12:14–26.

Jesus on Specific Responsibilities of a Business Manager

- The organization is to be God-oriented. It is to be a religious organization that commands all of the allegiance of the individual member of the company.[778]
- The organization is to be open about their allegiance to Yahweh.[779]
- The organization is to study and know Yahweh's laws and ordinances.[780]
- The organization is to remember Yahweh's laws and ordinances.[781]
- The organization is to value education as it teaches its younger members Yahweh's laws and ordinances.[782]
- The organization is to publicly display their allegiance to the Yahweh.[783]
- The organization is to commit their possessions to Yahweh.[784]

Achan the acculturating manager

> But the Israelites acted unfaithfully in regard to the devoted things; Achan . . . took some of them . . . And Joshua said, "Ah, Sovereign Lord, why did you ever bring this people across the Jordan to deliver us into the hands of the Amorites to destroy us?" . . . Yahweh said to Joshua, "Israel has sinned; they have violated my covenant which I commanded them to keep. They have taken some of the devoted things; they have stolen, they have lied, they have put them with their own possessions. That is why the Israelites cannot stand against their enemies." (Josh 7:1, 7, 10–12)

This is a most interesting passage concerning the sin of Achan. Achan was a leader in the organization. He was of the lineage of Zerah, the younger son of Judah and Tamar.[785] So he was a prominent acculturat-

---

778. Deut 6:4.
779. Deut 6:5.
780. Deut 6:6.
781. Deut 6:7–9.
782. Deut 6:7.
783. Deut 6:9.
784. Deut 6:10–11.
785. Gen 38:30.

ing manager. Achan took it upon himself to steal some of the "devoted things" that belonged to Yahweh. And what was the reaction? Yahweh's anger, Israel's defeat at the hands of the Amorites, a company-wide search for the offending party, and ultimate death for Achan and his entire family.[786] Why such a violent and non-proportional judgment on a leader of the tribe? The Bible seems to suggest that one flagrant lack of faithfulness in the organization will spread to others and have a company-wide deleterious effect. We see that in the repeated quaint phrase used by Moses, "the troubling of Israel," or the more contemporary phrase, "disaster on Israel."[787] Notice also that in Yahweh's judgment against Israel the sins are all plural not singular. It is not just Achan, but the entire tribe has sinned, and thus will be punished by Amorites. The reason for this swift and complete punishment of Achan the acculturating manager and his family is to prevent the rot of unfaithfulness from gaining a hold in the attitude of the rest of Israel. The culture of the tribe was to be faithfulness and a warring culture could not be permitted to exist and spread throughout the organization.

David the acculturating manager

> And behold, the Cushite came, and the Cushite said, "Good news for my lord the king! For Yahweh has delivered you this day from the hand of all who rose up against you . . . May the enemies of my lord the king and all who rise up against you for evil be like that young man [Absalom]." And the king was deeply moved and went up to the chamber over the gate and wept. And as he went, he said, "O my son Absalom, my son, my son Absalom! Would I have died instead of you, O Absalom, my son, my son." It was told Joab, "Behold the king is weeping and mourning for Absalom." So the victory that day was turned into mourning for all the people, for the people heard that day, "The king is grieving for his son." And the people stole into the city that day as people steal in who are ashamed when they flee in battle . . . Now the king arose and took his seat in the gate. And the people were all told, "Behold the king is sitting in the gate." And all the people came before the king. (2 Sam 18:31–19:3, 8)

786. Josh 7:24–25.
787. Josh 6:18; 7:24; 1 Chr 2:7.

This is a rather small example of a manager's ability to change the culture of an organization, but it shows how quickly the change can happen. In this story, Absalom, David's gifted but evil son, is killed in battle. David famously laments the death. Now, the lament for his evil, disloyal, king-hating son is because Absalom is forever lost to salvation and David knows it. But to those who engineered his death and secured victory over Absalom's army, it is inexplicable. The word goes out to the people in the organization that victory has turned to mourning because the manager is mourning, so they mourn. A victorious, celebrating cultural occasion has immediately been turned into a mourning, furtive one. Nobody can be happy if the manager is not happy. However, when David, at the behest of Joab, David's chairman of the joint chiefs of staff, changes his emotional posture, all the members of the organization change their emotional state and celebrate the well-earned victory.

- The main point to be taken from this brief episode in the managerial career of David is that followers will follow the leader, so the Christian manager must guard his emotions and public sentiments at all times.

David the acculturating manager

The "lament of the bow" in 2 Samuel 1:17–27 is another example of David requiring his organization to adopt a posture of mourning when he "orders" his company to lament the death of Saul and Jonathan. He is urging his organization to have an attitude adjustment about the man who, while anointed by God, was nevertheless David's fierce opponent seeking his destruction.

- One point to be taken from this "lament" is that there is to be no joy in the eradication of one's competition when that competitor is belongs to Yahweh.

Solomon the acculturating manager

> On a hill east of Jerusalem, Solomon built a high place for Chemosh the detestable god of Moab, and for Molech the detestable god of the Ammonites. He did the same for all his foreign wives,

> who burned incense and offered sacrifices to their gods. (1 Kgs 11:7–8)

> [King Josiah] also desecrated the high places that were east of Jerusalem on the south of the Hill of Corruption—the ones Solomon king of Israel had bult for Ashtoreth the vile goddess of the Sidonians, for Chemosh the vile god of Moab, and for Molech the detestable god of the people of Ammon. Josiah smashed the sacred stones and cut down the Asherah poles and covered the sites with human bones. (2 Kgs 23:13–14)

Solomon, for all his greatness, had a moral and spiritual blind spot with his harem of foreign women who did not follow Mosaic law. So, his royal acculturating example from the palace was as a sexual libertine.[788] We see the long-lasting national cultural and spiritual effect of King Solomon's moral deterioration in his organization in King Josiah's reforms four hundred years later in 600 BC in 2 Kings 23:7. Second Kings 23:13 specifically reiterates Solomon's apostasy mentioned in 1 Kings 11:7–8. It took four centuries to modify the destructive culture of Solomonic sin until Josiah worked his reforms, but it was too late to save the organization.

- The management lesson here is that the acculturating manager can destroy an organization's healthy and productive culture in just a few years. It then will take many years to rebuild the culture, if it can even be rebuilt.

> A righteous man is cautious in friendship, but the way of the wicked leads them astray.[789] (Prov 12:26)

Here is the negative influence that a bad employee can have on an organization. Solomon warns how dangerous the bad person can be to the moral and ethical health of a company. The good worker will have the opposite influence on the direction of the company. Solomon the acculturating manager also notes the power of words to give life or death to a company.

> The tongue has the power of life and death, and those who love it will eat its fruit. (Prov 18:21)

---

788. 1 Kgs 11:1–8 notes his "seven hundred wives" and his "three hundred concubines."

789. *Taah* = to seduce or deceive.

Here the language of the manager is empowered with the ability to kill or to give life to a coworker. The Hebrew literally has "the tongue has the hand of life and death"—a very strong picture of the value of encouraging managerial speech. Those that the manager encourages will eat the fruit of their encouraged labor. In sum, an encouraged worker is always more productive than a disheartened worker.[790] It is possible that the last phrase of verse 21, "those who love it will eat its fruit," refers to those who love the power of the tongue, and if the tongue is used for good purposes to enhance an individual then the community and the possessor of the good speech will harvest the blessed consequences. Social influence in a group is indicated in this proverb by saying that righteous people benefit not only themselves but also influence those around them. Christian acculturating managers are to lead their organization on the right path. Do not be deceived: bad company leads to destruction.[791]

> He who walks with the wise grows wise, but a companion of fools[792] suffers harm.[793] (Prov 13:20)

This Solomonic proverb teaches that the virtues and vices of the acculturating manager will rub off on those people around him. One will be like the company one keeps. The father is admonishing his son to associate with the wise because wisdom will rub off on to him. Companions are critical for the development of an individual and to associate with arrogant fools will lead to one's destruction. Pick your companions.

Jeroboam the acculturating manager

> And Yahweh will give Israel up because[794] of the sins Jeroboam has committed and has caused[795] Israel to commit. (1 Kgs 14:16)

---

790. "The implication is to make sure that our speech is used to build up rather than to tear down; to produce a good outcome rather than destructive consequences" (Wilson, *Proverbs*, 215).

791. Samson was not "cautious" in his friendships with the Philistines, and trouble ensued for his organization (Judg 14:11, 20; 15:2, 6).

792. *Kesil* = overly self-confident.

793. *Rua* = literally: shall be broken.

794. *Galal* = turning, circumstance, opportunity.

795. *Asah* = made.

Jeroboam enticed[796] Israel away from following Yahweh and caused[797] them to commit a great sin. The Israelites persisted in all the sins of Jeroboam and did not turn away from them. (2 Kgs 17:21–22)

The history of royal management in the Old Testament organization can be summed up in the awful phrase, "he had caused Israel to commit." Multiple times the narrative recites the result of bad management in shaping the culture of the Jewish organization with this destructive summation. The power of a manager to set the culture of an organization is reflected in the strong Hebrew terms translated "entice" but could also be translated "tear away" or "cut out." The Hebrew term translated "caused," could also be translated, perhaps even more accurately translated, "drove." Strong terms to describe the acculturating manager's influence in the organization. Almost all the kings of Israel and Judah after Solomon created a destructive culture in the organization which Yahweh had given them.

There is a character connection between managers and employees. The Bible teaches that the manager's actions influence the organization under him. Thus, the responsibility of a Christian acculturating manager is to take the lead in giving shape to the moral atmosphere of the company, of the character of one's employees. It will happen whether the manager wants it to happen or not. Jeroboam was not alone in leading his organization into sin and defeat. The Hebrew here is very strong—Jeroboam the acculturating manager "made" the organization commit sins! He is followed by nineteen sin-acculturating Israelite kings who did the same things, and all but the despicable Ahab were minor leaders.[798] Bad management leads to worse management.[799] In 1 Kings 14:14–15, Yahweh says he will not leave the uprooting of the bad manager and the bad company to chance. He will step in and clean out the swamp himself. Using strong language, Yahweh will "strike," "uproot," and "scatter" the organization all because of Jeroboam's management: "The king of Assyria invaded the entire land, marched against Samaria and laid siege to it for three years . . . and deported the Israelites to Assyria . . . All this took

---

796. *Qara* = to rend, cut out, tear, lacerate. Cf. 1 Kgs 13:33 for Jeroboam's general acculturating worldview.

797. *Nadah* = from the root "to toss" or "banish," meaning "drive out" or "put far away."

798. For example: Manasseh (Jer 15:4).

799. 1 Kgs 15 and 16.

place because the Israelites had sinned against Yahweh their God" (2 Kgs 17:5, 7).

Hezekiah the acculturating manager

I turn now to the management example of King Hezekiah and his organizational reforms in 2 Chronicles 29–32. The biblical narrative shows us how a dedicated acculturating manager can change the culture of an organization. The Chronicler thinks Hezekiah is so important that he devotes four chapters to his reign, more than any king other than David and Solomon. Hezekiah is important for us because he, as the acculturating manager, takes a floundering organization—Israel—and turns it into a successful organization without foreign wars or foreign interference. Previous managers like Jeroboam[800] and Ahaz[801] had almost ruined the company by bad management. Hezekiah worked with his fellow citizens to accomplish great things for not only Judah but even Israel. It is important to see that Hezekiah so changed the culture of the organization that where once failure reigned[802] now the coworkers worked overtime to make the company successful:[803]

- Hezekiah the acculturating manager began his managerial responsibilities by opening the sealed doors of the temple in Jerusalem and taking the time to repair them.[804] He quickly moved[805] to repair the damage done by his predecessors, thus publicly emphasizing the urgent effort of the organization to return to its original mission statement.

- Hezekiah the acculturating manager knew that it was important that the organization corporately and individually come to agreement with each other.[806] The manager himself would lead the group

---

800. 2 Chr 13:8–12, "500,000 casualties."
801. 2 Chr 28:22–24, "the downfall of all Israel."
802. Apostacy; "In his time of trouble King Ahaz became even more unfaithful to Yahweh. He offered sacrifices to the gods of Damascus . . . but they were his downfall and the downfall of all Israel" (2 Chr 28:22–23).
803. People brought in tithes and offerings to Yahweh in "huge heaps" (2 Chr 31:6).
804. 2 Chr 29:3.
805. "In the first month of the first year," 2 Chr 29:3, 17.
806. 2 Chr 29:5–11.

in publicly embracing the mission.[807] This action by the acculturating manager set forth a role model that comforted the people.[808]

- Hezekiah the acculturating manager sought coworker buy-in to the new era of his management by "assembling" the people from the very first.[809]

- Hezekiah the acculturating manager even took the people on a field trip to the "square on the east" to show them, firsthand, how unclean and disreputable the temple had been left by previous managers.[810] Thus, the goal of temple activity was seen by the people themselves.

- Hezekiah the acculturating manager pointed fingers at the previous managers by not shying away from blaming his predecessors for leading the people into failure and defeat. They had "turned their backs" on the mission of the company.[811] His commitment to undo the corporate damage was deep, genuine, and public, and he wanted to chart a new direction for the company.[812]

- Hezekiah the acculturating manager had a change of tone which was public, transparent, and thorough.[813] The new era was carefully planned and executed by management.[814]

- Hezekiah the acculturating manager began his new management style early in the morning by gathering all his lieutenants for a strategy meeting.[815] The result of such hard work, preparation, planning, and public display of leadership by the manager was that the entire company rejoiced and thanked the leadership.[816]

- Hezekiah the acculturating manager fully reestablished the original mission of the company[817] and set in order the founding princi-

---

807. 2 Chr 29:10.
808. 2 Chr 29:36.
809. 2 Chr 29:4.
810. Ahaz et al., 2 Chr 29:4.
811. 2 Chr 29:6–9.
812. "It is in my heart," 2 Chr 29:10.
813. "They brought out [the uncleanness] into the courtyard" and "carried it out to the Kidron Valley," 2 Chr 29:16.
814. "We have prepared and consecrated all the articles," 2 Chr 29:19.
815. 2 Chr 29:20.
816. "The whole assembly sang praises with gladness," 2 Chr 29:28, 30.
817. *Kun* = prepared, established, fixed.

ples.[818] The Chronicler again notes that all the current employees "rejoiced" in the return.[819] In fact, the reaction in the marketplace was so positive that past employees returned to the headquarters to participate in the new direction and leadership.[820]

- Hezekiah the acculturating manager took actionable counsel from his chief advisors and even the employees in general.[821]
- Hezekiah the acculturating manager then wrote the plan down and made it public,[822] and again there was "great rejoicing" and agreement among the employees.[823]
- Hezekiah the acculturating manager himself matched everything that his coworkers put in.[824]
- Hezekiah the acculturating manager built company procedures, protocols, and hiring policies to accommodate the workers' efforts.[825] The manager had picked men of appropriate skill and honesty to help manage the company.
- Hezekiah the acculturating manager saw how pleased everyone was with the new plan, so he extended the company holiday another week,[826] clearly showing he was sensitive to company culture. Unity reigned in the corporation.[827] The manager knew how to include every stakeholder in the company celebration.[828] The company buy-in

---

818. 2 Chr 29:35.

819. 2 Chr 29:36.

820. 2 Chr 30:1—31:1.

821. "The plan seemed right to both the king and to the whole assembly," 2 Chr 30:4; Jehoshaphat in 2 Chr 20:21, "After consulting the people, Jehoshaphat appointed men."

822. 2 Chr 30:6.

823. 2 Chr 30:21-23.

824. 2 Chr 31:3-9.

825. 2 Chr 31:11-19. The key administrative word here is *emuna*, translated "faithfully," 2 Chr 31:12, 15, 19 = dependable, reliable, sure = 1 Sam 2:35, as in the appointed managers "faithfully" carried out their fiduciary responsibilities.

826. 2 Chr 30:23.

827. 2 Chr 30:25.

828. Selman notes, "This is one of the most comprehensive examples in the Old Testament of the inclusion of non-worshippers of Yahweh among God's people, for neither the northerners nor the resident aliens would have had much accurate knowledge of the ways of the Lord" (Selman, *2 Chronicles*, 521).

to Hezekiah's leadership was so great that the employees gave more than required[829] to complete the mission.[830]

Obadiah the acculturating manager

> Now the famine was severe in Samaria, and Ahab had summoned Obadiah who was in charge of his palace. Obadiah was a devout believer in Yahweh. While Jezebel was killing off Yahweh's prophets, Obadiah had taken a hundred prophets and hidden them in two caves, fifty in each, and had supplied them with food and water . . . Elijah replied, "I have not made trouble for Israel, but you [Ahab] and your father's family have. You have abandoned Yahweh's commands and have followed the Baals." (1 Kgs 18:2–4, 18)

Obadiah the acculturating manager was in charge of the king's estate,[831] but for all his loyalty and access to Ahab he was not able to change the culture of Israel. Here is an example of management acculturating failure. In fact, Obadiah seems to acknowledge this in 1 Kings 18:13 as he speaks to Elijah, "Haven't you heard, my lord, what I did while Jezebel was killing the prophets of Yahweh?" That is to say, Ahab is more interested in feeding his cows than his citizens. Obadiah may even know that Ahab's apostasy is causing the famine, and he could have resigned in protest, signalling his virtue to the Jewish cohort, but he stayed in the service of the apostate king. Israel, under Ahab, was thoroughly rotten from boarder to boarder since the shrines of Baal were all over the country.[832] Christian managers don't always win.

---

829. There were abundant "freewill" offerings, that is, offerings above what was required. The people worked overtime.

830. 2 Chr 31:14.

831. For similar official governmental positions see 1 Kings 4:6; 16:9; 2 Kings 10:5; 18:18, 37; 19:2.

832. "Baals" is plural, 1 Kgs 18:18. Other Old Testament examples of Joseph, Daniel, Nehemiah, Mordecai (See Case, *Esther and Trump*), all give testimony of believers in management positions in an alien organization who were not able to impose their personal religious culture on the organization. Furthermore, there is no evidence that they even desired to do so. They were able to selectively influence the organization's culture at critical junctures to preserve the church and a godly perspective, but overall they did not fundamentally change the culture of their respective organizations, the state.

Isaiah the acculturating manager

> See, a king[833] will reign[834] in righteousness and rulers[835] will rule[836] with justice. Each man will be like a shelter[837] from the wind and a refuge[838] from the storm, like streams of water in the desert and the shadow[839] of a great rock in a thirsty land. (Isa 32:1–2)

Once again we have Isaiah the prophet speaking words of management but not modeling management skills. The point of this Isaiah passage is that managers set the tone for the organization. With good management practices there will be safety, rest, and flourishing for the employees. This is a beautiful picture of good management. Instead of oppressing the manager will be protecting from oppression.

- Isaiah the acculturating manager tells us the acculturating manager will provide steadfastness in a changing and unsteady environment.
- Isaiah the acculturating manager tell us the acculturating manager will provide the coworkers a place in which they can hide from the outside storm which is bearing down on them.
- Isaiah the acculturating manager tells us the acculturating manager will provide leadership like streams of water in an arid desert.
- Isaiah the acculturating manager tells us the acculturating manager will be a rock providing shelter, shade, and security for employees in a hostile environment.

Isaiah's thought is that in the ordinary course of business activity the manager is to be a refuge, a set of wings over the organization.[840] But the manager may not set the cultural tone for an entire organization. Perhaps just a corner of peace.

---

833. *Melek.*
834. *Malakh.*
835. *Sar.*
836. *Sarar.*
837. *Machabe* = hiding place.
838. *Cithrah* = covert, covering, protection.
839. *Tsel* = shade, defense.
840. Young. *The Book of Isaiah*, 2.386–387.

Mordecai the acculturating manager

> So the Jews agreed to continue the celebration they had begun, doing what Mordecai had written to them . . . Therefore, these days were called Purim, from the word *pur* . . . the Jews took it on themselves to establish the custom that they and their descendants and all who join them should without fail observe these two days every year, in the way prescribed and at the time appointed. These days should be remembered and observed in every generation by every family, and in every providence and in every city. And these days of Purim should never fail to be celebrated by the Jews—nor should the memory of these days die out among their descendants. (Esth 9:23, 26–28)

The establishment of Purim was an extraordinary achievement by Mordecai for the preservation of the Jewish church. The ten northern tribes had been obliterated by the Assyrians earlier and so the southern church was left by themselves in Persian exile. Being a member of the church was now voluntary and a personal choice in a hostile culture. Something needed to be done to bring the people together. It could be said that Mordecai reestablished the covenant between Yahweh and his people. The annual celebration of Purim was a reminder to the church that they could overcome a hostile government and flourish like Jeremiah promised they could.[841] Mordecai (and Esther) believing that it was good for his organization (Esth 10:3) broke with precedent and established a new holiday to energize, encourage, and rededicate his company to its historic mission of giving thanks to Yahweh in all circumstances.[842]

- Mordecai the acculturating manager led his organization to renew their culture and unite behind a common goal.

---

841. Jer 29:11–23.

842. Purim is a break from Moses' instructions not to add to his instructions (Deut 4:2).

THE ACCULTURATING MANAGER IN THE NEW TESTAMENT

Paul the acculturating manager

> In the name of the Lord Jesus Christ, we command you, brothers, to keep away[843] from every brother who is idle[844] and does not live according to the teaching[845] you received from us. (2 Thess 3:6)

Obviously Paul is referencing troublemakers in the church, but the principle is of separating because of lack of agreement in the organization. The context for this verse is laboring for the organization (2 Thess 3:10). The Greek word can also mean being disorderly and not following instructions. The penalty for those disorderly people is not excommunication but rather separation from the particular organization. Indeed, Paul calls these dissatisfied workers "brothers" (2 Thess 3:15). Green notes that the separation of the disorderly worker from the organization would be devastating. It is hard to imagine a more forceful way of bringing these people into harmony with the manager's teaching.[846]

Peter and John the acculturating managers

> On their release, Peter and John went back to their own people and reported all that the chief priests and elders had said to them . . . Now the full number of those who believed were of one heart and soul, and no one said that any of the things that belonged to him was his own, but they had everything in common. And with great power the apostles were giving their testimony to the resurrection of the Lord Jesus, and great grace was upon them all. There was not a needy person among them, for as many as were owners of lands or houses sold them and

---

843. *Stellomai* = avoid, withdraw; 2 Cor 8:20.

844. *Ataktos*.

845. *Paradosis* = tradition.

846. Green, *The Letters to the Thessalonians*, 345. Collins writes in *Built to Last*, "Visionary companies are so clear about what they stand for and what they're trying to achieve that they simply don't have room for those unwilling or unable to fit their exacting standards" (Collins, *Built to Last*, 9). He continues: "the crucial variable is not the content of a company's ideology, but how deeply it believes its ideology and how consistently it lives, breathes, and expresses it in all that it does" (Collins, *Built to Last*, 8).

brought the proceeds of what was sold and laid it at the apostles' feet, and it was distributed to each as any had need. Thus Joseph, who was also called by the apostles Barnabas (which means "son of encouragement"), a Levite, a native of Cyprus, sold a field that belonged to him and brought the money and laid it at the apostles' feet. (Acts 4:23, 32–35)

From the beginning of Acts until now and beyond, the managing partner of the organization has been Peter, with some help from John. In this wonderful passage we see the effects of the acculturating influence of Peter and John on the early Jerusalem organization.

Hebrews and the acculturating manager

And let us consider how we may spur[847] one another on toward love and good deeds. Let us not give up meeting together, as some are in the habit of doing, but let us encourage[848] one another—and all the more as you see the day approaching. (Heb 10:24–25)

In this famous passage, the preacher is exhorting Christians not to neglect the regular assembling together because by doing so they will "encourage" each other to do good works in the face of social pressure. This getting together is even more important, as an important day is approaching. I have covered the motivating manager of Hebrews 10:24 and elsewhere. Clearly the focus of the passage is on the cohort and assembling together to encourage the members to continue to do good works and to strengthen each other's commitment.[849] There are applicable management principles at work here for the culture of an organization to be positive and optimistic about the future:[850]

---

847. *Paroxysmos*. There is the negative use of arousing or motivating in Acts 15:39 where Paul and Barnabas have a "sharp disagreement" and split. A more positive use of the cognate is found in 2 Corinthians 13:5 and "love is not provoked."

848. *Parakaleo* = comfort, exhort, console.

849. What is a Christian manager to do when that manager has control and authority over the business organization's culture? Should a blatant, obvious religious message be promulgated in and through the secular organization with symbols, tracts, music, signs, etc.? The answer is a difficult and controversial one, and not directly addressed in this work.

850. In an interesting twist Hermas the Shepherd (ca. 150) wrote in his *Similitudes* about businessmen leaving church gatherings to attend to business affairs: "And

Jesus on Specific Responsibilities of a Business Manager

- The acculturating manager of an organization needs to be continually, if gently, "spurring on" the coworkers to accomplish the mission of the business.[851]

- The acculturating manager knows that organizational harmony and unity will be strengthened by gathering together. Gathering as an organization will keep the organization from splintering into different factions, and even those factions in the group that do not gather may be enticed by the prospect of unity to rejoin the company.[852]

- The acculturating manager of the organization needs to keep tabs on the coworkers so that they do not become lazy, unfocused, or weary and cease to be a part of the company.[853]

- The acculturating manager will cheerlead the organization in the face of marketplace pressures which can discourage coworkers from giving the company their best. It is important for organizational survival to remain united in the pursuit of a specific goal.[854]

- The acculturating manager keeps a specific goal before the company as a force for motivation.[855]

- The acculturating manager works for the welfare of the organization and fights against a lack of team spirit and self-centeredness that is dangerous for the health of the company.[856]

- The acculturating manager labors for a company culture which fosters encouragement.[857] It is only as the coworkers work together and

---

they who gave in their branches half green and half-withered, are those who are immersed in business, and do not leave to the saints" (Herm. *Sim.* 8.8.1). "There are some of them rich, and others immersed in much business. The thistles are the rich, and the thorns are they who are immersed in much business. Those, accordingly, who are entangled in many various kinds of business, do not cleave to the servants of God, but wander away, being choked by their business transactions; and the rich cleave with difficulty to the servants of God, fearing lest these should ask something of them" (Herm. *Sim.* 9.20.1).

851. Heb 10:24.
852. Heb 10:24–25.
853. Heb 10:25.
854. Heb 10:25.
855. Heb 10:25.
856. Heb 10:24.
857. The wildly successful professional football coach Pete Carroll of the Seattle Seahawks has created a team culture of celebration, not shame, for his players.

not individually, from home, can there be mutual support, comfort, encouragement, and exhortation. "Iron sharpens iron."[858]

- The acculturating manager realizes that all members of the organization will work best if they keep their eye on the ball—the goal(s) of the company. The workers should always work in light of the coming goal, as John says in Revelation 1:3, "because the time is near."[859]

- The acculturating manager understands that treating his coworkers with love and kindness is part of his productive labor ("good works").[860]

- The acculturating manager creates a work environment in which his coworkers exhibit a practical concern for each other. Critically important for the good of the organization is that "good works" not only applies to good productive working habits but also to active support and concern for each other in the company.

- The acculturating manager takes the responsibility to see that no one grows tired, depressed, or "weary" of persevering in doing a good job.[861]

THE WITNESSING MANAGER

> "You are my witnesses,"[862] declares Yahweh, "and my servant whom I have chosen, so that you may know and believe me and understand that I am he." (Isa 43:10)

> And we pray this in order that you may live a life worthy of the Lord and may please him in every way: bearing fruit[863] in every good work,[864] growing in the knowledge of God. (Col 1:10)

---

858. Prov 27:17. Hebrews 3:3 urges Christians to "encourage one another daily as long as it is called Today" (Hughes, *Commentary on the Epistle to the Hebrews*, 414–18).

859. Heb 10:25b.

860. Heb 10:24; *kalos* = good, appropriate.

861. *Kamno* = weary; cf. Heb 12:3.

862. *Ed* = This is a legal term meaning a person who has firsthand knowledge of an event and can testify to that event. It might refer to a person who can testify to a report he has received.

863. *Karpophoreo*.

864. *Ergon* = deed, business.

Is verbal evangelism the integrating characteristic of a Christian manager's professional life?[865] Probably not, because the Christian life is more complex. Paul in Colossians 1:10–12 tells us the things that "please the Lord in every way":

1. Bearing fruit in every "good work" as evidence of salvation.
2. Growing in the knowledge of God through the words of Jesus.
3. Being strengthened with all power through the Holy Spirit.
4. Giving thanks to the Father for his gifts and graces.

THE WITNESSING MANAGER IN THE GOSPELS

Jesus the witnessing manager

> Therefore, go and make disciples of all nations, baptizing them in the name of the Father and of the Son and of the Holy Spirit, and teaching them to obey everything I have commanded you. (Matt 28:19–20)

In the so-called "Great Commission" in Matthew 28, Jesus is giving the final instructions to his disciples, and tells them that their central responsibility is to reproduce themselves through evangelism, baptizing, and teaching. The teaching is not to be of information and facts, but of ethics, with the goal of obedience to God. Righteousness will be the hallmark of

---

865. One businessman author entitled a chapter of his book, "Be Obvious" (Bump, *How to Succeed in Business Without Being a Pagan*, 82–92). Some of his suggestions are keeping your Bible on your office desk (Wade and Kittler, *The Lord Is My Counsel*, 9. The great *New York Times* journalist John McCandlish Phillips kept a Bible on his desk in the newsroom), reading the Bible with your employees in the morning, distributing religious tracts through business channels, testifying at company-wide parties, public worship demonstrations such as invocations, prayers, eulogies, etc. In short, the Christian manager is to do any activity that "makes yourself obvious as a Christian on the job" (Bump, *How to Succeed in Business Without Being a Pagan*, 85). To prove the value of an unambiguous marketplace lifestyle Bump related the following story: "One day a man came into Don Mott's [Mott (1911–99) was a successful insurance executive in Orlando, Florida] office to insure his car. 'Why did you happen to come to us?' asked Don. 'Well,' the man explained, 'I'm new in town. I asked the people in my office where to get car insurance and they said, "Anywhere but Don Mott's agency. They're nothing but a bunch of religious fanatics." So, I came straight to you!'" (Bump, *How to Succeed in Business Without Being a Pagan*, 91). The moral drawn from this story: Religiosity may be risky, but it will lead to prosperity.

Jesus' disciples. The "going" is to be to everyone—"all nations." Various business managers have called for service, diligence, loyalty, and honesty on the part of a Christian businessperson,[866] and the reason for such personal qualities usually is to establish the atmosphere for the "Great Commission."[867]

---

[866]. Cf. Lev 19:36; Hos 12:7; Mic 6:10–11.

[867]. For instance, one author wrote, "I assumed in chapter 2 and in the introduction to this chapter that Christians actually believe that if God has called them to work in the marketplace, He has also called them to be missionaries in the marketplace. Without that assumption, there is no reason to talk about bringing 'the light of Christ' to the marketplace; there is no need to concern ourselves with Christian credibility; and there is surely no need to learn to articulate our faith" (Hybels, *Christians in the Marketplace*, 32–33). Stanley Tam, founder/owner of States Smelting and Refining Corporation and the subject of Anderson's *God Owns My Business*, states that he uses his business as a platform for witness (Tam and Anderson, *God Owns My Business*, 30, 49, 62, 155), and Larry Burkett maintains that the first function of a Christian businessman is the outreach of the unsaved (Burkett, *Using Your Money Wisely*, 128). In his biography, Ted DeMoss, president of the Christian Business Men's Committee of the USA (CBMC) wrote, "In the early 1960s [CBMC's] . . . purpose became redefined to what it is today: 'To present Jesus Christ as Lord and Savior to business and professional men, and to develop Christian business and professional men to carry out the Great Commission'" (DeMoss and Tamasy, *The Gospel and the Briefcase*, 51). Walt Meloon, an early executive of the boat manufacturing company Correct Craft, Inc., was quoted as saying, "Every businessman automatically is in danger of making money his god. Whenever he makes a decision in favor of his business as opposed to accepting an opportunity or obligation to witness for the Lord Jesus Christ, he has made money his god, for the moment, at least. He is favoring mammon, and his priorities are mixed" (Enlow and Enlow, *Saved from Bankruptcy*, 110). Bill Yeargin, the current president of the mammoth boat building company, enunciates a more nuanced vision: "To Make Life Better." Bailey Marks, a furniture store and future Cru executive, wrote, "I have found that it is impossible for me to be filled with the Holy Spirit unless I am regularly communicating my faith in Christ with others. If I fail to witness, I am being disobedient, and I certainly cannot be filled with the Holy Spirit while being disobedient" (Marks, *An Ordinary Businessman*, 18). Marks was a southern Presbyterian. He eventually became an executive with Cru. Myron Rush, the award-winning author who has written two helpful books on a Christian approach to the business arena, endorses the soteriological approach to developing a management theology. In *Lord of the Marketplace*, he wrote: "If God is our senior business partner, and we are committed to him, then His goals become our goals. As we saw in John 10:10, God's goal is to reach people with the Gospel. Therefore, as we seek to use our businesses to reach people in the marketplace with the Good News, and as we begin to actively pursue that goal, God has promised He will provide the monetary support we need to accomplish the goals of our business" (Rush, *Lord of the Marketplace*, 76); cf. Matt 6:32–33.

> My prayer is not that you take them out of the world[868] but that you protect them from the evil one. They are not of the world, even as I am not of it. Sanctify them by the truth; your word is truth. As you sent me into the world, I have sent them into the world. For them I sanctify myself, that they too may be truly sanctified. (John 17:15–19)

In this famous corollary passage Jesus marshals his "authority"[869] as he prays to the Father to protect his people as he sends them into spiritual battle. The objects of his sending are primarily the small group of disciples,[870] but by extension we can apply his words to present-day business managers. The "world" Jesus is referring to is not secular culture as is sometimes suggested but rather the hostile ethical world of secular thinking dominated by Satan, the "evil one." The call from Jesus is to "be dressed ready for service and keep your lamps burning."[871] Or as Isaiah said,

> He will strike the earth with the rod of his mouth; with the breath of his lips he will slay the wicked. Righteousness will be his belt and faithfulness the sash around his waist. (Isa 11:4–5)

Or as Paul said,

> Gird your loins with the belt of truth. (Eph 6:14)

Or as Peter said,

> Prepare your minds for action! (1 Pet 1:13)

Or as John said,

> Out of his mouth will comes a sharp sword with which to strike down the nations. He will rule them with an iron scepter. (Rev 19:15)

And so Jesus is praying that the Father and the Spirit will sanctify ("make holy") the managers' minds through the written word to engage in the upcoming ethical battle. The disciples have seen Jesus in action from the beginning of his ministry.[872] The Lord is now at the end of his

---

868. *Kosmos* = arrangement.
869. Matt 28:18.
870. Matt 15:27.
871. Luke 12:35.
872. John 15:27; 16:10.

ministry, and he is passing the baton to his vice-presidents who would pass the reconciling ministry on to their managers. Notice that Jesus does not pray that the Father take the managers out of the battle for the minds but that he prepares them for the coming intellectual fight. Jesus is not abandoning the world but seeks its agreement through the words and life of his ambassadors.[873] Our gracious God wants to deliver the world, so he sends the managers to present Jesus.[874]

Most of the Christian manager's responsibilities revolve around internal affairs, managing the organization God has given him. But there is an outside responsibility to the community that goes with managing. One's reputation in the community is important in the Bible: Moses,[875] Samuel,[876] David,[877] Hezekiah,[878] Jesus,[879] early Christians,[880] elders of the organization,[881] all Christians[882] are all to give evidence of a fine public reputation. Jesus commands us to live among our neighbors as full participants in our society and culture. That is, while the business of a business is profit, there is a sub-calling to be an instrument of eleemosynary activities. We are to be the "salt of the earth" and the "light of the world,"[883] and we can't fulfill that function if we separate ourselves from the political, economic, and social activities of the "world."[884]

Jesus tells the Jewish cohort the parable of the sheep and the goats in Matthew 25:31–46. The Lord is talking to the "goats" on his left, and he is telling them that because they did not indiscriminately feed "the hungry,"

---

873. 2 Cor 5:20.

874. Carson has a nice summary of Jesus' prayer for the Christian business leaders: "That Jesus' prayer for his disciples has as its end their mission to the world demonstrates that this Gospel is not introducing an absolute cleavage between Jesus and the world. Not only were the disciples drawn from the world (John 15:19), but the prayer that they may be kept safe in the world and sanctified by the truth so as to engage in mission to the world is ample evidence that they are the continuing locus of John 3:16" (Carson, *The Gospel According the John*, 566–67).

875. Cf. Exod 11:3.

876. Cf. 1 Sam 2:26; 1 Sam 8:7, 9, 22.

877. Cf. 1 Sam 18:5; 1 Chr 13:1, 4.

878. Cf. 2 Chr 30:2, 4, 23; 2 Chr 32:23.

879. Cf. Luke 2:52; Luke 13:20–21.

880. Cf. Acts 2:47.

881. Cf. 1 Tim 3:7.

882. Cf. Prov 3:4; 1 Cor 10:32; 1 Pet 2:15.

883. Cf. Matt 5:13–16.

884. Cf. John 17:18.

Jesus on Specific Responsibilities of a Business Manager

give drink to "the thirsty," show hospitality to "the stranger," clothe "the poor," care for "the sick," or visit "the imprisoned"—whoever the hungry, the thirsty, the stranger, the poor, the sick, the imprisoned were—they will not receive the blessings of the Lord. But rather, they will earn his harsh judgment: "Depart from me, you who are cursed, into the eternal fire prepared for the devil and his angels."[885] The reason for Jesus' anger? His solidarity with humankind: "For I was hungry . . . I was thirsty . . . I was a stranger . . . I needed clothes . . . I was sick and in prison!"[886] And so, to the extent the manager discriminates against the "needy," he discriminates against Jesus. These genuine incarnational Christian managers ask Jesus,

> Lord, when did we see you hungry or thirsty or a stranger or needing clothes or sick or in prison, and did not help you?

And he replies,

> I tell you the truth, whatever you did for one of the least of these brothers of mine, you did for me . . . Then they will go away . . . to eternal life. (Matt 25:37–39)

In John 7:45–52 there is a significant story in which the Pharisees send temple guards to arrest Jesus. The guards come back empty-handed and tell the Pharisees, "No one ever spoke the way this man does." The Pharisees, terribly angry, retort:

> Give us a break! No one of any education or sophistication[887] believes this guy. Only the common rabble, the mob,[888] those

---

885. Matt 25:41.

886. Matt 25:43.

887. "Rulers," "Pharisees."

888. *Ochlos*. Bietenhard wrote of *ochlos*, "In John 7:42, *ochlos* doubtless refers to the term *am ha Ares* or 'people of the land' . . . In the post-exilic age, it denoted the foreign or mixed population, as distinct from the returned exiles. It became a term of abuse, connoting ignorance of and lax attitude towards the law. Hence, the religious leaders with their strict attitude to the law regarded them as accursed" (Bietenhard, "Ochlos," 2.801). In the *Dictionary of the New Testament Theology*, we have further testimony to the separatistic nature of unambiguous thinking concerning the "common people." Rudolf Meyer wrote, "In post-exilic Old Testament books, the term *am ha Ares* obviously denotes the distinction between the temple community, decisively controlled by the returned exiles, and the Samaritans. In Rabbinic writings, however, the original sociological sense was completely lost, and the term became an exclusively religious and political one among the Jews themselves. As a slogan on the lips of the Pharisees it denotes the masses, or the individuals belonging to them, who in conduct

who don't know the religious way of life ("law")—only they believe him. And there is a curse on their life anyway! Besides, he comes from Galilee, and nobody who is anybody comes from Galilee. (John 7:47–48)

The temple guards were not secular policemen but rather theologically trained Levites who guarded the sacred Jewish buildings. So when the Pharisees mocked they were mocking theologically educated Levites who had fallen under the oratorical influence of Jesus. The Levites had joined the mob! Notice that the guards did not blame the power of public opinion but rather the power of Jesus' words on them. Interestingly, the assumption being made by the Pharisees is that public opinion influenced the guards, but it is the Pharisees who are sensitive to their public opinion ("Has any of the rulers or of the Pharisees believed in him?" John 7:48). The lesson for the Christian manager is that he needs to be aware that the received wisdom of the authorities may not be the truth, and he needs to think for himself, even if that puts him on the side of the "riff-raff." Doing so will earn the manager scorn and ridicule from the experts, so he had better have a thick skin. But it will also earn the manager admiration from his coworkers and his boss.

The charge from Jesus is to be in the world, closely identified with the world, partakers of the concerns of the world, yet not being of the same moral and spiritual nature as the world. The charge is given to the witnessing manager in the Lord's great prayer in John 17. Note in that prayer Jesus is not praying to protect the manager from "the world," but rather from "the evil one" who controls portions of "the world."[889] So to be the manager is to be one with the world, yet not be drawn into the evilness in the world by his own sinful natures. Resist the testing! Calvin stated,

> God does not take his people out of the world, because he does not want them to be soft and slothful; but he delivers them from evil that they may not be overwhelmed. For he wishes them to fight but does not allow them to be mortally wounded.[890]

---

do not live up to the nomistic ideal of the sanctification of all life (cf. the claim of Hillel, 20 BC: 'An uneducated man does not fear sin, and an *am ha Ares* is not pious')" (Meyer, "Ochlos," 5.589).

889. John 17:15.

890. Calvin, *The Gospel According to St. John and the First Epistle of John*, 145.

THE WITNESSING MANAGER IN THE OLD TESTAMENT

Moses the witnessing manager

> Impress [these commandments that I give you today] on your children. Talk about them when you sit at home and when you walk along the road, when you lie down and when you get up. Tie them as symbols on your hands and bind them on your foreheads. Write them on the doorframes of your houses and on your gates. (Deut 6:6–9)

God's word to Moses the witnessing manager was to form the framework of a holy worldview. The organization's cohort was to meditate on Yahweh's commandments to such an extent that the Scriptures would be part of their thinking and not a formal, legalistic approach to life. To accomplish this integration:

- The Scriptures were to be first a subject of conversation at home.
- The Scriptures were to permeate every aspect of a person's daily life.[891]
- The scriptural worldview was to animate one's public involvement in the community.

Taken metaphorically, the signs described indicate that the individual believer was to be characterized by obedience to God's word and a love for his gospel. Moses, the witnessing manager, was telling the company cohort that their testimony would be through their life. The coworkers were to wear the corporate gear to show their loyalty to the company.[892]

---

891. Cf. Prov 6:20–22.

892. "The individual was to be distinguished in their character by obedience to the commandments as a response of love for God" (Craigie, *The Book of Deuteronomy*, 171). Collins, in his book *Built to Last*, 123, writes about loyalty in a managerial setting: "Nordstrom presents an excellent example of what we came to call 'cultism'—a series of practices that create an almost cult-like environment around the core ideology in highly visionary companies. These practices tend to vigorously screen out those who do not fit with the ideology (either before hiring or early in their careers). They also instill an intense sense of loyalty and influence the behavior of those remaining inside the company to be congruent with the core ideology, consistent over time, and carried out zealously."

Isaiah the witnessing manager

> I, Yahweh, have called you in righteousness; I will take hold of your hand. I keep you and will make you to be a covenant for the people and a light[893] for the Gentiles, to open eyes that are blind, to free captives from prison and to release from the dungeon those who sit in darkness. (Isa 42:6–7)[894]

The message of Isaiah the witnessing prophet/manager is that his co-workers will be a vehicle of the company's message to their neighbors, especially their competitors.[895] The handicaps of both the company and the competitors will be resolved, and the limitations of both groups will be eliminated.[896] This will only happen as the corporate mission is promulgated.[897]

Jeremiah the witnessing manager

> This is what Yahweh Almighty, the God of Israel, says to all those I carried into exile from Jerusalem to Babylon: "Build[898] houses and settle down;[899] plant[900] gardens and eat[901] what they produce. Marry[902] and have sons and daughters; find wives for your sons and give[903] your daughters in marriage, so that they too may have sons and daughters. Increase[904] in number there; do not decrease. Also, seek[905] the peace and prosperity[906] of the

---

893. *Or* = illumination, enlightenment, brightness, happiness.
894. Cf. Ezek 34:11–16.
895. Isa 42:4; Acts 26:16–17.
896. Cf. Isa 9:2; 42:19–20; 43:8; 44:18–19.
897. Isa 2:1–4; 42:4, 18–20; 49:6; Ps 37:6, Mic 7:9.
898. *Banah.*
899. *Yashab* = sit down.
900. *Nata.*
901. *Akal.*
902. *Laqach* = take.
903. *Nathan.*
904. *Rabah* = to be many, multiplied.
905. *Darash* = inquire.
906. *Shalom* = peace, completeness.

Jesus on Specific Responsibilities of a Business Manager 359

city to which I have carried you into exile. Pray[907] to Yahweh for it, because if it prospers, you too will prosper." (Jer 29:4–7)

Yahweh's command to be deeply and significantly involved in our respective communities has Old Testament resonance. Indeed, in a wonderfully clear announcement to the exiled company cohort, Jeremiah the witnessing manager gave this cautionary (and yet impelling) message. Jeremiah's words are genuinely shocking because he is telling the organization that her mission statement does not depend on being in the promised land with all the accouterments of their religion, i.e., temple, holy places, memorials, etc. Rather, Jeremiah the witnessing prophet/manger is telling the coworkers that, in whatever circumstances they are in, and whoever they are with, they are to understand they are where they are because God has placed them there ("those I carried into exile"). Note the strong action verbs Jeremiah uses to make Yahweh's point: "build," "settle down," "plant," "eat," "marry," "find," "give," "increase," "seek," "pray," "prosper." Yahweh permits defeat and ruin for wise and salutary reasons unknown to humans. The member's houses are to be permanent and not tents or lean-tos, and the planting is to be done with the expectation of future harvests. The company is to create a model organization within the hostile community in order to effect a beneficial influence in the culture of the nation.[908] Domesticity and devotion, hard work and prayer, all contribute to peace in a hostile environment.[909] This would be a bitter pill for the company to take, so it needed stalwart and wise management to keep everyone in line.

Some management lessons to be learned from Jeremiah the witnessing prophet/manager:

- Witnessing managers are to seek the welfare of the specific community into which they have been placed, even if it is dominated by unbelievers.[910] The prophet is saying to endeavor to promote the prosperity of the community which God sends you. This brings us back to the divine call to bless the community of man in the Garden

---

907. *Palal* = entreat.

908. "Serve the king of Babylon and you will live" (Jer 27:17). This is civil religion at its very best and virtually unique in the Bible.

909. Prayerful conformity to Babylonian life! Carroll, *Jeremiah*, 556.

910. "Seek the peace and prosperity [welfare] of the city to which I have carried you." As Matthew Henry has written, "Every passenger is concerned in the safety of the ship" (Henry, *The Bethany Parallel Commentary on the New Testament*, 1595).

of Eden: "Yahweh took the man and put him in the Garden of Eden to work it and take care of it."[911]

- Witnessing managers are to take a long view of their cultural engagement. Jeremiah told the exiles that they will have grandchildren in Babylon.[912] There will not be the quick solution or dominant cultural influence forecast by false prophets such as Hananiah.[913]

- Witnessing managers must not despise the day of small things because the Jewish cohort had to start from scratch with building modest houses and planting private gardens for domestic use.[914]

- The witnessing manager must not let the false teaching and the current pieties of the age deceive him and his coworkers into thinking unrealistic thoughts. He must be grounded in reality.[915]

- The witnessing manager is to pray for his competitors with the implicit implication that God hears those prayers and will answer them and bless the competitors. No more *Schadenfreude!*[916] The difficult aspect of this is that the witnessing manager must be prepared for competitor success!

- Witnessing managers are to make the best of the contemporary situation God gives them, and they are not to live in the future, as outsiders or strangers to the present.[917]

- The witnessing manager is not to be a religious sociopath, but rather he is to fully penetrate and appropriately enjoy the multifaceted benefits of his respective secular communities because human culture is, after all, a result of Yahweh's common grace.[918]

---

911. Gen 2:15; *shamar* = to guard, protect, keep, manage.
912. "It will be a long time" (Jer 29:28).
913. Jer 27:16; 28:2-4.
914. Zech 4:10.
915. Jer 23:15-17. Jer 29:8-9. Prov 10:17.
916. Jer 29:7.
917. Jer 29:5-6.
918. Cf. Matt 5:45; elsewhere.

THE WITNESSING MANAGER IN THE NEW TESTAMENT

Paul the witnessing manager

> How then can they call on the one they have not believed in? And how can they believe in the one of whom they have not heard? And how can they hear without someone preaching[919] to them? And how can they preach unless they are sent? As it is written, "How beautiful are the feet of those who bring good news." (Rom 10:14)

Scholars have taken this passage to refer to the preaching of those formally commissioned to preach the gospel. Indeed, some even claim that to presume to take upon oneself the preaching duties with such a formal "sending" is arrogance and unbiblical. The context lends itself to this interpretation. However, the Greek word Paul the witnessing manager employs here, translated "preaching," means only to proclaim or publicly declare or even publish. So a non-ordained person, like a witnessing manager, is covered under Paul's quotation of Isaiah 52:7. And a couple of thousand years-worth of exegesis have suggested that ordinary non-ordained or commissioned persons can be motivated to share the good news of the gospel with their neighbors and have beautiful feet as a result. John Calvin wrote, "the Gospel does not fall from the clouds like rain, by accident, but is brought by the hands of men to where God has sent it."[920] There is the undeniable Pauline focus here on verbal proclamation, so the witnessing manager had better prepare himself for this with a short gospel presentation.

> Make it your ambition[921] to lead a quiet life, to mind your own business and to work with your hands, just as we told you, so that your daily life may win the respect of outsiders and so that you will not be dependent on anybody. (1 Thess 4:11–12)[922]

The focus now shifts to lifestyle evangelism and away from confrontational evangelism. In these two verses we have two more paradoxical Pauline statements: make it your ambition not to be ambitious and you are not to regard the opinion of the world, but you should strive to win

---

919. *Kerusso* = proclaim, declare, publish.
920. Calvin, *The Epistles of Paul to the Romans and Thessalonians*, 231.
921. *Philotimeomai* = to strive eagerly, to seek restlessly; Rom 15:20; 2 Cor 5:9.
922. Mic 4:4.

the opinion of the world. Paul the witnessing manager is telling the Thessalonians to work with their own hands to be about their own work and thus to provide for their own needs. The non-believing world will be looking on, and it has reasons enough to criticize the company. After all, the world doesn't need any help from lazy or busybody Christians. Particularly from a work ethic issue that is completely unnecessary and unbiblical. After all, Paul has repeatedly told the Thessalonians to get on with their lives of supporting themselves. Witnessing managers can take several pointers from Paul's letter to the Thessalonians:

- Witnessing managers are to take care of the business of his company and not dilute their attention or energies to outside activities. That is, he is a manager of a business, not a full-time evangelist, so he is to do what God has called him to do: effectively manage an organization.
- Witnessing managers are to conduct their business in a way that adorns their Christian convictions with competitors.
- Witnessing managers are to keep their obligations low so as not to be dependent on those outside the company.

> I urge you, then, first of all, that requests, prayers, intercession, and thanksgiving be made for everyone, for kings and all those in authority, that we may live peaceful and quiet lives in all godliness and holiness. This is good and pleases God our Savior who wants all people to be saved and to come to a knowledge of the truth. (1 Tim 2:1–4)

Another shift in focus, this time to prayers for the leaders of society. This Pauline passage is on the phrase "made for everyone" and not "prayers." Paul the witnessing manager is urging the cohort to remember that the offer of salvation is to everyone and not just a select few. In fact, Paul emphasizes this by mentioning four types of prayers: "requests," "prayers," "intercession," and "thanksgiving." There is a slight difference between each of these types, but that is not the point. The point is that "everyone" gets the same level of treatment. The mention of kings and authorities is a parenthetical mention and doesn't mean they get the most attention, but rather it is a matter of the corporate witness of the company to the outside world. It needs to be remembered that Nero was Roman emperor at the time, and he was no friend of the organization, so this injunction had power and controversy behind it. The concern for "everyone" is part of the Christian witnessing manager's life being "lived" out in the midst of a hostile political, religious and economic culture.[923] The four attributes of the Christian experience—"peaceful," "quiet," "godly," "holy"—are reflected in the life of the manager. Incidentally, Paul is not saying that the Christian life is to be conflict-free but rather belligerent-free. The Christian witnessing manager is to have a good reputation outside the organization.[924] Finally, in 1 Timothy 2:4, we get the motivation for our tranquil and dignified life of prayer and action: God's blessing would increase in the world.

> This is a trustworthy statement that deserves full acceptance: Christ Jesus came into the world to save sinners—of whom I am the worst. (1 Tim 1:15)

> This is a trustworthy statement that deserves full acceptance (and for this we labor and strive), that we have put our hope in the living God who is the Savior of all people and especially of those who believe. (1 Tim 4:10)

> For the grace of God that brings salvation has appeared to all people. (Titus 2:11)

In three short passages Paul the witnessing manager refers to the benefits of salvation through Christ to all people, not just the chosen few. Thus, once again, Paul throws the gauntlet down for the Christian business manager: Live such a good life among coworkers, suppliers, and customers that "all people" outside the Christian faith will benefit from one's lifestyle, maybe even becoming Christians in the process of them observing and hearing. In the meantime, the Christian witnessing manager is to be a force of tranquility and dignity in the community.[925]

Peter the witnessing manager

> Dear friends, I urge you, as aliens and strangers in the world, to abstain from sinful desires, which war against your soul. Live

---

923. Cf. Matt 10:16.

924. Mounce states it succinctly: "A Christian's life is not to be quiet of speech, but it should be quiet in nature, a tranquility stemming from a godly and reverent life" (Mounce, *Pastoral Epistles*, 82–83).

925. Cf. 1 Tim 3:4, 8, 11.

such good lives[926] among the pagans that, though they accuse you of doing wrong, they may see[927] your good deeds and glorify God on the day he visits us. Submit yourselves for the Lord's sake to every authority instituted among people: whether to the king as the supreme authority, or to governors, who went by him to punish those who do wrong and to commend those who do right. For it is God's will that by doing good[928] you should silence the ignorant talk of foolish people. (1 Pet 2:11–15)

Peter the witnessing manager strikes that lovely ambiguous balance between being "aliens and strangers in the world" and at the same time being the essential ingredients, the "salt" and "light" in the world, to the extent that God is glorified by our obedience to his commands, as do-gooders. Peter is encouraging the Christian witnessing manager to "live a good life" and "do good deeds among the pagans." The focus for the business manager, then, is to live a noble life in the company and the community in which God has placed him for the sake of the kingdom of God. Peter is very clear about the importance of "observable" conduct on the part of the Christian business manager. All thinking Christians understand that this deportment is not as easy as it might seem, since the "pagans" have a built-in hostility and suspicion of the Christian businessman, particularly when the alien Christian does not follow the lifestyle rules of the secular market game. The fact that the Christian business manager will abstain from "passions of the flesh" when others indulge themselves puts distance between the believer and the unbeliever.

John the witnessing manager

This we proclaim concerning the Word of life. The life appeared; we have seen it and testify to it, and we proclaim[929] to you the eternal life, which was with the father and has appeared to us. We proclaim to you what we have seen and heard, so that you also may have fellowship[930] with us. (1 John 1:1–3)

---

926. *Kalos* = noble, fair, honorable.
927. Scrutinizable.
928. *Agathopoieo* = behavior.
929. *Apaggello* = to tell.
930. *Koinonia*.

Jesus on Specific Responsibilities of a Business Manager

John the witnessing manager is telling his reader that he and his managerial colleagues were eyewitnesses to Jesus' earthly life and ministry. And because of this eyewitness experience ("heard," "seen," "beheld," "felt") they saw Jesus in the days of his flesh. The point is that readers can have fellowship with Yahweh through Jesus, but also fellowship with John and the other members of the company through Jesus. This "fellowship" is not a sentimental holding hands and singing "Kumbaya" by the campfire, but a relationship grounded on the truth of Jesus' life. The witnessing manager is to take an example of John's testimony.

It is a common understanding among the thoughtful that everything in society is downstream from culture, and that applies to a business as well. This basic solidarity with our neighbors implicitly and explicitly rejects social separatism. There must be a moral purity to our lives, but that is not the same as ceremonial purity. The Bible doesn't teach that separatism is prohibited only between the religious and the non-religious. It also teaches that separatism is prohibited between the hyper-religious and the genuinely interested folk, the "God-fearers."[931]

Solidarity, not separatism, with the world in which God has placed the witnessing manager is his divine port of call. Managing a small business involves the identification and solidarity with those around the organization. It is "taking the form" of our neighbors.[932] This is the basic definition of the incarnational lifestyle of the Christian witnessing manager.[933]

This solidarity with the sinful world must be genuine, but only in appearance and not nature. That is, the manager is not to free himself from the prescription of holiness and obedience given to him by Jesus.[934] John the witnessing manager tells the manager he or she is to participate in life as it exists in the culture in order to be the "salt" of society[935] and share the "blessings of the gospel . . . to those not having the law."[936] The

---

931. Cf. Acts 10:2.

932. Cf. Phil 2:7.

933. Berkouwer, in commenting on this solidarity of the incarnation with humanity, stated, "One can characterize Christ's entire life with the words, 'For this reason he had to be made like his brothers in every way (Heb 2:17a)'" (Berkouwer, *The Person of Christ*, 209).

934. Cf. Rom 13:8–10.

935. Cf. Matt 5:13.

936. Cf. 1 Cor 9:19–23. Grosheide commented on 9:21, "To the Gentiles, Paul is without the law (the Greek is the subjective condition, indicating that Paul is not

real danger for the witnessing manager who follows Jesus in the twenty-first century is not that he will become a Pharisee for the organization, erecting unbiblical barriers between the organization and society, but that he will soil his testimony by associating too closely with those outside "the Mosaic law."[937] The members of the Pharisaic group were concerned not only with their own status as a distinct group, but to their detached social relations with non-Pharisees, in the sense of staying away from them.

Because the world is so paradoxical, capricious, fickle, and ambiguous in its own approach to values and priorities,[938] the incarnational witnessing manager must likewise approach the world ambiguously in order to faithfully reflect the approach of Jesus. The world engages in religious acts without the circumcised heart,[939] and so the sifting of the wheat and the tares is impossible for the human mind.[940] That makes socializing only with the "pure" ones impossible! The fact that the witnessing manager is a spiritual "alien and stranger in his world"[941] does not mean he is a social, political, or economic "stranger" as well. The "spirit" of the world wars against the "Spirit" of God,[942] but it is a spiritual warfare and not an economic battle. Common revelatory reason,[943] resident in all but the insane and infant, can be helpful in establishing common ground with neighbors for the reflecting of a Christian management approach even in a fluid cultural environment.[944]

---

actually without law, but he is so in the opinion of the Gentiles), not because he is actually without any law, but because he is accommodating himself to the conduct of those who are not bound to the Mosaic law" (Grosheide, *Commentary on the First Epistle to the Corinthians*, 145).

937. Grosheide, *Commentary on the First Epistle to the Corinthians*, 311–313. Based on Colossians 3:2, the Fellowship of Companies for Christ (FCCI) have the conception that "Christian" companies are different, not better than, "non-Christian" companies. Case (1872–1947) argued that the term "separated" as it was applied to the Pharisees signified social, as well as religious and political, overtones (Case, *Jesus: A New Biography*, 311–312).

938. Cf. John 12:9-13; 18:38-40; 19:14-15.

939. Cf. Acts 17:22-23, 28; 2 Tim 3:5.

940. Cf. Matt 13:27-30.

941. Cf. Heb 11:13; 1 Pet 2:11.

942. Cf. Rom 12:1-2; Eph 6:10-12.

943. Cf. Rom 2:14-15.

944. Cf. West, *The Politics of Revelation and Reason*.

It is not for nothing that leaders in a local branch office must have a good reputation and be respectable in the surrounding community.[945] Luke records that the community at Lystra "spoke well" of Timothy.[946] Timothy, as a role model for the Christian manager, whose mother was Jewish and father was a gentile, had a foot in both segments of society.

CONCLUDING THOUGHT

The simple conclusion is that the incarnational, ambiguous Christian business manager must create and maintain a company culture of love which manifests itself by seeking the employee's best interests and by treating their ideas and values with respect, integrity, and importance. How the Christian business manager does that will depend on the circumstances and personalities involved. Trust the Holy Spirit and his inspired word.

I hope the exegetical emphasis of this book on management lessons taught and exemplified by biblical managers will prod today's managers to see practical wisdom and guidance from the hand of Jesus.

---

945. Cf. 1 Tim 3:2–3; 1 Pet 2:11–25.
946. Acts 16:2.

Appendix

"Rehoboam: A Study in Failed Management"
Presbyterion (Covenant Theological Seminary) Spring 1988

ROBERT CASE

IMMEDIATELY AFTER THE DEATH of King Solomon about 930 BC, with no powerful, charismatic king on the throne to hold all the tribes of Israel together, unity among Jacob's descendants was tenuous. The rightful heir to the throne was Solomon's son, Rehoboam. However, through a series of management lapses, Rehoboam threw away the opportunity to lead a united nation and instead precipitated a division between the northern tribes (Israel) and the southern tribes (Judah). Simply put, there was a window of opportunity which was forever lost due to Rehoboam's failure in leadership. The fact that this schism was part of God's foreordained plan does not mitigate Rehoboam's failure to provide godly leadership in a time of crises.

EXEGESIS OF 1 KINGS 12:1-20

When Rehoboam ascended to the throne in Jerusalem, it was important that all the tribes should recognize his legitimate kingship (cf. Deut 33). So he traveled to Shechem in the north to be crowned king of the northern tribes as well as the southern tribes headquartered in Jerusalem. However, before they crowned him king, the Israelites desired some political and economic concessions. They wanted Rehoboam to ease the economic and political repression Solomon had imposed. After conferring first with Solomon's advisors and then with his own younger aides, Rehoboam not only refused to make any concessions but in fact promised a tougher and more repressive public policy. In reaction the northern tribes refused to crown Rehoboam king and instead repudiated him and David's crown rights. In rebellion, the Israelites crowned Jeroboam, the renegade exile from Egypt, as their monarch! Furthermore, Rehoboam had so thoroughly antagonized his erstwhile northern subjects that they killed his labor representative and set up their own religious shrines and idols. Consequently, an absolute enmity was eventually established between the two regions of Abraham's inheritance (cf. 1 Kgs 14:30).

We will now take a closer look at the passage in order to observe King Rehoboam in action as he fails to exercise responsible management.

Verse 1: The fact that the tribes in the north (Israel) did not come down to Jerusalem to inaugurate Rehoboam as king should probably have signaled danger to the new king. When David was recognized as king over both Israel and Judah, he made Jerusalem the political capital, i.e., the "city of David" (2 Sam 5:1–10). Later, Solomon would make Jerusalem the permanent spiritual capital as well when he built the temple there (1 Kgs 6 and 7). So Jerusalem was the natural city in which to crown the successor to Solomon and David. It was not uncommon for the people to gather together to anoint a king. That had happened for Saul (1 Sam 9:15), David (2 Sam 2:4; 5:3), and Solomon (1 Chr 29:22). The difference here is that the people were dictating to the king where to be anointed. And the symbolism of Shechem portended problems. Shechem was in the territory of the tribe of Ephraim (Josh 24:1), and Jeroboam was an Ephraimite (1 Kgs 11:26)! Clearly, the Israelites seemed to be putting the new king on the defensive by making him come to unfamiliar turf to be crowned king. None of this should have been a surprise to Rehoboam, who knew the history of tribal conflict between Ephraim in the north and Judah in the south. As early as the time of Gideon, Shechem figured in opposition to the godly line of rulers when Abimelech refused to follow the line of Gideon and was crowned king in Shechem. It bears noting that Abimelech was Gideon's son through a Shechemite concubine (Judg 8:31–9:6). Later, while David was being crowned king of Judah at Hebron, Abner was being crowned king of Ephraim at Mahanaim (2 Sam 2:1–9). Further, in David's later years, Sheba, a Benjaminite from Ephraim (2 Sam 20:21), revolted against David's rule (2 Sam 20:1).

"Rehoboam: A Study in Failed Management"

Verses 2–3: Jeroboam "was a valiant warrior" whom Solomon recognized as a gifted leader. In 1 Kings 11:28 we read that the great king appointed Jeroboam "over all the forced labor" of the house of Joseph. In other words, Jeroboam was in charge of all public works projects in the northern tribes. Note that Joseph was buried in Shechem (Josh 24:32), and it was at Mt. Ebal that Moses spoke to the Israelites before crossing the Jordan River (Deut 27–28); so, despite a rebellious past, it was a hallowed region to all Israelites (Josh 24:30, 33). On his way from Jerusalem north to assume his new responsibilities, Jeroboam met the prophet Ahijah, who foretold of his kingship over the ten tribes of the north as a punishment against Solomon for his apostasy. Solomon, hearing of this prophecy, sought to kill Jeroboam, forcing him into exile in Egypt. He returned to lead the gathering at Shechem at which Rehoboam appeared. Consequently, the assumption can legitimately be made that Jeroboam had both the motivation and the following to lead the Israelites in revolt against the new king, the son of Solomon, his erstwhile benefactor and then enemy.

Verse 4: Rehoboam's dilemma was this: Should he ease up in the face of opposition led by his archrival Jeroboam and risk the appearance of weakness, or should he continue his father's harsh public practices, force his leadership on the Israelites, and thereby demonstrate that he is the undisputed king? It is important to see that the demand of the Israelites had nothing to do with redressing the spiritual defection of Solomon's later years. The Israelites were not complaining about Solomon's apostasy or his idolatry, which should have caused national grief. What angered the Israelites was their onerous civic obligations. They were more concerned about the good life than they were about the godly life! They were angry over the oppressiveness and not the religious declension of their national leaders. They were apparently totally indifferent toward faithlessness in the national character. Their sudden spiritual collapse under Jeroboam (1 Kgs 12:28; 2 Kgs 10:29; 17:15–16) is evidence of this uncircumcised national heart. There is little question that Solomon used a heavy hand in public works administration. Samuel had warned the Israelites of the drawbacks of a human king, but the people had insisted on having one (1 Sam 8:10–22). In 1 Kings 9:15–19 we read of Solomon's public projects, which required conscripted labor and taxation from all the tribes. That was the darker side of Solomon's rule. On the brighter side, the people lived in peace, prosperity, and respect under Solomon (1 Kgs 4:20–21—"they were eating and drinking and rejoicing," 24–25;

cf. 1 Kgs 10:27). Even the Queen of Sheba publicly acknowledged the benefits of Solomon's leadership (1 Kgs 10:8-9). Furthermore, while the "sons of Israel" were required to work on these massive building projects, they were not slaves, but rather laborers (1 Kgs 9:20-22). It is obvious, therefore, that the Israelites under Jeroboam were selective in their recollections when they focused on the negative "harsh labor and heavy yoke." They seemed to have forgotten the manifold benefits and blessings of a strong, vital, and secure monarchy.

Verse 5: In response to the demand of the Israelite assembly, Rehoboam did one wise thing. He gave himself some time to mull over his response. He replied, "Come back day after tomorrow for your answer."

Verse 6: During this period Rehoboam consulted with his father's advisors who had presumably benefited from Solomon's great wisdom (Cf. 1 Kgs 10:6-8, 23-24; 3:9-13). The Queen of Sheba referred to these advisors in 1 Kings 10:8. Robinson[1] maintains that Solomon probably was no more than sixty when he died (1 Kgs 3:7 and 11:42), so his "elders" may well have been of that age. It is to these wise counselors Rehoboam first turned for advice. It seems Rehoboam may have had correct, but weak, instincts, because he first turned to his father's elders for direction. Later in his administration he would also act wisely (1 Chr 11:23). He may have been a young man of a certain courage and determination, for he wanted to fight for his kingdom after the revolt under Jeroboam (1 Kgs 12:21), though later he was found cowering behind the walls of Jerusalem when King Shishak of Egypt attacked Judah (2 Chr 12:2-5). Rehoboam may even have been faithful to Yahweh, though weak in his faith, since he did refrain from attacking the northern tribes because "the word of the Lord" told him not to fight (1 Kgs 12:24). On the other hand, he could not or would not prevent Judah from apostasy and idolatry (1 Kgs 14:22-24). It is worth remembering at this point that Rehoboam had a Canaanite mother, "Naamah the Ammonitess" (1 Kgs 14:21; 11:3)—a perverse paternal legacy! The emerging picture of Rehoboam, then, is that of a well-intentioned but weak king.

Verse 7: Solomon's elders advised Rehoboam to do three things to head off a tragic rupture in the united kingdom: (1) "serve the people"; (2) "answer their petition" (i.e., address their concerns); (3) "speak good words to them." The last suggestion, "speak good words to them," deserves comment. The Septuagint translates "good" as *agathos*, which is

---

1. Robinson, "Solomon," 4.2823.

something "beneficial in effect." Andrew Bowling[2] states that the Hebrew term used here (*tob*) can either have a practical sense or suggest an economic benefit. The word is used earlier in 1 Kings to mean the right thing morally and spiritually (8:18), economic prosperity and wellbeing (10:7), and/or a moral and pious life before God (8:36). Consequently, the general meaning of "good" here seems to be that which benefits, pleases, and is agreeable to God. The elders' advice reported in verse 7 then means, "Do the right thing and tell them what they want to hear, that is, that the 'hard service' and 'heavy taxation' will be eased." Solomon himself would seem to so counsel his son in Proverbs 15:1 and 20:3. The general thrust of the elders' advice seemed to be appeasement and some moderation of the harsh public policies of Solomon. And this came from the very men who counseled Solomon during the period of "heavy yoking!" These men were apparently wise enough to see that what was good for one era may not be good and beneficial for another. On the other hand, the Solomonic elders were probably not unmindful of the political realities of the situation, for their counsel made profound political sense as well: give in "today" so that you can rule "forever." Or eat a little political crow today and feast on political pheasant tomorrow! These men knew how to rule a country. They knew that the people were ostensibly only asking for leniency and not independence from Rehoboam. By giving a little now, Rehoboam could satisfy the moderates, leaving the radical Jeroboam-backers isolated from the mainstream, and therefore without many followers.

Verses 8–9: However, Rehoboam apparently had his mind already made up, for he turned to his own advisors to get their opinion. Rehoboam seemed to have consulted the Solomonic elders as a political ploy, to keep those loyal to Solomon in the fold. As John Bright[3] points out, Rehoboam turned to "young men, like himself, born to the purple" for advice. First Kings 14:21 tells us Rehoboam was forty-one when he ascended to the throne, so "young men," then, is more than just the age of his trusted advisors. The reference may also be to the similarity of their thinking to his: probably they were "men who grew up with him" and were new to the power of the crown (2 Chr 10:8). We later learn that Rehoboam found it easier to be surrounded by "yes men" than to have independent critical thinkers as his advisors. Note the emphasis on

---

2. Bowling, *Theological Wordbook of the Old Testament*, 2.793.
3. Bright, *A History of Israel*, 230.

"serving him" as opposed to serving "his father Solomon." The Hebrew word translated "forsook" or "rejected" is *azab*, which Carl Schultz maintains has "three distinct emphases: to depart, to abandon, and to loose."[4] Clearly, the results, as well as the implication, of Rehoboam's actions indicate that he left the wisdom of Solomon behind as he turned to his own advisors for counsel. It is probable that Solomon, had he been consistent with his own advice and the advice of his counsellors, would have done what the elders suggested. The phrase "that we may answer this people" seems to indicate an official group of advisors composed of these "young men" who thought like Rehoboam. There is no "we" when Rehoboam addressed the "elders," perhaps indicating they were now detached from an official power base. The request for advice from Solomon's elders seems all the more perfunctory and *pro forma*.

Verses 10–11: The first thing one is struck with here is that the young advisors accepted the Israelites' complaint as true. They did not challenge the supposition of the request, that is, the harshness of Solomon's policies. Clearly, this statement by the Israelites should have been challenged and refuted by Rehoboam by pointing out the peace and prosperity enjoyed during the reign of Solomon which was brought about by higher taxes and some public labor service. This was a far lower price to pay than the death, destruction, and exile which was the consequence of the apostate reigns following Solomon. Nevertheless, the negotiating agenda had already been staked out by the Israelites. It is interesting to see the "young men," those supposedly loyal to Rehoboam, distance themselves from the responsibility of decision-making by telling him, "you shall say," whereas Rehoboam was looking for a "we may answer" response! The counsel from the "youngsters" was harsh, imprudent, and provocative. They told Rehoboam to reply that the weakest part of his body ("littlest finger") was stronger than Solomon's strongest part ("loin"). A better translation of "loin" might be "waist." What the young advisors were poetically suggesting was that Solomon was a mighty king, but his power and might was no match for his son's. Therefore, the people should not trifle with the new king. A raw and dangerous power play! To show that Rehoboam intended to use his presumed might, he was counseled to say further that while Solomon put a "heavy yoke" on the people, Rehoboam would impose ("load") an even heavier yoke of taxation. While Solomon kept the people in line with whips, Rehoboam would add barbed wire to the whips ("scorpions") to give added pain, suffering, and fear! What the

---

4. Schultz, "Azab," 2.658.

"young men" were apparently attempting was to show "all Israel" that they were the new power elite and would broach no opposition or resistance. However, they pulled back from personal involvement or responsibility for their power play. Clearly the advice given was insensitive to political reality and foolhardy in the extreme.

Verses 13–14: After three days, Jeroboam led the Israelites back to Rehoboam for his answer. Tragically, the new king had listened to the new power elite and not the wise men who were older and more experienced. The Scriptures say Rehoboam "answered the people harshly." They do not say he lied, or that he was evil, or that he was wrong—only that he was "harsh." At its extreme the Hebrew term can mean "cruel," "violent," "fierce."[5] Oehler terms Rehoboam's response to the Israelites' demands "perverse rejection."[6] Verse 13 implies then that he was "harsh" because he didn't follow the softer approach of servanthood counseled by the elders in verse 7.

Verse 15: Obviously, Rehoboam did not hear what the Israelites were really saying. Of course, the new king heard with his ears what the people were asking. But that is not what the narrator has in mind. He means that while Rehoboam may have heard the words, he missed the point! He heard the sounds but missed the meaning! This is crucial in the narrative because Rehoboam should have heard not only the words but also the intent, the emotion, the conviction being conveyed by the people. Had he done so he perhaps could have averted the tragic split of the nation.

Verse 16: The Israelites were dissatisfied when Rehoboam did not grant them relief from the load of heavy taxation and forced labor. To repeat, Rehoboam heard the people with his ears, but he had not "listened" to what they wanted. They were actually communicating something other than a simple request. Their "request" was an ultimatum, to which Rehoboam and his young advisors apparently were oblivious. So, if Rehoboam would not "answer" correctly the request of the Israelites, then they would "answer" correctly to Rehoboam! And they did "answer" by their own aphorism (See Sheba's words of revolt against David in 2 Samuel 20:1). With poetry, the Israelites rejected ownership and responsibility for David's kingly rule and tradition. If they were to be treated as slaves (verse 14), then they were going to act like slaves, that is, give

---

5. Coppes, "Qasha," 2.181. *Theological Wordbook of the Old Testament*, 2.818.
6. Oehler, *Theology of the Old Testament*, 385.

no loyalty or show no patriotism towards the crown. If the grandson of David was going to be extremely self-centered and self-preoccupied, so would the Israelites! Loyalty would apparently get them nothing but the dreaded scourge!

Verse 17: However, not everyone deserted Rehoboam. The Judeans in the south stayed loyal to the new king, just as Ahijah prophesied they would in 1 Kings 11:36.

Verse 18: Rehoboam was not pleased with the response of the northerners, so he apparently made an effort to woo them back, to placate their anger, by sending an emissary, perhaps intending to negotiate a return. He used a third-party intermediary to effectuate a reunion. Whether Rehoboam's emissary, Adoni-ram, is the same man who served David (2 Sam 20:24) and Solomon (1 Kgs 4:6; 5:14) as director of forced labor is problematic because of the length of time involved in such a term of service. Nevertheless, the important thing is that Rehoboam sent a government official who was responsible for the very area of anguish for the Israelites ("who was over the forced labor") to the Israelites to apparently seek a rapprochement. The fact that Adoni-ram even went on the mission might indicate there was some hope and expectation of success. It was clearly a suicide mission otherwise. It was a case of too little, too late. Adoni-ram was stoned to death by the angry Israelites. Rehoboam obviously did not expect trouble, for he was caught by surprise by the reaction and had to "flee back to Jerusalem." He had tragically misread the depth of the Israelites' outrage. Putting another face on Rehoboam's intention, one could say that Rehoboam sent Adoni-ram to the Israelites not to seek compromise but to enforce compliance with the forced labor laws, thereby adding gross insult to injury. This interpretation would indicate that Rehoboam still did not understand the depth of frustration and anger being expressed by the Israelites. He may not even have been aware that a revolt had taken place; so the mission of Adoni-ram may be interpreted as business as usual. In any case, the Israelites would have nothing to do with the enforcement attempt, and they killed the enforcer. In their fury the Israelites even threatened the king himself. Moisiman[7] rightly points out, "Rehoboam presumed too much on privilege not earned by service, and on power for which he was not willing to render adequate compensation."

---

7. Moisiman, "Rehoboam," 4.2551.

Verses 19–20: Even accepting the providential hand of God in this episode, one cannot excuse or overlook the grievous attitude of Rehoboam as the cause of this utterly catastrophic turn of events in the life of the tribes of Israel. Further, even if there was some premeditated scheme on the part of the Israelites to make Jeroboam king regardless of how Rehoboam answered, the fact is that Rehoboam gave them plenty of justification for revolt. There is some thought that Jeroboam was called back from Egypt not to lead an Israelite assembly request to Rehoboam (verse 3) but rather to lead them to independence from Davidic rule. In any case, we are now left with two kingdoms (note this first biblical reference to the "house of Judah" versus the "house of Israel" in verse 21 immediately following the rebellion narrative) and two kings—this bifurcation caused by Rehoboam's mismanagement of the pivotal episode in the history of God's people.

We now turn to look briefly at some modern management theories as they might bear upon this leadership crisis in church history. I now come to a brief integration of prominent management literature and Rehoboam's actions in 1 Kings 12:

POSITION POWER VERSUS PERSONAL POWER

From the very beginning of the relationship between Rehoboam and Israel there is tension caused by the ascendency through lineage of the new king without regard for the opinion of his subjects. This is a clear power struggle. Gary Yukl defines power as "an agent's potential at a given point in time to influence the attitudes and/or behavior of one or more specified target persons in the direction desired by the agent."[8] At stake in the beginning is not Rehoboam's capacity to exert power but rather his right to exert the power of Solomon. Put another way, the Israelites are not ostensibly questioning Rehoboam's power as much as his unilateral authority to rule as Solomon ruled. Management theory maintains that there are two major sources of power or influence a leader can use over "target persons": position power and personal power.[9] Position power is that power which comes inherently from the administration or organizational position of the occupant of that position, regardless of who the occupant is. Personal power is that power which comes from the

---

8. Yukl, *Leadership in Organizations*, 18.
9. See Etzioni, *A Comparative Analysis of Complex Organizations*.

characteristics and attributes of the person who occupies a position, regardless of the position. Rehoboam was depending on his position as king and son of Solomon to rule Israel and not his personal power base. Indeed, 2 Chronicles 13:7 speaks to his lack of personal charisma and credibility among his followers. It is notable at this point that Jeroboam had the opposite power source, i.e., personal and not positional. Due to Rehoboam's stupidity, Jeroboam's power source catapulted him into the kingship, deposing the rightful king (cf. 2 Chr 13:6–7; 1 Kgs 12:2–3, 20).

SIX POWER BASES OF FRENCH AND RAVEN

Analyzing a leader's power source in another way, one can use what numerous authors have elucidated as power bases or forms of influence which cause a follower to follow a leader. This power base typology was developed by J. R. French and B. H. Raven.[10]

French and Raven's six power bases are as follows:

1. Coercive power base (based on fear).
2. Legitimate power base (based on the position held by the leader).
3. Expert power base (based on the leader's possession of expertise, skill, and knowledge).
4. Reward power base (based on the leader's ability to provide rewards).
5. Referent power base (based on the leader's personal traits).
6. Information power base (based on the leader's possession of information).

Hersey and Blanchard[11] propose a seventh power base:

7. Connection power base (based on the leader's "connections" with influential persons).

It is fascinating to see which of these power bases Rehoboam appealed to in order to gain control over the Israelites. Rehoboam's response to the Israelites' request in verse 14 (adding "yoke" and "scorpions") was

---

10. Raven and French, "Studies in Social Power." See Hersey and Blanchard, *Management of Organizational Behavior*, 178–79; Yukl, *Leadership in Organizations*, 38–39; and Webber, Morgan, and Browne, *Management: Basic Elements of Managing Organizations*, 187–88.

11. Hersey and Blanchard, *Management of Organizational Behavior*, 178.

an appeal to coercive power. The sending of Adoni-ram in verse 18 might have been motivated from a similar power base. Reward power was behind the Israelites' request for leniency (verse 4) because they assumed Rehoboam had the power to grant relief from the oppressive labor and taxing policies of Solomon. A legitimate power base is evident from the fact that Rehoboam was designated successor king to Solomon by the Lord in 1 Kings 11:13 (cf. 1 Kgs 12:23). This power base was recognized by Israel because they "had come to Shechem to make [Rehoboam] king" (verse 1). Rehoboam's connection to David and to Solomon also generated a power base as the son and grandson of previous kings ("son of Solomon," 1 Kgs 12:23; "house of David," 1 Kgs 12:16, 19). Although Rehoboam later would "act wisely" (2 Chr 11:23) in public administration, it is evident that he did not act wisely in this particular instance. Combining this observation with the judgment of 2 Chronicles 13:7, it is clear that Rehoboam was without a referent power base. Finally, Rehoboam had access to an expert resource pool through the Solomonic elders, but he chose to disregard the expert opinion and thus lost that power source.

MANAGEMENT SYSTEMS OF RENSIS LIKERT

When Rehoboam sought the counsel first of the Solomonic elders and then of his own circle of advisors, he engaged in what Rensis Likert would term a "benevolent authoritative" system of leadership.[12] Likert develops four major systems of management, ranging from System 1, which is "exploitive authoritarian," to System 4, which is called "participative group." These systems range along a continuum of people-orientation, with System 1 being least people-oriented. The two middle systems are "benevolent authoritarian" (System 2) and "consultative" (System 3). Rehoboam initially used a "benevolent authoritarian" mode because he sought the advice of counsellors. He maintained control of the decision and did not delegate the verdict to anyone, yet he did seek to inform himself of other opinions. However, as Rehoboam talked with his younger advisors, he moved left, to System 1, "exploitive authoritarian"; Likert would characterize his attitude towards the Israelites as being "hostility towards peers and contempt for subordinates."[13] Likert maintains that leadership is gen-

---

12. Likert, *The Human Organization: Its Management and Value*.
13 Likert, *The Human Organization: Its Management and Value*, 15.

erally more successful as it moves right, to the more participatory mode, rather than left, to the more authoritarian style.

CONTINUUM OF LEADERSHIP BEHAVIOR (TANNENBAUM AND SCHMIDT)

Tannenbaum and Schmidt have a similar continuum which they call the "Continuum of Leadership Behavior." It also ranges from the far left—"Boss Centered Leadership," where the leader makes a decision and then announces it, to the far right—"Subordinate Centered Leadership," or laissez-faire style of leadership, where the leader permits "the subordinates to function within limits defined by the leader."[14] Rehoboam would clearly fall within the category of "Boss Centered" leadership on the far left of the continuum. There is a sense, of course, where any king will fall at this point in the continuum by the very nature of his responsibilities and expectations. However, Rehoboam initially moved towards the right when he opened himself up to some advice from subordinates that, if it had been taken, probably would have saved the day for him and the nation.

FORCE FIELD ANALYSIS (KURT LEWIN)

Another helpful leadership theory is advanced by Kurt Lewin, called "Force Field Analysis."[15] Basically, Lewin's theory is that in any given situation there are two major types of forces at work: driving forces and restraining forces. The amount of change possible in the situation is determined by the strength and number of these competing forces. A driving force is a force which pushes in a particular direction for a particular result. A restraining force is a force which resists change and fights to maintain the status quo. A leader's role is to know who and what the competing forces are and either to increase or decrease, add or eliminate, forces to move the situation (or organization) in the direction desired.

14. Tanenbaum and Schmidt, "How to Choose a Leadership Pattern," 162–80; cf. Hersey and Blanchard, *Management of Organizational Behavior*, 85–87, and Yukl, *Leadership in Organizations*, 204–06.

15. Lewin, "Frontiers in Group Dynamics: Concepts, Method and Reality in Social Science; Social Equilibria and Social Change"; cf. Hersey and Blanchard, *Management of Organizational Behavior*, 115–17, 269–72.

In Rehoboam's case a strong driving force was Jeroboam's ambition and Ahijah's prophecy concerning his kingship of Israel (1 Kgs 11:30–38). Another driving force against Rehoboam's kingship was the dissatisfaction of the Israelites over Solomon's forced labor and taxation policies. A third driving force was the apparent cavalier ambition for power of Rehoboam's young advisors. On the restraining side, Rehoboam desired to remain king over a united nation. Second, the Solomonic elders desired the house of David to continue to rule over a united kingdom. A third restraining force is the inclination of the Israelites to grant Rehoboam the benefit of his position when they came before him with the grievance and then gave him three days to formulate a position. A fourth restraining force is the loyalty of Judah and Benjamin (1 Kgs 12:21), the priests and the Levites (2 Chr 11:13–14), and all the faithful "who set their hearts on seeking the Lord God of Israel" (2 Chr 11:16). The equilibrium between the opposing forces was only destroyed when Rehoboam chose not to heed the Israelite request and another, stronger driving force was added—the rage of the Israelites. This new driving force destroyed the "force field" completely by pushing the equilibrium line beyond Rehoboam's grasp and into the clutches of Jeroboam, who then maintained equilibrium for twenty-two years (1 Kgs 14:20)!

TRANSFORMING LEADERSHIP VERSUS TRANSACTIONAL LEADERSHIP (JAMES M. BURNS)

James M. Burns[16] draws the distinction between transforming leadership and transaction leadership. Burns defines transaction leadership as that relationship between leader and follower which is basically a contract between the two where both parties "exchange gratification."[17] That is, one party "takes the initiative in making contact with others for the purpose of an exchange of valued things."[18] On the other hand, transforming leadership is that leadership which is an "elevating force."[19] The relationship can be characterized as more of a covenant than a contract in which it "raises the level of human conduct and ethical aspiration of both leader

---

16. Burns, *Leadership*.
17. Burns, *Leadership*, 258.
18. Burns, *Leadership*, 19.
19. Burns, *Leadership*, 166.

and led, and thus it has a transforming effect on both."[20] It would be expected that the son of Solomon would exercise transforming leadership, but such was not to be. Rehoboam failed to exercise such moral and uplifting leadership when the Israelites presented him with the contractual agreement: If you do this, then we will do this (verse 4). The Israelites had thus reduced the relationship between themselves and the "house of David" from a covenant obligation to a contractual arrangement. The fact of the matter is that Rehoboam never did ascend to transforming leadership. Rather, his was a perverse form of rule whereby he negatively influenced even the loyal Judeans, bringing them down. Though he ruled righteously for three years and led the Judeans in "the way of David and Solomon" (2 Chr 11:17), thereafter he led Israel to "forsake the law of the Lord" (2 Chr 11:17). Subsequently, there was a period of repentance for Rehoboam in which he led the nation of Judah into "good" times (2 Chr 12:12). But the overall evaluation of Rehoboam is given in 2 Chronicles 12:14, "And he did evil because he did not set his heart to seek the Lord." Josephus writes that Rehoboam was a proud and foolish man and that he "despised the worship of God, till the people themselves imitated his wicked actions."[21] Notice that the mention of Rehoboam's apostasy follows immediately after the mention of his mother! (2 Chr 12:15–16; cf. 1 Kgs 14:21). It took generations of heirs of Rehoboam to find a transforming king to lead Judah (e.g., sometimes Asa, 1 Kgs 15, 22; sometimes Joash, 2 Kgs 12:13; but preeminently Hezekiah: "So there was great joy in Jerusalem, because there was nothing like this in Jerusalem since the days of Solomon the son of David, king of Israel" [2 Chr. 30:26; cf. 2 Kgs 18–20].)

SITUATIONAL LEADERSHIP (HERSEY AND BLANCHARD)

Paul Hersey and Ken Blanchard[22] offer a helpful theory they call "Situational Leadership." Situational leadership can be defined as that leadership style which a "person should use with individuals or groups depending on the maturity level of the people the leader is attempting to influence."[23] "Maturity" is defined in situational leadership as "the ability and

---

20. Burns, *Leadership*, 20; See also Will, *Statecraft as Soulcraft*.
21. Josephus, *Ant.* 8.10.2.
22. Hersey and Blanchard, *Management of Organizational Behavior*.
23. Hersey and Blanchard, *Management of Organizational Behavior*, 151.

"Rehoboam: A Study in Failed Management" 383

willingness of people to take responsibility for directing their own behavior."[24] Follower maturity consists of two dimensions: "job maturity (ability) and psychological maturity (willingness)."[25] There is a maturity continuum (M1 to M4), beginning with "unable and unwilling to take responsibility" (M1) to "unable but willing to take responsibility" (M2) to "able but unwilling to take responsibility" (M3) to finally "able and willing to take responsibility" (M4). Turning to the leader, Hersey and Blanchard set forth two broad categories of leadership behavior: task-oriented behavior and relationship-oriented behavior. Task-oriented behavior is that in which a leader provides direction for people, that is, "telling" (Leadership Style #1) and "selling" (Leadership Style #2). Relationship-oriented leadership behavior is that which a leader engages in two-way communication with people, i.e., "participating" (Leadership Style #3) and "delegating" (Leadership Style #4). The unique contribution of Hersey and Blanchard is their contention that a leader must adapt his style of leadership behavior to the maturity level of the followers. So a leader is forced to know the group well so as to judge where they are on the maturity continuum. Having said this, what ought we to make of this situational leadership theory and Rehoboam? The Israelites were probably an M3, that is, able but unwilling to follow Rehoboam under the present circumstances. What was called for on Rehoboam's part was a participating style of leadership behavior (S3). This would have the king more relationship-oriented than task-oriented with an emphasis on communicating with the Israelites and facilitating a commonly-arrived-at decision which would move the nation along the desired path for both parties. However, Rehoboam misread the Israelites' maturity level by treating them as M1, needing specific directions, organized and specified goals, clearly imposed timelines, and a mechanism for reporting back to him. Rehoboam used a highly task-oriented leadership behavior style (that is, "telling," or S1) which was totally ineffective and resulted in a breakdown of the organization. Hersey and Blanchard would call his style of leadership "inappropriate to a given situation and extremely ineffective."[26] That's putting it mildly!

---

24. Hersey and Blanchard, *Management of Organizational Behavior*, 151.
25. Hersey and Blanchard, *Management of Organizational Behavior*, 157.
26. Hersey and Blanchard, *Management of Organizational Behavior*, 97–98.

THEORY Y, HUMAN POTENTIAL MOVEMENT, AND MANAGEMENT BY OBJECTIVES

Douglas McGregor[27] put forth the notion of "Theory Y" in leadership behavior and assumptions. These assumptions have been adopted into a concrete management system popularly called "management by objectives" (MBO).[28] The core of MBO convictions can be summarized as follows:

1. Most people possess high-level needs for power, autonomy, competence, achievement, and creativity that increasingly are motivating those who have satisfied their physiological and security needs.

2. People will want to satisfy these needs through their work if provided an opportunity to do so.

3. The educational, competency, and specialization levels of employees have increased to such an extent that they have substantial knowledge to contribute.

4. Organizations are facing increasingly complex and challenging conditions beyond the capacity of old-fashioned, centralized, authoritarian management.

5. People will work harder, satisfy their higher needs, manifest greater commitment, and perform better if they determine their own objectives.

6. Personal commitment and growth cannot be commanded by top management. It must be self-developed by individuals.

7. The best indicator of a superior's performance is subordinate's growth in capacity, aspirations, and performance.

In looking at these seven core beliefs of MBO and how they relate to the episode with Rehoboam and Israel, it can readily be seen that the relationship between the Israelites and Jeroboam can be characterized by MBO belief #1. Unfortunately for Rehoboam, he didn't perceive soon enough the expressed power and autonomy needs of the northerners. The belief expressed in #4 surely applies to this particular administrative

---

27. McGregor, *The Human Side of Enterprise*.

28. See Odiorne, *Management by Objectives*; Reddin, *Effective Management by Objectives: The 3-D Method*; Maslow, *Motivation and Personality*; Likert, *The Human Organization*.

decision of Rehoboam. We see later where he decentralized and delegated some of his leadership and thereby accomplished some political success (2 Chr 11:23). Conversely, belief #6 is evidenced by the reaction of the Israelites to Rehoboam's foolish response: "And the king answered the people harshly . . . So, the king did not listen to the people . . . When all Israel heard that the king did not listen to them, the people answered the king, saying, 'What portion do we have in David . . . ?" (1 Kgs 12:13, 15 16). In short, Rehoboam could not command a commitment to his goals. The Israelites' commitment had to be self-generated, and that opportunity was lost when Rehoboam gave his harsh answer. Finally, MBO belief #7 is perversely illustrated in the response of the Israelites to Rehoboam's harsh answer: "So Israel departed to their tents . . . Israel has been in rebellion against the house of David to this day. And it came about when all Israel heard that Jeroboam had returned, [they] made him king over all Israel. None but the tribe of Judah followed the house of David" (verses 16, 19–20). This indeed was an indicator of Rehoboam's performance as king over Israel, that is, the Israelites aspired and performed in a quite unexpected way—they left Rehoboam!

PASTOR PRINCIPLE OF LEADERSHIP (HOWARD BUTT)

Howard Butt[29] advances what he calls "Christian leadership in an age of rebellion" in which Christians are to emulate Christ as "Servant-king" by being "velvet covered bricks."[30] The brick stands for authority and the velvet symbolizes submission to the Holy Spirit. Richard Mouw[31] expresses the same thought when he states that a Christian can only lead if he is passive before God in order to be led by him. Butt introduces what he calls the "Pastor Principle." He writes that organizations demand leaders: "Leaders do not lead to lead; leaders lead to serve. They serve by leading; they lead by serving. In the Spirit of the Father and the Son."[32] Obviously, Rehoboam's example is not going to be found in Butt's book! Mouw's view of relating kingly administration of God's will to the peoples' felt needs would be apropos for our passage as well. The godly king is called to administer God's will in a transforming (as opposed to transactional)

---

29. Butt, *The Velvet Covered Brick*.
30. Butt, *The Velvet Covered Brick*, 20.
31. Mouw, *Politics and the Biblical Drama*.
32. Butt, *The Velvet Covered Brick*, 25.

manner in which the people are conformed to the will of God through a just, merciful, and righteous ruling structure and administration. Psalm 72:6 speaks about this kind of godly king: "He [the king] will be like rain falling on a mown field, like showers watering the earth" (see also verse 7; 1 Sam 12:14; Matt 9:36). A key Scripture verse in this servant/leadership idea is Matt 20:26: "But whoever wishes to become great among you shall be your servant" (see also Matt 23:11; Mark 9:35; and the awesome passage of Phil 2:3–11 which speaks of the great "servant-king" himself; cf. 2 Cor 8:9). Robert Greenleaf[33] postulates the same theory of leadership as Butt, but from a secular vantage point, deriving his view from a reading of Hermann Hesse's *Journey to the East*!

MYERS-BRIGGS INDICATOR OF TYPES

Finally, if one were to apply the Myers-Briggs Type Indicator to Rehoboam's type of leadership, it would give us a general understanding of how the new king's management style would be evaluated in today's management circles. In evaluating an individual, MBTI will mix and match eight stylistic preferences to arrive at four general types which will characterize an individual's way of deciding things:

1. Extrovert (E): relates more easily to the outer world of people and things than to the inner world of ideas.
2. Introvert (I): relates more easily to the inner world of ideas than to the outer world of people and things.
3. Sensing (S): rather work with known facts than look for possibilities and relationships.
4. Intuition (N): rather look for possibilities and relationships than work with known facts.
5. Thinking (T): bases judgments more on impersonal analysis and logic than on personal values.
6. Feeling (F): bases judgments more on personal values than on impersonal analysis and logic.
7. Judging (J): likes a planned, decided, orderly way of life better than a flexible, spontaneous way.

---

33. Greenleaf, *Servant Leadership*.

8. Perceptive (P): likes a flexible, spontaneous way of life better than a planned, decided, orderly way.

With these eight categories or preferences in mind, I believe Rehoboam could be characterized as an extroverted thinking type with sensing and judging as auxiliary qualities. Or, to put it in the nomenclature of Myers-Briggs, Rehoboam is an ESTJ.

I've only touched on a few management and leadership theories as they pertain to Rehoboam. This is a classic scriptural illustration of gross mismanagement, of failed and flawed leadership which resulted in catastrophic tragedy. Each one of these theories could be used by itself to analyze Rehoboam's actions. Indeed, 1 Kings 12 itself can be used as a guide to leadership principles. However one chooses to look at Rehoboam's leadership decisions, there is enough authoritative material to provide ample illustrations for any current management/leadership theory.

A BRIEF APPLICATION OF 1 KINGS 12 MANAGEMENT LESSONS

THE NEED FOR FOLLOWER CONFIRMATION OF LEADER

Verse 1 of our passage sets the tone for any discussion of the leader-follower relationship. The implication of this verse is that Rehoboam would not be the leader (king) unless the follower (Israel) "makes him" the leader! He cannot reign if there is no realm. This implication is borne out in the case of other Old Testament leaders (1 Sam 10:24–25; 2 Sam 3:17–21; 5:1–3; 1 Kgs 1:38–39). Consequently, the Old Testament Scriptures seem to indicate that any leader is leader only if the followers confirm or "make" his leadership. Thus, when Rehoboam went to Shechem to meet with the Israelites and be confirmed as their leader, this was not extraordinary, but rather a biblically accepted procedure for leaders to be confirmed as leaders by their followers. Indeed, it appears from this passage that if a leader is to be effective and thus achieve his goals as leader, he needs the confirmation and affirmation of the followers. He cannot lord it over his subjects. Peter gives good counsel to Rehoboam and all leaders in 1 Peter 5:1–3. After one becomes a leader of an organization, there is a period of peace but never calm because of the inevitable changes. Furthermore, there will be pockets of subtle opposition among members of the organization who still look elsewhere for leadership. One could call this the "Jeroboam Factor" in organizational conflict. This "Jeroboam Factor" of leadership opposition, however subtle within an organization, poses a persistent problem in small organizations. The ultimate solution to this "Jeroboam Factor" is to have the opposition "depart to their own tents." Firing or publicly rebuking a Jeroboam figure can have beneficial effects and may be the correct course of action. But that is radical surgery on the organization! It would seem better for all concerned if a continuity of relationship could be maintained between followers and leaders. That may mean some changes of style on the followers' part for which the leader could only be partially responsible, but it probably would also involve a different style of leadership on the leader's part for which he would be completely responsible! It appears from this passage that a biblically sound principle for leadership would be that when someone is elevated to management, business cannot be conducted as usual. Indeed, it would seem that one should not say, "There will be no immediate changes in operational or personnel procedures." In order to gain the loyalty of the people it might be necessary to give the people some degree of participation in the elevation of the new leaders so that the followers feel they have some control over their lives, some ownership of the changes. Consequently, it may be necessary to broaden peoples' participation in management at certain points or give them certain unaccustomed-to benefits from the new leadership, so they feel they are better off under the new leaders and that, in fact, they do have a stake, an "inheritance," in the organization. This appears to be the course of action the Solomonic elders were advising.

THE NEED FOR REFLECTIVE TIME AWAY FROM THE PRESSURES OF LEADERSHIP DECISIONS

A management principle coming out of this passage of Scripture is the need for a period of time away from the pressures of leadership. Here is an example of a biblical executive weekend retreat during which time the leader withdraws with his management team to seek their counsel (1 Kgs 12:5–6). The fact that Rehoboam rejected the counsel of the wise ones is irrelevant at this point. The fact is, Rehoboam did take time away to reflect. Practically, this would mean short conferences, management retreats, and "break-aways" for the organization's leadership.

THE NEED FOR HONEST, CRITICAL, AND FORTHRIGHT COUNSEL AND NOT JUST CONFIRMING COUNSEL

Rehoboam sought the counsel of two groups of advisors. He rejected one group's advice and accepted the other group's advice. In fact, it appears he rejected the first group's advice before he received the counsel from the second group (1 Kgs 12:7)! Wise enough to seek advice from two groups with different perspectives and experiences, Rehoboam was foolish enough to follow the advice of the group with which he had a natural affinity. Contrary counsel will inform the leader concerning the nature and needs of the followers to which he would otherwise be insensitive or unaware. It is comforting to hear corresponding opinion, but these opinions may not enlighten the leader, and it is crucial for the leader to know the followers. As James Appleton stated in his June 1986 Fuller Seminary lectures: "In order to be effective a leader must learn more about the people, learn more about the situation, and learn more about himself."[34] Wise counsel, even when contrary to the notions of the leader, will assist in this three-fold leadership goal. Solomon had advice in this regard for both Rehoboam and today's leaders: "Kings take pleasure in honest lips; they value a man who speaks the truth" (Prov 16:13; cf. also 26:28; 28:23; Ps 12:3).

THE NEED FOR LEADERS TO REALLY LISTEN TO WHAT THEIR FOLLOWERS ARE COMMUNICATING

Solomon wrote: "A wise man will listen (hear) and increase in learning, and a man of understanding will acquire wise counsel" (Prov 1:5). Before leaders can seek proper counsel, they need to know what to seek counsel about. To put it another way, before they can get any answers, they need to know the questions. The only way a leader is going to find out what the followers want and need is by listening to what they are saying and doing. In this regard Solomon says: "He who answers before listening—that is his folly and his shame" (Prov 18:13). In Psalm 46:8–10 we have a biblical definition of listening which applies pointedly to Rehoboam. In this passage, listening ("being still") is defined as observing ("come and see"), remembering ("He makes wars cease . . . he breaks the bow . . . he burns shields . . . ."), and understanding ("know"). In short, listening is not done

---

34. For similar advice refer to Hodgkinson, *The Philosophy of Leadership*, 210–11.

just with the ears, but it also involves the eyes, as well as all the sense organs, and the mind of the individual. This is borne out in our passage with Rehoboam. If Rehoboam had been more observant, he would have known what was really going on among the Israelites (cf. Jas 1:19).

The Need for Leaders to be Uplifting and Encouraging to Fellow Leaders

The advice Rehoboam was given by the Solomonic elders contained this phrase "speak good words to them." As I pointed out in the first section of this article, this means "edifying" and "encouraging" and "beneficial" words. Paul uses the same word (*agathos*) in Ephesians 4:29 when he writes, "Do not let any unwholesome talk come out of your mouths, but only what is helpful for building others up according to their needs, that it may benefit those who listen" (cf. also Col 4:6; Rom 15, and 1 Cor 12 on spiritual gifts). Note Solomon's words on this subject: "A man finds joy in giving an apt reply, and how good is a timely word" (Prov 15:23). If one subscribes to Howard Butt's view of leadership as detailed in the Pastor's Principle, then he sees edifying words as ministry tools to urge conformity to Christ's image in Christians and to urge salvation to non-Christians. Rehoboam rejected the milder and softer advice of the Solomonic elders for the harsh, threatening advice of the younger men. Our Great Leader did not use threats in his leadership: "When he suffered, he made no threats. Instead, he entrusted himself to him who judges justly" (1 Pet 2:23). Paul commands leaders to forsake threats in dealing with followers: "And masters, treat your slaves in the same way. Do not threaten them since you know that he who is both their Master and yours is in heaven, and there is no favoritism with him" (Eph 6:9). It is sad that Rehoboam did not have a copy of the New Testament at Shechem. Still, he should have known better.

The Need for Leaders to Encourage Genuine Participation in Leadership Responsibilities on the Part of the Followers

Without any input into the public policy discussion of the united kingdom, the Israelites believed they had no "ownership" of the kingdom of Rehoboam. They had no voice in how their lives would be affected by the new king. So, before they would confirm and recognize him as king, they wanted to extract from him a change in labor and tax laws. When Rehoboam foolishly refused to make any policy changes, even minor changes, the people realized the king was unsympathetic to their needs and that he had no intention of allowing them a voice in the counsels of power, so they revolted and established their own government in which they did have some control over their destiny. Paul's admonition to his brother in Christ, Philemon, concerning Philemon's slave, Onesimus, is instructive to a leader's relationship with those with whom he works: "So if you consider me a partner, welcome him as you would welcome me" (Phlm 17). Paul alludes to this self-determination in Colossians 4:1: "Masters, provide your slaves with what is right and fair, because you know that you too also have a Master in heaven."

THE NEED FOR LEADERS TO SERVE FELLOW LEADERS

> "If you will be a servant to this people today, will serve them . . . then they will be your servants forever."

Thus ran the advice to Rehoboam by the Solomonic elders. In many respects, this is the key to biblical leadership, for if Rehoboam had proceeded this way, the division probably would not have taken place (disregarding for the moment the "turning" of history by the Lord in order to accomplish his will). Myron Rush[35] defines biblical management as "meeting the needs of people as they work at accomplishing their jobs." Mouw refers to a biblical perspective on leadership as "wounded leaders" doing their job and quotes Luke 22:25–27 in support of this conception.[36] Ray Anderson, while defining Christian leadership in a more complex way than simply "service," does write at one point that Christian leadership is "first of all being a servant, and then finding a promise that can be attached to a crying need."[37] Ted Engstrom and Ed Dayton define Christian leadership as "leadership motivated by love and given over to service."[38]

---

35. Rush, *Management: A Biblical Approach*, 15.
36 Mouw, *Politics and Biblical Drama*.
37. Anderson, *Minding God's Business*, 81.
38. Engstrom and Dayton, *The Art of Management for Christian Leaders*, 27.

Regardless of how one precisely defines godly management, it seems clear from many passages of Scripture that service is an indispensable part of, and probably the foundation of, a genuine understanding and practice of any correct notion of leadership. A careful look at Rehoboam's leadership style and activity can be enormously instructive for any Christian leader in any arena of leadership in today's society. We only need to bend our will and our mind to learn and to be directed by God's holy word and his Holy Spirit.

Bibliography

a Kempis, Thomas. *Imitation of Christ*. 1470. Reprint, Notre Dame, IN: Ave Maria, 1989.
ABC News. "David Koch on the Plane Crash That Helped Change His Life." *ABC News*. https://abcnews.go.com/Entertainment/video/david-koch-plane-crash-helped-change-life-27598921.
Albright, W. E. *Matthew*. New York: Doubleday, 1971.
Alexander, J. A. *Acts*, vol. 2. London: Banner of Truth, 1960.
Alexander, John H. *Managing Our Work*. Downers Grove: InterVarsity, 1972.
Alinsky, Saul D. *Rules for Radicals*. New York: Vintage Books, 1972.
Allen, Leslie. *Psalms 101–150*. Word Biblical Commentary. Waco: Word, 1983.
Allen, Willoughby. *Gospel According to St. Matthew*. 1907. Reprint, Edinburgh: T. & T. Clark, 1947.
Anderson, John. *Managing Our Work*. Downers Grove: IVP, 1975.
Anderson, Ray. *Historical Transcendence and the Reality of God*. Grand Rapids: Eerdmans, 1975.
———. *Minding God's Business*. Grand Rapids: Eerdmans, 1986.
———. *On Being Human*. Grand Rapids: Eerdmans, 1982.
Archibald, Douglas. "Learning from the Liberal Arts." *The Wall Street Journal* December 23, 1981.
Aristotle. *Nicomachean Ethics*. Translated by W. D. Ross. Great Books of the Western World. Chicago: Encyclopedia Britannica, 1952.
———. *Rhetoric (Rhetorica)*. Translated by W. Rhys Roberts. Great Books of the Western World. Chicago: Encyclopedia Britannica, 1952.
Artapanus. "Fragment 3 (Moses)." In *The Old Testament Pseudepigrapha*, edited by James Charlesworth, 898–99. Garden City: Doubleday, 1985.
Armbruster, Wally. *It's Still the Lion vs. the Christian in the Corporate Arena*. St. Louis: Concordia, 1973.
Armerding, George D. *The Dollars and Sense of Honesty*. New York: Harper and Row, 1979.
Armerding, Hudson T. *Leadership*. Wheaton: Tyndale House, 1978.
Arnold, Matthew. "Dover Beach." poetryfoundation.org/poems/43588/dover-beach.
Athanasius. *The Incarnation of the Word of God*. In *Ante-Nicene Fathers*, translated by Alexander Roberts, 4.31–67. Grand Rapids: Eerdmans, 1987.
Bailey, Kenneth. *Poet and Peasant and Through Peasant Eyes*. Grand Rapids: Eerdmans, 1983.

Baldwin, Joyce. *Zechariah, Malachi: An Introduction and Commentary*. Tyndale Old Testament Commentary. Downers Grove: IVP, 1972.

Barber, Cyril J. *Nehemiah and the Dynamics of Effective Leadership*. Neptune, NJ: Loizeaux Brothers, 1976.

Barber, Cyril J., and Gary Strauss II. *Leadership: The Dynamics of Success*. Greenwood, SC: Attic, 1982.

Barbusse, Henri. *Jesus*. New York: Macaulay, 1927.

Barclay, William. *The Letters of James and Peter*. Philadelphia: Westminster, 1960.

Barnard, Chester, and Ken Andrews. *The Functions of the Executive*. Cambridge, MA: Harvard University Press, 1971.

Barron, Bruce. *The Health and Wealth Gospel*. Downers Grove: InterVarsity, 1987.

Barth, Karl. *Church Dogmatics*. Edinburgh: T. & T. Clark, 1962.

———. *Epistle to the Philippians*. Louisville: Westminster John Knox, 2002.

Bartholomew, Craig. *Ecclesiastes*. Baker Commentary on the Old Testament Wisdom and Psalms. Grand Rapids: Baker, 2009.

Barton, Bruce. *The Man Nobody Knows*. Indianapolis: Bobbs-Merrill, 1925.

Bauckham, Richard. *Jude–2 Peter*. Word Biblical Commentary. Grand Rapids: Eerdmans, 1983.

Bauer, Walter, et al. "Praytes." In *A Greek-English Lexicon of the New Testament*, 705–06. Chicago: University of Chicago Press, 1969.

Bay, Louise. *King of Wall Street*. New York: Louise Bay, 2016.

Beasley-Murray, George. *The Gospel of John*. Word Biblical Commentary. Grand Rapids: Zondervan, 1999.

Belloc, Hilaire. *This and That and the Other*. 1912. Reprint, New York: Dodd, Mead & Co., 1915.

Bennis, Warren. *Organization Development*. Reading, MA: Addison-Wesley, 1969.

Bennis, Warren, and Bert Nanus. *Leaders*. New York: Harper & Row, 1925.

Berkhof, Louis. *Systematic Theology*. Grand Rapids: Eerdmans, 1949.

Berkouwer, C. C. *The Person of Christ*. Grand Rapids: Eerdmans, 1969.

Bernbaum, John A., and Simon Steer. *Why Work?* Grand Rapids: Baker, 1986.

Berkouwer, G. C. *The Person of Christ*. Grand Rapids: Eerdmans, 1954.

Beyer, Herman Wolfgang. "Episkopos." In *Theological Dictionary of the New Testament*, edited by Gerhard Kittel, translated by Geoffrey W. Bromiley, 2.599–622. Grand Rapids: Eerdmans, 1974.

———. "Kubernesis." In *Theological Dictionary of the New Testament*, edited by Gerhard Kittel, translated by Geoffrey W. Bromiley, 3.1035–37. Grand Rapids: Eerdmans, 1974.

"Bibles in the Board Room." *Time* October 27, 1975.

Biederwolf, William E. *A Help to the Study of the Holy Spirit*. Grand Rapids: Baker, 1974.

Bietenhard, Hans. "Ochlos." In *Dictionary of New Testament Theology*, edited by Colin Brown, 2.800–805. Grand Rapids: Eerdmans, 1978.

Bissell, Herbert D. *Big Business—Your Life Within It*. Nashville: Thomas Nelson, 1973.

Bittlinger, Arnold. *Gifts and Graces*. Grand Rapids: Eerdmans, 1967.

Blackman, B. C. "Incarnation." In *The Interpreter's Dictionary of the Bible*, 2.691–97. Nashville: Abington, 1952.

Blanchard, Kenneth, and Phil Hodges. *Lead Like Jesus: Lessons from the Greatest Leadership Role Model of All Time*. Nashville: Thomas Nelson, 2002.

Bibliography

Blanchard, Kenneth, and Spencer Johnson. *The One-minute Manager*. New York: Berkley, 1981.
Blanchard, Kenneth, and Norman Vincent Peale. *The Power of Ethical Management*. New York: William Morrow, 1988.
Blanchard, Tim. *Finding Your Spiritual Gift*. Wheaton: Tyndale House, 1979.
Bland, Glenn. *Success: The Glenn Bland Method*. Wheaton: Tyndale House, 1972.
Block, Peter. *The Empowered Manager*. San Francisco: Jossey-Bass, 1987.
Bock, Darrell. *Acts*. Baker Exegetical Commentary on the New Testament. Grand Rapids: Eerdmans, 2007.
———. *Luke 1:1—9:50*. Grand Rapids: Baker, 1994.
———. *Luke: The New International Version Application Commentary*. Grand Rapids: Zondervan, 1996.
Boice, James. *The Parables of Jesus*. Chicago: Moody, 1983.
Bond, Doug. *Hold Fast*. Phillipburg, NJ: P & R, 2008.
Bonhoeffer, Dietrich. *Ethics*. New York: McMillian, 1955.
———. *Letters and Papers from Prison*. New York: Collier, 1971.
Bornkamm, Gunther. "Presbus." In *Theological Dictionary of the New Testament*, edited by Gerhard Kittel, translated by Geoffrey W. Bromiley, 6.651-83. Grand Rapids: Eerdmans, 1974.
Bowling, Andrew. "Messenger." In *Theological Wordbook of the Old Testament*, edited by R. Laird Harris, 1.464-65. Chicago: Moody, 1980.
Breasted, J. H. *Ancient Records of Egypt*. Chicago: University of Chicago Press, 1906.
Breton, Andre. *Manifestoes of Surrealism*. Ann Arbor: University of Michigan, 1969.
Bright, John. *A History of Israel*. Louisville: Westminster. 1971.
Brown, Colin, ed. *Dictionary of New Testament Theology*. Grand Rapids: Zondervan, 1978.
Brown, Raymond E. *The Gospel According to John, I-XII*. Anchor Bible. New York: Doubleday, 1966.
———. *The Gospel According to John, XIII-XXI*. Anchor Bible. New York: Doubleday, 1970.
Bruce, A. B. *The Synoptic Gospels*. The Expositor's Greek Testament. Grand Rapids: Eerdmans. 1980.
———. *The Training of the Twelve*. 1894. Reprint, Grand Rapids: Kregel, 1971.
Bruce, F. F. *The Epistle to the Romans*. Tyndale New Testament Commentary. Downers Grove: Eerdmans, 1985.
Brunner, Emil. *The Christian Doctrine of the Church, Faith and the Consummation*, vol. 3. Philadelphia: Westminster, 1968.
Brunner, Frederick. *A Theology of the Holy Spirit*. Grand Rapids: Eerdmans, 1970.
Buchanan, Pat. *Right from the Beginning*. Washington: Regnery, 1990.
Bultmann, Rudolph. *Theology of the New Testament*, vol. 2. London: SCM, 1955.
Bump, Glen Hale. *How to Succeed in Business without Being a Pagan*. Wheaton: Victor, 1975.
Bunyan, John. *The Pilgrim's Progress*. 1675. Reprint, London: Banner of Truth, 1977.
Burge, Gary. *John: The New NIV Application Commentary*. Grand Rapids: Zondervan, 2000.
Burkett, Larry. *Business by the Book: The Complete Guide of Biblical Principles for the Workplace*. New York: Thomas Nelson, 2010.

———. *Using Your Money Wisely: Biblical Principles under Scrutiny*. Chicago: Moody, 1990.
Burnham, James. *The Managerial Revolution*. Bloomington, IN: Indiana University Press, 1966.
Burns, James MacGregor. *Leadership*. New York: Harper & Row, 1978.
Buswell, J. Oliver. *Systematic Theology of the Christian Religion*, vols. 1–2. Grand Rapids: Zondervan, 1959.
Butt, Howard. *The Velvet Covered Brick*. New York: Harper & Row, 1973.
Cain, Herman. *This Is Herman Cain*. New York: Threshold Editions, 2011.
Calvin, John. *Commentary on the Book of the Prophet Isaiah*. 1852. Reprint, London: Forgotten Books, 2012.
———. *Commentary on the Book of Psalms*, vol. 4. Translated by James Anderson. Grand Rapids: Eerdmans, 1948.
———. *Commentary on Hebrews and I & II Peter*. Grand Rapids: Eerdmans, 1970.
———. *The Epistles of Paul to the Romans and Thessalonians*. Translated by R. Mackenzie. Grand Rapids: Eerdmans, 1973
———. *The First Epistle of Paul the Apostle to the Corinthians*. Grand Rapids: Eerdmans, 1960.
———. *The Gospel According to St. John and the First Epistle of John*. Grand Rapids: Eerdmans, 1961.
———. *Institutes of the Christian Religion*. Edited by John T. McNeill. Philadelphia: Westminster, 1960.
———. *Matthew, Mark, and Luke*. Translated by A. W. Morrison. Grand Rapids: Eerdmans, 1972.
———. *The Second Epistle of Paul to the Corinthians and the Epistle to Timothy, Titus and Philemon*. Grand Rapids: Eerdmans, 1960.
Camp, Donald. Review of *The Unfinished Presidency of Jimmy Carter* by Kai Bird. *American Diplomacy* August 2021.
Campbell, Thomas C., and Gary B. Reierson. *The Gift of Administration*. Philadelphia: Westminster, 1981.
Campolo, Anthony, Jr. *The Success Fantasy*. Wheaton: Victor, 1980.
Carnegie, Dale. *How to Win Friends and Influence People*. 1936. Reprint, New York: Open Library, 1970.
Carroll, Robert. *Jeremiah*. The Old Testament Library. Philadelphia: Westminster, 1986.
Carson, D. A. *From Sabbath to Lord's Day*. Grand Rapids: Zondervan, 1982.
———. *The Gospel According to John*. Grand Rapids: Eerdmans, 1991.
Case, Robert. *Esther and Trump*. Tacoma: Saluda, 2018.
———. "Human Resource Management: Aquarius or Aquinas?" Presentation given at Institute of Behavior and Applied Management Conference, Seattle, WA, October 1995.
———. "Pressures on Presbytery." *Presbyterion* 4.2 (Fall 1978) 84–90.
———. "Rehoboam: A Study in Failed Leadership." *Presbyterion* 14.1 (Spring 1988) 55–77.
———. "Socrates and the Small Businessman." *The Diary of Alpha Kappa Psi* September 1982.
Case, Shirley Jackson. *Jesus: A New Biography*. Chicago: The University of Chicago Press, 1927.
Catherwood, Fred. *On the Job: The Christian 9 to 5*. Grand Rapids: Zondervan, 1980.

Cathy, S. Truett. *How Did You Do It, Truett?* Decatur, GA: Looking Glass, 2007.
Chervokas, John V. *How to Keep God Alive From 9 to 5*. New York: Doubleday, 1986.
Chiles, Brevard. *The Book of Exodus*. Philadelphia: Westminster, 1974.
"Christ in the Newsroom." *Parade* July 11, 1982.
Chrysostom, John. *Homilies on the Epistles of St. Paul the Apostle to the Philippians, Colossians, and Thessalonians*. Homily 10. In *Nicene and Post-Nicene Fathers*, edited by Philip Schaff and Henry Wace, 13.323–98. Peabody: Hendrickson, 1995.
Clapp, Rodney. "Remonking the Church." *Christianity Today* August 12, 1988. 20-21.
Clark, Gordon. *The Incarnation*. Unicoi, TN: Trinity Foundation, 1988.
Clarke, Adam. *Commentary on the Bible*. London: Marshall, Morgan & Scott, 1960.
———. "Psalms 12:8: Clarke's Commentary and Critical Notes on the Bible." https://www.biblecomments.org/c/7/clarkes-commentary-and-critical-notes-on-the-bible/psalms/12/8.
Clemens, John, and Douglas Mayer. "The Classic Touch." *Best of Business Quarterly* 1987. 58–63.
———. *The Classic Touch: Lessons in Leadership from Homer to Hemingway*. Homewood, IL: Dow Jones-Irwin, 1987.
Clines, D. J. *Ezra, Nehemiah, Esther*. The New Century Bible Commentary. Grand Rapids: Eerdmans, 1984.
Cockerill, Gareth Lee. *The Epistle to the Hebrews*. New International Commentary on the New Testament. Grand Rapids: Eerdmans, 2012.
Coenen, Lothar. "Episkopos." In *Dictionary of New Testament Theology*, edited by Colin Brown, 1.188–92. Grand Rapids: Eerdmans, 1978.
Collins, Jack. *Genesis 1-4*. Phillipsburg, NJ: P & R, 2006.
Collins, Jim. *Good to Great: Why Some Companies Make the Leap and Other Don't*. New York: Harper Business, 2001.
Collins, Jim, and Jerry Porras. *Built to Last*. New York: Harper Business, 1994.
Compact Edition of the Oxford English Dictionary. Oxford: Oxford University Press, 1971.
Conn, Charles Paul. *Making It Happen*. Grand Rapids: Fleming H. Revell, 1981.
———. *The Possible Dream: A Candid Look at Amway*. Grand Rapids: Fleming H. Revell, 1977.
———. *An Uncommon Freedom*. Grand Rapids: Fleming H. Revell, 1982.
Conwell, Russell. *Acres of Diamonds*. Grand Rapids: Fleming H. Revell, 1968.
Cook, William H. *Success, Motivation and the Scriptures*. Nashville: Broadman, 1974.
Cooper, Lamar E. *Ezekiel*. The New American Commentary. Nashville: Broadman and Holman, 1994.
Copeland, Gloria. *God's Will Is Prosperity*. Tulsa: Harrison House, 1978.
Coppes, Leonard J. "Qasha." In *Theological Wordbook of the Old Testament*, edited by R. Laird Harris, 1.464–65. Chicago: Moody, 1980.
Cortines, John, and Gregory Baumer. *True Riches: What Jesus Really Said about Money and Your Heart*. Nashville: Nelson, 2019.
Cowles, Robert. "Manager's Memo: How Good Managers Motivate Salesmen." *The Rotarian* September 1935.
Craigie, P. C. *The Book of Deuteronomy*. International Commentary on the Old Testament. Grand Rapids: Eerdmans, 1976.
Crichton, James. "Gedaliah." In *The International Standard Bible Encyclopedia*, edited by James Orr, 2.1181. 1936. Reprint, Grand Rapids: Eerdmans, 1983.

Culbert, Samuel A., and John J. McDonough. *The Invisible War: Pursuing Self-interest at Work*. New York: John Wiley & Sons, 1980.

Culver, Robert. "Mashal." In *Theological Wordbook of the Old Testament*, edited by R. Laird Harris, 1.534–55. Chicago: Moody, 1980.

Dabney, Robert. *Lectures in Systematic Theology*. 1878. Reprint, Grand Rapids: Zondervan, 1976.

Dalrymple, Theodore. "The Choleric Outbreak." *The New Criterion* 38.10 (June 2020). Newcriterion.com/issues/2020/6/the-choleric-outbreak.

De Vries, Kets, and F. R. Manfred. "Managers Can Drive Their Subordinates Mad." *Harvard Business Review* November/December 1979.

Decker, Celia, and John Decker. *Planning and Administering Early Childhood Programs*. New York: Pearson, 2000.

Deal, Terrance S., and Allen A. Kennedy. *Corporate Cultures*. Reading, MA: Addison-Wesley, 1982.

Delitzsch, Franz. *Commentary on Isaiah*. Grand Rapids: Eerdmans, 1973.

DeMoss, Ted, and Robert Tamasy. *The Gospel and the Briefcase*. Wheaton: Tyndale House, 1984.

Denning, Steve. "The Best of Peter Drucker." *Forbes* July 29, 2014.

Dennison, James. *The Market Day of the Soul*. Morgan, PA: Soli Deo Gloria, 2001.

DePree, Max. *Leadership Is an Art*. East Lansing, MI: Michigan State University, 1987.

DeVaux, Roland. *Ancient Israel*. Translated by John McHugh. Grand Rapids: Eerdmans, 1997.

DeVos, Richard A. *Believe*. Grand Rapids: Fleming H. Revell, 1975.

Dickens, Charles. *A Christmas Carol*. London: Penguin, 1971.

Diehl, William E. *Thank God, It's Monday*. Philadelphia: Fortress, 1982.

Dillard, Raymond. *2 Chronicles*. Word Biblical Commentary. Waco: Word, 1987.

Dods, Marcus. *The Gospel of John*. The Expositor's Greek Testament. Grand Rapids: Eerdmans, 1980.

Douma, Douglas. *The Presbyterian Philosopher*. Eugene, OR: Wipf & Stock, 2016.

Douma, J. *The Ten Commandments: Manual for the Christian Life*. Phillipsburg, NJ: P & R, 1996.

Doriani, Dan. *Work: Its Purpose, Dignity and Transformation*. Phillipsburg, NJ: P & R, 2019.

Douty, Norman F. *Union with Christ*. Swengel, PA: Reiner, 1973.

Dreyer, Rod. *The Benedict Option*. New York: Penguin, 2017.

Drucker, Peter F. *The Effective Executive*. New York: Harper & Row, 1985.

———. *Management: Tasks, Responsibilities, Practices*. New York: Harper & Row, 1974.

———. *Managing in Turbulent Times*. New York: Harper & Row, 1980.

Durham, John. *Exodus*. Word Biblical Commentary. Waco: Word, 1987.

Dunn, James. *Romans 9–16*. Word Biblical Commentary. Grand Rapids: Zondervan, 1988.

Early Church History. "Peter's Home in Capernaum Found." https://earlychurchhistory.org/daily-life/peters-home-in-capernaum-found/.

Eckerd, Jack, and Charles Paul Conn. *Eckerd: Finding the Right Prescription*. Grand Rapids: Fleming H. Revell, 1987.

Edwards, James. *The Gospel According to Luke*. The Pillar New Testament Commentary. Grand Rapids: Eerdmans, 2015.

Egeria. *Diary of a Pilgrimage*. Ancient Christian Writers 38. Mahwah, NJ: Paulist, 1970.

Eldred, Ken. *God Is at Work: Transforming People and Nations Through Business*. Elevate Faith: Plano, TX, 2016.

Ellul, Jacques. *If You Are the Son of God*. 1991. Reprint, Eugene, OR: Cascade, 2014.

Engstrom, Ted W. *The Making of a Christian Leader*. Grand Rapids: Zondervan, 1976.

———. *The Pursuit of Excellence*. Grand Rapids: Zondervan, 1982.

———. *Your Gift of Administration*. Nashville: Thomas Nelson, 1983.

Engstrom, Ted W., and Edward R. Dayton. *The Art of Management for Christian Leaders*. Waco: Word, 1976.

Engstrom, Ted W., and David J. Juroe. *The Work Trap*. Grand Rapids: Fleming H. Revell, 1980.

Enlow, David, and Dorothy Enlow. *Saved from Bankruptcy*. Chicago: Moody, 1975.

Epictetus. *The Discourses of Epictetus*. Translated by George Long. Chicago: Encyclopedia Britannica, 1952.

Erickson, Millard J. *Christian Theology*, vol. 1. Grand Rapids: Baker, 1983.

Etzioni, Amitai. *Comparative Analysis of Complex Organizations*. New York: Free Press, 1975.

———. *Modern Organizations*. New York: Prentice Hall, 1964.

———. *The Moral Dimensions: Toward a New Economics*. New York: The Free Press, 1988.

Eusebius. *Church History*. In *Nicene and Post-Nicene Fathers*, edited by Philip Schaff and Henry Wace, 1.ix–405. Peabody: Hendrikson, 1995.

Fatjo, Tom. *With No Fear of Failure*. Waco: Word, 1979.

Fausset, Andrew. *The Jamieson, Fausset and Brown Commentary*. Bethany Parallel Commentary on the Old Testament. Minneapolis: Bethany House, 1985.

Fee, Gordon. *The First Epistle to the Corinthians*. New International Commentary on the New Testament. Grand Rapids: Eerdmans, 1987.

———. *Paul's Letters to the Philippians*. New International Commentary on the New Testament. Grand Rapids: Eerdmans, 1995.

Fensham, F. C. *The Books of Ezra and Nehemiah*. New International Commentary on the Old Testament. Grand Rapids: Eerdmans, 1982.

Fereday, William. *Samuel: God's Emergency Man and Jonathan and His Times*. London: John Ritchie, 1942.

Fernando, Ajith. *Leadership Lifestyle: A Study of 1 Timothy*. Wheaton: Tyndale House, 1985.

Filson, Floyd V. *The Gospel According to St. Matthew*. Peabody: Hendrickson, 1987.

Fitzmyer, Joseph A. *The Gospel According to Luke I–IX*. Anchor Bible. New York: Doubleday, 1981.

———. *The Gospel According to Luke X–XXIV*. Anchor Bible. New York: Doubleday, 1983.

Floubert, Gustave. "Thank You for Making Me Read Tolstoy's Novels." *New York Times* October 27, 1985.

Flynn, Leslie D. *19 Gifts of the Spirit*. Wheaton: Victor Books, 1974.

Fox, Michael. *Proverbs 1–9*. Anchor Bible. New York: Doubleday, 2000.

France, R. T. *The Gospel of Matthew*. New International Commentary on the New Testament. Grand Rapids: Eerdmans, 2007.

———. *Matthew*. Tyndale New Testament Commentary. Downers Grove: IVP, 1985.

Fraser, Donald. *The Metaphors of Christ*. 1885. Reprint, Minneapolis: Klock & Klock, 1985.

Freisen, Garry. *Decision Making & the Will of God*. Portland: Multnomah, 1980.
French, J. R. P., and B. H. Raven. *Leadership in Organizations*. New York: Pearson, 2018.
Funk, Robert W. "The Watershed of American Biblical Tradition: The Chicago School, First Phase, 1892–1920." *Journal of Biblical Literature* 95.1 (March 1976) 4–22.
Garland, David. *1 Corinthians*. Baker Exegetical Commentary on the New Testament. Grand Rapids: Baker, 2003.
Geldenhuys, Revel. *Commentary on the Gospel of Luke*. The New International Commentary on the New Testament. Grand Rapids: Eerdmans, 1975.
Geneen, Harold. *Managing*. New York: Avon, 1984.
Glass, Bill. *Expect to Win*. Waco: Word, 1981.
Gloag, Paton J. *Acts of the Apostles*, vol. 2. 1890. Reprint, Minneapolis: Klock & Klock, 1979.
Godin, Seth. *Purple Cow: Transform Your Business by Being Remarkable*. New York: Penguin, 2004.
Goppelt, Leonhard. *Theology of the New Testament*, vol. 1. Grand Rapids: Eerdmans, 1981.
Gratch, Alon. "Personality Makes the Manager." *The Rotarian* June 1986.
Gray, John. *1 and 2 Kings*. The Old Testament Library. Philadelphia: Westminster, 1970.
Green, David. *More Than a Hobby*. Nashville: Thomas Nelson, 2005.
Green, Gene. *The Letters to the Thessalonians*. The Pillar New Testament Commentary. Grand Rapids: Eerdmans, 2002.
———. *Jude & 2 Peter*. Baker Exegetical Commentary on the New Testament. Grand Rapids: Eerdmans, 2008.
Greenleaf, Robert K. *The Power of Servant Leadership*. Oakland: Berrett-Koehler, 1998.
———. *The Servant as Leader*. Suva, Fiji: Center for Applied Studies, 1973.
———. *Servant Leadership: Maxims of Life and Business*. New York: Paulist, 1977.
Grosheide, F. W. *Commentary on the First Epistle to the Corinthians*. The New International Commentary on the New Testament. Grand Rapids: Eerdmans, 1961.
Grounds, Vernon. "Pacesetters for the Radical Theologians of the 60s and 70s." *Journal of the Evangelical Theological Society* 18.3 (September 1975) 151–71.
Grover, T. R. *The Jesus of History*. New York: Paulist, 1977.
Guthrie, Donald. *Hebrews*. Tyndale New Testament Commentary. Downers Grove: IVP, 1983.
———. *The Pastoral Epistles*. Tyndale Bible Commentaries. Grand Rapids: Eerdmans, 1960.
Haenchen, Ernst. *The Acts of the Apostles*. Philadelphia: Westminster, 1965.
Haggai, John. *How to Win Over Worry*. Grand Rapids: Zondervan, 1959.
Hagner, Donald. *Matthew 1–13*. Nashville: Thomas Nelson, 1993.
———. *Matthew 14–28*. Nashville: Thomas Nelson, 1995.
Hallomon, J. Herbert. "Management and the Labor of Love." *Management Review* January 1983.
Halewood, William. *Six Subjects of Reformation Art: A Preface to Rembrandt*. Toronto: University of Toronto Press, 1982.
Hamann, J. G. *Writings on Philosophy and Language*. Cambridge, UK: Cambridge University Press, 2007.
Hamilton, Victor. *The Book of Genesis 18–50*. New International Commentary on the Old Testament. Grand Rapids: Eerdmans, 1995.

Hammond, Nicolas. *Alexander the Great: King, Commander and Statesman*. Chapel Hill: University of North Carolina Press, 1998.
Harris, R. Laird, ed. *Theological Wordbook of the Old Testament*, vols. 1–2. Chicago: Moody, 1980.
Harrison, R. K. "Edom." In *The Zondervan Pictorial Encyclopedia of the Bible*, edited by Merrill Tenney, 2.202–04. Grand Rapids: Regency, 1976.
Hart, David. *Organizational America*. New York: Houghton Mifflin, 1979.
Hazony, Yoram. *God and Politics in Esther*. Cambridge, UK: Cambridge University Press, 2016.
Heiges, Donald P. *The Christian's Calling*. Philadelphia: United Lutheran Church in America, 1953.
Hendricksen, William. *Exposition of Colossians and Philippians*. Grand Rapids: Baker, 1964.
———. *Exposition of the Gospel According to John*. Grand Rapids: Baker, 1972.
———. *Galatians*. Grand Rapids: Baker, 1971.
———. *I & II Timothy and Titus*. Grand Rapids: Baker, 1957.
———. *Philippians*. Grand Rapids: Baker, 1962.
Henry, Carl F. H. *Revelation and Authority*, 6 vols. Waco: Word, 1982.
Henry, Matthew. *The Bethany Parallel Commentary on the New Testament*. Minneapolis: Bethany, 1985.
———. *Commentary on the Whole Bible in One Volume*. The Bethany Parallel Commentary. 1960. Reprint, Minneapolis: Bethany House, 1985.
Herberg, Will. *Protestant-Catholic-Jew: An Essay in American Religious Sociology*. Chicago: University of Chicago Press, 1983.
Hersey, Paul, and Ken Blanchard. *Management of Organizational Behavior*. Englewood Cliffs, NJ: Prentice Hall, 1982.
Herzberg, Frederick. "One More Time: How Do You Motivate Employees?" *Harvard Business Review* January 2003.
———. *Work and the Nature of Man*. New York: Thomas Crowell, 1969.
Hesiod. *His Works and Days*. Translated by Richmond Lattimore. Ann Arbor: University of Michigan Press, 1984.
Hess, J. Daniel. *Integrity: Let Your Yea Be Yea*. Scottdale, PA: Herald, 1978.
Hill, Napoleon. *Think and Grow Rich*. New York: Hawthorn, 1966.
Hodge, Charles. *Exposition of the First Epistle to the Corinthians*. Grand Rapids: Eerdmans, 1974.
———. *Romans*. London: Banner of Truth, 1972.
———. *Systematic Theology*, vols. 1–3. Grand Rapids: Eerdmans, 1973.
———. *What Is Presbyterianism?* Philadelphia: Presbyterian Board of Publications, 1882.
Hodgkinson, Christopher. *The Philosophy of Leadership*. New York: St. Martin's, 1983.
———. *Towards a Philosophy of Administration*. New York: St. Martin's, 1983.
Howard, David. *Joshua*. The New American Commentary. Nashville: B. & H., 1998.
Hughes, Philip. *Commentary on the Epistle to the Hebrews*. Grand Rapids: Eerdmans, 1977.
Hybels, Bill. *Christians in the Marketplace*. Wheaton: Victor, 1988.
Iacocca, Lee. *Iacocca: An Autobiography*. New York: Bantam Books, 1984.
Irenaeus. *Against Heresies*. In *Ante-Nicene Fathers*, translated by Alexander Roberts, 352. Grand Rapids: Eerdmans, 1987.

Isaacson, Walter. *Steve Jobs*. New York: Simon & Schuster, 2011.
James, William. *Pragmatism*. Buffalo: Prometheus, 1991.
Jenkins, Daniel. *Christian Maturity and Christian Success*. Philadelphia: Fortress, 1987.
Jeremias, Joachim. *New Testament Theology*. London: SCM, 1971.
———. *The Parables of Jesus*. London: SCM, 1972.
Jerome. *Commentary on Jonah*. Ancient Christian Texts 1. Edited by Thomas Scheck. Downers Grove: IVP, 2016.
———. *The Homilies of St. Jerome*, vol. 1. Fathers of the Church 48. Washington, DC: Catholic University of America Press, 1964.
Johnson, Dave. *The Success Principle*. Irvine: Harvest House, 1976.
Johnson, Sharon. "A Biblical Philosophy Girds Godly Organization." *Spiritual Fitness in Business* 1985.
Johnson, James. *Profits, Power and Piety*. Irvine: Harvest House, 1980.
Johnson, John F. Review of *The Myth of God Incarnate* by John Hick. *Presbyterion* 4.2 (1978) 95–100.
Johnston, Jon. *Christian Excellence—Alternative to Success*. Grand Rapids: Baker, 1985.
Johnson, Paul C. *Grace: God's Work Ethic*. Valley Forge: Judson, 1985.
Johnston, Robert K. *Evangelicals at an Impasse*. Atlanta: Knox, 1979.
Johnston, V. W "Incarnation." In *The Zondervan Pictorial Encyclopedia of the Bible*, edited by Merrill Tenney, 3.271. Grand Rapids: Zondervan, 1976.
Jones, Charlie. *Life Is Tremendous*. Wheaton: Tyndale House, 1968.
Jones, Cliff C. *Winning through Integrity*. Nashville: Abingdon, 1985.
Jones, David Clyde. *Biblical Christian Ethics*. Grand Rapids: Baker, 1994.
———. "Character Education Movement." *Presbyterion* (Fall 2000) 84–92.
———. "Christ and Character." In *First Fruits of a New Creation*, edited by Doug Serven, 49–64. San Bernardino: White Blackbird, 2019.
———. Review of *The Truth of God Incarnate*, edited by Michael Green. *Presbyterion* 4.2 (1978) 100–103.
Jones, G. H. *1 & 2 Kings*. Grand Rapids: Eerdmans, 1984.
Josephus. *Antiquities*. Grand Rapids: Kregel, 1981.
Kaiser, Walter. *Hard Sayings of the Old Testament*. Downers Grove: InterVarsity, 1988.
Kant, Immanuel. *Metaphysical Elements of Justice*. Translated by John Ladd. New York: Prentice Hall, 1965.
Kanter, Rosabeth Moss, and Barry A. Stein. "Much Ado about Management." *The Rotarian* November 1986.
Kantrow, Alan M. "Why Read Peter Drucker?" *Harvard Business Review* January/February 1980.
Katzenstein, H. J. "The Royal Steward." *Israel Exploration Journal* 10.3 (1960).
Kendall, R. T. *The Parables of Jesus*. Grand Rapids: Baker, 2004.
Kierkegaard, Soren. *Training in Christianity*. Princeton: Princeton University Press, 1941.
Kirk, Russell. "The Inhumane Businessman." In *The Intemperate Professor*, 91–111. Peru: Sherwood Sugan, 1988.
Kirk, Thomas, and George Rawlinson. *Studies in the Book of Kings*, vol. 2. Minneapolis: Klock & Klock, 1983.
Kittel, Gerhard, ed. *Theological Dictionary of the New Testament*, 4 vols. Translated by Geoffrey W. Bromiley. Grand Rapids: Eerdmans, 1974.
Klein, George. *Zechariah*. The New American Commentary. Nashville: B. & H., 2008.

Kleinig, Vernon. "Confessional Lutheranism in Eighteenth-century Germany." *Concordia Theological Quarterly* 60.1–2 (January–April 1996) 97–127.
Klump, Ned L. "Executive Lifestyle: Stress: An Opportunity to Improve Performance." *The Rotarian* September 1986.
Knight, George A. *The Faithful Sayings in the Pastoral Epistles*. Nutley, NJ: Presbyterian & Reformed, 1968.
Knight, Phil. *Shoe Dog*. New York: Scribner, 2016.
Knowling, R. J. *The Acts of the Apostles*. The Expositor's Greek Testament. Grand Rapids: Eerdmans, 1980.
Korda, Michael. *Power: How to Get It, How to Use It*. New York: Ballantine, 1976.
Kostenberger, Andreas. *John*. Grand Rapids: Baker, 2004.
Kraus, C. Norman. *The Community of the Spirit*. Grand Rapids: Eerdmans, 1974.
Krieder, Carl. *The Christian Entrepreneur*. Scottdale, PA: Herald, 1980.
Kruger, David Delbert. *J. C. Penney: The Man, the Store, and American Agriculture*. Norman, OK: University of Oklahoma Press, 2017.
Kruse, Colin. *John*. Tyndale New Testament Commentary. Downers Grove: IVP, 2017.
Ladd, George Eldon. *A Theology of the New Testament*. London: Lutterworth, 1974.
Lane, William L. *Commentary on the Gospel of Mark*. The New International Commentary on the New Testament. Grand Rapids: Eerdmans, 1974.
Lane, William. *Hebrews 1–8*. Word Biblical Commentary. Grand Rapids: Zondervan, 1991.
Lasch, Christopher. *The Culture of Narcissism*. New York: Norton, 1979.
Leichner, Greg, and Bob Marsenich. "Manager's Memo: Bad Management Sometimes Works Too–for a While." *The Rotarian* August 1987.
Lencioni, Patrick. *The Five Dysfunctions of a Team: A Leadership Fable*. San Francisco: Jossey-Bass, 2002.
———. *Getting Naked*. San Francisco: Jossey-Bass, 2010.
———. *The Motive*. Hoboken: John Wiley, 2020.
Lenski, R. C. H. *The Acts of the Apostles*. Minneapolis: Augsburg, 1961.
LeTourneau, R. G. *Mover of Men and Mountains*. Chicago: Moody, 1967.
LeTourneau, Richard H. *Success without Compromise*. Wheaton: Victor, 1977.
———. *Success without Succeeding*. Grand Rapids; Zondervan, 1976.
Lewin, Kurt. "Frontiers in Group Dynamics: Method and Reality in Social Science; Social Equilibria and Social Change." *Human Relations* 1.1 (November 1947) 5–41.
Lewis, C. S. *The Great Divorce*. 1946. Reprint, San Francisco: Harper, 2001.
———. *Mere Christianity*. New York: HarperCollins, 2001.
Lewis, Michael. *Moneyball: The Art of Winning an Unfair Game*. New York: W. W. Norton, 2004.
Lightfoot, J. B. *Epistle to the Philippians*. Lynn, MA: Hendrickson, 1982.
———. *St. Paul's Epistle to the Colossians and to Philemon*. Lynn, MA: Hendrickson, 1982.
———. *St. Paul's Epistle to the Galatians*. Lynn, MA: Hendrickson, 1982.
Likert, Rensis. *The Human Organization*. New York: McGraw Hill, 1957.
Lillback, Peter A. *Saint Peter's Principles*. Phillipsburg, NJ: P. & R., 2019.
Lindell, Mike. *What Are the Odds*. Chaska, MN: Lindell, 2009.
Lloyd-Jones, Martyn. *Studies in the Sermon on the Mount*, vol. 2. London: InterVarsity, 1972.

Longman, Tremper. *Proverbs*. Baker Commentary on Old Testament Wisdom and Psalms. Grand Rapids: Baker, 2006.

Lucas, Ernest. *Daniel*. Apollos Old Testament Commentary. Downers Grove: IVP, 2002.

Lysius. *Against Eratosthenes*. Translated by W. R. M. Lamb. Cambridge, MA: Harvard University Press, 1930.

Maccoby, Michael. *The Leader*. New York: Ballantine, 1981.

Malloch, Theodore R. *Doing Virtuous Business: The Remarkable Success of Spiritual Enterprise*. New York: Thomas Nelson, 2011.

Maltz, Maxwell. *Psycho-Cybernetics*. Englewood Cliffs, NJ: Prentice Hall, 1968.

Manton, Thomas. *James*. The Geneva Series of Commentaries. 1693. Reprint, London: Banner of Truth, 1968.

Marcuse, Herbert. *Eros and Civilization*. Boston: Beacon. 1966.

Marks, Bailey. *An Ordinary Businessman*. San Bernardino: Here's Life, 1979.

Maslow, Abraham. *Motivation and Personality*. New York: Harper, 1954.

Marks, Peter. "Broadway Producer Scott Rudin Steps Aside Amid Accusations of Abusive Behavior Going Back Decades, Apologizes for Pain He Caused." *Washington Post* April 17, 2021. https://www.washingtonpost.com/entertainment/theater_dance/scott-rudin-broadway-producer-abuse-allegations/2021/04/17/f3d0ba88-9f0c-11eb-9d05-ae06f4529ece_story.html.

Marshall, Howard. *Commentary on Luke*. New International Greek Testament Commentary. Grand Rapids: Eerdmans, 1986.

Mattox, Robert. *The Christian Employee*. Plainfield, NJ: Logos International, 1978.

McFadyen, Joseph F. "The Life of Jesus Christ." In *The Abingdon Bible Commentary*, 891–904. New York: Abingdon, 1929.

McGregor, Douglas. *The Human Side of Enterprise*. New York: McGraw-Hill, 1960.

McKnight, Scot. *Letters of James*. New International Commentary on the New Testament. Grand Rapids: Eerdmans, 2011.

McLemore, Clinton W. *Good Guys Finish First: Successful Strategies from the Book of Proverbs for Business Men and Women*. Philadelphia: Westminster, 1983.

McManus, Michael J. "Businesses Try Christian Principles." *The Anniston Star* May 11, 1985.

———. "Executives Learn to Lead a Firm for Christ, Not Profit." *The Providence Journal Bulletin* May 11, 1985.

Menander. *Rhetor (Treatise 2), Dionysius of Halicarnassus*. Translated by William Race. Loeb Classical Library. Cambridge: Harvard University Press, 2019.

Merwin, John. "Have You Got What It Takes?" *Forbes* August 3, 1981.

Mettinger, Tryggve. *Solomonic State Officials: A Study in Civil Government Officials of the Israelite Monarchy*. Conietanea Biblica Old Testament Studies Series. San Francisco: Open Library, 1971.

Meyer, Heinrich A. W. *The Acts of the Apostles*. Winona Lake, IN: Alpha, 1979 (1906).

Meyer, Rudolph. "Ochlos." In *Theological Dictionary of the New Testament*, edited by Gerhard Kittel, translated by Geoffrey W. Bromiley, 5.582–90. Grand Rapids: Eerdmans, 1974.

Michaels, J. Ramsey. *The Gospel of John*. New International Commentary on the New Testament. Grand Rapids: Eerdmans, 2010.

Miles. Raymond. *Theories of Management*. New York: McGraw-Hill, 1975.

Miller, Julie, and Brian Bedford. *Culture without Accountability*. Austin: Criffel, 2013.

Milligan, William. *The Book of Revelation*. Cincinnati: Jennings & Graham, 1889.

Mills, Judy Ann. "Mixing Christianity and Business." *Yakima Herald Republic* November 3, 1980.
Minirth, Frank. *The Workaholic and His Family*. Grand Rapids: Baker, 1981.
Mintzberg, Henry. *Nature of Managerial Work*. New York: Prentice Hall, 1980.
———. "Planning on the Left Side and Managing on the Right." *Harvard Business Review* July/August 1975.
Moffett, Matt. "Fundamentalist Christians Strive to Apply Beliefs to the Workplace." *The Wall Street Journal* December 4, 1985.
Moisiman, S. K. "Rehoboam." In *International Standard Bible Encyclopedia*, edited by James Orr, 4.2551. 1936. Reprint, Grand Rapids: Eerdmans, 1983.
Montgomery, J. A. *A Critical and Exegetical Commentary on the Book of Daniel*. Edinburgh: T. & T. Clark, 1927.
Montgomery, John W. *The Suicide of Christian Theology*. Minneapolis: Bethany, 1971.
Moo, Douglas. *The Letter of James*. The Pillar New Testament Commentary. Grand Rapids: Eerdmans, 2000.
———. *The Letter to the Romans*. Grand Rapids: Eerdmans, 2018.
Moore, Russell. *Tempted and Tried*. Wheaton: Crossway, 2011.
Mouw, Richard. *Politics and the Biblical Drama*. Grand Rapids: Eerdmans, 1976.
Morris, Leon. *The First Epistle to the Corinthians*. Tyndale New Testament Commentary. Downers Grove: IVP, 1985.
———. *The Gospel According to Luke*. Tyndale New Testament Commentary. Grand Rapids: Eerdmans, 1974.
———. *The Gospel According to Matthew*. Tyndale New Testament Commentary. Grand Rapids: Eerdmans, 1992.
Motyer, Alec. *Isaiah*. Tyndale Old Testament Commentaries. Downers Grove: IVP, 1999.
Mouw, Richard J. *Called to Holy Worldliness*. Philadelphia: Fortress, 1983.
———. *Politics and the Biblical Drama*. Grand Rapids: Eerdmans, 1975.
Mounce, Robert. *The Book of Revelation*. New International Commentary on the New Testament. Grand Rapids: Eerdmans, 1977.
Mounce, William. *Pastoral Epistles*. Word Biblical Commentary. Nashville: Nelson, 2000.
Mulder, John M. "Critic's Corner: The Possibility Preacher." *Theology Today* July 1974.
Murray, John. *The Epistle to the Romans*. Grand Rapids: Eerdmans, 1959.
———. *The Sabbath Institution*. London: The Lord's Day Observance Society, 1953.
Nash, Laura. *Believers in Business*. Nashville: Thomas Nelson, 1994.
Newsom, Carol. *Daniel*. The Old Testament Library. Louisville: Westminster, 2014.
Niebuhr, H. Richard. *Christ and Culture*. New York: Harper Colophon, 1975.
Nolland, John. *The Gospel According to Matthew*. New International Greek Testament Commentary. Grand Rapids: Eerdmans, 2005.
———. *Luke 1—9:50*. Dallas: Word Books, 1989.
Nouwen, Henry. *In the Name of Jesus: Reflections on Christian Leadership*. New York: Crossroad, 1999.
Nunn, Henry. *The Whole Man Goes to Work*. New York: Harper, 1953.
Oates, Wayne E. *Confessions of a Workaholic*. Nashville: Abingdon, 1971.
Oehler, Gustaf *Theology of the Old Testament*. 1873. Reprint, Minneapolis: Klock & Klock, 1978.
Odiorne, George. *Management by Objectives*. New York: Pitman, 1972.

Origen. *Commentary on the Epistle to the Romans*. Translated by Thomas Scheck. Washington, DC: The Catholic University of America Press, 2017.

Oswalt, John. *The Book of Isaiah, Chapters 40–66*. New International Commentary on the Old Testament. Grand Rapids: Eerdmans, 1986.

O'Toole, James. *Vanguard Management*. New York: Doubleday, 1985.

Page, Ruth. *Ambiguity and the Presence of God*. Norwich, UK: SCM, 1985.

Paul, Bill. "Matters of Faith." *The Wall Street Journal* April 15, 1973.

Peabody, Larry. *Secular Work Is Full-Time Service*. Fort Washington, PA: Christian Literature Crusade, 1974.

Peale, Morgan Vincent. *The Power of Positive Thinking*. Grand Rapids: Fleming H. Revell, 1952.

Penney, James Cash. "The Challenge of Breeding Purebred Livestock: It Is Something to Bring Out the Best in a Man." *Hereford Journal* July 1, 1949.

———. *Fifty Years with the Golden Rule*. New York: Harper and Brothers, 1950.

Peters, Thomas J. "Leadership: Sad Facts and Silver Linings." *Harvard Business Review* November/December 1979.

———. *Re-Imagine!: Business Excellence in a Disruptive Age*. New York: DK, 2006.

Peters, Thomas J., and Robert H. Waterman. *In Search of Excellence*. New York: Harper & Row, 1982.

Peterson, Margaret. "These Christians Put Beliefs Where Office Is." *The Indianapolis News* November 23, 1987.

Phillips, J. B. *The New Testament in Modern English*. London: Geoffrey Bles, 1960.

Philo. *On Abraham. On Joseph. On Moses*. Translated by Francis H. Colson. Cambridge, MA: Harvard University Press, 1935.

———. *On the Confusion of Tongues. On the Migration of Abraham. Who is heir of Divine Things? On Mating with the Preliminary Studies*. Cambridge, MA: Harvard University Press, 1932.

———. *On the Embassy to Gaius*. Coppell, TX: Odin Library Classics, 2021.

Pindar. *The Complete Odes*. Translated by Anthony Verity. Oxford: Oxford University Press, 2008.

Piper, John. "He Must Manage His Household Well." https://www.desiringgod.org/messages/he-must-manage-his-household-well.

Plummer, Alfred. *Gospel According to St. Luke*. 1898. Reprint, Edinburgh: T. & T. Clark, 1981.

Plummer, William. *Psalms*. The Geneva Series of Commentaries. 1867. Reprint, Edinburgh: Banner of Truth, 1978.

Polhill, John. *Acts*. The New American Commentary. Nashville: B. & H., 1992.

Pratt, Richard. *1 & 2 Chronicles*. A Mentor Commentary. Greanies House, UK: Christian Focus, 1998.

Prior, David. *The Message of Joel, Micah & Habakkuk*. The Bible Speaks Today. Downer's Grove: IVP, 1998.

Proctor, William. "The Christian and Corporate Power." *Christian Herald* March 1979.

———. "An Entrepreneur's Gamble on God." *Power for Living* December–February 1979–1980.

Pulliam, Russ. "Putting God to Work in Pittsburgh." *Christianity Today* April 23, 1982.

Putnam, David. *Bowling Alone: The Collapse and Revival of American Community*. 2000. Reprint, New York: Simon & Schuster, 2020.

Rall, Harris Franklin. "The Teaching of Jesus." In *The Abingdon Bible Commentary*, edited by Frederick Carl Eiselen, Edwin Lewis, and David Downey, 904–14. New York: Abingdon, 1929.

Randolph, W. Alan, and Barry Z. Posner. "Manager's Memo: Managing Projects: How to Get the Job Done." *The Rotarian* April 1989.

Raven, Bertram, and John French. "Studies in Social Power." *Sociometry* 21.2 (1958) 83–97.

Real Estate Borkerage Council. "How to Manage a Real Estate Office Profitably." *Rocky Mountain Telegram* August 1984.

Reddin, W. J. *Effective Management by Objectives: The 3-D Method*. New York: McGraw Hill, 1971.

Rayburn, Robert. "A Neglected Chapter in the History of Redemption: The Forty Days." April 11, 2021. https://vimeo.com/535688335

Reddin, W. J. *Effective Management by Objectives: The 3-D Method*. New York: McGraw-Hill, 1971.

Redpath, Alan. *The Making of a Man of God*. London: Pickering & Inglis, 1962.

———. *Victorious Christian Service*. London: Pickering, 1978.

Renan, Ernest. *The Life of Jesus*. 1863. Reprint, Buffalo: Prometheus, 1991.

Reymond, Robert. *A New Theology of the Christian Faith*. Nashville: Thomas Nelson, 1998.

Richter, Paul. "Can Bible, Business Mix?" *Los Angeles Times* July 13, 1986.

Ridderbos, Herman. *The Coming of the Kingdom*. Philadelphia: Presbyterian and Reformed, 1959.

———. *Matthew*. Grand Rapids: Zondervan, 1987.

Ridenour, Fritz. *How to Be a Christian in an Unchristian World*. Glendale, CA: Regal, 1971.

Rieff, Philip. *The Triumph of the Therapeutic*. New York: Penguin, 1973.

Ries, Eric. *The Lean Startup*. New York: Currency/Random House, 2011.

Ringer, Robert. *Winning through Intimidation*. New York: Funk & Wagnalls, 1975.

Robertson, A. T. *Word Pictures in the New Testament*, 6 vols. Nashville: Broadman, 1931.

Robinson, George. "Solomon." In *International Standard Bible Encyclopedia*, edited by James Orr, vol. 4.2822–25. 1936. Reprint, Grand Rapids: Eerdmans, 1983.

Robinson, John A. T. *Honest to God*. London: SCM, 1963.

Rogers, Jack. *Biblical Authority*. Waco: Word, 1977.

Ross, Alexander. *The Epistle of James and John*. Grand Rapids: Eerdmans, 1954.

Ross, Allen. "7. The Scribes." *Bible.org*. https://bible.org/seriespage/scribes.

Rousseau, Jean-Jacques. *Emile*. 1758. Everyman's Library. Reprint, New York: Dutton, 1969.

———. *First Discourse*. New York: Harper Torchbooks, 1990.

Rush, Myron. *Lord of the Marketplace*. Wheaton: Victor, 1986.

———. *Management: A Biblical Approach*. Wheaton: Victor, 1983.

Rushdoony, Rousas. *Institute of Biblical Law*. Philadelphia: Presbyterian & Reformed, 1977.

Ryken, Leland. "Puritan Work Ethic: The Dignity of Life's Labors." *Christianity Today* October 19, 1979.

———. *Worldly Saints*. Grand Rapids: Zondervan, 1986.

Ryle, John Charles. *Expository Thoughts on the Gospels*, vols 1–4. Grand Rapids: Baker, 1982.
Sanders, J. Oswald. *Spiritual Leadership*. London: Marshall, Morgan and Scott, 1967.
Sanderson, John W. *The Fruit of the Spirit*. Grand Rapids: Zondervan, 1972.
Sasse, Harmann. "Kosmos." In *Theological Dictionary of the New Testament*, edited by Gerhard Kittel, translated by Geoffrey W. Bromiley, 3.867–98. Grand Rapids: Eerdmans, 1974.
Schaeffer, Francis. *Genesis in Time and Space*. Downers Grove: IVP, 1972.
———. *The God Who Is There*. London: Hodder & Stoughton, 1968.
———. "Transcript and Video of Francis Schaeffer Speech in 1983 on the Word 'Evangelical.'" *The Daily Hatch*. https://thedailyhatch.org/2014/07/25/transcript-and-video-of-francis-schaeffer-speech-in-1983-on-the-word-evangelical/
Schaller, Lyle E. *The Change Agents*. Nashville: Abingdon, 1972.
Schein, Edgar H. *Organizational Culture and Leadership*. San Francisco: Jossey-Bass, 1986.
Schmidt, K. L. "Threskos." In *Theological Dictionary of the New Testament*, edited by Gerhard Kittel, translated by Geoffrey W. Bromiley, 3.155–59. Grand Rapids: Eerdmans, 1974.
Schnackenburg, Rudolf. *The Johannine Epistles*. Chicago: Crossroad, 1992.
Schneider, Walter, and Colin Brown. "Peirao." In *Dictionary of New Testament Theology*, edited by Colin Brown, 3.798–808. Grand Rapids: Eerdmans, 1978.
Schreiner, Thomas. *1, 2 Peter, Jude*. The New American Commentary. Nashville: B. & H., 2003.
Schoonenoerg, Piet. *The Christ*. New York: Herder & Herder, 1971.
Schrader, Ann. "Republic Air CEO Puts His Faith to Work." *Denver Post* November 13, 2009.
Schreiner, Thomas R. *Romans*. Baker Evangelical Commentary on the New Testament. Grand Rapids: Baker, 1998
Schroeder, Alice. *The Snowball: Warren Buffett and the Business of Life*. New York: Bantam, 2009.
Schuller, Robert. *Move Ahead with Possibility Thinking*. Grand Rapids: Fleming H. Revell, 1967.
Schultz, Carl. "Azab." In *Theological Wordbook of the Old Testament*, edited by R. Laird Harris, 2.658–59. Chicago: Moody, 1980.
Schweizer, Eduard. *The Good News According to Luke*. Atlanta: Knox, 1984.
———. *The Good News According to Mark*. Atlanta: Knox, 1970.
———. *The Good News According to Matthew*. Atlanta: Knox, 1975.
Scott, J. B. "David." In In *The Zondervan Pictorial Encyclopedia of the Bible*, edited by Merrill Tenney, 2.31–43. Grand Rapids: Zondervan, 1976.
Sears, Richard P. "The Biblical Concept of Work and American Industry in 1975." *The Presbyterian Guardian* January 1979.
Seaver, Paul S. *Wallington's World*. Stanford, CA: Sanford University Press, 1985.
Selman, Martin. *2 Chronicles*. Tyndale Old Testament Commentary. Downers Grove: IVP, 1994.
Sendry, Alfred. *Music in Ancient Israel*. New York: Philosophic Library, 1969.
Seneca. *Moral and Political Essays*. Edited by John Cooper and J. F. Procope. Cambridge, UK: Cambridge University Press, 1995.
Senior, Donald. *The Gift of Administration*. Collegeville: Liturgical, 2016.

Serven, Doug, ed. *First Fruits of a New Creation*. San Bernardino: White Blackbird, 2019.
Shearer, Darren. *Marketing Like Jesus: 25 Strategies to Change the World*. Houston: High Bridge, 2021.
Shelly, Judith Allen. *Not Just a Job*. Downers Grove: InterVarsity, 1985.
Sherman, Doug, and William Hendricks. *Your Work Matters to God*. Colorado Springs: Nav Press, 1987.
Sherrill, John, and Elizabeth Sherrill. *The Happiest People on Earth*. Waco: Word, 1975.
Shinn, George. *The American Dream Still Works*. 1977. Reprint, Wheaton: Tyndale House, 1987.
———. *The Miracle of Motivation*. Wheaton: Tyndale House, 1987.
Shoemaker, Dennis E. "Critic's Corner: Schuller Shooting." *Theology Today* 31.4 (January 1, 1975) 350–55.
Sifford, Darrel. "Put Your Company to 10-point Enlightenment Test." *Yakima Herald Republic* December 22, 1985.
Silvoso, Ed, and Laurie Jones. *Anointed for Business*. Grand Rapids: Chosen/Baker, 2009.
Simon, Herbert. *Administrative Behavior*. New York: Free Press, 1997.
Simonides. "Plato Republic." In *Greek Lyric III: Stesichorus, Ibycus, Simonides, and Others*, 368–592. Loeb Classical Library. Cambridge, MA: Harvard University Press, 1991.
Sinek, Simon. *Leaders Eat Last*. New York: Portfolio/Penguin, 2014.
Slavin, Stewart. "God Is 'Senior Partner' in Knife Firm." *Yakima Herald Republic* January 14, 1980.
Sloan, Allan. "Killer Monopoly and Other Fun Games." *Forbes* August 3, 1981.
Sloan, Harold S., and Arnold J. Zurcher. *A Dictionary of Economics*. New York: Harper Collins, 1971.
Slocum, Robert E. *Ordinary Christians in a High-Tech World*. Waco: Word, 1986.
Smedes, Lewis. *Choices*. New York: HarperOne, 1981.
———. *Love Within Limits*. Grand Rapids: Eerdmans, 1978.
———. *Mere Morality*. Grand Rapids: Eerdmans, 1983.
Smith, Barrie T. "Running on People Power." *The Rotarian* July 1985.
Smith, Charles Merrill. *The Case of a Middle-Class Christian*. Waco: Word, 1973.
Smith, David. *The Days of His Flesh*. London: Harper & Brothers, 1905.
———. *The Epistles of John*. The Expositor's Greek Testament. Grand Rapids: Eerdmans, 1980.
Smith, Donald Gregor. *J. C. Hamann*. London: Collins, 1968.
Smith, Gary. *Isaiah 1–39*. The New American Commentary. Nashville: B. & H., 2007.
Smith, Frank. *Amos, Obadiah, Jonah*. The New American Commentary. Nashville: B. & H., 1995.
Smith, Robert. "The Christian Foundations of Work in America." *The Counsel of Chalcedon* October 1988.
Sorenson, Laurel. "Oregon Bank Tries to Exploit Christian Ethic." *The Wall Street Journal* July 22, 1981.
Southard, Samuel. *Ethics for Executives*. Nashville: Thomas Nelson, 1975.
Spurgeon, Charles. *The Treasury of David*, vol. 2. McLean, VA: MacDonald, 1885.
Stanley, Arthur P. *Lectures on the History of the Jewish Church*, vol. 2. Miami: Hardpress, 2017.

Stearns, Richard. *Lead Like It Matters to God.* Downers Grove: IVP, 2021.
Steele, Richard. *The Religious Tradesman (The Tradesman Calling).* 1684. Reprint, Harrisonburg, VA: Sprinkle, 1989.
Steinbeck, John. *The Winter of Our Discontent.* New York: Penguin, 1961.
Stepansky, Robert. *Thoughts on Leadership from a Higher Level.* Bloomington, IN: iUniverse, 2011.
Stevens, George Barker. *The Christian Doctrine of Salvation.* New York: Charles Scribner, 1905.
Stone, Brad. *The Everything Store: Jeff Bezos and the Age of Amazon.* New York: Back Bay, 2014.
Storms, Samuel. "Jesus: God the Son." https://www.samstorms.org/all-articles/post/Jesus:-god-the-son.
Stuart, Doug. *Exodus,* vols. 1–2. The New American Commentary. Nashville: B. & H., 2006.
Swift, Allan. "Christian Witness in the Business World." *Decision* December 1983.
Tam, Stanley, and Ken Anderson. *God Owns My Business.* Waco: Word, 1976.
Tannenbaum, Robert, and Warren Schmidt. "How to Choose a Leadership Pattern." *Harvard Business Review* May 1973.
Tappan, Arthur. *The Life of Arthur Tappan.* New York: Hurd and Houghton, 1870.
Taylor, Frederick. *The Principles of Scientific Management.* 1911. Reprint, New York: Norton, 1967.
Thielicke, Helmut. *Between God and Satan.* 1938. Reprint, Farmington Hills, MI: Oil Lamp, 2010.
———. *The Evangelical Faith,* vols. 1–3. Translated by Geoffrey W. Bromiley. Grand Rapids: Eerdmans, 1971.
Thiessen, Henry C. *Introductory Lectures in Systematic Theology.* Grand Rapids: Eerdmans, 1949.
Thomas, Dave. *Dave's Way.* Seattle: Amazon, 2016.
Tillich, Paul. *Systematic Theology.* Digwells Place, Hertfordshire, UK: James Nisbet, 1969.
Torrance, Thomas. *Incarnation.* Downers Grove: IVP, 2008.
Towner, Phillip. *The Letters to Timothy and Titus.* New International Commentary on the New Testament. Grand Rapids: Eerdmans, 2006.
Trench, Richard C. *Synonyms of the New Testament.* Grand Rapids: Eerdmans, 1973.
Trueblood, Elton. *Your Other Vocation.* New York: Harper & Brothers, 1952.
Trueman, Carl. *The Rise and Triumph of the Modern Self.* Wheaton: Crossway, 2020.
Turner, David. *Matthew.* Baker Exegetical Commentary on the New Testament. Grand Rapids: Baker, 2008.
Van Gemeren. *New International Dictionary of Old Testament Theology and Exegesis,* vols. 1–5. Grand Rapids: Zondervan. 1997
Vance, Ashlee. *Elon Musk: Tesla, SpaceX, and the Quest for a Fantastic Future.* New York: Ecco, 2017.
Vawter, Bruce. *This Man Jesus.* New York: Doubleday, 1973.
Vincent, Marvin R. *Word Studies,* vols. 1–2. 1886. Reprint, MacDill AFB, Florida: Creative Media Partners, 2015.
Vine, William. *Expository Dictionary of New Testament Words.* Ada, MI: Revell, 1966.
Vischer, Phil. *Me, Myself and Bob: A True Story about Dreams, God and Talking Vegetables.* Nashville: Thomas Nelson, 2008.

Bibliography

Von Rad, Gerhard. *Theology of the Old Testament*, vol. 2. New York: Harper & Row, 1965.
Wade, Marion E., and Glenn Kittler. *The Lord Is My Counsel*. Englewood Cliffs, NJ: Prentice Hall, 1966.
Waltke, Bruce. *The Book of Proverbs*, vols. 1–2. New International Commentary on the Old Testament. Grand Rapids: Eerdmans, 2004.
Walton, Sam, and John Huey. *Sam Walton: Made in America: My Story*. New York: Bantam, 1992.
Wanamaker, John. *Maxims of Life and Business*. Mechanicsburg, VA: Executive Books, 2004.
Warfield, Benjamin B. "Person of Christ." In *The International Standard Bible Encyclopedia*, edited by James Orr, vol. 4.2338–48. 1936. Reprint, Grand Rapids: Eerdmans, 1983.
―――. *The Person and Work of Christ*. Philadelphia: Presbyterian and Reformed, 1950.
Warn, Richard S. "Management." *Western World* May/June 1984.
Warner, Gary. *Competition*. Elgin, IL: David C. Cook, 1979.
Watts, John. *Isaiah 1–33*. Word Biblical Commentary. Nashville: Thomas Nelson, 2005.
Waugh, Evelyn. *Robbery under Law*. London: Catholic Book Club, 1939.
Webber, Robert. *The Secular Saint*. Grand Rapids: Zondervan, 1979.
Webber, Ross A., Marilyn A. Morgan, and Paul C. Browne. *Management: Basic Elements of Managing Organizations*. Homewood, IL: Richard D Irwin, 1985.
West, John. *The Politics of Revelation and Reason*. Lawrence, KS: University Press of Kansas, 1996.
Westermann, Claus. "Nagid." In *Theological Lexicon of the Old Testament*, edited by Ernst Jenni and Claus Westermann, translated by Mark Biddle, 2.714–18. Peabody: Hendrikson, 2004.
Westminster Confession of Faith. Applecross, Scotland: Free Presbyterian Church of Scotland. 1970.
Whitcomb, J. C. "Darius the Mede." In *The Zondervan Pictorial Encyclopedia of the Bible*, edited by Merrill Tenney, 2.26–29. Grand Rapids: Zondervan, 1976.
White, Jerry, and Mary White. *Your Job: Survival or Satisfaction*. Grand Rapids: Zondervan, 1977.
White, John. *Excellence in Leadership*. Downers Grove: InterVarsity, 1986.
White, William. "Rosh." In *Theological Wordbook of the Old Testament*, edited by R. Laird Harris, 2.852–53. Chicago: Moody, 1980.
Wilkins, Michael. *Matthew*. The New NIV Application Commentary. Grand Rapids: Zondervan, 2004.
Will, George. *Statecraft as Soulcraft*. New York: Touchstone, 1984.
Wilson, Lindsay. *Proverbs*. Tyndale Old Testament Commentaries. Downers Grove: IVP, 2018.
Wilson, Robert E. "He Emptied Himself." *Journal of the Evangelical Theological Society* 19.4 (September 1976) 279–81.
Wilson, William. *Wilson's Old Testament Word Studies*. McLean, VA: MacDonald, 1870.
Winston, Bruce E. *Be a Leader for God's Sake*. Vancouver, BC: School of Global Leadership, 2002.
Woelfel, James W. *Bonhoeffer's Theology: Classical and Revolutionary*. Nashville: Abingdon, 1970.
Wolff, Richard. *Is God Dead?* Wheaton: Tyndale House, 1966.

Wright, N. T. *After You Believe: Why Christian Character Matters.* New York: Harper One, 2010.

Wroe, Ann. *Pontius Pilate.* New York: Random House, 1999.

Xenophon. *Memorabilia. Oeconomicus. Symposium. Apology.* Translated by E. C. Marchant. Cambridge, MA: Harvard University Press, 2013.

Yarbrough, Robert. *1–3 John.* Baker Exegetical Commentary on the New Testament. Grand Rapids: Baker, 2008.

———. *The Letters of Timothy and Titus.* The Pillar New Testament Commentary. Grand Rapids: Eerdmans, 2010.

Yeager, Randolph V. *The Renaissance New Testament,* vol. 3. Bowling Green, KY: Renaissance, 1978.

Young, Edward J. *The Book of Isaiah,* vols. 1–2. Grand Rapids: Eerdmans. 1969.

Young, Edward J. "Sabbath." In *The New Bible Dictionary,* 2nd ed, 1042–43. Wheaton: Tyndale, 1982.

Yukl, Gary. *Leadership in Organizations.* New York: Pearson. 2008.

Zabloski, Jim. *The Twenty-five Most Common Problems in Business.* Nashville: Broadman & Holman, 1996.

Ziglar, Zig. *Confessions of a Happy Christian.* Gretna, LA: Pelican, 1979.

———. *See You at the Top.* Gretna, LA: Pelican, 1977.

Zitzman, Susan. "I Found the Source of Happiness." *Power for Living* December–February 1979–80.

Author Index

a Kempis, Thomas, xxivn13
Aaron, xxiiin8, 42n116, 124, 238
Abba, 168n771
Abda, 299n568
Abednego, 147, 149, 153, 153n665, 154
Abel, 104
Abiathar, 123, 124, 124n445
Abiezer, 279n474
Abigail (wife of Nabal), 34, 35, 282–85
Abimelech, 119n405, 166n754, 369
Abiram, 184n82
Abishag, 109n347
Abishai, 35
Abner, 369
Abraham, 32n34, 57n17, 107–8, 107n337, 126n458, 175, 176, 229, 244, 264–65, 332n769, 369
Absalom, 37n62, 43n117, 132, 299n568, 305n607, 336, 337
Acbor (son of Micaiah), 158
Achan, 335–36
Adah, 103, 104
Adam, xxvin20, 22, 23, 332
Adoni-jah, 299n568
Adonijah, 299n568
Adoni-kam, 299n568
Adoni-ram, 123n441, 127–28, 132, 168, 168n764, 168n771, 299n568, 375, 378
Adoni-zedek, 299n568
Adoram, 127n462
Agrippa, 171n4
Agur (son of Jakeh), 303n592

King Ahab, 43n117, 139, 140, 140n581, 146n626, 157n693, 168n771, 200, 340, 344
King Ahaz, 341, 341n802, 342n810
Ahijah, 131, 132, 271, 375, 380
Ahikam, 158–59, 159n706
Ahilud, 123
Ahimaaz, 131, 133
Ahimelech (son of Abiathar), 123, 124, 125
Ahinadab, 132
Ahishar, 132, 139n580, 168n771
Ahithopel, 305n607
Ahitub, 123
Alexander, 39n77
Alexander, John H., 82n191, 82n192
Alexander the metal worker, 324n726
Allen, Leslie, 300, 300n574
Amaziah, 142n591
Amnon, 299n568
Amos, 287
Ananas, 180
Anderson, John, 42n112
Anderson, Ray, 82, 82n192, 83, 352n867, 390, 390n37
Apollos, 190
Appleton, James, 388
Aquila, 189–90
Aquinas, xii, xiii
Archibald, Douglas, xiin12
Aristotle, xii, 70, 75n191, 94n255, 102n308
Armerding, George D., xivn20
Arnold, Matthew, xiiin12, 79n177
Artapanus, 113n372

413

King Artaxerxes, 154, 201
Arza, 139n580
Asa, 381
Asaiah, 158
Asaph, 45, 195, 302
Ashpenaz, 146n624, 147n628, 151
Athanasius, 19
Augustine, xii, xiii, 24
Azariah, 109n346, 129n479, 131, 132, 133, 141–42, 142n591
Azra, 168n771

Bacon, Francis, 80
Bailey, Kenneth, 6n14
Balaam, 203n80
King Balak of Moab, 203n80
Baldwin, Joyce, 52n179
Barak, 118, 122, 323n717
Barber, Cyril J., 156n688
Barclay, William, 205n90
Barnabas, xin4-7, 10n39, 180–82, 183, 193, 254, 288, 348, 348n847
Barth, Karl, 3n13, 18n80, xxxn39, 329n750
Bartholomew, Craig, 138
Basemath (daughter of Solomon), 133
Bathsheba, 43
Bauckham, Richard, 94n256
Bauer, Walter, 70n110
Bay, Louise, 25n114
Bedford, Brian, 236n254
Bedford, Bryan, xiin13
Beeckman, 295n543
Belloc, Hilaire, 79n177
Belshazzar, 145n622
Ben-Abinadab, 132
Benaiah (son of Jehoiada), 123, 124, 124n450, 131, 131n502
Ben-Geber, 132
Berkouwer, G. C., 1n2, 99n289, 365n933
Beyer, Herman Wolfgang, 89n240, 90n240, 241n278
Bezalcel, 198
Bezalel, 116–17, 116n395, 136n557
Biederwolf, William E., 59n31
Bietenhard, Hans, 355n888

Blanchard, Ken, 377, 377n10, 377n11, 379n14, 379n15, 381, 381n22, 381n23, 382, 382nn24–26
Bland, Glenn, 257n352
Boaz, 38n70, 299n568
Bock, Darrell, xxivn9, 179n46
Bond, Doug, 145n620
Bonhoeffer, Dietrich, 4n13, xxxn39, 102, 102n312
Bornkamm, Gunther, 184n82
Bowling, Andrew, 372, 372n2
Boyle, 295n543
Breasted, J. H., 110n349
Breton, Andre, 222n175
Bright, John, 372n3
Lord Brooke, xxxin39
Brown. Colin, 39n80, 65n73
Browne, Paul C., xxviiin32, 377n10
Bruce, A. B., 49n155, 78n175, 334m775
Bruce, F. F., 83
Brunner, Emil, 18n80
Buchanan, Pat, 325n730
Buffet, Warren, xxxn38
Bulfinch, Thomas, xiiin16
Bump, Glen Hale, 351n865
Bunyan, John, 25n114
Burkett, Larry, 352n867
Burnham, James, ixn1
Burns, James M., 380
Burns, James MacGregor, 380nn16–19, 381n20
Butt, Howard, 384–85, 384nn29–30, 384n32, 389

Cain, 103–5
Cain, Herman, 209n107
Calvin, John, xii, 1, 1n3, 10n35, 44n120, 79, 79n176, 90n240, 94n256, 100, 100n296, 205, 205n91, 213, 213n126, 231n231, 310n642, 356, 356n890, 361, 361n920
Campbell, John, xiiin16
Campbell, Thomas C., 92n253
Carnegie, Dale, 257n352
Carroll, Pete, 349n857
Carroll, Robert, 359n909

Author Index

Carson, D. A., 194n17, 354n874
Case, Robert, xiin10, xiin11, 60n43, 250n320, 344n832, 366n937
Cathy, S. Truett, xivn20, xxxn38, 236n253
Cavett, Dick, 325n730
Chiles, Brevard, 114n376
Chrysostom, John, 309n636
Churchill, Winston, xin6
Chuza (husband of Joanna), 6n17, 7n17
Clapp, Rodney, 56n9
Clark, xxvn15
Clarke, Adam, 78n174
Clemens, John, xin5, xiiin15
Clines, D. J., 201n73
Cockerill, Gareth Lee, 255n349
Coenen, Lothar, 93n254
Collins, Jim, ixn2, 12n43, xxixn33, 257n352, 258n352, 319n700, 347n846, 357n892
Conaniah, 109n346, 129n479
Conn, Charles Paul, 257n352, 260n361, 320n708
Conrad, 299n568
Cook, William H., 257n352
Cooper, Lamar E., 51n175
Copernicus, 295n543
Coppes, Leonard J., 374n5
Cornelius, 57n18, 180
Craigie, P. C., 357n892
Crane, Steve, 208n107
Crichton, James, 160n714
Culver, Robert, 126n458
King Cyrus of Persia, 40n93, 160
Cyrus the Zoroastrian, 200

Dabney, Robert, 22n102
Dalrymple, Theodore, 78n173
Daniel, 32n34, 58, 145–54, 147n626, 147n629, 148n631, 149n637, 153n665, 157n693, 200–201, 269n421, 344n832
King Darius of Persia, 148n631
Dathan, 184n82
David, xxin4, 32–43, 32n34, 37n62, 40n93, 41n97, 44, 60n43, 73, 79n177, 109n347, 121, 123–26, 125n454, 125n457, 126n460, 128, 128n474, 129, 130, 130n482, 131, 132, 136n557, 196–97, 198n42, 205n97, 211n117, 226, 227, 230n230, 237–40, 266–67, 269n419, 279–81, 280n478, 280n479, 282, 283, 283n488, 284, 286n505, 299n568, 301–3, 302n586, 315–16, 323n717, 329n752, 336–37, 341, 354, 369, 374, 375, 378, 381, 384
Dayton, Edward R., 82n191, 390, 390n38
de Mirabeau, xxviin30
Deborah, 118, 118n402, 122, 123n438
Decker, Celia, 60n43
Decker, John, 60n43
Deliah, 42n116
DeMoss, Ted, 352n867
Denning, Steve, xxixn34
DePree, Max, 86n219, 311n644
DeVos, Richard A., 257n352
Diaconus, Petrus, 240n277
Dickens, Charles, 10n35, xiiin15
Dillard, 224n196
Diotrephes, 42n116
Dives, 174–76
Dods, Marcus, 19n82
Dorcas, 53n186, 178n31
Doriani, Dan, 12n40, xviin28, 192n1, 290n515, 331n766
Douma, Douglas, xxvn15
Douma, J., 22n102
Douty, Norman F., 102n313
Dreyer, Rod, 56n9
Drucker, Peter F., xxix, xxiin5, xxixn35, xxixn37, xxxn38, 209n108
Dunn, James, 262n373
Durant, Will, xiiin15
Durham, John, 117n397, 266n397

Ebenezer Scrooge, 10n35
Eckerd, Jack, 260n361, 320n708
Edwards, James, 175n20, 216n142, 219n153, 232n238, 313n659
Egeria, 240n277
Eleazar (son of Aaron), 89n240, 109n346, 115n386, 237, 238

Eliab, 279–80, 280n478, 280n479
Eliahim, 168n771
Eliakim, 139n580, 165–67
Eliam (mother of Bathsheba), 43
Eliezer of Damascus, 126n458, 264, 265
Elihoreph, 131
Elijah, 73, 140, 234, 344
Elisha, 73
Elizabeth, 21, 21n96, 53n186
Elliott, Charles W., xin6
Engstrom, Ted W., 82n191, 92n254, 93n254, 390, 390n38
Enlow, David, 236n253
Enlow, Dorothy, 236n253
Enoch, 28n11, 103, 104, 105
Epictetus, 70n119
Erastus, 262n373
Esau, 42n116, 276
Esther, 145, 149, 201–2, 202n75, 346
Etzioni, Amitai, 264n382, 311n643, 376n9
Eusebius, 84n203, 171, 171n5
Eve, xxvin20, 22
Ezekiel, 50–52, 147n626
Ezra, 123n438, 162, 201, 238

Fausset, Andrew, 147n629
Fee, Gordon, 72n135, 328n746
Felix, 171n4, 327n743
Felix, Marcus, 172
Fensham, F. C., 155n681, 161n725
Fereday, William, 122n430
Festus, 171n4, 327n743
Filson, 25n114
Fitzmyer, Joseph A., 2n9, 219n154, 219n157
Flaubert, 79n177
Fox, Michael, 267, 267n403
France, R. T., 243n291
Fraser, Donald, 326m738, 327n738
French, J. R., 377, 377n10

Emperor Gaius, 171
Galileo, 295n543
Garland, David, 57n19
Geber, 133

Gedaliah, 159–60, 159n706, 160n714, 169n773
Geldenhuys, Revel, 297n560
Geneen, Harold, xxixn32, xxviiin32
Gideon, 118–19, 119n410, 122, 126n460, 269n414, 278–79, 278n471, 279n473, 279n474, 323n717, 369
Gilead, 119
Gladwell, Malcom, xin6
Goliath, 33, 280
Green, David, 95n282, 235n253, 257n352
Green, Gene, 95n271, 347n846
Greenleaf, Robert, xxxi, xxxin40, 257n352, 385, 385n33
Grosheide, F. W., 241n280, 365n936, 366n936, 366n937
Grounds, Vernon, xxxn39
Guthrie, Donald, 93n254

Haarbeck, 39n80
Haenchen, Ernst, 204n86
Haggai, 44n125, 161
Hagner, Donald, 214n135
Haldane, Richard, xiiin16
Halewood, William, 80, 80n183
Haman, 156, 157
Hamann, J. G., 4n13, 61, 307, 307n620
Hamilton, Victor, 265n393
Hammond, Nicolas, 39n77
Hammurabi, 40n93
Hananiah, 142n591
Hannah, 195n22
Hannibal, 170n3
Hanun (son of Nahash), 36
Harrison, R. K., 161n720
Hart, David, xviin27
Harvey, 295n543
Hazony, Yoram, 158n700
Hegesipus, 84n203
Hendricksen, William, 18n79, 67n86, 71, 71n121, 76, 76n158, 216n141, 328n748
Henry, Matthew, 202n75, 359n910
Hermas the Shepherd, 348n850, 349n850

Author Index

King Herod, 6n17, 7n17, 171, 172, 334m775, 334
Herodotus, 7n17
Hersey, Paul, 377, 377n10, 377n11, 379n14, 379n15, 381, 381n22, 381n23, 382, 382nn24-26
Herzberg, Frederick, 260n361
Hesiod, 312n658
Hesse, Hermann, 385
King Hezekiah, 32n34, 109n346, 129n479, 142-44, 144n613, 165, 168, 168n771, 169, 341-44, 354, 381
Hilkiah, 158, 166
Hill, Napoleon, 257n352
Hiram, 133, 136
Hodge, Charles, 1, 1n4, 22n102, 55, 55n7, 64n70, 207n99, 241n280, 291, 291n520
Hodgkinson, Christopher, 60n43, 108n340, 199n58, 388n34
Homer, 7n17, 122n429
Howard, David, 32n35
Howard, John A., xiin12
Hughes, Philip, 350n858
Huldah (prophetess), 159
King Huram, 136n557
Huram-Abi, 116, 136n557, 137, 198
Hushai the Archite, 132n507
Hybels, Bill, 352n867
King Hyram of Tyre, 196, 197

Immer, 129n479
Ira the Jairite, 125n454
Irenaeus, 179n44
Isaac, 265
Isaacson, Walter, 222n180
Isaiah, 49-50, 84n203, 147n626, 169, 271, 283n491, 305, 316-17, 345, 358
King Ish-baal, 132
Ishmael, 264
Ithamar, 237

Jabal, 103
King Jabin, 118
Jacob, 42, 57n17, 276-77, 301, 368
Jacob Marley, 10n35

Jael, 42n116, 118
Jairus, 194
Jakeh, 303n592
James, 24n112, 68, 84-87, 84n203, 86n218, 211, 211n117, 214, 229-31, 264, 288-89, 294
James, William, 257n352
Jehiel, 109n346
King Jehoiachin, 149, 161
Jehoiada, 123, 223n190
Jehoshaphat, 131, 286-87, 299n568, 343n821
Jehoshaphat (son of Ahilud), 123, 124
Jeiel, 141n590, 142n591
Jephthah, 119-20, 122, 323n717
Jeremiah, 84n203, 147n626, 159n710, 160, 226, 257n352, 272, 346, 358-60
Jeremias, Joachim, xxvin22
Jeroboam, 168, 224n191, 224n193, 225n202, 270-71, 339-41, 369, 370, 371, 374, 377, 380, 383, 384
Jerome, 199n53, 300, 300n574
Jesse, 283n488
Jesse of Bethlehem, 41n98
Jethro, 113n370, 237
Jezebel, 140, 146n626, 344
Joab, 123, 124, 131, 336, 337
Joanna (wife of Chuza), 6n17, 7n17
Joash, 223n190, 381
Job, 149n637, 230n230, 314
Jobs, Steve, xin6, 222n180
John, 24n112, 42n116, 68, 99-102, 189, 211, 214, 274, 293n532, 294, 347-48, 350, 353, 364-67
Johnson, David, 257n352
Johnson, Sharon, 235n250
Johnston, V. W., 20n84
Jonah, 43n117, 199-200, 199n53
Jonathan, 35, 36, 126n460, 281-82, 337
Jones, David Clyde, xvin24, 27n3, 257n352, 262n373, 333n773
Joseph, xvii, xxin4, xxivn9, 29, 32n34, 108-10, 109n346, 109n347, 110n349, 126n458, 130n482, 146n625, 157n693, 200, 220, 222n178, 265, 269n420,

(Joseph continued)
270, 277, 277n459, 299–301, 327n743, 332n769, 344n832, 370
Joseph (called Barnabas), 180, 348
Joseph (religious leader of Judah), 161n719
Joseph of Arimathea, 172–74
Josephus, 7n17, 28n8, 112, 112n366, 113n372, 302, 302n589, 381, 381n21
Joshua, 31–32, 117, 184n82, 237, 247–48, 299n568, 332n769, 335
Joshua the Levite, 163
King Josiah, 144–45, 158, 159, 159n710, 226–27, 338
Jubal, 103
Judah, 335
Judas, 179, 330

Kaiser, Walter, 53n185
Kant, Immanuel, xxvin20
Katzenstein, H. J., 158n703
Kendall, R. T., 219n151
Kepler, 295n543
Kirk, Russell, x–xii, xiin8, xiin9
Kirk, Thomas, 140n581
Kittel, Gerhard, 19n82
Kittler, Glenn, xvin23, 31n34, 83n194, 83n195, 351n865
Klein, George, 52n178
Kleinig, Vernon, 61n49
Knight, George A., 90n240
Knowling, 204n85
Koch, David, 209n107
Korda, Michael, 257n352
Kruger, David Delbert, 235n253

Lane, William, 330n758
Lasch, Christopher, xviin27
Lazarus (begger), 175
King Lemuel, 303n592
Lencioni, Patrick, 261n367
Lenski, R. C. H., 177n25, 204n86
LeTourneau, R. G., xivn20, 209n107, 329n751
Lewin, Kurt, 379–80, 379n15
Lewis, C. S., 3n12, 317n687

Lightfoot, J. B., xxxin39, 68, 68n89, 318n692
Likert, Rensis, 378, 378n12, 378n13, 383n28
Lindell, Mike, xivn20, 210n110
Locke, John, xxvin20
Longman, Tremper, 221n171
Lucas, Ernest, 150n643
Luke, xxii, xxiii, 190n117, 288, 292m522, 294, 367
Luther, Martin, 18n80
Lysias, 312, 312n658

Maaseiah, 142n591
Maccabees, 238
Malachi, 154n674
Maltz, Maxwell, 257n352
Manaen, 7n17
Manasseh, 340n798
Manton, 84n203
Marcuse, 60n43
Mark, 291, 292m522
Marks, Bailey, 352n867
Marks, Peter, 49n154
Marley, Jacob, 10n35
Marshall, Howard, 312n653
Marx, Karl, xxvi, xxvin20, xxvn20
Maslow, Abraham, 260n361, 383n28
Matthew [Levi], 2, 292m522
Matthias, xxiv
Mayer, Douglas, xin5, xiiin15
McGregor, Douglas, 383–84, 383n27
McKnight, Scot, 230n230
McLemore, Clinton W., xvin24, 257n352
Mead, George W., xin5
Meloon, Walt, 352n867
Meloons, 236n253
Menander, 94n255
Mephibosheth, 36, 126n460
Meshach, 147, 149, 153, 153n665, 154
Mettinger, Tryggve, 166n753
Meyer, Rudolf, 355n888, 356n888
Micah, 52–53, 84n203, 317–19
Micaiah, 158
Miles, Ray, 260n361
Miller, Julie, 236n254
Milligan, William, 189n114

Author Index

Milton, 317n687
Mintzberg, Henry, xxviiin30
Miriam, 42n116
Moisiman, S. K., 375n7
Montgomery, J. A., 146n625
Moo, Douglas, 86n214, 229n225, 262n373, 321n712
Moore, Russell, 22n104
Mordecai, 156–58, 168n771, 200, 201–2, 202n75, 269n422, 344n832, 346
Morgan, Marilyn A., xxviiin32, 377n10
Morris, Leon, 20n86, 25n113, 174n18, 213n125, 241n280
Moses, xvii, 27n1, 29, 30, 31, 42n116, 43n117, 62n58, 73, 75, 89n240, 110, 111–15, 112n364, 113n372, 114n376, 115n386, 117, 126n458, 141n590, 147n629, 172, 184n82, 198n42, 203n80, 225, 230n230, 235–37, 244–47, 246n304, 265–66, 268n413, 277–78, 288, 298, 315, 332, 332n769, 333, 334–35, 346n842, 354, 357, 370
Mott, Don, 351n865
Motyer, Alec, 79n176
Mounce, Robert, 189n113
Mounce, William, 363n924
Mouw, Richard, 384, 384n31, 390, 390n36
Murphy, Charles H., Jr., xin5, xiiin15
Murray, John, xxxn39, 55n6, 66n80, 320n710

Naamah the Amonitess, 371
Naaman, 43n117
Nabal, 34, 282, 283, 285
Naboth, 43n117, 146n626
Nahash, 36
Naomi, 38n70
Nash, Laura, xiv, xivn18, xviiin30
Nathan, 269n419
Nathan (David's son), 131
Nebo-Sarsekim, 146n624
Nebuchadnezzar, 145, 147, 147n628, 148, 150, 151, 151n653, 154, 159, 159n706, 159n712, 160, 169n773, 200, 202–3
Nehemiah, 147n626, 149, 154–56, 154n674, 155n680, 155n681, 156n685, 249–50, 299n568, 344n832
Nehmiah, 145
Nergal-Sharezer of Samgar, 146n624
Newsom, Carol, 150n644
Newton, 295n543
Nicanor, 176
Nicolas, 176, 179n44
Niebuhr, Richard, xxv, xxvn18, xxxn39
Noah, 28, 28n9, 28n11, 56n13, 87n225, 105–6, 149n637
North, Thomas, xin5, xiiin15
Nouwen, Henri, 25, 25n116, 26nn117–119

Obadiah, 139–41, 157n693, 200, 234, 344
Obil, 239n276
Odiorne, George, 383n28
Oehler, Gustaf, 374n6
King Og of Bashan, 132, 133
Oholiab, 116, 136n557
Onesimus, 185n86, 205n95, 390
Oreb, 278, 279
Origin, 273n442
Oswalt, John, 79n176

Parmenas, 176
Pashhur (son of Immer), 129n479
Paul, 3n10, 5, 10n39, 20n84, xxviin24, xxxin39, 41n106, 45, 54, 55–79, 68n90, 85, 87, 89n239, 89n240, 90n240, 92n254, 93n254, 94, 95, 101n298, 178n39, 180, 180n54, 181, 182–89, 185n86, 190, 191, 193, 202–7, 211n117, 214n130, 227–28, 236n254, 238, 240–42, 241n278, 250–54, 254n340, 262n373, 273–74, 273n442, 288, 289, 291, 297n561, 306–9, 312, 312n657, 320–30, 328n748, 347, 348n847, 351, 353, 361–63, 365n936, 389, 390

Paulus, Sergius, 7n17
Peale, Norman Vincent, 257n352
Penney, James Cash, 62n55, 197n33, 235n253
Peter, 18, 25, 26, 45, 57n18, 68, 68n94, 85, 86, 87–99, 89n239, 101n298, 173, 176–80, 179n45, 205n90, 240, 256–58, 290, 291, 293n532, 310, 310n642, 312n652, 324, 331, 347–48, 353, 363–64, 386
Peters, Thomas J., 85n205, 186n86
Philemon, 185n86, 214n130, 390
Philip, 19, 176, 179, 234n245
Phillips, J. B., 66n81
Phillips, John McCandlish, 351n865
Philo, 113n372, 172, 172n9, 229, 229n226
Phoebe, 190–91
Pilate, 170–72, 173, 327n743
Pindar, 312n658
Piper, John, 41n106
Plato, xii, 251n324
Plummer, William, 267n402, 302n586
Plutarch, xin5
Polhill, John, 179n44
Porcorus, 176
Porras, Jerry, ixn2, 12n43
Potiphar, 108, 109n346, 110, 110n349
Pratt, Richard, 144n613, 286n506
Pricilla, 189–90
Prior, David, 318n692
Priscilla, 190n117
Putnam, David, xxviiin31
Pyrrhus, 170n3

Queen of Sheba, 371

Raven, B. H., 377, 377n10
Rayburn, Robert, 291n520
Rebekah, 265
Reddin, W. J., 383n28
Redpath, Alan, 41n107, 156n688
Rehoboam, xix, 60n43, 123n441, 127, 128, 132, 135, 167–68, 250, 299n568, 305n607, 309n639, 368–91
Reierson, Gary B., 92n253
Reymond, Robert, 61, 61n50

Ridderbos, Herman, 2n5, 22n103
Rieff, Philip, xviin27
Ringer, Robert, 257n352
Robertson, A. T., 308n633
Robinson, George, 371, 371n1
Rollin, xxviiin30
Ross, Alexander, 99, 99n288
Ross, Allen, 292m522
Roswell, Penney, 235n253
Rousseau, Jean-Jacques, 79n177, 274n447
Rowlinson, George, 140n581
Rudin, Scott, 49n154
Rush, Myron, xivn20, 82n191, 208n107, 209n107, 352n867, 390, 390n35
Rushdoony, Rousas, 8n22, 22n102
Ryle, J. C., 18, 18n79

Samson, 42n116, 119, 323n717, 339n791
Samuel, 37n62, 73, 121–22, 121n423, 132n510, 196, 323n717, 332, 332n769, 354, 370
Sanderson, John W., 59n31
Sapphira, 180
Sarai, 107n337
Sasse, Hermann, 19n82
Satan, 24, 25, 57, 98, 353
King Saul, 32, 33, 35, 36, 43n117, 119, 124, 126n460, 129, 196, 279, 281, 282, 337
Saul/Paul, 181, 254
Schaeffer, Francis, 3, 3n13, 57, 57n20
Schmidt, K. L., xxxin39, xxxn39
Schmidt, Warren, 379, 379n14
Schnackenburg, Rudolf, 100n292
Schneider, Walter, 39n80, 65n73
Schrader, Ann, xiin13
Schreiner, Thomas, 65n76, 95n271
Schultz, Carl, 373, 373n4
Scott, J. B., 302n589
Scrooge, Ebenezer, 10n35
Selman, Martin, 343n828
Sendrey, Alfred, 122n429
Senior, Donald, xviin28, 182n70, 208n104, 262n373
King Sennacherib, xxin4, 169

Author Index

Seraiah, 123, 124, 124n448, 131
Shadrach, 147, 149, 153, 153n665, 154
Shalmaneser, 198
Shaphan, 158, 159, 159n706, 159n710
Shealtiel, 161n718, 242
Sheba, 369, 374
Shebna, 165, 166, 167, 168–69, 169n773, 169n775
Shemaiah, 73
Sheva, 124n448
Shimei, 109n346, 129n479
Shinn, George, xivn20, 257n352
Shisha, 124n448
Shisha (Seraiah), 131
King Shishak of Egypt, 371
King Sihon, 120
Silas, 202
Simeon, Charles, xivn17
Pharisee Simon, 2, 2n9
Simon (briber), 180
Simon Peter, 98, 232n239
Simonides, 312n658
Sinek, Simon, 21n94, xxixn33
Sisera, 42n116, 118
Sloan, Harold S., xxviiin32
Smedes, Lewis, 16n64, 80, 80n184, 81n185, 88n235
Smith, Adam, xii
Smith, David, 101n298, 234n245
Smith, Frank, 287n508
Smith, Gary, 169n776
Socrates, xii, 70, 95n263
Solomon, xxi, xxii, xxin4, 32n34, 41n97, 43n117, 45–49, 60n43, 123n441, 124, 125, 126n460, 127, 128–34, 128n474, 130n482, 133n518, 135, 136, 136n551, 136n557, 137, 138, 139, 145, 154n674, 169, 197–99, 197n36, 220–23, 221n171, 224n191, 226, 227, 228n218, 230, 239, 248–49, 265n393, 267–70, 271, 285, 286n505, 299n568, 303–4, 316, 323n717, 337–39, 341, 368, 369, 370, 371, 372, 373, 375, 376, 377, 378, 381, 388, 389
Spurgeon, Charles, 195n24, 302n586
Stanley, Arthur P., 140n581

Stearns, Richard, xin6, 10n38, 155n682, 253n329, 333n774, 334m774
Steele, Richard, xivn19
Stepansky, Robert, xiv, xivn18, 274n448
Stephen, 112, 176, 179, 240
Admiral Stockdale, James, 257n352, 258n352
Storms, Samuel, 169, 169n777
Stuart, Doug, 115n386

Tam, Stanley, 208n107, 209n107, 352n867
Tamar, 335
Tamasy, Robert, 352n867
Tannenbaum, Robert, 379, 379n14
Taphath (daugher of Solomon), 132
Tappan, Arthur, 235n253, 236n253
Tattenai, 161n719
Taylor, Frederick W., xxixn34
Tertullian, 179n44
Thielicke, Helmut, 2, 2n7, 18n80, 19n80, 20n84, 292m524
Thiessen, Henry C., 99n289
Emperor Tiberius, 171, 172
Timon, 176
Timothy, 55, 69, 73, 74, 75, 76, 77, 89n240, 90n240, 92n254, 254n340, 367
Titus, 90n240, 184, 184n85, 185
Torrance, Thomas, xxiiin8, xxxn39
Towner, Phillip, 73n137
Trench, Richard C., xxxin39, 86n219
Trueman, Carl, 78n173
Tubal-Cain, 103
Turgenev, Ivan, 79n177
Turner, David, 20n88, 21n88, 21n95

Uri, 133
Uriah the Hittite, 43
Uzziah (Azariah), 141–42, 141n590, 223–26, 223n184, 223n189, 223n190, 224n193, 224n194, 224n198, 225n201

Van Gemeren, 318n694
Vincent, Marvin R., 88n232

Vine, William, 310n641
Vischer, Phil, xxxn38, 202n78, 208n105, 252n327
Vitellius, Lucius, 172
Von Rad, Gerhard, 53n186

Wade, Marion E., xviin23, 31n34, 83n194, 83n195, 325n734, 351n865
Walters, Barbara, 209n107
Waltke, Bruce, 221n168
Walton, Sam, xvin21, 252n327
Wanamaker, John, 257n352
Warfield, Benjamin B., xxiv, xxivn12
Waterman, Robert H., 186n96
Watts, John, 50n162, 271n433
Waugh, Evelyn, 79n177
Webber, Ross A., xxviiin32, 377n10
West, John, 366n944
Westermann, Claus, 128n474
Whitcomb, John, 148, 148n631
White, William, xviiin29
Will, George, 381n20
Wilson, Lindsay, 339n790
Woelfel, James W., 18n80
Wright, N. T., xin6, 257n352, 262n373
Wroe, Ann, 170n2

Xenophan, 95n263

King Xerxes, 156, 157, 200, 202, 269n422

Yarbrough, Robert, 73, 73n139, 77n171, 101n307
Young, Edward J., 50n161, 79n176, 169n773, 272, 345n840
Yuki, Gary, 376, 376n8, 377n10, 379n14

Zabloski, Jim, 252n327
Zabud, 131
Zachariah, 21
Zadok, 123, 124, 124n445, 125, 128, 128n474, 131
Zebedee, 211
Zechariah, 21n96, 44n125, 52, 53n186, 142n591, 161, 223, 225
King Zedekiah, 159
Zeeb, 278, 279
Zerah, 335
Zerubbabel, 154n674, 160–65, 161n718, 161n719, 161n722, 161n723, 242, 264n385
Zeruiah, 123
Ziba (servant), 35, 36, 126n460
Ziglar, Zig, 257n352
Zillah, 103, 104
Zurcher, Arnold J., xxviiin32

Subject Index

Abednego, 147, 153, 153n665
Abigail, as peacemaking manager, 282–85
abilities of each employee, releasing, 253n329
ability, outweighing birthright, 221n171
Abimelech, 369
abolition, of sexual codes in their entirety, 78n173
Abraham, 107–8, 229, 244, 264–65
Absalom, 37n62, 43n117, 336, 337
abundance, 47, 220, 335–36
abuse, 312, 324
academics or pastors, without real marketplace experience, xv
accommodation
    between Jews and gentiles, 180
    using discerning spirit about, 58
    with the world, 57
accountability
    attached to individual stewardship, 252
    management with, 327n743
    managerial, 61
    between the organization and its members, 236
    showing no partiality, 236n254
accounting
    of employees, 60
    of managers, 61–62
    for the work of the coworker, 263
acculturating manager, 331–50
    Achan as, 335–36
    culture of an organization and, 338

David as, 336–37
in the Gospels, 332–34
Hebrews and, 348–50
Hezekiah as, 341
Isaiah as, 345
Jeroboam as, 339–41
Jesus as, 333–34
John as, 347–48
Mordecai as, 346
Moses as, 334–35
in the New Testament, 347–50
Obadiah as, 344
in the Old Testament, 334–46
Paul as, 347
Peter as, 347–48
providing direction and vision, 334
shaping the moral atmosphere, 340
Solomon as, 337–39
virtues and vices of, 339
acculturation, principle of, 332
Achan, as acculturating manager, 335–36
actions
    loving with, 101
    morally unacceptable becoming acceptable, 78
    of organizing and administration, 242
    reevaluating our own, 326
    speaking louder than words, 260n362
Adam, xxvin20, 22
administration, 82n191, 108n340, 241–42

423

administrative acts, as decisional, 60n43
administrative decisions, made by Moses, 114
administrative districts, of Solomon, 132
administrative functions, defining, 60n43
administrative managers, organized by David, 239
administrative victories, of Daniel, 147–48
administrators, David delegating and empowering, 38–39
admirable, whatever is, 72
Adoni-Jah, incompetent as a manager, 299n568
Adonijah, leader of the people during Nehemiah's governorship, 299n568
Adoni-kam, led a group of exiles back to Jerusalem, 299n568
Adoni-ram
 in charge of forced labor, 168n771
 continued to manage the forced labor, 132
 death of, 168n764
 dispatched to his death by Rehoboam, 168
 as manager, 123n441, 127–28, 299n568
Adoni-zedek, defeated by Joshua, 299n568
advisers, Rehoboam took advice of less qualitied, 168
agape, 77n163, 96, 97
agribusinessman, 173, 305
King Ahab, 43n117, 140, 140n581, 200, 344
Ahijah, 131, 271, 370
Ahikam, as manager, 158–59
Ahimaaz, 133
Ahimelech (Abiathar), 124
Ahimelech (son of Abiathar), 123
Ahinadab, 132
Ahishar, 132, 168n771
alcohol, not drinking too much, 262n373

Alexander, managing his organization, 39n77
the alien, leaving what remains for, 245
alienation, xxvin20
"alienation of labor," for the worker, xxvin20
"all Israel," no opposition or resistance from, 374
"all nations," "going" to be, 352
"all people," benefiting from one's lifestyle, 363
allurements, fleeing, 73
Amalekite raiding party, defeated by David, 125n457
ambiguity
 of Christian business managers, 100
 as critical in staffing, 206
 in the ministry of Jesus, 20
 as part of the environment, 1–2
 theology of, xxxn39
Ammonites, humiliation of David's mighty men, 36
Amos, as peacemaking manager, 287
Ananias/Sapphira situation, handled by Peter, 180
anarchy, 80n177
Anderson, Ray, 82, 390
angels, repudiating the worship of, xxxin39
anger, 97n279, 262n373
animal behavior, destroying everyone, 325
animal breeding, oversight of Solomon over, 138
animal kingdom, illustrating industrious workers, 46n132
animals, Noah managed the gathering of, 106
animosity, between Pilate and Herod, 171–72
anti-Marxist biblical defense, of the managerial class, xxvi
Apollos, Aquila and Pricilla hosted, 190
apostasy, of Rehoboam, 381

Subject Index

apostasy and idolatry, Rehoboam not preventing, 371
apostles, 193, 199n58, 291. *See also* disciples
"apostolic ministry," increasing the staff of, 177n24
appeasement, as advice, 372
appointing people, to carry on the work, 82n191
"appointment history," 237
appreciation, of the beautiful, 72
aqueduct, constructed by Pilate, 171
Aquila and Pricilla, as managers, 189–90
Aristotle, 75n151, 94n255
ark, Noah managed, 106
ark of the covenant, recovered by Samuel, 121, 121n427
army
 of Abraham, 107, 244
 equipped and organized by Uzziah, 141, 224
 of Roman occupation, 171
Arnold, Matthew, xiin12
art
 leadership as, 86n219
 management as, 42n112, 81
 of war, 302
art of the deal! by Abraham, 108
Artapanus, on Moses, 113n372
King Artaxerxes, 201
Asaph, 45, 195
ascendency, through lineage, 376
ascension, period of training of disciples prior to, 306
Ashpenaz, 146n624, 147n628
assembling together, exhorting Christians not to neglect, 348
attitude
 having same as that of Christ Jesus, 61
 towards our competition, 330
attributes
 certain present in each company colleague, 204
 of the Christian experience, 363
Augustine, 24
authorities

received wisdom of may not be the truth, 356
 submitting to, 273, 274
authority
 Jesus delineated lines of, 234
 Jesus marshaling his to protect his people, 353
 in a position and in a person, 235n252
 respect for proper, 126n458
Azariah, 131, 133
Azra, 168n771

Babylonian citizens, Daniel's fine reputation with, 148n631
Babylonian idols, food offered to, 152n653
bad company, leading to destruction, 339
bad employee, negative influence of, 338
bad ideas, morphing into bad company policy, 297
bad management, leading to worse management, 340
bad managerial motivation, example of, 250
bad planning managers, 226
bad teaching, leading to an unproductive career, 212
bad tree, cannot bear good fruit, 212
Balaam, 203n80
Balak king of Moab, 203n80
Barak, 118, 122
barbarism, as never finally defeated, 79n177
barbed wire, Rehoboam add to whips, 373–74
Barclay, William, 205n90
Barnabas
 hashing out differences, 288
 management activities of, 183
 as manager, 180–81
 as motivating manager, 254
Barnabas effect, 254
"barren externalism," 327n738
Barth, Karl, 3n13
Basemath, daughter of Solomon, 133

Bathsheba, wife of Uriah the Hittite, 43
Bedford, Bryan, xiin13
believers
  first state persecution of recorded in Scripture, 140
  impulse of a Christian manager to hire only, 202
  in management positions, 344n832
  working for an unbelieving boss, 141
belligerent-free, Christian life as, 363
Belloc, Hilaire, 79n177
Ben-Abinadab, 132
Benaiah, 124–25, 131, 131n502
benchmarks, for the Christian business manager, 50
"benevolent authoritative" system, of leadership, 378
Benjamin, loyalty of, 380
Bereans, on management, 54–55
Bezaleel, skillful artisan, 198
Bezalel, as manager, 116–17
biblical approach, to managing one's business, xxiv
biblical defense, of the managerial class, xxvi
biblical material, on business management, xxvii
biblical teaching, human rules and business customs overriding, 296
biblical way of life, embracing, 66
bitterness, 97n279
Blanchard, Ken, 381–82
blessing, 245, 320, 331
blind man leading a blind man, parable of, 292–93
boasting, about the God who saves, 64
Boaz, 38n70, 299n568
boldness, Mordecai a man of, 157
Bonhoeffer, Dietrich, 4n13, 102
books, on management and leadership, xxixn33
boss, 109n347, 140, 156
"Boss Centered Leadership," of Rehoboam, 379
brain, as a programmable computer, 257n352

Breton, Andre, 222n175
Bright, John, 372
"brotherhood," of a Christian manager and employee, 91
"brotherly kindness," as the penultimate virtue, 96
Browne, Paul C., xxviiin32
Buffet, Warren, xxxn38
Bulfinch, Thomas, xiiin16
Bulfinch's Mythology, author of, xiiin16
burglaries, happening when one least expects it, 214
burial plot, of Joseph of Arimathea, 174
Burkett, Larry, 352n867
Burnham, James, ixn1
Burns, James M., 380–81
business
  Christian self-help books on, 257n352
  conducting in a way adorning Christian convictions, 362
  operating at the pleasure of Yahweh, 30
business management, 8
business managers
  David's plea to be sent in against Goliath and, 33–34
  "discerning" and "wise" sleeping soundly, 48n151
  emulating the lifestyle of the Savior, 1
  God the Father patient with, 42n117
  having God's blessing, 49
  Jesus liked, ix
  Jesus loved, x, xxx
  Jesus on specific responsibilities of, 192
  on planning for the future, 230
  thinking about "doing the right thing," 15
business organization
  as a community formed around a mission, xxviii
  definite calling in the kingdom of God, 10

as not a family or a congregation of believers, 5n14
as a para-parochial organization, 83
business practices, 251, 307, 315
business transactions, 349n850
business world, moral and ethical dangers, 22
businessmen
 making money as their god, 352n867
 not equipped for intellectual and political leadership, x
 rejecting false teaching, 95
 without serious theological training, xv–xvi
Butt, Howard, 384, 389

cabinet, of Solomon, 129
Cain, 103–5, 108
Cain, Herman, 209n107
"callings," 205, 206
Calvin, John
 on God not taking his people out of the world, 356
 on God's image appearing in us, 100
 on the Gospels as brought by the hands of men, 361
 on he who wishes to live innocently, 79
 on the "Jacobian condition," 231n231
 on the obligation of a Christian in business, 10n35
 observation on, 94n256
 pastoral comfort for the foreordained manager, 213
 on Peter denying wickedness, 310n642
 on theology of vocation, 205
Campbell, John, xiiin16
Canaanites, hired by Solomon, 197, 198
"cannibalism in the marketplace," 325n734
"captain," of the temple guard in Acts, 128n474

career pattern of preparation, of managers, 60n43
careful life, living before a watching God, 53
Carroll, Pete, 349n857
Carson, D. A., 354n874
cash flows, discounting for quicker payment, 16
Cathy, S. Truett, xvn20, 236n253
causation, Paul noting the principle of, 228
cause-and-effect relationship, in God's economy, 210–11
Cavett, Dick, 325n730
Central Washington University, courses taught by the author, xii
centralized, authoritarian management, 383
"chamber of commerce supporter," Jesus as, x
character
 of the Christian business manager, 21
 connection between managers and employees, 340
 counting for a business manager, 327n743
 creating bad, 102n308
 of David the manager, 35
 defining for a Christian manager, 63–66
 described, 16n64
 example of persons of, 21–22
 found only in Paul's writings, 65
 hallmarks of quality, 39–40
 of Hoah, 28
 leading to hope, 65
 managers as people of, 287
 as a matter of obedience to God's law, 97–98
 as more important than skills, 97
 of Moses, 30–31
 Paul's definitions of Christian, 66
 Paul's testimony of his, 76
 producing hope, 64
 as a result of "working out one's salvation," 98
 of Timothy, 55, 73

character-building process, of refining fire, 66
charge, from Jesus to be in the world, 356
cheerleader, 254, 349
Chick-fil-A, closed on Sunday, 236n253
"chief of sinners," Paul as, 328n748
chief of staff, Azariah the manager as, 131
Christ. *See* Jesus
Christian(s)
  encouraging one another daily, 350n858
  following the pattern of their Lord, 100
  as "letters of recommendation from Christ," 61
  making yourself obvious as on the job, 351n865
  needing social connections in the world, 58
  receiving preferential treatment from each other, 101
  treating like family members, 5
Christian business managers
  characteristics of in Nehemiah, 155–56
  code of ethics for, 51
  companionship of non-believers and, 67
  company culture of love, 367
  knowing what is expected of them by the Lord, 251
  radah applying to, 62n58
  sagan applying to, 147n626
  "sent" by God, 112
  shepherding the workers, 40n93
  spurring one another on toward love and good deeds, 255
  urging coworkers to be constantly diligent, 13
  wandering away from a godly management practices, 79
Christian Business Men's Committee of the USA (CBMC), 352n867
Christian doctrine and morality, consideration of, 326–27n738

Christian literature (*studia divinitatis*), business managers of old schooled in, xiii
Christian managers
  advised to follow the pattern of Jesus, xxiv
  asking God to show favor on competitors, 331
  boasting in God's love, 64
  character transformation of, 67
  characteristics of, 12
  continuing to walk as Jesus did, 99
  guarding emotions and public sentiments, 337
  habit of acting Christian, xvii
  Jesus anointing, 4
  not having a life-long, continual obligation of care and responsibility, 6–7n14
  Peter calling to be courteous and respectful to all people, 92
  praying for the love of Christ to be manifested, 11
  speaking truth to coworkers, 71
  as vulnerable with an outstretched hand, 313
Christ-likeness, Christians character as, 67
A Christmas Carol (Dickens), 10n35
Chuza, managed the royal estate of Herod, 7n17
circumstances, patience with respect to, 77
cisterns, dug by Uzziah, 224
civil peace and tranquility, keeping, 333
clan leader-managers (*allups*), from Philistia joining Judah, 161n720
classical literature (*studia humanitatis*), business managers of old schooled in, xiii
clear conscience, 284
climate, Abraham setting for his organization, 108
clothes, of Dives, 175
clouds, having our heads in, 19
code of conduct, not going along with Nebuchadnezzar's, 154

Subject Index

code of ethics, Ezekiel providing a, 51
coercive power, 377, 378
command staff loyalty, within the organization of Jesus, 234
commandment, greatest in the Laws, 11
commerce, hand-to-hand combat of, xvii
commitment, 46, 383, 384
the "common people," 355–56n888
communication methodology, of Rehoboam, 250
communication needs, motivation from the manager meeting, 256–58
communion of the Holy Spirit, 59n31
community
  as a business organization, xxviiin31
  of faith, 5n14
  of man, 359
  management organized by David, 239
  managers promoting a sense, xxviii
"community specific," church as a parish as, 82n192
companions, selecting well, 339
companionship, 287
company life, David organizing, 239
company mission statement, workers buying in to, 256
compassion, of Dives as limited, 175
compassion to his competitors, of Hezekiah, 143
compensation for managers, standard from Samuel, 122
competing manager, 311–31
  David as, 315–16
  in the Gospels, 311–13
  Hebrews and, 330
  Isaiah as, 316–17
  Jesus as, 311–13
  Job as, 314
  Micah as, 317–19
  Moses as, 315
  in the New Testament, 319–31
  in the Old Testament, 314–19
  Paul as, 320–30
  Peter as, 331
  Solomon as, 316
competing neighbors, helping carry the burden of, 328
competition
  manager not to devalue, 328
  in market economies, 311
  no joy in the eradication of, 337
  in the private marketplace, 326
  striking out at, 281
competitive attitude, Isaiah defining limits to, 316
competitive boasting, Paul attempting to reduce, 326
competitive business manager, 284
competitive Christian managers, 323
competitive endeavor, bringing justice, mercy, and faithfulness to, 326
competitiveness, unfettered, 319, 320–23
competitors
  beating as enjoyable, 320n708
  doing what is right for, 322
  Job not rejoicing in the troubles besetting, 314
  looking for the good and positive qualities in, 329
  reasons for asking God to bless, 331
  rejoicing over the troubles of wicked, 314n666
  retribution and retaliation against, 86n218
  ruthless defined, 312–13
  treating with care, 316
  witnessing manager praying for, 360
compliment, of Paul as full of meaningful content, 253
compromises, trifling, 24n112
concessions, Rehoboam refused, 369
condescension
  of God, 20n84
  of Jesus, 18n80
connection power base, 377
conscience, 39, 273n442
construction
  Solomon excelled in, 135

(construction continued)
   Zerubbabel planning and recording, 162, 163
"consultative" management system, 378
contingencies, Abraham prepared for future, 244
continuance, persisting until the end, 83
continuing education, Jesus incarnational call for, 293
continuity, between followers and leaders, 387
continuum of leadership behavior (Tannenbaum and Schmidt), 379
contractors, Jesus comparing two, 213
conversation, tried by Jephthah, 120
copper coins, minted by Pilate, 172
Cornelius situation, handled by Peter, 180
corporate chieftains, humanely educated, xin5
corruption, Nehemiah drained the royal swamp of, 155
cost, counting before engaging in any project, 216
Council of Jerusalem, 240, 288–89
counsel
   Hezekiah took, 343
   need for, 388
court prophet, Zadok as, 124
"covenantal thinking" approach, to the marketplace, 311
coveting, tenth commandment against, 315
coworkers
   acculturating manager keeping tabs on, 349
   Bezalel taught, 116, 116n395
   buy-in sought by Hezekiah, 342
   calling their superiors "father," 308
   consistency in treatment of, 272
   "fair" and square treatment of, 63
   giving what they deserve, 274
   hidden emotions and aspirations of, 15
   loving, 11, 46
   manager's relationship with, 68
   needing to train, 263
   planning to accomplish but failing to implement, 219
   providing a place to hide from the outside storm, 345
   reciprocal obligation on the part of, 111
   Samuel establishing guilds for, 122
   strengthening, 98
   teaching to be subject to their managers, 307
   tending and loving as "the Chief Shepherd," 18
   training manager knowing, 293
   wanting the manager's affection but not his competence, 26
   warned not to plan evil, 220
Crane, Steve, 208n107
creation, came into existence from a divine plan, 214
Creator, ordained each worker in his right place, 204
Creator/Savior, Christian business manager imitating, 29
creditor, not permitted to go into the house of the debtor, 30
criminal class, in every nation, 79n177
crisis management, in the Old Testament, 135
"cultism," example of, 357n892
cultural involvement, 58
"cultural mandate," in the Old Testament, 62n58
culture, 331–32, 337, 343
cursing, 115n386, 320
customers, 15, 315
cybernetics, Christianized version of Maltz's, 257n352
Cyrus, as Yahweh's manager (*raah*), 40n93
Cyrus the Zoroastrian, Persian "hiring," 200

Daniel
   "asked" the "chief official" for a different diet, 150
   exceptional qualities of, 269n421

Subject Index

formal management training of, 148
as manager, 145–54
ran the day-to-day operations of the government, 152
as staffing manager, 200–201
third in Babylon, 157n693
trained in the learning of the Chaldeans, 147n629
King Darius of Persia, 148n631
David
  Abigail's counsel to, 283
  as acculturating manager, 336–37
  as competing manager, 315–16
  dignifying the offspring of his deadly enemy, 36
  equitable stance of for plunder distributions, 34
  as evaluating manager, 266–67
  exercised kindness and had his men's back, 36
  hired by Yahweh, 196
  Jonathan covenanting with, 282
  lamenting the death of Absalom, 337
  on management, 32–43
  as manager, 123–26
  managing the political apparatus of Israel, 37n62
  noted Yahweh's protection from barbarians, 79n177
  as organizing manager, 237–40
  as peacemaking manager, 279–81
  planning following the written instructions by, 227
  responding to his big brother, 280
  as a shepherd, 33
  as staffing manager, 196–97
  strong central administrative organization, 129
  as training manager, 301–3
  on the wicked freely strutting about, 78
Dayton, Ed, 390
deacons, Titus appointing, 185
Deborah, 118, 118n402, 122
deception, 101, 221

decision making, God providing wisdom and insight for, 201
deeds, eventually one is repaid for one's, 272
"defilement" issue, clearing up Daniel's, 149
delegation
  by Hezekiah, 143
  by Moses, 115
  understanding of, xxvii
descendants, of Cain, 104
details, "careful attention" to, 222
deus ex machina, viewing God as, xxxn39
"devoted things," Achan took it upon himself to steal, 336
dietary restrictions, not worrying about, 232
dignity and respect, treating every person with, 310
diligence, of Berean management, 54–55
diligent manager, following the plan, 220
diplomacy
  success of Gideon's, 279
  tried by Jephthah, 120
discerning manager, 9n33, 80–81
discernment
  as a character trait, 46
  coming from experience and practice, 45
  coming through "testing" and "trials," 85
  commended in Hebrews, 80
  of Daniel, 149, 153
  defined, 80
  demonstrated by Jesus the manager, 8–9
  of false teachers, 212
  helping Paul determine when to tell bad news, 59
  Jesus grew and improved in, 294
  lack in the dreamer, 222n178
  of Moses, 114
  of Nehemiah, 156
  Paul urging, 56–57
  Rehoboam failed to use, 250

(discernment continued)
  using to make the right decision, 58
disciples, 193, 233, 306. *See also* apostles
discretion, as an Old Testament character quality, 44n121
dishonest manager, commended for acting shrewdly, 15, 297
disorderly people, penalty of separation, 347
distribution of rewards and sanctions, requiring formally structures, 264n382
district offices, organized by Solomon, 130
districts, land in Judah not divided into, 133
Dives, as manager, 174–76
divine command, to love our enemies and do good to them, 324
divine endowments, three groups of, 68
divine grace, asking for, 331
divine practical gifts, of Bezalel, 116
divorce, Lord's instructions concerning, 333
doctoral dissertation, by the author, xv
dog-eat-dog atmosphere, true picture of, 325
double-mindedness, precluding, 211n117
"Dover Beach," 79n177
dreamer, the mind of, 222n175
driving forces, 379, 380
Drucker, Peter, xxix, xxiin5, xxxn38
dust, shaking free from, 232n238
"duty," to be loyal to God, 96

Early Christians, as a sect of the Jewish religion, 57
early decisions, of Rehoboam, 167–68
earthly life, imitating Christ's, xxiv
earthy authorities, moral responsibility to obey, 273
Ecclesiastes, 45–46, 47n148
economic enemy, being in love with, 330

economic murder, seeking, 319
economic power, using to destroy others, 317
Edom, 161n720
education, as critical for believers, 290
educational system, Cain's descendants creating the first, 105
Egeria, 240n277
Egyptian managers, Joseph training, 301
Elath, revolted under Jeroboam, 224n191
"elder managers," men as young as thirty called, 184n82
"elders," as older persons or an official position, 182n67
elders' advice, 372
Eleazar son of Aaron, 109n346, 115n386, 238
"elevating force," leadership as, 380–81
Eliab, 279, 280, 280n478
Eliahim, 168n771
Eliakim, as manager, 165–67
Eliezer of Damascus, 126n458, 264, 265
Elihoreph, son of Shisha (Seraiah), 131
Elijah, 140
Elizabeth and Zachariah, as righteous, 21–22
Elliott, Charles W., xin6
employees. *See also* workers
  all having respect of the manager, 89–90
  as divinely appointed, 207
  engaged in productive work, 46n132
  every business looking for good, 329
  expressing their gifts and graces, x
  giving an account of their labor, 60
  good management focused on service to, xxxi
  hiring the right, 193
  needing more than words to change behavior, 260

Subject Index

showing mercy and compassion to, 52
taking care of managers, 115n386
told to be alert and to watch, 13
treating as equal, 308
treating with love, 97
trustworthiness of, 69
employments in life for all persons, under God's sovereignty, 206
encouragement
　company culture fostering, 349–50
　giving to employees, 253, 339
end justifying the means, sin of, 25
endurance, 74, 77, 87
enemies, 77, 101n298, 311, 316
"enemy-occupied territory," world as, 3n12
Engstrom, Ted, 390
Enlows, on Correct Craft making 400 boats in 14 days, 236n253
Enoch, 28n11, 105
Ephesian managers, 186, 188
Ephraim, tribe of Jephthah responded to in peace, 120
Ephraimites, furious with Gideon, 278–79
error, arising from a ruler (*shatlar*), 146n625
Erza, as staffing manager, 201
Esau, 161n720, 276
Esther, 149, 157, 201–2, 346
ESTJ, Rehoboam as an, 386
ethic, of the Lord contradicting fallen human culture, 20n88
ethnic divisions, countering in society, 177
Etzioni, Amitai, 311
Eusebius, on Pilate, 171
evaluating manager, 258–74
　Abraham as, 264–65
　David as, 266–67
　in the Gospels, 258–64
　Isaiah as, 271
　Jeremiah as, 272
　Jeroboam as, 270–71
　Jesus as, 258–64
　John as, 274
　Moses as, 265–66
　in the New Testament, 273–74
　not responsible for the worker forever, 259
　in the Old Testament, 264–72
　Paul as, 272–74
　Pharaoh as, 265
　Solomon as, 267–70
evaluation, 260, 273
evangelical monasticism, as not the answer, 56
evangelical writings, superficial philosophies of wealth, xiv
evangelicals, responses to traditional moral conflicts, xviiin30
evangelism, 194, 361
Eve, xxviin20, 22
"everyday life," Paul on, xxviin24
evil
　feeding on itself and spawning greater evil, 323
　not repaying with evil, 321, 324n726, 331
　overcoming with good, 319, 322
　seeking public approval for doing, 78
evil companions, corrosive effect of, 67
evil competing manager, assaulting his competitor, 318
evil fighting warriors, not willing to share spoils of war, 34
evil persons, managers to beware of, 5
evildoers, not satisfied with the freedom to do evil, 78
excellence, seeking for, 72
executive ability or skill, to lead, 82n191
executive committee, appointed by Jesus, 234
executive management training program, of Paul, 187
executive team, Jesus hand-picked, 233
executive weekend retreat, example of a biblical, 387
executives, leading and encouraging branch offices, 85

Subject Index

exiles, told they will have grandchildren in Babylon, 360
expectations, of Paul as high, 228
experience
    attributes of Christian, 363
    as the schoolmistress of fools, xin5, xiiin15
expert opinion, disregarded by Rehoboam, 378
expert power base, based on expertise, skill, and knowledge, 377
experts, bad teachers presenting themselves as, 212
"exploitive authoritarian" management system, 378
external "testing," of persecution, 86
extrinsic reward path, 261
Extrovert (E) stylistic preference, 385
Ezekiel, on management, 50–52
Ezra, 123n438, 238

"fair" person, proper evaluation of, 142n595
fairness, laid down for all business managers, 306–7
faith
    in letters to Timothy, 74
    men of who were "managers of justice," 323n717
    of Paul, 76
    testing of producing steadfastness, 84
    as a virtue, 94–95
faithfulness, 69, 189, 336
faithlessness, Yahweh not always punishing, 267
false prophets, 212, 212n119
false teachers, 96, 101, 212n119
false theology, leading to a false life, 212
families, prominent following Jesus, 7n17
fantasies, 222, 222n176
the fatherless, leaving what remains for, 245
feasts and epicurean delights, Dives celebrating with, 175
Fee, Gordon, 241n278

feeding of thousands, 211n115, 234
Feeling (F) stylistic preference, 385
Felix, Marcus, 172
fellowship, 75
Fellowship of Companies for Christ (FCCI), 366n937
Fensham, F. C., 155n681
field managers, appointed by David, 239
"fight the good fight of faith," as an imperative for Timothy, 75
finances, Paul careful of, 188
financial corruption, as a disqualifier for being a judge, 266
fired manager, discounted the outstanding debts to his rich boss, 16
firing
    biblical example of, 196
    lazy workers, 259
first-hired workers, complained they were treated "unfairly," 7
"Five Whys," 176, 176n24
Flaubert, Gustave, 79n177
"flee," as an imperative for Timothy, 73
"focus," as [Steve Jobs] management mantra, 222n180
follower maturity, dimensions of, 382
followers, 77, 386, 387, 388
food, Noah managed, 106
fool, God's privilege to call somebody a, 219n151
foolish virgins, excluded from the celebration, 215
footnotes, in this book, xix
"Force Field Analysis," advanced by Kurt Lewin, 379
forced labor, Adoni-ram managed, 127
forces, types of in any given situation, 379
foreign workers, hired by Solomon, 198
foreordaining, by God, 220
forgiveness, of Joseph, 277
fortified towers, built by Uzziah, 224
Fraser, Donald, 326n738

Subject Index

freedom, 206
Frey, Donald N., xin5
"friend," synonym for "chief advisor" in Hebrew, 132
friends, of Daniel, 148
friendship-selling, as the setting-the-stage promotion, 232
fruit, recognizing by, 212
"fruit of the Spirit," 59
"fruits of the spirit" portion, of Galatians 5, 68
functions, comprising a management paradigm, xxix
future, 143, 208, 230–31, 360
future change, organizing manager managing for, 240

Galatian manager, being like Christ, 67
gathering together, harmony and unity strengthened by, 349
Gedaliah, 159–60, 160n714
"generalists," denial of conflicting impulses, xviiin30
generations, organic unity in, 229
generosity
 of Hezekiah, 143
 of Moses, 111
 of Nehemiah, 155
"gentleness," as an imperative for Timothy, 75
Gideon, 118–19, 122, 278–79
gift, management as, 9
The Gift of Administration (Senior), on "institutional" management, 262n373
gift of helps, preceding the gifts of management, 241n278
gifts of leadership, *sigenin* having, 147n626
gifts of management, 241n278
Gilead, father of Jephthah, 119
gleaning commands, given by Moses, 245
glory, Barak not seeking, 118
goal(s). *See also* objectives
 accomplishment of, 255
 of all Christians, 67

as a force for motivation, 349
Nehemiah set, 156
organizing manager and, 236n253
Paul pursuing, 227
social costs of, 211
unswerving directedness towards a, 267
working in light of coming, 350
God
 allotting specific people to manage, 204
 brought the Babylonians to Judah, 144
 commanded David to manage, 40n93
 as constantly evaluating, 266
 Daniel remaining loyal to, 150n643
 gave the Israelites favor in the eyes of the Egyptians, 113n369
 giving Christians an example of a holy life, 99n289
 glorified by our obedience to his commands, 364
 interest in the stewardship of the manager's responsibilities, 92
 love of, 267
 Nehemiah's commitment to the word of, 156
 as the origin of all authority, 126n458
 people of, 113
 as a planning God, 220
 positioning his people under Paul and Silas, 203
 revealing Himself in Christ, xxv
 seeking guidance from, 208n107
 on who gains power, 195
 wrath of, 322
God Owns My Business (Tam), 209n107
Godliness, 74, 96, 97
godly character, 50, 262–63n373
godly king, called to administer God's will, 384–85
godly management, 88
godly manager, told four things by Zechariah, 52

"God's emergency man," Samuel as, 122
going "into the world," drawing attention for Dietrich Bonhoeffer, 102
"Golden Rule," 62, 313
Goliath, David using of the sword of, 125
good
  doing to everyone, 330
  Micah defining, 52–53
good breeding, characteristics of, 54–55
"good deeds," applying to the business operation, 255
good job, persevering in doing, 350
"good judgment," required by Peter's management team, 179
good news of the gospel, sharing with neighbors, 361
good Samaritan, parable of, 5n14
good shepherd, laying down his life for the sheep, 17
good things, doing for "all people," 5
good tree, cannot bear bad fruit, 212
good will of God, bestowed on Christian managers, 207
good works, 189, 260n361, 350
goodness, 69, 95
Gospels
  acculturating manager in, 332–34
  competing manager in, 311–13
  evaluating manager in, 258–64
  Jesus on management in, 1–26
  motivating manager in, 243
  organizing manager in, 231–35
  peacemaking manager in, 275–76
  planning manager in, 210–19
  staffing manager in, 193–95
  training manager in, 290–98
  witnessing manager in, 351–56
governmental advisors, surrounding David, 239
"grace of continuance," insistence on, 83
"Great Commission," of Jesus, 351
"Mr. Great-Heart," 25n114
greed, making the sin of the miser so hateful, 318n692

greedy, not being, 263n373
Greek-speaking employees, in the minority, 178
Greek-speaking men, appointing seven, 178
Greenleaf, Robert, xxxi, 385
grudges, not harboring against co-workers, 111
guilds, for secular musicians, 122n429
the guilty, 268, 271

Haggai, 161
Halewood, William, 80
Haman, 156, 158
Hamann, J. G., 307
Hammurabi, called "shepherd," 40n93
hands-on managers, 177, 286
"Hanoi Hilton," 258n352
hardness of heart, causing unfaithfulness, 333
harem of foreign women, Solomon's blind spot for, 338
"harm," 283–84
harmony, 276, 289, 321
"Harvard Classics," in fifty-one books, xin6
"health and wealth" gospel, xvin22
healthy environment, creating in an organization, 307
healthy work environments, 290
hearts of men, as in the hand of God, 207n99
heavenly Father, patterning your live after, 21
Hebrew herdsmen, Egyptian pharaoh requesting the services of, 265n393
Hebrews
  acculturating manager and, 348–50
  competing manager and, 330
  on management, 80–84
  motivating manager and, 255
  planning manager and, 228–29
  training manager and, 309–10
helmsman, importance of, 241n278
Hendricksen, William, 328n748
Hermas the Shepherd, 348n850

Subject Index

Herod, as an acculturating manager, 334
Hersey, Paul, on situational leadership, 381–82
Herzberg, Frederick, 260n361
Hezekiah, 142–44, 341, 381
high priest, xxiiin8, 171
Hodge, Charles, 55, 207n99, 291
Hodgkinson, Christopher, 60n43, 199n58
hokma man, wisdom displayed by, 133–34
Holy Spirit, 59, 102, 208n107
Homer, singers of, 122n429
honest men, Josiah hiring as purchasing agents, 145
honor, rendering to all, 310n642
hope, 65, 66
hostile community, creating a model organization within, 359
hostile environment, managers sent into, 4
hostility, 284, 325, 378
"house of Judah," versus the "house of Israel," 376
Huldah the prophetess, 159
human beings
　cannot exalt ourselves, 195
　as different from all other creation, 3
human relations model, 260n361
human resource model, 260n361
humanitarian concern, of the Christian business manager, 30
humanitas, American businessmen no longer knew the arts of, xi
humankind, Jesus' solidarity with, 355
humility, as a character trait, 47
King Huram, 136n557
Huram-Abi, 116, 136n557, 198

identification, of Jesus with the human situation, 330
idolatry, of marketplace success, 22
idols, eating food sacrificed to, 57, 58
image of God, our true nature defined by our bearing the, xii
impartiality, of God, 63

improvement, seeking constant, 12n43
In Search of Excellence: Lessons from America's Best-Run Companies (Peters and Waterman), 186n96
incarnation, 20n84, 61
incarnational lifestyle, imitation of, xxiv
incarnational love, 11, 101n298
incompetent manager, 15–16, 17
incrementalism, Zerubbabel practiced, 162
individual workers, flourishing of under Eliakim, 166
individuals
　God using, 285
　treating with freedom and respect, 329
information power base, 377
inheritance, turning our thoughts to our, 213
innocence, of the Christian manager, 5
innocent, condemning, 271
"inquiring" of God, before decisions are made, 208n107
integrity
　of Abraham, 107
　of Ahikam, 158
　as a character trait, 47
　of the Christian business manager, 21
　corporate, 155n682
　as the goal for the business manager, 87
　of Nehemiah, 155
　organizing requiring, xxxn38
　showing under duress and unfairness, 312
　types of, 155n682
intelligence, Mordecai a man of, 158
The Intemperate Professor (Kirk), x
internal motivation, 273
internal promotion, by Peter's management team, 178
"internship" period, of Jesus, 294
interpersonal relations, management of in an organization, 190

intransigence, temptation to recant of, 154
Introvert (I) stylistic preference, 385
intruders, plan for safety against, 214
Intuition (N) stylistic preference, 385
irascibility, as senseless, 97n279
iron scepter, ruling the nations with, 353
Isaiah
    as acculturating manager, 345
    as competing manager, 316–17
    as evaluating manager, 271
    on management, 49–50
    as training manager, 305
    as witnessing manager, 358
Israel, Obadiah not able to change the culture of, 344
Israelites
    able but unwilling to follow Rehoboam, 382
    angered by onerous civic obligations, 370
    dissatisfaction over Solomon's forced labor and taxation policies, 380
    having no "ownership" of the kingdom of Rehoboam, 389–90
    under Jeroboam as selective in their recollections, 371
    plundered the Egyptians, 298
    rejected ownership and responsibility for David's kingly rule and tradition, 374–75
    response to Rehoboam's harsh answer, 384
Ithamar managers, gifts in temple management, 238

Jacob, pursuing peace with Esau, 276
Jacob Marley, on the ocean of business, 10n35
"Jacobian condition," "If it is the Lord's will," 231
Jael, Sisera killed by, 118
James, 84–87, 229–31, 288–89
James, William, 257n352
King Jehoiachin, 149, 161
Jehoiada, 223n190
Jehoshaphat, 123, 124, 286–87
Jehovah, 140, 214
Jephthah, 119–20, 122
Jeremiah
    Ahikam protected, 158
    commitment to Babylonian peace and stability, 159
    as evaluating manager, 272
    on habitual thinking, 257n352
    as planning manager, 226
    as witnessing manager, 358–60
Jeroboam
    as acculturating manager, 339–41
    in charge of public works projects, 370
    as evaluating manager, 270–71
    Israelites crowned as their monarch, 369
    led the Israelites back to Rehoboam, 374
    met the prophet Ahijah, 370
    personal and not positional power, 377
"Jeroboam Factor," in organizational conflict, 386–87
Jerome, on Jonah, 199n53
Jerusalem
    attacked and destroyed because of cast lots, 202
    bowed to godless power and cared for their own interest, 334n775
    Nehemiah rebuilt the wall of, 155
    Nehemiah seeking to restore the glory of, 249
    opposition to the coming Messiah, 334
    planning points in Jesus lamenting over, 216
    repaired and fortified by Uzziah, 141
Jerusalem Council, on Barnabas, 180–81
Jesus
    as acculturating manager, 333–34
    as always available and ready to receive miraculous intervention, 211
    as chief manager, xxiv

Subject Index

commanding us to live among our neighbors, 354
as competing manager, 311–13
continued submission to the Father's will, 294
"enfleshing" himself, xxii–xxiii
as evaluating manager, 258–64
on everything as possible, 257n352
final evaluating word from, 274
finding here in the world, 19
having Scriptures memorized, 24
as history's perfect manager, xxii
humanity's "mannishness" in, 3
as the ideal example, 1
on management in the New Testament, 54–102
as motivating manager, 243
not spurning socializing with anyone, 2–3
as organizing manager, 231–35
as patient with all, 69
Paul's love for, 76
as peacemaking manager, 275–76
as planning manager, 210–19
praying to protect from "the evil one," 356
presence in the world necessary, 19n82
promising persecution, 77
on selected managers in the New Testament, 170–91
on selected managers in the Old Testament, 103–69
on specific responsibilities of a business manager, 192
spoke in parables as a storyteller, xxvi–xxvii
as staffing manager, 193–95
susceptible to all the temptations, 330n758
taught us how to successfully manage a business, ix
took upon himself our humanity, 18n80
as training manager, 290–98
truth of his life, 365
as witnessing manager, 351–56

Jethro, as consultant to Moses, 113n370
Jewish church, bigotry of, 6n14
Jewish rebels, assassinated Gedaliah, 160
Jews, hated Pilate, 172
Jezebel, 140, 146n626
Joab, 123, 124
Joash, having a wise counsellor, 223n190
Job, as competing manager, 314
job description and responsibilities of each coworker, under the control of God, 204
job maturity (ability), of followers, 382
John, 99–102, 274, 347–48, 364–67
Jonah, 43n117, 199–200
Jonathan, as peacemaking manager, 281–82
Joseph
  earned the respect of Pharaoh, 299–300, 299n568
  on management, 29
  as manager, 108–10
  as peacemaking manager, 277
  as second in Egypt, 157n693
  seeking reconciliation with his brothers, 277
  should have kept his dream to himself, 222n178
  as a sovereign administrator, 146n625
  as a supreme example of a successful manager, 110
  teaching through lifestyle as well as words, xxivn9
  as training manager, 299–301
  wisdom (*Sophia*) of, 327n743
Joseph (earthly father of Jesus), Jesus' years of training under, 294
Joseph of Arimathea, as manager, 172–74
Josephus, 113n372, 381
Joshua, 31–32, 117, 247–48
Joshua the Levite, 163
Josiah, 144–45, 159, 226–27
Jotham, 168n771

Subject Index

Judah, 380, 384
Judaism, scribes sought to preserve, 292n522
Judas Iscariot, replacement discussion for, xxiii
Judeans, in the south stayed loyal, 375
Judging (J) stylistic preference, 385
judgment, of Jesus on the non-excellent worker, 259
"just" and "fair" treatment, with "a sincere heart," 63
just workplace, managing, 52
justice
    in correctly evaluating workers, 268
    David administering, 124
    giving back to each coworker what is due him, 53
    human judge dispensing true, 126n459
    managed or administered to communities, 323n717
    only God dealing out lasting, 284
justification, is of God, 230n230
"justifiers," denial of conflicting impulses, xviiin30

Kant, Immanuel, xxvin20
kenosis passage, love characterized by, 88n235
key performance indicators ("KPIs"), gauging performance over time, 267
kind manager, David as, 42
kindness, managers showing towards their workers, 69
king of Assyria, invaded and deported the Israelites to Assyria, 340–41
king of Babylon, serving, 359n908
King of Wall Street (Bay), 25n114
Kingdom Advisors, bankruptcy counseling for Christian business people, 236n253
kingdom of God, 83, 208
kingdom of heaven, being citizens of as mattering most, 71
kings
    example of international relations between two, 136
    forced to make a tough decision by making a plan, 217
    list of the managers of the business of, 37n62
    Obadiah as manager of the palace, 139
1 Kings 12 management lessons, brief application of, 386–91
1 Kings 12:1-20, exegesis of, 368–76
Kirk, Russell, x–xi
knowledge, 95, 383
Koch brothers, "good works" done by, 209n107

labor pool, acquired by Solomon, 136
"labor theory of value," xxvin20
lack of faithfulness, spreading to others, 336
Lamb of God, seeing Jesus primarily as, 1
language of the manager, killing or to giving life, 339
laughingstock, being in Jesus' day, 216n142
law
    knowing the application of, 266
    looking behind, 21
laws and regulations, inscribing, 123n438
Lazarus, Dives and, 175
"leader" (*shaphat*), Deborah called a, 118n402
leader-follower relationship, discussion of, 386
leaders
    adapting style of leadership, 382
    elevation of new, 387
    encouraging participation by followers, 389–90
    leading to serve, 384
    listening to followers, 388–89
    needing follower confirmation of, 386–87
    obeying, 81
    qualifications for given to Titus by Paul, 185
    serving fellow, 390–91

Subject Index

setting the tone for the organization, xxxn38
testing of by Ephesian organization, 189
leadership
  as an art, 86n219
  categories of behavior, 382
  compared to managing people, xviii
  effect of old age on, 246
  gift of, 92n254
  "humanely" educated people fit for, xii
  Joseph as a teacher of, 300
  like streams of water in an arid desert, 345
  managers given the recognition of, 238
  needing reflective time away from decisions, 387
  not always in ecclesiastical contexts, 93n254
  of Peter's management team, 179
  of Solomon, 136–37
  wisdom required in good, 130n482
  Yahweh establishing and sustaining, 195
learning, Daniel's aptitude for, 147
leaven, metaphor of the influence of, 296–97
leaving behind, reminding that land and produce belong to Yahweh, 245
legal precedents, managers needing to know, 266
legitimate power base, 377, 378
Lencioni, Patrick, 261n367
lending, graciously advised by Moses, 111
Lenski, R. C. H., 204n86
lessons, for the peacemaking manager, 276–77
lethargy, result of as ruin and "destruction," 268
LeTourneau, R. G., 209n107, 329n751
Levites, building of the house of Yahweh, 163n736
Levitical family, of Eleazar, 238

liberty, not harming or injuring anyone, 310n642
life
  ambiguity and uncertainty of, 230
  Christian, 4n13, 189
  of virtue, 94
life-and-death authority, of Pilate, 171
lifestyle
  of ambiguity, xxv
  of the Christian manager, 21
  exhortation about from Paul, 67
  God the Son set the example, 59n31
  one unified to all people, 211n117
  of Paul, 76, 187
"light of the world," being, 354
Lightfoot, J.B., 68
Likert, Rensis, 378–79
limitations, Solomon knew his, 136
limited liability, in the parable of the good Samaritan, 5n14
Lindell, Mike, xvn20, 210n110
line of authority, establishing and maintaining, 235
listening, biblical definition of, 388–89
lives, laying down for our brothers, 100
local church, as a community of people, 82n192
local helps, temptation to accept as, 164
long-range planning, Jesus believed in, 210
longsuffering, 68, 84n203
Lord of the Marketplace (Rush), 352n867
"lots," God sovereignly working with, 199–200, 202
love
  allowing for self-sacrifice, 88n235
  coming from God, 88n235
  of coworkers, 46
  definition of, 88n235
  given to Paul by the Holy Spirit, 77
  as the last virtue listed by Peter, 96
  in letters to Timothy, 74

(love continued)
   for those managed as well as competitors, 11, 324
   treating coworkers with, 350
   without Jesus as hollow and a lie, 100
   yoke of binding us to our fellows, 49n155
lovely, whatever is, 72
low position, associating with people of, 321
loyalty
   of Daniel to his boss, 152
   display of company, 196
   to the organization, 96, 235
   within a business organization as a two-way street, 236n253
Lysias, on doing harm to one's enemies, 312

"malicious accusation," of treason, 153
"man of God," Paul calling Timothy, 73
man of principle, Mordecai as, 157
"a man of standing," of the administrative class of individuals, 38n70
management
   as an art, 82n191
   author's understanding of, xvii–xviii
   Bereans on, 54–55
   biblical description of good, xxi
   changing hands to Joshua from Moses, 246
   David on, 32–43
   dealing with the normal stresses of, xiii–xiv
   defining, xxviii, xxviiin32, 82n191, 391
   as described by Peter, 92
   essential in a business endeavor, 194
   etymology of the word, xxvii
   as an example of "faith" in Yahweh, 323n717
   Ezekiel on, 50–52
   as first task-oriented and secondarily definitional, xxix
   as a gift, 9
   gifts of, 241n278
   goal of all good, xxi–xxii
   good outcomes for, xxii
   Hebrews on, 80–84
   Isaiah on, 49–50
   James on, 84–87
   Jesus on in the Gospels, 1–26
   Jesus on in the Old Testament, 27–53
   John on, 99–102
   Joseph on, 29
   Joshua on, 31–32
   as a long-term, continual process, 309
   Micah on, 52
   Moses on, 29–31
   Noah on, 27–28
   over all material goods of a master, 126n458
   Paul on, 55–79
   Peter on, 87–99
   in the plan of God from the very beginning, 213
   psalmist on, 44–45
   Rehoboam fails to exercise responsible, 369–76
   seeking a better understanding of the "science" of, 307n620
   Solomon on, 45–49
   Zechariah on, 52
management ability, as one of the gifts of the Holy Spirit, 42n112, 82n191
management activities
   of Josiah, 144–45
   of Nehemiah, 155
   of Paul and Barnabas, 183
management advice, given by Solomon, 134
management approach, of Barnabas, 181
management authority, 179, 269
"management by objectives" (MBO) management system, core beliefs of, 383–84
management by wandering around ("MBWA"), 186, 186n96

Subject Index 443

management decisions
  made by Pilate, 170, 171
  of Obadiah, 140
management effectiveness, of the Ephesian overseer/managers, 188–89
management issues, faced by Jesus, x
management lessons
  from the administration of Zerubbabel, 162–65
  from Adoni-ram, 127
  from Barak, 118
  from Eliakim, 166–67
  from Jeremiah, 359–60
management points, Petrine, 177–80
management principles, from Joseph of Arimathea, 173–74
management qualities, of Gideon, 119
management skills
  evidenced by Solomon and by Joseph, xxin4
  ignorance as no excuse or protection for a Christian, 263–64
  of Peter's management team, 179
  Scripture stressing, 93n254
management style, of Barnabas, 180
management systems, of Rensis Likert, 378–79
management theories, modern, 376
management tips, for the peacemaking manager, 280
management training
  of David, 302
  of Joseph, 110
management training regimen, of Joseph for Egyptian workers, 299
management traits, of Mordecai, 157–58
management-labor relations, parable of, 7
manager(s). *See also* acculturating manager; business managers; Christian business managers; Christian managers; competing manager; evaluating manager; motivating manager; organizing manager; peacemaking manager(s); planning manager; staffing manager; training manager; witnessing manager
  Abraham as, 107–8
  accountable to the owner, 61–62
  accused of malfeasance or mismanagement, 16
  administrative tasks of, xxiin5
  Adoni-ram as, 127–28
  Ahikam as, 158–59
  applying truth and love to complexities, 81
  appointed by Jehoshaphat, 286
  Aquila as, 189–90
  Barak as, 118
  Barnabas as, 180–81
  Bezalel as, 116–17
  biblical providing management lessons, 103
  "bourgeoisie," xxvin20
  Cain as, 103–5
  of character, qualities of, 44
  criteria for all, 263
  Daniel as, 145–54
  David as, 123–26
  David chose excellent, 238
  Dives as, 174–76
  effective, xxxi
  Eliakim as, 165–67
  expecting to be persecuted and suffer, 77
  free from constraints, 91
  Gedaliah as, 159–60
  Gideon as, 118–19
  Hezekiah as, 142–44
  hiring the unemployed, 7
  Jephthah as, 119–20
  Jesus loved, xxx
  Joseph as, 108–10
  Joseph of Arimathea as, 172–74
  Joshua as, 117
  Josiah as, 144–45
  Mordecai as, 156–58
  Moses as, 111–15
  needing to be teachable and not quarrelsome, 308
  Nehemiah as, 154–56
  as a new ruling class, ixn1

(manager continued)
  New Testament company followed the Old Testament company in organizing around, 7n17
  New Testament examples of non-patient, 68
  Noah as, 105–6
  not taking advantage of the managed, 89n239
  Obadiah as, 139–41
  over the tribes of Israel, 37n62
  Paul as, 182–89, 306
  Peter as, 176–80
  Phoebe as, 190–91
  Pilate as, 170–72
  Pricilla as, 189–90
  providing the right atmosphere, xxviii
  qualifications for those selected by Moses, 266
  Rehoboam as, 167–68
  as representatives of the whole people, 184n82
  reprograming through a lifelong struggle of obedience, 67
  responsibilities in an organization, 209n108
  roles of the modern, xxviiin30
  sagan, 146n626
  Samuel as, 121–22
  sensing into the marketplace, 4
  setting the tone for the organization, 345
  Shebna as, 168–69
  Solomon as, 128–39
  taking pleasure in other's victories, 321
  temptations as part of the life of, 98
  types of, 60n43
  Uzziah as, 141–42
  walking by faith, 56
  wanting to do something spectacular, 26
  watching over their coworkers, 81
  Zerubbabel as, 160–65
manager development program, conducted by Paul, 187

managerial accomplishments, of Solomon, 137–38
managerial actions, of David, 239
managerial acumen, in the midst of evil, 4–5
managerial authority, of Paul over Titus, 185–86
managerial creativity, extent of Solomon's, 138
managerial discernment, manager's prayer for, 45
managerial duties, under the power of the Spirit and Scripture guidance, 97
managerial effectiveness, of Solomon, 128–29
managerial impatience, in the Old Testament, 43n117
managerial patience, with respect to people, 76
managerial philosophy of Paul, qualities of, 76–77
managerial practices, all benefiting from good, 93n254
managerial responsibilities, 239–40, 275
The Managerial Revolution (Burnham), ixn1
managerial staff, Solomon's key, 130
managerial team, for David, 124
managerial training, of Solomon, 135
manager-shepherd, watching and guarding coworkers, 41
man-made idol, temptation to "bow down and worship," 153
"mannishness of man," created in God's image, 3
Marcuse, Herbert, 60n43
marketplace
  being missionaries in, 352n867
  constant pressure not to eat "gentile" food, 57
  God mitigating damages, 330
  idolatry of success, 22
  managing as a ministerial function, 10
  problem with exodus from, 326–27
  "religious" approach to, xxxn39

Subject Index

set of punishments for failure, xvii
viability as temptation, 325
Marks, Bailey, 352n867
marriage, as a sacred institution, 333
Marx, xxv–xxvin20, xxvi
Marxism, business antidote to a recurrent, xxv–xxvi
Maslow, Abraham, 260n361
master builder, assigning tasks to, 59–60
material loss, obedience to the word of God causing, 25
Matthew's [Levi's] house, Jesus having dinner at, 2
Matthias, continuity of exposure to Jesus, xxiv
maturation process, from testing to perseverance, 85
maturity
　in Christian character, 87
　in situational leadership, 381–82
"MBWA," 186, 186n96
McGregor, Douglas, on Theory Y, 383–84
Mead, George W., II, xin5
meat, purchasing in the market, 57–58
mediating situation, peacemaking manager in, 275–76
mediating skills, of Barnabas, 180
mediation, 276, 278
meekness, in dealing with coworkers, 70
Meloon family business, 236n253
Menander, on virtues, 94n255
mental images, succeeding through, 257n352
Mephibosheth, 36, 126n460
"mercy," loving, 53
Meshach, 147, 153, 153n665
messianic kingdom, management results of, xxii
metallurgy, one of Cain's descendants created, 104
Micah, 52, 317–19
"mighty men," of David, 196
"mighty" men (*gibbor*), also "substantial" or "honored" men, 37n62

Miles, Ray, 260n361
military managers, organized by David, 239
minds, preparing for action, 353
mindset, having the same as Jesus, 61
mines, dug by Solomon for silver and gold, 138
ministering, to high officials, 109n347
ministry, of Jesus as concealed, xxv
mission, 164, 235n251, 252
mistreatment, at the hands of the competitors, 312
modesty, required in business practices, xxv
money, 16, 82
moral compass, a Christian manager's internal, 68
moral courage, under duress and unfairness, 312
moral deterioration, effect of King Solomon's, 338
moral perversion, ethical rightness and, 271
moral restraint, combining with endurance and steadfastness, 96n269
Mordecai, 156–58, 201–2, 269n422, 346
Morgan, Marilyn A., xxviiin32
Moses
　as acculturating manager, 334–35
　adjudicated difficult cases himself, 115
　as competing manager, 315
　cultural agreement getting more specific with, 332
　as evaluating manager, 265–66
　highly regarded by Egyptian officials, 113
　on how to treat people in general, 115n386
　lack of self-control, 43n117
　led God's people to plunder the Egyptians, 112–13
　on management, 29–31
　as manager, 111–15
　as motivating manager, 244–47

(Moses continued)
  needed wise advice of an outsider, 113
  as organizing manager, 235–37
  as peacemaking manager, 277–78
  permitting divorce prohibited by Yahweh, 333
  sent by Yahweh as manager and deliverer, 112
  setting the cultural framework, 334–35
  on showing loyalty, 357
  as training manager, 298
  as witnessing manager, 357
motivating manager, 242–58
  Abraham as, 244
  Barnabas as, 254
  in the Gospels, 243
  Hebrews and, 255
  Jesus as, 243
  Joshua as, 247–48
  Moses as, 244–47
  Nehemiah as, 249–50
  in the New Testament, 250–58
  in the Old Testament, 244–50
  Paul as, 250–54
  Peter as, 256–58
  Rehoboam as, 250
  Solomon as, 248–49
motivation, 244, 256
motivational writers, on Morgan Vincent Peale, 257n352
motivation/evaluation, coming from within, 273
motivator, Nehemiah as, 156
mourning, 320–21, 337
Mouw, Richard, 390
moving on, in obedience towards the goal, 245
Murphy, Charles H., Jr., xin5, xiiin15
Murray, John, xxxn39
mutual service, Paul stressing the concept of, 63
Myers-Briggs Type Indicator (MBTI), 385

"Naamah the Ammonitess," Rehoboam's Canaanite mother, 371

Naaman, impatience of, 43n117
Nabal, refusing to help David, 283
Nash, Laura, xiv
natural resources, aggressive management of, 138
Nebo-Sarsekim, a chief officer, 146n624
Nebuchadnezzar
  appointed Gedaliah governor of Judah, 159
  Daniel as manager of, 145
  hiring Daniel, 200
  killed many of the Judean managers, 159n712
  as staffing manager, 202–3
  volcanic and mercurial temper of, 150
needs, 260n361, 383
negative stir-up passages, in Proverbs, 249
negotiation and success in a hostile environment, Joseph of Arimathea used to, 173
Nehemiah, 149, 154–56, 249–50
Nergal-Sharezer of Samgar, 146n624
Nero, as no friend of Christians, 362
New Testament
  acculturating manager in, 347–50
  competing manager in, 319–31
  evaluating manager in, 273–74
  Jesus on management in, 54–102
  Jesus on selected managers in, 170–91
  motivating manager in, 250–58
  organizing manager in, 240–42
  peacemaking manager in, 288–89
  planning manager in, 227–31
  relationship between employer/manager and employee/co-worker, xxivn11
  staffing manager in, 203–7
  training manager in, 306–10
  witnessing manager in, 361–67
Nicolas, as a possible apostate, 179n44
Niebuhr, Richard, xxv
Noah, 27–28, 105–6
nobility, applied to *chor*, 146n626
noble, whatever is, 71

Subject Index

noble life, living, 364
non-believers, 67, 304, 321
non-Christians, commending ourselves before, 321n712
non-worshippers of Yahweh, including among God's people, 343n828
Nouwen, Henri, 25–26

Obadiah, 139–41, 157n693, 344
obedience, to the commandments, 357n892
objectives, 209n108, 235, 263, 383. *See also* goal(s)
obligations, witnessing managers keeping low, 362
"observable" conduct, importance of, 364
Oehler, Gustaf, 374
officials (*sar*), of the king of Babylon, 146n624
Oholiab, 116
oil, unprepared girls scrambled around to find, 215
Old Testament
    acculturating manager in, 334–46
    competing manager in, 314–19
    evaluating manager in, 264–72
    examples of unkind managers, 42n116
    Jesus on management in, 27–53
    Jesus on selected managers in, 103–69
    law forbidding divorce, 333
    motivating manager in, 244–50
    organizing manager in, 235–40
    peacemaking manager in, 276–87
    planning manager in, 220–27
    staffing manager in, 195–203
    training manager in, 298–305
    witnessing manager in, 357–60
opponents, thinking how to make "stumble," 284–85
opportunities, to help a competing colleague, 328
opposition, 173, 386, 387
oppression, manager protecting from, 345

optimists, died of a broken heart in prison, 258n352
oral tradition, as authoritative, 296
organization, pecking order in any, 62n58
organizational communicating, by Joshua, 248
organizational life, no aspect of bereft of God's gracious sovereignty, 205
organizational management authority, important to Paul, 185
organizational power, not corrupting Eliakim, 167
organizational principles, of Jesus, 233–34
organizational problem, negotiating in good faith to solve, 125n457
organizational relationships, God as sovereign over, 205
organizational sovereignty, Paul appreciating Yahweh's, 204
organizational structures, developing, 240
organizing manager, 231–42
    David as, 237–40
    in the Gospels, 231–35
    Jesus as, 231–35
    Moses as, 235–37
    in the New Testament, 240–42
    in the Old Testament, 235–40
    Paul as, 240–42
    Peter as, 240
Origen, on "conscience," 273n442
others, 156, 327, 328
overbearing, not being, 262n373
ownership, versus stewardship, 218

pagan sailors, casting lots, 199
"pagans," hostility and suspicion of the Christian businessman, 364
pain and suffering, as manifestations of God's benevolent and beneficent character, 64
parables
    blind man leading a blind man, 292–93
    good Samaritan, 5n14

(parables continued)
  of Jesus, xxvii, xxvin22
  Jesus spoke in, xxvi–xxvii
  management-labor relations, 7
  rich foolish farmer, 217–19
  sheep and the goats, 354–55
  shrewd manager, 15, 297
  sower and the reaper, 194
  talents, 9–10, 12–13, 243, 258–59, 260, 294
  virgins, 215
  watchfulness, 263
  wealth creation, 7
  weather patterns, discernng, 295
  wedding feast, 214
  workers in the vineyard, 6–8, 260
paradox, of the Christian life, xxv
the paralytic, Jesus' healing of, 6n14
parochial church organizations, 82–83, 82n192
partiality, 248, 267
participating style of leadership behavior, 382
"participative group" management system, 378
"passions of the flesh," Christian business manager abstaining from, 364
password protection, instituted by Jephthah, 120
"Pastor Principle," of Howard Butt, 384
pastors, without real marketplace experience, xv
patience
  also "long-suffering" or "steadfast," 84
  of David, 281
  leading to character, 65
  Mordecai a man of, 158
  of Paul, 76–77
  as a people-oriented quality, 86
  tribulations leading to, 64
Paul
  as acculturating manager, 347
  admonishing Philemon, concerning Onesimus, 390
  on all barriers to be broken down, 3n10
  "appointing" managers of the branch offices, 182
  Barnabas having his back, 254
  commanding leaders to forsake threats, 389
  as competing manager, 320–30
  conduct of, 76
  encouraging Timothy to seek management responsibilities, 90n240
  as evaluating manager, 272–74
  explicit definitions of Christian character, 66
  on the gift of leadership, 92n254
  giving nine particular virtues in no discernable order, 75–77
  on God's marriage bond, 206
  hashing out differences from Antioch managers, 288
  his own training session in Arabia, 291
  implying a shepherd-sheep relationship, 89n240
  innocence of, 5
  introduced by Barnabas, 181
  on management, 55–79
  as manager, 182–89
  on a manager needing to be a person of character, 90n240
  on managing a family, 41n106
  on managing branch offices "well," 184
  as motivating manager, 250–54
  on not letting unwholesome talk, 389
  as organizing manager, 240–42
  as peacemaking manager, 289
  as planning manager, 227–28
  as staffing manager, 203–7
  on things that "please the Lord in every way," 351
  on those who are not bound to the Mosaic law, 366n936
  as training manager, 306–9
  using *agape* in every one of his letters, 77
  as witnessing manager, 361–63

Subject Index

peace, 277, 289, 322
peacemaking manager(s), 274–89
   Abigail as, 282–85
   Amos as, 287
   Council of Jerusalem as, 288–89
   David as, 279–81
   Gideon as, 278–79
   in the Gospels, 275–76
   Jacob as, 276
   James as, 288–89
   Jehoshaphat as, 286–87
   Jesus as, 275–76
   Jonathan as, 281–82
   Joseph as, 277
   Moses as, 277–78
   in the New Testament, 288–89
   in the Old Testament, 276–87
   Paul as, 289
   Solomon as, 285
Peale, Morgan Vincent, 257n352
Penney, James Cash, 62n55, 197n33, 235n253
Pentecost, explained by Peter, 179
people, working with, 82n191
"people of light," often unwise in conduct toward others, 297–98
perception, of Jesus, 8–9
Perceptive (P) stylistic preference, 386
perfect love, manifesting, 21
"perfection," the Lord commanding for the Christian manager, 20–21
performance
   measuring, 209n108
   Paul concentrating on his own, 227
performance parameters, setting for employees, 274n448
permissible activities and expenditures, organization setting limitations on, 236n255
persecutions, of Paul, 77
perseverance
   of a Christian business manager, 96
   defined, 64
   of Dives, 176
   Paul calling for against the flesh and the world, 75
   process of developing, 86
   producing character, 63

personal advantages, connected to temptations, 23
personal ambition, James and John failing the test of, 24n112
personal expenses, Nehemiah not using tax receipts for, 155
personal integrity, 155n682
personal life, of Solomon, 139
personal manager, of Paraoh, 110
personal power, 376–77
personal stewardship, of what God has given, 324
personal "works," benefiting those who receive them, 255
personnel decisions, 193–94, 199–200
Peter. *See also* Simon Peter
   as acculturating manager, 347–48
   as competing manager, 331
   on continual progress and improvement, 94n256
   first post-resurrection sermon, 290–91
   on management, 87–99
   as manager, 176–80
   as motivating manager, 256–58
   as organizing manager, 240
   temptation and denial story of, 98–99
   as training manager, 310
   as witnessing manager, 363–64
Pharaoh
   delegated training responsibilities to Joseph, 299
   as evaluating manager, 265
   hiring Joseph, 200
   putting Joseph in charge, 109n347, 269n420
   recognized the discretion and wisdom of Joseph, 29
   Solomon asked for advice in managing his realm, 130
Pharisees, 2, xxxin39, 355–56, 366
Philemon, 185n86, 214n130
Philip, 19
Philo, 113n372, 172, 229
Phoebe, as manager, 190–91
physical world, perceiving with our senses, 295

Pilate, as manager, 170–72
Pilgrim's Progress (Bunyan), 25n114
planning
  all over the Old Testament, 208n106
  as a character trait, 46
  emphasized by Paul, 187
  God blessing with skills, 218
  involving the organization members, 210
  leading to abundance, 220
  protecting the organization, 208
  seeking stability and reliability and effectiveness, 209
  warning about not, 219
planning manager, 208–31
  in the Gospels, 210–19
  Hebrews and, 228–29
  James as, 229–31
  Jeremiah as, 226
  Jesus as, 210–19
  in the New Testament, 227–31
  in the Old Testament, 220–27
  Paul as, 227–28
  Solomon as, 220–23
  Uzziah as, 223–26
plans, 209, 214, 217, 230
Plato, 251n324
pleroma of God, as divine perfections, 59n31
policy changes, Rehoboam refused to make, 390
political advancement, of Joseph, 110
political decision, to publicly decide who is for the organization, 164–65
political districts, created by Solomon, 138
political manager, of Pharaoh, 110
political position, Daniel not enriching himself through, 152
political process, managers coming to their office by way of, 60n43
the poor, remainder is theirs, 245
poor stewards, of time and resources, 260
population, divided into groups by Moses, 114

position power, versus personal power, 376–77
positive thinking, power of, 257n352
post-Christian era, marketplace valuing narcissism and materialism, xvii
Potiphar, 108–9, 109n346
power, 318n694, 376
power bases, of French and Raven, 377
power play, advocated by the young advisors, 373
pragmatism, of Dives, 176
"praiseworthy," whatever is, 72
prayers, types of, 362
predecessors, Hezekiah blaming his, 342
preparation, 214–15, 284
pride, of Uzziah led to his downfall, 142, 225
"prince of this world," will not give in to the "Prince of Peace," 23
The Principles of Scientific Management (Taylor), xxixn34
prize, entering the race and receiving, 252
problems, Daniel solving difficult, 152
product, creating as a blessing from God, 48
professional lives, conducting with discipline and training, 251
"profit," xxvin20, 243
prohibitions, as part of biblical organization, 236
promotion, Old Testament example of untimely and ill-advised, 203n80
prosperity, 32, 32n34, 351n865
proverbial planning manager, 220
Proverbs
  avoiding a superficial analysis of life, 221
  guideposts to a description of character, 45–46
  on human beings without special revelation, xvin24
  not praising the worthless employee, 249

Subject Index

providential care of God, temptation to distrust/disbelieve, 23
prudence, 221n169
the prudent, wisdom of, 215n138
prudent approach, as a character trait, 46
prudent man, giving thought to his steps, 221
prudent manager, saving a foolish business owner, 221
Psalm for managers, for managers subject to temptations, 40
psalmist, on management, 44–45
psychological maturity (willingness), of followers, 382
public peacemaking role, of David, 280
public works projects, construction manager of, 127
pure, whatever is, 71–72
"pure" religion, *threskos* used to connote, xxxin39
Purim, 346, 346n842
purpose, of Paul, 76
"pursue," as an imperative for Timothy, 74
pursuit of managerial virtue, as never ending, 75

qualifications, for God's "manager," 262n373
questions, leaders needing to know, 388
quick success, Satan offering, 23
quorum of ten men, to settle an issue, 146n626

raah/manager, Joshua as, 117
rab, designating a chief of executive of a group, 146n624
rabrab, as abundant, 146n624
racial discrimination, among early Christians, 177
radah, treading down as in a winepress, 62n58
rage, becoming a great and incurable sin, 97n279
rational faculties, using shrewdly, 298

reality, witnessing manager grounded in, 360
Rebekah, found by Eliezer, 265
reciprocity, begetting reciprocity, 285
reconciliation, 275, 276
recorder, Jehoshaphat as, 131
referent power base, 377, 378
refining (*dokimion*), of gold and silver, 86–87
refuge, manager as, 345
Rehoboam, 368–91
  "answered the people harshly," 374
  depending on his position and not his personal power base, 377
  as an ESTJ, 386
  failed to exercise moral and uplifting leadership, 381
  gave himself time to mull over his response, 371
  knew the history of tribal conflict, 369
  left the wisdom of Solomon behind, 373
  as manager, 167–68
  misread the depth of the Israelites' outrage, 375
  as motivating manager, 250
  not acting wisely, 378
  not commanding a commitment to his goals, 384
  overall evaluation of, 381
  precipitating a division between tribes, 368
  sent a third-party intermediary Adoni-ram, 128, 375
  turned to his own advisors, 372
rejection, 20, 232
rejoicing, with those who rejoice, 320
relational integrity, 155n682
relationship-oriented behavior, 382
relief mission to Judea, organized by Barnabas, 181
religion, limited as a rule to the "spiritual," xxxin39
"religionless Christianity," Bonhoeffer on, 4n13, xxxin39

religious convictions, as secondary when staffing for marketplace work, 197
religious outcasts, Jesus not afraid to socialize with, 2
remuneration, of honest, 63
reputation, of Christian managers to those outside the faith, 298
rescue mission, accomplished by Obadiah, 140
respect, 71, 89
responsibilities
　continual "preparation" for, 294
　Eliakim firm and resolute in, 167
　handling your own, 326
　Jesus delegated, 232, 234
　of Joseph, 299
　of managers, 192, 209n108, 239–40, 275
　trust in small leading to trust in big, 304n601
restraining forces, 379
return of Jesus, mini-parable on, 12
revenge, 283, 284, 312, 322
revolt, Rehoboam gave plenty of justification for, 376
reward paths, types of, 260–61
reward power, behind the Israelites' request for leniency, 378
reward power base, based on ability to provide rewards, 377
reward-based management, as flawed, 261n367
rewards, internal path to, 261
the rich, 318, 349n850
rich foolish farmer, parable of, 217–19
rich man's possessions, manager accused of wasting, 15–16
riches, 130n482, 222
Ridderbos, Herman, 2n5
right, whatever is, 71
"right judgments," 14
the righteous, 44n120
righteous man, Noah as, 28
righteous manager, David as, 41
righteous people, influencing those around them, 339
righteousness, 22, 39, 74, 351–52

rivalry, Paul attempting to reduce, 326
role model, of the acculturating manager, 342
Roman military shields, set up in Jerusalem, 171
Rousseau, Jean-Jacques, 79n177, 274n447
royal chaplain, Azariah as, 131
royal food, 149, 151
royal guard, Nehemiah kept control of, 155
royal heresy, not agreeing to, 153
royal palace managers, in the Bible, 139n580
royal property, someone in charge of, 262n373
royal steward, tomb of thought to be the tomb of Shebna, 169n775
ruler (*shalat*), Daniel described as a, 147n629
Rush, Myron, xvn20, 352n867, 390
ruthlessness, 313, 317, 322
Ryle, J. C., 18

Sabbath, value of keeping, 235n253
salary negotiations, by Solomon, 137
"salt" of society, sharing the blessings of the gospel, 365
"salt of the earth," being, 354
salvation, benefits of through Christ to all people, 363
salvation history, planned by Yahweh, 229
Sam Walton: Made in America (Walton), xvin21
Samaritan businessman
　loved his Jewish neighbor, 5n14
　returned to the inn as a good "Christian," 6n14
Samaritans, gathered on Mt. Gerizim, 172
Samnites, wars with the Roman Republic, 170n3
Samson, 339n791
Samuel, 121–22, 196
sanctification, of character development, 67

Subject Index

Sanhedrin, Joseph of Arimathea as a member of, 173
Satan, 23, 24, 25
King Saul
  firing of as decisive and permanent, 196
  ignoring God's timetable, 43n117
  looking for someone to confront Goliath, 33
  organized the twelve tribes into a loose confederation, 129
  wanting to kill David, 282
Saul and Jonathan, lamenting the death of, 337
Schadenfreude, 325n730, 360
Schaeffer, Francis, 3, 57
schemes, of Jephthah the manager, 120
Schreiner, Thomas, 65n76
"science," defined, 307n620
"science of politics," of Burnham, ixn1
scribes, 292, 292n522
Scriptures
  Dives failed to understand, 175
  not prohibiting the Christian manager from socializing, 3
  permeating every aspect of a person's daily life, 357
  teaching we are to be like Jesus, 2
  "scum" and "refuse," Paul remaining to his opponents, 324
seamless robe, 211n117
secular calling, 207
secular character education movement, 66
secular communities, multifaceted benefits of, 360
secular culture, 202–3
secular forces, ruining anyone who shuns evil, 78
secular marketplace, business manager competing in, 2
secular society, saw the courage of Peter and John, 293n532
secular songs, as important to Jewish church life, 122n429
secular thinking, hostile ethical world of dominated by Satan, 353

seed, sowing much in order to reap much, 228
"seekers," awareness of conflicting values, xviiin30
self-affirmation and motivation, treading lightly, 257n352
self-centeredness, fighting against, 349
self-control, 70, 95, 237n255
self-discipline, process of, 251
self-interest, 325
selfish ambition, 311, 328
self-righteousness, "revenge" and, 322
self-sacrificing love, of the Christian business manager, 101
self-sufficiency about life, arrogantly presuming, 23
self-worth, as internal reward, 261
"sense of oughtness," 99n288
senselessness, 97n279
Sensing (S) stylistic preference, 385
sensitivity, of Jesus to his surroundings, 9
separatism, 56, 365
Seraiah, disseminating the royal edicts, 124
"a servant leader," Phoebe as, 190
"servant leadership," books on, xxxi
"servant shepherd," David described as, 41
"Servant-king," Christians emulating Christ as, 384
service, x, 17, 48, 384
sex, Solomon's obsession with, 139
sexual codes, transgression of traditional, 78n173
sexual libertine, 338
Shadrach, 147, 153, 153n665
Shalmaneser, Assyrian military general and king, 198
Shaphan, 158, 159n710
shared leadership, by Peter's management team, 178
"sharing in our humanity," by Jesus, 18n80
Queen of Sheba, 371
Shebna, 165, 166, 167, 168–69
Shechem, 369, 370
sheep, Peter feeding the Lord's, 18

sheep and the goats, parable of, 354–55
shepherd, 17, 164
shepherd paradigm, of management, 90
shepherding, 26, xviiin29, 33, 92
shepherding manager, 26, 42, 91
shepherding task, in the marketplace, 83
shepherds, being of God's flock, 89–90
Shinn, George, xvn20
King Shishak of Egypt, attacked Judah, 371
shrewd conduct, managers training themselves in, 296
shrewd manager, parable of, 15, 297
shrewd public front, of Mordecai, 158
shrewdness, of Abigail, 35
Simeon, Charles, xivn17
Simon bribe situation, handled by Peter, 180
Simon Peter, 232n239. *See also* Peter
sin, 73, 79, 103, 257n352
sinful desires, abstaining from, 363
singers, guild of in primeval times, 122n429
singlemindedness, of Paul, 76
sinless life, led by Jesus, xxiii
General Sisera, Barak led the charge against, 118
situational leadership, defined, 381
slaves, providing with what is right and fair, 390
sleepless nights, for business managers, 81
sleeplessness, pursuit of wealth causing, 48
slothful workers, supervising, 259
small business, management of, 10
smaller groups, organizational principle of, 234–35
Smedes, Lewis, 80
social guidelines, any organization needing, 162
social harmony, preserving, 333
social relationships, importance of, 58
social separatism, 365
Socrates, 95n263

Sodom, Abraham negotiated the fate of, 108
solidarity, incarnational ethic of, 101n298
Solomon
  as acculturating manager, 337–39
  on answering before listening, 388
  as competing manager, 316
  David passing the baton to his son, 38–39
  equated lack of self-control to a city in collapse, 43n117
  evaluating Jeroboam and rewarding him, 270–71
  as evaluating manager, 267–70
  exhibiting initial humility before his sovereign God, 126n460
  on finding joy in an apt reply, 389
  heavy hand in public works administration, 370
  made Jerusalem the permanent spiritual capital, 369
  on management, 45–49
  management policies of, xxi
  as manager, 128–39
  as motivating manager, 248–49
  as no more than sixty when he died, 371
  peace, prosperity, and respect under, 370
  as peacemaking manager, 285
  planning following the written instructions by, 227
  as planning manager, 220–23
  portrayed as a man in charge, 137
  right to exert the power of, 376
  sought to kill Jeroboam, 370
  as staffing manager, 197–99
  as training manager, 303–4
  on valuing a man who speaks the truth, 388
  verses on prudential living, 303
  on a wise man listening and increasing in learning, 388
Solomon's elders, 371, 380
sons, of David as priests in the order of Melchizedek, 125

Subject Index

sovereignty of God, clear expression of, 231
sower and the reaper, parable about, 194
sowing season, 228
"special abilities," 265, 266
speech, using to build up, 339n790
spirit of an age, scrutinizing, 296
"spirit" of the world, warring against the "Spirit" of God, 366
Spirit of your Father, speaking through you, 211n115
spiritual challenges, residing in wealth creation, 22
spiritual collapse, under Jeroboam, 370
spiritual crime, of Uzziah, 225
spiritual gifts, comments on, 68–70
spiritual task, of managing Christian organizations, 83
spoils of war, Moses distributing among the Israelites, 30
staffing, God's providential care over, 204
staffing decision, of Jesus, 193
staffing lessons, Pauline passages teaching, 205
staffing manager, 192–207
   Asaph as, 195
   Daniel as, 200–201
   David as, 196–97
   Esther as, 201–2
   Ezra as, 201
   in the gospels, 193–95
   Jesus as, 193–95
   Jonas as, 199–200
   Mordecai as, 201–2
   Nebuchadnezzar as, 202–3
   in the New Testament, 203–7
   in the Old Testament, 195–203
   Paul as, 203–7
   Samuel as, 196
   Solomon as, 197–99
Mr. Steadfast, 25n114
steadfastness, 47, 95, 187, 345
Stearns, Richard, xin6, 11n38, 333n774
Steele, Richard, xivn19
Stepansky, Robert, xiv
Stephen, describing Moses, 112
stewardship
   accountability attached to individual, 252
   as a character trait, 46
   lack of good as serious business, 268
   personal, 253
   planning as a high form of, 208–9
   resulting in "profit" for the organization, 263
   in secular society, 270
   still, small voice, spoken of in Scripture, 210n110
Stockdale paradox, 258n352
Stockwell, James, 257–58n352
storehouses, set up by David, 239
Storms, Samuel, 169
"straining," of Paul toward the goal, 227–28
strategy meeting, Hezekiah gathering his lieutenants for, 342
"strike your cheek," those who, 313
the strong, looking out for the weak, 92
stylistic preferences, mixing, 385–86
"Subordinate Centered Leadership," 379
subordinate's growth, as best indicator of a superior's performance, 383
"substantial" men, of Israel, 37n62
success, 32, 321
suffering, 64, 77, 86
   producing perseverance, 63
suicide mission, by Adoni-ram, 375
superficiality, xxviiin30
superiority, religion with its in-group of the elect, xxxn39
supervisors, hundreds reporting to Adoni-ram, 127
supply officer, Jesus entrusted Philip with, 234n245
"surplus value," of Marx, xxvin20
symbol management, for the artistic organization manager, 85n205
"synapsis," of the mind as wired for sin, 257n352

tabernacle, Bezalel as hands-on manager of, 117
talents, parable of, 9–10, 12–13, 243, 258–59, 260, 294
Tam, Stanley, 209n107, 352n867
Taphath, the daughter of Solomon, 132
Tappan, Arthur, 235–36n253
task-oriented behavior, described, 382
task-oriented leadership behavior style, of Rehoboam, 382
tasks, [coworkers] entrusted with, 219
taxation, Rehoboam would impose even more, 373
taxes, Josiah assigned people to collect, 144
Taylor, Frederick W., xxixn34
teachableness, as a character trait, 46
teachers, contrasting false with true, 212
teaching, 76, 291, 296
teamwork, essential in a business endeavor, 194
temper, not arousing another's, 276
temperament, having a generous, 75
temple
    activity, 342
    David prohibited by Yahweh from building, 237
    Hezekiah opening the sealed doors of, 341
    high quality of construction, 163
    restoring the beauty of Solomon's, 145
    Zerubbabel completing the reconstruction of, 161
temple guards, 356
temptations
    business managers encountering, x
    expecting, 22
    fleeing, 73
    of the Lord, 22–23
    as not, in and of themselves, sinful, 24
    nothing random and chaotic about, 98
    of the surrounding culture, 153–54

Ten Commandments, organizational values in, 235–36
tension, being a servant to multiple human bosses, 17
testing, 84, 85, 87, 258
Thayer-Case Realtors, author as owner/broker of, xxxii
theological doctrine, referring to as "food," 80
"the theology of ambiguity," xxx
Theories of Management (Miles), 260n361
"Theory Y," 383
Thessalonians, compared to Bereans, 54
Thielicke, Helmut, 2
Thinking (T) stylistic preference, 385
thinking causally, 295–96
Thummim, precious stones of Aaron's breast piece, 20n86
"Thy will be done," saying to God, 317n687
Emperor Tiberius, appointed Pilate, 171
Tiglath-Pileser, Assyria under, 224n193
timing, of personnel decisions, 203
Timothy, 69, 73, 367
Titus, 184–85, 184n85
tone, setting for an organization, 12
tools, provided by the Lord, 232, 233n239
tough love, as Joseph's management style, 300
towns
    Ben-Geber managed fortified, 132
    rebuilt by Uzziah, 224
The Tradesman Calling (Steele), xivn19
traditional model, assuming that work is inherently distasteful, 260n361
trained men, under the military management of Abraham, 107
training
    to be godly, 297n561
    as a character trait, 46
    of Jesus, 294
    as a modeling lifestyle activity, 293

Subject Index

simple steps to early, 303
  for success, 303, 309n636
training manager, 290–310
  David as, 301–3
  in the Gospels, 290–98
  Hebrews and, 309–10
  Isaiah as, 305
  Jesus as, 290–98
  Joseph as, 299–301
  Moses as, 298
  needing to use available resources, 303
  in the New Testament, 306–10
  in the Old Testament, 298–305
  Paul as, 306–9
  Peter as, 310
  Solomon as, 303–4
tranquility, of Christian life, 363n924
transforming leadership, versus transactional leadership, 380–81
transparency, xxviii, 246–47, 249
traveling together, conditions for, 287
treasurer, Judas as, 234n245
treatment, "everyone" getting the same level of, 362
Trench, Richard, xxxin39
trials, short-circuiting or hindering, 85
trials and testing, producing a different mindset, 64
tribal boundaries, Solomon dividing the land according to, 132
tribulations, 64–65
trouble, planning for, 213
true, whatever is, 71
true believers, aristocracy of, xxxn39
Trump, Donald, telephone call to Mike Lindell, xvn20
trust, 325
truth, 257n352, 353
the Twelve, called as "apostles," 193

unambiguous approach, to management, xxxn39
unbelievers, 78, 90n240, 298
under-shepherd, motivation of, 49n155

understanding friend, Satan coming as, 24
unfaithfulness, preventing the rot of, 336
unity, founded on Christ's love, 4n13
unjust, rewarded and indulged, 45
unkind managers, examples of, 42n116
unprepared girls, not accused of sin or unfaithfulness, 215
Uriah, death of, 43
utilitarianism, 271
Uzziah, 141–42, 141n590, 223–26, 223n189

vain conceit, 311, 328
"Mr. Valiant-for-Truth," 25n114
value management, the art of, 85n205
value-free managerial climate, of the twenty-first century, 97
"velvet covered bricks," Christians being, 384
vengeance, bringing the guilt of competitive, 284
vengeful manager, putting in the place of God, 322
vices, shunning, 79n176
violence, not practicing, 263n373
virgins, parable of, 215
virtue(s)
  [Peter's] selection of, 94n256
  as the faculty of conferring benefits, 94n255
  Paul is telling the managers to "practice," 72–73
  Pauline list of unique, 70–71
  rising out of Christian faith, 94
Vischer, Phil, 208n105
vision
  of Jesus, 233
  parts of, 333–34n774
  transference from the manager, 252
visionary companies, ixn2, 347n846
Vitellius, Lucius, 172
vocational education, 116

Wade, Marion E., xvi, xvin23
"walk of life," of Paul, 76

"walked with God," Enoch and Noah, 28, 28n11
"walking," as Jesus did, 99
Walton, Sam, xvin21
"wandering," in a workplace, 186n96
wars, Uzziah waged successful, 224
watchful manager, constantly surveilling dangers, 12
watchfulness, parable on, 263
Waugh, Evelyn, 79n177
"way of life," 75, 76
wealth
  Abraham knew how to manage, 107n337
  business managers provided, x
  "evils" of the pursuit of, 47
  as like sand in one's hand, 49
  pursuit as a ball and chain, 48
  seduction coming from the ability to amass, 219
wealth creation, parable of, 7
wealth creator, 47, 48, 327
weapons of war, made by Uzziah, 225
weather patterns, parable on discerning, 295
weather-watching activity, as a gift from God, 14
Webber, Ross A., xxviiin32
wedding feast, parable of, 214
Westminster Confession Faith, on the Holy Scriptures, xvin24
"whatever" virtues, Paul emphasizing at Philippi, 71–72
Whitcomb, John, 148
"who knows" uncertainty, expressing the ambiguity of life, 206
wickedness, 78n174, 257n352
the widow, leaving what remains for, 245
wisdom
  calling for planning and prudence, 221
  concerned with responsible excellence, 270
  of Joseph, 301
  required in good leadership, xxin4
  of Solomon, 130n482, 135, 137–38, 197n36, 285

"wise men," Daniel appointed, 147
witnessing, how Jesus lived his life, xxiii–xxiv
witnessing manager, 350–67
  in the Gospels, 351–56
  Isaiah as, 358
  Jeremiah as, 358–60
  Jesus as, 351–56
  John as, 364–67
  Moses as, 357
  in the New Testament, 361–67
  not diluting attention to outside activities, 362
  in the Old Testament, 357–60
  Paul as, 361–63
  Peter as, 363–64
  seeking the welfare of the specific community, 359
words, 254, 271, 338–39
work environment, creating a kindly, 52
workaholic, becoming, 49
workers. *See also* employees
  Christian managers attracting good, 192n1
  encouraged as more productive, 339
  exhorting to accomplish honest, productive work, 222
  lifting up, 52
  needing to know their importance, 256
  not ruling over ruthlessly, 62
  organizing, 209n108
  ownership and buy-in of objectives, 252
  products of labor of, xxvin20
  as "proletariat," xxvin20
  relationships of, 275
  separating lazy from the organization, 259
  using all the resources, 13
  as a vehicle of the message to their neighbors, 358
  in the vineyard, 6–8, 260
  ways of failing in their tasks, 60
workforce, David appointed a manager of his, 239

working hard with skill, 304
workmanship, 163, 197
workplace, 63, 194n16, 229
the world, 6, 19n82, 101–2, 362
worldliness, 23, 102
"worldly" image, 100
worldly wealth, using to gain friends, 15, 297
worldly wisdom, to achieve selfish aims, 297n560
worship process, violated by Uzziah, 225
worthless employee, 268, 272
worthy employee, 272
wrath, 97n279

King Xerxes, trusted Mordecai, 157, 200

Yahweh
  causing Daniel to enjoy "favor and sympathy," 153
  characterized by attributes of strength and love, 267
  commending Solomon for his attitude toward competitors, 316
  employed various managers, 103
  evaluating and exalting, 195
  fired Saul as king and hired David, 196
  as the Great Motivating Manager, 242
  instituting curses and blessings, 264
  Jesus claimed to be, xxv
  as the master of plans, 229
  to Nathan concerning David, 269n419
  permitted multiple temptations, 154
  permitting defeat and ruin for reasons unknown to humans, 359
  personnel decisions confirmed using lots, 199–200
  "planned" and executed a construction blueprint, 217
  plunder belonging to in the first place, 34
  as "sovereign" (*shatlar*) over men, 146n625
  sovereignty over staffing changes, 200–201
  speaking through an unbeliever, 114
  took man and put him in the Garden of Eden, 62n58
  Uzziah inflicted with a skin disease of leprosy, 225
  as a vocational ag teacher, 305
  watching the upright business manager, 39
  Zerubbabel dedicated the work to, 162
Yeargin, Bill, 352n867
"yes men," Rehoboam surrounded by, 372–73
young advisors, 373, 380
Yukl, Gary, 376

Zabud, Solomon's personal advisor, 131–32
Zadok (son of Ahitub), 123, 124
Zechariah, 52, 161
Zechariah (Uzziah's advisor), 223, 225
Zeitgeist, scrutinizing, 296
Zerah, Achan of the lineage of, 335
Zerubbabel, 160–65, 161n723
Ziba, 36, 126n460

Scripture Index

OLD TESTAMENT

Genesis

1:26	62n58
1:26–28	62n58, 138
1:28	62n58
2:15	62n58, 144n614, 360n911
2:25	332
3:6	22
3:24	62n58
4:17	103, 104n319
4:20	xviiin29, 104n321
4:20–21	103
4:21	104n320, 105n322
5:22–24	28n11
6:5	257n352
6:5, 11	28n8
6:8–9	28
6:9	28n10, 87n225
6:11	28n8
6:14	105
6:19	105
6:19–20	106n328
6:21	106n329
6:21–22	105
7	56n13
7:1	28n9
7:4–5	105
7:16	105, 106n330
8	56n13
8:6–8,	105
8:6–11	106n331
8:13	105, 106n332
8:20	105, 106n333
9:5–6	30n22
11	105n322
12:16	107n337
13:2	107n337
14:14	244
14:14–16	107
14:15	107n335, 244n294
14:18	42n111
14:23–24	107n336
15:2	126n458, 265n387
15:7–18	111n358
17:1	28n10
18:14	200n69
18:18	108n341
18:19	108n339
18:22–33	3n11
19:28 LXX	230n229
20:2	166n754
20:8	166n754
20:13	53n183
22:8	290n515
23:5–6	136n557
23:16	28n6
24	32n34, 265n388
24:2	126n458, 264
24:29	53n183
25:27	42n116
25:29–34	43n117
26:14	63n61
27:1—28:9	161n720
29	xviiin29
31:7	284n493
32:8	276n456

461

Scripture Index

(Genesis continued)

32–33	276	3:11	136n554
33:4	276n457	5:6	141n590
36:15–19	161n720	5:10–14	141n590
36:15–29	291n518	5:13–14	46n132
37	222n178	6–12	31n24
37:2	110n352	7:7	113n373
39	32n34	8:1–2	268
39:4	109n347, 110	11:3	113n368, 354n875
39:4–5	109n346	12:25–27	108n340
39:5	109	12:35–36	112, 298
39:11	146–47n626	13:17	327n743
39:80–9	109n347	14:10	244
40:1	300n573	14:15	244
41	200n60	15:15	161n720, 291n518
41:8	134n528, 304n594	16:35	262n373
41:21	284n493	18	114
41:33	29n12	18:13	114n377
41:34	109n346	18:13–26	112, 112n364, 113, 114, 237n256
41:39–40	269	18:14	114n379
41:39–41	29	18:15–16	114n377
41:39–45	277n458	18:17–24	235n252
41:41	109n347	18:18	114n380
41:43	146n625, 157n693	18:21	161n720, 266
41:46	110n353, 301n577	18:23	112n362, 113n375, 115n385
41:55–57	146n625	18:24	114n378
42:6	146n625	18:25–26	114nn382–383
42:10	299n568	18:26	115n384
42:24	277n459, 277n460	18:27	115n385
43:30	277n459	19	114
44:5	284n493	20:4–6	235n252
45:1–3	277n459	20:7	236n253
45:2	277n459	20:8–12	235n253
45:8	126n458	20:10	298n567
45:15	277n459	20:12	308n630
46:29	277n459	20:13–17	236n255
47:6	265, 265n392	20:15	51n174
47:29	53n183	21:17	115n386
49:10	123n438	22	51n174
49:29	38n70, 296n551	22:28	115, 115n386
49:33	38n70, 296n551	22:28–29	115n386
50:15–21	277n461	23:4–5	324n725
50:19	220n161, 220n165	23:9	298n565
		25	113n367
Exodus		25:1–8	31n28, 31n29
		25:3	xxin4, 130n482
1:11	37n62	25:8–9	198n42
2:23	113n374	26–27	51n174
3:10	112		

28:3	134n525, 137n564, 198n50	12:13	31n30
31:1–6	136n557	13	104n318
31:3	xxin4, 130n482, 134n525, 137n565	13:2	115n386
		14:5–9	248n307
31:3–6	116	14:19	31n30
31:6	xxin4, 130n482, 137n565	16:1–3	236n253
32	113	16:8–11	31n27
34:6	42–43n117	16:15	284n493
34:23	299n568	16:19–21	236n253
34:31	115	16:20–21	209n109
35	113n367	16:22	31n30
35:10	134n525, 301n576	16:25	184n82
35:30–35	116n395	16:46	31n30
35:30—36:2	136n557	17:1–6	115n386
		20:10–12	43n117
		21:27	122n429
		22:17	203n80

Leviticus

4	45n131	22–24	203n80
11	149n638	22:30	169n773
11:44	29	25:12–13	124n445
19:2	20n87, 29n18	27:12–23	237n258
19:13	253n329	27:15–23	117n401
19:13–16, 35–36	51n174	31:4	161n720
19:18	18n76, 331n762	31:8	203n80
19:35–36	51n174	31:14	89n240
19:35–37	315n672	31:25–28	30
19:36	352n866	31:30	30
20:26	29n18	34:18–29	115
25:35–37	44n120	35:21–22	284n494
25:39	63n61		
25:43	62	## Deuteronomy	
25:46	155n680	1:9–18	237n259
27:1–8	146n626	1:15	141n590
		1:16–17	277

Numbers

		3:4	132n512
1:16	161n720	4:2	346n842
3:24–37	115	4:39–40	332
3:32	109n346, 115n386, 238n264	6:1–7	108n340
4:16	90n240, 109n346	6:4	335n778
4:16 LXX	89n240	6:4–9	334
6:22–26	331n764	6:5	335n779
7:11–84	115	6:6	335n780
11:1–25	237n257	6:6–7	290n514
11:23	200n69	6:6–9	357
12:1	112n366	6:7	335n782
12:1–3	42n116	6:7–9	335n781
12:1–15	31n26, 31n27	6:9	335n783
12:3	31n25, 75n152	6:10–11	335n784

Scripture Index

(Deuteronomy continued)

6:11	194n12
6:16–18	31n34
6:20–25	108n340
7:10	266
10:17	299n568
13:6	22n101
15:7–11	111
15:9	284n493
15:11	51n174
16:13–14	194n15
16:19	50n160
18:13	20n87, 28n10
19:12	146n626
20:10–11	128n470
21:19	301n579
23:19–20	51n174
24:1–5	333n772
24:6, 19–22	51n174
24:7	155n680
24:10	30n21
24:10–11	30
24:15	253n329
24:19–22	51n174, 245
25:13–16	51n174, 315
27–28	370
28:30	194n13
31:1–7	246
31:28	141n590
33:21	123n438
34:9	134n527, 138n567
34:10	30
38:30	335n785

Joshua

1	32, 117
1:4–6	117
1:6–11	248
1:7	31n32
1:8	31
1:10–11	248
1:16	117, 248
6:18	336n787
7:1	335
7:6	184n82
7:7	335
7:10–12	335
7:14	199n55
7:24	336n787
7:24–25	336n786
8:10	184n82
10	299n568
10:24	46n132
20:4	182n67
20:4 LXX	184n82
22:30	115
24:1	184n82, 369
24:13	194n12
24:14	41n102
24:30, 33	370
24:31	247n306
24:32	370
24:33	370

Judges

3:15	118n402
4	118n403
4:15–16	118
4:18–23	42n116
5:9	123n438
5:14	123n438
5:31	122n433
6	119n410
6–8	119
6:11	279n474
6:15	119n411, 126n460
6:35	278n472
7:2	283n492
7–8	268
7:15–18	248n307
7:17–18	118
7:21	248n307
7:24	278n472
8	279n473
8:1–3	278
8:3	279n475
8:28	122n433
8:31—9:6	369
9:16	41n102, 119n405
9:19	41n102
9:28	89n240
10:18	112n362
11:6	46n132
11:11	46n132
11:27	120n414
11:32–33	119

12:1	120n415	10:5	122n429
12:3	120n416	10:10	122n429
12:5	120n418	10:20–21	199n54
12:6	120n419	10:24–25	386
14:11	339n791	12:1–4	122n432
14:20	339n791	12:11	119n412, 122n433
15:2	339n791	12:14	385
15:6	339n791	13:8	43n117
15:11	312n654	13:14	38n70, 129n479
16:4–22	42n116	13:19	125n457
16:10	101n306	13:19–20	224n198
16:13	101n306	14:42–43	199n57
16:15	101n306	15:23	196n28
16:31	112n359	15:24	196n28
19:4–9	218n149	15:28	196
20:9	199n56	16:8	132n511
		16:18	32n36, 33n40, 41n98, 196n27
Ruth		16:21–22	196n26
2:1	38n70	17:13	132n511
2:9	38n70, 296n551	17:17	280n478
2:13	299n568	17:20	38n70, 296n551
4:2	146n626, 182n67, 184n82	17:28–31	279
		17:29	280n479
1 Samuel		17:31	280n481
1:1–20	173n11	17:34	33n39, 33nn43–44, 33n46
1:15	285n500	17:34–37	32, 41n101
2:7	195n23, 195n24	17:35	33n45
2:7–8	192n1	17:35–37	34n47
2:26	354n876	17:55—18:2	302n588
2:35	343n825	18:5	354n877
4:11	121n424	18:5–6, 14–15	32n34
7:1–2	121n427	18:14	xxin4, 130n482
7:1–6	121n425	18:14–15	32n34
7:5	121n426	18:14–16	32n36
7:13–17	121n428	18:18	136n554
7:15–17	121	19:20	122n429
8:3	42n116	20:1–2	281
8:7	42n116, 354n876	20:12–13	282
8:9	354n876	20:30	282
8:10–11	332	20:32	282
8:10–18	132n510	21:5	125n452
8:10–22	370	21:8–9	125
8:20	112n359	22:2	196
8:22	354n876	22:14	124n451
9:1	38n70	23:13	197n29
9:15	369	25:3	35
9:21	126n460	25:10	283n488

Scripture Index

(1 Samuel continued)

25:13	34n48
25:23-25	35
25:26	283
25:28	284
25:28-29	284
25:28-31	283
25:31	284
25:33	283, 285
26	35, 35n59
26:9	35n56, 35n58
26:9-11	35, 35n55, 35n57
27	329n752
29	329n752
30:9-18	125n457
30:21-25	33
30:25	34

2 Samuel

1:17-27	337
2:1-9	369
2:4	369
2:8	132n514
3:4	299n568
3:17-21	386
4:1	132n511
4:5	131n504, 132n507
4:6	132n509, 132n510
4:13	132n512
4:14	132n513
5:1-3	386
5:1-10	369
5:2	40n93
5:3	369
5:11	196
5:14-15	131n504
7:14	269
7:18	126n460, 136n554
8:15	37n62, 125n457, 323n717
8:15-18	123, 129n480
8:16	131n500
8:17	131n498
8:18	123n439, 131n505
9	126n460
9:1-3	35
9:10	126n460
9:12	126n460
10:2	36

10:4-5	36
11:2-4	43
12:22	206n97
13:17	93n254
14:20	134n527, 138n567
14:29	43n117
15:27	124n446
15:29	131n495
15:36	131n495
15:37	132n507
16	126n460
16:14	53n183
16:16	132n507
17	208n106, 305n607
17:24	132n515
18:15-18	239n273
18:31—19:3	336
19:8	336
19:41-43	37n62
20:1	369, 374
20:21	369
20:22	134n524
20:23	124n442
20:23-25	129n480
20:23-26	123n440, 239n273
20:24	127, 127n463, 131n500, 375
20:25	124n448
20:26	123n439, 125n454
21:14	38n70, 154n673, 296n551
23:3	126n459
23:3-4	126
23:8-39	196
23:20-21	124n450

1 Kings

	234n249
1	299n568
1:2	109n347
1-2	125n453
1:4	109n347
1:15	109n347
1:38-39	386
2	299n568
2:2-3	370
2:3	32n34
2:11	302n587
2:27	124n445
2:35	124n447, 131n502

Scripture Index

3:1	130n483	8:36	372
3:7	371	8:39	272n440
3:7–9	135n549	9:4–7	41n97
3:9–13	371	9–10	239n274
3:11	316	9:15	127n464
3:16—4:34	135n548	9:15, 24	270n430
3:25–28	285	9:15–19	370
4:1–6	123n440	9:20–22	371
4:1–19	123n441, 129n481, 130, 133n517	9:23	271n432
		9:24	270n430
4:2	131n496	10:4	130n482
4:3	124n444, 124n448, 124n449	10:4, 24	xxin4
		10:6–8	371
4:4	125n453	10:7	372
4:5	133n518	10:8	371
4–5	239n274	10:8–9	371
4:6	127n469, 139n580, 168n771, 169, 262n373, 299n568, 344n831, 375	10:9	323n717
		10:15	154n674
		10:18	28n6
4:15	133n516	10:23–24	xxin4, 130n482, 371
4:20, 25	xxi	10:24	xxin4, 130n482
4:20, 28	130	10:27	371
4:20–21	370	11:1–3	139n577
4:21	133n518, 197	11:1–8	338n788
4:24–25	370	11:3	371
4:25	xxi	11:7–8	338
4:28	130	11:9	139n579
4:29, 30–34	197n36	11:9–14	139n578
4:29–34	135n541	11:13	378
4:30–34	197n36	11:26	270n429, 369
4:32	138n574	11:27	270n430
4:33	138n570	11:28	270, 370
5	194n16	11:30–38	380
5:5–6	198n41	11:31	271
5:7	134n527, 145n621	11:36	375
5:12	133	11:37	271
5:13	127n465	11:42	371
5:14	299n568, 375	12	250, 309n639, 386
5:15	127n466, 270n431	12:1	369, 378, 386
5:16	135n545	12:1–20	368–76
6	369	12:2–3	377
6:16	46n132	12:3	376
7	369	12:4	167, 370, 378, 381
7:1–12	135n548	12:5	371
7:13–14	116n394	12:5–6	387
7:14 LXX	205n88	12:6	167, 371
7–19	138n573	12:7	371–72, 388
8:18	372		

(1 Kings continued)

12:8	167, 208n106, 250, 305n607
12:8–9	372–73
12:10–11	373–74
12:11	167
12:13	305n607, 374, 384
12:13–14	374
12:14	375, 377
12:15	374, 384
12:16	374–75, 378, 384
12:17	375
12:18	127n468, 132n510, 299n568, 375
12:19	378
12:19–20	376, 384
12:20	377
12:21	371, 376, 380
12:23	378
12:24	371
12:28	370
12:33	225n202
13	73
13:33	340n796
14:14–15	340
14:16	339
14:20	380
14:21	371, 372, 381
14:22–24	371
14:30	369
15	340n799, 381
16	340n799
16:9	132n508, 139n580, 168n771, 344n831
16:30–32	140n581
18	200n62
18:2–4	344
18:3	132n508, 139, 157n693
18:4	140n582
18:13	234, 344
18:18	344, 344n832
18:44	14n52, 295n544
20:24	154n674
21	318
21:1	43n117
21:8	146n626
22	381

2 KINGS

2:3	122n429
2:12	308n631
5:11–12	43n117
5:13	308n631
6:21–23	324n725
10:5	132n508, 139n580, 168n771, 344n831
10:29	370
11:15	89n240
12:11	262n373
12:13	381
15	223n184
15:4	225n201
15:5	132n508, 168n771
15:6	223n188
15:20	38n70
17:5	341
17:7	341
17:15–16	370
17:21–22	340
17:24	162n731
17:33	164n744
18:18	123n438, 139n580, 168n771, 262n373, 344n831
18:18–37	132n508
18–20	381
18:24	154n674
18:37	139n580, 168n771, 344n831
18:56	32n34
19:2	132n508, 139n580, 168n771, 344n831
22:4–7	144
22:11–13	159n708
22:12	158
22:14	159n707
22:19–20	158n704
23:7	338
23:13	338
23:13–14	338
23:22	112n359
25:8	146n624
25:18	129n479
25:19	123n438
25:22	169n773
25:22–24	159
25:25	160n715
25:27–30	149n639

Scripture Index

34:14–21	159n710

1 Chronicles

	37n62
1:43–54	291n518
1:51–54	161n720
2:7	336n787
3:17—5:26	161n718
5:26	242n283
6:3–9	124n445
6:9	131n495
11:6	124n443
11:23	371
13:1	161n720, 354n877
13:4	354n877
14:17	224n193
15:21	163n736
16:4	123n437
18:5	140n583
18:7–9	140n584
18:14	125n457
18:14–17	129n480, 239n273
18:17	125n455, 131n505
22:12	135n547
22:13	32n34
23:2–3	163n739
23:4	163n736, 286n505
23:4–5	164n740
24	237, 238
24:4	237
24:4–5	237
24:5	237n261, 238
26:13–19	199n58
26:20–32	37n62
26:27	262n373
26:29	286n505
26:32	37n62
27:1	109n347, 161n720, 238
27:1–15	239
27:5	124n450
27:16–24	239
27:25–34	37n62, 239
27:32–34	239
27:34	239
28	37n62, 38, 38n70
28:1	37n62, 38, 38n72, 238, 239
28:1–3	38n71
28:3	39n76
28:4–10	38n73
28:10	39n75
28:11–18	198n42
28:18	28n6
28:21	38n74
29:4	28n6
29:14	126n460, 136n554
29:15	230n230
29:22	128, 128n474, 369
29:23	32n34, 128n475, 129n478
29:24	129n479
29:25	128n476, 129n477

2 Chronicles

1:2	286n505
2	198
2:1	115n386
2:1–2	136n551
2:1–14	135n547
2:3	136n552
2:3–10	136n553
2:5	136n551
2:5–14	198n39
2:6	126n460, 136n555, 136n556
2:7	136n557, 137n559, 137n560
2:8	137n558
2:9	136n551
2:10	137n561
2:13–14	136n557, 198n45
2:14	137n559
2:17–18	198n44
9:17	28n6
10:4	128n471
10:8	168n762, 372
10:10–11	168n763
10:16	168n766
10:18	128n472, 168n764
11:13–14	380
11:13–17	168
11:16	380
11:17	381
11:23	378, 384
12:2–5	371
12:12	381
12:14	381
12:15–16	381
13:6–7	377
13:7	377, 378

Scripture Index

(2 Chronicles continued)

13:8–12	341n800
16:14	169n775
17:8	299n568
19:4–7	286
19:8–11	42n117
20:21	343n821
20:32–33	286n507
21:16	242n283
23:18	109n346
24:2	223n190
24:11	109n346
24:22	123n437
26	141, 223n189, 225
26:1	223n189
26:1–2	141, 223
26:3	225nn204–205
26:4	225n200
26:5	223n186
26:7	142n592, 223n187
26:10	141n588, 223n186, 224n195, 224n197
26:11	123n438, 141n590
26:11–13	223n186
26:11–15	141n590
26:15	141, 142, 223n185, 223n186, 225n199
26:16	142n593
26:19	225n203
27:2	225n200
28:9–15	324n725
28:22–23	341n802
28:22–24	341n801
29:2	142n597
29:3	341n804, 341n805
29:3–36	142n598
29:4	342n809, 342n810
29:5–11	341n806
29:6–9	342n812
29:10	342n807
29:16	342n813
29:17	341n805
29:19	342n814
29:20	342n815
29:28	342n816
29:28–30	143n599
29:30	342n816
29–32	341
29:35	343n818
29:36	143n599, 342n808, 343n819
30:1–2	143n600
30:1—31:1	343n820
30:2	354n878
30:4	143n608, 343n821, 354n878
30:6	143n600, 343n822
30:6–12	143n601
30:18–19	143n601
30:21–23	343n823
30:22	143n602
30:22–23	143n600
30:23	343n826, 354n878
30:24	143n603
30:25	343n827
30:26	381
31:2	143n604, 143n605
31:3	143n606
31:3–9	343n824
31:4–8	143n607
31:6	341n803
31:11	143n608
31:11–19	343n825
31:12	343n825
31:13	109n346, 129n479
31:14	344n830
31:15	343n825
31:16–19	143n607
31:19	343n825
31:20	142
32:3	143n609
32:3–4	143n610
32:5	143n608
32:6	143n605
32:7–8	143n602
32:23	354n878
32:25	144n613
32:28–29	143n608
32:30	143n610, 144n611
32:33	169n775
35:4	226

Ezra

1:1	242n283
1:6	164n745
2:1–2	160
2:62	149n643
2:64	162n732

Scripture Index

3:2	161n718, 162n729	4:14	146n626, 156n688, 248n307
3:6	162n730, 163n733	4:23	155n682
3:7	163n734	5:1–6, 9–10	156n686
3:7–9	163n735	5:5	318n694
3:8	161n718, 163n736	5:7–12, 16	155n677
3:8–9	163n737, 164n741	5:8	155n680
3:12–13	164n742	5:8, 15	155n680
3:89	163n736	5:9–10	156n686
4:1–3	164n743	5:9–12	155n682
4:3	164n745	5:12–15	155n679
4:3–4	165n746	5:14	154, 154n674
4:4	162n730	5:14–19	155n682
4:4–5	165n747	5:15	146n625, 155n680
4:23	165n748	5:16	155n677
4:24	165n747	5:17	155n681
5, 6	32n34	5:18	155n679
5:2	161n718, 165n747	6:1	156n688
6	32n34	6:2–4	156n687
6:14–18	162n727	6:8	156n684
6:15	163n738	6:10–13	156n687
7	201	6:15	127n467
7:1	238n265	7:2	38n70
7:6	269n423, 304n601	7:3	155n678
7:14–15	165n747	7:8	299n568
7:25	201	8:9	156n683
7:27–29	201n74	8:9–10	155n682
7:28	165n747	8:13	123n438
8:25	165n747	9:12	327n743
		10:1	155n682
		10:16	299n568
		10:32–39	155n682

NEHEMIAH

1	32n34	11	156n685
1:4–11	156n686	11:1–3	156n685
2	32n34	11:9	89n240, 156n685
2:1	149n641	11:19	156n685
2:1–6	154n675	11:24	156n685
2:1–8	156n684	12:1	161n718
2:5	156n687	13:4–28	155n682
2:8	138n570	13:18	156n686
2:12–13	156n685		
2:12–17	156n687		
2:16	146n626, 147n626	**ESTHER**	
2:17–18	156n688, 249	1:8	262n373
3:1–16	155n676	2:3	109n346
3:12	155n678	2:7	157n695
3:17–19	155n678	2:10	157n696
3:29	155n678	2:11	157n695
4:6	156n688	2:19–20	157n695
4:13–23	155n678	2:21	157

(Esther continued)	
2:22	157n694
3:2	157
3:2–4	157n697
4:8–14	157n698
4:13–14	201
5:4–5	149n640
5:8	157n697
5:13	157n697
6:1–3	158n699
6:13	134n531, 304n594
8	200n64
8:2	157
8:7–8	157n694
8:9	154n674, 169n771
8:9–10	158n700
9:3	154n674
9:3–4	157
9:20–23	158n700
9:23	346
9:26–28	346
10:3	157, 269, 346

Job

	35n59, 134
1:1	20n86
1:3	63n61
2:6	62n58
4:8	228n218
5:12	200n69, 215n138, 226n208
7:7	230n230
7:9	230n230
7:16	230n230
10:12	109n346
12:4	28n10
12:7	46n132
15:3	169n773
21:27	215n138, 226n208
22:2	169n773
22:19–20	314n666
22:21	169n773
23:10	65n72
29:16	166n754
31:8	228n219
31:24	47n148
31:29	325n730
31:29–30	314, 324n725
31:39	50n160

34:4	169n773
35:3	169n773
36:11	32n34
37:12	134n535, 134n536

Psalms

1:1	193n2
1:3	31n34
8:6	62n58, 126n458
11	39
11:7	39
12:3	388
12:6	86n221
12:8	78
15	262n373
15 LXX	323n717
15:1	40
15:1–5	40
15:2	28n10
15:3	42n117
17:17	311n645
18:24	28n10
22:16	284n493
24:3–6	51n173
26:4–5	193n2
34:10	31n34
35:11–16	324n725
37:6	358n897
37:7–8	281
37:13	228n222
37:25	32n34
37:30	44n121
37:37	20n86
39:5–6	230n230
40:5	220n162
45:1	xxviin27, 249, 269n423, 304n601
49:6	47n148
49:14	62n58
52	316
52:6	314n666
52:7	315
58	320n710
58:11	314n666
62:11–12	266
64:5–6	78n174
68:27	62n58
72:6	385

Scripture Index

72:7	385	1:5	41n99, 134, 134n536, 135n540, 241n278, 388
73:9–12	45		
75	195	1:5 LXX	241n279
75:6–7	195, 195n24	1:7	66n78, 108n340
78:53	41n100	1:26	314n666
78:70–72	41, 212n122, 302	3:4	354n882
90:4–6	230n230	3:9–10	48n152
90:12	134n523	3:16	48n152
90:17	290n517	3:21	48n151
91	24	3:24	48n151
94:1	215n138	3:27	269
94:11	226n208	4:16	284n498
101:3–4	44n127	4:25–27	267
101:7	262n373	6:6–8	46n132
105:16–22	xxin4, 130n482	6:6–11	268n412
105:21–22	299	6:7	46n132, 146n625
105:23	xxivn9	6:20–22	357n891
106.10	311n645	8:6	71n124
107:27	198n48	8:12	221n169
107:42	314n666	8:18	48n152
108:8	90n240	8:33	133n522
109:6–20	314n666	9:9	46n133
110:4	42n111	10:3	316n676
111:5	262n373	10:4	46n134
112:5	42	10:4–5	269
112:5–9	44	10:12	249n313, 285n502
118:7	314n666	10:15	32n34
119	45	10:17	360n915
119:54	xxviin27	10:26	268n412
119:66	45	11:1	315n672
119:67	45n130	11:5	28n10
119:113	211n117	11:12	41n106
119:115	193n2	11:14	41n99, 134n536, 135n540, 241n278
124:6	79n177		
137:8–9	314n666	11:28	47n148
139	9n32	12:1	304n596
139:3	169n773	12:2	281n484
139:14	261n369	12:5	44n121, 134n536, 135n540
143:12	314n666	12:11	222
144	302	12:15	241n278
144:1	302	12:24	126n458, 268n412, 269
144:6	314n666	12:26	338
		12:27	268n412
PROVERBS		13:1	108n340
	xvin24, 134	13:4	268n412, 269
1:2–3	303	13:6	46n135
1:4	220, 221	13:11	215n138, 221n171
		13:16	221n170, 304n597

Scripture Index

(Proverbs continued)

13:18	304n599	19:11	285n502
13:20	193n2, 339	19:21	198n51, 215n138, 216n138, 221n171
13:21	48n152	20:3	372
14:3	215n138	20:4	268n412
14:7	193n2	20:10	315n672
14:8	221	20:14	284n493
14:15	215n138, 221	20:18	134n536, 135n540, 215n138, 226n208
14:17	281n484		
14:20	47n149	20:22	331n762
14:23	268n412	20:23	315n672
14:24	48n152	20:25	216n138, 221n171
14:29	41n104	20:27	14n53, 296
15:1	249n313, 285n502, 372	21:1	198n51
15:6	48n152	21:5	208, 215n138, 220
15:18	249n312, 285n502	21:15	44n121
15:21	41n105	21:21	48n152
15:22	215n138, 221n171	22:3	46n138, 216n138, 221n171
15:23	389	22:6	303
15:27	50n160	22:8	228n218
16:1	198n51	22:13	268n412
16:7	284n495, 285n502	22:29	46n139, 269, 270n424, 304
16:9	198n51	23:19	133n522
16:11	315n672	24:3–4	48n152
16:13	388	24:3–6	217n145
16:26 Living Bible	261n366	24:6	41n99, 134n536, 135n540, 241n278
16:28	285n502		
16:33	199n58	24:17–18	316, 325n730
17:2	221	24:21	88n236
17:3	65n72	24:23–25	268, 268n409
17:5	316n677, 321n711, 324n725, 325n730	24:27	219n152, 304n600
		24:29	331n762
17:15	248, 249n312, 267n406, 271	24:30–34	268n412
		25:4	28n6
17:17	46n136	25:8, 21–22	285n502
18:5	248, 267n406	25:21–22	284n497, 285n502, 324n725
18:9	147n626, 268		
18:11	47n148	25:28	43n117
18:13	285n502, 388	26:4–5	280n480
18:15	268n412	26:13–16	268n412
18:18	199n58	26:28	388
18:19	285n502	27:1	230
18:21	249n312, 338, 339	27:6	47n140
18:24	268n412	27:11	133n522
18:25	33n41	27:17	304n595, 350n858
19:2	46n137	27:18	115n386
19:4	48n152	27:21	28n6, 86n221
19:4–6	47n149	27:23–27	222, 304n600

28:6	47n141	12:13	49n156
28:16	41n106, 50n160		
28:19	221, 222, 268n410, 268n412	**SONG OF SONGS**	
28:20	220n160	2:15	24n112
28:21	267n406, 268		
28:23	388	**ISAIAH**	
28:25	220n160, 249n313, 285n502	1:1	223n184
		1:22	65n71
29:2, 25	285n502	2:1–4	358n897
29:4	44n121	2:11	195n24
29:19	260n362	2:16	195n24
29:22	249n313	3:3 LXX	59n36
29:23	47n142	5:8	317n686
29:25	285n502	5:8–10	316
30:1	303n592	5:9	317n683
30:24–30	46n132	5:10	317n684, 317n688
30:25	219n152	5:15	195n24
31:1	303n592	5:20	271, 283n491
31:23	301n579	5:23	271
90:12	133n520	6:1	223n184
		9:2	358n896
ECCLESIASTES		9:6	23n106
		10:3	134n526
2	137, 138	10:13	137n566, 198n49
2:3	138n568	11:4–5	353
2:4	138n569	11:5	299n570
2:4–8	137n562	16:5	304n601
2:5	138n570	19:3	208n106
2:7	138n572	19:14 LXX	101n305
2:8	138n571, 138n573, 138n574, 139n577	20:35	36n61
		22:11	217n143
2:9	138n568	22:13	218n149
2:9–11	139	22:15	132n508, 168, 169n773
2:12	138n568	22:16	169n774
2:13	138n568	22:19	168, 262n373
2:24	218n149	22:20	166n755
3:2	161n723	22:20–25	165
3:13	218n149	22:21	166n756
5:7	208n105	22:22	167n757
5:10–11	47n149	22:23	167n758
5:10–11a	47	22:24	167n757, 167n759, 167n760
5:10–15	47		
5:12	47, 48n150, 48n151	22:25	167n761
5:14	49	23:8	37n62
5:18	218n149	24:23	182n67
5:19—6:2	48	25:1	208n106
8:15	218n149		
10:5	146n625		

Scripture Index

(Isaiah continued)		3:15	xviiin29, 40n93
28:23–29	305	4:11–12	14n52, 295n546
29:13	296n552	4:19a LXX	80n181
32:1–2	345	5	32n34
33:14–17	51n173	5:28	112n359
33:15–16	50	10:9	134n525
33:18	123n438	11:19	161n720
33:22	123n438	11:20	314n666
36	146n624	12:3	314n666
36:3	123n438, 132n508, 262n373	13	32n34
		13:23	257n352
36:16–18	xxin4	14:21	23n107
37	146n624, 165	15:4	340n798
37:2	132n508	17:9	257n352
37:26	208n106	17:10	272
40:20	169n773	18:12	215n138, 226
41:2	62n58, 242n283	18:15	285n499
42:4	358n895, 358n897	18:18	133n521
42:6–7	358	20:1	129n479
42:18–20	358n897	22	32n34
42:19–20	358n896	22:1–5	51n173
43:8	358n896	23:13 LXX	101n302
43:10	350	23:15–17	360n915
43:24	93n254	26:24	158n705, 159n710
44:18–19	358n896	27:16	360n913
44:25	134n529, 304n594	27:17	359n908
44:28	40n93, 200n63	28:2–4	360n913
45:5	63n63	29:4–7	359
49:6	358n897	29:4–8	3n11
49:10	14n52, 295n546	29:4–14	159n711
50:2	200n69	29:5–6	360n917
52:7	361	29:7	298n566, 360n916
54:9–10	28n8	29:8–9	360n915
55:8–9	xxvn17	29:11–23	346n841
57:17	319n696	29:26	129n479
58:7	51n174	29:28	360n912
59:1	200n69	30:10	xxin3
59:15	78, 79	31:18	257n352
60:3–13	197n32	31:20	257n352
60:17	89n240	31:31–34	257n352
63:14	327n743	31:33	257n352
65:1–5	21n92	32	32n34
65:8	3n11	32:17	200n69
65:10	239n275	32:27	200n69
		33:3	xvn20
JEREMIAH		33L8	257n352
		36:4–32	123n438
2, 5, 13, 22, 32	32n34	37:15	123n438
2:25	226, 226n209		

Scripture Index

38:4	165n747	2:48	147n626, 147n629, 152n655, 152n656
39:3	146n624	2:48–49	147, 153n665, 153n666
39:6	146n626	2:49	152n657, 152n658
40:5	159	3	32n34
40:10	160n713	3:2	147n626
40:12	160n713	3:2–3	147n629
43:25 LXX	160n714	3:3	147n626
50:9	242n283	3:4–7	153n667
51:1	242n283	3:8–12	153n668
51:11	242n283	3:12, 30	152n657
52:9–11	159n712	3:16–18	154n669
52:24–27	159n712	3:19	154n670
52:25	123n438	3:19–20	149n647
		3:20	154n671
Lamentations		3:27	147n626, 147n629
3:26–27	159n711	3:30	152n657, 154n672
		4:17	146n625, 192n1, 200n69
Ezekiel		4:32	200n69
2:63	162	5:12	152n654
5:2	162	5:17	152n659
14:12–23	149n637	5:22–23	152n660
14:14	28n8	5:29	157n693
14:20	28n8	6	32n34
18:5–9	51	6:1	152n655
21:21–2	202	6:2–3	148n631
21:27	202n77	6:3	269
22:30	3n11	6:7	147n626, 147n629
24	40n93	6:22	152n661
28:3	145, 149n637	6:24	152n662
28:4–5	134n530, 138n567	6:28	152n655
34:11–16	358n894	7:28	152n663
46:2–8	115n386	8:27	153n664
		9:14	147n629
Daniel		10:3	151n653
1	147	11:18	46n132
1:3	146n624, 194n16		
1:4	147n628, 147n629	**Hosea**	
1:4–5	148n630	1:1	223n184
1:8	149	2:13 LXX	101n303
1:10	149n645, 149n648	8:7	228n218
1:12–13	151	10:11	302
1:16	149	12:1	295n545
2	200n61	12:7	315n672, 352n866
2:5	145n622		
2:12	149n647		
2:21	192, 200, 200n69		

Joel

1:6	xn3
2:14	206n97
3:3	199n59

Amos

1:1	223n184, 224n194
2:8	51n174
3:3	258n353, 287
3:15	317n688
4:1	317n682
5:3	161n720
5:11	317n688
5:12	318n693
5:19	33n41
6:4–7	317n688
8:5	315n672
9:13	194

Obadiah

12	314

Jonah

1:7	199
3:9	206n97
4:8–9	43n117

Micah

2:1–2	318
2:2	318n692
2:4	316n678
2:12	318
3:1	44n121, 318n693
3:9	318n693
4:4	xxi, 130n482, 361n922
5:8	44n121
6:8	28n11, 52, 53
6:10–11	352n866
6:11	315n672
6:15	194n13, 228n219
7:9	358n897

Nahum

3:10	199n59
3:19	314n667

Habakkuk

	163n736
3:19	163n736

Haggai

1	165n749
1:1	154n674, 161n718
1:1–15	160n717
1:6	164n745
1:9–11	164n745
1:12	161n718
1:14	161n718, 242
2:2	161n718
2:3	164n742
2:15–17	164n745
2:23	161n718, 264n385

Zechariah

3:7	112n359, 144n614
3:10	xxi
4:6	161n721
4:7	161n722
4:8	161n724
4:9	165n750
4:10	123n438, 161n720, 164n742, 360n914
7:8–10	52
7:10	220n164
8:10	162n726
9:7	161n720
11:13	28n6
14:5	223n184

Malachi

1:7	149n643
1:8	154n674
1:12	149n643
3:5	253n329

Scripture Index

DEUTEROCANONICAL BOOKS

Jubilees

22:16	57n17

1 Maccabees

5:19	93n254
12:10, 17	5n14
12:17	5n14

2 Maccabees

2:28 LXX	88

4 Maccabees

5:34	70n116
9:23	5n14
10:3, 15	5n14
10:15	5n14

Sirach

4:30	63n61
40:28	16n67
46:13–14	121n423
49:11	161n723

Wisdom of Solomon

3:6	65n72
11:16	xxxin39
14:16, 18, 27	xxxin39
14:18	xxxin39
14:27	xxxin39

Pseudepigrapha (Old Testament)

Psalms of Solomon

10:1–2	64n65

ANCIENT JEWISH WRITERS

Artapanus

"Fragment 3 [Moses]"	113n372

Josephus

Jewish Antiquities

1.3.1	28n8
2.10	112n366
2.9.6	113n372
7.15.2	302n589
8.10.2	381n21

18.6.6	7n17

Philo

On the Confusion of Tongues

181	229n226

On the Embassy to Gaius

38.299–301	172n9

On the Life of Moses I,

V.18–24	113n372

NEW TESTAMENT

Matthew

1:6–20	102n311
2:3	334
2:4	292n523
2:6	327n743
3:10	255n345
3:17	23n107
4:1–11	22
4:6	24n110
4:18–19	261n370
4:18–22	8n30, 193n8
4:21	211, 293n531
5	61n50
5:3–5	319n699
5:9	274

Scripture Index

(Matthew continued)

5:13	365n935	12:30	268n412
5:13–16	354n883	12:35	261n366
5:16	319n703	12:38	25n115
5:17–18	27	13:21	77
5:21–26	319n695	13:21–35	xxviin25
5:23–25	275	13:27–30	366n940
5:38	319n702	13:57	88n235
5:43	20	15:1	334n776
5:43–48	101n298	15:9	296
5:44	89n238, 319n698, 319n702	15:14	293n530
		15:23	68n93
		15:27	353n870
5:44–48	5	16	295, 296
5:45	360n918	16:1	25n115
5:46	72n134	16:2–3	295
5:48	20, 29n19	16:3	9n34
6:10	231n281	16:11–12	296, 297
6:19–20	12n42	16:21	184n82, 334n776
6:19–24	47n148	16:25	xxvn16
6:33	219n155	17:1	234
7:1–20	212	17:20	297n561
7:12	62n55	18:4	319n699
7:17–20	xxviin26	18:12	91n250
7:24	213	18:15–17	261n368, 333n773
7:24–27	60n40	18:15–19	276
8:19	102n311	18:15–20	275n455
9:1–8	6n14	18:21–35	68n94
9:6	6n14	19	333
9:6–7	6n14	19:3	25n115, 333
9:10–13	2, 292	19:7	333
9:36	385	19:8	333
10	233	19:16–22	102n311
10:1–2a	233	19:26	297n561
10:2	193n7	20:1	194n14
10:5a	233	20:1–6	8n23
10:14–15	329n749	20:1–16	6, 260n363
10:16	232n237, 298n562, 325n728, 363n923	20:2	8n26
		20:3	8n27
10:16–17	4	20:3, 5, 6	8n25
10:19–20	211n115	20:4	63n60
10:22	6n15	20:5	8n25
10:24	24n108	20:6	8n25
10:40	2n6, 233	20:8	6
11:12	25n114	20:12	8n24
11:29	18n78, 70n111, 70n113, 319n699	20:13	8n28, 8n29
		20:13–15	7
12:19	320n709	20:15	8n28
12:29	12n42	20:16	194n14

Scripture Index

20:17–18	334n776	25:41	355n885
20:20–28	24n112	25:43	355n886
20:21–35	xxviin25	26:3	184n82
20:23	203n79	26:9	263n378
20:26	385	26:42	231n281
21:1	334n776	27:2	170
21:5	70n111	27:24–25	334n776
21:10	334n776	27:41	184n82
21:22	xvn20	27:57–60	173
21:33	9	27:59	174n14
21:33–44	10	27:60	174nn15–17
21:42	237n262	28	351
22:4	214	28:18	353n869
22:15–22	83n196	28:19	182n62
22:18	25n115	28:19–20	351
22:21	333n774		
22:35	25n115	**Mark**	
22:36–40	11		
23	2n7	1:11	97n278
23:11	385	1:19	293n531
23:12	319n699	3:2	193n7
23:23	69n105, 326n738	3:13	207n100
23:37	334n776	4:2	xxviin23
24:42–43	12	4:34	xxvin21
24:43	214	5:37	194n10
24:44	215n136	8:31	184n82
25:9	215	9:7	97n278
25:10	215	9:23b	257n352
25:14	12, 259n357	9:35	385
25:14–29	261	9:40	165n746
25:14–30	12, 236n254, 243, 260n364	9:50	319n706
		10:13–16	69n100
25:15	212n122, 259n356, 294n539	10:35–44	8n30
		10:40	213n124, 294
25:16	323n717	10:42–45	319n699
25:16–17	243n288	11:27	184n82
25:18	243n289	13:9	319n698
25:21	243n292, 263n375	13:32	294n538
25:23	243, 243n292, 253n328, 258, 259n358	13:33–37	13, 81
		13:34	205n88
25:24–25	259n357	13:35	13n46
25:25	243n290	15:43	173n12
25:26–27	258	15:45	174n13
25:26–30	259n360		
25:28–29	261n371	**Luke**	
25:31–46	101n298, 354	1:6	21n96
25:34	213	1:71	311n645
25:37–39	355	2:52	294, 354n879

481

(Luke continued)

3:13	184n83	12:16	218
3:23	294n536	12:16–19	17n69
4:22	294n534	12:16–21	218
4:23	8n31	12:17–18	218
5:6	233n239	12:19	218
5:21	xxv	12:20	214n130, 219
5:22	8n31	12:21	218
6	293, 313	12:34	261n366
6:8	8n31	12:35	353n871
6:13	193	12:35–48	263
6:27–28	319n698, 322n714	12:42	263
6:27–30	312	12:43	262n373
6:27–36	312	12:45	262n373
6:28	319n702	12:46	16, 17, 262n373
6:29–30	330n755	12:47	219, 262n373, 263n376, 263n380
6:33	72n133	12:47–48	263n377
6:35	312, 313n660, 322n714	12:48	45n131, 263n379, 264n381, 264n382
6:39–40	292, 293n528		
6:43–45	212n121	12:54–57	14
6:46–49	210n113	12:54–59	83n196
7:36	2n9	12:56	9n34, 295n541
7:40	8n31	12:57	112n359
8:3	6n17	13:1–2	171n6
9:14	234	13:20–21	354n879
9:22	184n82	13:24	320n709
9:28	8n30	13:32–33	215
9:28–36	193n9	14	216
9:46–50	8n30	14:1	2n8
9:47	8n31	14:26–27	193n6
9:54	68n95	14:28–30	216
9:62	76n159	14:28–33	211n114, 211n115
10:1	231	14:31–32	217
10:5	231	14:33	193n6
10:7	194n14	15:11–13	330n753
10:8	231	15:13	15n62
10:10–11	232n238	16	15
10:25–37	5n14	16:1	15n58, 16n65, 17
10:30	6n14	16:1–2	15
10:35	5n14	16:2	16n63
11:7	333n774	16:2–4	15n59
11:17	8n31	16:3	15n58
11:23	333n774	16:3–4	16
11:31	xxin4	16:5–7	16
11:37	2n8	16:6	15n58, 16n68
12	263	16:7	16n68
12:13–15	83n196	16:8	17
12:14	184n81, 185n87	16:8–9	15, 297

Scripture Index

16:13	15n60, 17, 17n72	10:30	xxv
16:19	174	12:4–6	234n245
17:2	82n190	12:9–13	366n938
17:7–10	313n659	12:41	xvin24, 27n2
18:9–14	292n523	13	18
19:11–27	xxviin25	13:14–15	18
20:1	184n82	13:27	330n754
21:12	319n698	13:29	234n245
22:25–27	390	13:34–35	5n14, 11n38
22:31–34	98	13:35	4n13, 18n76
22:32	177n27	14:7–9	102n309
22:40	98	14:9	xxvn19
22:45–46	98	14:9–10	19
23:6–7	172n8	14:11	xxvn19
23:12	172n7	14:14	xxvn19
23:24	312n655	14:16	xxivn10, 324n723
23:34	322n714	14:30	23n105
24:45	291	15	99
24:45–49	306	15:4–5	2
25:14–30	xxviin25	15:7	xvn20
		15:12	11n38
JOHN		15:18	91n250
		15:18–25	6n15
	291	15:19	20, 354n874
1:14	xxiiin8	15:27	353n872
1:14a	xxii	16:2	319n698
1:29	1n2	16:10	353n872
3:16	97n278, 354n874	17	3n13, 19n82, 356
4:36–38	194	17:11	24n109
4:37	194, 228n219	17:15	356n889
4:38	194, 194n18	17:15–19	353
4:46	102n311	17:16	6
6:5	234n245	17:18	19n82, 56n14, 354n884
6:8	234n245	17:21–23	19n82
6:27	323n717	17:22–23	4n13
6:52	320n709	17:25	19
7:1	210, 210n112	17:25–26	19
7:12	101n304	18:10–11	68n94
7:42	355n888	18:36	320n709
7:45–52	355	18:38–40	366n938
7:47–48	356	19:14–15	366n938
7:48	356	19:19–22	172
8:34	257n352	19:23	211n117
8:56	xvin24, 27n2	19:36	21n89
10:10	352n867	20:21	19n82
10:11	17, xviiin29, 40n93	20:25–28	88n235
10:11–18	17	21:11	232n239
10:24	xxvn14	21:15–17	18n74
10:28	xxvn19		

Scripture Index

(John continued)

21:15-19	25
21:16	89n239
21:17	11n37
21:22	18, 18n75

Acts

	291
1	178n40
1:11	19n81
1:15-17	306
1:15-26	179n47, 199n58
1:20	90n240
1:21	xxiii, 177n24, 193n4
1:24-26	177n24
1:25	177n24
2	306
2:14	290
2:14-36	179n48
2:19	230n229
2:47	354n880
3:16	87
4:1	128n474
4:5	182n67
4:8	182n67
4:13	293n532
4:23	182n67, 348
4:32-35	348
4:34	177n26
4:35	177n27
4:36-37	180
5:1-11	180n49, 327n739
5:29	179n45
6	182n69, 183
6:1	176, 176n24, 178n30, 178n33
6:1-5	176
6:2	177n24, 178n32, 178n34
6:2-3	178n35
6:3	89n240, 179n42, 243n286
6:3-4	177n24, 178n37, 178n38
6:5	177n28, 178n39, 179n43
6:9	177n29
6:12	182n67, 184n82
7	112
7:10	xxin4, 29n17, 130n482, 327n743
7:22	29n16, 112n364, 113n372, 147n629
7:26	320n709
7:30	113n370, 113n373
7:35	112n364, 112n365
7:36	113n371
7:60	312n656, 322
8:1	78n172
8:14-25	180n50
9:27	181n57
9:27-28	254
9:36	53n186
10:1-8	180n51
10:2	365n931
10:28	57n18
10:35	323n717
11	179n44, 240
11:2-3	57n18
11:19-20	240
11:20-24	181n58
11:24	180n55
11:26	242n281
11:27-30	181n60
11:30	183n78
13:1	7n17
13:1-3	181n59
13:7	7n17
13:12	7n17
13:48-52	77n169
14:1-7	77n169
14:8-20	77n169
14:19-20	182n71
14:21	183nn73-74
14:21-23	182
14:22	183nn75-76
14:23	182n67, 183n77, 183n79, 242n281
14:27	242n281
15	180, 181, 240
15:1-2	288
15:2	182n67, 242n281
15:4	182n67
15:6	182n67
15:6-21	180n52
15:19-20	289n509
15:22	182n67
15:22-29	181n61
15:23	182n67

Scripture Index

15:25	181n56	22:3	xxxiin39
15:28–29	288	22:3–5	328n748
15:36–41	11n39, 178n39, 329n752	23	171n4
		23:6–8	5
15:39	255n343, 348n847	23:14	182n67
15:41	242n281	23:23	214n130, 219n152
16:2	367n946	24:1	182n67
16:5	242n281	24:16	5
16:6	182n67	24:17	327n739
16:21	71	24:25	70n117
16:37	71	25	171n4
17	204, 324n724	25:15	182n67
17:4	55, 204	26	171n4
17:5	54	26:5	xxxiin39
17:11	54	26:12	6n17
17:12	55	26:16–17	358n895
17:22–23	366n939	26:26	102n310
17:26	203	27:10	326n737
17:28	366n939	27:11	135n540, 241n278
18:1–2	189	27:39	217n144
18:2–3	190n116		
18:19	190n118	**Romans**	
18:21	231n281		
19:31	7n17		289
20	189	1:8	253n334
20:13	184n83, 242n281	1:10	231n281
20:17	182n67, 183n72, 187n101	1:14	20n83
		1:17	97n278
20:17–18	186	1:18	322
20:17–35	186	1:28	65n73
20:18	186n96, 187n97	1:32	78, 79
20:19	187n98	2:4	77
20:20	186, 187n99	2:7	95n265
20:21	187n100	2:14–15	366n943
20:23	187n102	2:18	14n48, 65n73
20:24	187n103	5:2	64
20:27	186, 187n99	5:2b–5a	64
20:28	89n240, 187n101, 187n104	5:3	64
		5:4	65n72
20:28–31	187n102	5:5	66, 66n80, 88n235
20:30	187n105	5:8	21n90
20:31	186, 187n98, 187n99, 187n106, 188n107	5:10	324n727
		6:19–20	257n352
20:33–34	188n108	7	252n325
20:35	187n98, 188n109, 241n278	7:6	67n84
		8	55, 85n204
21:14	231n281	8:3	xxii
21:18	182n67	8:15–17	1n1
		8:29	1n1, 55, 99n287

485

(Romans continued)		4:12	331n762
9:21	203n79	4:12–13	324
10:11	66n79	4:17	75n153, 76n158
10:12	3n10	4:19	231n281
10:14	361	5:6–8	297n556
12	92n254	5:11	193n2
12:1–2	366n942	5:11–13	261n368
12:2	66, 332	7	205
12:8	92n254, 241n278	7:9	251n323
12:9	5n14	7:13–14?	57
12:14–19	319	7:15–16	206
12:15–21	284n497	7:16	56n12, 206
12:17	331n762	7:17	242n281
12:17–18	275	7:17–24	206
12:17–21	324n726	7:19b	206n94
12:20	322n715	7:20–24	205
12:21	14n48, 319	8:1–13	180n54
13:1	91n248	8:9–13	57n19
13:4	274n446	9:7	89n239
13:5	91n248, 273	9:10	76n159
13:6–7	326n736	9:14	242n281
13:7	274	9:19–23	365n936
13:8–10	49n156, 237n255, 365n934	9:21	365n936
		9:24–27	70n118, 251
14:18	308n623	9:25	320n709
14:19–20	289	9:25–26	320n709
15	389	10	57
15:10	65n74	10:4	xvin24, 27n2
15:14	69n102, 253	10:25	58n22
15:20	361n921	10:25–27	56
16:1–2	190, 253n328	10:27	67
16:3	190	10:27–28	58n22
16:23	262n373	10:32	354n882
		11:1	61n46
1 CORINTHIANS		11:13	307n621
	241n278	11:28	14n48, 261n369, 273n444
1:6	64n69	12	241n278, 389
1:12–13	211n117	12:7	188n110
2:6	87n227	12:14–26	334n777
2:11	14n53, 273n442, 296n547	12:18	240
		12:28	135n540, 240n278
3:1	100n295	12:29	241n278
3:2	58, 58n26	13	96n276
3:8	194n14	13:6	78n172
3:10	59, 59n37, 60nn38–40	13:7	69n105
3:11	60n41	13:12	56n10
3:12–13	60n42	14:29	189n112
3:14	194n14		

14:33	231
14:34	91n248
14:40	231
15:9	328n748
15:33	67, 193n2
15:49	103n313
16:1–3	327n739
16:7	231n281
16:13–18	183n72
16:15–18	242n281
16:16	91n248
16:19	189n115
16:22	312n657

2 Corinthians

1:6	85n204
2:2	218n150
2:6–7	261n368
2:9	55, 65n71
3:1–3	61n45
3:18	67n87, 102n313
4:2	321n713
4:10	103n313
5:7	56n11
5:9	254n342, 361n921
5:11	209n109
5:20	184n82, 354n873
6:3–10	77n165
6:6	68n92, 69n98, 76n162
6:8	72nn130–131
6:14	193n2
6:14–15	211n117
6:15	34n49
7:5	320n709
8:2	55
8:2–3	65n71
8:9	385
8:10–21	208n107
8:13	327n739
8:19	182n66, 185n89, 242n281, 308n624
8:20	347n843
8:21	308
9:2	254
9:3	236n254
9:6	228, 274n448
9:8–10	309n636
9:9	44n126
9:13	55, 65n72
10:5	70
10:16	273n445
11:23–33	77
11:32–33	327n743
12:10	77n170
13:3	65n72
13:5	258, 273n444, 348n847

Galatians

1:6	85n204
1:8–9	312n657
1:10	273n444
1:12	291n519
1:16	208n107
1:17–18	291n519
2:11–13	101n298, 329n752
2:11–14	180n53
2:19–20	59n29
3:15	xxviin24
3:28	194n16
3:29	3n10
4:2	6n17
4:4	20n84
4:6	59n30
4:16	69n107
4:19	59n29, 66, 67
4:29	xxiiin7
5	68, 85n204, 96n276
5:7–8	260n365
5:10	236n254
5:15	317n688, 325
5:20	70n115
5:22	21n93, 68, 84, 88n235
5:22—6:10	75n154
5:23	95n264
5:26	328n745
6:4	273n443
6:4–5	326
6:5	326
6:10	56n8, 96n273, 330n760

Ephesians

1:4–6	261n369
1:11	204n85
1:15	5n14

(Ephesians continued)		2:19–30	69n108
2:4–10	69n103	2:22	55, 65n71
3:8	328n748	2:24	231n281
3:16–19	59n31	3:12	227
4:2	68n92	3:12–22	252n326
4:11–12	309n636	3:13	290n516
4:12	63n63, 309	3:13–14	227
4:13	87n227	3:15	87n227
4:23	61n48	3:21	71n120
4:24	67n87	4:8	95, 308n623
4:28	292n525	4:8–9	70
4:30	327n739		
5:1	61		
5:1–2	61n48		

Colossians

5:3	307n621	1:9–10	58n28
5:9	69n102	1:10	350
5:15	297n561	1:10–12	351
5:21–22	91n248	1:11	68n92, 103n313
5:23	238n263	1:15–20	20n83
5:24	91n248	1:19	59n31
6:5, 9	63n62	1:28	87n227
6:5–9	xxivn11, 89n240	1:29	320n709
6:9	63, 63n62, 389	2:6–8	211n117
6:10–12	366n942	2:12	262n373
6:14	353	2:18	xxxin39
6:20	184n82	2:22	296n553
6:21	74n147	3:2	31n31, 273n444, 366n937
		3:10	67n87
		3:11	3n10, 194n16

Philippians

		3:12	68n92, 69n99
1:1	183n72, 242n281	3:13–14	289n512
1:9	95n261	3:17	31n31
1:9–10	58n27	3:18	91n248
1:9–11	68n90	3:22—4:1	89n240
1:10	254	3:22–25	xxivn11
1:17	328	3:23	242
1:27	71n120, 320	4	308
2	61, 329n750	4:1	61, 71n126, 306, 308
2:2	5n14	4:6	389
2:3–4	311, 327	4:10	11n39
2:3–8	88n235	4:12	320n709
2:3–11	385		
2:5	61, 328n747		

1 Thessalonians

2:5–8	xxiv		309n636
2:7	xxii, 365n932	2:4	273n444
2:12	98n283	2:7	70n112
2:12–13	97n281	3:12	96n275
2:13	207n101	4:11	292n525
2:19, 24	231n281		

4:11–12	361	3:8	363n925
4:12	254n342	3:11	363n925
5:12	92n254, 93n254, 242n281	3:16	74n143
5:12–22	75n154	3:22	92n254
5:12–24	183n72	4:7	74n143, 297n561
5:14	241n278, 309n636	4:8	74n143
5:15	331n762	4:10	363
5:19	323n716	4:12	74n146
5:21	189n112, 273n444	5	93n254, 178n31
5:23	87n224	5:8	292n525, 317n685
		5:17	92n254, 183n72, 241n280, 242n281

2 Thessalonians

		5:18	194n14
1:11	69n102	5:20	207n98
2:12	78n172	6:1–2	xxivn11
3:5	87n222	6:3	74n143
3:6	207n98, 347	6:5	74n143
3:10	347	6:6	74n143
3:14–15	207n98, 312n657	6:9	85n211
3:15	347	6:10	47n148, 83n196
		6:11	74n146, 77n166, 85n204

1 Timothy

		6:11–12	73
	73	6:12	73, 320n709
1:2	74n147		
1:3	74n149	## 2 Timothy	
1:5	74n146		
1:14	74n146	1:13	74n146
1:15	328n748, 363	2:2	184n84
1:16	69n96, 77	2:5	320
1:20	273n443	2:15	65n73, 254n342
2:1–4	362	2:22	74, 74n146
2:2	74n143	2:23–24	320n709
2:4	363	3:1	63n63
2:10	307n621	3:5	366n939
2:15	74n146	3:10	68n92, 74n146, 74n150
2:22	73n138	3:10–11	75
3	93n254	3:12	77n167
3:1	89n240	3:17	290, 309
3:2	90n240	4:2	68n92
3:2–3	367n945	4:7	320n709
3:2–7	254n340, 308	4:11	11n39
3:3	90n240	4:14	324n726
3:4	92n254, 108n339, 363n925		
3:4–5	41n106, 90n240	## Titus	
3:5	92n254		
3:6	90n240	1	307
3:7	90n240, 354n881	1:5	183n72, 184, 185n89, 242n281
3:7–8	298n562	1:6–8	254n340

Scripture Index

(Titus continued)		11:2	253n328
1:6–9	185n88, 308	11:13	366n941
1:7	262n373	11:26	xvin24, xviin26,
1:8	70n117		27n1, 27n2
2:1	307	11:27	31n23, 31n24
2:2	74n146	11:33–34	323n717
2:5	91n248	11:38	101n300
2:6–10	307	11:40	228
2:9	91n248	12	309
2:9–10	xxivn11	12:1	255n348
2:10	69n105, 69n106,	12:3	350n861
	74n147	12:7	41n96, 41n100
2:11	363	12:11–12	309
2:12	100n295	12:24	41n96, 41n100
3:1	91n248	13:1–6	255n346
3:8	93n254	13:7	327n743
3:8 MNT	93n254	13:17	81
3:9	320n709	13:21	63n63
3:10	193n2		
3:14	93n254, 292n525	**JAMES**	
			291
PHILEMON		1:2	85
8	185n86	1:3–4	84
10–13	206n95	1:6–8	87n228, 211n117
17	390	1:12	65n71
22	214n130, 219n152	1:19	389
		1:26–27	xxxin39
HEBREWS		2:1	85n206
		2:8	89n238
2:14	18n80	2:14	85n206
2:17	330n757	2:22	229
2:17a	365n933	3:1	85n206, 264n383,
3:3	350n858		309n639
3:14	226n206	3:4	123n438, 327n743
4:13	9n32	3:9	89n237
4:15	330	3:10	85n206
5	80	3:10–12	92n252
5:7	xxiii, xxiiin8	3:12	85n206
5:7–10	xxiiin8	4:1–2	320n709
5:14	80, 87n227	4:11	85n206
6:1–3	58n24, 255n347	4:13	83n196
6:12	68n92, 83, 84	4:13–14	218n148
8:6	254n340	4:13–15	230
10:24	255, 348, 349n851,	4:13–16	209n108
	349n856, 350n860	4:14	230
10:24–25	348, 349n852	5	68
10:25	349nn853–855	5:4	194n14, 253n329
10:25b	350n859	5:7	68, 85n206

5:9–10	85n206	*2 Peter*	
5:10	68n92, 84	1:3–4	95n258
5:11	35n59	1:5–8	93, 94
5:12	85n206	1:7	94n256
5:14	183n72	2:2	95n266
5:19	85n206	2:3	230n227
		2:10	95
1 Peter		2:13	95
1	85n204	2:13–17	96n277
1:6	70n117	2:14	95
1:6–7	86n220	2:14–19	78n172
1:7	65n72	2:19	95
1:13	353	3:1	256
1:14	90n245	3:18	97n280
1:14–15	97n281		
2	180n54	*1 John*	
2:9	261n369, 331n765	1:1–3	xxiv, 364
2:11	366n941	2:1–2	xxivn10
2:11–15	364	2:6	88, 99, 100n294, 101n298
2:12	308n623, 319n704		
2:12–17	3n11	2:19	165n746, 329n752
2:13	91n248, 92n252	2:26	78n172, 101
2:13–17	308n632	3:3	100n294
2:15	354n882	3:7	102
2:15–17	298n562	3:16–18	101
2:16–17	310	3:17	155n681
2:16–17a	91	4:1	189n112, 208n105
2:17	88	4:2	100
2:18	xxivn11, 91n248	4:2–3	xxiii, xxiiin8
2:19–21	312n652	4:7	88n235
2:21	87	4:7–21	4n13
2:23	389	4:17	100
2:25	101n301	4:19	324n727
3:1–7	90n244		
3:8	331	*2 John*	
3:8–9	91n246	1	183n72, 242n281
3:9	324n726, 331	7	xxiii, xxiiin8
3:17	231n281		
4:12	86n213	*3 John*	
5	91		
5:1	183n72	1	183n72, 242n281
5:1–2	242n281	9–10	42n116
5:1–3	386		
5:1–4	18n76		
5:2–3	89n240, 90		
5:3	205		
5:5	90, 91n248		
5:9	91n248		

JUDE

	291
5	xvin24, xviin25, 27
8	208n105
11	83n196

REVELATION

1:3	350
2	179n44
2:1–7	188
2:2	188n111
2–3	286n507
5:9	194n16
13:18	216n141
18:17	135n540, 241n278, 323n717
19:15	353
20:12	273n443
22:8–9	xxxin39
22:12	274

APOCRYPHA (NEW TESTAMENT)

GOSPEL OF THOMAS

91	14n48

EARLY CHRISTIAN WRITINGS

A KEMPIS
Imitation of Christ,

Book Three	xxivn13

CHRYSOSTOM, JOHN
Homilies on the Epistles of St. Paul the Apostle in the Philippians, Colosians, and Thessalonians

13.366–67	309n636

DIDACHE

4:10	63n61

EUSEBIUS
Church History

2.7.100	171n5

Ecclesiastical History

2.23	84n203

IRENAEUS
Against Heresies

1.26.3	179n44

JEROME
Commentary on Jonah

1.7	199n53

Homilies

1.1–59	300n574

ORIGEN
Commentary on the Epistle to the Romans

5.100	273n442

SHEPHERD OF HERMAS
Mandate

34:4	97n279

Similitudes

8.8.1	348–49n850
9.20.1	349n850

GRECO-ROMAN LITERATURE

ARISTOTLE
Nicomachean Ethics

	102n308
2.7.1108a	75n151

RHETORIC

1366	94n255

HESIOD
The Works and Days

lines 340–57	312n658

LYSIUS
Against Eratosthenes

9.20	312n658

MENANDER
Rhetoric

373	94n255

PINDAR

"Ode #2," line 83	312n658

SIMONIDES
"Plato Republic"

paragraph 642	312n658

XENOPHON
Memorabilia

1.5	95n263

REFORMATION

CALVIN, JOHN
Commentary on Hebrews
and I & II Peter

272–73	310n642
332	94n256

Commentary on the Book
of the Prophet Isaiah

4.261	79n176

The Epistles of Paul to the
Romans and Thessalonians

231	361n920

The Gospel According to St. John
and the First Epistle of John

145	356n890
295	100n296

Institutes of the Christian Religion

1.408–11	10n35
1.411	10n35
2.724	205n91
3.7.4–7	44n120

Matthew, Mark, and Luke

3.114	213n126
3.303	231n281

The Second Epistle of Paul to
the Corinthians and the Epistle
to Timothy, Titus and Philemon

227–28	90n240

Westminster Confession of Faith

1.5	xvin24
Q & A 1.	xiin14